INTEGRATION AT THE BORDER

A recent development in the immigration policies of several European states is to make the admission of foreign nationals dependent upon criteria relating to their integration. As the practice of 'integration testing abroad' becomes more widespread, this book endeavours to clarify the legal implications that have hitherto remained poorly understood and studied.

The book begins by looking at the situation in the Netherlands, which was the first EU Member State to introduce pre-entry integration requirements. It explores the historical and political origins of the Dutch Act on Integration Abroad and explains how, in this national context, integration has become a criterion for the selection of immigrants. It then examines how integration requirements must be evaluated from the point of view of European and international law, including human rights treaties, EU migration directives and association agreements and the law on non-discrimination. The book identifies the legal standards set by these instruments with regard to integration testing abroad and draws conclusions as to the lawfulness of the Dutch approach.

Volume 44 in the series Studies in International Law

Studies in International Law

Recent titles in this series

Reflections on the UN Declaration on the Rights of Indigenous Peoples
Edited by Stephen Allen and Alexandra Xanthaki

Contracting with Sovereignty: State Contracts and International Arbitration
Ivar Alvik

Multi-Sourced Equivalent Norms in International Law
Edited by Yuval Shany and Tomer Broude

The Distinction and Relationship between *Jus ad Bellum* and *Jus in Bello*
Keiichiro Okimoto

International Humanitarian Law and Terrorism
Andrea Bianchi and Yasmin Naqvi

The Militarisation of Peacekeeping in the Twenty-First Century
James Sloan

Accounting for Hunger: The Right to Food in the Era of Globalisation
Edited by Olivier De Schutter and Kaitlin Y Cordes

Promises of States under International Law
Christian Eckart

Multilevel Regulation of Military and Security Contractors: The Interplay between International, European and Domestic Norms
Edited by Christine Bakker and Mirko Sossai

Europe and Extraterritorial Asylum
Maarten den Heijer

The Practice of International and National Courts and the (De-) Fragmentation of International Law
Edited by Ole Kristian Fauchald and André Nollkaemper

The Politics of International Criminal Justice: A Spotlight on Germany
Ronen Steinke

Fighting Corruption in Public Procurement: A Comparative Analysis of Disqualification or Debarment Measures
Sope Williams-Elegbe

The Interception of Vessels on the High Seas: Contemporary Challenges to the Legal Order of the Oceans
Efthymios Papastavridis

For the complete list of titles in this series, see 'Studies in International Law' link at www.hartpub.co.uk/books/series.asp

Integration at the Border

The Dutch Act on Integration Abroad and International Immigration Law

Karin de Vries

•HART•
PUBLISHING
OXFORD AND PORTLAND, OREGON
2013

Published in the United Kingdom by Hart Publishing Ltd
16C Worcester Place, Oxford, OX1 2JW
Telephone: +44 (0)1865 517530
Fax: +44 (0)1865 510710
E-mail: mail@hartpub.co.uk
Website: http://www.hartpub.co.uk

Published in North America (US and Canada) by
Hart Publishing
c/o International Specialized Book Services
920 NE 58th Avenue, Suite 300
Portland, OR 97213-3786
USA
Tel: +1 503 287 3093 or toll-free: (1) 800 944 6190
Fax: +1 503 280 8832
E-mail: orders@isbs.com
Website: http://www.isbs.com

British Library Cataloguing in Publication Data
Data Available

ISBN: 978-1-84946-410-9

Typeset by Hope Services, Abingdon
Printed and bound in Great Britain by
TJ International Ltd

MIX
Paper from responsible sources
FSC® C013056

Table of Contents

B. Integration Requirements, EU Law and International Agreements

Table of Cases

Netherlands

Supreme Court

Administrative Jurisdiction Division of Council of State (AJD)

Central Appeals Tribunal

District Court (The Hague)

District Court (The Hague, Aliens Affairs Legal Uniformity Chamber)

Court of Justice of the European Union

European Commission of Human Rights

European Court of Human Rights

Human Rights Committee

Table of Legislation

NATIONAL LEGISLATION

EU LEGISLATION

Treaties, Agreements, Conventions, Charters

Directives

Regulations

INTERNATIONAL LEGISLATION

1

Introduction

I. OBJECT AND PURPOSE OF THE STUDY

A. Integration as a Condition for Immigration: the Act on Integration Abroad

THIS BOOK ASKS if states, and the Netherlands in particular, may enact integration tests as a condition for the admission of aliens. Such a test was introduced in the Dutch Act on Integration Abroad (*Wet inburgering buitenland*), which entered into force on 15 March 2006.[1] Since then, several groups of immigrants – in particular family migrants from non-Western countries – have only been granted admission to the Netherlands if they can demonstrate proficiency in the Dutch language and a certain amount of knowledge about the country. Their ability to do so is assessed by means of the integration exam abroad (*inburgeringsexamen in het buitenland*), which is taken in their country of origin before the visa application is made.

The Act on Integration Abroad (AIA) is an instrument of Dutch integration policy. This policy seeks to ensure that, among the Dutch population, there exist a level of social cohesion and a degree of economic participation that are considered necessary for the continued viability of the welfare state as a political and economic institution. From the late 1970s until approximately the turn of the century, Dutch integration policy was primarily directed towards persons who had already been admitted. It aimed to achieve an equal position for these immigrants compared to that of the non-immigrant population and, at a later stage, to ensure their active participation in various domains of mainstream society, notably education and the labour market. For the past 10 years, however, integration measures have increasingly been directed towards excluding immigrants of whom it is expected that they will not successfully integrate.[2] This new

[1] *Bulletin of Acts and Decrees* 2006, 28; entry into force *Bulletin of Acts and Decrees* 2006, 75.

[2] Schinkel points out that the term 'integration' necessarily refers to a process involving different actors or elements; hence it would be wrong to state that a single person can either integrate or not integrate (Schinkel 2008, 39–40). In fact, what is required will often be a certain degree of participation, adjustment or adaptation, depending on how the concept of integration is understood at the time. Although I subscribe to this view, I was unable to find a suitable term to replace 'integration' as a general descriptor of what states expect

line of thinking has been described as a 'reversal of citizenship concepts': whereas integration (in the sense of learning the language of the host state and developing a commitment towards its society) was previously expected to follow admission and the granting of rights, the current understanding is that immigrants should integrate before they are admitted or access to rights is granted.[3] At the same time, integration policy became increasingly directed towards cultural adaptation of immigrants and their identification with Dutch society.

Besides the AIA, the augmented prevalence of this new perspective on integration has inspired several new measures, including an (advanced) integration exam which also serves as a condition for the acquisition of a permanent residence permit (the Integration Act 2007), a naturalisation test (introduced in 2003) and a legislative proposal to make the granting of social assistance dependent on demonstrated proficiency in the Dutch language.[4] Similar developments can be seen in other European countries, which have also introduced integration conditions into their immigration and nationality legislation.[5] In particular Germany, France, Denmark, the United Kingdom and Austria have introduced integration tests as a condition for the admission of family or other migrants.[6] The possibility of making residence rights dependent on integration requirements has also been expressly included in a number of EU migration directives (notably the Family Reunification Directive and the Long-term Residents Directive).[7]

With the introduction of the AIA and similar measures in other countries, language proficiency and country knowledge have become part of the criteria used to determine whether immigrants, and specifically family migrants, are granted the right of admission to the territory of the states concerned. Within liberal democracies, the use of such criteria can be seen as a democratically legitimated expression of self-determination, aiming to preserve unity and solidarity within the state. On the other hand, integration requirements can be at odds with the principles of individual freedom and equality, to which liberal democratic states are also

immigrants to do (or be). I therefore continue to refer to 'integration' as something that immigrants can do, although I try to minimise this use of the term. For reasons of readability I refrain from using quotation marks.

[3] Vermeulen 2010a, 87–89. See also Groenendijk 2004, 111–13 and Carrera and Wiesbrock 2009, 2.

[4] On the introduction of the naturalisation test see Van Oers 2010, 60–62. The proposal to introduce an integration requirement into the Social Assistance Act (*Wet werk en bijstand*) was submitted by the Liberal Party (*VVD*) in 2010 and was still pending before the Dutch Parliament at the time of writing, see *Parliamentary Papers II*, No 32, 328.

[5] Guild et al 2009a; Van Oers et al 2010a; Groenendijk 2011.

[6] Groenendijk 2011, 9–20. The Austrian requirement is laid down in Art 21a of the Settlement and Residence Act (*Niederlassungs- und Aufenthaltsgesetz*), see www.bmi.gv.at.

[7] Groenendijk 2004, 117–25; Carrera 2009, 145–225; Carrera and Wiesbrock 2009, 5–11; Groenendijk 2011, 5–9.

committed. These principles, which are considered to be of a universal nature, may stand in the way of erecting barriers for the admission of immigrants and distinguishing between those who are and those who are not considered capable of successful integration. They also impose limitations on the extent to which immigrants are asked to conform to the integration norms of the receiving state, in particular where culture and moral values are concerned.[8] This book aims to see how the law, both at the national and international level, finds a balance between these competing claims. More specifically, it clarifies the legal framework concerning integration requirements for the admission of immigrants and identifies the criteria determining their legality. To do this, relevant legal instruments are analysed and suggestions offered for their interpretation. Throughout the investigation, the Dutch Act on Integration Abroad serves as a point of departure and conclusions are drawn as to its lawfulness.

B. Approach

This book is divided into two parts. The first part, which can be read separately or as a prelude to the second part, investigates the integration exam abroad and its role in Dutch integration policy. It gives a description of the Act on Integration Abroad, including the target group, the contents of the exam and the effects measured to date, and explains the historical and political context in which the Act was introduced. To this end, a historical overview is given of Dutch integration policy, with particular attention being paid to the introduction and development of language courses and civic education for immigrants. An analysis of parliamentary documents focuses more directly on the objectives of integration policy, as defined by the Dutch legislator, and the changes in the Dutch concept of integration. At the end of this analysis, both the integration objectives pursued and the suitability of the AIA as a means to achieve them are made subject to some preliminary objections.

The second part of this study examines the legal norms and standards with which integration requirements must comply. This part of the investigation addresses the legal effect of integration tests, which is the temporary and sometimes even permanent exclusion of immigrants seeking to enter a state of which they are not nationals. The specific question examined is which standards are set by (mostly international) immigration rules regarding non-admission of aliens on the grounds that they have

[8] On the inherent contradiction between the principles of self-determination and freedom and equality see, eg, Tholen 1997; Bosniak 2006, esp 1–9; Joppke 2008, 533–36 and Vermeulen 2010, 46. See also Benhabib, who describes this stand-off as 'the constitutive dilemma at the heart of liberal democracies: between sovereign self-determination claims on the one hand and adherence to universal human rights principles on the other', Benhabib 2004, 2.

failed to meet an integration requirement. The examination covers various areas of immigration law, including legal rules on family reunification, labour migration and the right to free movement in the EU. Legal instruments on asylum are not included, the reason being that there is clearly no scope for states to enact integration requirements in relation to requests for international protection.[9] In the Netherlands, as in other states where integration is a prerequisite for admission, asylum seekers have been excluded from this condition. On the other hand, as religious servants form a specific target group of the Act on Integration Abroad, the relevance of the right to freedom of religion for the admission of aliens is considered. Lastly, given that the AIA does not apply to all immigrants alike, integration requirements are assessed in relation to the right to equal treatment.

The objective of the above examination is twofold. The first aim is to describe and analyse the legal standards that states, and the Netherlands in particular, must take into account when enacting integration requirements as part of their immigration rules. A second but related aim is to construct a comprehensive argument concerning the lawfulness of the AIA in relation to relevant norms of international and Dutch constitutional law. To the extent that such lawfulness is found to be lacking, adjustments to the Act, or its application, will be needed to ensure that the legal obligations assumed by the Netherlands are duly respected and the rights of immigrants protected.

As part of the objective of this study is to evaluate the lawfulness of the AIA, the scope and contents of the examination in the second part of the book are, to a large extent, determined in relation to this Act. By taking the (Dutch) integration exam abroad as a point of reference, it will be possible to formulate more specific legal standards (concerning, for example, the target group or the contents of the test) than if a more abstract definition of integration requirements were to be used. Nonetheless, much of the legal framework developed in this study is equally applicable to integration requirements adopted or to be adopted by other states. In particular, the interpretation of various provisions of human rights treaties – including the European Convention on Human Rights – and the EU migration directives will be equally pertinent to other EU Member States. It is hoped, therefore, that the relevance of this study will not remain limited to the national context of the Netherlands.

[9] For an overview of relevant instruments and their contents see Boeles et al 2009, 253–361.

C. Relation to Other Research

Developments in the integration policy and legislation of various EU Member States and at the EU level over the past 10 years have formed an important topic of academic research. One matter that has attracted considerable attention has been the redefining of the concept of citizenship in various EU states and the manifestation of these changes in actual integration measures, in particular naturalisation tests.[10] A prevailing theoretical perspective in this literature concerns the compatibility of these developments with liberal political theories on citizenship and integration.[11]

As far as the Netherlands is concerned, the evolution of the concept of citizenship has been quite extensively described and evaluated by different authors.[12] This literature mostly analyses the normative conception of citizenship or integration as it has been formulated in the Dutch political debate. An important strand of criticism expressed in various publications concerns the shift that has taken place, especially since 2003, towards the unilateral adaptation by immigrants to the cultural norms and values of the majority population and the presentation of these norms and values as forming part of a static and exclusive national identity. Another, related objection formulated by various researchers concerns the fact that responsibility for a successful integration process has been placed wholly or largely on the immigrant population.[13]

Given their close connection to the topic of this study, this book also includes an analysis and assessment of the conceptualisation of citizenship and integration in the Dutch political debate. The findings from the abovementioned literature are thereby taken into account. Adding to the developments that have already been described, this study also explains how the concept of integration continued to evolve between 2007 and 2011, with special attention being paid to the relationship between the political or ideological concept of integration in the Netherlands and the legal requirements of the Act on Integration Abroad. Lastly, while mindful of the comments that have already been made, this study aims to provide a brief individual assessment of the objectives of Dutch integration policy and the suitability of the AIA as a means to achieve these objectives.

[10] Michalowski 2011; Guild et al 2009a; Van Oers et al 2010a.

[11] See, esp, Joppke 2008; Michalowski 2011; Guild et al 2009a; Bauböck and Joppke 2010.

[12] Spijkerboer 2007; Driouichi 2007; WRR 2007; Schinkel 2008; Klaver and Odé 2009; Fermin 2009; Van Gunsteren 2009 and Vermeulen 2010. For earlier analyses see also Fermin 2000 and Van Blom and Van Schilt-Mol 2001, 21–31.

[13] See, esp, Driouichi 2007; Klaver and Odé 2009 and Vermeulen 2010. See also Fermin 2006.

Meanwhile another strand of academic research concerns the reinforced connection between integration and immigration measures in Europe. This linkage has been seen to represent a key development in integration policies, both at the EU level and in various Member States (including the Netherlands).[14] The introduction of integration requirements for the acquisition of residence rights and nationality has been criticised by several authors on the grounds that the objective and/or effect of such requirements is to function as instruments of exclusion and immigration control rather than as a tool for integration.[15]

This study argues that the predominant purpose of the AIA is indeed to function as a selection criterion and thus to exclude those immigrants who do not pass the integration exam abroad. It then attempts to take the discussion one step further by asking whether this 'exclusive' conception of integration is acceptable in view of the competing interests of the residents of the receiving state and those of the immigrants seeking admission. As mentioned above, a primary objective of this study is also to assess the legality of integration requirements for the admission of aliens and specifically of the Act on Integration Abroad.

Although the issue of legality has been raised on various occasions,[16] a comprehensive legal framework regarding integration requirements has not yet been formulated. Thus far the available literature has mostly provided a limited evaluation of the compatibility of integration requirements with the right to family life, the prohibition of discrimination and the EU migration directives.[17] Naturally the results that emerged from these previous inquiries have been included in this study. The legal description and analysis presented in this book are, however, more encompassing and produce a number of different outcomes.

Finally, an important question concerning integration requirements is whether those requirements actually contribute to achieving the objectives for which they were introduced. Although this is an empirical question that does not as such pertain to the object of this study, we will see that the effectiveness of the AIA is a relevant factor in determining both the political legitimacy of the integration exam abroad and its legal validity. An evaluation of these effects was conducted in 2009, three years after the Act entered into force.[18] In the same year Klaver and Odé provided a more general overview of the effects of various integration measures

[14] See notably Groenendijk 2004; Carrera 2009; Vermeulen 2010.

[15] Carrera 2009; Carrera and Wiesbrock 2009; Van Oers et al 2010; Groenendijk 2011. For a different view, see Vermeulen 2010.

[16] eg, Guild et al 2009b, 9–11; Van Oers et al 2010b, 326–29.

[17] See notably ACVZ 2004a; Oosterom-Staples 2004; Groenendijk 2004; Boeles and Lodder 2005; De Vries 2006; Groenendijk 2006b; Groenendijk 2011; Van Dam 2008; Human Rights Watch 2008; Carrera 2009; Carrera and Wiesbrock 2009; Lodder 2009 and Vermeulen 2010.

[18] Brink et al 2009.

adopted in the Netherlands.[19] This book includes the outcomes of both studies.

II. INTEGRATION REQUIREMENTS AND LEGAL RULES ON THE ADMISSION OF ALIENS

A. Scope of the Investigation

As mentioned above, the primary purpose of this book is to describe and analyse the legal standards applying to the Act on Integration Abroad and to determine whether the Act is in compliance with these standards. To this end this study examines legal instruments that are of relevance to immigration law and the admission of aliens. Limitations to the power of states to control immigration can be found in human rights treaties, as well as in the law of the European Union. Also relevant are bi- and multilateral treaties containing agreements between states on the admission of each other's nationals. As far as international instruments are concerned, the investigation is limited to treaties to which the Netherlands is a party. Finally, restrictions to the Dutch legislator's power to regulate immigration can be found in the human rights provisions of the Dutch Constitution.

The question of whether the admission of aliens to the Netherlands may be conditioned upon fulfilment of integration requirements is preceded by the question of whether any right to admission exists at all. Such a right is expressly laid down in several legal instruments, in particular in the field of EU law (see, for example, Art 21 TFEU). In many other situations, however, the existence of a right of admission is not self-evident. This is the case, for instance, with regard to most of the human rights provisions discussed in this study, as well as in the Association Agreement concluded between the EU (then EEC) and Turkey. To give an example from the human rights arena, it is not immediately evident whether Article 8 of the European Convention on Human Rights (ECHR), which protects the right to respect for family life, also includes a right of admission for aliens in situations where the members of one family do not share the same nationality. A relatively large part of the examination in the second part of this book consequently focuses on determining the scope of the provisions under investigation. Only when it has been established that a right to admission exists is it necessary to determine whether this right may be restricted and, if so, whether an integration exam in the country of origin constitutes a lawful restriction.

[19] Klaver and Odé 2009.

B. Sources of Immigration Rules

As stated above, legal rules regarding the admission of aliens can be found in different instruments of national and international law. The sources of immigration rules addressed in this study are listed below, together with some general remarks on their interpretation and legal effect. A distinction is made between instruments of international law, EU law and Dutch constitutional law.

i. International Law

a. Instruments

For the purpose of this study, the main sources of immigration rules in international law are the human rights treaties concluded at the level of the United Nations (UN) and the Council of Europe (CoE). These include the ECHR and the (revised) European Social Charter (ESC), the International Covenant on Civil and Political Rights (ICCPR), the Convention on the Elimination of All Forms of Racial Discrimination (CERD) and the Convention on the Rights of the Child (CRC). None of these treaties are directly concerned with the admission of aliens. Nevertheless, some provisions can be (or have been) interpreted to include admission rights. Furthermore, the equality norms laid down in some of the above treaties, including the CERD, are also applicable in the field of immigration. In addition to the above instruments, some relevant legal standards can be found in treaties that are more specifically concerned with the regulation of international migration. These include the European Convention relating to the Legal Status of Migrant Workers (ECMW) and various bilateral treaties concluded between the Netherlands and other states.

b. Legal Effect

Self-executing provisions (*een ieder verbindende bepalingen*) of international law have direct effect in the legal order of the Netherlands and take precedence over national law.[20] This means that such provisions may be relied upon by individuals before Dutch courts and administrative bodies and can provide grounds for invalidating Dutch immigration legislation and any decisions based upon it. Whether an international provision is self-executing is ultimately determined by the court before which it is invoked. The criterion that has traditionally been applied in this respect is whether the provision is formulated sufficiently specifically to allow it to be

[20] Arts 93 and 94 of the Dutch Constitution.

applied without prior intervention by the legislator.[21] To date, the Dutch courts have labelled most of the relevant provisions in the above treaties (including the provisions in the ECHR and ICCPR) as self-executing. Where, however, this is not the case, the existence of direct effect has been assessed separately.

c. Interpretation

The meaning of the above treaty provisions has been determined in accordance with the interpretation rules laid down in Articles 31 to 33 of the Vienna Convention on the Law of Treaties (VCLT).[22] In itself this Convention applies only to treaties concluded after it entered into force for the states concerned.[23] However, its rules on treaty interpretation are generally regarded as corresponding to rules of customary international law.[24] The same rules may therefore be applied to treaties concluded before the VCLT entered into force.

Where available, decisions and comments by treaty-monitoring bodies have been taken into account to aid the process of interpretation. In this regard the case law of the European Court of Human Rights (ECtHR) has been especially significant.[25] Final judgments by the ECtHR are legally binding on the State Parties involved in the particular case.[26] In addition, it has been assumed for the purpose of this study that all State Parties to the ECHR are legally bound by the Court's interpretations of the Convention's provisions. This seems reasonably to follow from the fact that the Court is ultimately authorised to decide whether the Convention has been correctly interpreted and applied.[27] To take an example from chapter 4 of this study, the ECtHR has repeatedly held that Article 8 ECHR (on the right to respect for family life) may give rise to an obligation to admit aliens for the purpose of family reunification. Given this case law, it would appear rather pointless (from a legal perspective) for a State Party not involved in these proceedings to maintain that it is not bound by such an obligation until such time as the Court decides otherwise. In this

[21] Dutch Supreme Court 3 May 1986, case no 12698, LJN: AC9402 (*Spoorwegstaking*), para 3.2; Dutch Supreme Court 14 April 1989, case no 13822, LJN: AD5725 (*Harmonisatiewet*), para 5.3.

[22] UNTS Vol 1155, 331, *Treaty Series (Traktatenblad)* 1972, 51 and following, entry into force for the Netherlands on 9 May 1985.

[23] Art 4 VCLT.

[24] Dixon and McCorquodale 2003, 64. See also Battjes 2006, 14–15 with references to relevant case law.

[25] Before 1998 the admissibility of complaints about violations of the ECHR was decided by the European Commission of Human Rights (EComHR), see Harris et al 2009, 5. In this study some references are made to EComHR decisions.

[26] Art 46(1) ECHR.

[27] cp Battjes 2006, 23–24 and Gerards 2010, 231–33. Battjes claims that the binding effect of the interpretations provided by the ECtHR is supported by state practice (23).

connection it is also relevant to note that the ECtHR considers itself bound to follow its own case law unless there are 'cogent reasons' to the contrary.[28] This being said, it is often not easy to determine the extent to which previous interpretations by the Court are also relevant with regard to new and different situations. This requires careful consideration of the judgments and the arguments and formulations employed, which is precisely what this study sets out to do.[29] Inevitably, the interpretations provided will be subject to discussion. However, whatever the content of these interpretations, it follows from the above that failure by the State Parties to the ECHR to respect the provisions of the Convention will be considered a failure to comply with a legally binding obligation.

Other interpretations by treaty-monitoring bodies that have been used to clarify the provisions discussed in this study include the general comments and recommendations, communications and concluding observations issued by the Human Rights Committee (for the ICCPR), the Committee on the Elimination of Racial Discrimination (for the CERD) and the Committee on the Rights of the Child (for the CRC).[30] None of the aforementioned treaties provides for these statements to be legally binding, and so state actions cannot be considered violations of these treaties solely on the grounds that they are not in accordance with the interpretations of the monitoring bodies. Nevertheless, the specific function and expertise of these bodies endow them with a guiding role in establishing the meaning of the various treaty provisions. For this reason it may be assumed that any divergence from the interpretations proposed by the treaty-monitoring bodies needs to be explicitly substantiated.[31]

ii. *European Union Law*

a. Instruments

At the time of writing, European Union (EU) law has become one – if not the most – important source of rights for immigrants to the Netherlands (and to other EU Member States). Since the Lisbon Treaty entered into force on 1 December 2009, the core of EU law has been formed by the Treaty on European Union (TEU) and the Treaty on the Functioning of the European Union (TFEU).[32] The latter contains provisions concerning both the free movement of EU citizens and third-country nationals within the

[28] Battjes 2006, 23; Harris et al 2009, 17–18.

[29] As Harris et al put it: 'Any statement by way of interpretation of the Convention by the Court, and formerly the Commission, is significant, although inevitably the level of generality at which it is expressed or its centrality to the decision on the material facts of the case will affect the weight and influence of any pronouncement'. Harris et al 2009, 17.

[30] The competence of these treaty-monitoring bodies is laid down in Art 40(4) ICCPR, Art 5(4) Optional Protocol to the ICCPR, Arts 9(2) and 14(7)(b) CERD and Art 45(d) CRC.

[31] cp Battjes 2006, 22.

[32] [2010] OJEU C 83.

EU and the immigration of third-country nationals from outside the Union.[33] In addition to these treaty provisions, various instruments of secondary EU law have been adopted in these areas.[34] For the purpose of this study, the main instruments of secondary law discussed are the Family Reunification Directive, the Long-term Residents Directive, the Residence Directive and the Blue Card Directive.[35]

For some categories of immigrants, entitlement to admission and residence stems from international agreements concluded between the EU (sometimes together with the Member States) and third countries. This study considers those agreements that most closely reflect the provisions of the TFEU concerning the free movement of persons. These include, first of all, the Agreement on the European Economic Area and the EC-Switzerland Agreement on the free movement of persons. Account is also taken of the provisions of the Association Agreement between the EEC and Turkey (including its Additional Protocol and the decisions adopted on the basis of the Agreement) and the Stabilisation and Association Agreements concluded with several Western Balkan countries (Macedonia, Croatia, Albania and Montenegro).

When investigating EU law as a source of rules concerning integration requirements and the admission of aliens, account must also be taken of the EU Charter of Fundamental Rights (CFR) and the general principles of EU law. The CFR gained legally binding force in 2009 with the entry into force of the Lisbon Treaty.[36] Its scope of application is limited to the sphere of EU law: the CFR is directed towards the EU institutions as well as to the Member States when they are implementing EU law.[37] Article 6(1) TEU explicitly states that 'the provisions of the Charter shall not extend in any way the competences of the Union as defined in the Treaties'.[38] It can be inferred from this clause that individuals cannot, for example, rely on the freedom of assembly as protected by the Charter of Fundamental Rights

[33] The term 'third-country nationals' is used here to indicate persons with a nationality of a state that is not a Member State of the European Union.

[34] Under Art 79(4) TFEU, the EU also has competence to enact measures to provide incentives and support for the action of Member States with a view to promoting the integration of third-country nationals residing legally in their territories. However this provision has not served as a legal basis for any instruments of secondary law examined as part of this study.

[35] Council Directive 2003/86/EC of 22 September 2003 on the right to family reunification, [2003] OJ L251/12; Council Directive 2003/109/EC of 25 November 2003, [2004] OJ L16/44, as amended by Directive 2011/51/EU of the European Parliament and the Council of 11 May 2011, [2011] OJ L132/1; Directive 2004/38/EC of the European Parliament and of the Council of 29 April 2004 on the right of citizens of the Union and their family members to move and reside freely within the territory of the Member States, [2004] OJ L158/77 and Council Directive 2009/50/EC of 25 May 2009 on the conditions of entry and residence of third-country nationals for the purposes of highly qualified employment, [2009] OJ L155/17.

[36] Art 6(1) TEU.

[37] Art 51(1) CFR.

[38] See also Art 51(2) CFR, which states that 'The Charter does not extend the field of application of Union law beyond the powers of the Union or establish any new power or task for the Union, or modify powers and tasks as defined in the treaties'.

to invoke a right to admission where such a right does not already have a legal basis elsewhere in EU law. Where, however, the Union does have competence to act, it will have to do so in accordance with the Charter. In addition, the EU institutions and the Member States, when acting within the scope of application of EU law, must respect the general principles of EU law established in the case law of the Court of Justice of the European Union (CoJ).[39] These general principles include the fundamental rights, as guaranteed by the ECHR and as resulting from the constitutional traditions common to the Member States.[40] At the time of writing, it is still unclear as to whether the fundamental rights as general principles of EU law will remain of significance in addition to the guarantees laid down in the CFR.[41] At present, however, it seems plausible that the CoJ case law with regard to these rights will serve as a point of departure for interpreting the corresponding CFR provisions.

Lastly, the general principles of EU law also include several principles regarding good governance or administrative legality. The principle of most relevance to this study is the principle of proportionality. At a general level, the requirement of proportionality requires measures adopted by the EU institutions, or by the Member States when acting within the scope of EU law, to be suitable and necessary to achieve the objective pursued and not to impose an excessive burden on the individual concerned. The contents of the principle vary, however, depending on the nature of the case and the interests involved.[42] It must also be observed that, like the rights laid down in the CFR, the general principles of EU law do not constitute an independent source of rights for individuals, including aliens seeking admission. Instead they are viewed in this study as interpretative guidelines for establishing the meaning of the above provisions of primary and secondary EU law and EU agreements with third countries.

b. Legal Effect

Regarding the legal effect of the above instruments, the CoJ has long since held that EU law constitutes an autonomous legal order that applies in the

[39] The question of when exactly a member state is 'acting within the scope of application of EU law' is still subject to discussion. Part of this discussion concerns the relationship of this criterion to the seemingly narrower criterion used in Art 51(1) CFR ('the member states when implementing EU law'). For an overview, see Toner 2004, 125–27; Craig and De Búrca 2008, 395–402 and Chalmers et al 2010, 252–56.

[40] Art 6(3) TEU.

[41] According to its preamble, the CFR 'reaffirms' both the rights that result from the constitutional traditions of the Member States and those laid down in the ECHR, as well as the case law of the ECtHR. Moreover, where overlap exists between the rights protected by the Charter and those laid down in the ECHR or resulting from the constitutional traditions of the Member States, the Charter itself stipulates that it is not to be interpreted in a more restrictive way (Art 52 CFR).

[42] Craig and De Búrca 2008, 544–51; Chalmers et al 2010, 367–72.

Member States of its own accord (regardless of the constitutional arrangements of those states) and takes precedence over national law.[43] This stance is accepted by the Supreme Court (*Hoge Raad*) of the Netherlands.[44] Provisions of EU law have direct effect, providing they are sufficiently clear, precise and unconditional, in which case individuals may rely on them before the national courts of the Member States to challenge national measures concerning integration requirements. As far as directives are concerned, the possibility of direct effect occurs when the time limit for their implementation has expired and no adequate implementation has taken place.[45]

With regard to the above international agreements between the EU and third countries, the CoJ has held that they belong to the EU legal order.[46] Consequently these agreements also form part of the domestic legal orders of the Member States in the same way as other EU law and take precedence over national law. The agreements examined in this study can moreover be considered as agreements creating 'special relations of integration' with the EU.[47] According to the CoJ, the provisions of such agreements can be directly effective, providing they meet the above criterion of being sufficiently clear, precise and unconditional.[48]

c. Interpretation

While the national courts of the EU Member States are competent and even obliged to apply EU law, the responsibility for interpreting EU law ultimately lies with the Court of Justice of the European Union.[49] The Court itself has held that, at least in the context of preliminary rulings, its judgments establish the meaning of EU legal instruments from the moment of their entry into force. These interpretations must therefore be followed by the national authorities of the Member States, to the extent that these authorities are bound by the legal instruments concerned.[50]

As regards the means of interpretation, the CoJ has determined that the EU does not constitute a regular treaty-based organisation, but instead a

[43] CoJ 15 July 1964, C-6/64 [1964] ECR 585 (*Costa/ENEL*), 593–94.

[44] Dutch Supreme Court 2 November 2004, case no 00156/04E, LJN: AR1797, para 3.6.

[45] Craig and De Búrca 2008, 268–303.

[46] CoJ 30 April 1974, C-181/73 [1974] ECR 449 (*Haegeman*), para 5.

[47] CoJ 23 November 1999, C-149/96 [1999] ECR I-8395 (*Portugal v Council*), para 42.

[48] Craig and De Búrca 2008, 206–13.

[49] Arts 267 and 274 TFEU, cp Chalmers et al 2010, 149–50. The Court of Justice of the EU comprises the Court of Justice, the General Court (formerly the Court of First Instance) and the specialised courts (Art 19(1) TEU). Cases resulting in interpretations relevant for this study will normally be decided by the Court of Justice. Often such cases will concern preliminary rulings requested by national courts (Art 267 TFEU). Relevant interpretations of questions of EU law can also, however, be given in the context of enforcement actions brought by the Commission or other Member States (Arts 258 and 259 TFEU) or requests for judicial review (Art 263 TFEU).

[50] Craig and De Búrca 2008, 466–74; Chalmers et al 2010, 169–71.

'new legal order', characterised by a (limited) transfer of sovereignty by the Member States.[51] Consequently the CoJ does not apply the interpretation rules of Articles 31–33 VCLT (see above) when explaining EU law, except in regard to international agreements between the EU and third countries.[52] Instead the Court applies a combination of textual, contextual (or systematic), historical and teleological arguments to support its explanations of provisions of EU law.[53] In general the CoJ tends to put considerable emphasis on the purpose of the instrument or provision concerned. Nevertheless, when faced with more detailed provisions (especially in secondary legislation) it is easier for the Court also to rely on textual and contextual arguments.[54] Moreover, as commented above, instruments of EU law need to be interpreted in conformity with the Charter of Fundamental Rights and the general principles of EU law.

To determine the purpose of instruments of secondary EU law (including the directives examined in this study) regard may be had to the text of those instruments, including the considerations of the preamble, as well as to the underlying treaty provisions.[55] Contextual arguments may be drawn from a variety of sources, specifically including the preamble, references to instruments of international law or systematic interpretations in relation to other provisions (within the same directive or in other directives relating to the same subject matter).[56] Furthermore, regard may be had to the preparatory acts (*travaux préparatoires*) of instruments of EU law, where available, as a means of historical interpretation.[57] Such acts function as subsidiary means of interpretation and are mostly used to confirm interpretations reached on the basis of other arguments.[58] Their use is possible only if the content of the preparatory acts is reflected in the actual text of the instruments concerned.[59] If, however, these preparatory

[51] CoJ 5 February 1963, C-26/62 [1963] ECR 1 (*Van Gend & Loos*).

[52] Battjes 2006, 42; Dhondt and Geursen 2008, 282.

[53] Battjes 2006, 42–46; Dhondt and Geursen 2008, 282–83.

[54] Dhondt and Geursen 2008, 283. See, eg, CoJ (Grand Chamber) 25 July 2008, C-127/08 [2008] ECR I-6241 (*Metock and others*), paras 49–54 and 82–90 and CoJ 4 March 2010, C-578/08 [2010] ECR I-01839 (*Chakroun*), paras 42–48 and 59–62.

[55] It will often be possible to discern multiple objectives, some of which will be formulated at different levels of abstraction. See, eg, the case of *Metock and others*, where the CoJ referred both to the objective of 'strengthening the right of free movement and residence of all Union citizens' (as laid down in the preamble to the Residence Directive) and to the broader aim of creating an internal market (formulated in Art 3(1)(c) of the EC Treaty). In such situations, the outcome of the interpretation exercise is obviously likely to be influenced by the objective chosen as a point of reference. Where multiple objectives are available, it is arguably up to the interpreting body (or scholar) to decide which interpretation is the most persuasive, taking into account the various objectives and other means of interpretation.

[56] See, eg, *Metock and others* (n 54), paras 52–53, 69 and 83; CoJ (Grand Chamber) 23 February 2010, C-310/08 [2010] ECR I-01065 (*Ibrahim*), paras 45–46, 48 and 56–57 and CoJ 4 March 2010, C-578/08 [2010] ECR I-01839 (*Chakroun*), paras 48 and 62.

[57] For an overview of relevant documents, see Battjes 2006, 44–45.

[58] cp *Ibrahim* (n 56), para 47 and *Chakroun* (n 56), para 62.

[59] Battjes 2006, 45 and Dhondt and Geursen 2008, 282–83, both with reference to case law.

acts are to be relied on, the information derived from them must be sufficiently clear and unambiguous. The mere fact, for instance, that a Member State has either supported or objected to a particular interpretation of a term in a directive is insufficient to confirm or dismiss that interpretation if the reaction of the other Members States remains unknown.

As a final remark, it should be noted that the different language versions of EU legal instruments are equally authentic.[60] Interpretations must take these different versions into account; where disparities occur, these must be reconciled in the light of the 'purpose and general scheme' of the instrument concerned.[61] Where necessary, this study has compared the different language versions within the limits of my linguistic capabilities.

iii. The Dutch Constitution

Integration requirements in the immigration legislation of the Netherlands must also remain within the limits set by the Dutch Constitution (*Grondwet*). The relevance of this instrument for the purposes of this study is, however, rather limited. The Constitution does not contain any material norms regarding the admission of aliens, nor does it lay down a fundamental right to respect for family life (which is one of the main legal standards examined in this book). Two constitutional norms are nevertheless discussed in this study: the right to equal treatment and the prohibition of discrimination (Art 1 Constitution) and the right to freedom of religion and belief (Art 6 Constitution).

According to Article 120 of the Dutch Constitution, laws enacted by the parliament and government acting together as the national legislator (*wetten in formele zin*) are not subject to judicial review. Instead the compatibility of this legislation, which includes the AIA, with the Constitution is decided by the legislator itself. As a result, there is no extensive body of case law in which the meaning of the above constitutional provisions is explained in relation to individual situations. The fact that the legislator has adopted the AIA also implies that it has thereby interpreted the Constitution, in a legally binding manner, so as to allow for the conditions laid down in that Act. This study examines how this interpretation fits into the broader legal context of the relevant provisions. To this end, where possible, it examines how the said provisions have been interpreted in related situations. In addition consideration is given to interpretive statements by the Dutch government and to relevant case law of the Dutch courts (concerning legislation not enacted by the national legislator).

[60] Art 55(1) TEU and Art 358 TFEU.

[61] Battjes 2006, 45–46, with reference to case law.

III. STRUCTURE OF THE BOOK

The first part of this study, concerning Dutch integration policy and the Act on Integration Abroad, is made up of chapters 2 and 3. Chapter 2 contains a description of the AIA and of the effects measured to date. This same chapter includes a historical overview of integration programmes in the Netherlands, which has thus far largely not been provided.[62] Chapter 3 focuses on the objectives of Dutch integration policy (including the integration exam abroad) and the reasons why integration has been made into a requirement for admission.

The second part of the book focuses on formulating legal standards for integration requirements in immigration law and on assessing the Act on Integration Abroad in relation to these standards. Section A examines various provisions of international human rights treaties, as well as corresponding provisions of EU law and the Dutch Constitution. These provisions concern the right to family life and family reunification (chapter 4) and the right to freedom of religion (chapter 5).

Section B concerns integration requirements in relation to EU law and other international agreements. It addresses the rules of EU law on the right to free movement of EU nationals, their family members and (other) third-country nationals (chapter 6). Given their close connection to these rules, the EEA Agreement and the EC-Switzerland Agreement on the free movement of persons are discussed in the same chapter. Chapter 7 then examines a number of international agreements concluded at a European or Dutch national level and containing rules on the entry and/or residence of aliens, including the EEC-Turkey Association Agreement.

Thirdly, Section C reviews integration requirements in relation to the right to equal treatment as guaranteed in international human rights treaties, EU law and the Dutch Constitution. As well as explaining the general legal framework regarding equal treatment, chapter 8 sets out specific standards regarding direct differential treatment on the grounds of nationality and residence purpose. Chapter 9 addresses indirect differential treatment on the grounds of racial or ethnic origin. Lastly, chapter 10 examines the issue of 'reverse discrimination' that arises when nationals of one EU Member State have fewer rights than nationals of other EU Member States due to the workings of EU law. Chapter 11 concludes.

As noted above, this study sets out to evaluate the lawfulness of the Act on Integration Abroad and to formulate legal standards regarding integration requirements for the admission of aliens that are also relevant out-

[62] An exception concerns the report of the parliamentary committee of enquiry that investigated the Dutch integration policy in 2003 (*Commissie Blok*), *Parliamentary Papers II* 2003–2004, 28 689, No 9. An abridged version of this history can also be found in Odé and De Vries 2010, 15–17.

side the Dutch context. For this reason the chapters in the second part of this book mainly begin with a general assessment of the legal norms under examination and their relevance to integration requirements. The compatibility of the AIA with these norms is then addressed in a separate section.

The book manuscript was concluded on 31 August 2012. Later developments could only be taken into account in exceptional cases.

PART I

Integration and Immigration in the Netherlands

2

Dutch Integration Policy and the Act on Integration Abroad

I. INTRODUCTION

THIS CHAPTER PROVIDES a brief historical account of Dutch integration policy, as well as a description of the Act on Integration Abroad (AIA). Its aim is to serve as background information for the examination conducted in the rest of this study. Sections II to V present an outline of the main developments in Dutch integration policy since the Second World War, with special attention being paid to measures and events paving the way for the introduction of the integration exam abroad, in particular measures relating to language teaching and the reception of new immigrants.

The historical description of the integration policy is divided into different time periods, corresponding to the developments that took place. Until 1979 the only integration policy in the Netherlands was the assimilation policy for Indonesian-Dutch repatriates (section II). Subsequently, in the 1980s, an integration policy was devised for a number of immigrant groups, the so-called 'ethnic minorities' (section III). After a while various language courses and other educational programmes designed specifically for immigrants were developed. Once these programmes were in place, the idea of making them compulsory began to gain ground. This occurred against the background of a new vision, outlined in 1994, on the integration of ethnic minorities, in which citizenship became a central theme (section IV). Eventually, the policy of compulsory 'civic integration' (*inburgering*) for immigrants led to the enactment of the Newcomers Integration Act (*Wet inburgering nieuwkomers*) in 1998 and the Act on Integration Abroad (*Wet inburgering buitenland*) in 2006 (section V).

Following this description of Dutch integration policy, section VI addresses the Act on Integration Abroad, with attention being paid to the target group and the integration exam, as well as to the effects identified thus far. An analysis of the objectives of the Act and the concepts of integration and citizenship in the Dutch context is not included in this chapter, but can be found in chapter 3.

II. BEFORE 1979: AN AMBIGUOUS APPROACH TO INTEGRATION

A. Immigration to the Netherlands

In the period immediately following the Second World War, the Netherlands was primarily an emigration country. Between 1945 and 1961 many Dutch nationals left the Netherlands, actively supported by the government, to try their luck overseas in countries such as Australia, Canada and the United States. Nevertheless some immigrants also came to the Netherlands[1] as post-colonial migration brought in new residents from the former Dutch East Indies (today's Indonesia), followed by immigrants from Suriname and the Netherlands Antilles. Immigration from 'the West' initially occurred only on a small scale, but became more substantial in the 1970s (Suriname) and 1980s (Netherlands Antilles).[2]

Apart from post-colonial immigration, the Netherlands also received people coming for political or economic reasons. Refugees arrived primarily from Eastern Europe, but only in small numbers.[3] Numerically more important was the arrival of guest workers, who were recruited to compensate for shortages of Dutch labour, firstly from Spain and Italy and later from other countries including Turkey and Morocco. Such recruitment ended in 1973 because of the oil crisis, but was followed by the immigration of guest workers' family members, mostly from Turkey and Morocco, which reached its peak in 1980.[4] Lastly, there were also noticeable influxes of immigrants from other Member States of the European Economic Community (EEC), as well as from the United States, Canada and Japan.[5]

B. Integration or Return Migration?

The various immigrant groups mentioned above were subject to divergent policies with regard to their reception or integration.[6] Most of the immigrants were expected to be in the Netherlands only temporarily, and therefore a policy aimed at their integration or assimilation was not con-

[1] Here I use 'the Netherlands' to refer to the European part of the Kingdom of the Netherlands, which, after Indonesian independence, also included Dutch New Guinea (until 1962), Suriname (until 1975) and the Netherlands Antilles.

[2] On migration to and from the Netherlands after 1945, see, eg, Entzinger 1984, 71–83 and Lucassen and Penninx 1994, 10 and 39–44. On post-colonial migration, see Jones 2007, 106–16, 137–67, 198–252 and 270–99.

[3] Lucassen and Penninx 1994, 44–46.

[4] Entzinger 1984, 78–94; Lucassen and Penninx 1994, 57.

[5] Penninx 1979, 5; Lucassen and Penninx 1994, 27 and 60.

[6] Van Praag 1973; Lucassen and Penninx 1994, 140–41; WRR 2001a, 168.

sidered necessary. The main exception to this rule concerned the repatriates from the former Dutch East Indies, who were subjected to an active assimilation policy.[7]

The assimilation policy stood in stark contrast to the approach taken towards the Moluccan immigrants, who were housed in camps separated from the Dutch population. The segregation policy adopted towards them was founded on the belief, both on the part of the government and of the Moluccans themselves, that their stay would be temporary.[8] This presumption of temporariness also existed with regard to guest workers and immigrants from the Netherlands Antilles and Suriname.[9] As it was expected that these immigrants would eventually return home, the government limited its involvement to providing certain reception facilities, such as housing and social work services. Meanwhile, immigrants from the EEC and non-European industrialised countries were not subject to any policy on reception or integration.[10]

In 1970, the Dutch government still took the view that the Netherlands was not an immigration country.[11] In the years to come, however, it became more and more clear that many immigrants were in fact there to stay. This led the government to pursue a two-track policy: facilitating participation in Dutch society, while at the same time encouraging return migration.[12] The objective of this policy was to integrate immigrants, while at the same time helping them to maintain their (assumed) ethnic or cultural identity. A typical policy measure in this respect was the introduction of 'Native Language and Culture' courses (*Onderwijs in eigen taal en cultuur* or *OETC*) as part of the school curriculum for immigrant children. Such measures were primarily perceived as a means to facilitate the immigrants' return to their countries of origin.[13] However, they could also be construed as supporting their integration into Dutch society through collective emancipation. This ambiguity blurred the direction of the government's policy on immigrant integration towards the end of the 1970s and allowed the presumption of return migration to co-exist alongside the growing awareness that most immigrants would stay.[14]

Despite the above support for immigrant groups to preserve their own identity, the reception facilities also included Dutch language lessons.[15] Such lessons were usually provided by volunteers and migrant

[7] On this policy, see Godeschalk 1990, Mak 2000 and Jones 2007, 173–77.

[8] Entzinger 1984, 76; Lucassen and Penninx 1994, 141; Jones 2007, 116–22.

[9] Entzinger 1984, 78–79 and 85–86; Lucassen and Penninx 1994, 140; WRR 2001a, 168.

[10] Penninx 1979, 6.

[11] Nota Buitenlandse Werknemers, *Parliamentary Papers II* 1969–1970, 10 504, Nos 1–2, 9.

[12] Entzinger 1984, 87–92; Struijs 1998, 11.

[13] Lucassen and Penninx 1994, 140.

[14] Penninx 1979, 148–52; Entzinger 1984, 88.

[15] *Parliamentary Papers II* 2003–2004, 28 689, Nos 8–9 (*Rapport Commissie Blok*), 110–12; WRR 2001b, 46.

organisations such as the Interdenominational Contact Committee for Moluccans (*Interkerkelijk Contact Comité Ambon-Nederland*) or the Dutch Refugee Council (*VluchtelingenWerk Nederland*), whereas language courses for guest workers were also provided by their employers. Subsidies for the courses could be obtained from the Department of Social Work.

III. AN INTEGRATION POLICY FOR ETHNIC MINORITIES (1979–1989)

A. Developments in the Fields of Immigration and Integration

In 1979, the Dutch government abandoned the assumption that the presence of many immigrants in the Netherlands was merely temporary and decided to adopt a policy which, though still mindful of the cultural identities of immigrants, was univocally geared towards integration and no longer towards return.[16] This policy became known as the Ethnic Minorities policy (*Etnische Minderhedenbeleid*) and was coordinated by the Home Affairs Minister.[17] The policy comprised a number of measures and programmes designed to ensure equal access to different segments of Dutch society, including health care, housing, education and the labour market.[18]

The Ethnic Minorities policy replaced the group-specific reception and assimilation policies described earlier. It was directed towards a number of ethnic and/or immigrant communities in the Netherlands that were considered to experience comparable social problems, such as discrimination, high unemployment and a weak legal position.[19] These communities were henceforth referred to as 'ethnic minorities'. The largest groups affected by the policy were guest workers and their families (over 200,000 people), Surinamese (around 130,000 people), Antilleans (some 25,000 people) and Moluccans (around 32,000 people). Also included were several smaller groups, including refugees, caravan dwellers and gypsies, who were considered to experience problems similar to those of the larger groups.[20] Despite various discussions, Chinese immigrants were never included in the Ethnic Minorities policy.[21] The policy also did not apply to

[16] *Parliamentary Papers II* 1980–1981, 16 102, No 6, 4–7. These changes were prompted by a report prepared by the Scientific Council for Government Policy (*WRR*) on the basis of a preparatory study conducted by Penninx (WRR 1979).

[17] After an elaborate draft published in 1981 by the Department of Home Affairs (*Ontwerp-minderhedennota*), the Ethnic Minorities policy was eventually outlined in *Parliamentary Papers II* 1982–1983, 16 102, No 21 (*Minderhedennota*).

[18] For an overview of these measures and programmes, see the *Ontwerp-minderhedennota* and *Minderhedennota* (n 17). The integration objectives of the Ethnic Minorities policy are discussed in ch 3.

[19] WRR 1979, X.

[20] *Minderhedennota* (n 17), 11.

[21] See *Parliamentary Papers II* 1984–1985, 16 102, No 89, 3 and *Parliamentary Papers II* 1988–1989, 20 856, No 2, 7.

immigrants from EEC Member States and other industrialised countries. Meanwhile, again following the recommendations of the Scientific Council for Government Policy (*WRR*), the Dutch government subscribed to the need to pursue a restrictive policy on immigration.[22] While the government did not wish to limit the reunification of existing families, there was concern about the fact that ethnic minority youths were starting new families by bringing over partners from their countries of origin. It was claimed that these partners arrived at an age at which it was difficult for them to participate in education or the labour market. Their chances of becoming structurally unemployed were high and their arrival thus put pressure on the integration process of ethnic minorities already in the Netherlands and of future generations.[23] As seen in chapter 3, the same argument was used more than 20 years later to support the introduction of the Act on Integration Abroad. As yet, however, family reunification was not subjected to specific integration requirements.

B. A Patchwork of Language Courses

One concrete proposal made by the *WRR* in 1979 was to offer Dutch language courses to foreign workers and their families. The *WRR* considered the existing courses on offer to be too non-committal and not suited to the situation of the guest workers, who often worked in shifts and performed heavy labour. It was suggested to follow the example of Sweden, where foreign workers were granted paid leave in order to learn the language. Another proposal was to provide 'orientation courses' for new immigrants upon their arrival so as to 'acquaint them with the elementary characteristics of the receiving society'. Educational facilities were also deemed necessary for the wives of foreign workers who did not have jobs and, according to the *WRR*, risked becoming socially isolated.[24]

The notion that immigrants should learn Dutch and become acquainted with Dutch society was also put forward by the Dutch government, which recognised that the motivation of immigrants to learn Dutch could well have been restrained by the presumption – both on the part of the government and of the immigrants – that their stay would be temporary.[25] In the 1980s, the rejection of this presumption made way for the realisation that an insufficient command of the Dutch language could form a barrier

22 eg, *Parliamentary Papers II* 1980–1981, 16 102, No 6, 14; *Minderhedennota* (n 17), 144–50. For the *WRR*'s proposals on immigration see WRR 1979, XXXV–XXXVIII.

23 *Minderhedennota* (n 17), 148–50. The relationship between the Dutch policy on family migration and considerations relating to integration during the period in question is described in more detail in Van Walsum 2008, 169–76.

24 WRR 1979, XXXIII.

25 *Ontwerp-minderhedennota* (n 17), 22.

preventing immigrants from participating in education, the labour market and society at large.

The *WRR*'s suggestion to organise language courses was not followed, however.[26] Instead, during the first half of the 1980s, the provision of adult education to members of ethnic minority groups was mainly characterised by a lack of structure and infrastructure. The extensive array of courses existing at the time has been described as a 'patchwork' or even an 'inextricable jumble'.[27] Most of these courses included Dutch lessons (in some form) and/or some kind of social orientation. Many differences existed however, including with regard to content, objectives, duration and educational methods. Some projects also received government funding, whereas others depended on private financing. Examples of projects run in the 1980s included literacy training and educational activities targeted specifically towards ethnic minorities,[28] as well as the 'Dutch on the work floor' (*Nederlands op de werkvloer*) project, where in-company language courses were provided for foreign workers. Melkunie, for example, a large Dutch dairy company, provided language classes for its foreign employees between 1982 and 1984.[29] Yet, despite the variety, the availability of the language courses on offer was insufficient to meet the demand.[30] This problem persisted into the 1990s and became a major bottleneck in Dutch integration policy.

In 1986, the system for basic adult education became more streamlined due to the adoption of the Regulation concerning Basic Education (*Rijksregeling Basiseducatie*).[31] Under this regulation, municipalities could obtain contributions from the central government for implementing and supporting basic adult education.[32] Although the regulation was not directed specifically at ethnic minorities, they constituted an important target group. Literacy courses and educational activities for ethnic minorities were continued on the basis of this regulation. The introduction of this regulation furthered the professionalisation of this type of education: henceforth courses could only be given by or under the supervision of licensed instructors.[33]

[26] During the parliamentary debate of the government's reaction to the *WRR* report, a representative of the Reformed Political Alliance (*GPV*) asked if the government would consider imposing an obligation for immigrants to receive education in Dutch language, history and form of government. This question remained unanswered, see *Parliamentary Papers II* 1980–1981, 16 102, No 5, 6.

[27] WRR 2001b, 47 and Verhallen 1986, 203. The latter provides an extensive overview of the available courses.

[28] Van den Berg 1992, 10–18; see also *Minderhedennota* (n 17), 36.

[29] Verhallen 1986, 182–89; see also *Minderhedennota* (n 17), 60.

[30] *Minderhedennota* (n 17), 36–37; Van den Berg 1992, 16.

[31] *Bulletin of Acts and Decrees* 1986, 433; for a detailed description of this regulation and how it came about, see Van den Berg 1992, 3–8.

[32] *Parliamentary Papers II* 1986–1987, 19 705, No 2, 16; *Parliamentary Papers II* 1987–1988, 20 260, No 2, 23.

[33] Van den Berg 1992, 34.

C. Reception of Refugees and Other Protected Persons

In addition to the courses and educational facilities described above, integration courses were also offered as part of the measures for receiving refugees and other protected persons.[34] In the early 1980s the Department of Welfare developed a special programme, the 'in-house model' (*in-huis-model*), for receiving resettled refugees.[35] Under this programme refugees were hosted at a central reception centre for a maximum of three months, during which time they had to follow an introduction programme consisting of Dutch lessons and social orientation.

The aim of the programme was to help the refugees to become self-reliant. An educational programme ('*Zeg nu zelf*') was developed specifically for this purpose: topics covered included 'introducing oneself', 'the market', 'shopping', 'the post office', 'the bank', 'public transport' and 'health care'. Information was also provided on social security legislation, the educational system, cultural differences, contacts with various agencies and other topics suggested by the refugees themselves. The programme entailed 25 hours of tuition a week, over a period of six weeks. Normally refugees would leave the reception centre after this period and move into permanent, independent accommodation. However, if no such accommodation was available, the refugee would continue the introduction programme at the reception centre. A second module would then be started, covering the topics of 'living', 'the weather', 'budgeting', 'education', 'employment', 'recreation' and 'traffic'.[36]

Responsibility for receiving other refugees and protected persons was vested in the municipalities.[37] The municipal reception tasks included organising various activities, such as language and literacy courses, coaching and social orientation.[38] A financial contribution was available from the Department of Welfare, providing the municipal reception programmes included social orientation, as well as 480 hours of literacy courses (in Dutch) for illiterate participants or 400 hours of Dutch lessons for literate participants.[39] Several volunteer organisations, such as the

[34] The term 'other protected persons' is used to indicate aliens who did not qualify as refugees, but who had been granted residence permits on humanitarian grounds (*B-status*); see Art 1(2) of the Regulation concerning Welfare Facilities for Minorities *(Rijksregeling welzijn minderheden), Bulletin of Acts and Decrees* 1985, 68.

[35] Between 1981 and 1989 several thousands of refugees, including many Vietnamese 'boat people', were admitted to the Netherlands for resettlement. See Lucassen and Penninx 1994, 46–47.

[36] *Parliamentary Papers II* 1983–1984, 18 100 XVI, No 150, 3–7; *Parliamentary Papers II* 1985–1986, 19 637, No 2, 31–32.

[37] *Parliamentary Papers II* 1983–1984, 18 100 XVI, No 150, 8; *Parliamentary Papers II* 1985–1986, 19 637, No 2, 34.

[38] *Parliamentary Papers II* 1985–1986, 19 637, No 2, 35.

[39] This was stipulated in Art 12(4) of the Regulation concerning Welfare Facilities for Minorities. Before this regulation entered into force, contributions were granted on the basis

Association of Vietnamese Refugees in the Netherlands (*Associatie van Vietnamese Vluchtelingen in Nederland*) and the Dutch Refugee Council (*VluchtelingenWerk Nederland*), were involved in implementing the reception programmes, both in the centres and in the municipalities.[40]

Lastly, integration courses were not made available to asylum seekers. The number of asylum applications in the Netherlands rose sharply throughout the 1980s, from 832 in 1981 to 13,898 in 1989. Asylum seekers came from many different countries around the world, including Suriname, Pakistan, Turkey, Ghana, Somalia, Romania and Sri Lanka.[41] Their exclusion from the reception programmes was motivated by the argument that participation in integration activities would create false expectations concerning their chances of being allowed to stay in the Netherlands and thus interfere with the immigration policy.[42]

IV. PREPARING THE GROUND FOR A COMPULSORY INTEGRATION POLICY (1989–1998)

A. Developments in the Fields of Immigration and Integration

In 1989 the *WRR* reported that the Netherlands had 623,537 foreign nationals, of whom 160,448 were from other Member States of the European Community (EC). The largest group of aliens consisted of Turkish nationals (177,297), followed by Moroccans (139,749). The report also mentioned the presence of 210,000 Surinamese (including 194,189 with Dutch nationality), 66,000 persons from the Netherlands Antilles and Aruba and 40,000 Moluccans.[43] Ten years after the introduction of the Ethnic Minorities policy, the *WRR* observed not only that those who had arrived in the 1960s and 1970s were still there, but also that the immigrant population would continue to grow in the future, despite a restrictive admission policy.[44]

Despite the efforts made in the 1980s, the social position of many members of ethnic minority groups was still found to be far from satisfactory. In 1993, the Social and Cultural Planning Office (*Sociaal en Cultureel Planbureau, SCP*) issued a report on the position of the four main minority groups in the Netherlands (Turks, Moroccans, Surinamese and Antilleans)

of the Regulation concerning Facilities for Refugees (*Faciliteitenregeling vluchtelingen*), *Government Gazette* 1983, 99.

[40] *Parliamentary Papers II* 1983–1984, 18 100 XVI, No 150, 15–16; *Parliamentary Papers II* 1985–1986, 19 637, No 2, 36.

[41] Lucassen and Penninx 1994, 46–48; Puts 1995 (34) mentions somewhat different (mostly higher) numbers.

[42] *Parliamentary Papers II* 1985–1986, 19 637, No 2, 43; see also Puts 1995, 37.

[43] WRR 1989, 67; all figures are as at 1 January 1989.

[44] ibid, 19–20.

in the fields of employment, education and housing.[45] This report concluded that disadvantages continued to exist among minority groups in each of the investigated areas. Although there were some positive developments, these were often blurred by the persistent influx of new immigrants. While the number of family migrants was slightly declining, the number of asylum seekers had increased. With regard to labour market participation, minorities' disadvantaged position was reinforced by the disappearance of the low-skilled jobs they had traditionally occupied.[46]

B. A New Integration Policy

In view of the above developments, the need for an effective approach to immigrant integration was felt to remain high. For several years after publication of the 1989 *WRR* report, the integration policy was subject to debate both in and outside parliament.[47] In retrospect, the years 1989 to 1994 can be seen as a transitional period, during which the government moved away from the Ethnic Minorities policy of the 1980s towards the so-called 'Integration policy',[48] the outlines of which were formulated in 1994.[49] Compared to the Ethnic Minorities policy, the new approach put a stronger emphasis on achieving active participation in society and individual self-reliance (see section III.A. of chapter 3). Henceforth the principal focus was on achieving socio-economic integration, with enhanced efforts being made primarily in the fields of (adult) education and employment.[50] Meanwhile policy measures actively supporting cultural expressions of ethnic minorities were no longer foreseen. This change in focus was based on the presumption that successful socio-economic integration would allow ethnic minority groups to express their cultural identities on an equal basis with the majority population.[51]

It is against the background of the principles formulated in the 1994 policy paper that compulsory language and social orientation courses were eventually advocated and implemented. During the same period the groundwork for these measures in terms of infrastructure was also laid.

[45] SCP 1993.

[46] ibid, 241–67.

[47] For the parliamentary discussion see, eg, *Proceedings II* 1993, UCV 19.

[48] Van Walsum 2000, 113–14.

[49] *Parliamentary Papers II* 1993–1994, 23 684, No 2 (*Contourennota Integratiebeleid etnische minderheden*).

[50] *Parliamentary Papers II* 1989–1990, 21 472, No 2, 14–29. See also the policy paper 'Investing in integration' (*Investeren in integreren*), published by the Department of Welfare in 1994. In addition to supporting integration through work and education this paper also stressed the need to intervene, in the very first phase of the integration process, and address young immigrants or those who had only just arrived in the Netherlands (1–7).

[51] *Parliamentary Papers II* 1989–1990, 21 472, No 2, 33–34. This approach had been advocated by the *WRR*, see WRR 1989, 13, 23–24 and 49–50.

Important developments included the institutionalisation and professionalisation of opportunities for adult education, specifically in Dutch as a second language, and the creation of a reception structure for newly arrived immigrants. The experience gained during this period was used to shape the policy on 'civic integration' (*inburgering*) that was implemented in 1996 and eventually led in 1998 to the adoption of the Newcomers Integration Act (*Wet inburgering nieuwkomers*) in 1998. These developments are described in more detail in sections IV.C and IV.D below.

With regard to the target group of the integration policy, the WRR had recommended adopting a policy addressing not only designated ethnic minorities, but all 'foreign born persons' (*allochtonen*).[52] The Dutch government chose not to follow this suggestion. Instead the policy continued to be directed towards specific ethnic minority groups 'for the admission of which the Dutch government bore a particular responsibility, or who were tied to the Netherlands by our colonial past'. Nationals of other EC Member States, however, were no longer targeted by the integration policy because they were not in a disadvantaged position.[53] In other words, guest workers from Italy, Greece, Portugal and Spain were no longer deemed to be in need of special consideration.

Lastly, it was decided to maintain a restrictive policy on immigration, particularly with regard to labour migrants.[54] In respect of family reunification the *WRR* had stated that additional limitations on this form of migration could substantially lower the number of immigrants to the Netherlands. However, introduction of such restrictions was opposed on the grounds that this would negatively affect the integration process (see also section II.A of chapter 3). For the same reason it was also considered undesirable to impose admission criteria relating to new immigrants' ability to integrate. Instead, unskilled spouses or children who were not ready to participate in the Dutch labour market would have to be allowed to benefit from reception facilities in the Netherlands.[55]

C. Learning Dutch as a Second Language: Towards Compulsory Education for Adult Immigrants

The *WRR* specified proficiency in Dutch as an absolute condition for successful integration of immigrants. Lack of language proficiency was considered a problem, especially among first-generation Turkish and

[52] By this term, the *WRR* meant all immigrants, as well as their offspring (up to the third generation, as long as they defined themselves as 'foreign born'). See WRR 1989, 10, 24–25.

[53] *Parliamentary Papers II* 1989–1990, 21 472, No 2, 8–9.

[54] ibid, 9–10.

[55] WRR 1989, 89.

Moroccan immigrants and youths who had not been born in the Netherlands.[56] In order to address this problem it was specifically proposed entitling all adult members of ethnic minority groups to free basic education, in particular Dutch lessons and an introductory course on Dutch society. For some immigrants, it was added, this entitlement should be complemented by an obligation to obtain a basic level of education (*basiseducatieplicht*). Such an obligation was primarily to be targeted towards immigrants with little education and receiving social security benefits.[57]

The Dutch government recognised that education and language training in particular were important for improving the position of ethnic minorities, also on the labour market.[58] Meanwhile members of ethnic minority groups continued to participate increasingly in both basic and secondary adult education.[59] Throughout the 1990s various efforts were made to increase the adult education on offer and to eliminate the waiting lists for Dutch language courses.[60] Additional financial means were provided to municipalities for this purpose, on the condition that they created a differentiated range of language courses to suit participants' varying needs. It was also suggested introducing contracts in which participants would undertake to take part in the courses, while the municipalities would guarantee their availability.[61]

Meanwhile, the realisation occurred that teaching Dutch as a second language (*Nederlands als tweede taal* or *NT2*) required specific expertise and that the existing infrastructure needed to be improved. A project group was set up in 1989 for this purpose, teachers were trained and new

[56] ibid, 22 and 115.

[57] ibid, 43–45.

[58] *Parliamentary Papers II* 1989–1990, 21 472, No 2, 3 and 19–20.

[59] *Parliamentary Papers II* 1989–1990, 21 301, No 2, 16; *Parliamentary Papers II* 1990–1991, 21 971, No 2, 9–10. At the time the activities in the field of adult education could be divided into four categories: basic education (*basiseducatie*), secondary education at evening schools (*Voortgezet Avondonderwijs voor volwassenen, VAVO*), vocational education (*scholing*) and socio-cultural education (*vormings- en ontwikkelingswerk*), see WRR 1989, 166–72. Basic education was primarily meant for adults who had had a maximum of two years of secondary education; those who had already had education above the basic level were expected to enrol in secondary education institutions, where they could obtain a diploma (*MAVO, HAVO, VWO*), see *Parliamentary Papers II* 1992–1993, 22 809, No 9, 7–8.

[60] *Parliamentary Papers II* 1989–1990, 21 472, No 2, 20; *Parliamentary Papers II* 1995–1996, 24 401, No 2, 40 and especially *Parliamentary Papers II* 1991–1992, 22 656, No 1 (*Notitie 'Weg met de wachtlijsten'*). The issue of waiting lists became an important topic of debate in parliament, specifically in respect of the availability of courses for immigrants who had been in the Netherlands for longer periods of time. These immigrants did not fall under the reception policy discussed in section IV.D and risked being 'pushed off the waiting lists' by the newcomers. See, eg, *Parliamentary Papers II* 1994–1995, 23 901, No 20, 4–5 and 7; *Parliamentary Papers II* 1996–1997, 25 001, No 11, 32–33 and *Proceedings II* 1997, No 14, 978–79 and 983–84. An evaluation in 1997 showed that this effect did indeed occur in some municipalities, but others managed to reduce waiting lists by using funds left over from the reception policy to fund the cost of educating resident immigrants (Brink et al 1997, 120–21).

[61] *Notitie 'Weg met de wachtlijsten'* (n 60), 10–13.

educational methods developed.[62] Another important advancement was the creation of *NT2* certificates, which non-native speakers could use to prove that they had reached a certain level of proficiency in Dutch.[63]

The first *NT2* certificates were issued in July 1992.[64] As of 1 January 1996 *NT2* courses were provided by so-called 'Regional Education Centres' (*Regionale Opleidingen Centra*) under the Act on Adult and Vocational Education (*Wet educatie en beroepsonderwijs*).[65]

Despite these efforts, the Dutch government rejected the *WRR*'s proposal to make basic education obligatory for certain groups of immigrants. It argued that no obligation could be imposed as long as the availability of language courses was insufficient to meet the demand.[66] The then Home Affairs Minister, Ien Dales, also believed that most members of ethnic minority groups were eager to learn Dutch and that it was unnecessary to create an obligation.[67] Finally, the government declared that the existing legislation provided enough sanctions for those refusing to participate in the labour market or in activation programmes and that directing such coercion towards one specific section of the population (ethnic minorities, *KV*) would be unacceptable.[68]

Notwithstanding these arguments the idea of obligatory Dutch language education for adult immigrants steadily gained support. It became commonly accepted among the various factions in the Dutch Parliament that members of ethnic minorities had a personal responsibility to obtain the necessary skills and qualifications to participate in Dutch society.[69] The primary target group in this respect was that identified earlier by the *WRR*: unemployed people in receipt of social security benefits and lacking basic education.[70] For the time being, however, the government declined to introduce new measures on the grounds that the proposed obligations could already be imposed under existing social security legislation.[71]

[62] *Parliamentary Papers II* 1989–1990, 21 472, No 2, 16; *Parliamentary Papers II* 1990–1991, 21 971, No 2, 12 and *Parliamentary Papers II* 1991–1992, 22 314, No 2, 17.

[63] *Parliamentary Papers II* 1991–1992, 22 314, No 2, 17 and No 4, 7.

[64] *Parliamentary Papers II* 1992–1993, 22 809, No 3, 19.

[65] *Bulletin of Acts and Decrees* 1995, 501.

[66] *Proceedings II* 1990, UCV 48, 45–46 and 69.

[67] *Proceedings II* 1991, UCV 13, 28.

[68] *Parliamentary Papers II* 1992–1993, 22 809, No 3, 9; see also *Parliamentary Papers II* 1989–1990, 21 472 and 20 941, No 5, 23 and *Parliamentary Papers II* 1993–1994, 23 409, No 2, 18.

[69] See, eg, *Parliamentary Papers II* 1992–1993, 22 809, No 3, 9; *Proceedings II* 1990, UCV 48, 18–19, 24, 27 and 57 and *Proceedings II* 1991, UCV 38, 8–9, 11, 26 and 30.

[70] *Proceedings II* 1990, UCV 48, 27. It was added that, if necessary, the obligation would also extend to persons belonging to the Dutch majority.

[71] *Proceedings* 1990, UCV 48, 67 and *Proceedings II* 1992, UCV 11, 29. See also *Parliamentary Papers II* 1992–1993, 22 800 VIII and 22 656, No 26, 11.

D. Reception and Integration of Newly Arrived Immigrants

In the late 1980s, several proposals were made to set up a reception programme for newly arrived immigrants (other than refugees or other protected persons).[72] These proposals were inspired by concerns about the integration of those expected to come to the Netherlands in the coming years for family reunification purposes, especially from Turkey and Morocco. It was suggested setting up an introductory programme for immigrants, including a Dutch language course. The *WRR* again proposed making the programme obligatory for those who had become dependent on the state in any way and who had not received the equivalent of Dutch basic education. Such an obligation was felt to be justified by the fact that many immigrants had not received the 12 years of compulsory education that they would have received in the Netherlands and had arrived without the necessary skills and knowledge to find employment. For immigrants who were not dependent on the state, the *WRR* suggested making introduction programmes available on a voluntary basis.[73]

i. Building up Experience: Reception Programmes between 1990 and 1995

The reception of new immigrants subsequently became a task of the Department of Welfare, together with the Dutch municipalities. It was decided that new immigrants should be contacted as soon as possible after their arrival so that their needs could be assessed and they could be directed towards relevant service providers in the fields of education, employment or welfare. Additionally, newcomers would be offered courses, including Dutch as a second language and an introduction to Dutch society.[74] Two experimental reception projects were started in 1990 in the municipalities of Tilburg and The Hague.[75] Over the subsequent years the number of projects increased substantially.[76] As, however, the reception projects drew on existing facilities in the field of adult education, they were equally affected by the problem of waiting lists (see

[72] *Parliamentary Papers II* 1988–1989, 20 941, No 2, 14–15; WRR 1989, 44–47.

[73] WRR 1989, 44–47.

[74] *Parliamentary Papers II* 1989–1990, 21 472, No 2, 12–13.

[75] *Parliamentary Papers II* 1989–1990, 21 301, No 2, 24. See also *Parliamentary Papers II* 1989–1990, 21 301, No 8, 23, *Parliamentary Papers II* 1990–1991, 21 971, No 15, 2–3 and *Parliamentary Papers II* 1991–1992, 22 456, No 1, 27.

[76] By 1994, 235 of the 289 municipalities were offering reception programmes to newcomers. However the largest cities, which received most of the new immigrants, showed quite diverse pictures: in Rotterdam 75% of newcomers were offered a programme, versus 25% in The Hague (*Parliamentary Papers II* 1994–1995, 23 901, No 2, 10 and 79–81). Throughout the first half of the 1990s, the Welfare Minister was hard-pressed to expand the number of reception programmes and to make them available on a structural basis. See *Proceedings II* 1991, UCVs 13, 38 and 55; *Proceedings II* 1992, UCV 11 and *Proceedings II* 1993, UCV 19.

section IV.B).[77] The success of the reception policy depended partly, therefore, on the efforts made to reduce these lists.

As mentioned above, one of the main functions of the reception programmes was to redirect newly arrived immigrants to other service providers in the fields of adult education, labour market orientation and welfare.[78] After their arrival newcomers were contacted and invited for an intake interview, during which their needs and capabilities were assessed. If necessary, a personal reception plan was drawn up and individual coaching (*trajectbegeleiding*) provided. Coaches were expected to motivate newcomers, to arrange social support (through, for example, voluntary organisations) and to signal problems (in, for example, the domestic sphere) that could cause newcomers to quit the programmes.[79]

Once their reception plans had been completed, newcomers started their introduction programme with a social orientation course in their own language. This course could include an introduction into 'Western concepts and ways of thinking', as well as information on topics such as child support, social security, education, health care and the labour market. Next came a Dutch language course (*NT2*), combined with social and labour market orientation. The average duration of the introduction programmes was initially set at 400 course hours and later increased to 500 hours.[80] The level to be achieved within this time depended on newcomers' starting levels and their personal objectives. Three final levels were distinguished: educational self-reliance (for those wishing to pursue some form of additional education), professional self-reliance (for those seeking employment) and social self-reliance (for elderly newcomers or those caring for a family). Newcomers pursuing social self-reliance had to learn Dutch to at least level *CITO-2*, whereas educational or professional self-reliance required level *CITO-3* as a minimum.[81] For those opting for educational or professional self-reliance, the final phase of the reception programme involved transferring to an educational institute or to the labour market. The entire programme took an average of two years to complete,[82] although implementation of the reception projects varied considerably from one municipality to another.[83]

[77] *Parliamentary Papers II* 1990–1991, 21 971, No 15, 6.

[78] An overview of the reception model developed was presented to parliament in February 1995, as an Annex to *Parliamentary Papers II* 1994–1995, 23 901, No 10.

[79] *Parliamentary Papers II* 1992–1993, 22 809, No 9, 17.

[80] *Parliamentary Papers II* 1990–1991, 21 971, No 11, 2 and *Parliamentary Papers II* 1992–1993, 22 809, No 9, 10 and 15–16.

[81] *CITO* stands for the Central Institute for Test Development *(Centraal Instituut voor Toetsontwikkeling)*. In 1986 this institute, together with the University of Nijmegen, developed an entry test for Dutch as a second language. This test could be taken at five levels, ranging from *CITO-1* to *CITO-5*. See WRR 2001b, 68–69.

[82] *Parliamentary Papers II* 1992–1993, 22 809, No 9, 10.

[83] Brink et al 1997.

ii. The Introduction of Integration Contracts . . .

The reception policy continued being further developed and improved in the second half of the 1990s.[84] As was the case with regard to adult education (section IV.C), the question of whether participation in the reception programmes should be made obligatory for newcomers (or some groups of them) was widely discussed. Again, it was argued that no obligations should be imposed as long as the availability of language courses was insufficient to meet the demand.[85] Although it had been announced in 1996 that the length of the waiting lists had declined and that the problem was 'under control', some 11,000 people were then still waiting for a course.[86] Waiting lists thus remained a concern, and the government was continuously being pushed to make more financial resources available.[87] At the end of 1997 the battle against the waiting lists was integrated into the reception policy, which had by then become known as the policy on 'civic integration' (*inburgering*).[88]

Despite the waiting lists, the idea of making reception programmes obligatory gained widespread support.[89] In May 1994 the Home Affairs Minister commissioned an advisory report by two experts, professors Entzinger and Van der Zwan.[90] This report contained a proposal for an integration programme (*inburgeringstraject*) for new immigrants, including mandatory integration contracts. Although the government did not adopt the proposal in its entirety, integration contracts were eventually introduced on 1 January 1996. In these contracts, municipalities undertook to offer integration programmes including social orientation, Dutch as a second language, labour orientation and counselling. In return, newcomers committed themselves to participating in the integration programmes. The contracts were expected to provide more clarity, ensure an adequate range of courses on the part of the municipalities and prevent participants from dropping out halfway through the programme.[91]

[84] *Parliamentary Papers II* 1994–1995, 23 901, No 2, 81; *Parliamentary Papers II* 1995–1996, 24 401, No 2, 63–64; *Parliamentary Papers II* 1996–1997, 25 001, No 2, 22–23; *Parliamentary Papers II* 1997–1998, 25 601, No 2, 20–23.

[85] *Proceedings II* 1991, UCV 13, 15; 1993, UCV 19, 5.

[86] *Parliamentary Papers II* 1996–1997, 25 001, No 2, 56–57.

[87] *Parliamentary Papers II* 1994–1995, 23 901, No 20; *Parliamentary Papers II* 1995–1996, 24 401, No 15 and *Parliamentary Papers II* 1996–1997, 25 001, No 11, 7–8, 32–33 and 52–53.

[88] *Parliamentary Papers II* 1997–1998, 25 601, No 2, 59.

[89] *Proceedings II* 1990, UCV 48, 24; *Proceedings II* 1991, UCV 13, 15, 21 and 34 and UCV 55, 13–14; *Proceedings II* 1993, UCV 19, 25; *Parliamentary Papers II* 1993–1994, 23 409, No 6, 1–5.

[90] Van der Zwan and Entzinger 1994.

[91] *Parliamentary Papers II* 1994–1995, 23 901, No 10, 5–6. From 1 January 1996, funding for integration programmes was also available under the Welfare Regulation on Civic Integration for Newcomers (*Welzijnsregeling inburgering nieuwkomers, Government Gazette* 1995, 246) and the Education Regulation on Civic Integration for Newcomers 1996 (*Onderwijsregeling inburgering nieuwkomers 1996, Explanatory Notes* 1995, No 31a, later replaced by the *Onderwijsregeling inburgering nieuwkomers 1997, Government Gazette* 1996, 225).

The government had intended to introduce integration contracts for all newcomers at risk of ending up in a disadvantaged position. However mandatory contracts, enforced by sanctions, could not be imposed without a sufficient legal basis. At the time, such a legal basis existed only with regard to newcomers who were dependent on social assistance. Under the Social Assistance Act (*Algemene Bijstandswet*), benefit recipients could be forced to undertake labour activation activities, including participating in an integration programme. If they refused, the municipal social services could reduce or even suspend payment of their benefits. For other newcomers, however, no similar sanctions could be imposed.[92]

iii. . . . and the First Integration Act

In 1997 the reception policy – by then known as the civic integration policy – was evaluated. An important outcome of this evaluation was that the introduction of mandatory integration contracts could not be established to have positively influenced the participation of newcomers. Most municipalities did not actively enforce the contracts, on the grounds that most newcomers who dropped out of the programme had a legitimate reason for doing so, such as illness, pregnancy, moving to a different municipality or finding a job. Only 15 out of 120 'drop-outs' indicated that they were simply not interested in following the programme.[93] The evaluation also showed that the effects of the civic integration policy had thus far been limited: it was estimated that only 45 to 60 per cent of the target group finished the entire integration programme, with most participants not reaching the minimum level of language proficiency required for professional self-reliance (see section IV.D.i).[94]

The results of the evaluation did not, however, preclude the adoption of an Act providing a legal basis for making the integration programme compulsory for all newcomers, including those not covered by the Social Assistance Act. In November 1996 a legislative proposal for the Newcomers Integration Act (*Wet inburgering nieuwkomers* or '*Win*') was submitted to parliament.[95] Under this Act, integration contracts would be replaced by administrative decisions taken by municipalities.

The procedure laid down in the Act was very similar to that developed in the course of the reception policy. After their arrival newcomers were required to report to the municipal administration for an intake interview, during which it would be established whether they were at risk of ending up in a 'disadvantaged position'. This would be determined on the basis of criteria such as the newcomer's proficiency in the Dutch language and

92 *Parliamentary Papers II* 1994–1995, 23 901, No 10, 6–7 and No 16, 1–3.
93 Brink et al 1997, 38, 96–97 and 102–06.
94 Brink et al 1997, 108–10.
95 *Parliamentary Papers II* 1996–1997, 25 114, Nos 1–2.

knowledge about Dutch society and the Dutch labour market. Those considered to be in need of assistance would have to participate in an integration programme. Within a year after enrolment newcomers would be given the opportunity to take a test, which was not set at a particular level, but was meant to determine the participant's progress.

By the time the Newcomers Integration Act was discussed in parliament, there was barely any opposition to the idea that participation in the integration programmes should be obligatory and subject to sanctions.[96] The Newcomers Integration Act allowed an administrative fine to be imposed on newcomers who did not report to the municipal administration or did not participate in the integration programme.[97] The option to impose sanctions on residence rights or naturalisation was nevertheless rejected[98] as it was argued that such sanctions would be difficult to enforce and that a clear distinction had to be maintained between immigration and integration.[99] Residence-related sanctions were also considered unsuitable because they would not affect all newcomers in the same way.[100]

The Newcomers Integration Act was eventually adopted in April 1998 and entered into force on 30 September that year.[101]

iv. Target Group of the Reception and Civic Integration Policy

The reception programmes set up in the first half of the 1990s initially targeted newcomers aged 18 or older and legally staying in the Netherlands. Immigrants were designated as 'newcomers' if they had been in the Netherlands for less than one year and were expected to stay permanently.[102] A memorandum issued in late 1992 specified that the reception projects were primarily meant for people without a high level of education and unable to find their way in the Netherlands by themselves.[103] The number of newcomers considered to be in need of reception was estimated at 12,000 in 1991 and 20,000 in 1993.[104]

The majority of those addressed by the reception programmes belonged to the four main immigrant groups, originating from Turkey, Morocco,

[96] The only faction in parliament to express doubts on this point was the Green party (*GroenLinks*), *Parliamentary Papers II* 1996–1997, 25 114, No 5, 4–5.

[97] The level of the fine was specified in the Decree concerning Fines for the Civic Integration of Newcomers (*Boetebesluit inburgering nieuwkomers*), *Bulletin of Acts and Decrees* 1998, 330.

[98] *Parliamentary Papers II* 1994–1995, 23 684 and 23 901, No 3, 7.

[99] *Parliamentary Papers II* 1994–1995, 23 901, No 20, 2–3, 10.

[100] *Parliamentary Papers II* 1996–1997, 25 114, No 6, 65.

[101] *Bulletin of Acts and Decrees* 1998, 261; entry into force *Bulletin of Acts and Decrees* 1998, 533.

[102] *Parliamentary Papers II* 1992–1993, 22 809, No 7, 13.

[103] *Parliamentary Papers II* 1992–1993, 22 809, No 9, 3.

[104] *Parliamentary Papers II* 1990–1991, 21 971, No 11, 2 and *Parliamentary Papers II* 1992–1993, 22 809, No 9, 4–6.

Suriname and the Netherlands Antilles and Aruba. Although there were several thousand other newcomers from countries such as the United States, Peru, Sweden, Indonesia and Japan, most of these immigrants were not considered in need of reception. The same was true with regard to immigrants from other EU Member States.[105] How target groups were determined also varied from one municipality to another.[106]

When the Newcomers Integration Act was subsequently enacted the delineation of the target group gave rise to debate. These discussions specifically concerned the inclusion or exclusion of immigrants from the Netherlands Antilles and Aruba (who are Dutch nationals) and citizens of other EU states. In the end, the definition of 'newcomers' was made to include all aliens and Dutch nationals who had reached the age of 18 and were first-time residents of the Netherlands. An exemption applied to aliens whose residence purpose was defined as temporary (such as students and labour migrants). EU citizens were also exempted, on the grounds that the obligation to participate in an integration programme would be contrary to EU law and because most of these individuals were not in disadvantaged positions.[107] Lastly, with regard to Antilleans and Arubans, it was decided that highly educated immigrants would be exempted from the integration programme because they, too, were not at risk of marginalisation.[108] In practice, the target group consisted mostly of family migrants from outside Europe and Dutch citizens from the Antilles or Aruba.

E. Reception of Refugees and Other Protected Persons

The reception programmes developed during the first half of the 1990s did not involve refugees or other protected persons. Section III.C describes how reception programmes for refugees in the 1980s were organised through the 'in-house model'. In 1990 the Netherlands Court of Audit (*Algemene Rekenkamer*) reported that this model did not sufficiently prepare all refugees for continued education or for the labour market. Various improvements were thereupon realised: the introduction of a qualification structure (for Dutch as a second language and for social orientation),

[105] *Parliamentary Papers II* 1992–1993, 22 809, No 9, 4–6.

[106] Brink et al 1997, 65. Some municipalities only targeted immigrants from Morocco, Turkey and Suriname, whereas others excluded newcomers who had a Dutch partner or came from OECD countries.

[107] *Parliamentary Papers II* 1996–1997, 25 114, No 6, 8. Meanwhile, some members of parliament queried whether the exclusion of EU citizens was compatible with the prohibition of discrimination and encouraged the government to make integration programmes available to these citizens on a voluntary basis. This discussion served to illustrate the ambiguity of the Act, which treated the integration programme as an obligation, as well as an instrument for improving immigrants' position in society.

[108] *Parliamentary Papers II* 1996–1997, 25 114, No 9.

the development of a social orientation course and the combination of Dutch lessons with jobs so that refugees could apply their knowledge in practice.[109] Overall, the reception programme was intended to focus more on education, vocational training and employment.[110] Lastly, the reception programme developed for refugees was also made available to other protected persons (holders of a permanent residence permit; *vergunning tot verblijf* or *VTV*).[111] Since these persons were not accommodated in central reception centres (section III.C) the reception programme was to be implemented by municipalities at a local level.

Given the many similarities existing between them, the Department of Welfare encouraged municipalities to merge the reception facilities for refugees and protected persons with those for other newcomers.[112] The integration contracts introduced in 1996 could also be entered into with refugees and protected persons. Refugees and protected persons were subsequently included in the target group of the Newcomers Integration Act in 1998.

The numbers of asylum applications remained high throughout the period described in this section, with 21,208 applications in 1990 and 21,615 in 1991.[113] In 1992 a new reception system was introduced whereby asylum seekers would initially be accommodated in a central reception centre (*onderzoek- en opvangcentrum, OC*). From there, only those whose claims were likely to be accepted would be transferred to an asylum seekers' centre (*asielzoekerscentrum* or *AZC*), where education and integration activities were organised to prepare the asylum seekers to participate in Dutch society.[114] In May 1993 the government announced that Dutch lessons were given in all asylum seekers' centres, with the help of volunteer

[109] *Parliamentary Papers II* 1989–1990, 19 637, No 69, 11–13, and No 77, 16.

[110] *Parliamentary Papers II* 1989–1990, 21 301, No 2, 24; *Parliamentary Papers II* 1989–1990, 19 637, No 60, 13–14 and No 62, 9–11; *Parliamentary Papers II* 1990–1991, 21 971, No 2, 19. From September 1993 onwards funding for the reception of refugees and other protected persons was granted under the Regulation concerning Contributions for Reception Programmes for Protected Persons (*Bijdrageregeling opvangprogramma's verblijfsgerechtigden*), *Government Gazette* 1993, 165. The term 'reception programmes' was later replaced by 'integration programmes' (*integratieprogramma's*) so as to align the terminology with that of the Welfare Act (*Welzijnswet*); see *Government Gazette* 1994, 177.

[111] In 1993 the reception programme was also extended to people holding a conditional residence permit (*voorwaardelijke vergunning tot verblijf, VVTV*): asylum seekers who were not eligible for protection, but who could not be deported because of the situation in their country of origin. Their reception was originally financed under the Regulation for the Reception of Asylum Seekers (*Regeling opvang asielzoekers, Government Gazette* 1994, 10), but was later integrated into the Regulation for Protected Persons (n 110); see *Government Gazette* 1994, 177. When the Newcomers Integration Act was adopted it was decided that holders of a *VVTV* would become eligible for the integration programmes once they received a permanent residence permit. See *Parliamentary Papers II* 1996–1997, 25 114, No 14 and *Proceedings II* 1997, No 22, 1666.

[112] *Parliamentary Papers II* 1991–1992, 19 637, No 82, 21; *Parliamentary Papers II* 1992–1993, 22 809, No 2, 39–40 and No 14, 14.

[113] *Parliamentary Papers II* 1991–1992, 19 637, No 82, 14.

[114] *Parliamentary Papers II* 1991–1992, 19 637, No 80, 18 and No 82, 17–18.

organisations.[115] Later, in 1997, asylum seekers residing in the centres became entitled to a daily programme of activities, including Dutch language and social orientation lessons.[116] Apparently the idea that asylum seekers' uncertain residence status should bar them from any activities aimed at integration had been abandoned. Instead, it was considered more important to prevent integration backlogs among those asylum seekers who would eventually be allowed to stay.[117]

F. Integration in the Country of Origin

In addition to the policy measures described above, one idea that arose in the period under discussion was that immigrants had to be informed about the Netherlands before they were admitted. In 1991, the Dutch government issued a brochure containing information to be distributed to (potential) immigrants in Turkey and later also Morocco.[118] It was explained that the brochure was designed to provide 'a realistic picture of the possibilities and impossibilities that existed in the Netherlands in the fields of education, employment, living and welfare'. Immigrants who decided to come 'despite this information' would be encouraged to learn Dutch as soon as possible and become familiar with Dutch society.[119]

One member of parliament stated that providing information in the country of origin would prevent potential immigrants from having 'too rosy expectations' about life in the Netherlands. She added that such information should also be provided to Antillean youths, who were immigrating with 'exaggerated expectations'.[120] In 1997 the government announced that it had set up a centre in the Netherlands Antilles to inform potential immigrants about life in the Netherlands *(Centrum Voorlichting Antillianen)*.[121] At the time, the *GPV* (Reformed Political Alliance) even suggested that family migrants wanting to come to the Netherlands should be obliged to take a Dutch language course in their country of origin before immigrating.[122] This proposal was rejected as being difficult to execute and enforce.[123] However, the then Home Affairs Minister, Hans

115 *Parliamentary Papers II* 1992–1993, 22 809, No 14, 4.

116 See Art 5 of the Regulation on Facilities for Asylum Seekers and Other Categories of Aliens 1997 (*Regeling verstrekkingen asielzoekers en andere categorieën vreemdelingen 1997*), *Government Gazette* 1997, 246.

117 *Parliamentary Papers II* 1996–1997, 25 001, No 8, 4–5.

118 *Parliamentary Papers II* 1991–1992, 22 314, No 4, 13 and *Parliamentary Papers II* 1993–1994, 23 409, No 2, 56–57.

119 *Proceedings II* 1991, UCV 13, 30.

120 ibid, 11.

121 *Parliamentary Papers II* 1996–1997, 25 114, No 6, 12.

122 *Proceedings II* 1992, No 4, 183 and 214; see also *Parliamentary Papers II* 1996–1997, 25 114, No 6, 7 and *Proceedings II* 1997, No 21, 1584.

123 *Parliamentary Papers II* 1992–1993, 22 809, No 19, 7.

Dijkstal, indicated that he would investigate the possibility of offering integration courses on the Antilles.[124]

V. COMPULSORY INTEGRATION IN THE NETHERLANDS AND ABROAD (1998–2007)

A. Developments in the Fields of Immigration and Integration

Immigration to the Netherlands continued after 1998 and immigrant integration remained an issue of concern. Between 2000 and 2007, the total number of immigrants in the Netherlands (including the second generation) rose from 2,775,302 to 3,170,406, while the number of 'non-Western allochthones' (*niet-westerse allochtonen*) increased from around 1,260,000 in 1998 to 1,738,452 in 2007.[125] Although the traditional ethnic minority groups (Turks, Moroccans, Surinamese and Antilleans) remained the largest groups, the population had become increasingly diverse. New minority groups included Iraqis, Afghans and people from the former Yugoslavia. In 2004 Statistics Netherlands observed that the influx of labour and asylum migrants had decreased in recent years and family migration had become the largest immigration category. The majority of these family migrants came to the Netherlands to form new families (*gezinsvorming*) rather than for family reunification (*gezinshereniging*).

While there were signs that the second generation of immigrants was doing better than the first, the socio-economic position of those designated as non-Western allochthones continued to be perceived as problematic. Compared to Western allochthones and to the majority population, non-Western allochthones continued to suffer high levels of unemployment and low levels of labour market participation and to be overrepresented in the lower segments of the education system (*vbo/mavo/vmbo*). Non-Western allochthones belonging to the first generation moreover made relatively high use of social assistance and disability benefits.[126]

In 2003, a parliamentary committee (*Commissie Blok*) was set up to conduct an inquiry about the Dutch integration policy over the previous 30 years. This committee concluded that the integration of many immigrants ('allochthones') had been wholly or partly successful, but that it was difficult to say whether this was the result of the integration policy. In

[124] *Proceedings II* 1997, No 21, 1597.

[125] The classification 'non-Western allochthones' is used by Statistics Netherlands (*Centraal Bureau voor de Statistiek* or *CBS*). Countries of origin considered as 'non-Western' are Turkey, Morocco, Suriname, the Dutch Antilles and Aruba and all other countries in Africa, Asia (excluding Indonesia and Japan) or Latin America, whereas the term 'immigrant' is used for every person with at least one foreign-born parent. See www.cbs.nl.

[126] The data in this section have been derived from the CBS, see CBS 1995–2004 and www.cbs.nl.

general it was advised to continue the integration policy in a way requiring the commitment of all those involved. Interestingly the committee also concluded that, for a long time, both parliament and the government had underestimated the importance of learning Dutch. In this respect it was recommended to improve the implementation of the Newcomers Integration Act of 1998 (section V.C.i). In addition to language proficiency, the committee also mentioned respect for legally established norms and values and a knowledge of unwritten social rules as conditions for successful integration.[127]

B. The 'New Style' Integration Policy

During the period discussed here, immigrant integration became one of the main topics on the Dutch political agenda and the integration policy continued to be subject to new developments.[128] In 1998 the second coalition government under Prime Minister Kok (*Paars II*) outlined the integration policy for the period 1999–2002.[129] Throughout those years, achieving active participation of members of ethnic minority groups remained a primary objective.[130] However, the government did not want to focus solely on economic participation. In this respect it deviated from the recommendations made by the *WRR* in 2001.[131]

Given the relatively high level of immigration, the increasingly diverse population and the need to maintain the welfare state, the WRR had repeated its earlier position that integration policy should primarily aim to further the economic participation of immigrants rather than their full cultural inclusion (section IV.B). Nevertheless the Dutch government also sought to address the socio-cultural dimension of the integration process, stating that integration required efforts on the part of the host society and that it was up to the administration, individuals and institutions of civil society to create the circumstances under which immigrants would be able to fully develop their capacities. Where necessary, procedures and structures would have to be altered to create space for immigrants, while active policy measures would be taken with regard to 'processes of identity and interaction and the adaptation of existing social structures to the

[127] *Parliamentary Papers II* 2003–2004, 28 689, No 9 (*Rapport Commissie Blok*) 522–24.

[128] This was illustrated by the appointment of a separate minister for the integration portfolio, which was transferred from the Department of Home Affairs to the Department of Justice in 2002, to the Department of Housing and Spatial Planning in 2007 and then back to Home Affairs in 2010.

[129] This coalition consisted of the Labour Party (*PvdA*), the Liberals (*VVD*) and the Liberal Democrats (*D66*).

[130] *Parliamentary Papers II* 1998–1999, 26 333, No 2 (*'Kansen krijgen, kansen pakken'*).

[131] WRR 2001a.

reality of the multi-ethnic society'.[132] Increased consideration was also given to the role played in the integration process by religion and other beliefs.[133]

In 2002 the government announced that integration policy would no longer be directed towards designated ethnic minorities. Instead the target groups of particular policy measures would be determined according to the issue at stake, and immigrant minorities would only be specifically targeted if their migration background was deemed a relevant factor in relation to the problem to be addressed.[134] In this respect, it was assumed that processes of identification and socio-cultural integration would take more time in the case of immigrants 'at a greater distance from the Western culture'.[135]

Lastly, the government agreed with the *WRR* that immigration and integration policy could not be formulated separately from each other. It was therefore proposed that integration policies would henceforth need to take account of the continuing influx of new immigrants, while the immigration policy should be designed so as to keep the integration process manageable.[136]

Meanwhile, Dutch language education continued to represent an important priority. As far as immigrants were concerned, a command of the Dutch language was not seen only as an instrument for socio-economic integration, but also as a crucial condition for communication and mutual acceptance between different groups in the population.[137] Between 1998 and 2002, therefore, much effort was devoted to consolidating the civic integration policy and implementing the Newcomers Integration Act 1998. In addition, the increased attention for religion as a factor of integration resulted in the compulsory integration programmes being extended to religious servants.

However, the revision of integration policy in general and civic integration policy in particular did not stop there. In 2002 a new government took office under the leadership of Prime Minister Balkenende (the *Balkenende I* cabinet, which was soon followed by *Balkenende II*).[138] The coalition agreements of 2002 and 2003 proposed making the integration policy more coercive and restricting the immigration of family migrants

[132] *Nota 'Kansen krijgen, kansen pakken'* (n 130), 7–9 and *Parliamentary Papers II* 2001–2002, 28 198, No 2 (*Nota 'Integratie in het perspectief van immigratie'*), 48.

[133] *Nota 'Kansen krijgen, kansen pakken'* (n 130), 51 and *Parliamentary Papers II* 1998–1999, 26 333, No 13.

[134] *Nota 'Integratie in het perspectief van immigratie'* (n 132), 58.

[135] *Nota 'Integratie in het perspectief van immigratie'* (n 132), 13–14 and 21.

[136] *Nota 'Integratie in het perspectief van immigratie'* (n 132).

[137] *Nota 'Kansen krijgen, kansen pakken'* (n 130), 7–9.

[138] The *Balkenende I* government was a short-lived coalition of the Christian Democratic party (*CDA*), the Liberals and the *LPF* (the populist party led by Pim Fortuyn) that quickly fell apart, due to internal strife, after the elections. It was succeeded by a coalition consisting of the *CDA*, *VVD* and *D66* parties.

in the interests of integration.[139] In 2003 the government also presented a renewed integration policy. In what was referred to as the 'New Style' Integration policy (*Integratiebeleid 'Nieuwe Stijl'*), great importance was attached to individual responsibility and adherence to basic Dutch norms and values (section III.B of chapter 3).[140] While it was noted that the position of ethnic minorities in the labour market and the education system was improving, the government still found too many immigrants to be too distanced from Dutch society in both cultural and economic terms. It also believed, however, that integration was not something that could be achieved through legislation. Responsibility for the integration process was therefore attributed primarily to the citizens themselves (immigrants and non-immigrants), whereas the government was seen as being responsible for offering incentives and removing obstacles so as to allow civic initiatives to succeed.

Despite this emphasis on individual responsibility, the 'New Style' Integration policy imposed additional obligations and conditions on immigrants in and to the Netherlands. This included a complete overhaul of the structure for civic integration, which had become the main instrument of overall integration policy. A proposal was made for a new Integration Act (*Wet inburgering*), which eventually replaced the Newcomers Integration Act of 1998. In 2006 the obligation to pass a basic integration exam was also integrated into Dutch immigration law as a condition for the admission of certain categories of aliens. This condition, which was enacted through the Act on Integration Abroad (*Wet inburgering in het buitenland*), forms the main object of this study and is therefore described in more detail in section VI.

C. Civic Integration between 1998 and 2007

i. Implementation of the Newcomers Integration Act 1998 and Integration Contracts for Resident Immigrants

The Newcomers Integration Act eventually entered into force on 30 September 1998.[141] During the initial years, however, the Act did not bring about the desired results. In part, this was caused by a lack of cooperation between municipalities and the other parties involved in organising the integration programmes. Another problem was that the waiting lists continued to exist and the integration courses on offer were insufficiently tailored to newcomers' needs, while many newcomers also continued to

[139] *Parliamentary Papers II* 2001–2002, 28 375, No 5 (*Strategisch Akkoord 2002*), 15–17 and *Parliamentary Papers II* 2002–2003, 28 637, No 19 (*Hoofdlijnenakkoord 2003*), 14.

[140] *Parliamentary Papers* 2003–2004, 29 203, No 1.

[141] *Bulletin of Acts and Decrees* 1998, 533.

drop out before or during the programme and those who finished often failed to meet the minimum level of social self-reliance.[142]

In order to address these problems and support the implementation of the civic integration policy, a taskforce was instituted in 2000 (*Taskforce inburgering*). Apart from its primary task, which was to eliminate the waiting lists, this taskforce identified several areas of concern (such as the non-availability of child care) and developed and distributed a series of best practices and solutions to common problems. It also encouraged the creation of 'dual programmes' combining language courses with work, vocational training or educational support.[143] Projects of this kind were set up with various companies.[144] The taskforce continued operating until the end of 2002, when a final document with recommendations was presented to the then Integration Minister, Hilbrand Nawijn. After the taskforce was dismantled, its supporting task was taken over by the Front Office for Civic Integration (*Frontoffice inburgering*).

From 1999, civic integration policy was no longer restricted to newcomers, but was expanded to include immigrants who had already been living in the Netherlands for longer periods.[145] Although they were not new residents, these immigrants were considered to be in a disadvantaged position due (partly) to a lack of proficiency in Dutch. As the available financial resources were limited, priority was given to unemployed people and those with school-age children (sections III.B and III.C. of chapter 3)[146] The lack of a legal basis meant participation in the integration programmes could not be made obligatory for all resident immigrants.[147] From 2001, however, integration contracts were introduced, as previously with newcomers, to ensure that those who started a programme also finished it.[148] Several years later, resident immigrants' participation in

[142] See Brink et al 2002. See also the report on the civic integration policy published by the Court of Audit (*Algemene Rekenkamer*) in 2000: *Inburgering en taalonderwijs allochtonen, Parliamentary Papers II* 1999–2000, 27 275, No 2.

[143] eg, *Parliamentary Papers II* 2001–2002, 28 006, No 2, 19–20.

[144] Brink et al 2002, 62–63. The introduction of dual programmes was proposed in the 1998 coalition agreement to improve newcomers' chances on the labour market; see *Parliamentary Papers II* 1997–1998, 26 024, No 10, 68. The *WRR* also stressed that language acquisition would be more effective in a context-related setting, WRR 2001a, 150–55.

[145] Integration programmes for these immigrants were funded under a number of different regulations (known as *oudkomersregelingen*). These included the *Bijdrageregeling sociale integratie en veiligheid G25, Government Gazette* 1999, No 162, *Bijdrageregeling inburgering oudkomers, Government Gazette* 1999, No 230 and *Bijdrageregeling inburgering oudkomers 12 gemeenten, Government Gazette* 2001, No 44.

[146] In 2001 the Social and Cultural Planning Office (*Sociaal and Cultureel Planbureau*) estimated that this target group consisted of approximately 465,000 people, which was much higher than had originally been thought. See SCP 2001, 53.

[147] For unemployed people, however, the Unemployment Act (*Werkloosheidswet*) could serve as a legal basis for imposing mandatory integration courses as part of the reintegration programme.

[148] See, eg, the *Regeling aanvullende bijdrage inburgering oudkomers 54 gemeenten, Government Gazette* 2001, No 231.

integration programmes became compulsory under the Integration Act 2007.

ii. Compulsory Integration for Religious Servants

As indicated in section V.B, the role of religion in the integration process was increasingly recognised from 1998 onwards. In the same period concerns were raised about public statements by imams that were considered expressions of religious intolerance.[149] Religious servants (*geestelijke bedienaren*), such as ministers, other clergymen and teachers of religion, were able to exert significant influence on the integration process, and it was therefore deemed important that they, too, should participate in integration programmes.[150]

On 1 January 2002, religious servants who immigrated to the Netherlands were brought into the target group of the Newcomers Integration Act 1998.[151] That meant they had to complete the regular integration programme, followed by a specific programme geared towards their pastoral care activities. Although the amendment applied to all religious servants irrespective of their denomination, the majority of the target group consisted of imams.[152] Soon afterwards the government was asked to further extend the civic integration policy to imams already resident in the Netherlands.[153] A new course, with a strong emphasis on the meaning of the Dutch Constitution and the way democracy functioned in the Netherlands, was also requested for this group.[154] Both proposals were included in the revision of the civic integration policy (see section V.D below).[155] In the meantime, religious servants were designated a priority group, alongside unemployed people and parents of school-age children, under the integration regulations for resident immigrants.[156]

Before the Newcomers Integration Act was amended, parliament discussed whether other categories of professionals should also be brought under the Act on the grounds that they had a specific role to play in the integration process.[157] The Council of State had already suggested that this

[149] One well-known example is the case of imam El Moumni, who spoke out against homosexuality on Dutch television in 2001. See, eg, *NRC Handelsblad* of 7 May 2001, 'Van Boxtel wil snel in gesprek met imams'.

[150] *Parliamentary Papers II* 1997–1998, 25 919, No 2, 24; *Parliamentary Papers II* 1999–2000, 26 333, No 13, 9 and *Parliamentary Papers II* 1999–2000, 27 000, No 3, 2.

[151] *Bulletin of Acts and Decrees* 2001, 351; *Government Gazette* 2001, No 247.

[152] *Parliamentary Papers II* 1999–2000, 27 000, No 3, 2. In June 2003 it was reported that 18 imams had participated in the integration programme, of whom 16 had obtained a certificate (*Parliamentary Papers II* 2002–2003, 27 083, No 37, 2).

[153] *Parliamentary Papers II* 2001–2002, 28 006, No 14; *Proceedings II* 2002, No 91, 5451.

[154] *Parliamentary Papers II* 2002–2003, 27 083, No 30; *Proceedings II* 2002, No 34, 2538–39.

[155] *Parliamentary Papers II* 2002–2003, 27 083, No 37, 2–3.

[156] Art 2 *Regeling inburgering oudkomers* and Art 2.b *Regeling inburgering oudkomers 54 gemeenten*.

[157] *Parliamentary Papers II* 1999–2000, 27 000, No 4, 1–4.

could be the case with regard to nurses and teachers.[158] At the time, however, the government chose to extend the Act only to religious servants.[159]

iii. Adjustment of the Course Objectives for Social Orientation

Section IV.D.i describes how the integration programmes included a course in social orientation in addition to Dutch as a second language. As the goal of this course was to provide newcomers with the necessary knowledge and skills to become self-reliant in Dutch society, the main focus was on practical information. The social orientation course addressed a variety of topics classified as 'need to know' and 'nice to know'. The 'need to know' topics were 'legal status', 'work and income', 'social security', 'housing', 'health', 'traffic and transport', 'education', 'health care', 'insurances', 'the right to vote', 'leisure', 'children' and 'taxes'. 'Nice to know' topics included information about geography, economics, Dutch history, holidays and memorial days and the Dutch population.[160] In 2002 the overall political opinion, however, was that the existing course contents put too much emphasis on self-reliance and not enough on participation and citizenship. There was a call to include topics such as norms and values, social codes and culture within the 'need to know' category, together with Dutch history and constitutional law.[161] In January 2004 a committee of experts (*Commissie Franssen*) was set up to advise on the contents of the integration courses, including social orientation.[162] The committee's report was later taken into account in the revision of the civic integration policy described below (section V.D).

iv. Integration Abroad for Antillean Youths

In 1998, the government signalled that the immigration of disadvantaged youths from the Netherlands Antilles was leading to problems in several Dutch cities.[163] One of the measures proposed to address these problems was to set up integration programmes on the Antillean islands. In January 1999 a 'cooperation protocol' was signed with the Antillean government, with the aim of introducing a voluntary integration programme on the Antilles for youths aged under 25. This programme should include realistic information about the Netherlands ('social orientation') and

[158] *Parliamentary Papers II* 1999–2000, 27 000, A, 2.

[159] *Parliamentary Papers II* 1999–2000, 27 000, No 5, 11. Ch 5 of this study examines the position of religious servants in the Dutch integration legislation against the background of the right to freedom of religion and the right to equal treatment.

[160] Brink and Tromp 2003, 9.

[161] ibid, 10; *Parliamentary Papers II* 2002–2003, 28 600 VI, No 48; *Proceedings II* 2002, No 31, 2240.

[162] *Government Gazette* 2004, No 14.

[163] *Parliamentary Papers II* 1998–1999, 26 283, No 1, 2.

Dutch language classes. A pilot project was started in late 1999.[164] In reaction to some comments by members of parliament, the Integration Minister stated that the measure was not meant to curb immigration, but to ensure actual participation of Antilleans in the integration programmes.[165] Nevertheless, the Antillean government refused to adopt the legislation needed to make participation in the integration programmes compulsory. Alternative plans were then made to include integration courses in the compulsory education programme for Antilleans aged under 25 who planned to move to the Netherlands, but these, too, were never realised. Eventually the Dutch government decided to abandon the project and to allocate the reserved funds to the Antillean community already present in the Netherlands.[166]

D. Reform of the Civic Integration Policy

As early as 2000, when the Newcomers Integration Act had been in force for less than two years, calls were heard for substantial changes to be made to the civic integration policy. It was proposed replacing the obligation of effort to participate in a course by an obligation of result (in other words, to pass an exam) and requiring integration programmes to start in immigrants' countries of origin.[167] Around the same time the government was asked to investigate the possibilities of making the granting of a permanent residence permit dependent on completion of the integration programme, while plans were made to make the partners of family migrants bear part of the costs of those programmes.[168] The proposed changes were inspired by the disappointing results of the Newcomers Integration Act, including the high drop-out rates.

Although not initially receiving much support, these proposals eventually gained ground. In 2003 a thorough revision of the civic integration policy was proposed as part of the 'New Style' Integration policy.[169] As well as reflecting the call for more coercive measures, these proposals also placed a strong emphasis on the immigrant's personal responsibility. The main features of the reforms are briefly set out below.[170]

[164] *Parliamentary Papers II* 1999–2000, 26 283, No 6, 6–7.

[165] *Parliamentary Papers II* 1998–1999, 26 283, No 4, 5.

[166] *Parliamentary Papers II* 2000–2001, 26 283, No 10, 5.

[167] *Proceedings II* 2000, Nos 70 and 71, 4713. See also the resolution adopted in 2002 (*Motie Sterk*), in which the government was asked to submit proposals concerning civic integration for family migrants in their countries of origin, *Parliamentary Papers II* 2002–2003, 27 083, No 25; *Proceedings II* 2002, No 34, 2538.

[168] *Parliamentary Papers II* 1999–2000, 26 732, No 77 and *Parliamentary Papers II* 2001–2002, 28 198, No 4, 1–2.

[169] *Parliamentary Papers II* 2003–2004, 29 203, No 1.

[170] *Parliamentary Papers II* 2003–2004, 29 543, No 2 (*Contourennota Herziening van het inburgeringsstelsel*).

Firstly, they provided for integration to become compulsory for all aliens and Dutch citizens – newcomers *and* resident immigrants – born outside the EU/EEA and who came to live in the Netherlands on a non-temporary basis. This definition of the target group raised a number of (legal) problems and could not be maintained.[171] In the end, the compulsory integration policy would apply only to third-country nationals, with a number of exemptions.[172]

A second reform involved replacing the obligation to participate in an integration programme by the obligation to pass an integration exam at a certain level. This exam was designed to test applicants' knowledge of Dutch society, as well as their Dutch language proficiency. Anyone who did not pass the exam within a set period of time would have to pay an administrative fine. The responsibility for obtaining the required skills was also placed on the immigrants themselves. Integration programmes would no longer be provided by the municipalities and it would be up to the immigrants to decide how to prepare for the integration test. They would also have to pay the costs of preparing for and taking the exam, although under certain conditions a partial refund could be granted.

Lastly, immigration conditions would firmly link the obligation to integrate to the right to reside in the Netherlands. From then on, all those applying for an independent or permanent residence permit (*vergunning voortgezet verblijf* or *vergunning onbepaalde tijd*) would have to show that they had passed the above integration exam. In addition, a basic integration exam would be introduced for family migrants and religious servants in their countries of origin as a condition for admission to the Netherlands.

The proposed changes were realised by way of two Acts. The obligation to pass the integration exam in the Netherlands was provided for in the Integration Act (*Wet inburgering*), which replaced the Newcomers Integration Act on 1 January 2007. This Act also introduced the integration exam as a condition for independent and permanent residence in the Netherlands. In addition, the basic integration exam as a condition for the admission of certain categories of aliens (the integration requirement abroad) was established through the Act on Integration Abroad (*Wet inburgering buitenland*). The latter Act is discussed in more detail below.

[171] For an overview of the various proposals and arguments made concerning the target group, see De Vries 2006, 278–80.

[172] See Arts 3 and 5 Integration Act 2007.

VI. THE ACT ON INTEGRATION ABROAD

A. The Requirement of Integration Abroad in Dutch Immigration Law

The Act on Integration Abroad (AIA) entered into force on 15 March 2006.[173] This Act does not stand alone but instead constitutes an amendment to the Dutch Aliens Act (*Vreemdelingenwet 2000*), which contains the main rules concerning the admission of aliens to the Netherlands. Since the adoption of the AIA, the Aliens Act sets the requirement of integration abroad as a condition for acquisition of a residence permit. This condition applies in principle to residence permits issued for the first five years of residence on non-asylum-related grounds (*verblijfsvergunning bepaalde tijd regulier*).[174] More specific regulations and administrative guidelines concerning the integration requirement abroad are laid down in the Aliens Decree (*Vreemdelingenbesluit 2000*), Aliens Regulations (*Voorschrift Vreemdelingen 2000*) and Aliens Circular (*Vreemdelingencirculaire 2000*).

As a rule, applications for a residence permit can normally be made after the applicant has lawfully entered the Netherlands on a long-stay visa (*machtiging tot voorlopig verblijf*).[175] Applications for such visas are assessed on the basis of the same conditions as those applying to the residence permit. It follows in effect that immigrants seeking to obtain a Dutch residence permit must first meet the integration requirement abroad before they can be admitted. This was also the aim of the Dutch legislator, who wanted immigrants to prepare for integration before coming to the Netherlands (section V.D). Once applicants have passed the exam and have been admitted to the Netherlands, they do not have to take the exam again in order to obtain a residence permit.

i. A Contested Legal Basis

In July 2008, the Amsterdam District Court decided that admission could not be refused to family migrants on the grounds that they did not meet the integration requirement abroad. The Court's decision was based on the grounds that this requirement had insufficient basis in law.[176] The Court pointed out that the Aliens Act itself did not state that applications for residence *had* to be refused if the applicant had not passed the integration exam abroad, but merely granted discretionary powers to do so.

[173] *Bulletin of Acts and Decrees* 2006, 28; entry into force *Bulletin of Acts and Decrees* 2006, 75.

[174] Art 16(1)(h) Aliens Act.

[175] Art 16(1)(a) Aliens Act.

[176] District Court of The Hague sitting in Amsterdam 15 July 2008, case no AWB 07/18932, LJN: BD7189 and District Court of The Hague sitting in Amsterdam 15 July 2008, AWB 07/20102.

Meanwhile, Article 3.13 of the Aliens Decree stated that residence permits for family reunification *would be* granted if the conditions set out in that provision were met. Since the integration requirement abroad was not mentioned, the Court concluded that the application of this requirement was not based on law. At the same time, it also recognised that it had clearly been the legislator's intention to apply the integration requirement in situations involving family reunification. However, the Court found that it was unclear as to how the legislator wished to include this requirement in the immigration legislation and the lack of a legal basis could not, therefore, be repaired by the judiciary.

The Dutch government appealed against the Amsterdam Court's judgments, which were subsequently overruled by the Administrative Jurisdiction Division of the Council of State (*Afdeling bestuursrechtspraak Raad van State*, hereafter AJD).[177] Although the AJD's judgment did not directly address the integration requirement as a condition for a residence permit, it found that there was a sufficient legal basis for refusing applications for long-stay visas on the grounds that applicants had not passed the integration exam in their countries of origin. The AJD stated that this legal basis could be found in Article 7 of the Royal Decree (*Souverein Besluit*) of 1813, in conjunction with Article 1(h) Aliens Act and Article 3.71a(1) Aliens Decree, and taking into account the legislative history of the AIA and the consistent practice of the Foreign Affairs Minister to apply the integration requirement to applications for family reunification.[178] In practice, the decision by the AJD meant that family migrants would still need to meet the integration requirement abroad before being admitted to the Netherlands. The decision was confirmed in a number of later judgments.[179]

I previously argued that the reasoning followed by the AJD is not entirely convincing.[180] Nevertheless, it follows from the above judgment that, as a matter of Dutch national law, the requirement of integration abroad has a legal basis and can serve as grounds for refusing applications for family reunification. In my view, the legislative history of the AIA also clearly shows both that and how the Dutch legislator intended to

[177] AJD 2 December 2008, case no. 200806120/1.

[178] Under Art 7 Royal Decree 1813 aliens entering the Netherlands shall subject their passports to the visa of the State Secretary; this provision still functions in Dutch immigration law as the legal basis for the competence of the Foreign Affairs Minister to decide on visa applications. Art 1(h) Aliens Act gives the definition of a long-stay visa (*machtiging tot voorlopig verblijf*), whereas under Art 3.71a(1) Aliens Decree aliens are deemed to meet the integration requirement if they pass the integration exam abroad within one year before submitting their visa application. Neither of these provisions states that a visa may be refused because the integration requirement has not been fulfilled.

[179] eg, AJD 9 February 2009, case No 200806121/1, para 2.2; AJD 2 April 2009, case no 200808062/1/V1, para 2.2 and District Court of The Hague sitting in Utrecht 29 June 2009, case no 08/39827, para 2.12.

[180] De Vries 2009, para 5.

add this requirement to the conditions for the admission of family migrants and that the requirement was consistently applied from the moment the AIA entered into force. Hence, from the perspective of legal certainty and democratic legitimacy, the outcome of the AJD's judgment should not be considered problematic.

B. Personal Scope of the Act on Integration Abroad

i. Main Target Group: Family Migrants from Non-Western Countries

As mentioned above, the requirement of integration abroad applies only to aliens wishing to obtain a residence permit on non-asylum-related grounds (*verblijfsvergunning regulier*). This means that asylum seekers do not have to meet the requirement as a condition for obtaining international protection, whether they are in the Netherlands or abroad. Also excluded are aliens whose residence purpose is qualified as temporary under Dutch legislation; hence the requirement of integration abroad does not apply to inter alia students, highly skilled workers (*kennismigranten*) and other labour migrants.[181] This limitation, which also existed under the Newcomers Integration Act 1998 (section IV.D.iv), is motivated by the consideration that integration is a matter primarily concerning immigrants seeking to remain in the Netherlands for a longer or indefinite period of time.[182] In practice the vast majority of immigrants falling within the target group of the AIA are those seeking admission for the purpose of family reunification.[183] This concerns both new and existing families (*gezinsvorming* and *gezinshereniging*). As of 1 October 2012, only members of the nuclear family are eligible for family reunification. These are the spouse or registered partner and minor children belonging to the family.[184]

In addition to the residence purpose, another important criterion used to determine the target group of the AIA is nationality. The requirement of

[181] Art 16(1)(h) Aliens Act in conjunction with Art 3(1)(a) Integration Act 2007. As a matter of Dutch immigration law, a temporary residence *purpose* (*tijdelijk verblijfsdoel*) is not the same as a temporary residence *permit* (*verblijfsvergunning bepaalde tijd*). Although the two may go together, a temporary residence permit may be issued for a non-temporary residence purpose (such as international protection). In that case the alien will be able to apply for a permanent residence permit after five years, which is not the case if the permit is issued for a temporary purpose. A list of residence purposes qualifying as temporary under the Integration Act 2007 can be found in Art 2.1(1) Integration Decree (*Besluit inburgering*) and Annex 1 to the Integration Regulations (*Regeling inburgering*).

[182] *Parliamentary Papers II* 1996–1997, 25 114, No 3, 4–5; *Parliamentary Papers II* 2003–2004, 29 700, No 3, 7.

[183] See www.ind.nl.

[184] *Bulletin of Acts and Decrees* 2012, 148; entry into force *Bulletin of Acts and Decrees* 2012, 326.

integration abroad does not apply to aliens who are nationals of an EU or EEA Member State, nor to nationals of a select number of economically developed countries.[185] Nationals of these states do not need a long-term visa to be admitted to the Netherlands and are therefore not subject to prior control before entering Dutch territory. The Dutch government estimated that subjecting these nationals to the AIA could harm the diplomatic and economic relations of the Netherlands. It also declared that the above countries were 'comparable to the Netherlands in social, economic and political terms' so that immigration from these countries would not lead to major problems in the field of integration.[186] It follows that the requirement of integration abroad applies only to aliens who are nationals of non-Western countries. In 2010 and 2011, the integration exam abroad was most often taken by nationals of Turkey and Morocco, followed by China, Thailand and Indonesia (section VI.D).

Lastly, the AIA does not apply to nationals of EU/EEA Member States or Switzerland and their family members if they are entitled to free movement within the EU (chapter 6).[187] This exclusion ground was included in order to ensure respect for the obligations of EU law.[188]

ii. Additional Target Group: Religious Servants

In addition to family migrants, the Act on Integration Abroad also addresses religious servants.[189] According to Article 1(1)(g) of the Integration Act 2007, a religious servant is a 'person who holds a spiritual or religious office, who works as a minister, religious teacher or missionary or who conducts activities of a predominantly spiritual, ideological or religious nature on behalf of a spiritual or religious congregation'. Section V.C.ii explains that religious servants were brought under the Newcomers Integration Act of 1998 because of the particular role they were believed to play in the integration process.[190] For the same reason, religious servants were also covered in the AIA even though they are not normally eligible for permanent residence in the Netherlands.[191] To date, the number of

[185] Art 16(1)(h) in conjunction with Art 17(1)(a) Aliens Act. Apart from the EU/EEA Members States, the exempted countries are Australia, Canada, Japan, Monaco, New Zealand, South Korea, Switzerland, the United States and Vatican City (see the Aliens Regulations, Annex 2).

[186] *Parliamentary Papers II* 2003–2004, 29 700, No 3, 19 and *Parliamentary Papers II* 2004–2005, 29 700, No 6, 31–32. These arguments are discussed in detail in ch 8 on the right to equal treatment.

[187] Art 16(1)(h) in conjunction with Art 17(1)(b) and Art 1(e) Aliens Act. For nationals of the EU/EEA Member States and Switzerland, these grounds for exemption overlap the above exemption on the grounds of nationality.

[188] *Parliamentary Papers II* 2003–2004, 29 700, No 3, 19.

[189] Art 16(1)(h) Aliens Act read in conjunction with Art 3(1)(b) Integration Act 2007.

[190] See also Van der Winden 2006, 85–86, with further references.

[191] See paras B19/4 and 7 Aliens Circular.

religious servants seeking admission to the Netherlands has not been substantial.[192]

iii. Exemptions

Dutch immigration law contains several exceptions to the rule that all aliens belonging to the target group of the AIA must pass the integration exam abroad. Exemptions may be granted on a categorical or individual basis. The grounds for exemption are briefly reviewed below.

a. Categorical Exemptions

The requirement of integration abroad does not apply to nationals of Suriname who can demonstrate that they received their primary education in Dutch in the Netherlands or in Suriname.[193] This exemption was added on the grounds that many Surinamese nationals already speak Dutch and are familiar with Dutch society.[194]

The AIA furthermore does not apply to immigrants who, after arriving in the Netherlands, would be exempted under the Integration Act 2007 from the obligation to pass the advanced integration exam.[195] In so far as relevant here, these are:

a. people younger than 16 or 65 years or older;[196]
b. people who resided in the Netherlands – lawfully or unlawfully – for at least eight years during the period of compulsory education (5–16 years of age);
c. people with a diploma, certificate or other document demonstrating that they have already obtained the skills and knowledge needed to pass the integration exam;[197]
d. people subject to compulsory education or training (*leerplicht* or *kwalificatieplicht*);
e. people who cannot be subjected to compulsory integration because of provisions of international or EU law.

As regards the ground mentioned above under 'e', the Central Appeals Tribunal (*Centrale Raad van Beroep*), the highest Dutch court to rule on the application of the Integration Act 2007, decided on 16 August 2011 that

[192] The number of admission applications by religious servants was 55 in 2006, 23 in 2007 and 46 in 2008. See Lodder 2009, 24.

[193] Art 16(3) Aliens Act. See also Art 3.13 Aliens Regulations.

[194] See Van der Winden 2006, 65–67 with further references.

[195] Art 16(1)(h) Aliens Act in conjunction with Art 5 Integration Act 2007.

[196] Note that persons aged 16 and 17 will necessarily be covered by one of the exemptions under Art 5(1)(c) or (d). In practice, therefore, the AIA does not apply to people younger than 18.

[197] A list of relevant documents is included in Art 2.3 Integration Decree and Annex 2 to the Integration Regulations.

Turkish nationals falling under the scope of the EEC-Turkey Association Agreement must be exempted from the requirements of that Act.[198] In a letter to parliament, the Home Affairs Minister (then responsible for integration) subsequently confirmed that Turkish nationals were, from then on, also exempted from the obligation to pass the integration exam abroad.[199] According to this letter, the exemption applies to all Turkish nationals and their family members.

In addition to the above, Article 3.71a Aliens Decree mentions two more exempted categories. First, the requirement of integration abroad does not apply if the applicant is a family member of a person who has been granted a residence permit in the Netherlands on asylum grounds.[200] Also exempted are persons who have already complied with an integration requirement in another EU Member State in order to acquire the status of long-term resident under the EU Long-term Residents Directive (chapter 6, section VI.C).[201] It may be observed that the second exemption is superfluous, given that EU long-term residents do not need a long-stay visa to be admitted to the Netherlands. Hence, they are in any case exempted from the obligation to pass the integration exam abroad even if they have not already fulfilled an integration requirement in the first Member State. The latter grounds for exemption also apply to the spouse and minor children of the long-term resident, providing the family already existed in the first Member State.

b. Individual Exemptions

Article 3.71a Aliens Decree also contains an exemption for persons who are 'lastingly unable to take the integration exam due to a mental or physical disability'.[202] Disabilities covered by this provision include, but are not limited to, blindness, deafness and deaf-muteness and serious speech impediments.[203] Case law shows that this ground for exemption does not apply if the applicant is illiterate, has had little or very little education or has little capacity for learning.[204] This does not change when these problems occur in combination with medical complaints that are not in

[198] Central Appeals Tribunal 16 August 2011, case nos 10/5248, 10/5249, 10/6123 and 10/6124, LJN: BR4959). On the EEC-Turkey Association Agreement see further section II of ch 7.

[199] *Parliamentary Papers II* 2011–2012, 31 143, No 89.

[200] Art 3.71a(2)(a) Aliens Decree.

[201] Art 3.71a(2)(b) Aliens Decree.

[202] Art 3.71a(2)(c) Aliens Decree and Art 3.10 Aliens Regulations. On these grounds for exemption, see also Van der Winden 2006, 69–73.

[203] See also para B1/4.7.1.2 Aliens Circular. The President of the Haarlem District Court ruled that disabilities that may warrant an exemption are not limited to those expressly mentioned in the Circular, see President District Court of The Hague sitting in Haarlem 10 April 2008, case no 07/43197, LJN: BE9559, para 2.14.

[204] AJD 2 December 2008, case no 200806120/1, para 2.3.2; AJD 9 February 2009, case no 200806121/1, para 2.4.2.

themselves sufficient to necessitate application of the exemption clause,[205] or when it is shown that the lack of education is due to external factors not attributable to the applicant's own choice (*in casu*, the fact that she was a woman raised in a part of Afghanistan controlled by the Taliban).[206]

As of 1 April 2011, an exemption can be granted if refusal to admit the applicant would be evidently unreasonable.[207] This ground for exemption was added in connection with the introduction of a reading test as part of the integration exam abroad (section VI.C.ii). Its applicability is determined by the Integration Minister on an individual basis. It has been announced, however, that exemptions will only be granted in the event of very specific individual circumstances that result in the applicant being lastingly unable to pass the exam despite having made substantial efforts to that effect.[208] No case law regarding this ground for exemption is available to date.

Moreover, several exemptions deserve to be mentioned that are not directly related to the requirement of integration abroad but are nonetheless relevant to its application. First, persons who are already in the Netherlands when applying for a residence permit can, under certain circumstances, be exempted from the obligation to travel back to their country of origin in order to obtain a long-stay visa (section VI.A).[209] Where this exemption applies, applicants are also no longer required to pass the integration exam abroad.[210] The exemption will be granted, inter alia, if applicants can demonstrate that returning to their country of origin would separate them from their family members in violation of Article 8 ECHR, or if the requirement to return would be 'decisively unreasonable'.[211] Conversely, applicants who are not exempted will not be able to re-enter the Netherlands until they have fulfilled all the conditions for a long-stay visa, including the requirement of integration abroad. Dutch case law shows several examples of applicants seeking exemption from the long-

[205] District Court of The Hague 17 July 2008, case no 08/4788, para 7; District Court of The Hague sitting in 's-Hertogenbosch 12 January 2009, case no 08/7556, LJN: BG9517, paras 15–18.

[206] AJD 15 August 2011, case no 201007300/1/V2, para 2.2–2.2.2.

[207] Art 3.71a(2)(d) Aliens Decree; *Bulletin of Acts and Decrees* 2010, 679; entry into force *Bulletin of Acts and Decrees* 2010, 844. The introduction of a hardship clause was one of the recommendations made following the evaluation of the AIA in 2009, see the Principal findings and conclusions of the evaluation of the Act on Integration Abroad (*Evaluatie Wet inburgering in het buitenland. Centrale bevindingen en conclusies*), Annex to *Parliamentary Papers II* 2008–2009, 32 005, No 1, 14.

[208] *Bulletin of Acts and Decrees* 2010, 679, 14.

[209] This situation can occur when the applicant has entered the Netherlands unlawfully, or has been initially admitted for a purpose other than family reunification (eg on a short-stay visa or to seek asylum).

[210] Art 16(1)(h) Aliens Act. The grounds for exemption are listed in Art 17(1) Aliens Act and Art 3.71(2) Aliens Decree.

[211] Art 3.71(2)(l) and 3.71(4) Aliens Decree. Whether the obligation to return to the country of origin would be 'decisively unreasonable' is to be determined by the minister responsible for Aliens Affairs. On Art 8 ECHR see ch 4, section II.

stay visa requirement mainly or partially because of the efforts involved in having to pass – and prepare for – the integration exam abroad.[212] In each of these cases, however, the refusal to grant an exemption was upheld by the courts.

Article 4:84 of the General Administrative Act (*Algemene wet bestuursrecht*) furthermore grants Dutch administrative bodies a discretionary power not to apply administrative regulations (*beleidsregels*) if, due to unforeseen circumstances, the consequences for the individuals concerned would be disproportionate in relation to the aims pursued. This also applies to the rule that applications for a long-stay visa *must* be refused if the integration requirement abroad is not met, which is laid down the Aliens Circular.[213] This exemption clause has been invoked before the Dutch courts on several occasions, including on the grounds that the applicant was illiterate, the exam could not be taken in the applicant's country of origin or there were no course materials available for preparing for the exam. So far, however, the clause has been interpreted restrictively by the courts and the appeals have been rejected.[214] Lastly, the Aliens Circular also provides that applications for family reunification shall not be refused if such refusal would violate Article 8 ECHR.[215] In these cases, the applicants must be admitted even if they have not passed the integration exam abroad. Relevant Dutch case law is discussed in section II.E of chapter 4.

To avoid confusion, a schematic overview of the different possibilities for individual exemption is included in the table on the next page.

The application of the AIA by the immigration authorities has been subject to criticism by the Dutch Ombudsman (*Nationale ombudsman*). In a report issued in May 2011, the Ombudsman asserted that the Act was enforced too rigidly and the existing possibilities for exemption – other than on grounds of disability – were not applied in practice. In particular, the Immigration and Naturalisation Service (*Immigratie- en Naturalisatiedienst*) failed to consider the various circumstances of each case in combination and so did not get a good picture of the difficulties faced by some applicants. The Ombudsman advised the assessment of individual cases in a more comprehensive manner, taking into account factors enabling applicants to pass the integration exam abroad (including education and

[212] District Court of The Hague sitting in Maastricht 6 October 2010, case nos 09/33430 and 10/9629; District Court of The Hague sitting in Maastricht 29 December 2010, case nos 09/38308 and 10/10071; District Court of The Hague sitting in Amsterdam 8 March 2011, case nos 10/23459 and 10/23449, paras 3.2 and 5.3–5.5; District Court of The Hague sitting in Rotterdam 22 September 2011, case no 10/31223, para 4.3.2.

[213] Para B1/4.7.1 Aliens Circular.

[214] eg, District Court of The Hague sitting in Middelburg 16 August 2007, case no 07/30015, LJN: BB3524, para 6; District Court of The Hague sitting in Groningen 10 November 2009, case no 08/34677, paras 2.14–2.16.

[215] Para B2/10 Aliens Circular.

social support) as well as factors reducing their ability to do so (health problems, lack of educational or financial means, etc).[216]

Table 1. Individual exemptions

Legal basis	Ground for exemption	Result
Applicant is still abroad		
Art 3.71a (c) Aliens Decree	mental or physical disability	exemption from integration exam abroad
Art 3.71a (d) Aliens Decree	very specific individual circumstances; refusal of application 'evidently unreasonable'	exemption from integration exam abroad
Art 4:84 General Administrative Act	obligation to pass exam 'disproportionate' due to 'unforeseen circumstances'	exemption from integration exam abroad
Para B2/10 Aliens Circular	violation of Art 8 ECHR (right to family life)	failure to pass integration exam abroad does not lead to refusal of application
Applicant has already entered the Netherlands		
Art 16(1)(h) Aliens Act read together with Art 3.71(2)(l) Aliens Decree	obligation to return to country of origin and pass exam violates Art 8 ECHR (right to family life)	exemption from long-stay visa requirement and hence from integration exam abroad
Art 16(1)(h) Aliens Act read together with Art 3.71(4) Aliens Decree	obligation to return to country of origin and pass exam 'decisively unreasonable'	exemption from long-stay visa requirement and hence from integration exam abroad

In response to the Ombudsman report, the Home Affairs Minister (then responsible for integration) referred to the new exemption clause enacted on 1 April 2011 (see above). The creation of a special 'decision-making team' to put this clause into operation was also announced. The decision-making team would apply the assessment criteria suggested by the Ombudsman.[217] Between 1 April and 31 December 2011, 19 requests for exemption were examined, of which seven were granted and seven

[216] *Inburgering in het buitenland,* report issued by the Dutch Ombudsman (report no 2011/135), 33–38, available at www.nationaleombudsman.nl.

[217] See the Annex to *Parliamentary Papers II* 2010–2011, 31 143, No 88, 3–4.

denied. In five more cases an exemption was eventually granted on medical grounds.[218]

C. The Integration Exam Abroad

In order to be granted admission to the Netherlands, aliens belonging to the AIA target group and not qualifying for an exemption must demonstrate that they have a basic knowledge of Dutch language and Dutch society. This knowledge is tested by means of an exam (the basic integration exam or the integration exam abroad), which can be taken at the Dutch embassy or consulate in the applicant's country of origin or habitual residence.[219]

i. Contents of the Exam before 1 April 2011

Prior to 1 April 2011, the integration exam abroad consisted of two parts: a spoken Dutch language test (*Toets Gesproken Nederlands*) and a test examining applicants' knowledge of the Netherlands (*Kennis van de Nederlandse Samenleving*).[220] The language test consists of several exercises designed to assess applicants' listening and speaking skills; for instance, the applicant has to repeat a number of (simple) phrases spoken in Dutch or answer several basic questions. The 'Knowledge of the Netherlands' test requires applicants to answer 30 out of 100 questions about the film 'To the Netherlands' (*Naar Nederland*), which they have to watch before the exam. All 100 questions and answers are known in advance and can be learned by heart. The questions cover the topics 'topography, history and the constitutional system of the Netherlands', 'housing, education, employment, health care and integration', 'rights and obligations after arrival in the Netherlands', 'rights and obligations of others' and 'Dutch social norms and conventions'. Examples of questions asked in this part of the exam include: 'Where is the Dutch government based?' (correct answer: The Hague), 'Do newspapers, radio and television enjoy freedom of expression?' (correct answer: yes) and 'Why is it good for children to watch Dutch television?' (correct answer: to learn Dutch).[221]

[218] See the Monitor of the Integration Exam Abroad (*Monitor inburgeringsexamen buitenland*) of 7 May 2012, published as Annex to *Parliamentary Papers II* 2011–2012, 32 175, No 32, 41.

[219] Art 16(1)(h) Aliens Act and Art 3.71a (1) Aliens Decree.

[220] Art 3.98a(2)–(7) Aliens Decree, as they read before 1 April 2011. See also Van der Winden 2006, 105–08.

[221] An overview of all 100 questions and the different types of exercises included in the language test is provided in the exam programme devised by the Integration Minister. This programme is included in the preparation package developed by the Dutch government, see section VI.C.iv.

To pass the exam, applicants needed to be able to speak and understand Dutch at the A1-minus level of the Common European Framework of Reference (CEFR).[222] This is a very basic level, which implies that they can use a limited array of words and well-known expressions in contexts directly relating to their everyday life. This level was recommended by the Committee of experts (*Commissie Franssen*), which was set up specifically for this purpose, on the grounds that any higher level would result in the exclusion of large groups of persons who were illiterate or had received little education. The Committee took into account that the government would not organise preparatory courses in countries of origin and that candidates would need to prepare themselves by means of self-tuition (see also section VI.C.iv). According to the Committee, candidates would need between 100 and 300 hours of study to reach the exam level, depending on their previous education and the availability of support.[223] The government itself stated that the purpose of the exam was to select potential immigrants on the basis of their motivation to integrate, rather than on their educational level (see also section II.B.iii of chapter 3). Interestingly it was also asserted that a higher exam level could be problematic in view of international legal norms, in particular Article 8 of the ECHR and the EU Family Reunification Directive (chapter 4). While it was recognised that the A1-minus level itself would not be sufficient to allow immigrants to function independently in the Netherlands, it was nevertheless believed that those who passed the exam at this level would be better prepared for further integration upon arrival.[224]

The 'Knowledge of the Netherlands' test is taken in Dutch.[225] This goes against the recommendations made by the Committee of experts, which found such an examination to be 'unrealistic'. According to the Committee, the very basic language level (A1-minus) of the test meant that candidates could obtain only 'very superficial information' about life in the Netherlands, whereas testing candidates in their own language would require large investments and increase the possibility of fraud. The Committee also pointed out that a cognitive test would not be enough to actually familiarise applicants with 'the Dutch way of life', as such familiarity is gained through experience rather than study. It was consequently suggested not to test applicants' knowledge of the Netherlands, but instead to provide them with information (in their own language) preparing them for their stay.[226] This suggestion was not, however, adopted by the Dutch government.[227]

[222] Art 3.98a(3) Aliens Decree, as it read before 1 April 2011.

[223] Commissie Franssen 2004, 21–22 and 34–35. See also Van der Winden 2006, 94–97.

[224] Van der Winden 2006, 95–97, with references to parliamentary documents.

[225] Art 3.98a(7) Aliens Decree.

[226] Commissie Franssen 2004, 40–41.

[227] *Parliamentary Papers II* 2003–2004, 29 700, No 3, 13. See also Van der Winden 2006, 110–11.

ii. Contents of the Exam after 1 April 2011

Despite the above considerations, the Dutch government decided in late 2009 to make the integration exam abroad more difficult. The proposed changes entered into force on 1 April 2011.[228] As of this date the required level of language proficiency was raised from A1-minus to A1 of the CEFR. Candidates are now also required to pass a reading comprehension test (*toets Geletterdheid en Begrijpend Lezen*) in addition to the other two tests. This means that immigrants to the Netherlands must not only demonstrate oral language skills, but must also be able to read and understand Latin script.

In support of the above changes, the government asserted that the effects of the AIA had so far been insufficient. Because of the basic level of the exam, newcomers who had passed the integration exam abroad still had little command of the Dutch language. In addition, the knowledge obtained abroad was not retained for long enough to have a positive effect on newcomers' further integration in the Netherlands (section VI.D.ii). It was expected that a higher level of proficiency in Dutch and the ability to read (Latin script) would enable immigrants to integrate more rapidly and participate more easily in the labour market.[229] The government announced several measures to assist candidates in obtaining the necessary language skills, including the development of additional study materials to support the introduction of the reading test (section VI.C.iv).[230]

In the government's view, the increased exam requirements would not result in large groups of family migrants being excluded from immigration to the Netherlands. It was stated that, given the availability of extra preparation facilities, the majority of applicants, including illiterate persons and those with very little education, would have 'a reasonable chance' of passing the exam. By way of illustration, the government pointed out that prior to the changes almost 74 per cent of exam candidates passed the test at the A1 level. Lastly, it was claimed that the AIA left enough scope for individual exemptions in situations where the integration exam abroad would make family reunification permanently impossible.[231] Hence, contrary to what it had said earlier (section VI.C.i), the government now claimed that a more difficult exam was not incompatible with Article 8 ECHR or the Family Reunification Directive.[232]

[228] *Bulletin of Acts and Decrees* 2010, 679; entry into force *Bulletin of Acts and Decrees* 2010, 844. The new exam programme is published in *Government Gazette* 2011, 1433.

[229] *Parliamentary Papers II* 2009–2010, 32 175, No 1, 9; *Bulletin of Acts and Decrees* 2010, 679, 3 and 5.

[230] *Parliamentary Papers II* 2009–2010, 32 175, No 1, 22; *Bulletin of Acts and Decrees* 2010, 679, 9–10.

[231] *Bulletin of Acts and Decrees* 2010, 679, 4–6 and 9–11.

[232] ibid, 10–12. The government stated that the wish not to exclude large groups of family migrants was one reason why it had chosen not to introduce a written test, see *Bulletin of Acts and Decrees* 2010, 679, 7–8.

Before the more difficult integration exam was introduced, objections to the proposed changes were raised by the Advisory Committee on Aliens Affairs (*Adviescommissie voor Vreemdelingenzaken* or *ACVZ*) and the Council of State (*Raad van State*). In particular the *ACVZ* stated that little information was as yet available about the effects of the AIA, both on the integration process in the Netherlands and on the extent to which the Act resulted in the exclusion of family migrants. The Committee consequently claimed that no changes to the Act should be made without further research.[233] The Council of State, moreover, was not convinced that the proposed changes would not have the effect of a priori excluding certain groups of immigrants, in particular those who were illiterate or unfamiliar with Latin script, given also that the government offered only minimal support to candidates wishing to prepare themselves for the exam and that adequate Dutch language tuition was not always available in countries of origin (section VI.C.iv). In view of these objections, the Council of State doubted whether the new exam would be consistent with the Family Reunification Directive.[234]

iii. The Examination

The integration exam abroad is conducted on a computer equipped with speech recognition technology.[235] Each attempt to take the exam costs €350.[236] The exam can be taken at Dutch embassies and consulates in immigrants' countries of origin.[237] In 2009 the exam could be taken at 119 locations around the world. In some countries, including several countries whose nationals are not exempted from the AIA (Afghanistan, Iraq, Qatar and Pakistan, for example), there was no opportunity to take the exam.[238] Applicants who cannot take the exam at an embassy or consulate in their own country have to travel to a neighbouring country and take the exam there.[239]

The results of the integration exam abroad are also determined by the computer and no appeal is possible.[240] Applicants can, however, appeal against the decision on their application for admission to the

233 ACVZ 2010a, 4–5. See also ACVZ 2010b.

234 *Government Gazette* 2010, 13998, 14–16.

235 Art 3.98c(2) Aliens Decree. For a detailed discussion of the exam and the technology used, see Van der Winden 2006, 87–119.

236 Art 3.98b(2) Aliens Decree. The evaluation conducted in 2009 showed that candidates spent an average of €721 on the exam, including preparations; see the Principal findings and conclusions of the evaluation of the Act on Integration Abroad (*Evaluatie Wet inburgering in het buitenland. Centrale bevindingen en conclusies*), Annex to *Parliamentary Papers II* 2008–2009, 32 005, No1, 8.

237 Art 3.98c(1) and (2) Aliens Decree.

238 Lodder 2009, 18–19.

239 See www.minbuza.nl.

240 Art 3.98c(3) and Art 3.98d(1) Aliens Decree.

Netherlands.[241] In this procedure they can also address the requirement of integration abroad. There is no limit on the number of times applicants can retake the exam.[242]

iv. Preparing for the Exam

Before the AIA was adopted, the Committee of experts advising on the exam requirements (*Commissie Franssen*) had warned that the availability of Dutch language courses and study materials in countries of origin was still limited, especially for those with little education, and that course providers in the Netherlands did not seem very eager to close this gap. The Committee also found that many study materials were available in the Netherlands, but that these were not suitable for learning Dutch abroad or without the guidance of a language teacher.[243] It advised the government to develop adequate course materials and argued that the integration exam abroad could not be introduced without sufficient facilities to make it reasonably possible for candidates to prepare for the exam.[244] Similar concerns were voiced by the Advisory Committee on Aliens Affairs and the Council of State, which argued that the government should ensure the availability of suitable study materials in countries of origin or at least monitor their development by private actors.[245]

These recommendations, however, were not followed by the government. As mentioned in section V.D, one of the principles behind the reform of the civic integration policy and the introduction of the Act on Integration Abroad was that immigrants to the Netherlands are primarily responsible for their own integration. The government consequently decided not to take responsibility for the availability of integration programmes or study materials in countries of origin and to leave this to the market. Exam candidates could choose from the courses or materials already available or that would be developed to meet their needs. Where necessary they could be helped by family members in the Netherlands or, in the case of religious servants, by the organisation seeking their admission.[246] The government did, nevertheless, develop a preparation package to inform candidates about the requirements of the exam. This also contains the film 'To the Netherlands' (*Naar Nederland*) and a photo book that

[241] Art 72(2) Aliens Act.

[242] Art 3.98d(2) Aliens Decree.

[243] Commissie Franssen 2004, 22–23.

[244] ibid, 26.

[245] ACVZ 2004a, 44–45 and *Parliamentary Papers II* 2003–2004, 29 700, No 4, 4–5. In this respect the Council of State referred to Art 19(6) of the European Social Charter, which states that the Contracting Parties shall facilitate the family reunification of migrant workers. On this provision see section IV.C of ch 7.

[246] *Parliamentary Papers II* 2003–2004, 29 700, No 3, 13–14; *Parliamentary Papers II* 2004–2005, 29 700, No 6, 18 and 27–30. See also Van der Winden 2006, 97–100.

candidates can use to prepare for the 'Knowledge of the Netherlands' test (section VI.C.i). The package was first made available in 13 and later 18 languages and can be bought in bookshops in the Netherlands and on the internet at a cost of €63.90.[247]

The 2009 evaluation showed that integration courses had been set up in immigrants' main countries of origin, including Turkey and Morocco. Of the candidates, 41 per cent indicated that they had taken a course in their own country; however, the quality of these programmes was said to vary from professional language training to 'inferior classes taught in someone's living room'.[248] A majority of the candidates (87 per cent) used the preparation package devised by the government to study for the exam. This package was generally found to provide adequate preparation for the 'Knowledge of the Netherlands' test, but less so for the Dutch language test. Interestingly some candidates found that the package did not prepare them sufficiently for the language test, whereas others found the level of the test to be too low.[249] Finally, some candidates (15 per cent) prepared themselves by taking an integration course in the Netherlands. While some of these candidates had already resided in the Netherlands at an earlier stage, others requested admission on a short-stay visa so as to be able to study for the exam.[250] Although the available case law shows that such requests may be successful, in other cases requests for visas were denied because candidates were found to have insufficiently demonstrated their intention to return home.[251]

As far as the time required for preparation is concerned, the majority of applicants stated that they had studied for less than three months (40 per cent) or between three and six months (35 per cent), while 7 per cent indicated that they had prepared for more than one year. Two-thirds of the candidates stated that they found preparation to be 'difficult' or 'very difficult', whereas the others stated that it was 'not so difficult'.[252]

It can be concluded that the opportunities to prepare for the integration exam abroad differ depending on a number of factors. Some candidates can prepare themselves by taking an integration course in the Netherlands or in their country of origin. For others, however, such courses may not be available or may be too costly or of insufficient quality. The preparation package alone also does not seem sufficient to prepare candidates for the language test, particularly those with little previous education. One of the

[247] Art 3.11 Aliens Decree. See also the website www.naarnederland.nl.

[248] Brink et al 2009, 23–25.

[249] ibid, 25–27.

[250] ibid, 24–25.

[251] See President District Court of The Hague sitting in Amsterdam 28 May 2009, case no 08/34330, LJN: BI8787 (admission granted in appeal) and President District Court of The Hague sitting in Amsterdam 17 September 2009, case nos 09/29111 and 09/25711, LJN: BJ9690 (admission denied).

[252] Brink et al 2009, 27.

recommendations made following the above evaluation was that the government could do more to make adequate preparation facilities available to those wishing to take the integration exam abroad.[253]

Case law to date contains several examples of applicants who requested to be exempted from the integration exam abroad on the grounds that they could not prepare for it. In these cases the applicants claimed that they did not have access to integration courses or study materials (including a computer) and/or that no preparation materials were available in their own language. Nevertheless all the appeals were rejected on the grounds that preparation for the exam was the responsibility of the applicants.[254] In one case, the District Court of The Hague stated that applicants could ask others to help them and to translate the preparation package into a language they could understand.[255]

On 1 April 2011 the level of the integration exam abroad was increased and a reading test introduced. In view of these changes the government decided to make additional preparation materials available in order to increase the effect of the integration exam and ensure that it would not result in the exclusion of large groups of family migrants (section VI.C.ii).[256] In particular, a language module, consisting of instructions, an illustrated exercise book, a CD and an e-learning tool, was added to the existing preparation package. There are two varieties of the module, one specifically designed for people who are illiterate or cannot read Latin script. It was also stated that candidates without a computer could prepare themselves equally well using the exercise book and the CD.[257] Lastly, the government announced that it would improve the supply of information about available preparation materials and seek to promote new initiatives for learning Dutch abroad. It continued to maintain, however, that preparation for the exam remained the primary responsibility of applicants and that it was not the government's responsibility to set up integration courses abroad.[258]

[253] Principal findings and conclusions of the evaluation of the Act on Integration Abroad (*Evaluatie Wet inburgering in het buitenland. Centrale bevindingen en conclusies*), Annex to *Parliamentary Papers II* 2008–2009, 32 005, No 1, 13.

[254] District Court of The Hague sitting in Middelburg 16 August 2007, case nos 07/30015 and 07/31032, LJN: BB3524; District Court of The Hague sitting in Breda 13 November 2007, case no 07/18500; District Court of The Hague 21 October 2009, case no 09/5145, LJN: BK5782; District Court of The Hague sitting in Groningen 10 November 2009, 08/34677; District Court of The Hague sitting in Maastricht 6 October 2012, case nos 09/33430 and 10/9629. In the latter case the applicant was already in the Netherlands and claimed an exemption from the long-stay visa requirement.

[255] District Court of The Hague 21 October 2009, case no 09/5145, LJN: BK5782, para 6.2.

[256] *Parliamentary Papers II* 2009–2010, 32 175, No 1, 9–10 and 22; *Bulletin of Acts and Decrees* 2010, 679, 4.

[257] *Bulletin of Acts and Decrees* 2010, 679, 9–10.

[258] *Bulletin of Acts and Decrees* 2010, 679, 4 and 10.

D. Effects of the Act on Integration Abroad

To the extent that information is available, this section briefly addresses the effects to date of the Act on Integration Abroad. The impact and effects of the Act were measured in an evaluation conducted in 2009 and covering the period between 15 March 2006 and 1 September 2008.[259] Additional data are available from the Monitor of the Integration Exam Abroad (*Monitor inburgeringsexamen buitenland*), which has been regularly published since the AIA entered into force.[260] The Monitor shows that, between 15 March 2006 and 31 December 2011, the integration exam abroad was taken 45,954 times by some 42,951 candidates.[261] Most of the candidates are women: between 2006 and 2011 the share of female participants rose from 60 to 72 per cent. About half of the candidates were between 26 and 35 years of age. Older candidates are less well represented, with only around 5 per cent of candidates being older than 46. In terms of education, the share of candidates having received some form of secondary schooling varied between 43 and 52 per cent, whereas 26–29 per cent was highly educated and 20–25 per cent had had no more than primary education. The available data do not show how many candidates were illiterate. After 1 April 2011, when the reading comprehension test was introduced (section VI.C.ii), the share of highly educated candidates rose to 35 per cent. The most common nationalities taking the exam were Turkish (+/–21 per cent), Moroccan (+/– 15 per cent), Chinese (+/– 6 per cent) and Thai (+/– 6 per cent).[262]

In so far as the effects of the AIA are concerned, a distinction can be made between the effects on the level and nature of immigration to the Netherlands and the effects on further integration after arrival. Both are discussed below.

i. Effects on Immigration

As explained above, the obligation to pass the integration exam abroad functions as a condition for admission to the Netherlands. Those who fail the exam are not allowed to immigrate. In addition, some people who may have wanted to come to the Netherlands may decide not to take the exam at all, either because they do not expect to pass or because they are not prepared to make the effort.

[259] Brink et al 2009, esp 35–70.

[260] The Monitors are available from the Immigration and Naturalisation Service website (www.ind.nl) or as annexes to the *Parliamentary Papers*.

[261] The Monitors for 2007 and 2008 do not indicate whether the candidates had already taken the exam in a previous year; some candidates may therefore have been counted more than once.

[262] As of September 2011 Turkish nationals no longer belong to the target group of the AIA, see section VI.B.iii.

Between 15 March 2006 and 1 September 2008, 96 per cent of the exam candidates passed the integration exam abroad, with 91 per cent of them passing on their first attempt. The latter percentage fell to 88 per cent in 2009, then rose to 92 per cent in the first quarter of 2011. The pass rates for the 'Knowledge of the Netherlands' test are up to 5 per cent higher than those for the language test. After the introduction of the reading comprehension test, the share of candidates passing the exam at their first attempt dropped significantly, to 75 per cent in the period between 1 April and 31 December 2011. The chances of passing the exam are not heavily affected by the age, gender, nationality or educational level of the candidate. However, candidates with no or only primary schooling are somewhat less likely to pass the exam than candidates with secondary or higher education. The same is true for older compared to younger candidates. After 1 April 2011, an increased divergence can be observed between candidates with no or little education (pass rate of 61 per cent) and highly educated candidates (pass rate of 87 per cent). The available data moreover show variation between candidates of different nationalities, ranging from 74 per cent (Yugoslavians [?, *KV*] in 2010) to 100 per cent (South Africans in 2011). As mentioned above, the results achieved by illiterate exam candidates are not indicated separately, which makes it impossible to say whether this group is in effect excluded from family migration to the Netherlands.

The number of applications for admission to the Netherlands decreased strongly following the introduction of the Act on Integration Abroad, from 20,221 in 2005 to 13,796 in 2006.[263] It rose again after 2006, but thus far has not reached the same level as before the AIA entered into force: the available data show that 18,621 applications were made in 2010 and 15,540 in 2011.[264] The introduction of the AIA has not resulted in any significant shifts in the composition of immigrant groups, specifically with regard to age, gender, nationality or level of education. Again, however, there is evidence that those who applied for admission after 15 March 2006 were slightly younger and better educated than those applying before. This could indicate a certain level of self-selection among older persons and those with less education.[265] In 2009, the committee appointed to evaluate

[263] Lodder 2009, 21. For the year 2006, the numbers cited by this author are somewhat lower than those provided in the Monitor of the Integration Exam Abroad (14,230).

[264] These figures concern applications for admission by applicants belonging to the target group of the AIA. As of 2009, more specific data are available, indicating the number of applicants belonging to the target group of the AIA and who are not subject to exemptions (section VI.B.iii). These figures show a total of 13,679 applications in 2010 and 10,553 in 2011; however, a comparison with the situation before 2009 cannot be made.

[265] Brink et al 2009, 60–62. In order to measure these differences, researchers made a comparison with immigrants applying for admission before 15 March 2006. The comparison concerned immigrants who, given their residence purpose and nationality, would have fallen within the target group of the AIA if they had applied after the Act entered into force (Brink et al 2009, 45–47). On the effect of 'self-selection' see also Odé 2009, 289–90.

the AIA concluded that the introduction of the integration exam abroad had thus far not had a 'strong or unacceptable' selective effect on potential immigrants.[266] However, in the second half of 2011, after the exam requirements had been raised (section VI.C.ii), the number of applications by persons belonging to the target group of the AIA dropped by one-third, from approximately 1500 to 1000 applications per month. It remains to be seen whether this trend will persist, and whether the tougher exam requirements will result in a decreased share of applicants who are illiterate or have little education.

ii. Effects on Further Integration in the Netherlands

With regard to further integration in the Netherlands, the studies conducted to date have not been able to establish any effects. As the AIA was introduced fairly recently, most of the immigrants who took the integration exam abroad have not yet taken the advanced integration exam in the Netherlands and it is not possible to say whether they will do better than immigrants who did not study Dutch before their admission.[267] It is also still too early to examine whether those who passed the exam abroad have done better in terms of participating in society, for instance in terms of labour market participation or employment levels.[268] Any assessment of the effects of the AIA on further integration will clearly also raise complicated questions of how 'integration' or 'participation' should be defined and measured.[269]

What has been shown thus far is that candidates who obtain high results on the integration exam abroad also do better when they are tested again upon arrival. The latter results tend, however, to be lower than those obtained in the exam abroad, which may indicate that knowledge acquired in the country of origin dwindles rapidly. In addition, immigrants who pass the exam abroad hardly perform better upon arrival in terms of oral language skills (listening and speaking) than those who did not take the exam, which can be attributed to the very basic level of the exam (until 1 April 2011). Interestingly, however, they do slightly better in terms of written skills (reading and writing), which, at the time of the evaluation, were not tested under the AIA. According to the researchers,

[266] Principal findings and conclusions of the evaluation of the Act on Integration Abroad (*Evaluatie Wet inburgering in het buitenland. Centrale bevindingen en conclusies*), Annex to *Parliamentary Papers II* 2008–2009, 32 005, No 1, 10.

[267] Under the Integration Act 2007 (section V.D) immigrants to the Netherlands must pass an advanced integration exam within 3.5 years of being granted a residence permit.

[268] Brink et al 2009, 48–49. The same goes, a fortiori, for the effects of the changes introduced on 1 April 2011 (section VI.C.ii).

[269] See, eg, the report of the pilot investigation into the effects of the civic integration policy, *Eindrapport Pilotonderzoek Volgsysteem inburgering, effect van inburgering op participatie* (Annex to *Parliamentary Papers II* 2010–2011, 32 321, No 3).

this may be an effect of the preparation for the test or the fact that immigrants who took the exam were better educated than those who did not (section VI.D.i).[270] Candidates themselves indicated that they expected the exam to help them with their further integration, but that their language proficiency was still too limited to make a real difference.[271]

The effects of the AIA on immigrant integration to date appear overall to have been mostly of an intangible nature. Professionals involved in implementing the AIA and integration programmes in the Netherlands have indicated that immigrants are now better prepared for their arrival and that family members in the Netherlands have become more involved in the integration process. Candidates also state that they are motivated to continue studying Dutch after they have been admitted. According to the committee that conducted the evaluation, these signals could translate into more active participation of immigrants in the Netherlands. The committee warned, however, that immigrants need to be able to enrol on an integration programme soon after arriving, whereas long waiting periods will reduce the motivation of newcomers, as well as their freshly acquired language skills.[272]

VII. SUMMARY

This chapter traces the history of the Dutch policy on immigrant integration, with a focus on the events that eventually led to the adoption of the Act on Integration Abroad in 2006. Notwithstanding variations in numbers, residence purposes and countries of origin, immigrants came to the Netherlands throughout the period described above. From the 1970s onwards there was a growing awareness that immigrants would remain in the Netherlands and that they needed to be included in the Dutch society. This resulted in the formulation of the Ethnic Minorities policy in the 1980s, later followed by the Integration policy and the 'New Style' Integration policy. For the most part, Dutch integration policy has not been directed towards all immigrants, but towards those whose socio-economic and / or socio-cultural integration was perceived as problematic (the so-called ethnic minorities, later referred to as 'non-Western allochthones').

Ever since the Ethnic Minorities policy came into existence, language education and social orientation for immigrants formed part of the Dutch

[270] Brink et al 2009, 62–68.

[271] Principal findings and conclusions of the evaluation of the Act on Integration Abroad (*Evaluatie Wet inburgering in het buitenland. Centrale bevindingen en conclusies*), Annex to *Parliamentary Papers II* 2008–2009, 32 005, No 1, 8.

[272] Brink et al 2009, 69–70; Principal findings and conclusions of the evaluation of the Act on Integration Abroad (*Evaluatie Wet inburgering in het buitenland. Centrale bevindingen en conclusies*), Annex to *Parliamentary Papers II* 2008–2009, 32 005, No 1, 8–9 and 14.

approach towards integration. Over time, however, these elements gained importance and more policy measures were taken to support them. In the 1980s, no organised structure for immigrant adult education existed other than the reception programmes for refugees and other protected persons. At the time, language and social orientation courses were taught on an ad hoc basis by a variety of institutions and with a variety of methods. Meanwhile the courses on offer were insufficient to meet the demand. In the early 1990s the structure for adult basic education became more streamlined and specific facilities – including a state exam – were established for education in Dutch as a second language (*NT2*). Around this time the government also began developing reception programmes for newcomers other than refugees with the aim of making these people more self-reliant. This aim tied in well with the new vision on immigrant integration, formulated in 1994, which emphasised the need for active participation of all citizens.

As the reception policy developed further (and became known as the civic integration policy), it became generally accepted that participation in the reception programmes had to be mandatory. A legal basis for such mandatory participation was eventually introduced in 1998 in the form of the Newcomers Integration Act. Several years later, with the introduction of the 'New Style' Integration policy, the approach towards immigrant integration became yet more stringent and integration conditions were also introduced into immigration policy as a condition for admission and permanent or independent residence in the Netherlands. The integration exam abroad as a condition for admission was laid down in the Act on Integration Abroad, which entered into force on 15 March 2006.

The AIA is discussed in detail in section VI of this chapter. As outlined there, the target group of the Act consists mostly of family migrants from non-Western countries. In addition, religious servants are also subject to the condition of integration prior to admission. Although several exemption grounds are available, until recently individual exemptions were never or rarely granted for illiteracy or other forms of hardship. It is the responsibility of the candidates themselves (and their family members) to prepare for the integration exam abroad; some study materials are provided by the Dutch government, but these are not available in all languages and – until recently – did not prepare for the language test. While the requirements of the integration exam abroad were originally rather basic, the level was raised on 1 April 2011 and a reading comprehension test introduced to complement the examination of candidates' oral language skills.

After the introduction of the AIA, the number of immigrants in the target group remained lower than before. There are no signs as yet that the exam has the effect of excluding particular groups of persons, although older and less educated immigrants tend to be less well represented and no information is available regarding the effects on illiterate persons. It is, furthermore, still too early to say whether the AIA has had a positive effect on the integration process in the Netherlands. The evaluation conducted in 2009 shows that immigrants who pass the exam tend to be more prepared and motivated and have slightly better written language skills than those who came before the AIA entered into force. It remains to be seen, however, whether these results will also have an effect in the longer term, and how the above results will be affected by the increased exam requirements.

3

Concepts of Integration and Citizenship in the Netherlands

I. INTRODUCTION

THE PREVIOUS CHAPTER gave an overview of Dutch integration policy up until the adoption of the Act on Integration Abroad. Since the early 1990s the objective of this policy has often been formulated in terms of citizenship. Yet both citizenship and integration are rather abstract concepts that lend themselves to differing interpretations.[1] It is worthwhile, therefore, to analyse in more detail the meaning given to these concepts in Dutch integration and immigration policies. This analysis serves two aims. The first is to show how the Dutch understanding of integration and citizenship has developed over time. The second is to gain better insight into the objectives pursued by the Act on Integration Abroad.

This chapter focuses on two distinct themes. One concerns the relationship between immigration and integration policy and the construction of integration as an exclusionary concept. Section II explains how the integration exam abroad, as a *requirement for admission*, is expected to contribute to better integration in the Netherlands. The second theme is the changing meaning of integration throughout different stages of Dutch integration policy. Section III traces developments in the definition of integration, and hence in the objectives of the integration policy, both before and after the introduction of the Act on Integration Abroad. At the end of each section, a limited normative assessment is provided of the Dutch integration objectives and of the integration exam abroad as an instrument to achieve them.

The findings presented in this chapter are primarily based on parliamentary documents expressing the views of the Dutch government. Where useful, other sources, such as the reports of the Scientific Council for Government Policy (*WRR*), are used to illustrate specific developments.

[1] See, amongst others, Fermin 2000, 17–25; Bosniak 2006, 19–20; Klaver and Odé 2009, 13–24.

II. INTEGRATION AS AN ADMISSION REQUIREMENT

A. Integration as a Ground for Exclusion before 2003

Before the proposal for the Act on Integration Abroad was submitted in 2003, considerations of integration policy already played a role in the formulation of Dutch immigration rules. Under the Ethnic Minorities policy (chapter 2, section III), a restrictive policy on immigration was seen as a condition for successful integration.[2] This position was confirmed in a 2001 policy paper, where the Dutch government stated that the number of immigrants that could be admitted was limited by the capacity of Dutch society to absorb new arrivals. This capacity was said to be 'dependent on many factors, including employment opportunities, social infrastructures, the availability of reception and housing, but also the mental preparedness of Dutch nationals to live together with new citizens'.[3] The paper moreover highlighted the potentially negative economic and social consequences of immigration, especially with regard to immigrants who were 'at a larger distance from Western culture'.[4] This illustrates that both the scope and nature of immigration flows were considered relevant factors in determining the impact of immigration on the integration process.

Initially, however, considerations of integration did not point unequivocally in the direction of a restrictive immigration policy. Specifically where family migration was concerned, it was also recognised that family reunification could have a positive effect on the well-being of migrants already living in the Netherlands.[5] From this perspective, the right to family reunification was viewed as an element of a strong legal status and in turn as a prerequisite for successful integration.[6] Nevertheless, family reunification and especially family formation were at the same time also perceived as both symptom and cause of a faltering integration process. The fact that some immigrants in the Netherlands chose to marry someone from their country of origin was seen as a sign that they were not oriented towards the Netherlands. Concerns were also raised about a lack of participation of family migrants in Dutch society and the effects of this on their children.[7] These concerns eventually resulted in the introduction of new criteria for regulating family migration, including age and income

[2] Van Walsum 2008, 169–70.

[3] *Parliamentary Papers II* 2001–2002, 28 198, No 2 (*Nota 'Integratie in het perspectief van immigratie'*), 7. In the same vein, see *Parliamentary Papers II* 2003–2004, 28 689, No 17 (*Kabinetsreactie rapport Commissie Blok*), 15.

[4] *Nota 'Integratie in het perspectief van immigratie'* (n 3), 13–14.

[5] ibid, 45–46; WRR 2001a, 225.

[6] Van Walsum 2008, 226–27.

[7] WRR 2001a, 75 and 225; *Nota 'Integratie in het perspectief van immigratie'* (n 3), 45–46.

requirements.[8] Some years later these requirements were followed by the integration exam abroad, which is discussed below.

B. The Act on Integration Abroad: from Inclusion to Exclusion

i. Inclusion: Preparing for Life in the Netherlands

The idea for the integration exam abroad was introduced in 2003 as part of the 'New Style' Integration policy (section V.D of chapter 2). Initially, the exam was presented primarily as an instrument for the inclusion of newcomers. It was argued that integration abroad would enable immigrants to be better prepared for their future life in the Netherlands and to experience a greater degree of autonomy immediately upon their arrival.[9] Clearly, this argument was based on the assumption that those having to take the exam would eventually be admitted. In the government's view, taking the integration exam abroad would allow the integration process to start earlier: before being admitted, immigrants would already be obliged to obtain basic knowledge of the Dutch language and society. It was anticipated that this early preparation would make their integration in the Netherlands both faster and more effective. This connection between integration abroad and further integration in the Netherlands is also reflected in the target group of the AIA. According to the government, 'it would not be useful to impose the integration exam abroad on aliens who will not be subject to integration obligations in the Netherlands'.[10] Consequently, the Act applies only to immigrants who will also be subject to compulsory integration after being admitted.

The integration exam abroad – and the sanction of non-admission for those failing the exam – was thus originally seen as an incentive for those who would not prepare themselves for life in the Netherlands of their own accord.[11] It may be recalled in this respect that one of the principal features of the 'New Style' Integration policy was a strong emphasis on individual responsibility (chapter 2, section V.B). Implicit in the view of the exam as an 'incentive', however, is that all applicants for admission can eventually pass and enter the Netherlands. Yet, as was pointed out by the Dutch Council of State, application of the AIA would also result in the

[8] Van Walsum 2008, 226–38.

[9] *Parliamentary Papers II* 2003–2004, 29 543, No 2 (*Contourennota 'Herziening van het inburgeringsstelsel')*, 5–6; *Parliamentary Papers II* 2003–2004, 29 700, No 3, 4, 6 and 16; *Parliamentary Papers II* 2004–2005, 29 700, No 6, 1–2, 8, 11 and 13.

[10] *Parliamentary Papers II* 2004–2005, 29 700, No 6, 33.

[11] *Parliamentary Papers II* 2003–2004, 29 203, No 1, (*Brief Integratiebeleid Nieuwe Stijl*), 16; *Contourennota 'Herziening van het inburgeringsstelsel'* (n 9), 7; *Parliamentary Papers II* 2004–2005, 29 700, No 6.

exclusion of those immigrants who would not pass the exam.[12] The explanatory memorandum to the AIA (*memorie van toelichting*) was subsequently revised so as to include reasons why failure to pass the exam should result in non-admission.

ii. Exclusion: the Threat of Continuing Immigration

In the above memorandum the government reinforced its earlier stance that immigration could cause problems in the field of integration (section II.A), claiming that the continuing immigration to the Netherlands resulted in a constant repetition of the integration process 'at the macro level' as all new immigrants had to start their integration from the beginning. This was deemed to have a negative influence on social cohesion in Dutch society, as well as on the resident population's acceptance of new migrants.[13] Additionally, it was feared that continual immigration and delayed integration would marginalise certain groups in the population and result in their having a reduced capacity for social participation, poor opportunities in the labour market and structural dependence on social security benefits. Such marginalisation could in turn increase the chances of immigrants turning away from society and becoming susceptible to anti-Western feelings or radical ideologies. Lastly, since many new immigrants were family migrants who would raise their children in the Netherlands, there were concerns that these problems would be transferred from one generation to the next.[14]

Against the background of these expected problems, the integration exam abroad was proposed as a selection criterion for distinguishing between those immigrants whose integration into Dutch society was likely to be successful and others who would likely prove unable to integrate successfully.[15] Even as an immigration requirement, therefore, the exam still pursued an integration objective. However, whereas the earlier arguments in support of the AIA were based on the assumption that applicants for admission would eventually be *included*, the current argument assumes that unsuccessful immigrants will be *excluded*. In this reasoning, the integration of those already present in the Netherlands will improve because others, who could disturb this process, will be kept out. The lasting influence of this line of argumentation on Dutch immigration policy was illustrated several years after the AIA had been adopted. While recognising that immigration to the Netherlands is unavoidable and

[12] *Parliamentary Papers II* 2003–2004, 29 700, No 4, 1.

[13] *Parliamentary Papers II* 2003–2004, 29 700, No 3, 3; *Parliamentary Papers II* 2004–2005, 29 700, No 6, 3.

[14] *Parliamentary Papers II* 2003–2004, 29 700, No 3, 4; *Parliamentary Papers II* 2004–2005, 29 700, No 6, 4.

[15] *Parliamentary Papers II* 2003–2004, 29 700, No 3, 6.

sometimes also desirable (notably in the case of labour migration), the government nevertheless asserted that

> the arrival of migrants whose convictions and behaviour differ from, and sometimes clash heavily with, the convictions and behaviour of resident Dutch citizens has led to social tensions and discussions. The everyday effect of cultural diversity, in combination with the arrival of low-educated migrants who are insufficiently equipped for life in the Dutch society, has exerted severe pressure on the quality of life particularly in the larger cities.[16]

The need for a selective immigration policy was subsequently reconfirmed, together with the intention to increase the level of the integration exam abroad.[17]

iii. Selection: from Motivation to Education

It was submitted in section II.A that both the scope and nature of family migration to the Netherlands gave rise to concerns with regard to integration. Contrary to what has been asserted by other authors, however, the legislative history of the AIA shows that the integration exam abroad was primarily intended to act as a selection mechanism rather than as a mere barrier to immigration.[18] As explained above, the purpose of the exam is to select those immigrants for admission whose integration in the Netherlands is likely to be successful. Meanwhile, it was acknowledged that introducing the AIA would also have the effect of restricting immigration.[19] However reducing the number of immigrants was not presented as a goal in itself. In the words of the Dutch government:

[16] *Parliamentary Papers II* 2009–2010, 31 268, No 25 (*Integratiebrief*), 2.

[17] *Parliamentary Papers II* 2009–2010, 32 175, No 1 (*Kabinetsaanpak huwelijks- en gezinsmigratie*). See also, more recently, *Parliamentary Papers II* 2010–2011, 32 824, No 1 (*Nota 'Integratie, binding, burgerschap'*), 5 and 12–13.

[18] See Spijkerboer 2007, 30–31 and Carrera and Wiesbrock 2009, 12–13. The latter authors argue that a reduction in the number of immigrants was a 'hidden' but nonetheless 'crucial' objective of the AIA. They claim, first of all, that the exclusionary effects of the AIA were not explicitly addressed by the Dutch legislator in the explanatory memorandum (*memorie van toelichting*) to the Act. In support of this statement the authors refer to the advisory opinion of the Dutch Council of State (section II.B.i). However, this opinion concerned the draft explanatory memorandum (*ontwerp-memorie van toelichting*), which is sent to the Council of State before being made public (Art 15(1)(a) of the Act on the Council of State (*Wet op de Raad van State*)). By contrast, the final memorandum, to which the authors also refer, includes the comments of the Council of State and expressly acknowledges the exclusionary effects of the AIA (*Parliamentary Papers II* 2003–2004, 29 700, No 3). In another argument the authors state that the level of the integration exam abroad was raised in March 2008 because 'candidates had a higher level of language proficiency than expected', which resulted in 'too many applicants' passing the test. From the parliamentary documents, however, it appears that the exam was adjusted not because the pass rate was considered too high, but because the test turned out to measure a lower level of language proficiency than agreed on before the AIA entered into force (*Parliamentary Papers II* 2006–2007, 29 700, No 40, 5–6).

[19] *Parliamentary Papers II* 2003–2004, 29 700, No 3, 15.

> The new integration requirement does not primarily aim to reduce the influx of new immigrants. The most desirable situation would be one in which every potential immigrant would become sufficiently acquainted, in the country of origin, with the language and the society of the country in which he wishes to settle.[20]

From this statement it can be concluded that the integration exam abroad was regarded as a measure of qualitative rather than quantitative immigration control. While it was expected that the exam would result in a reduction of immigration to the Netherlands, this was not presented as a solution for integration-related problems or as one of the reasons for the enactment of the AIA. Nevertheless, to the extent that this effect remained within the limits set by international law, it was considered 'preferable to the situation in which the integration process is hampered immediately after [the] arrival [of the immigrant]'.[21] In other words, the fact that fewer immigrants would be admitted was considered acceptable in view of the importance of the integration objective.[22]

This being said, the observation that the integration exam abroad was intended to act as a selection mechanism raises the question of the selection criterion to be used. In this respect the Dutch legislator's position appears to have developed since the AIA was adopted. Initially, it was suggested that the main criterion for selection would be the immigrant's motivation or determination to successfully integrate. It was claimed that the level of the integration exam abroad would be 'reasonably attainable for all those who make sufficient efforts' and that no one would be a priori excluded from coming to the Netherlands.[23] To pass the exam immigrants would be required to demonstrate their readiness to make substantial efforts to integrate in the Netherlands, whereas those not willing to do so would not be eligible for admission.[24] By contrast, it was expressly stated that the purpose of the AIA was not to select immigrants on the basis of their education and that both highly skilled and less-educated immigrants would be able to pass the integration test.[25]

Yet, despite the wish to use immigrants' willingness to integrate as the primary selection criterion, the integration exam abroad was formulated as an obligation of result.[26] Instead of having to complete an integration

[20] *Parliamentary Papers II* 2004–2005, 29 700, No 6, 43.

[21] *Parliamentary Papers II* 2003–2004, 29 700, No 3, 14.

[22] *Parliamentary Papers II* 2004–2005, 29 700, No 6, 13 and 41.

[23] ibid, 10. See also section VI.C.i of ch 2.

[24] *Parliamentary Papers II* 2003–2004, 29 700, No 3, 11 and 16; *Parliamentary Papers II* 2004–2005, 29 700, No 6, 7, 11, 17 and 41.

[25] *Parliamentary Papers II* 2003–2004, 29 700, No 3, 11; *Parliamentary Papers II* 2004–2005, 29 700, No 6, 10–11, 18, 40 and 44.

[26] A nice illustration of the distinction between obligations of effort and obligations of result is provided by Bonjour, who compares the Dutch and French systems of 'integration abroad', Bonjour 2010, 303–07.

programme or invest a certain number of hours to prepare for life in the Netherlands, immigrants are asked to pass an exam at a specified level. This means that those with little education or learning capacity will have to show more effort and determination than those who are highly educated or learn easily. Additionally, the level of persistence needed to pass the exam depends on other factors, such as the availability of learning materials and the candidate's financial means. These differences were accepted on the grounds that the basic knowledge required to pass the integration exam abroad was minimally necessary for successful integration in the Netherlands.[27] By setting this standard, however, the legislator agreed to a measure that would select immigrants not only on the basis of their motivation to integrate, but also on their ability.[28] Even if the exam was set at such a low level that those without any formal education were able to pass, such people still had to make more effort than others and were probably more easily deterred from seeking admission at all.

More recently, the government explicitly changed its earlier position and claimed that education was an important factor in determining immigrants' chances of successful integration. Towards the end of 2009, several years after the AIA entered into force, it was asserted that 'the long-term effects of the integration exam abroad are still limited and 25 per cent of family migrants who take the exam have not received more than primary education in their country of origin'.[29] It was then concluded that the level of the exam had to be raised so as to ensure that immigrants who were admitted would be better prepared for their further integration in the Netherlands. A reading comprehension test was also introduced, on the grounds that the ability to read the Latin script also enhanced the prospects of successful integration.[30] These changes, which took effect on 1 April 2011, show that a certain level of education or literacy has replaced the motivation to integrate as the primary criterion for selection under the AIA.

C. The Legitimacy of Exclusion: a Balancing of Interests

The previous subsections describe how the notion of integration has been conceptualised in relation to the admission of immigrants to the

[27] *Parliamentary Papers II* 2003–2004, 29 700, No 3, 11 and 14.

[28] It appears that this was also recognised by the Dutch government, which stated at one point that the exam would entail 'a selection of persons who are willing *and able* to invest in their own integration' (emphasis added), *Parliamentary Papers II* 2004–2005, 29 700, No 6, 17. The distinction between education and motivation as grounds for selecting family migrants is also noted by Spijkerboer in his analysis of the political debate that preceded the adoption of the AIA, see Spijkerboer 2007, 31–32.

[29] *Kabinetsaanpak huwelijks- en gezinsmigratie* (n 17), 3.

[30] ibid, 3 and 9–10. See also ch 2, section VI.C.ii.

Netherlands and demonstrate that the integration exam abroad, as a requirement for admission, has been supported largely by arguments of exclusion. For immigrants eventually admitted to the Netherlands, preparation for the exam can be seen as a first step in the integration process. However, the exam mainly functions as a requirement for admission on the assumption that the integration process in the Netherlands will benefit from a selective immigration policy.

The exclusionary purpose and effects of the AIA led Groenendijk to conclude that the integration exam abroad aims to control immigration rather than facilitate integration.[31] However, these objectives do not necessarily contradict each other. Instead, as the above analysis shows, the aim of integration, as understood in the context of the AIA, includes facilitating a smooth integration process within the Netherlands that is not interrupted by the arrival of new immigrants whose prospects for integration are considered problematic.[32] The aim of the integration exam abroad can thus be described as 'integration through exclusion'. Arguably this is not merely a terminological issue. By recognising that certain immigrants are excluded in order to make integration easier for those who are already in the Netherlands, the interests of the receiving state are made visible. The question to be asked, then, is not *if* the aim of the AIA is to enable integration, but whether the Act constitutes a suitable measure to achieve this aim and whether the interests of the receiving state outweigh those of the individuals (immigrants and their family members) who are seeking admission.

Regarding the latter question, different authors have argued that the acceptability of immigration conditions must be determined by balancing the competing interests (the interest of the state versus that of the individual), with an important consideration being the reasons for which admission is sought. Vermeulen has submitted that the case for admission is particularly strong in situations where a person seeks international protection – thus leaving little or no room for requirements in the field of integration. On the other hand, states have a greater amount of discretion in cases of labour migration or family reunification, to decide the terms under which admission may be granted. In the latter type of cases, such requirements may be imposed as are necessary to protect national interests, including the interest of social unity or integration.[33]

[31] Groenendijk 2011, 27–28.

[32] cp Bonjour 2010, 307, who states that the AIA is intended to 'assuage the "problem" of social cohesion by reducing the inflow of "problematic" migrants'.

[33] Vermeulen 2010a, 140–42. See also Benhabib 2004, 137; ACVZ 2004b, 20–21 and Tholen 1997, 194–95. The latter author, while not explicitly pleading for the admission of asylum seekers, refers to a 'responsibility to offer help' as a criterion for the just regulation of immigration. It may be assumed that application of this principle will also result in a prioritisation of those seeking international protection. Lastly, see Groenendijk 2011, 29–30, who states that language requirements may well be legitimate for selecting labour migrants or

In my view it is indeed plausible to maintain that the legitimacy of integration conditions depends, to a large extent, on the grounds on which admission is sought. It can also be accepted that states are entitled to a certain amount of discretion where the regulation of family migration is concerned. Nevertheless, the individual interest involved in cases of family reunification should not be underestimated. Family reunification cases differ from asylum cases in that the family members will usually also have the opportunity to live together in their country of origin, in which case denying admission will not impact on the freedom to live as a family. However, people have a strong interest in being able to live together with their (immediate) family in the state of which they are nationals or with which they otherwise have strong ties.[34] It is submitted that the Dutch legislator, in adopting the Act on Integration Abroad, has failed to give this interest sufficient weight. The extent to which integration requirements for the admission of family members fit into the legal framework for family reunification is addressed in chapter 4 of this study.

Lastly, it is argued that the legitimacy of integration requirements for the admission of immigrants is greater if it can be established that such requirements actually contribute to the realisation or preservation of social unity. In most cases it is obviously not possible to establish the effect of integration measures before they are adopted. However, the longer these measures have been in force, the more weight has to be given to evidence (positive or negative) of their effectiveness. Thus, when considering the legitimacy of the AIA, the results of the 2009 evaluation (and further evaluations) must be taken into account (see chapter 2, section VI.D).

III. THE INTEGRATION EXAM ABROAD AS AN INSTRUMENT OF CITIZENSHIP

A. Integration and Citizenship in the Netherlands before the Introduction of the Act on Integration Abroad[35]

Chapter 2 explained that the issue of immigrant integration in the Netherlands was first comprehensively addressed in the Ethnic Minorities

co-ethnics (persons belonging to an ethnic group with strong ties to the host state, such as the German *Aussiedler*), but is more critical as regards language or integration requirements in the case of family reunification.

[34] See also De Hart 2009, 251 and Groenendijk 2011 (n 33).

[35] The description and analysis in the following subsections (III.A–III.C) are based on primary sources, mainly parliamentary documents and reports by public advisory bodies. The developments signalled largely correspond to those described by other authors; see notably Driouichi 2007, 18–47; Spijkerboer 2007, 13–17; Klaver and Odé 2009, 42–55; Fermin 2009, 16–19 and 22–25 and Van Gunsteren 2009. Where applicable, references to this literature are made to support or complement the analysis in this chapter or to highlight relevant differences.

policy, which came into being in the 1980s. In terms of integration objectives, this policy primarily sought to improve the legal and socio-economic position of immigrants compared to Dutch residents and to further their political engagement by granting them voting rights at a local level and adopting lenient laws on citizenship.[36] At the same time, although members of ethnic minority groups were expected to respect 'basic Dutch norms and values' and make efforts to learn Dutch, these aspects of the integration process received relatively little attention. As far as ethnic minorities' cultural identities were concerned, the Dutch government rejected both forced assimilation and segregation as possible policy approaches. Instead it was claimed that minority groups had to be enabled to experience and develop their identity in relation to Dutch society, which in turn would be changed by these new cultural influences. The government saw it as its task to create the conditions for this interaction to take place.[37]

In the early 1990s the concept of 'integration' – and consequently of the objectives of the integration policy – was reconsidered (chapter 2, section IV.B). This reconsideration was inspired by continuing concerns about immigration and the position of migrant minorities, as well as the ongoing restructuring of the welfare state and a changing philosophy on the relationship between the state and its citizens.[38] The reformulated integration policy emphasised that integration was not only a matter of rights, but also of duties, and that the objective of integration (thereafter referred to as 'citizenship') required active participation in the public domain. As the government put it, citizens were 'free, autonomous and active human beings who have a responsibility for their own well-being as well as for the society in which they live'.[39] Concern was expressed that the Ethnic Minorities policy had treated immigrants too much as 'needy categories', thus making them dependent on the state.[40] By contrast, the notion of 'citizenship' entailed immigrants being expected to 'become judicious and mature citizens able to cope in the competitive Dutch society'.[41]

[36] *Parliamentary Papers II* 1993–1994, 23 684, No 2 (*Contourennota Integratiebeleid etnische minderheden*), 10.

[37] Draft memorandum on minorities policy published by the Department of Home Affairs in 1981 (*Ontwerp-minderhedennota*), 18–20, 37–38; *Parliamentary Papers II* 1982–1983, 16 102, No 21 (*Minderhedennota*), 11, 107–108.

[38] Fermin 2009, 16.

[39] *Contourennota Integratiebeleid etnische minderheden* (n 36), 24; *Parliamentary Papers II* 1998–1999, 26 333, No 2 (*Nota'Kansen krijgen, kansen pakken'*), 3–4 and 8–9. The move towards 'active citizenship' is also visible in two reports published by the Scientific Council for Government Policy, see WRR 1989 and WRR 1992.

[40] WRR 1989, 17. See also the position paper published by the Department of Welfare entitled 'Investing in integration' (*Investeren in integreren*), in which it was stated that future integration policy should aim to reinforce the independent participation of immigrants in society (in particular through work and education) in order to prevent their marginalisation and dependence on communal facilities (Ministerie van WVC, *Investeren in integreren*, 1994, 1–7).

[41] *Contourennota Integratiebeleid etnische minderheden* (n 36), 24–25.

The notion of 'citizenship', as introduced in 1994, also, however, assumed a shared commitment of all Dutch residents (immigrant and non-immigrant), civil society and the government for the integration process. Immigrants' responsibilities were balanced by responsibilities on the part of non-immigrant residents, the government and various social institutions and organisations (schools, housing corporations, employment agencies and so on) to enable immigrant participation by creating an open and receptive society.[42] Integration was thus perceived as a two-sided process.

The focus of integration policy in the 1990s was primarily on socio-economic integration,[43] with immigrants' participation in education and the labour market often seen as key factors for achieving the citizenship objective. It was in order to achieve such participation that immigrants were expected to learn Dutch and to acquire basic knowledge about the Netherlands.[44] As discussed in the previous chapter, attaining educational, professional or social self-reliance was also the objective of the Newcomers Integration Act adopted in 1998 (chapter 2, section IV.D).[45]

In the meantime, cultural expressions by ethnic minorities or interactions between minorities and the majority population did not feature prominently in the newly formulated notion of citizenship, especially in the first few years after it was introduced. This absence may be explained by two factors. Firstly, the idea of government support for ethnic minority cultures had been criticised. In September 1991 Frits Bolkestein, a Member of Parliament for the liberal *VVD* party, called for a more 'daring' integration policy, in which cultural relativism made way for the dominance of certain liberal principles that Bolkestein claimed to be universal and fundamental to the Dutch legal order (notably the separation of church and state, freedom of speech, tolerance and non-discrimination). According to Bolkestein, these principles had to be defended against what he perceived as illiberal practices occurring particularly in Muslim cultures, including discrimination of homosexuals, forced marriages and calls for the death of the writer Salman Rushdie.[46]

Although these remarks spurred a great deal of protest Bolkestein's central thesis – the prevalence of liberal values and principles over cultural relativism – was eventually generally accepted.[47] During the ensuing 'national integration debate' (*maatschappelijk debat integratie*) the Dutch Home Affairs Minister (then responsible for integration policy) stated that

[42] ibid, 24–27.
[43] Fermin 2009, 16.
[44] WRR 1989, 43–47.
[45] Fermin also pointed out that, in line with the perspective of the 'activating welfare state', an important target group of civic integration policy consisted of newcomers dependent on social security benefits. See Fermin 2009, 23.
[46] Prins 2000, 27–30; Struijs 1998, 17.
[47] Prins 2000, 29; Driouichi 2007, 22; Van Gunsteren 2009, 45.

certain values were non-negotiable within Dutch society.[48] The revised Integration policy also stated that citizenship required respect for norms described as fundamental to the Dutch constitutional system, including the democratic legal order, freedom of expression, the individual right to self-determination, equality between the sexes and the separation of church and state.[49]

The above focus on respect for liberal principles can help explain why support for ethnic minority cultural expressions waned. In addition, the prevailing view was that socio-cultural integration would come about after, and as a result of, successful social-economic integration, which would be achieved primarily through labour participation and (language) education.[50] The stated aim of the integration policy was primarily, therefore, to achieve results in these latter fields. As far as civic integration was concerned, Dutch history and information on national holidays were taught as part of the social orientation course, but only as 'nice to know' topics.[51] It was also expressly stated that members of ethnic minority groups were not expected to give up their own (ethnic) identity as this was regarded as a matter of personal choice.[52] Compared to the Ethnic Minorities policy, however, the revised Integration policy did increase the pressure on individual immigrants to 'fit in' and adapt to mainstream society.[53]

From 1998 onwards, elements of culture and ethnicity began to play a more significant role in the way integration was conceptualised in the Netherlands.[54] Although active citizenship remained the core objective of integration policy and responsibility for achieving this objective continued to be placed on immigrants and the receiving society alike,[55] the government also expressed an increased awareness of the role of cultural differences – including minority religions – in the integration process.[56] Initially, it was proposed accommodating these differences in the Dutch constitutional order, while interaction between different ethnic and cultural groups was to be promoted.[57] Gradually, however, the scope for

[48] *Parliamentary Papers II* 1991–1992, 22 314, No 9, 2.

[49] *Contourennota Integratiebeleid etnische minderheden* (n 36), 25..

[50] ibid, 24–25; WRR 1989, 23–24, 49–50. See also Driouichi 2007, 23 and Fermin 2009, 17.

[51] Ch 2, section V.C.iii. On the contents of the social orientation course and the way in which these topics were taught, see also Van Huis and De Regt 2005, 397–400.

[52] *Contourennota Integratiebeleid etnische minderheden* (n 36), 25.

[53] Driouichi 2007, 25 (citing Fermin 1997, 226). This development was also observed by Schinkel, see Schinkel 2008, 39–40.

[54] See also Van Huis and De Regt 2005, 382–83.

[55] *Nota 'Kansen krijgen, kansen pakken'* (n 39).

[56] ibid, 6–7; *Parliamentary Papers II* 1999–2000, 26 333, No 13. See also section V.B of ch 2. As mentioned there, the government's policy on socio-cultural integration went against the approach proposed by the *WRR* (WRR 2001a).

[57] *Nota 'Kansen krijgen, kansen pakken'* (n 39), 7–8; see also *Parliamentary Papers II* 2003–2004, 29 614, No 2 (*Nota 'Grondrechten in de pluriforme samenleving'*).

cultural, ethnic and religious differences diminished as a more comprehensive concept of citizenship was formulated.[58]

In 2000, the publicist Paul Scheffer called for more commitment to the integration process and for a stronger 'national consciousness' that could serve as guidance for immigrants seeking to integrate. In the ensuing parliamentary debate his ideas were rejected by several (liberal or leftist) political parties (*GroenLinks*, *D66* and *SP*), but defended by the Christian Democratic party (*CDA*).[59] After the 'Scheffer debate', issues of socio-cultural integration, including processes of identity and interaction, continued to play an increasingly important role in integration policy. At this stage it was reaffirmed that immigrants needed scope to experience their own identities. The government also, however, presented a rather wide-ranging view on what integration entailed, declaring that 'immigrants must learn the Dutch language, adopt Dutch values, norms and social codes, qualify for the labour market, internalise the legal order and – most importantly – eventually feel at home'.[60]

As the notion of citizenship thickened, minority groups' affiliations with their own cultures or religions increasingly came to be seen as an obstacle to citizenship, particularly in the case of non-Western immigrants, who were considered to be 'at a greater distance from Western culture', and Muslims.[61] This development was reinforced in the years to come by events such as the attack on the New York Twin Towers in 2001 and the murder of the Dutch filmmaker Theo van Gogh by a Muslim extremist in 2004.[62]

B. The 'New Style' Integration Policy: from 'Active' to 'Shared' Citizenship

In 2003, the Dutch government once again reformulated its position on integration under the heading of the 'New Style' Integration policy (chapter 2, section V.B). At this point the objective of the integration policy, which was then labelled as 'shared citizenship', was described as a series of duties and responsibilities. Rather than fostering or supporting affiliations to minority cultural identities, the government sought to promote unity and social cohesion by emphasising commonalities between citi-

[58] See also Driouichi 2007, 95–96.

[59] *Proceedings II* 2000, No 70, 4700–28 and No 71, 4731–92. Driouichi notes that an important theme in the *CDA's* political programme at the time was that of shared 'norms and values' (*normen en waarden*). After 2002, when the *CDA* came to power, this theme came to play an important role in the integration policy (section III.B). Driouichi 2007, 41–42.

[60] *Parliamentary Papers II* 2001–2002, 28 198, No 2, 13–14.

[61] ibid, 13. See also Fermin 2009, 17–18. In the words of this author 'problems in the field of integration were increasingly defined in terms of cultural conflicts, whereby the Islamic religion was perceived as the main source of division'.

[62] Spijkerboer 2007, 17; Fermin 2009, 17; Van Gunsteren 2009, 46; Vermeulen 2010a, 85–87.

zens. To this end, it was asserted, citizens had to actively participate in Dutch society, speak Dutch and comply with the Dutch Constitution and 'basic Dutch norms'.[63] Although no exhaustive account of these norms was provided, they were said to include

> attempting to sustain oneself financially; complying with laws and regulations; caring for one's environment; respecting the physical integrity of others, including within a marriage; accepting the right of every person to freedom of speech; accepting the sexual preferences of others and recognising the equality of men and women.[64]

At the same time, the ideal of 'shared citizenship' involved achieving individual autonomy and the freedom for citizens to shape their lives as a matter of personal choice. However, the prevailing view at the time was that such freedom and autonomy could not be accomplished unless the above norms were respected.[65]

Under the 'New Style' Integration policy, immigrant participation in education and the labour market continued to be seen as important elements of integration. Immigrants receiving social security benefits and also 'non-active migrant women' (often housewives) were consequently designated as being specific target groups of the (civic) integration policy.[66] In addition, immigrants were expected to orientate themselves towards Dutch society, to adjust to the dominant social norms, to be aware of or even accept the dominant ethical principles and to familiarise themselves with elements of Dutch culture (including the history and geography of the Netherlands, its constitutional system and the monarchy).[67]

[63] *Brief Integratiebeleid Nieuwe Stijl* (n 11), 8–9; see also *Parliamentary Papers II* 2002–2003, 28 637, No 19 (*Hoofdlijnenakkoord 2003*), 14.

[64] *Brief Integratiebeleid Nieuwe Stijl* (n 11), 8–9. See also *Kabinetsreactie Rapport Commissie Blok* (n 3), 7. It may be observed that, throughout the period concerned, the definition of 'Dutch norms and values' remained subject to debate, (also) at the political level. See, eg, *Parliamentary Papers II* 2003–2004, 29 700 VI & 29 203, No 94. There is also evidence that the government tried to avoid an essentialist concept of what Dutch culture entailed (Driouichi 2007, 105–06). However, this did not preclude it from formulating a concept of citizenship in which these elements were included.

[65] *Brief Integratiebeleid Nieuwe Stijl* (n 11), 8–9; *Contourennota 'Herziening van het inburgeringsstelsel'* (n 9), 1.

[66] See, eg, *Brief Integratiebeleid Nieuwe Stijl* (n 11), 10; *Contourennota 'Herziening van het inburgeringsstelsel'* (n 9), 9–10 and 15–16 and *Kabinetsreactie Rapport Commissie Blok*, 29. The aim of getting migrant women to participate in paid labour can be qualified both as a form of economic integration and as the setting of a cultural norm reflecting female emancipation and sex equality, see also section III.C. Spijkerboer shows how this aim eventually became one of the primary stated objectives of the AIA, see Spijkerboer 2007, 35–36.

[67] *Contourennota 'Herziening van het inburgeringsstelsel'* (n 9), 2. As Fermin noted, the formulation of a 'thick public morality' also entailed abstract moral or constitutional principles being translated into specific behavioural norms (see Fermin 2009, 18). Thus, the then Integration Minister Verdonk once publicly rebuked an imam who refused to shake her hand. In the view of the Minister (and several MPs), the imam's action demonstrated a lack of respect for the principle of equality of the sexes and thus constituted a sign of insufficient integration. See NRC Handelsblad 22 November 2004, *Imam geeft Verdonk geen hand.*

This new direction was reflected in the contents of the integration programmes and exams (in the Netherlands and abroad), which subsequently included topics such as Dutch history, social norms and conventions and the rights and obligations of others.[68] Lastly, the need to learn Dutch was presented both as a means towards participation in education and the labour market and as an element of a common culture that would enable social cohesion.[69]

It follows from the above that, by the time the AIA was enacted, the Dutch perception of 'integration' or 'citizenship' had become more encompassing than before and that it became more focused on immigrants' unilateral adaptation to what was portrayed as 'Dutch culture' or 'the Dutch identity'. A distinct, but related and simultaneous development was the shifting of responsibility for the integration process towards individual citizens and immigrants in particular. This shift resulted from concerns that too much facilitation would reduce the initiative and motivation of individuals to contribute to the integration process. In the words of the government,

> A policy that is primarily aimed at providing services carries with it the risk that participation will be considered more important than results. This adds to an atmosphere with regard to integration in which commitment is lacking [. . .]. The emphasis that the government places on the individual responsibility of allochthones and autochthones for the integration process is in line with the ambition to stop the lack of engagement that has surrounded the integration process until this date.[70]

Elsewhere it is stated that '[We must move] away from the often non-committal and service-oriented approach, which has diminished the initiative of those concerned, by aiming for an obligation of integration that will unambiguously activate individual responsibility'.[71]

Thus, to become integrated, immigrants not only had to meet the standards of 'shared citizenship', but also had to do so of their own accord and without government support. This prompted Driouichi to remark that the success of the integration policy was apparently expected to be commensurate with the efforts immigrants had to make.[72] One practical consequence of this approach was that integration programmes were no longer offered, as they had been under the Newcomers Integration Act 1998, either abroad or in the Netherlands, except for some specific groups (see also section V.D of chapter 2).[73]

[68] See ch 2, sections V.C.iii. and VI.C.i. On the contents and function of integration programmes in the Netherlands, see for more detail Van Huis and De Regt 2005.

[69] *Kabinetsreactie Rapport Commissie Blok* (n 3), 9 and 13.

[70] ibid, 11.

[71] *Contourennota 'Herziening van het inburgeringsstelsel'* (n 9), 1.

[72] Driouichi 2007, 90.

[73] See also Fermin 2009, 24 and Vermeulen 2010a, 92.

C. After Enactment of the Act on Integration Abroad: Citizenship in Turmoil

When the AIA entered into force on 15 March 2006, the idea of 'shared citizenship' still constituted the leading integration objective in the Netherlands. As shown above, this objective was reflected in the contents of the integration exam abroad and in the fact that the government did not organise any integration programmes to prepare candidates for the exam. However, the meaning of citizenship, as the leading concept of the integration policy, continued evolving after the Act was adopted, pushed by the rapidly shifting political climate. In 2007, a centre-left government (*Balkenende IV*) took office, consisting of the Christian Democratic party (*CDA*), the Labour Party (*PvdA*) and the smaller Social-Christian *ChristenUnie*. In 2010, this coalition was succeeded by a right-wing government (*Rutte I*), including the Liberal (*VVD*) and Christian Democratic parties and relying for majority support on the far-right Freedom Party (*PVV*). Both coalitions put forward a vision on integration in which participation and social cohesion were key objectives to be achieved. Clearly different attitudes were taken, however, regarding the room allowed for cultural diversity and the role of immigrants in the integration process.

The integration policy of the *Balkenende IV* coalition in many ways echoed the concept of 'active citizenship' devised in the 1990s, but with additional attention for commonality and immigrants' identification with the Netherlands.[74] Immigrants were still expected to learn Dutch and to participate in education and the labour market, besides actively contributing to the communal interest through volunteer work, political participation or other forms of community involvement.[75] With respect to cultural adaptation, however, greater emphasis was placed on reciprocity instead of unilateral adaptation to a dominant 'Dutch identity', with the 'norms and values' of the majority population being presented as objects of discussion and not as benchmarks for migrant minorities.[76] Although a strong focus on unity remained from the previous period, this time unity was defined primarily in terms of 'a shared commitment to common interests such as safety, the education of children and care for fellow residents'.[77] Thereby the existence of cultural and religious differences were considered less of an obstacle to integration than it had been before. Also, a return could be observed to the idea of integration as a two-sided

[74] *Parliamentary Papers II* 2007–2008, 31 268, No 2 (*Integratienota 2007–2011*) and *Integratiebrief* (n 16). See also Fermin 2009, 18 and Van Gunsteren 2009, 49.

[75] *Integratienota 2007–2011* (n 74), 18.

[76] ibid. This turn in the integration policy was likely inspired by the report of the Scientific Council for Government Policy issued in 2007, entitled *Identificatie met Nederland* ('Identification with the Netherlands'), WRR 2007.

[77] *Integratienota 2007-2011* (n 74), 17–18.

process, engaging the responsibility of immigrants as well as the government and the receiving society. This approach was translated into a renewed commitment by the government to improving the organisation of integration programmes under the Integration Act 2007.[78]

Of course the above change of direction was not absolute. Concerns remained that too much facilitation would result in a lack of commitment to the integration process; hence, the individual responsibility of immigrants continued to be stressed.[79] In some areas a call for immigrants to adapt to dominant social norms could also still be heard. It was asserted, for instance, that the principle of equality of the sexes did not allow for the creation of separate facilities for men and women, including where integration programmes were concerned.[80] In the context of family migration, traditional marriage patterns whereby the wife stays at home and is financially dependent on the husband were described as irreconcilable with 'the Dutch principle of equality within marriage'.[81] Lastly, a strong focus was put on the role of citizens as the educators of the next generation. Citizens (and immigrants in particular) were expected to overcome the barriers to their own participation so as not to pass them on to their children.[82] Overall, however, between 2007 and 2011 the tone of the integration policy was more relaxed and the ideal of citizenship more open and attainable for immigrants with different means and backgrounds.

By contrast, the integration memorandum of the *Rutte I*-coalition signalled a return to a monocultural idea of citizenship and a coercive integration policy, with a renewed emphasis on immigrants' 'individual responsibility' for the integration process.[83] More explicitly than before, the Dutch government renounced multiculturalism as the leading model for integration policy. Instead, Dutch society was posited as a historically determined society to which immigrants would have to adapt:

> The fundamentals shaping social life in the Netherlands are historically determined and form markers of identification that are shared by many Dutch people and cannot be given up. . . . Integration means integration into Dutch society. A society that was formed through the dedication, the efforts, the expectations

[78] See notably *Parliamentary Papers II* 2006–2007, 31 143, No 1 (*Deltaplan inburgering*). See also Fermin 2009, 24 and Vermeulen 2010a, 137–38.

[79] *Integratienota 2007–2011* (n 74), 20–21.

[80] *Integratiebrief* (n 16), 7.

[81] *Kabinetsaanpak huwelijks- en gezinsmigratie* (n 17), 4–5. To a large extent the problems signalled in this paper concern acts prohibited by Dutch law, notably polygamy, forced marriage and domestic violence. However, the paper also addresses situations not involving unlawful behaviour, such as women assuming a subservient role in relation to their husbands or not engaging in any activities outside the home. Despite the 'grey area' often existing, the objective of the integration policy in these cases is clearly not limited to compliance with legal norms.

[82] *Integratiebrief* (n 16), 6; *Kabinetsaanpak huwelijks- en gezinsmigratie* (n 17), 4–5. The above concerns became more pronounced as of 2009, when Integration Minister Ella Vogelaar was replaced by Eberhard van der Laan.

[83] *Nota 'Integratie, binding, burgerschap'* (n 17).

> and convictions of the generations that preceded us, which are also the foundations on which it will further develop through the dedication, efforts, expectations and convictions of all who seek to turn our society into a lasting home. Despite the unmistakable presence of social change and cultural development, society is based on a fundamental continuity of values, beliefs, institutions and customs that form the leading culture of Dutch society and are co-determining of its recognisability. [my translation, *KV*][84]

As the 'markers of identification' of Dutch society the government mentioned not only the core values of the Dutch Constitution, but also historically or culturally defined elements such as the Dutch language, monuments and architecture and unwritten behavioural codes. Immigrants were expected to know the Dutch language and customs and to respect and share the Dutch constitutional values of freedom, responsibility, equality, tolerance and solidarity. These demands came together with the recognition that Dutch society would change, partially as a consequence of migration. It was stated that assimilation or the realisation of a uniform identity were not objectives of the integration policy and that room for diversity and plurality were among the achievements of the Dutch Constitution.[85] It remains unclear, however, what this room for diversity still entailed and where it was to be found.

In addition to the above, the integration memorandum put great emphasis on autonomy, commitment and solidarity, and on the duty of all citizens to participate and contribute to the common interest. The government claimed, however, that the envisaged ideal of citizenship would not come about by itself. A coercive civic integration policy was therefore considered justified, to prevent social segregation and a sense of non-belonging.[86] As regards the Integration Act 2007, the revised notion of citizenship informed proposals to discontinue government support for civic integration and to make all immigrants fully responsible for paying and organising their own integration course. In addition, it was confirmed that a requirement to learn Dutch would be introduced into the Social Assistance Act (chapter 1, section I.A) and it was proposed to revoke the (non-permanent) right of residence of immigrants who did not pass the advanced integration exam within the statutory period.[87] As of 1 July 2011, one of the course objectives for civic integration programmes in the Netherlands is that participants must be able to recognise the Dutch national anthem.[88]

As mentioned earlier, the above redefinitions of the Dutch concept of citizenship occurred after the AIA entered into force. For the most part,

[84] ibid, 7–8.
[85] ibid, 7–9.
[86] ibid, 9–10, 16–20.
[87] ibid, 11–12.
[88] *Government Gazette* 2011, 7426.

however, they did not result in actual changes to the integration exam abroad. For instance, the renewed recognition of the government's (partial) responsibility for the integration process, between 2007 and 2011, did not result in additional preparation facilities or in integration programmes being set up in countries of origin.[89] The contents of the 'Knowledge of the Netherlands' test also remained the same. Nevertheless, the language requirements were increased on 1 April 2011 (chapter 2, section VI.C.ii), while, as of 2009, the integration exam abroad appears mainly to have been positioned as a means of ensuring that (family) migrants coming to the Netherlands are able to actively participate in the labour market and in other areas of the public domain.[90] This fits with the objective of improving the socio-economic position of migrant minorities, but also with a culturally defined norm that expects married women to get out of the house and not be dependent on their partner. Lastly, seen within the context of the 2011 integration memorandum, passing the integration exam abroad also becomes the first step in the immigrant's adaptation to a more encompassing, historically determined Dutch identity.

D. Assessment: Citizenship in the Netherlands and the Act on Integration Abroad

The previous subsections describe how Dutch thinking on integration evolved from the 1980s until 2011. During this period the concept of integration, or 'citizenship', as it was termed after 1994, was endowed with different meanings: from participation in education and the labour market, to adaptation to a 'Dutch identity' primarily defined in relation to certain designated norms and values and to a shared commitment to common interests such as safety and child education. Different perspectives also prevailed with regard to the responsibility for successful integration, which was sometimes seen as a burden shared between immigrants and the receiving society and sometimes as something of concern to immigrants alone.

The various dimensions of Dutch citizenship are discussed and assessed below. Firstly, this assessment includes an evaluation of the integration

[89] In 2010 the Dutch government announced that it would expand the existing preparation package and stimulate initiatives for learning Dutch abroad; see section VI.C.iv of ch 2. However, this occurred after it had been established that, without such changes, many candidates would not be able to pass the exam (which became more difficult on 1 April 2011); this was considered problematic, partly because of the applicable legal norms. Meanwhile the government has consistently maintained that preparation for the integration exam abroad is primarily a responsibility of the candidates themselves and their family members in the Netherlands. See *Bulletin of Acts and Decrees* 2010, 679, 10.

[90] *Kabinetsaanpak huwelijks- en gezinsmigratie* (n 17), 3–5 and 9; *Bulletin of Acts and Decrees* 2010, 679, 3. See also *Nota 'Integratie, binding, burgerschap'* (n 17), 12–13.

objectives encountered (section III.D.i). The Dutch approach to integration has been criticised recently for its exclusive potential and perceived tendency towards a model of cultural assimilation. Where applicable, the discussion includes the arguments made by other authors in this regard. Secondly, section III.D.ii considers whether and to what extent the realisation of the above integration objectives is likely to be furthered by the Act on Integration Abroad.

i. Citizenship in the Netherlands

a. Cultural Adaptation

A first dimension to be distinguished in the Dutch conception of citizenship concerns adaptation to various aspects of national culture: legal norms, but also moral values, customs and unwritten social rules. This dimension is especially prevalent in the notion of 'shared citizenship', developed in 2003 and which has been quite widely criticised as being too 'thick' or amounting to a form of 'cultural assimilation',[91] and in the monocultural ideal of citizenship defended in the latest integration memorandum. It is not entirely clear as to what extent the Dutch government expects immigrants to adapt in order to become proper citizens, in particular whether immigrants are actually expected to internalise particular values or norms or to accept them as being morally correct.[92] Clearly this is something a liberal state cannot demand. After all, the principle of individual freedom on which liberal democracies are based means that people are free to determine their own aims in accordance with their moral perception of 'how to live'.[93] As there is no objective, external source for such moral beliefs, they cannot be prescribed by the state.

Beyond the impossibility of requiring acceptance of moral principles, however, lies a greyer area as far as cultural adaptation is concerned. May a state seek to enforce cultural unity by demanding that citizens *know about* the dominant norms and values of the receiving society or that they *act* in accordance with them (actively or passively)? The answer to these questions seems less straightforward. To start, a state may of course require its citizens to respect its laws, which presupposes (fictitiously or not) that they are familiar with the content of those laws. This requirement would obviously apply not only to immigrants, but to all citizens alike. On the other hand, it would be less evident to ask citizens to respect norms or conventions that are based only on social consensus. Examples would include shaking hands with members of the opposite sex, role

[91] eg, Driouichi 2007, 96–99; Spijkerboer 2007, 67–72; Fermin 2009, 25–26 and Vermeulen 2010a, 136–39.

[92] Spijkerboer 2007, 39–41, with references to parliamentary documents.

[93] Joppke 2008, 541–42; Vermeulen 2010a, 137.

patterns that families ought to comply with or caring for one's physical environment. Arguably, the enforcement of such conventions in the form of integration requirements goes beyond what is necessary to maintain public order.[94] Moreover, a liberal state cannot enforce certain norms or forms of behaviour on the grounds that they are morally superior to others.[95]

To be distinguished from the above is the situation where citizens are not asked to behave in a particular way, but merely asked to acquire certain knowledge. This may be awareness that certain norms or values are supported by a majority of the population, but also knowledge about the receiving country's history, geography, customs and so on. It could be argued that a merely cognitive concept of integration is not as such at odds with the above requirements of liberalism. On the other hand, the value of mere common knowledge as an integration objective may be queried (what is actually gained by all citizens knowing who William of Orange was?).[96] There is also a risk that cognitive integration requirements relating, for example, to prevailing values and social conventions will nevertheless obtain a certain normative function in practice.[97]

Lastly, a different but related problem with regard to cultural adaptation as an integration objective is that it is based on an essentialist understanding of culture.[98] By designating certain norms or values that immigrants must respect or at least be aware of, the disagreement that exists about those norms and values among members of the non-immigrant population is disregarded. Another related risk is that setting 'cultural benchmarks' for integration, whether behavioural or cognitive, will always have an exclusionary effect towards those who do not comply or do not have the right knowledge and who are consequently marked as 'not integrated'. This occurs especially when the norm for cultural adaptation is formulated in terms of what immigrants are *not* (for example,

[94] Vermeulen speaks in this respect of 'ideological paternalism'; see Vermeulen 2010a, 143.

[95] Spijkerboer 2007, 67–72. The impossibility of saying that certain rules are right from a moral point of view obviously applies to legal norms as well as to non-legal conventions. Such legal norms constitute reflections of what is considered right by a majority of the population at a particular time. However since laws do restrict the freedom of all those falling under their jurisdiction, they should also not go any further than is necessary to set the conditions for secure and fair interaction between citizens. Also, (migrant) minorities should be able to participate in the law-making process. It follows that the requirement of compliance with legislation is perhaps not as self-evident as suggested above. Nevertheless, compared to social conventions, legal norms do have a stronger degree of objectivity, consistency and accessibility.

[96] cp Vermeulen 2010a, 138.

[97] Michalowski 2011, 759–60. By way of example this author mentions certain elements of the Dutch naturalisation test whereby candidates must show that they are aware of unwritten social rules, such as that people are expected to keep their front garden tidy and should know that the way in which certain women are dressed in public should not be misunderstood as unchaste or inviting.

[98] Driouichi 2007, 97–99.

Western, non-religious or non-Islamic). The description in the previous sections shows that the Dutch vision on integration has tended to fall foul of this trap, in particular around the turn of the century. By definition, such developments result in the exclusion of minorities rather than the creation of unity.[99]

It can be concluded that respect for, or knowledge of, particular cultural elements (norms, values, conventions, history and so on) is not to be recommended as an integration objective in itself. Nevertheless, a certain amount of knowledge or awareness about the receiving society can serve other objectives of integration, such as economic participation or a commitment to the host country, and this possibility is included in the discussion below.

b. (Economic) Participation

Besides cultural adaptation, another aspect of the Dutch concept of integration is participation: in the labour market, in education or in other domains of social life. This integration objective also includes maintaining contacts with fellow citizens belonging to other ethnic, cultural or religious groups of the population (interethnic contacts). In one way or another, the objective of participation has played an important role in the Dutch vision on citizenship since it was first introduced in the mid-1990s.

Compared to cultural adaptation, the objective of participation has been subject to less criticism in academic literature. Here, too, however, care must be exercised as participation requires citizens to actively contribute to the general interest and as such interferes with their freedom to arrange their lives as they see fit. Participation is also not a culturally neutral concept. This was seen above, for example, where it was stated that the requirement for migrant women to find work reflects a cultural norm that rejects traditional role patterns within the family (section III.C).[100]

It is submitted that the objective of economic participation is acceptable to the extent that such participation is necessary to maintain the viability of the welfare state.[101] This means that citizens may in principle be required to be financially self-reliant and to contribute to the institutions of the welfare state by paying taxes. In addition, it is submitted that the capacity for financial self-reliance is so strongly influenced by having at least a minimum level of education and by the ability to speak the (or a) common language of the host society that requirements may also be imposed with regard to these factors. Empirical research shows that both education and language proficiency are important factors in enabling economic

[99] Spijkerboer 2007, 63–64; Schinkel 2008, 43–48; Fermin 2009, 25.
[100] Compare also the illuminating analysis by Van Walsum (Van Walsum 2008).
[101] See also WRR 2001a, 228 and following; Vermeulen 2010a, 138.

participation.[102] Nonetheless, education and language proficiency do not form integration objectives in and of themselves; integration measures should therefore provide exemptions for citizens able to be self-reliant even though they do not possess these assets. Groenendijk points out, for example, that in some situations knowledge of English may be more conducive to economic participation in the Netherlands than proficiency in Dutch.[103] Finally, finding a job is likely to be easier if the person concerned is acquainted with certain institutions, facilities and conventions of the labour market (how to apply for jobs, what to wear to a job interview, etc). In this respect the purpose of economic participation may be served by cognitive integration requirements.

A more difficult issue concerns other forms of participation, in particular maintaining contacts with people from different groups of the population. It seems realistic to suppose that states with a high level of segregation have a greater risk of conflicts and perhaps even of falling apart. The existence of social networks is also a factor influencing the economic participation of minority groups.[104] However, interethnic contacts and social cohesion are not objectives that easily lend themselves to being translated into demands on individual citizens. Rather they place a responsibility on the government and on the institutions of the civil society to ensure accessibility for minorities and to erase barriers such as the occurrence of ethnic discrimination.

c. Commitment

A third dimension of the Dutch concept of citizenship, which has become increasingly dominant from 2007 onwards, concerns a sense of commitment to or emotional identification with the state and the community of people living in it. This is the least tangible element of citizenship, which arises at the psychological level and consists of a feeling of belonging to a particular group and being connected to other citizens in a consequential way, despite the absence of actual interpersonal contacts.[105] The existence of such a connection is of course highly subjective and difficult to measure, as is its influence on citizens' actual behaviour or on the condition of society as a whole.

It does not seem unreasonable to assume that citizens' emotional identification with the national community (and the ensuing feelings of loyalty and solidarity) will have a positive effect on the experience of living together, as well as fostering support for social security structures, preventing interethnic tensions and conflicts, aiding the observance of

[102] Klaver and Odé 2009, 39–40 and 185–87.
[103] Groenendijk 2011, 28.
[104] Klaver and Odé 2009, 40.
[105] cp Anderson 2006, 6–7.

state laws and more generally endowing the state with a certain level of authority. However, this form of commitment is also something belonging to the emotional or moral domain of the individual and which the liberal state should not seek to enforce (regardless of whether that would be possible). In the words of Van Gunsteren, such enforcement would come down to a form of 'brainwashing' or 'mind control' characteristic of totalitarian states.[106] Another related objection is that a liberal state may not demand its citizens to forfeit their commitment to other communities (such as the national community of the country of origin or cultural or religious communities). In this respect, it is unfortunate that a call for a unilateral commitment to the national community of the Netherlands seems to echo in the Dutch debate on multiple nationalities.[107] Finally, it may be observed here again (as with regard to demands for cultural adaptation), that a requirement for (exclusive) commitment to the receiving state risks resulting in the exclusion rather than the inclusion of immigrants, since the existence of emotional ties is not something that individuals can change at will.[108]

Despite the above, states may seek to foster emotional identification and commitment through non-coercive means, for example through dialogue and education (including about national history and traditions) or through rituals (such as citizenship ceremonies or commemoration of historical events).[109] Indeed, prior to 2007, various authors claimed that integration policy would be more effective if more attention were paid to the role of emotional ties with the Netherlands.[110] However, an obligation of emotional identification is at odds with the principles of citizenship in a liberal state.[111]

d. Individual Responsibility

We have seen that, from the mid-1990s onwards and especially since 2003, the Dutch conception of citizenship has placed strong emphasis on the individual responsibility of immigrants for successful integration. At a theoretical level, this approach can be criticised because it fails to recognise the equality of all citizens. Another point of criticism is that the one-sided focus on the role of immigrants is not likely to make the integration process more effective. The chances that migrant minorities will participate in various domains of public life and feel committed to the receiving society are increased if efforts are also made by the non-immigrant

[106] Van Gunsteren 2009, 48.
[107] eg, Vermeulen 2010a, 135.
[108] eg, Driouichi 2007, 97–99.
[109] Vermeulen 2010a, 143.
[110] Driouichi 2007, 102–07, with further references.
[111] Van Gunsteren 2009, 49.

population and facilities are provided by the government or non-governmental institutions.[112] Furthermore, as seen above, some aspects of integration (notably interethnic contacts and mutual acceptation) simply cannot be achieved by immigrants alone. It would consequently be better to perceive integration as a two-sided process.[113]

ii. The Act on Integration Abroad as an Instrument of Citizenship

The foregoing provides a review of the concepts of citizenship that have inspired Dutch integration policy. Next, I discuss the extent to which the Act on Integration Abroad, as a tool of that integration policy, is a suitable instrument to achieve the envisaged integration objectives, while taking into account that the integration exam abroad can work both as an instrument of inclusion and of exclusion (section II.B).

Firstly, it may be observed that the main function of the integration exam abroad is to assess the fulfilment of certain cognitive requirements. It was argued above that liberal states should not seek to make their citizens accept the moral rightness of legal or social norms or ethical principles or require them to feel emotionally attached to the national community. It is also impossible to test such moral views or feelings by means of an exam, as such testing would necessarily remain limited to testing the candidates' *awareness* of culturally defined norms and values or, perhaps, their capacity to learn things by heart. While such awareness may eventually contribute to creating a sense of belonging, 'giving the right answers' in a social orientation test is not as such proof of normative or emotional identification.[114] In the same vein, an integration exam also does not constitute an adequate instrument to test or predict individual behaviour. Again, what can be tested is whether candidates are aware of the existence or prevalence of certain social and legal norms. However, such awareness does not guarantee that candidates will act accordingly outside the exam situation. When asked about their own behaviour in particular situations, candidates may also be tempted to provide socially desirable answers.[115]

It follows that the scope of the integration exam abroad is by and large limited to testing the possession of cognitive skills, which, as submitted earlier, do not constitute a very relevant integration objective. It was also assumed, however, that having certain knowledge about the host country may contribute to achieving other objectives. Education and language

[112] Klaver and Odé 2009, 86.
[113] See also Vermeulen 2010a, 136.
[114] Driouichi 2007, 108.
[115] ibid, 43–44; Klaver and Odé 2009, 88. Before the AIA was enacted, the committee that advised on the exam requirements (*Commissie Franssen*) had already warned that the impact of the integration exam abroad on the behaviour of immigrants would be only limited, Commissie Franssen 2004, 37.

proficiency are important factors in determining a person's chances of economic participation. Arguably, the same is true with regard to knowledge about the structure and conventions of the Dutch labour market. For this reason, excluding immigrants with little education, language proficiency or prior awareness of the Dutch labour market may well increase the rates of economic participation in the Netherlands and reduce the numbers of immigrants who are not financially self-reliant. In this sense, the integration exam abroad could potentially constitute a relevant instrument of citizenship.

Two remarks deserve to be made, however. Firstly, the available empirical research shows that the effects of the Act on Integration Abroad have thus far been rather limited (section VI.D of chapter 2). In general, immigrants who were admitted to the Netherlands after the AIA entered into force had slightly higher levels of education than those arriving before. However, the exam had only a very limited effect on their level of Dutch language proficiency, which moreover tended to disappear quickly. Meanwhile no evidence is yet available regarding the long-term effects of the Act, including on the level of immigrants' economic participation. With regard to civic integration in the Netherlands, however, Klaver and Odé showed that integration programmes have only a limited effect on the integration process. These authors have warned that successful integration results from a combination of factors, including the facilities provided by the government and the attitude of the receiving society, and that not too much should be expected of integration programmes and exams alone.[116]

A second remark concerns the potential negative effects on the integration process that may result from excluding immigrants who are unable to pass the integration exam abroad. The non-admission of unsuccessful applicants creates a disadvantage for Dutch residents (nationals and non-nationals), who face significant obstacles to the exercise of their family life (or, in the case of religious servants, their religious freedom). This may well have repercussions for their sense of inclusion and their commitment to the Netherlands,[117] especially if it is felt that the exam (in particular the 'Knowledge of the Netherlands' test) is designed to reflect the cultural norms of the majority population and does not take minority perspectives into account.

Presumably, the effects of the integration exam abroad are influenced by its contents. Thus, the selection of immigrants who will participate successfully in the labour market will likely be more effective if the level of the exam is raised, as occurred on 1 April 2011 (section VI.C.ii of chapter 2). However, more stringent requirements will also increase the

[116] Klaver and Odé 2009, 179 and 185–87. See also Bloemraad 2006 and Groenendijk 2011, 24.

[117] Groenendijk 2011, 27–28.

exclusionary effect of the exam and thus strengthen the negative effects on the dimension of emotional identification. It was remarked earlier that knowledge of certain characteristics of the host country (such as its history and geography) may help foster a sense of belonging. Such knowledge cannot, however, be properly taught at a very low level of language proficiency.[118] A study of integration programmes in the Netherlands has also shown that participants with higher levels of education tend to be more interested in topics without immediate practical relevance than those who are less educated.[119]

Apart from testing cognitive skills, the integration exam abroad can be seen as an instrument for testing immigrants' willingness and determination to make an effort towards successful integration in the Netherlands (section II.B.iii). Seen from this perspective, it is not so much the contents of the exam that count, but rather the process of preparation and participation that shows candidates' motivation to succeed. As the previous chapter shows, this perception also explains why, in Dutch case law on the AIA, the existence of obstacles or difficulties on the part of the applicant is not readily qualified as grounds for exemptions (section VI.B.iii of chapter 2).

Although the assumption that the integration exam abroad functions as a 'motivation test' is not implausible in itself, it has not yet been shown that excluding non-motivated immigrants also has a positive effect on the integration process in the Netherlands. Moreover, the effort needed to pass the exam will vary greatly among candidates, depending, for example, on their education and learning capacity and on the circumstances in their country of origin. It follows that, as a motivation test, the integration exam abroad does not set the same standard for all applicants. Hence, to the extent that the exam is indeed meant to test candidates' willingness to integrate, it is not the most suitable instrument. Other alternatives, such as the obligation to participate in an integration course or an exam designed to test the progress someone has made, would be more appropriate in this respect.

IV. CONCLUDING OBSERVATIONS

This chapter describes and, to a certain extent, assesses the conceptualisation of integration and citizenship in the Netherlands. The description and assessment focus firstly on the connection created between immigration and integration policy. It was established that the Act on Integration Abroad was designed to further the integration process in the Netherlands,

[118] Commissie Franssen 2004, 40–41.
[119] Brink and Tromp 2003, 31–44.

through the exclusion of new immigrants with poor prospects for integration. The exclusionary effect of the Act was further emphasised when the exam requirements were raised on 1 April 2011, with the result that the integration exam abroad is now used primarily to test the educational level or literacy of candidates rather than their willingness to integrate. The fact that the integration requirement is formulated as an obligation of result also corresponds to its purpose of selection.

As an instrument of exclusion rather than inclusion, the Act on Integration Abroad marks an important change in the thinking on integration. As regards the desirability of this change, it has been argued that the appropriateness of an exclusive policy depends (at least in part) on the reason why admission is sought. With regard to people looking for international protection, there is no or very little scope to make admission dependent on considerations relating to the interests of the host state. With regard to family or labour migration, the host state has more discretion. Nevertheless, it has been submitted that this discretion should also be limited in family migration situations where the person (or persons) residing in the receiving state has close ties to it, be it through nationality, long-term residence or other relevant factors. The question to what extent integration requirements for family reunification are compatible with the legally guaranteed right to family life will be addressed in the following chapter.

Section III investigates how the ideal of an integrated society has been depicted in the Dutch political debate. This investigation showed that the concept of integration (or citizenship) has been continually subject to change and re-interpretation. From 1994 onwards, however, the citizenship concept has always been rather 'thick', encompassing not only entitlements and rights, but also the duty to actively contribute to society.

One danger of this 'thick' ideal of citizenship is that the Dutch state risks infringing upon one of the fundamental principles of its own political system, namely the liberal principle that a state should not interfere with the individual freedom of its citizens to hold their own moral views and to arrange their life accordingly. This risk is inherent in all obligations imposed by the state (including the obligation to abide by the law), all of which necessarily entail a certain normative component, but increases as those obligations become more encompassing. Furthermore, formulating norms of good citizenship always carries the risk of neglecting differences existing among the population and excluding those who do not conform to the norm and are subsequently regarded as 'non-integrated'.

Given these objections, it has been argued that the objective of the integration policy should go no further than is necessary to maintain public order and to enable the continuation of the welfare state. This implies that demands may be made with regard to the economic self-reliance of citizens, as well as the qualifications necessary to enable this (notably education, linguistic skills and an understanding of the labour market, and also maybe an awareness of prevailing social conventions). However, a state may not require its citizens to morally subscribe to certain norms or values, to be emotionally committed to the national community or to give up their commitment to other (cultural, ethnic or religious) communities. Another problematic issue is the requirement to act in accordance with social norms or conventions other than those prescribed by law. Lastly, it is submitted that the equality of all citizens requires the responsibility for successful integration not to be placed solely on the migrant population. The focus on the 'individual responsibility' of immigrants has played a significant role in the Dutch conception of citizenship from 2003 onwards, and even more so in the past year.

The introduction of integration requirements in the form of conditions for admission is not necessarily tied to one particular conception of citizenship. Depending on the contents of the exam and the choice for an obligation of effort or result, such integration requirements may be directed towards achieving various integration objectives. It is not surprising, therefore, that the Act on Integration Abroad has remained in force despite the changes affecting the Dutch conception of citizenship after 2006.

Nevertheless, the effectiveness of the integration exam abroad as a means to achieve the Dutch integration objectives is arguably only limited. In any case, the exam does not represent an adequate instrument for testing the moral opinions or behaviour of potential future citizens. Although it is plausible that the exam can be used to assess whether immigrants possess certain knowledge or skills that will increase their chances of successful economic participation, results achieved so far have not proved the exam to be very effective. Additionally, the emotional identification of people within the Netherlands may be negatively affected by the exam preventing them from bringing in their family members or, even more generally, by the perception that '(certain) immigrants are not welcome'. Lastly, to the extent that the integration exam abroad is meant to test candidates' willingness to integrate, it was submitted that an obligation of effort would be a more suitable instrument than an obligation of result.

PART II

Integration Requirements in Immigration Law

A. Integration Requirements and Fundamental Rights

4

Family Life and Family Reunification

I. INTRODUCTION

IN THE NETHERLANDS family migrants make up the majority of the target group of the Act on Integration Abroad. If a family member fails to pass the integration exam and is consequently denied admission, both he or she and the family member(s) in the Netherlands are obstructed in the enjoyment of their family life. This chapter examines whether this situation is in accordance with the right to family life, as protected by various human rights treaties. Firstly the legal standards that can be derived from these treaties with regard to the admission of aliens for the purpose of family reunification are examined. The initial issue addressed in this respect is whether the right to family life includes a right for family members to be admitted to the state where the rest of their family is living. Where such a right is found to exist, the next question examined is whether its exercise may lawfully be made subject to the fulfilment of integration requirements.

The provisions examined in the course of this chapter include, first and foremost, Article 8 of the European Convention on Human Rights (ECHR).[1] European Court of Human Rights case law has with some regularity addressed the question of whether refusing to grant legal residence to an alien violates the right to respect for family life. This case law is discussed in section II. The right to family life is also protected by Articles 17 and 23 of the International Covenant on Civil and Political Rights (ICCPR).[2] While these provisions have not given rise to the same amount of interpretative activity by international monitoring bodies as Article 8 ECHR, the Human Rights Committee has been asked on several occasions to comment on Articles 17 and 23 ICCPR in immigration contexts (section III). Thirdly, standards concerning the admission of family migrants can be found in the Convention on the Rights of the Child (CRC).[3] In

[1] European Convention for the Protection of Human Rights and Fundamental Freedoms, CETS No 5; *Treaty Series* 1951, 154 and following, entry into force for the Netherlands on 31 August 1954.

[2] UNTS Vol 999, 171; *Treaty Series* 1969, 99 and following, entry into force for the Netherlands on 11 March 1979.

[3] UNTS Vol 1577, 3, entry into force on 2 September 1990; *Treaty Series* 1990, 46 and following, entry into force for the Netherlands on 2 September 1990.

particular, Articles 9 and 10 CRC guarantee the right of children not to be separated from their parents, which may also be at stake in immigration cases (section IV).

In addition to the above guarantees a right to family reunification is laid down in the EU Directive on Family Reunification (section V).[4] Unlike the above human rights provisions, the Family Reunification Directive (FRD) explicitly mentions the possibility of imposing integration requirements. The examination of this directive therefore focuses on determining the possible contents of such requirements, as well as the criteria relating to their application.

Where available and relevant, Dutch case law with regard to the Act on Integration Abroad is taken into account in relation to each of the legal instruments discussed in this chapter. Section VI gives a summary of the legal standards encountered. Next, section VII examines whether the Act on Integration Abroad is in accordance with these standards. The chapter closes with some concluding observations on integration requirements and the right to family life.

II. ARTICLE 8 OF THE EUROPEAN CONVENTION ON HUMAN RIGHTS

Article 8 of the European Convention on Human Rights states that everyone has the right to respect for their family life. This provision is especially relevant for the Netherlands as the right to family life is not mentioned as such in the Dutch Constitution. Its relevance has moreover increased as the European Court of Human Rights (ECtHR) has clarified the scope and meaning of Article 8 ECHR in what has become a substantial body of case law. The following examination focuses on those cases in which the Court was asked to decide whether a Contracting State's refusal to admit family members of legal residents in that state violated the right to family life as protected by Article 8 ECHR (hereafter referred to as 'admission cases'). Given the purpose of this study, this examination aims to determine whether and under which circumstances violation of Article 8 ECHR could occur if admission is refused on the grounds that the person concerned has not complied with integration requirements set by the Contracting State. To answer this question, it is necessary to describe the Court's approach to admission cases in some detail.

[4] Council Directive 2003/86/EC of 22 September 2003, [2003] OJ L251/12.

A. Scope of Article 8 ECHR – Family Life

Before considering the significance of Article 8 ECHR for admission cases, some general remarks regarding the scope of this provision are in order. The concept of 'family life' has been defined by the ECtHR in rather broad terms, referring to factual rather than legal relationships between family members.[5] As far as couples are concerned, family life is considered to exist between unmarried as well as married partners, providing the relationship has a certain degree of intensity and durability.[6] Family life is furthermore taken to exist between parents and minor children from the moment of the child's birth, save in exceptional circumstances.[7] Relationships other than those between partners or parents and minor children (the 'core family') may also qualify as 'family life' under Article 8 ECHR. However, the ECtHR has held that, in immigration cases, there is no family life between parents and adult children unless 'additional elements of dependence' surpassing the existence of 'normal emotional ties' are demonstrated.[8]

As to the contents of the right to family life, Article 8 ECHR clearly encompasses the right to live together and to enjoy each other's company.[9] In situations where parents live separated from the children, for example after a divorce, they are nevertheless entitled to maintain access to their children in the form of regular contacts and visits.[10] In both cases it follows that the exercise of family life may be hindered if one of the family members is not admitted to a Contracting State in which another family member is living. This was recognised for the first time in the case of *Abdulaziz*, which concerned three women who were lawful residents of the United Kingdom and sought to be reunited with their husbands in that country. The ECtHR acknowledged that, under certain circumstances, 'measures taken in the field of immigration may affect the right to respect for family life'.[11] However, as demonstrated below, this does not mean that the right to family life also implies a right for family members to be admitted to the territory of a Contracting State.

[5] For a detailed discussion, see Boeles et al 2009, 145–48, with references to further case law. See also Forder 2003, 4.

[6] ECtHR 20 June 2002, app no 50963/99 (*Al-Nashif*), para 112.

[7] ECtHR 21 June 1988, app no 10730/84 (*Berrehab*), para 21.

[8] ECtHR 7 November 2000 (admissibility decision), app no 31519/96 (*Kwakye-Nti & Dufie*) ('l'existence d'éléments supplémentaires de dépendence, autres que les liens affectifs normaux'); ECtHR 9 October 2003, app no 48321/99 (*Slivenko*), para 97 and ECtHR 12 January 2010, app no 47486/06 (*A.W. Khan*), para 32. In the absence of an explanation by the Court, it seems rather odd that the concept of 'family life' is defined differently in immigration cases than in other contexts.

[9] eg, ECtHR 28 May 1985, app nos 9214/80, 9473/81 and 9474/81 (*Abdulaziz, Cabales & Balkandali*), para 62; ECtHR 27 June 1996, app no 17383/90 (*Johansen*), para 52.

[10] eg, ECtHR 21 June 1988, app no 10730/84 (*Berrehab*), paras 22–23. See also Forder 2005, 49–54, with references to further case law.

[11] *Abdulaziz, Cabales & Balkandali* (n 9), para 60.

B. Family Life and the Admission of Aliens: the Approach of the European Court of Human Rights

ECtHR case law on the right to family life has consistently held that states have the right to control the entry of non-nationals into their territory and that Article 8 ECHR does not impose a general obligation on states to respect the choice by married couples of the country of their matrimonial residence.[12] Article 8 ECHR does not, therefore, entail a general right to family reunification in the state where one of the family members is living. However, this has not precluded the ECtHR from examining, in the cases brought before it, whether there existed special circumstances that meant that a Contracting State's refusal to admit the family members of lawful residents constituted a violation of Article 8 ECHR. The Court's approach in these cases is set out below. For a better understanding of the case law, some attention is paid first to the distinction between 'positive' and 'negative' obligations and the criteria applied by the ECtHR to determine whether Article 8 ECHR has been violated.

i. Positive or Negative Obligation, Fair Balance or Necessity?

Conceptually, a distinction can be made between 'positive' and 'negative' obligations, both of which are inherent in a state's duty to safeguard human rights. A negative obligation is usually defined as a duty on the part of the state to abstain from acting where such action would interfere with the exercise by individuals (or groups of individuals) of their human rights (such as the obligation not to break up a demonstration). By contrast, a positive obligation entails a duty on the state to take action to ensure that human rights are effectively secured (such as the obligation to hold regular elections).[13]

Related to the distinction between positive and negative obligations, at least in the context of Article 8 ECHR, is the way in which the ECtHR approaches the question of whether the Convention has been violated. Where a negative obligation is involved, the Court first establishes whether the state has interfered with this obligation (by, for example, taking children out of the family and placing them in a home). If interference is found, the Court then examines whether this interference is justified because it complies with the criteria in the second paragraph of Article 8 (in which case there has been no violation). These criteria entail that the interference must be prescribed by law and must be 'necessary in a demo-

[12] eg, *Abdulaziz, Cabales & Balkandali* (n 9), paras 67–68; ECtHR 1 December 2005, app no 60665/00 (*Tuquabo-Tekle and others*), para 43; ECtHR 28 June 2011, app no 55597/09 (*Nunez*), paras 66 and 70.

[13] Harris et al 2009, 18–19.

cratic society' in order to achieve one of the legitimate aims mentioned in the provision (the 'necessity test'). It is up to the respondent state to show that sufficient justification is available.

On the other hand, where a positive obligation is at stake, the ECtHR does not seek to establish whether there has been an interference, nor whether the alleged lack of state action is justified under Article 8(2) ECHR.[14] Instead the existence or non-existence of a positive obligation is determined by the 'fair balance' test, whereby the interests of the individual applicant(s) are weighed against the general interests of the Contracting State. Where the latter outweigh the former, the Court will conclude that the state was not under a positive obligation to secure the right to family life. By contrast, where the individual interest prevails it will be concluded that there was a positive obligation that was not fulfilled and that the right to family life has been violated. Hence, unlike in the case of a negative obligation, the extent of the state's obligation and the existence of justification are determined by means of a single test,[15] with the criterion being that a fair balance must be struck between the general and the individual interests.

Both the above tests require there to be a certain relationship of proportionality between the interests of the state and the obstacle created for individuals in enjoying their family life. Nevertheless, the 'fair balance' test is less precise than the necessity test because it does not specify which state interests can justify interference with the right to family life and does not require the respondent state to demonstrate that the interference was necessary to achieve a 'pressing social need' (which is part of the 'necessary in a democratic society' criterion). Perhaps even more significant is that, under the fair balance test, the Court does not conduct the proportionality test on the assumption that the interests of the individual amount to a fundamental right. For these reasons, it is generally contended that a violation is less likely to be found when the 'fair balance' test is used and, therefore, that this test offers a lower level of protection to those applying to the Court.[16]

ii. Admission of Family Members: Still Searching for the Right Approach

The distinction between positive and negative obligations is not always easy to make in practice: often a decision taken by state authorities can be defined both as an action and as a refusal to act. With regard to admission

[14] ECtHR 13 June 1979, app no 6833/74 *(Marckx)*, para 31.

[15] See the Court's often repeated formula in admission cases that 'the extent of a State's obligation to admit to its territory relatives of settled immigrants will vary according to the particular circumstances of the persons involved and the general interest'. eg, ECtHR 28 October 1996, app no 21702/93 (*Ahmut*), para 67.

[16] Forder 1992, 624 and 630; Lawson 1995a, 566–67 and Lawson 1995b, 728.

cases this is due in part to factual circumstances. To illustrate this, compare the situation of a person who is outside the state where his or her family lives and is seeking to be admitted with the situation of a person who is already present illegally within the state and is asking not to be removed. While the latter case can more readily be portrayed as one involving a negative obligation, both applicants are in essence seeking the same thing, namely leave to reside. However, the problem also exists on a more fundamental level as, theoretically, requiring people to ask for permission to reside in a particular state can be considered as the creation of an impediment to such residence, while refusing to grant permission can be seen as a failure to enable it.[17]

It is perhaps, therefore, no surprise that the ECtHR has thus far steered a rather wobbly course concerning both the determination of the nature of the obligations involved in admission cases and the test to be applied. Originally, the Court treated these cases as involving a potential positive obligation on the part of the Contracting State and refrained from testing whether the lack of state action was justified under the second paragraph of Article 8 ECHR.[18] This approach, however, was subject to criticism both in and outside the Court.[19] Later ECtHR judgments have often – though not always – refrained from qualifying obligations to admit family members as either negative or positive, stating instead that 'the boundaries between [both types of obligation] do not lend themselves to precise definition'. To this the Court has added that the 'applicable principles' are, nevertheless, similar:

> In both contexts regard must be had to the fair balance that has to be struck between the competing interests of the individual and of the community as a whole; and in both contexts the State enjoys a certain margin of appreciation.[20]

As could be seen above, however, the fair balance test can be distinguished from the necessity test in several ways. From an analysis of the case law, it appears that the ECtHR most often decides admission cases using some form of the fair balance test. With only a few exceptions, the Court has consistently established that the relationship between the family members constituted family life for the purpose of Article 8 ECHR and then proceeded directly to balancing the different interests involved, without

[17] See also Forder 1992, 619–22.

[18] *Abdulaziz, Cabales & Balkandali* (n 9), para 67.

[19] See the concurring opinion of Judge Bernhardt in *Abdulaziz*, para 1 and Forder 1992, 630–31. Also illustrative is the dissenting opinion of Judge Martens in the case of *Gül* (where the Court had already changed its approach): ECtHR 19 February 1996, app no 23218/94, diss opinion para 7.

[20] eg, ECtHR 19 February 1996, app no 23218/94 (*Gül*), para 38; ECtHR 6 November 2001 (admissibility decision), app no 50568/99 (*Adnane*); *Tuquabo-Tekle and others* (n 12), para 42; ECtHR 14 February 2012, app no 26940/10 (*Antwi and others*), para 89.

establishing the existence of an interference.[21] In 2008, after the majority of the Court had found an interference in the case of *Omoregie*, Judge Jebens issued a concurring opinion in which he argued that, in cases where the person concerned had not been granted lawful residence, the Court should always frame the case in terms of failure to comply with a positive obligation and refrain from applying the necessity test.[22] This approach was subsequently followed by the Court in the case of *Narenji Haghighi*.[23] Since then, however, it seems that the Court increasingly mingles the two tests. Recent case law shows several examples where the ECtHR applied the fair balance test, but also checked whether the impugned measure was 'prescribed by law' and served one of the 'legitimate aims' of Article 8, paragraph 2.[24]

In summary, the ECtHR is still searching for the right way to qualify and examine the claims of aliens seeking admission for the purpose of family reunification. This seems to result from unwillingness on the part of the Court to recognise a right to family reunification as part of the right to family life, while at the same time not wanting to exclude entirely the possibility that a claim for family reunification could come within the scope of the Convention. This has led to a somewhat muddled approach, at the core of which the fair balance test can nonetheless be distinguished as the instrument most often used for examining admission cases (even where the obligation at stake is not expressly identified as positive). Section II.C examines the arguments used by the Court to determine whether a fair balance has been struck between the interests of the individual and those of the community in family reunification cases. In this way it attempts to establish a better idea of how to conduct the fair balance test in situations where the admission of family members is made subject to integration requirements. Firstly, however, the margin of appreciation is considered.

[21] Cases in which an interference was found are ECtHR 5 September 2000 (admissibility decision), app no 44328/98 (*Solomon*); ECtHR 31 July 2008, app no 265/07 (*Darren Omoregie and others*), para 55 and ECtHR 15 May 2012, app no 16567/10 (*Nacic and others*), paras 73–76. In the latter case, the finding of an interference was related to the fact that the applicants were already living together as a family before they entered the respondent state. It is noteworthy that, in each of the above cases, the fair balance test was still applied at the proportionality stage: instead of examining whether the interference had been 'necessary in a democratic society', the Court checked whether a fair balance had been struck between the different interests involved.

[22] *Darren Omoregie and others* (n 21), concurring opinion of Judge Jebens.

[23] ECtHR 14 April 2009 (admissibility decision), app no 38165/07 (*Narenji Haghighi*). In this judgment the ECtHR repeated its standard formula that 'in the case of both positive and negative obligations the State must strike a fair balance between the competing interests of the individual and of the community as a whole'. There is no indication, however, that anything like the necessity test was in fact applied.

[24] ECtHR 11 October 2011 (admissibility decision), app no 25579/09 (*A.Y. c France*); ECtHR 3 April 2012 (admissibility decision), app no 1722/10 (*Biraga*), para 56 and ECtHR 10 May 2012 (admissibility decision), app no 111859/03 (*Olgun*), para 42 (legitimate aim not specified). See also *Nacic and others* (n 21).

iii. Margin of Appreciation

When applying the fair balance test the ECtHR usually states that Contracting States have a 'certain margin of appreciation'.[25] This margin serves to determine the intensity of the judicial review conducted by the Court: where a margin is granted, the review is less intense and it is left to the Contracting State to appraise the various interests at stake. In this respect the margin of appreciation doctrine must be distinguished from other instruments of interpretation used by the ECtHR, such as the fair balance test or the necessity test. Unlike the latter instruments, the margin of appreciation doctrine does not set the criteria for determining whether a particular state measure is compatible with Article 8 ECHR (for example, that there must be a fair balance or that the measure must be necessary in a democratic society). Instead it determines the scope of the review to be performed; in other words, whether the Court will conduct an intensive examination or whether it will defer to the judgment of the respondent state.[26]

Consequently, the margin of appreciation doctrine is not, strictly speaking, relevant to the primary purpose of this section, which is to identify the standards governing the application of Article 8 ECHR in relation to integration requirements for family reunification. However, it is good to be aware that the criteria formulated by the ECtHR are not all-encompassing, but that there is scope for choices to be made by the national authorities of Contracting States. Hence the standards articulated by the ECtHR must be perceived as minimum standards.[27]

The scope of the margin of appreciation is determined by a number of different circumstances and can therefore vary from case to case. Relevant circumstances include the nature of the right at issue, the nature of the aim pursued by the contested measure or of the general interest involved and the extent to which there is common ground between the laws of the Contracting States concerning the topic before the Court.[28] This was confirmed by the ECtHR Grand Chamber in two judgments, both of which involved positive obligations under Article 8 ECHR.[29]

[25] eg, *Gül* (n 20), para 38; *Tuquabo-Tekle and others* (n 12), para 42 and *Narenji Haghighi* (n 23).

[26] On the margin of appreciation, see Schokkenbroek 1996; Schokkenbroek 2000, 18–30; Van Dijk and Van Hoof 1998, 82–95 and Arai-Takahashi 2002. Useful reflections on the margin of appreciation and the intensity of judicial review in general can also be found in Gerards 2002, notably 79–100 and 165–97.

[27] Gerards 2010, 226.

[28] See, eg, Schokkenbroek 1996, 205–09, Van Dijk and Van Hoof 1998, 87–91 and Gerards 2002, 169–97.

[29] In the case of *Evans*, the Grand Chamber held that 'a number of factors to be taken into account when determining the breadth of the margin of appreciation to be enjoyed by the State in any case under Article 8 [include] whether there is at stake a particularly important facet of an individual's existence or identity; whether there is consensus between the

The various elements determining the scope of the margin of appreciation may all point in the same direction. However, it can also occur that one element supports the application of a narrow margin, whereas another requires a wide margin. With regard to cases involving integration requirements for family reunification, immigration and integration are arguably matters of general policy and a wide margin should, therefore, be granted.[30] On the other hand, a narrow margin may be appropriate in, for example, cases involving very young children, whose right to be with their parents can be considered an essential element of the right to family life.[31] Where both factors play a role, the applicable margin of appreciation will ultimately depend on the particular circumstances of the case.[32]

C. Balancing Family Life and Immigration Control: the Criteria Used by the Court

As stated above, the fair balance test examines whether the impediment to applicants' family life, caused by refusal to allow family reunification, is proportionate to the state interest served by this refusal. The lawfulness of the state's decision will therefore depend on the reasons why family reunification was refused, as well as on the applicants' personal circumstances

Member States of the Council of Europe, either as to the relative importance of the interest at stake or as to the best means of protecting it, particularly in cases involving sensitive moral or ethical issues and whether the State is required to strike a balance between competing private and public interests or Convention rights' (ECtHR (Grand Chamber) 10 April 2007, app no 6339/05, para 77). In *Hatton and others* the Court added that a wide margin of appreciation was to be granted in situations where the interest invoked by the Contracting State concerns a 'matter of general policy, on which opinions within a democratic society may reasonably differ widely', such as environmental policy and social and economic policies (ECtHR (Grand Chamber) 8 July 2003, app no 36022/97, paras 97–101).

[30] The ECtHR has found on several occasions that a wide margin of appreciation exists in admission cases. See *Abdulaziz, Cabales & Balkandali* (n 9), para 67. See also ECtHR 12 February 2008 (admissibility decision), app no 33831/03 (*M.F.S. v Bulgaria*), para 1. In the latter case the Court stated: 'La Cour rappelle que le mécanisme de sauvegarde des droits fondamentaux institué par la Convention revêt un caractère subsidiaire par rapport aux systèmes nationaux et que ce principe s'applique pleinement en matière d'immigration'. Finally, the following passage can be found in a recent decision of the Court regarding an alleged violation of Art 10 ECHR (ECtHR 20 April 2010 (admissibility decision), app no 18788/09 (*Le Pen*), para 1): 'En l'espèce, la Cour note que les propos du requérant s'inscrivent dans le cadre du débat d'intérêt général relative aux problèmes liés à l'installation et à l'intégration des immigrés dans le pays d'acceuil. Quant au contexte de ce débat en ce qui concerne la France, la Cour a précisé [. . .] que [ces problèmes] font actuellement l'objet d'amples débats dans les sociétés européennes, tant sur le plan politique que sur le plan médiatique. [. . .] Elle a rappelé à cet égard l'ampleur variable des problèmes auxquels les Etats pouvaient faire face dans le cadre des politiques d'immigration et d'intégration, qui commande de leur laisser disposer d'une marge d'appréciation assez large pour déterminer l'existence et l'étendue de la nécessité de pareille ingérence'.

[31] Compare the cases of *Sen* and *Rodrigues Da Silva* described in the following section.

[32] ECtHR (Grand Chamber) 8 July 2003, app no 36022/97 (*Hatton and others*), para 103.

and the effect of the refusal on their opportunities to enjoy family life. This will also apply if the decision is based on an applicant's failure to pass an integration test. This section analyses ECtHR case law in admission cases in an attempt to get more insight into how the Court assesses both individual and state interests and weighs them against each other. Firstly, considerations relating to the state's interests are considered. Next, the interests of applicants will be considered, with a distinction being made between arguments relating to the situation of the family members and arguments relating to the nature and effect of the disputed immigration measures.

i. Interests of the State

The fair balance test requires the interests of the individual applicants to be weighed against the general interests of the state. With regard to admission cases, this would imply that the ECtHR not only examines the situation of family members, but also the conditions by which family reunification is refused or restricted and the reasons underlying these conditions. Indeed, the Court has often stated that one of the factors to determine whether Article 8 ECHR requires that a family member be admitted is 'whether there are factors of immigration control (eg, a history of breaches of immigration law) or considerations of public order weighing in favour of exclusion'.[33] So far, however, the Court has been rather reticent in formulating more specific criteria with regard to immigration rules applied by Contracting States.

As stated above (section II.B.i), the 'pure' fair balance test does not involve an examination of whether the state's refusal to allow family reunification serves one of the legitimate aims mentioned in Article 8(2) ECHR. Especially in its early case law, the Court often did not explicitly consider the grounds on which admission was refused. In the case of *Gül*, for instance, the Court concluded that there was no obstacle preventing the family from exercising its family life in the country of origin and then immediately went on to find that there had been no violation of Article 8 ECHR, without mentioning which state interest would be served if the son were not admitted.[34] In other cases, the Court found – and accepted – that refusal of family reunification pursued the rather broadly formulated state interest of 'controlling immigration', which is not as such mentioned

[33] eg, ECtHR 22 June 1999 (admissibility decision), app no 27663/95 (*Ajayi and others*); *Darren Omoregie and others* (n 21), para 57; *Nunez* (n 12), para 70; *Olgun* (n 24), para 43.

[34] *Gül* (n 20), paras 42–43 (by contrast, see the dissenting opinion of Judges Martens and Russo, paras 10–15). Other examples of cases in which the Court did not address the reasons underlying the refusal of admission include ECtHR 19 January 1999 (admissibility decision), app no 39322/98 (*Cincil*), ECtHR 9 November 2000 (admissibility decision), app no 50065/99 (*Shebashov*) and, more recently, ECtHR 24 June 2008 (admissibility decision), app no 25087/06 (*M. v United Kingdom*). This element of the Court's approach was criticised by Forder for its lack of transparency; see Forder 2005, 40.

in the Convention. It has done so even in cases where the respondent state indicated that the immigration measures were taken with regard to one or more of the 'legitimate aims' of Article 8(2) ECHR.[35]

Of late, however, the Court has begun to refer to these aims more explicitly. In several, more or less recent, cases, the ECtHR specified that the refusal of admission was in the interest of the 'protection of economic well-being' and/or the 'prevention of disorder and crime'.[36] On some occasions, the reference to these aims seems to have been inspired by the fact that specific conditions for admission had not been met. For example, in *Konstatinov*, the applicant had been convicted of various criminal offences, whereas her partner failed to meet the income requirement set by the respondent state (the Netherlands). The Court subsequently held that the refusal of admission had been in the interest of 'controlling immigration and public expenditure and the prevention of disorder or crime'.[37] However, it has also invoked these aims in cases where the refusal apparently resulted from an overall restrictive immigration policy (the applicants simply did not belong to a category of aliens eligible for admission) or from the failure to meet a formal requirement (eg the possession of a valid visa or passport).[38] Specifically, in *Nacic and others*, the Court clarified that it considered the economic well-being of the respondent state to be served by the effective implementation of immigration control.[39]

As regards the proportionality of immigration measures in relation to the public interest at stake, ECtHR case law provides little guidance: in the majority of cases these issues are simply not addressed. Several judgments deserve to be mentioned, however. In the cases of *Haydarie* and *Konstatinov*, the applicants were refused residence because, inter alia, the family members seeking their admission did not meet the income requirements imposed by the respondent state. In both cases, the ECtHR stated that

> in principle the Court does not consider unreasonable a requirement that an alien who seeks family reunion must demonstrate that he/she has sufficient

[35] eg, *Ahmut* (n 15), para 73 and ECtHR 21 December 2001, app no 31465/96 (*Sen*), para 41. In both cases the respondent state (the Netherlands) argued that it pursued a restrictive immigration policy for reasons of inter alia the availability of employment. This aim can easily be understood as serving the interest of 'protecting the economic well-being of the country'.

[36] eg, ECtHR 31 January 2006, app no 50435/99 (*Rodrigues Da Silva & Hoogkamer*), para 44; ECtHR 26 April 2007, app no 16351/03 (*Konstatinov*), para 53; *A.Y. c France* (n 24) and *Biraga* (n 24), para 56.

[37] *Konstatinov* (n 36), paras 50–51 and 53, I take it that the aim of 'controlling public expenditure' can be subsumed under 'protection of the economic well-being' of the state.

[38] eg, *Rodrigues Da Silva & Hoogkamer* (n 36), para 44; *A.Y. c France* (n 24) and *Biraga* (n 24), para 56.

[39] *Nacic and others* (n 21), para 79: 'The Court further accepts that the legitimate aim pursued was to ensure an effective implementation of immigration control and *hence* to preserve the economic well-being of Sweden' (emphasis added).

> independent and lasting income, not being welfare benefits, to provide for the basic costs of subsistence of his or her family members with whom reunion is sought.[40]

It may be derived that, at least *in abstracto*, states' economic interest in not having to support family members from abroad is considered sufficiently weighty to justify the introduction of the income requirements concerned. With regard to the public interest of immigration control, the Court stated in *Nunez* and *Antwi* that the possibility for states to expel family members constitutes an 'important means of general deterrence against gross or repeated violations of the Immigration Act'. Having established that such violations existed in the cases concerned, the ECtHR went on to find that 'the public interest in favour or ordering the applicant's expulsion weighed heavily in the balance when assessing the issue of proportionality'. Additionally, in *Nunez*, the Court rejected the argument made by the applicant, to the effect that 'the public interest in an expulsion would be preponderant only in instances where the person concerned had been convicted of a criminal offence'. Yet, in *Antwi*, it indicated that longer re-entry bans can be imposed when the breaches of the state's immigration laws have been more serious in nature.[41]

On the other hand, in its judgment in *Rodrigues Da Silva & Hoogkamer*, the ECtHR found that the decision by the Netherlands to refuse admission had been disproportionate. In the Court's view, the state had indulged in 'excessive formalism' by attaching 'paramount importance' to the fact that Mrs Rodrigues had been residing in the Netherlands illegally at the time of her daughter's birth. The Court had regard, therefore, for the fact that the Dutch government itself had indicated that Mrs Rodrigues could have obtained lawful residence on the basis of her relationship with the child's father, if only she had applied for it.[42] Thus, the mere fact that a person fails to apply for a residence permit, even though the requirements for obtaining such a permit are met, is apparently not regarded by the Court as a very important contravention of the state's immigration rules. Given that Mrs Rodrigues was moreover unable to continue her family life with her young daughter in her country of origin, the Court decided that the interests of the state did not outweigh those of the applicants. A similar type of reasoning was followed in the case of *Nunez*, where the ECtHR held it against the respondent state that it had not acted fast enough in reacting to Mrs Nunez' unlawful stay. According to the Court, the expulsion of Mrs Nunez did not 'to any appreciable degree [fulfil] the interests of swiftness and efficiency of immigration control that was

[40] ECtHR 20 October 2005 (admissibility decision), app no 8876/04 (*Haydarie and others*) and *Konstatinov* (n 36), para 50.

[41] *Nunez* (n 12), paras 71–73; *Antwi and others* (n 20), paras 90 and 104.

[42] *Rodrigues Da Silva & Hoogkamer* (n 36), paras 43–44.

the intended purpose of such administrative measures'. Consequently, the state interest served by the expulsion could not tip the balance.[43]

In *Biraga*, however, the Court again attached rather a lot of weight to the respondent state's interest in compliance with a mainly formal immigration measure. In this case, a decision had not yet been taken on the applicant's request for admission, hence it had not been established that she failed to meet any of the applicable conditions. She had, however, already entered the respondent state (Sweden) as an asylum seeker, whereas Swedish immigration law required her to apply for a residence permit for family reunion from abroad. The ECtHR found that the applicant's expulsion was not contrary to Article 8 ECHR.[44] A comparison with *Rodrigues Da Silva* suggests that the situation in the latter case was really quite exceptional, insofar as the mother's eligibility for a residence permit was not disputed. Moreover, in admission cases, the outcome of the fair balance test is not only determined by the interests of the state but also by those of the applicants. The ECtHR's considerations relating to these interests are discussed below.

ii. *Interests of the Applicants*

a. Considerations Relating to the Situation of the Family Members

An assessment of admission cases handled by the ECtHR shows that many different circumstances play a role in determining the weight to be accorded to family members' interest in establishing or continuing their family life in the respondent state. To start with, the Court itself distinguishes between 'those [family members] seeking entry into a country to pursue their newly established family life and those who had an established family life before one of the spouses obtained settlement in another country'.[45] In general, the interests of the family members will weigh more heavily if family life had already been created before one of them moved abroad. This may reflect a reasoning to the effect that, when admitting a person who already has a family in his or her country of origin, states can expect to be asked to admit that family as well, whereas this is not the case if the family did not exist at that time. However, as discussed below, the differentiation between family life created before or after migration should not be overstated: in both situations the Court has often found there to be reasons why Article 8 ECHR does not require family reunification in the respondent state.

[43] *Nunez* (n 12), paras 82–84. By contrast, see *Antwi and others* (n 20), para 102.

[44] *Biraga* (n 24).

[45] *Sen* (n 35), para 37; ECtHR 6 July 2006 (admissibility decision), app no 13594/03 (*Priya*). This distinction corresponds to the distinction made in Dutch law between family formation (*gezinsvorming*) and family reunification (*gezinshereniging*). This chapter uses the term 'family reunification' or 'family reunion' to cover both types of cases, unless otherwise indicated.

The majority of cases in which family life already existed before migration concern children left behind in their country of origin when (one of) their parents went to settle abroad. The ECtHR held in several of these cases that

> it may be unreasonable to force the parent to choose between giving up the position which they have acquired in the country of settlement or to renounce the mutual enjoyment by parent and child of each other's company which constitutes a fundamental element of family life.[46]

Yet this is not to say that a right to family reunification always exists in such situations. Case law shows that the Court takes various factors into account when determining the weight to be given to individual interests, including the age of the children and their situation in the country of origin, the extent to which the children are dependent on their parents, whether the separation was the result of a conscious and voluntary decision by the parents and whether there are any obstacles preventing the enjoyment of family life elsewhere.[47]

To give some examples, in the cases of *Sen* and *Tuquabo-Tekle* the ECtHR held that the Netherlands was under a positive obligation to admit the children because the rest of the family could not be expected to join them in the country of origin. In both cases the parents had not only settled in the Netherlands, but also had children who had been born and raised there and who had no or only minimal ties to the country of origin.[48] The Court also held that family reunification was 'particularly exigent' in view of the young age or otherwise vulnerable position of the children.[49] By contrast, the ECtHR found no positive obligation for the state in *Chandra* and *I.M.* because it considered that family life could also be exercised in the country of origin, and in *Magoke* because the applicant was not prevented from maintaining the same degree of family life with his daughter as they had enjoyed before his migration.[50]

A somewhat different scenario occurred in the case of *Nacic and others*: family life had been created before migration and all the family members

[46] eg, ECtHR 9 January 2001 (admissibility decision), app no 38047/97 (*I.M.*); ECtHR 6 November 2001 (admissibility decision), app no 50568/99 (*Adnane*); ECtHR 18 March 2003 (admissibility decision), app no 59186/00 (*Ismail Ebrahim and Serhan Ebrahim*) and *Haydarie and others* (n 40).

[47] eg, *Ahmut* (n 15), paras 69–73; ECtHR 5 September 2000 (admissibility decision), app no 39003/97 (*Knel & Veira*); *Sen* (n 35), paras 37–41; ECtHR 6 July 2004 (admissibility decision), app no 53675/00 (*Ramos Andrade*); ECtHR 5 April 2005 (admissibility decision), app no 43786/04 (*Benamar and others*) and *Tuquabo-Tekle and others* (n 12), paras 44–52.

[48] *Sen* (n 35) and *Tuquabo-Tekle and others* (n 12).

[49] In *Tuquabo-Tekle* (n 12), the ECtHR considered it relevant that the daughter had been taken out of school and had reached an age where she could be married off, contrary to the wishes of her mother.

[50] ECtHR 25 March 2003 (admissibility decision), app no 41226/98 (*I.M.*), ECtHR 13 May 2003 (admissibility decision), app no 53102/99 (*Chandra and others*) and ECtHR 14 June 2005 (admissibility decision), app no 12611/03 (*Magoke*).

(the parents and their two sons) had moved to Sweden together to apply for asylum. Eventually one son was granted a residence permit on medical grounds, while the other family members' applications were rejected. The ECtHR treated the case as one involving an interference instead of a potential positive obligation (para II.B.ii), but nevertheless found that neither the son's health nor the applicants' ties to Sweden constituted insurmountable obstacles for the family to return the country of origin. As a result, the Court concluded that Article 8 ECHR had not been violated.[51]

The second category of cases under Article 8 ECHR includes those in which family life was created after migration. These cases normally concern families that were formed in the respondent state while one of the parents or partners was residing there illegally or on a temporary residence permit (for example, while awaiting a decision on an asylum claim). In such cases, the circumstances considered by the ECtHR in relation to the individual interests of the applicants include 'the extent to which family life is or will be effectively ruptured, the extent of the ties in the Contracting State and whether there are insurmountable objective obstacles for exercising the family life in the country of origin'. Another important element is

> whether family life was created at a time when the persons involved were aware that the immigration status of one of them was such that the persistence of the family life within the host state would from the outset be precarious.[52]

The Court has indicated that, where the latter condition is met, a violation of Article 8 ECHR will occur only 'in the most exceptional circumstances'.

To date such exceptional circumstances have been found to exist only twice. In *Rodrigues Da Silva*, the respondent state (the Netherlands) sought to expel the mother of a very young girl who depended on her care. As the parents had separated and custody had been granted to the father, there was no possibility for the mother to take her daughter with her to her country of origin (Brazil).[53] Very similar facts emerged in *Nunez*, in which case the ECtHR also attached relevance to the disruption and stress already experienced by the children on account of their parents' separation and the pending expulsion of their mother.[54] More often, however, the Court has found there to be no positive obligation because the family relationship started at a time when one of the persons concerned had a weak immigration status and/or because family life could also be exercised in the country of origin.[55]

[51] *Nacic and others* (n 21), notably para 85. A partially dissenting opinion was issued by Judges Spielmann and Power-Forde.

[52] eg, *Ajayi and others* (n 33), ECtHR (admissibility decision) 11 April 2006, app no 61291/00 (*Useinov*); *Darren Omoregie and others* (n 21), para 57 and *Olgun* (n 24), para 43.

[53] *Rodrigues Da Silva and Hoogkamer* (n 36).

[54] *Nunez* (n 12), notably para 84.

[55] eg, ECtHR 24 November 1998 (admissibility decision), app no 40447/98 (*Mitchell*); *Solomon* (n 21); *Antwi and others* (n 20).

Looking at the above, three elements seem to play an important role in the Court's evaluation of a family's situation in admission cases. The first is whether family reunification is called for, either in the country of origin or in the respondent state. With regard to this point, the Court may consider that reunification is not necessary because the children are no longer in need of parental care,[56] or because the applicants can maintain their family life by means of regular visits across the border. The second element concerns the alternative of family reunification in the country of origin. This is normally considered possible, unless there are particularly strong ties binding the family, or some members of it, to the respondent state. Although the Court has never stated so explicitly, it seems likely that it would also consider family reunification to be precluded in the country of origin if one or more family members were at risk of persecution there.[57] Finally, the third element concerns the family members' own role in causing the separation, which may weigh against their claim for family reunification. This is reflected in the argument that the parent(s) consciously decided to leave their child behind in the country of origin, and in the argument that family life was created at a time when the immigration status of one of the family members was precarious.[58]

b. Considerations Relating to the Effect of Immigration Measures

The extent to which the applicants' interests are affected also depends on the nature of the immigration measures taken by the respondent state. As mentioned before, these measures are not often subject to express consideration by the ECtHR. The Court has, however, on several occasions considered the duration of re-entry bans imposed by the Contracting State, whereby it has found temporary re-entry bans of up to five years to be acceptable.[59] By contrast, in *Nunez*, the interests of the children put so much weight on the scale that a re-entry ban of two years was already considered disproportionate.[60]

[56] eg, *Knel & Veira* (n 47).

[57] See, *a contrario*, the judgment in *Gül* (n 20), para 41, where the Court held that the reasons why the father had applied for asylum were apparently no longer valid as he had visited his son in their country of origin several times. Asylum-related grounds probably also played a role in the case of *Haydarie* (n 40), where the Court referred to 'the possible existence of an objective obstacle for the applicants' return to Afghanistan'.

[58] Conversely, in *Tuquabo-Tekle* (n 12), para 47, the ECtHR considered that 'it is questionable to what extent it can be maintained [. . .] that Mrs Tuquabo-Tekle left Mehret behind of "her own free will", bearing in mind that she fled Eritrea in the course of a civil war to seek asylum abroad'. This also shows that asylum-related arguments can play a role here, as well as in determining whether family life is possible in the country of origin.

[59] *Konstatinov* (n 36), para 52; *Darren Omoregie and others* (n 21), paras 67–68; *Antwi and others* (n 20), para 104.

[60] *Nunez* (n 12), para 81.

As regards income requirements, it has already been mentioned that the Court does not, in principle, consider it unreasonable for states to demand that

> an alien who seeks family reunion must demonstrate that he/she has sufficient independent and lasting income, not being welfare benefits, to provide for the basic costs of subsistence of his or her family members with whom reunion is sought.[61]

It follows that applicants may normally be expected to make the efforts necessary to comply with this requirement. In *Konstatinov*, the Court considered that it had not been demonstrated, over a period of eight years, that the applicant's husband in the Netherlands had ever complied or at least made any efforts to comply with the minimum income requirement.[62] A similar situation was found in *Haydarie*: although it was established that the applicant had been taking language and sewing courses, which may have increased her employability, there was no indication that she had actively sought gainful employment. Instead she had preferred to stay at home to care for her disabled sister, which, according to the respondent government and the Court, she could also have left to a professional agency.[63] In both the above cases, the Court concluded that the state authorities had not failed to strike a fair balance between the applicant's interests on the one hand and its own interests in controlling immigration and public expenditure on the other.

In *Haydarie* the Court did, however, take into account the respondent government's statement that it would not have maintained the income requirement if Mrs Haydarie could demonstrate to have made, during a period of three years, serious but unsuccessful efforts to find gainful employment, 'also bearing in mind the possible existence of an objective obstacle for the applicant's return to Afghanistan'. This suggests that, at least where the option of exercising family life in the country of origin does not exist, states may not indefinitely continue to refuse admission to applicants who are willing but unable to meet the income requirements imposed.

Additional considerations relating to the proportionality of immigration requirements can be found in the ECtHR's decision in *M.F.S. v Bulgaria*.[64] This case concerned a Ukrainian national, Mrs M.F.S., who wished to reside in Bulgaria with her Bulgarian husband. During the first two years of her marriage she had to pay between €100 and €250 in administrative charges every six months in order to obtain and renew her residence permit. The applicant claimed that the annual sum to be paid by

[61] *Haydarie and others* (n 40) and *Konstatinov* (n 36), para 50.
[62] *Konstatinov* (n 36), para 50.
[63] *Haydarie and others* (n 40).
[64] ECtHR 12 February 2008 (admissibility decision), app no 33831/03 (*M.F.S. v Bulgaria*).

her equalled four times the Bulgarian minimum wage, while at the same time she was not permitted to work in Bulgaria. Although the Court held that a residence permit allowing a family member to reside in the respondent state was normally an adequate measure to meet the requirements of Article 8 ECHR, it nevertheless went on to examine 'whether the legal and factual conditions regarding this residence permit were not such as to disturb the fair balance between the interests of the applicants and those of the community'.[65] In doing so, it conceded that the amount to be paid by Mrs M.F.S. was substantial for Bulgarian standards, but found that she had not proven that the financial burden was too heavy, given her personal circumstances. The Court also recalled that the applicant's situation was temporary, as she would be able to apply for permanent residence status after two years. In summary, the Court concluded that the applicant's interests did not outweigh the financial considerations underlying the administrative charges imposed by the respondent state.

iii. Final Observations Regarding the Fair Balance Test in Admission Cases

ECtHR case law regarding admission cases is discussed above, with the aim of providing greater insight into how the Court applies the fair balance test. From this discussion, a number of criteria emerged that are used by the Court to assess whether a fair balance has been struck between the interests of the applicants and those of the Contracting States. It should be noted, however, that the Court's application of these criteria is highly casuistic and does not follow a fixed argumentative pattern, which means that their significance may vary in each individual case. It cannot, for example, be deduced from case law how the fact that family reunification is not possible in the country of origin will be weighed against the fact that family life was started at a time when the residence status of one of the partners was insecure, or that the applicant has made too few efforts to comply with income requirements.[66] It is, furthermore, unclear why the Court addresses the proportionality of immigration measures in some detail in some cases, but not in others. Lastly, the Court does not always seem to act consistently in the way it evaluates the facts of a case. In this respect, it is not obvious why the Court found that, in the *Sen* case, the decision by the parents to leave their daughter behind was not meant to be final, whereas the same decision was seen as definite and held against the parents in *Gül* and *Ahmut*.[67]

[65] 'Encore faut-il s'assurer que les conséquences de droit et de fait découlant du titre de séjour accordé à la personne concernée ne rompent pas le juste équilibre à ménager entre les intérêts de l'individu et ceux de la communauté', *M.F.S. v Bulgaria* (n 64), para 1.

[66] On the latter question cp Boeles et al 2009, 169–79.

[67] See *Sen* (n 35), para 40, *Gül* (n 20 above), para 41 and *Ahmut* (n 15 above) para 70. These and other inconsistencies in ECtHR case law in admission cases are discussed in Spijkerboer 2009, 276–80. According to this author, the 'structural instability' of the Court's decision-

The above inconsistencies and the interplay between the different criteria used by the Court affect the level of certainty with which it can be determined whether immigration decisions taken by a Contracting State are compatible with Article 8 ECHR. The following section nevertheless attempts to establish how Article 8 ECHR affects Contracting States' competence to make family reunification dependent on the fulfilment of integration conditions.

D. Article 8 ECHR in Relation to Integration Requirements

It has been established that, according to the ECtHR's interpretation, Article 8 ECHR does not grant individuals a general right to family reunification in the territory of a Contracting State. It follows that states are, in principle, allowed to make family reunification dependent on the fulfilment of certain conditions and to refuse admission in cases where those conditions are not met. Hence, measures aiming to control immigration of family members are not a priori incompatible with Article 8 ECHR. Nonetheless, a Contracting State may be under an obligation to allow family reunification in individual cases, where the interests of the applicants outweigh the general interests of the state. The previous section identifies criteria that are relevant for assessing these interests. It is now time to apply these criteria to situations where family reunification is made subject to integration requirements.

i. Integration Requirements and the Interest of the State

Thus far, the ECtHR has not been asked to pass judgment in any cases involving integration requirements. The Court has consequently not pronounced on the legitimacy of the aim of promoting integration. Nevertheless, it appears unlikely that this objective would be deemed incompatible with Article 8 ECHR. Possibly, the aims pursued through integration requirements can be subsumed under the interests already regarded as legitimate by the ECtHR, which are usually formulated in rather broad terms. The Court could accept, for example, that integration requirements are meant to prevent disorder (for example, by promoting peaceful relations between different groups of the population) or to protect the economic well-being of the country (by encouraging economic self-reliance and ensuring that immigrants have the necessary labour market skills). Alternatively, given the ECtHR's reticent attitude in this

making is inevitable due to the normative conflict between cosmopolitanism and communitarianism and the conflict between the 'ascending' and 'descending' positions in international legal argument. I believe, however, that the existence of these conflicts does not necessarily prevent the Court from addressing them in a more structured and consistent way.

regard, it is not unlikely that the Court will regard integration as a legitimate public interest in itself, leaving it to the Contracting States to determine more specifically what this objective entails. Lastly, as demonstrated earlier, the Court has accepted that admission requirements are necessary to 'control immigration', without going into the underlying purpose of such immigration control.

There are, nevertheless, some limitations to the objectives that Contracting States may pursue through integration measures. These objectives should not conflict with the fundamental rights guaranteed by the ECHR. Consequently, the purpose of integration measures may not be to abolish or restrict religious or ethnic pluralism.[68] It was also submitted in chapter 3 (section III.D.i) that states may not seek to make immigrants agree with particular moral values or beliefs. Arguably, this criterion translates into a legal norm through Article 9 ECHR, which protects the freedom of thought. Also relevant in this regard is the ECtHR's judgment in *Kjeldsen, Busk Madsen and Pedersen*, in which the Court stated that the Contracting States were not permitted to pursue an aim of indoctrination. While this case concerned the right to freedom of education as protected in Article 2 of the First Protocol to the ECHR, the Court expressly stated that it considered its interpretation to be consistent with 'Articles 8, 9 and 10 of the Convention and with the general spirit of the Convention itself, an instrument designed to maintain and promote the ideals and values of a democratic society'.[69] It moreover held that, to be in conformity with the ECHR, information or knowledge included in the curricula of state schools had to be conveyed 'in an objective, critical and pluralistic manner'.[70] It is submitted that this criterion may well also be applied in the context of integration requirements.

Another judgment with potential relevance for the issue at hand was issued in the case of *Tănase*. Here, the ECtHR qualified as a legitimate aim the need to ensure loyalty to the state. The Court explained that such loyalty 'in principle encompasses respect for the country's Constitution, laws, institutions, independence and territorial integrity'. However, it also stated that 'the notion of respect in this context must be limited to requiring that any desire to bring about changes to any of these aspects must be pursued in accordance with the laws of the state'.[71] The judgment

[68] This is not to deny that restrictions to such pluralism are sometimes allowed in, eg, the interest of public order (see Art 9(2) ECHR). However, the abolition or restriction of religious or ethnic pluralism as an objective in itself would be incompatible with the ECHR. The ECtHR has often indicated that the existence of such pluralism (or diversity) is protected by the Convention; see, eg, ECtHR (Grand Chamber) 22 December 2009, app nos 27996/06 and 34836/06 (*Sejdić and Finci*), paras 43–44 and ECtHR 10 June 2010, app no 302/02 (*Jehovah's Witnesses of Moscow and others*), para 99.

[69] ECtHR 7 December 1976, app nos 5095/71, 5920/72 and 5926/72 (*Kjeldsen, Busk Madsen and Pedersen*), para 53. See also, more recently, ECtHR (Grand Chamber) 18 March 2011, app no 30814/06 (*Lautsi and others*), para 62.

[70] *Kjeldsen, Busk Madsen and Pedersen* (n 69), para 53.

[71] ECtHR (Grand Chamber) 27 April 2010, app no 7/08 (*Tănase*), paras 166–67.

concerned a complaint under Article 3 First Protocol ECHR (the right to free elections), regarding a requirement in the legislation of Moldova that precluded citizens with dual nationality from becoming a member of parliament. This is, of course, a different context from the one examined in this book. Nevertheless, it is reasonable to believe that, where states enact integration requirements with the aim of ensuring the loyalty of immigrants to the host state (for instance, through a declaration), they should at least remain within the limits described above.

Another factor to be considered in relation to the interests of the state is the effectiveness of integration requirements in improving immigrant integration in the host society. It is observed that, with the exception of the *Nunez* case (section II.C.i), the ECtHR has so far refrained from testing the suitability of the immigration measures at stake to realise the public interests pursued, and it may well be that an assessment of the effectiveness of those measures would go beyond the scope of the Court's review. If, however, it is established that integration requirements do not have much effect, it follows that the interests of the state would not be strongly affected if those requirements were to be disregarded. Conversely, if the requirements are highly effective, the state interests will clearly benefit from their application. Consequently, where evidence of the effectiveness of integration requirements is available, it will be relevant to the question of whether a 'fair balance' has been struck between the interests of the state and those of the applicants in the individual case.

ii. Integration Requirements and the Interests of the Applicants

Turning now to the interests of the applicants, it can be inferred from the above analysis that these interests must be given increased weight when reunification is clearly in the best interests of the children involved (because, for instance, the children are still young), when there are obstacles to the exercising of family life in the country of origin and when the separation of family members could not be attributed to their own choice or to the fact that they started their relationship when the immigration status of one of them was precarious. Where one or more of these circumstances play a role, there will normally be less scope for a Contracting State to refuse to admit a family member on the grounds that he or she has not met an integration requirement.

In addition to the above circumstances, the nature and effect of integration requirements can play a role. From the ECtHR's judgments in *Haydarie, Konstatinov* and *M.F.S. v Bulgaria,* it can be derived that the interests of the applicants will weigh more heavily when family reunification is delayed for a longer period of time or even made permanently impossible. This will depend, to an important extent, on the burden imposed by the integration requirements and the efforts required from the applicants.

It should be noted that, in each of the above judgments, the ECtHR not only considered whether the disputed immigration conditions were acceptable *in abstracto,* but also assessed their effect in the case at hand, given the particular circumstances of the applicants.

While the Court has not yet ruled on this, it is suggested that several elements are significant in assessing the extent to which the possibility of family reunification is affected by integration requirements, such as the contents of the integration exam or programme, the level of knowledge or skills required, whether course materials or study facilities are provided by the Contracting State and the costs for the applicants. The effect of integration requirements on the applicants will also be influenced by individual circumstances, such as the education and learning capacity of the person concerned, the existence of any physical or psychological disabilities and the actual accessibility of course materials and the programme or exam (taking into account the financial situation of the applicants, as well as possible obstacles existing in the country of origin). Lastly it will make a difference whether the immigration regulations of the Contracting State contain an exemption clause for applicants who, despite making the necessary efforts, have not been able to comply with the integration requirements. As stated in section II.C.ii, the existence of such an exemption clause seems to have played a role in the Court's decision in *Haydarie*.

In the judgments in *M.F.S.* and *Haydarie,* the fact that the applicants faced substantive costs or efforts was not enough to render the immigration measures disproportionate. Translated into integration measures, the latter judgment may mean that Article 8 ECHR does not, in principle, prevent Contracting States from requiring the applicant to make an effort to meet an integration requirement throughout a fixed period of time (*in casu* three years). Yet, the ECtHR's reasoning in *Haydarie* and *Rodrigues Da Silva & Hoogkamer* supports the statement that the level of the demands that may be placed on applicants is also determined by the situation of the family members (although, in the former case, even the 'possible existence of an objective obstacle for the applicant's return to Afghanistan' was not enough to outweigh the substantial effort imposed on Mrs Haydarie). Thus, even where the separation of family members is temporary, the admissibility of the integration requirement will depend on the circumstances of the case.[72]

[72] Consider, for instance, the situation in *Tuquabo-Tekle* (n 12), section II.C.ii, where family reunification was found necessary because the daughter was about to be married off by her grandmother. In such a situation, even a temporary prolongation of the separation would have had irreversible consequences for the family life of the applicants. In this connection, Van der Winden referred to ECtHR case law stating that delays to family reunification, caused by state measures, cannot be such as to result in the de facto termination of family life. See Van der Winden 2006, 127.

E. Dutch Case Law with Regard to Article 8 ECHR and Integration Requirements

Unlike the ECtHR, Dutch courts have been asked on several occasions to review the compatibility of integration requirements with Article 8 of the ECHR. Although case law on this topic is not substantial, some contours of the courts' approach are emerging, as outlined below. The purpose of this section is twofold. Its primary aim is to establish how Dutch courts interpret Article 8 ECHR in relation to integration requirements and which criteria have been developed in this respect. Secondly, the question of whether these criteria are compatible with Article 8 ECHR, as interpreted by the European Court of Human Rights, is considered.

i. Positive Obligation and Fair Balance Test

Firstly it may be noted that, in the cases examined, the courts have consistently asked whether the refusal to admit a person on the grounds that the integration requirement had not been met amounted to a violation of a positive obligation under Article 8 ECHR. This approach is motivated by the argument that the refusal does not have the effect of withdrawing a residence permit that allowed the applicant to exercise his or her family life in the Netherlands and, therefore, does not constitute interference with the right to family life.[73] As seen above, the ECtHR itself does not consistently distinguish between positive and negative obligations. However, the 'positive obligation' doctrine followed by the Dutch courts is not as such contrary to Article 8 ECHR. More important is the test that is applied.

It was established in section II.B that Article 8 ECHR does not include a general right to family reunification in the state where one of the family members is living. Whether such a right exists in an individual case depends on the interests of the family members, as well as the general interests of the state. Like the ECtHR (in most cases), the Dutch courts determine the existence of a right to family reunification in a particular case by means of the fair balance test.[74] The following subsections discuss how this test has thus far been conducted in cases concerning integration requirements, with attention being paid first to the general interests

[73] eg, AJD 2 December 2008, case no 200806120/1, para 2.4.1; AJD 9 February 2009, case no 200806121/1, para 2.5.1; District Court of The Hague sitting in 's-Hertogenbosch 19 May 2010, case no 09/44517, paras 12–13; District Court of The Hague sitting in Rotterdam 22 September 2011, case no 10/31223, paras 4.2.1–4.2.2.

[74] eg, President District Court of The Hague sitting in Middelburg 16 August 2007, case nos 07/30015 and 07/31032, LJN: BB3524, para 8; District Court of The Hague 21 October 2009, case no 09/5145, LJN: BK5782, para 6.3; AJD 15 August 2011, case no 201007300/1/V2, para 2.3.1.

served by integration requirements. After that, case law on the proportionality of integration requirements is discussed and some consideration given to the intensity of the review conducted by the Dutch courts. Lastly, the extent to which Dutch case law provides more specific criteria for integration requirements than ECtHR case law is considered, as is the question of whether there are any points on which the approach of the Dutch courts may not meet the requirements set by Article 8 ECHR.

ii. State Interests Served by Integration Requirements

Under the fair balance test, the interests of family members have to be weighed against the general interests of the state. As far as the latter are concerned, it was argued above that integration requirements may pursue a variety of more or less specifically formulated state interests. So far, the ECtHR has generally accepted that public interests such as 'controlling immigration' or 'preserving the economic well-being of the state' can, in principle, justify immigration measures, including expulsion of family members or the application of income requirements. In several more recent cases, however, the ECtHR did have regard for arguments to the effect that the state interests were not deeply affected or served by the immigration measure at stake, with the result that they weighed less heavily in the balance (section II.C.i).

To date, the Dutch courts' approach in cases concerning integration requirements has been yet more reticent. In the majority of cases brought before them, the courts did not address the interests of the state at all, or merely claimed that the individual interests had to be weighed against the 'general interest' or the 'interests of the defendant', without specifying what these entailed. In only two cases was the general interest addressed in more detail. In these judgments, the courts, referring to the legislative history of the AIA, found that

> in this specific case the general interest consists, inter alia, of the need to stop the repeating process of lagging integration paired with continuing immigration so as to diminish the marginalisation of particular groups of the population – with all its consequences for the economic well-being of the Netherlands, public order and public safety and the rights and freedoms of others.[75]

Despite the above judgments it can be concluded that, overall, the nature of the general interests or the aims pursued by the state are not taken into account in the examination conducted by the Dutch courts in cases involving integration requirements. Consequently, both the definition of the general interests involved and the definition of the weight to be attached

[75] District Court of The Hague 21 October 2009, case no 09/5145, LJN: BK5782, para 6.3 and District Court of The Hague sitting in Haarlem 24 November 2010, case no 10/18883, LJN: BO5381, para 2.13.

thereto are left to the discretion of the legislative and administrative authorities. This also implies that it is not assessed whether or to what extent the integration exam abroad is a suitable or necessary instrument to achieve the aims pursued.

iii. Proportionality of Integration Requirements

From an examination of the available case law on integration requirements, the outcome of the fair balance test appears mainly to be determined by two criteria. One of these criteria, which is also taken into account by the ECtHR, is whether family life can be exercised in the country of origin. To a somewhat lesser extent, the courts also have regard to whether the obligation to pass the integration exam abroad makes the exercise of family life in the Netherlands permanently impossible.[76] With regard to the second question, the courts assess whether there are reasons to assume that the person seeking admission is lastingly unable to pass the integration exam abroad. It was suggested above (section II.D.ii) that the latter element could be of relevance in assessing the proportionality of integration requirements.

The Dutch courts use the above criteria to determine whether the obligation to pass an integration exam – and the denial of admission in the event of non-compliance – are proportionate to the general interests. However, case law shows that the scale does not easily tilt in favour of the applicants. To date there have only been two cases in which a court found the requirement of integration abroad to be disproportionate, both of which were overruled on appeal.[77] To illustrate the strictness with which the above criteria are applied some of the cases that have been decided thus far are described below.

One case that came before the District Court of The Hague (sitting in Middelburg) concerned an applicant of Eritrean nationality who sought admission for the purpose of family reunification with his Dutch wife.[78] The applicant stated that he was residing illegally in Sudan and that he was at risk of being sent back to Eritrea, from where he had previously

[76] eg, AJD 9 February 2009, case no 200806121/1, para 2.5.1; AJD 15 August 2011, case no 201007300/1/V2, para 2.3.1; District Court of The Hague sitting in Rotterdam 23 April 2008, case no 07/35128, *JV* 2008/282, annotated by KM de Vries, para 2; District Court of The Hague sitting in 's-Hertogenbosch 12 January 2009, case no 08/7556, LJN: BG9517, para 42; District Court of The Hague sitting in Utrecht 26 June 2009, case no 08/39827, para 2.20 and District Court of The Hague sitting in Maastricht 6 October 2010, case nos 09/33430 and 10/9629.

[77] District Court of The Hague sitting in Haarlem 24 November 2010, case no 10/18883, LJN: BO5381, overruled by AJD 1 December 2011, case no 201012538/1/V4; District Court of The Hague 30 June 2010, case no 09/46478, overruled by AJD 15 August 2011, case no 201007300/1/V2.

[78] President District Court of The Hague sitting in Middelburg 16 August 2007, case nos 07/30015 and 07/31032, LJN: BB3524.

fled. The applicant consequently maintained that he could not be expected to pass the integration exam abroad within a reasonable time. He also stated that no study materials for the exam were available in his mother tongue and that he would, therefore, have had to learn English before being able to learn Dutch.

Despite these circumstances, the court found that the decision by the Foreign Affairs Minister to refuse the applicant's admission did not fail to strike a fair balance between the interests of the applicant and the general interest of the state. Thereby the Court considered that the applicant's arguments relating to his situation in Sudan had to be examined in the course of an asylum procedure and could not be taken into account under Article 8 ECHR. The difficulties faced by the applicant with regard to the integration exam appear not to have been considered sufficient to justify concluding that he had to be admitted without having to meet the integration requirement.

A second case concerned a Moroccan applicant wishing to live in the Netherlands with her partner. She claimed that she would never be able to pass the integration exam abroad because she was illiterate. A residence permit had already been granted to the applicant's two minor children, meaning that she was the only member of the family who was not allowed to live in the Netherlands.

The Administrative Jurisdiction Division of the Council of State (AJD) found that the above case presented no special circumstances that made the Netherlands obliged to admit the applicant. In reaching this conclusion, it considered that the existence of an objective obstacle to the exercise of family life in the country of origin had not been demonstrated and that the applicant had not shown that she was lastingly unable to pass the integration exam, which meant that a refusal to exempt her from this exam would not permanently deprive her of the possibility to exercise her family life in the Netherlands. With regard to the latter consideration, the AJD accepted that the exam had been designed by the Dutch legislator in such a way that illiterate persons should also be able to pass (chapter 2, section VI.C). It did not, however, address the consequences of the applicant's illiteracy in terms of the efforts and costs that she would be required to make and the time that it would take her to reach the level required to pass the exam.

The third case concerned two Somali children seeking to be reunited with their mother and her husband in the Netherlands.[79] The mother had previously entered the Netherlands as an asylum seeker and had since obtained Dutch nationality. By the time a decision was taken on their application, both children were no longer minors. According to reports issued by two non-governmental organisations (Defence for Children

[79] District Court of The Hague 21 October 2009, case no 09/5145, LJN: BK5782.

International and the Red Cross), the applicants were living in dire circumstances in their country of origin. They did not have a home of their own and were living under the overhang of someone else's house. They were living off gifts from other people and did not have a computer or money to buy materials to prepare for the exam. It was therefore submitted that the applicants could not reasonably be expected to pass the integration exam abroad and had to be granted an exemption.

The above case was brought before the District Court of The Hague. With regard to the difficulties faced by the applicants in respect of preparing for the integration exam, the court stated that:

> [It is] primarily the responsibility of the applicants and their mother to obtain the necessary study materials and the required knowledge of the Dutch language and society in the country of origin. Thereby the applicants and their mother can let themselves be assisted by the non-governmental organizations that have also helped them earlier on in the procedure – by paying the administrative charges and enabling the application for family reunification to be made [. . .]. More specifically, the minister was justified in considering that the fact that the applicants do not speak any of the 13 languages in which study materials are available and that they do not have a computer does not present an obstacle for imposing the obligation to pass the integration exam. In view of the legislative history the applicants may be expected to let themselves be assisted by their mother or by third parties, who can arrange the translation of the study materials into a language which they do understand. Moreover, it was established during the court hearing that a computer is not a necessary asset for the preparation for and the participation in the exam [my translation, *KV*].[80]

In view of the above, the court found that the exercise of family life by the applicants was not made permanently impossible by the integration requirement and that the Minister had provided sufficient reasons why the refusal to admit the applicants was not contrary to Article 8 ECHR.[81] The court's decision was upheld in appeal in a non-reasoned judgment by the AJD.[82]

The above examples illustrate that the obligation to pass the integration exam abroad is not easily found to constitute a violation of Article 8 ECHR. In particular, Dutch case law shows that substantial efforts may be required of applicants and that the existence of specific obstacles – such as

[80] ibid, para 6.2.

[81] Later the court also stated that the protection of Art 8 ECHR did not extend to family relationships between parents and adult children unless there were 'more than normal emotional ties' (cp section II.A). Given this statement, it is submitted that the court should have found that Art 8 ECHR was not applicable instead of conducting a fair balance test. Meanwhile it is possible that the applicants' age played a role in the court's finding that Art 8 ECHR had not been violated; however, this was not explicitly mentioned.

[82] AJD 29 January 2010, case no 200908815/1/V2. Under Art 91(2) Aliens Act the AJD can refrain from motivating its judgment if the appeal is unfounded and if the complaints submitted by the applicant 'do not raise any questions that need to be answered in the interest of the unity or development of the law or of legal protection in general'.

illiteracy or the unavailability of study facilities – has not to date led to the conclusion that the obligation to pass the exam was disproportionate.[83]

As stated earlier, however, the proportionality of the integration exam abroad is also influenced by the situation of the family members and whether it is possible to exercise family life in the country of origin. In one case this situation led the court to conclude that the obligation to pass the integration exam abroad was disproportionate. The applicants in this case were an Afghan family (the parents and three children), who sought admission to join their son or brother who had been admitted to the Netherlands on asylum grounds when he was nine-years-old.[84] The family had been recognised as refugees by the United Nations High Commissioner for Refugees and was living irregularly and under very difficult circumstances in Turkey. Some of the children were still minors and the family had been trying for 10 years to be reunited in the Netherlands, where other close relatives were also living. Lastly, it had been established that the mother suffered from depression and post-traumatic stress syndrome. On the basis of these conditions, the District Court found that the interests of the applicants outweighed the integration interest underlying the AIA and ruled that the Netherlands had a positive obligation under Article 8 ECHR to admit the family.[85] This judgment was, however, overruled by the AJD on procedural grounds.[86] Moreover, in at least two of the other cases described above there was also no possibility of reunification in the country of origin because at least one of the family members feared persecution there. Yet this was either disregarded or not found substantial enough to conclude that the applicants had to be admitted to the Netherlands.

iv. Intensity of Review

Just like in cases before the ECtHR, the outcome of proceedings before the Dutch courts also depends on the intensity of the review conducted. Whereas the ECtHR sometimes leaves a certain margin of appreciation to the Contracting States, the national courts can defer to the assessment

[83] See also District Court of The Hague sitting in Rotterdam 23 April 2008, case no 07/35128, *JV* 2008/282, annotated by KM de Vries; District Court of The Hague sitting in Rotterdam 22 September 2011, case no 10/31223; District Court of The Hague sitting in Maastricht 6 October 2012, case nos 09/33430 and 10/9629 and District Court of The Hague sitting in Amsterdam 8 March 2011, case nos 10/23459 and 10/23449.

[84] Several years later the asylum permit was withdrawn and a non-asylum permit was granted, which is why the family members were not exempted from the integration exam under Art 3.71a (2)(a) Aliens Decree (section VI.B.iii of ch 2).

[85] District Court of The Hague sitting in Haarlem 24 November 2010, case no 10/18883, LJN: BO5381, paras 2.13–2.14.

[86] AJD 1 December 2011, case no 201012538/1/V4. The case was thereafter referred to the Immigration Minister to be decided anew; it is unknown whether admission was eventually granted.

made by the legislature or the administrative authorities. In this respect it appears that, at least at the district court level, the Dutch courts' approach to cases involving integration requirements has not always been consistent. Case law provides examples of judgments in which the courts conducted a full review of the decision to refuse admission in the light of Article 8 ECHR, as well as judgments in which only a marginal review took place.[87]

Reviews conducted by the AJD have been somewhere in between full and marginal. In the judgments delivered to date in which it assessed the AIA in relation to Article 8 ECHR, the Division twice held that 'the Minister was not wrong to find' that there were no special facts or circumstances to justify a finding that Article 8 ECHR had been violated, and once that 'it cannot be maintained that the Minister could not reasonably have let [the interests of the Dutch state] prevail over those of [the applicant]' [my translation, *KV*].[88] In one case, however, the AJD took into account that 'the applicant had not substantiated her statement that the medical problems suffered by her spouse effectively constituted an objective obstacle to the exercise of family life outside the Netherlands'.[89] In another case the Division added that

> it is [furthermore] taken into account that the applicant has not substantiated the existence of an objective obstacle to the exercise of family life in the country of origin [nor that] she is permanently unable to meet the integration requirement; [hence] the refusal to exempt her from this requirements does not imply that she will never be able to exercise family life in the Netherlands.[90]

It appears from the above considerations that the AJD supplemented the balancing of interests conducted by the Minister, indicating that it found that the above circumstances should have been taken into account even if they did not lead to a different conclusion. This approach is apparently confirmed in other case law (not concerning integration requirements), where the AJD has repeatedly stated that, when applying the fair balance test of Article 8 ECHR, the courts must establish whether the Minister has taken all the relevant facts and circumstances into account and whether, given the 'fair balance' criterion, he was 'not wrong to find that the interference with the applicant's right to respect for family life was justified' [my translation, *KV*].[91]

[87] Compare, eg, District Court of The Hague sitting in Utrecht 26 June 2009, case no 08/39827, para 2.20 (full review) and President District Court of The Hague sitting in Middelburg 16 August 2007, case nos 07/30015 and 07/31032, LJN: BB3524, para 8 (marginal review).

[88] See AJD 2 December 2008, case no 200806120/1, para 2.4.1; AJD 9 February 2009, case no 200806121/1, para 2.5.1 and AJD 15 August 2011, case no 201007300/1/V2, para 2.3.2.

[89] AJD 2 December 2008, case no 200806120/1, para 2.4.1.

[90] AJD 9 February 2009, case no 200806121/1, para 2.5.1.

[91] eg, AJD 1 May 2012, case no 201101008/1/V1, LJN: BW4897, para 2.4.2. See also the annotation by KE Geertsema in *JV* 2012/311.

v. Approach of the Dutch Courts in Relation to Article 8 ECHR

The above overview shows that the test conducted by the Dutch courts to determine whether, in a particular case, a refusal to allow family reunification in the Netherlands is compatible with Article 8 ECHR is largely similar to the test conducted by the ECtHR. Unlike the ECtHR, however, the Dutch courts have been asked on several occasions to rule on cases where the refusal of admission was based on the fact that the applicant had not passed the integration exam abroad. In determining the proportionality of this particular measure, the Dutch courts took into account the personal capacity of the applicants (including illiteracy and learning capability) and circumstances relating to their preparation for the exam (the availability of study materials or a computer, for example), as well as the existence of obstacles to reunification outside the Netherlands and other conditions amounting to a situation of hardship. Nonetheless, findings of disproportionality rarely occurred. It is not yet clear whether there are any circumstances that would lead the courts to find that an applicant is not able to pass the exam and, if so, what these circumstances would be. It also cannot be said with certainty that such a finding would necessarily lead to the conclusion that the obligation to pass the exam was disproportionate in that particular case, or whether this would depend on other circumstances as well.

It is not easy to say whether, overall, the standard of proportionality used by the Dutch courts is less strict than that used by the ECtHR (meaning that a violation is less likely to be found) or whether there are specific circumstances that the ECtHR clearly weighs differently from the national courts. In general, particularities pertaining to the situation of the family members seem to be given somewhat less attention in Dutch case law, whereas these often play a decisive role in ECtHR case law. This could result in judgments at a national level that are incompatible with Article 8 ECHR. In particular, it is questionable whether sufficient weight is always given to the position of settled migrants and the existence of asylum-related obstacles precluding the exercise of family life in the country of origin. It is also submitted that the standard imposed on applicants by the Dutch courts in terms of the efforts expected to be made to pass the exam is very high. It is not inconceivable that, in some of the situations considered in section II.E.ii above, the ECtHR would not find it reasonable to conclude that applicants could successfully take the exam before being admitted. Lastly, whereas the Dutch courts have so far been reticent to examine in any detail the public interest served by the Act on Integration Abroad, section II.C.i shows that the ECtHR has displayed a tendency lately to give more careful consideration to the interests of the state and the weight to be attached thereto.

III. ARTICLES 17 AND 23 OF THE INTERNATIONAL COVENANT ON CIVIL AND POLITICAL RIGHTS

The right to family life is also protected in Articles 17 and 23 of the International Covenant on Civil and Political Rights (ICCPR). Article 17(1) ICCPR provides that 'no one shall be subjected to arbitrary or unlawful interference with his [. . .] family', while the second paragraph adds that 'everyone has the right to the protection of the law against such interference or attacks'. Article 23(1) ICCPR moreover declares the family to be 'the natural and fundamental group unit of society [which] is entitled to protection by society and the State'.

At first sight, these provisions do not indicate whether the right to family life also includes a right to family reunification and, if so, whether this right may be made dependent on the fulfilment of integration requirements. To answer these questions, we need to examine how the above articles have been interpreted by the relevant bodies. Unlike the ECHR, the ICCPR is not monitored by an international court or other body competent to issue binding decisions on the interpretation and application of the Covenant. This means that it is ultimately left to the States Parties themselves to determine the contents of the rights and freedoms laid down therein. Nevertheless, some important guidelines for interpreting the Covenant are provided by the ICCPR monitoring body, the Human Rights Committee (HRC).[92] The HRC's jurisprudence on Articles 17 and 23 ICCPR is examined below, with particular regard to the Committee's General Comments and Communications issued in individual cases.[93] Additionally, case law of the Dutch courts is taken into account. While these sources do not, in general, provide more specific criteria with regard to integration requirements than those discussed above in relation to Article 8 ECHR, they do help to provide a more complete picture.

A. Scope of Articles 17 and 23 ICCPR – Family Life and Family Reunification

With regard to the relationships protected by Articles 17 and 23 ICCPR, the HRC supports a broad interpretation that leaves scope for the different concepts of the family that may exist in the societies and legal systems

[92] Art 28 and following ICCPR.

[93] The Optional Protocol to the ICCPR entitles individuals to the right of complaint before the HRC. After the ICCPR has declared a complaint admissible, it issues its views on the alleged infringement to the State concerned (Art 5 Optional Protocol ICCPR). General Comments and Communications issued by the HRC are not legally binding; see section II.B.i of ch 1.

of the States Parties to the Covenant. Thereby those groups of persons regarded as a family by the national legislation and practice of a state are in any case entitled to protection of their family life.[94] The HRC has determined that the concept of the family includes the relationships between married couples and between parents and their children, the latter continuing when the parents are divorced.[95] However, the Committee has also found that the mere existence of these relationships is not enough to qualify for protection unless there is some form of actual family life, such as life together, economic ties or a regular and intense relationship.[96]

An essential element of the right to family life is the right of members of a family to live together and to enjoy each other's company. This has been recognised on several occasions by the HRC.[97] The Committee has also found that this element of the right to family life may be affected by immigration measures adopted by the States Parties to the ICCPR. In its General Comment on the position of aliens, the HRC acknowledged that the Covenant does not contain a right for aliens to enter or reside in the territory of a State Party and that in principle states are allowed to decide who they will admit to their territory. Nevertheless, the HRC stated that 'in certain circumstances an alien may enjoy the protection of the Covenant even in relation to entry or residence, for example, when considerations of [. . .] respect for family life arise'.[98] The Committee has also issued a number of views in which it applied Articles 17 and 23(1) ICCPR in immigration matters, including cases concerning the admission of aliens to a State Party for the purpose of family reunification.[99]

Nevertheless, not every claim for family reunification automatically comes within the scope of Articles 17 and 23 ICCPR. To attract the protection of the above articles it must be established that the refusal to admit a family member either constitutes an interference with the family (under Art 17(1) ICCPR) or a failure on the part of the state to provide the necessary level of protection (under Art 23(1)). In this respect, the HRC has observed that

> there may indeed be cases in which a State Party's refusal to allow one member of a family to remain in its territory would involve interference in that person's

[94] Joseph et al 2004, 587, with references to General Comments 16, paras 5 and 19, para 2 of the HRC.

[95] HRC 9 April 1981, No 35/78 (*Aumeeruddy-Cziffra and others v Mauritius*), para 9.2(b)2(i)1 and HRC 12 August 1988, No 201/85 (*Hendriks v The Netherlands*), para 10.3, cited in Joseph et al 2004, 587–88.

[96] HRC 31 March 1981, No 68/80 (*A.S. v Canada*), para 8.2(b) and HRC 29 July 1994, No 417/90 (*Balaguer Santacana v Spain*), para 10.2, both cases cited in Joseph et al 2004, 588–89.

[97] *Aumeeruddy-Cziffra and others v Mauritius* (n 95), para 9.2(b)2(i)2 and General Comment 19, para 5.

[98] CCPR General Comment No 15 of 11 April 1986, para 5.

[99] See, eg, *Aumeeruddy-Cziffra and others v Mauritius* (n 95), HRC 16 August 2001, No 930/2000 (*Winata and Li v Australia*) and HRC 22 July 2008 (inadmissibility decision), No 1513/2006 (*Vital Maria Fernandes et al v The Netherlands*).

family life. However, the mere fact that one member of a family is entitled to remain in the territory of a State Party does not necessarily mean that requiring other members of the family to leave involves such interference.[100]

Thus far, the HRC has not provided a general criterion for deciding whether the exclusion of a family member from the territory of a State Party does or does not come within the scope of Article 17(1) and/or Article 23(1) ICCPR. In both *Winata and Li* and *Madafferi*, however, the Committee found there to be interference caused by the fact that the planned deportation by the State Party of one of the family members would necessarily result in 'substantial changes to long-settled family life'.[101] These two cases concerned similar situations where the parents (or one of the parents) were unlawfully residing in the receiving state, whereas one or more children had been born in that state, had lived there for more than 10 years and had even obtained that state's nationality. The state's intention to deport the unlawfully residing parent(s) consequently compelled them to choose between leaving their child(ren) behind, thus causing a separation of the family, or taking them away from the country where they had been born and lived all their lives to be reunited with their parents in their country of origin.[102]

The HRC's decision in *Winata and Li* was criticised in a dissenting opinion by a minority of the Committee's members, who found, amongst other things, that there had been no interference because the State Party was not forcing the parents to be separated from their child. After all, the son could have joined his parents in Indonesia, the country to which they were to be returned.[103] While the decision in *Madafferi* shows that this criticism was not followed by the majority, the issue of forced separation did play a role in the more recent case of *Gonzalez*. Here, the Guyanese authorities refused to grant a residence permit to the Cuban husband of a Guyanese national, as a result of which the couple could not continue to live together in Guyana. The HRC found that they could not live in Cuba either, while the State Party had not indicated any other place where the couple could exercise their family life. Under these circumstances the Committee took the view that denying legal residence to the husband also constituted interference with the applicants' family life.[104]

[100] *Winata and Li v Australia* (n 99), para 7.1 and HRC 26 August 2004, No 1011/2001 (*Madafferi v Australia*), para 9.7.

[101] *Winata and Li v Australia* (n 99), para 7.2 and *Madafferi v Australia* (n 100), para 9.8.

[102] Note that these cases show the HRC adopting a different approach to that of the ECtHR. Given that the parents in *Winata* and *Madafferi* were not legally resident migrants, the ECtHR would most likely have treated these cases as involving a potential positive obligation rather than as interference with a negative obligation. For a comparison of ECtHR and HRC case law on this point, see also Forder 2003, 9–10.

[103] *Winata and Li v Australia* (n 99), individual (dissenting) opinion by Committee members Bhagwati, Khalil, Kretzmer and Yalden, para 3.

[104] HRC 25 March 2010, No 1246/2004 (*Gonzalez v Guyana*), para 14.3. Note also the HRC's decision in *Nakrash and Liu Qifen v Sweden* (HRC 30 October 2008, No 1540/2007), where the

In the above examples, the family members seeking admission were already (unlawfully) present within the territory of the receiving state. Where this is not the case, however, an issue may also arise under Articles 17 and/or 23 ICCPR. This follows from the Communication in the case of *Ngambi and Nébol*, which concerned the denial of an entry visa to a woman who wanted to join her partner in France. Here the HRC stated that 'Article 23 of the Covenant guarantees the protection of family life including the interest in family reunification'.[105] Nevertheless, the Committee found the complaint in *Ngambi* to be inadmissible because the applicants had not demonstrated the existence of a family relationship.

Meanwhile, it may be observed that the HRC itself does not seem to be very strict about whether it treats cases concerning the admission of family members under Article 17(1) or 23(1) ICCPR. From the wording of both provisions, Article 17(1) appears to contain a negative obligation for the state not to interfere with the family, whereas Article 23(1) reflects a positive obligation to provide protection. However, as remarked in section II on Article 8 ECHR, it is not always self-evident whether a state's duty to allow family reunification must be qualified as a negative or a positive obligation. It may be observed that the above case of *Ngambi & Nébol*, in which the applicant had not yet entered the territory of the State Party, was dealt with under Article 23(1) ICCPR. This could be a sign that the HRC regarded the refusal to admit a family member from abroad as a failure to comply with a positive obligation rather than as an interference under Article 17(1). However, the Committee has also at least once applied Article 23(1) in a situation concerning the removal of an unlawfully residing family member from the receiving state.[106] Other admission cases in which the family member was already present on the territory of the receiving state have been dealt with under Article 17(1) alone[107] or under Articles 17(1) and 23(1) together.[108]

applicants' claim was found inadmissible because they had not demonstrated that the family would be unable to reunite in the country of origin of one of the partners or in a third country. Unlike in *Winata* and *Madafferi*, the applicants in this case also did not have 'long-settled family life' in the receiving state. The HRC's decision does not reveal whether the finding of inadmissibility was based on the conclusion that there was no interference, or that there was an interference which was considered lawful and justified (see para 7.4).

[105] HRC 16 July 2004, No 1179/2003 (*Ngambi and Nébol v France*), para 6.4. See also the HRC's Concluding Comments on Switzerland (UN doc. CCPR/C/79/Add.70, para 18) and Israel (UN doc. CCPR/C/79/Add.93, para 26 and CCPR/CO/78/ISR, para 21), in which it criticised these states' policies on reunification with family members from abroad. All comments are cited in Joseph et al 2004, 591–93.

[106] HRC 28 March 2003, No 893/99 (*Sahid v New Zealand*), para 8.2.

[107] eg, *Nakrash and Liu Qifen v Sweden* (n 104), paras 3.4 and 7.4.

[108] eg, *Winata and Li v Australia* (n 99), para 8.

B. Limitations to the Right to Family Reunification

While Articles 17 and 23(1) ICCPR also protect the right to family life in situations involving family reunification, these provisions do not entail an absolute right to enjoy family life on the territory of a State Party. As far as Article 17(1) is concerned, the wording of this provision already indicates that it forbids only those interferences with family life that are arbitrary or unlawful. The meaning of these standards has been specified to a certain extent by the HRC, especially in its General Comment no 16 on the interpretation of Article 17 ICCPR.

According to the Committee, the requirement of lawfulness entails that the interference must be envisaged in the law of the State Party and that this law must itself comply with the provisions, aims and objectives of the Covenant. The law must moreover be precise and circumscribed and each interference must be based on a decision taken by a designated authority on a case-by-case basis.[109] With regard to the concept of arbitrariness, the Committee stated that this was 'intended to guarantee that even interference provided for by law should be in accordance with the provisions, aims and objectives of the Covenant and should be, in any event, reasonable in the particular circumstances'.[110] Taking into account this General Comment, as well as the HRC's views in individual cases, it can be assumed that limitations to family life must in any event pursue a valid aim, as well as meet a certain standard of proportionality.[111]

With respect to admission cases, the application of a proportionality test is also clearly visible in the HRC's Communication in *Madafferi*. There the Committee stated that

> in cases where one part of the family must leave the territory of the State party while the other part would be entitled to remain, the relevant criteria for assessing whether or not the specific interference with family life can be objectively justified must be considered, on the one hand, in light of the significance of the State party's reasons for the removal of the person concerned and, on the other, the degree of hardship the family and its members would encounter as a consequence of such removal.[112]

Neither Article 17 nor any other provision of the ICCPR specifically enumerates the aims considered legitimate for the purpose of restricting the right to family life. However, as mentioned above in section III.A, the HRC has taken the view that states are entitled in principle to control the entry and residence of aliens. HRC case law does not provide examples of

[109] CCPR General Comment No 16 of 8 April 1988, paras 3 and 8, cited in Joseph et al 2004, 481.

[110] ibid, para 4.

[111] Joseph et al 2004, 483–84.

[112] *Madafferi v Australia* (n 100), para 9.8.

admission cases in which a violation of Article 17(1) ICCPR was found on the grounds that the decision not to admit a family member did not pursue a valid objective.

As far as the proportionality test is concerned, HRC case law indicates that states will normally be allowed to deny admission to a family member if the conditions for residence are not met.[113] Nonetheless, the Committee has held that, in extraordinary circumstances, the State Party may be required to adduce additional reasons to support its decision. Such extraordinary circumstances were deemed to exist in the above case of *Winata and Li*, in which Australia sought to remove the unlawfully residing parents of a 13-year-old Australian boy who had lived all his life in that country. The HRC stated that

> In the present case, both authors have been in Australia for over 14 years. The author's son has grown in Australia from his birth 13 years ago, attending Australian schools as an ordinary child would and developing the social relationships inherent in that. In view of this duration of time, it is incumbent on the State Party to demonstrate additional factors justifying the removal of both parents that go beyond a simple enforcement of its immigration law in order to avoid a characterisation of arbitrariness.[114]

The Committee's decision was not altered by the fact that the parents were able to (and also did) apply for 'parent visas' which, if granted, would have allowed them to return to Australia after a certain period of time.[115]

Other factors that have played a role in HRC case law concerning family reunification have been medical or psychological problems suffered by one or more of the family members (especially when these result from measures taken by the State Party, such as immigration detention), as well as difficulties they would face in relation to their integration in the country of origin.[116] The existence of such circumstances will weigh in favour of family reunification being allowed in the State Party. Nevertheless the difficulties will have to be demonstrated by the applicants; mere statement that relocation would lead to problems is not enough.[117]

Lastly, the available case law does not provide much information on the HRC's evaluation of the immigration criteria applied by the States Parties to the ICCPR. Nevertheless, the interests of the respondent state in *Madafferi* were found to weigh less heavily than the interests of the family members. *In casu* Mr Madafferi had been denied residence on the grounds

[113] See *Sahid v New Zealand* (n 106), para 8.2 and *Vital Maria Fernandes et al v The Netherlands* (n 99), para 6.3.

[114] *Winata and Li v Australia* (n 99), para 7.3.

[115] ibid, para 4.3.

[116] *Madafferi v Australia* (n 100), para 9.8 and HRC 6 November 2003, No 1069/2002 (*Bakhtiyari v Australia*), para 9.6.

[117] *Vital Maria Fernandes et al v The Netherlands* (n 99), para 6.3.

of his illegal presence and his alleged 'bad character', as he had committed several criminal acts in Italy. However the HRC considered that the acts had been committed 20 years earlier, that Mr Madafferi's outstanding sentences in his country of origin had been extinguished and there was no outstanding warrant for his arrest.[118] This decision suggests that the reasons for refusing to admit a family member must represent an actual interest and not be of a merely formal nature.

Unlike Article 17(1), Article 23(1) ICCPR does not expressly indicate the extent to which States Parties must protect the family or the conditions under which this protection may be limited. It follows, however, from the nature of the obligation laid down in this article that such protection cannot be absolute. This was also acknowledged by the HRC in *Aumeeruddy-Cziffra*, where it stated that 'the legal protection or measures a society or a State can afford to the family may vary from country to country and depend on different social, economic, political and cultural conditions and traditions'.[119] In *Sahid,* the Committee applied the criterion of 'arbitrariness', as prescribed by Article 17(1), also under Article 23(1).[120]

C. Articles 17 and 23 ICCPR and Integration Requirements

The previous sections show that a state's refusal to allow family reunification on its territory may come within the scope of the right to family life as protected by Articles 17(1) and 23(1) ICCPR. This can also be the case when the refusal is based on the grounds that the applicant for family reunification has failed to comply with an integration requirement. HRC case law indicates, however, that not every refusal to admit a family member amounts to interference with the right to family life. Whether this is so depends on the circumstances of the case, in particular on whether the state's decision amounts to a disruption of long-settled family life and whether it is possible to exercise family life in another country.

Moreover, even if interference has been established, the protection afforded to the right to family life under the ICCPR is not absolute. The States Parties to the Covenant remain entitled to regulate the entry and residence of aliens and to introduce conditions for the admission and residence of non-national family members, including in the form of integration requirements. Such conditions must, however, meet the criteria of lawfulness and non-arbitrariness. This means that integration requirements must, first of all, have a basis in the legislation of the State Party. Although the ICCPR does not specify how or by which body this legislation is to be drawn up, the HRC has indicated that it must be sufficiently

[118] *Madafferi v Australia* (n 100), para 9.8.
[119] *Aumeeruddy-Cziffra and others v Mauritius* (n 95), para 9.2(b) 2 (ii) 1.
[120] *Sahid v New Zealand* (n 106), para 8.2.

precise and circumscribed. A decision to reject a claim for admission because of non-compliance with integration requirements must furthermore be taken by a designated authority and on a case-by-case basis.

In addition to being lawful, integration requirements for the admission of family members must also not be arbitrary, which implies that they must serve a valid aim and be proportionate in relation to that aim. While it could be accepted that integration requirements are necessary to control immigration, it was submitted earlier that they could also be taken to serve other legitimate general interests, such as the protection of public order or the economic well-being of the state or the promotion of immigrant integration (section II.D.i). Again the integration objectives pursued by the States Parties to the ICCPR must respect the rights and freedoms laid down in the Covenant, including the freedom of thought and religion (Art 18 ICCPR). In this respect, however, the Covenant does not provide any more specific standards.

As to the question of proportionality, this depends on the specific circumstances of the case. HRC communications show that states are in principle entitled to refuse a request for family reunification on the grounds that the applicant has not complied with the relevant immigration rules, including failure to meet an integration requirement. Nevertheless, in each case it has to be assessed whether any exceptional circumstances require increased weight to be attached to the interests of the family. On the question of which circumstances can be regarded as exceptional, the available communications seem to indicate some gradual differences between the HRC's approach and that of the ECtHR and the Dutch courts in relation to Article 8 ECHR. It is doubtful, for example, whether the ECtHR would also have found a violation of the right to family life in the case of *Winata and Li*, given that the boy concerned was already 13-years-old and could have moved with his parents to Indonesia.[121] The HRC also appears to attach more weight to the difficulties that would be faced by applicants upon return to their country of origin.

Where additional weight is given to the interests of the family, the state has to put forward stronger reasons to justify its decision to refuse admission on the grounds of non-compliance with an integration requirement. In assessing the proportionality of this decision, however, account must also be taken of the immigration measure and the burden it imposes on applicants for family reunification, both *in abstracto* and in the particular case. In this respect neither the ICCPR itself nor the comments and communications of the HRC have provided any useful criteria thus far, either with regard to

[121] This case bears some resemblance to the case of *Rodrigues Da Silva and Hoogkamer*, in which the ECtHR found a violation of Art 8 ECHR (section II.C.i). However, in that case the Court expressly gave weight to the fact that the child was very young and, because custody had been granted to the father, that she could not have moved to Brazil with her mother if the latter were to be expelled.

immigration measures in general or with regard to integration requirements. Nevertheless, it is submitted that the various factors mentioned in section II.C above (such as costs, the level of the exam and the availability of study materials) are equally relevant in relation to the proportionality of integration requirements under Articles 17 and 23 ICCPR.

D. Dutch Case Law with Regard to Articles 17 and 23 ICCPR and Integration Requirements

Articles 17 and 23 ICCPR have not to date played a significant role in legal proceedings in the Netherlands concerning the compatibility of the Act on Integration Abroad with the right to family life. In one case before a district court, Article 17 ICCPR was invoked, along with Article 8 ECHR, by an alien who sought admission for the purpose of family reunification and had been refused an entry visa because he had not complied with the integration requirement abroad.[122] However, in its judgment, the Court dealt with the complaint only under Article 8 ECHR and did not address Article 17 ICCPR at all.

In a judgment in a later admission case, which did not concern integration requirements, the Administrative Jurisdiction Division (AJD) of the Council of State held that 'Articles 17 and 23 ICCPR do not give rise to any further reaching entitlements than Article 8 ECHR'.[123] Although the judgment reveals very little about the particular circumstances of the case, it clearly involved an alien who claimed the right to reside in the Netherlands with his spouse and their minor children. He was subsequently asked to apply for an entry visa (*machtiging tot voorlopig verblijf*), which meant he had to return to his home country and would be separated from his family at least temporarily. While it is not clear whether the AJD's statement was meant to apply to admission cases in general or only to this specific situation, it is submitted that claims for family reunification should not be assessed solely in the light of the standards of Article 8 ECHR. Instead account should also be taken of Articles 17 and 23 ICCPR and the interpretations issued by the HRC.

IV. ARTICLES 3, 9 AND 10 OF THE CONVENTION ON THE RIGHTS OF THE CHILD

As explained above, the mutual enjoyment by children and their parents of each other's company is foremost among the forms of family life

[122] President District Court of The Hague sitting in Middelburg 16 August 2007, case nos 07/30015 and 07/31032, LJN: BB3524, para 3.

[123] AJD 17 March 2008, case no 200706542/1, LJN: BC8001, para 2.4.1.

protected by the ECHR and the ICCPR. In addition, specific protection for the family life of children can be found in the Convention on the Rights of the Child (CRC). Article 7 of this Convention proclaims that 'the child shall . . . have . . . as far as possible, the right to know and be cared for by his or her parents'. This rather generally formulated right is made more specific by Articles 9 and 10 CRC, which concern the right of children not to be separated from their parents and the issue of family reunification.[124] Also relevant is the general obligation laid down in Article 3(1) CRC, which proclaims that the best interests of the child shall be a primary consideration in all actions concerning children.[125]

The implementation of the CRC by the States Parties is monitored by the Committee on the Rights of the Child (the Committee).[126] This Committee is not entitled to receive individual complaints concerning violations of the Convention. However, it may issue suggestions and general recommendations to the States Parties on the basis of the information presented to it in accordance with the CRC (including through state reports).[127] Where relevant, the comments provided by the Committee will be taken into account in interpreting the meaning of Articles 3, 9 and

[124] Art 9(1) CRC reads:

> States Parties shall ensure that a child shall not be separated from his or her parents against their will, except when competent authorities subject to judicial review determine, in accordance with applicable law and procedures, that such separation is necessary for the best interests of the child. Such determination may be necessary in a particular case such as one involving abuse or neglect of the child by the parents, or one where the parents are living separately and a decision must be made as to the child's place of residence.

Art 10(1) CRC reads:

> In accordance with the obligation of States Parties under article 9, paragraph 1, applications by a child or his or her parents to enter or leave a State Party for the purpose of family reunification shall be dealt with by States Parties in a positive, humane and expeditious manner. States Parties shall further ensure that the submission of such a request shall entail no adverse consequences for the applicants and for the members of their family.

In addition, Art 10(2) provides that children whose parents reside in different states shall have the right to maintain personal relations and direct contacts with both parents. While this provision may create an obligation for the state to admit a child or his or her parents to enable the contact to take place, such visits will by their nature be temporary. It is therefore not necessary to consider Art 10(2) CRC further in the course of this study.

[125] A very similar provision can be found in Art 24(2) of the EU Charter of Fundamental Rights, which states that: 'In all actions relating to children, whether taken by public authorities or private institutions, the child's best interests must be a primary consideration'. Thus far the EU Court of Justice has not provided any interpretations of this provision that would be of particular relevance to the topic of this study, see Reneman 2011, 356–58. The obligation to let the best interests of the child form a primary consideration has however been implemented (at least partly) in provisions of secondary EU law, including in Art 5(5) Family Reunification Directive. The directive will be discussed in section V.

[126] Art 43 CRC.

[127] Art 44 and 45 CRC.

10 CRC with regard to integration requirements for family reunification. Case law of the Dutch courts is discussed in section IV.F.

A. Scope of Articles 9 and 10 CRC – the Right of Children not to be Separated from their Parents and Family Reunification

i. Applicability of Article 9 CRC to Immigration Cases

According to Article 9(1) CRC the States Parties to the CRC must ensure that children shall not be separated from their parents against their will unless this is necessary for the best interests of the child. The issue of family reunification is expressly covered in Article 10(1) CRC, which states that applications for admission by children or their parents shall be dealt with by States Parties in a 'positive, humane and expeditious manner'.

From a declaration made by the chair of the open-ended Working Group that drafted the CRC, it can be derived that only Article 10 was intended to apply to immigration matters, whereas it was considered that domestic situations would be covered by Article 9.[128] However, there are good reasons why this interpretation cannot be maintained. This is because Article 10 concerns only applications to enter (or leave) a State Party for the purpose of family reunification and thus applies only to situations where the child or the parents have not yet been lawfully admitted. Yet, a separation between children and parents may also occur when one of them is expelled after having held legal residence (for reasons of public order or economic well-being, for instance).

The latter situation (expulsion after termination of legal residence) is clearly not addressed by Article 10 CRC. However, the idea that the Convention offers protection against separation in admission cases, but not in cases involving expulsion would seem an unlikely assumption. Such a result would be difficult to reconcile with the core obligation, under Article 9(1) CRC, not to separate children from their parents, as well as with the standards laid down in other human rights instruments, including the ECHR and the ICCPR.[129] In this respect, ECtHR case law indicates that Article 8 ECHR affords a higher level of protection to family

[128] Detrick 1992, 181. The declaration, which was made after Art 9 had been adopted in its current form, reads as follows:

> It is the understanding of the Working Group that article 6 [Art 9, *KV*] of this Convention is intended to apply to separations that arise in domestic situations, whereas article 6 *bis* [Art 10, *KV*] is intended to apply to separations involving different countries and relating to cases of family reunification. Article 6 *bis* is not intended to affect the general right of States to establish and regulate their respective immigration laws in accordance with their international obligations.

[129] See also Forder 2005, 31.

members who have already been lawfully admitted than to those for whom this is not the case.[130]

In light of the foregoing, it is submitted that Article 9(1) CRC applies also to immigration cases, in particular to cases involving the expulsion of legally resident aliens.[131] Given this assumption, it is not immediately clear whether the situation of aliens (children or parents) who are on the territory of a State Party, but who have not been lawfully admitted would fall under Article 9 or 10 CRC. While their removal would amount to a de facto separation within the meaning of the former provision, it is also argued that distinguishing between a claim to be admitted and a claim not to be removed may be rather arbitrary (section II.B.ii). It is consequently submitted that applications made by unlawfully residing aliens should be treated under Article 10(1) CRC.

ii. The Right not to be Separated

At the essence of Articles 9 and 10 CRC is the right of children not to be separated from their parents against their will. As far as Article 10(1) is concerned, the words 'in accordance with the obligation of States Parties under Article 9 (1)' indicate that the obligation to treat applications for family reunification in a positive, humane and expeditious manner is one way of ensuring that separation does not take place.

This right not to be separated is formulated in nearly absolute terms, subject only to the exception that the separation is in the best interests of the child. However, neither Article 9 nor Article 10 provides that family reunification must always take place on the territory of the State Party concerned. Consequently, Article 9(1) does not create an absolute obligation for the States Parties to allow legal residence to a child or his or her parents whenever the maintenance of family unity is not contrary to the best interests of the child.

Yet, before expelling or refusing to admit a child or parent, States Parties must consider whether family reunification would also be possible elsewhere (section IV.B). If the family can also be together outside the State Party, there will be no obligation under Article 9(1) to allow the family to reside in its territory. However, if there is no alternative for family life outside the State Party and a refusal to allow residence would necessarily result in a separation, the option of family reunification within the state's territory will have to be considered. This appears also to be the view taken by the Committee on the Rights of the Child.[132]

[130] The expulsion of a legally resident family member will normally be considered by the ECtHR as an interference with a negative obligation under Art 8 ECHR, which must meet the conditions of Art 8(2) in order to be justified. See section II.B.i.

[131] See also Steenbergen et al 1999, 239–40.

[132] See CRC General Comment No 6 of 1 September 2005 on the treatment of unaccompanied and separated children outside their country of origin, para 83, available at www.un.org.

It is submitted that, where family life cannot be exercised elsewhere and legal residence has already been granted, the obligation under Article 9(1) entails that states are not allowed to terminate such residence and/or expel the parent or child. Exceptions to this rule are possible only if it is shown that separation would be in the best interests of the child. If, on the other hand, the parent or child has not yet been legally admitted, the obligation of Article 10(1) comes into play. In such cases the application for admission will have to be considered as prescribed in that article, taking into account the question of whether family life is also possible elsewhere.

Two further issues regarding Articles 9 and 10 CRC are addressed below, namely the possibility of exercising family life elsewhere and the requirement that applications for family reunification must be dealt with in a positive, humane and expeditious manner.

B. The Possibility to Exercise Family Life Elsewhere

It is argued above that the States Parties to the CRC have an obligation to consider applications for family reunification in accordance with Article 10(1) CRC if it is not possible for the applicants to exercise their family life elsewhere, notably in the country of origin of (one of) the family members. However, this raises the question of when such an impossibility can be said to exist.

In this respect, it is submitted that Articles 9 and 10 CRC do not guarantee a right for children or parents to be reunited in the country of their choosing. Such a right would go well beyond what is required to avoid separation and would therefore entail an unfounded restriction of the power of states to control immigration in accordance with the general interest. However, there are situations in which obstacles to reunification in the country of origin can clearly be assumed to exist, including situations where the home state refuses to admit one or more family members, or where, if they were to return, the child or parents would risk serious human rights violations that would give rise to a claim for international protection.

According to the Committee on the Rights of the Child, the answer to the question of whether family reunification can take place in the country of origin should take into account the best interests of the child.[133] The Committee thus confirmed what was stated above, namely that a child should not be returned to the country of origin if this would amount to *refoulement*. It also stated that other (lower-level) risks that the child may face in the country of origin, such as the risk of being affected by the indiscriminate effects of generalised violence, 'must be given full attention and

[133] ibid, para 82, available at www.un.org.

balanced against other rights-based considerations, including the consequences of further separation. In this context, it must be recalled that the survival of the child is of paramount importance and a precondition for the enjoyment of any other rights'.[134]

In addition to the above considerations, the Committee has mentioned a number of other circumstances that it finds should be taken into account to determine whether returning a child to the country of origin would be in his or her best interests. To the extent that these are relevant here they include the safety, security and other conditions, including socio-economic conditions, awaiting the child upon return; the views of the child as expressed when exercising his or her right to do so under Article 12 CRC, and those of the persons caring for the child; the child's level of integration in the host country and the duration of absence from the home country; the child's right 'to preserve his or her identity, including nationality, name and family relations' (*cf* Art 8 CRC) and the 'desirability of continuity in a child's upbringing and to the child's ethnic, religious, cultural and linguistic background' (*cf* Art 20 CRC).[135] It is clear from this enumeration that these circumstances may weigh both in favour of or against reunification in the country of origin.

Lastly, the CRC Committee has noted that children may exceptionally be returned to their home country even though this is not in their best interests, provided that a careful balancing has taken place and other rights-based considerations support the decision to return. By way of example, the Committee mentions situations in which the child constitutes a serious risk to the security of the state or to the society.[136] Although this argument is understandable from the perspective of protecting the general interest, it cannot be sustained as Article 9(1) CRC does not leave scope for restrictions to the right set forward therein other than those necessary in the best interests of the child.

C. The Obligation to Treat Requests for Admission in a 'Positive, Humane and Expeditious Manner'

It was submitted above that Article 10(1) CRC applies to situations in which a parent or child has not yet been legally admitted to a State Party and in which it has been established that family life cannot be exercised elsewhere. In such situations, applications for admission made by the child or the parent(s) must be dealt with in 'a positive, humane and expeditious manner'.

[134] ibid.

[135] ibid, para 84.

[136] ibid, para 86, available at www.un.org. In this same paragraph the Committee also notes that arguments relating to general migration control are not sufficient to override the best interests of the child.

During the drafting process of the CRC the question arose as to whether the term 'positive' in Article 10(1) contained an element of prejudgment as regards the decision to be taken on the application. The representative of the United Kingdom believed this to be the case and therefore suggested replacing it by 'objective'. However, the word 'positive' was kept in the text after the delegate of the United States indicated that it 'only obliged States to act positively and in no way prejudged the outcome of their deliberations on questions of family reunification'.[137] Given this history, it may be assumed that the term 'positive' in Article 10(1) must be understood in the sense of 'actual', 'definite' or 'effective' rather than 'favourable'.[138] This also corresponds with the procedural nature of the obligation laid down in this provision.

To date the Committee on the Rights of the Child has not provided much guidance on the requirements stemming from Article 10(1). Nevertheless, it has indicated that the protection afforded to separated children is hampered in countries where the conditions for family reunification are so restrictive as to make such reunification virtually impossible to achieve.[139] Given that the right of children not to be separated from their parents is protected in the CRC, it is submitted that limitations to this right should be based on sound reasons and should strike a fair balance between the general interests and the interests of the applicants. Where overly restrictive conditions make family reunification effectively impossible, this standard is unlikely to be met.

As far as procedural guarantees are concerned, it may be derived that applications for family reunification should in any case be dealt with within a reasonable time period ('expeditious'). It is also submitted that the term 'humane' implies that applicants must be able to obtain information on the status of their application and, in the event of a rejection, about the reasons for it. Lastly, it is observed that nothing in the CRC indicates that children should follow their parents to their place of residence rather than the other way around.[140]

D. Article 3 CRC – the Obligation to Let the Best Interests of the Child be a Primary Consideration

Article 3(1) CRC prescribes that 'in all actions concerning children, whether undertaken by public or private social welfare institutions, courts of law, administrative authorities or legislative bodies, the best interests of

[137] Detrick 1992, 206.

[138] cp the online Oxford American Thesaurus of Current English at www.oxfordreference.com.

[139] CRC General Comment No 6 of 1 September 2005, on the treatment of unaccompanied and separated children outside their country of origin, para 3, available at www.un.org.

[140] Steenbergen et al 1999, 240 and 242.

the child shall be a primary consideration'. This provision applies not only to state actions directly related to the application of the Convention (such as a court deciding whether refusal to admit a parent would be contrary to Art 9 or 10 CRC), but to all actions concerning children. This means that the child's best interests should form a primary consideration in all legislative measures, administrative and judicial decisions concerning the family reunification of children, even if such cases are not within the scope of Article 10(1).[141]

Article 3(1) CRC does not require applications for family reunification by children and their parents always to be granted, even if this would be in the best interests of the child. In the view of the Committee on the Rights of the Child, the provision functions rather as a general principle, requiring state bodies and institutions systematically to consider how children's rights will be affected by their decisions and actions.[142] Accordingly, the Dutch government has taken the position that the interests of the child are not absolute or always decisive, but that they should form the primary consideration and determine the outcome in the event of a conflict of interests.[143] This interpretation seems compatible with the requirements of Article 3(1) CRC. Lastly, Steenbergen et al point out that Article 3(1) also functions as a procedural guarantee: where decisions are taken that affect children, including decisions concerning family reunification, their reasoning should show that the best interests of the child have been established and taken into account and how these interests have been weighed against other factors.[144]

E. Articles 3, 9 and 10 CRC in Relation to Integration Requirements

It may be derived from the above that, like Article 8 ECHR, the above provisions of the CRC do not contain an absolute right for parents or children to be admitted to the country where one of them resides for the purpose of exercising family life. Nevertheless, they do lay down a number of guarantees that must be respected by the States Parties in relation to applications for family reunification. This section examines how these guarantees affect the possibility of imposing integration requirements.

[141] In determining the best interests of the child in a particular case regard also has to be had to Art 12 CRC, which requires due weight to be given to the views of the child in accordance with his or her age and maturity.

[142] CRC General Comment No 5 of 27 November 2003 on general measures of implementation of the Convention on the Rights of the Child, CRC/GC/2003/5, 3-4, available at www.un.org.

[143] *Memorie van Toelichting bij de Goedkeuringswet, Parliamentary Papers II* 1992–1993, 22 855, No 3, 14, cited in Steenbergen et al 1999, 230–31.

[144] Steenbergen et al 1999, 231.

As indicated above, the core obligation of Articles 9 and 10 CRC is to ensure that children are not separated from their parents. With regard to applications for family reunification, whether made by a child or a parent, it consequently always has to be established whether the child and his or her parents can also live together outside the State Party. Thereby the standard to be applied is arguably stricter than that prescribed by the ECHR and possibly also the ICCPR: apart from the possibility that the child will be subjected to persecution or other forms of violence, regard also has to be had to other circumstances that may seriously and negatively affect the child's development. Examples of such circumstances would probably include the absence of any form of education or of special medical or psychological care required by the child. Also to be taken into account are the child's chances of integrating in the society where it will be living and of maintaining or building up family relationships.

If it can be established, in a particular case, that the child can also live with his or her parents elsewhere and that refusing admission will not result in separation, Articles 9 and 10 CRC do not impose any further obligations on the State Party concerned. In this situation, the Convention does not preclude permission for family reunification being made dependent on the fulfilment of integration requirements.

If, on the other hand, the child and his or her parents cannot be reunited elsewhere, the guarantee of Article 10(1) CRC comes into play (in admission cases). This article provides that applications for family reunification must be dealt with in a positive, humane and expeditious manner. This is a procedural obligation, which at first sight does not affect the possibility for the State Party to impose integration requirements. Nevertheless, it can be argued that the procedure surrounding such integration requirements should not inflict an unnecessary burden on the applicant. This may mean, for instance, that the applicant should not be required to repeatedly travel long distances in order to visit the embassy or another exam location, that course or study materials should be reasonably available and that exam results should be communicated within a satisfactory time limit.

It has also been submitted that, in view of the obligation of States Parties not to separate children from their parents, conditions for admission should not be such that they render family reunification effectively impossible. This would also be true with regard to integration requirements. Earlier in this chapter several factors are mentioned that affect the achievability of integration conditions, such as the level of knowledge required or the availability of preparation facilities (section II.C).

It follows from Article 3(1) CRC that the best interests of the child must be taken into consideration in all actions concerning children, including legislation as well as administrative and judicial decisions. With regard to integration requirements, the best interests of the child must consequently play a role in the legislative process where it is decided to introduce such requirements as conditions for admission, as well as in applying these requirements in individual cases and in the review conducted by the courts. Each of these measures or decisions will need to explain that and how the best interests of the child formed a primary consideration. This obligation is also not limited to situations coming within the scope of Articles 9 and 10 CRC (where the unity of children and parents is at stake), but extends to all decisions regarding family reunification, including those where admission is denied because of failure to fulfil integration requirements.

Compared to the provisions of the ECHR and the ICCPR discussed earlier in this chapter, the CRC at some points offers different standards with regard to admission requirements, including integration requirements, for family members. Whereas the former treaties protect the right to family life in rather general terms, Articles 9 and 10 CRC specifically oblige the States Parties not to separate children from their parents. The criteria to be applied to determine whether the child can also live with his or her parents in the country of origin are more rigorous than those developed in relation to Article 8 ECHR or Articles 17 and 23 ICCPR, reflecting the vital importance of the child's well-being.

In addition to this increased standard, Articles 3(1) and 10(1) CRC set forth some guarantees not explicitly included in the ECHR or the ICCPR. These concern the way in which applications for family reunification are dealt with by the receiving State Party and the primary significance to be attached to the best interests of the child. While the existence of these differences does not mean that children and their parents will always be entitled to more protection under the CRC than under the other provisions concerning the right to family life, the former does offer an autonomous legal framework for examining applications for family reunification that States Parties will need to apply, also in relation to implementing and applying integration requirements.

F. Dutch Case Law with Regard to Articles 3, 9 and 10 CRC and Integration Requirements

Proceedings before the Dutch courts, including cases regarding the removal or admission of non-national children or their parents, have called on Articles 3, 9 and 10 CRC with some regularity.[145] The interpretations that have been developed in this case law, where relevant for admis-

[145] For an overview of relevant case law see Steenbergen et al 1999, 246–49 (to 1999) and Ruitenberg 2003, 60–85, 101–26, 185–90 and 195–99 (to 2001).

sion cases, are briefly discussed below. So far there have been only two occasions on which the above provisions were applied in relation to the Act on Integration Abroad. These judgments are considered in section IV.F.iii.

i. Dutch Case Law with Regard to Articles 9 and 10 CRC

Dutch courts have not expressly determined that Articles 9(1) and 10 (1) CRC are self-executing (*een ieder verbindend*), to the effect that they can be called upon by individuals. Nevertheless, both provisions have been applied by the courts on various occasions. With regard to Article 9(1) CRC, it has been ruled on several occasions that this provision does not cover situations where separation between children and parents results from a refusal to grant admission.[146] In other cases, it was held that Article 9(1) does not grant parents a right to remain with their children in a State Party[147] and does not preclude the application of admission requirements (*in casu* the obligation to obtain a long-term visa) in cases where the interests of children are involved.[148]

Concerning Article 10(1) CRC, Dutch policy and legislation on family reunification have generally been considered to be in conformity with the requirements of this provision.[149] Whether these requirements have also been respected in the particular case at hand has not been examined.[150] The criterion that applications for family reunification must be dealt with in a 'positive, humane and expeditious manner' has not been further specified.

On several occasions the courts considered that Articles 9 and 10 CRC did not contain any obligations extending beyond those contained in Article 8 ECHR.[151] It is argued above, however, that this statement cannot be maintained (section IV.E). In addition to the procedural guarantees laid

[146] eg, District Court of The Hague (Alien Affairs Legal Uniformity Chamber) 25 September 1997, case no 96/9718, para 11.1; President District Court of The Hague sitting in 's-Hertogenbosch 19 December 2006, case nos 06/51734 and 06/51732, LJN: AZ5104, para 27.

[147] District Court of The Hague sitting in Haarlem 29 April 2004, case nos 03/19211, 03/19517 and 02/24266, para 2.27.

[148] District Court of The Hague sitting in Amsterdam 7 September 2006, case nos 05/18443, 05/52726 and 06/01750, para 7.10.

[149] eg, District Court of The Hague (Alien Affairs Legal Uniformity Chamber) 25 September 1997, case no 96/9718, para 11.3; District Court of The Hague sitting in 's-Hertogenbosch 30 June 2006, case no 05/23256, para 7.

[150] For an exception see District Court of The Hague sitting in Haarlem 29 April 2004, case nos 03/19211, 03/19517 and 02/24266, para 2.27. In this judgment the court held that 'it has not appeared that the application has not been dealt with in a positive and expeditious manner'.

[151] eg, District Court of The Hague (Alien Affairs Legal Uniformity Chamber) 25 September 1997, case no 96/9718, para 11.3; District Court of The Hague sitting in Haarlem 29 April 2004, case nos 03/19211, 03/19517 and 02/24266, para 2.27; District Court of The Hague sitting in Maastricht 29 December 2010, case nos 09/38308 and 10/10071.

down in Article 10(1), the CRC also provides a more stringent standard for determining whether a child can return to the country of origin. In this respect it must be noted that there have also been cases where the Dutch courts decided that it had to be established whether the child could join the parents outside the Netherlands. Also noteworthy is a recent judgment, where it was held that account had to be taken of a number of factors, including the child's integration in the Netherlands, the psychological problems suffered by the mother and her (in)capacity to provide a safe home for the child in the country of origin.[152]

ii. Dutch Case Law with Regard to Article 3 CRC

Dutch case law offers different interpretations of Article 3(1) CRC, both with regard to its legal effect (*een ieder verbindendheid*) and to its contents.[153] According to the Administrative Jurisdiction Division (AJD) of the Council of State, the highest judicial body to decide in admission cases, Article 3(1) CRC merely obliges states to take the best interests of the child into account when deciding on applications for family reunification. However, as far as the weight to be attached to these interests is concerned, the AJD has held that the provision is insufficiently specific to be self-executing and thus to be applied by the courts.[154] The AJD also found that, given its formulation, Article 3(1) CRC requires the interests of the child to be a primary consideration, but allows them to be balanced against other interests.

There have been several cases to date in which (district) courts ruled decisions taken by the Dutch immigration authorities to be unlawful because of their taking insufficient account of the interests of the child.[155] Nevertheless, it is submitted that the approach taken by the AJD does not entirely do justice to the requirements of Article 3(1) CRC. After all, by stating that the best interests of the child must form 'a primary consideration', this provision indicates that those interests must be given relatively heavy weight and that it is not enough for the State Party simply to mention the best interests of the child in its decision.[156] Where those interests

[152] District Court of The Hague sitting in Amsterdam 25 June 2010, case nos 08/37726 and 08/37729, LJN: BM9523, para 4.12. In this judgment the court did not apply the CRC directly, but assumed that the norms laid down in this Convention were equally applicable under Art 8 ECHR.

[153] Ruitenberg 2003, 60–85, 101–26, 185–90 and 195–99.

[154] eg, AJD 23 September 2004, case no 200404485/1, para 2.1.2; AJD 7 February 2012, case no 201103064/1/V2, LJN: BV3716, para 2.3.8. Note that in other cases the AJD decided that Art 3(1) CRC was not generally applicable at all; see, eg, AJD 15 February 2007, case no 200604499/1, LJN: AZ9524, para 2.4.1 and AJD 22 February 2012, case no 201107168/1/A2, LJN: BV6578, para 2.4.

[155] eg, District Court of The Hague sitting in Amsterdam 25 June 2010, case nos 08/37726 and 08/37729, LJN: BM9523, paras 4.11–4.12.

[156] cp District Court of The Hague sitting in Zutphen 24 July 2008, case no 07/43969, para 2.7.

do not prevail, this will have to be justified by substantial reasons.[157] While it is admitted that it may be difficult, in practice, to determine the existence of sufficient reasoningwithout actually conducting a renewed balancing test, it is maintained that this is what is required to meet the obligation of Article 3(1) CRC.

iii. Dutch Case Law with Regard to the CRC and Integration Requirements

As mentioned above, there have to date been only two cases in which Dutch courts ruled on whether the application of the Act on Integration Abroad (AIA) was compatible with Articles 3, 9 and 10 CRC.[158] In both cases the applicants were mothers who sought to join their husbands and children in the Netherlands. In the first case the claim concerning the CRC was first addressed in appeal, where the AJD considered that 'to the extent that they could be considered self-executing', the above provisions did not entail anything other than that 'in procedures such as those at issue, the interests of the children have to be taken into account' and that 'the disputed provisions did not contain any norm as to the weight to be attached to these interests'. As the situation of the applicant's children had been included in the examination of the claim, no violation was found to have occurred.[159] This consideration was later repeated in the second case.[160]

Since it was established in the above judgments that family life could also have been exercised in the country of origin, it seems unlikely that application of the CRC would have led to a different outcome. In the second case, the court addressed this issue by considering that the children were still very young, that they spoke Romani as well as Dutch and that they would be able to attend school in Croatia. Nonetheless, it follows from the arguments in the previous subsections that the AJD's interpretation of the CRC cannot be followed and that it should have been established whether the interests of the children had formed a 'primary consideration', taking into account the obstacle to family reunification resulting from the AIA.

[157] See also Ruitenberg 2004, paras 3–5.

[158] A claim was also made under Art 10 CRC in District Court of The Hague 21 October 2009, case no 09/5145, LJN: BK5782; in this case, however, the court found the CRC not to be applicable because the applicants had already reached the age of majority.

[159] AJD 9 February 2009, case no 200806121/1, para 2.6.1.

[160] District Court of The Hague sitting in Maastricht 6 October 2010, case nos 09/33430 and 10/9629.

V. THE FAMILY REUNIFICATION DIRECTIVE

A. Object and Purpose of the Directive

The Family Reunification Directive (FRD)[161] is an EU directive with its legal basis in Article 79(2)(a) TFEU (formerly Art 63(3)(a) TEC). The directive entered into force on 3 October 2003 and had to be implemented in the Member States by 3 October 2005. According to its first article, the purpose of the directive is 'to determine the conditions for the exercise of the right to family reunification by third-country nationals residing lawfully in the territory of the Member States'. Within the scope of the directive, the term 'family reunification' concerns both the entry and residence of family members in the EU Member States in order to preserve the family unit. The directive moreover applies irrespective of whether the family relationship arose before or after the sponsor entered the Member State where he or she lawfully resides.

For the purposes of this study, it is interesting to observe that the preamble to the FRD expresses the notion that family reunification is a means to enhance the integration of third-country nationals in the Member States in both legal and social terms. Reference is made to the Conclusions of the 1999 Tampere European Council, in which it was stated that 'a more vigorous integration policy' should aim to grant third-country nationals rights and obligations comparable to those of EU citizens.[162] It is also stated that family reunification can create socio-cultural stability, which 'facilitates the integration of third country nationals and also serves to promote economic and social cohesion, a fundamental Community objective stated in the Treaty'.[163]

At the same time, however, the directive makes provision for integration requirements to be imposed before family reunification is granted. This reflects a recognition of the idea that family reunification can also lead to integration-related problems if newly admitted family members have trouble settling in. It thus appears that the drafters of the FRD were working with different and contradicting conceptions of the relationship between integration and family reunification, one of which is reflected in the preamble and the other in the text of the directive.

In November 2011, the European Commission issued a Green Paper with the aim of initiating a public debate on certain aspects of the Family Reunification Directive, including integration requirements.[164] According

[161] Council Directive 2003/86/EC of 22 September 2003 on the right to family reunification, [2003] OJ L251/12.

[162] Preamble FRD, recital 3.

[163] Preamble FRD, recital 4.

[164] *Green Paper on the right to family reunification of third-country nationals living in the European Union (Directive 2003/86/EC)*, COM(2011) 735 final, 1–2.

to the Commission, the integration requirement had been 'one of the most controversial and debated requirements during the negotiations'.[165] In the Green Paper, stakeholders are asked to comment on the effectiveness of integration requirements, the need for further definition at the EU level and the desirability of pre-entry measures.[166] At the time of writing, a follow-up to this inquiry had not yet occurred.

B. Eligibility for Family Reunification

Sponsors (third-country nationals residing in a Member State) are eligible for family reunification if they hold a residence permit issued by a Member State with a validity of at least one year and have reasonable prospects of obtaining a right of permanent residence. The status of the family members is not relevant, but they must be third-country nationals.[167] The FRD does not apply to asylum seekers who have not yet received a final decision on their application, to people who have been granted or have applied for temporary protection status or to people who have been granted or have applied for a subsidiary form of protection.[168] The directive also does not apply to family members of EU citizens, who are instead covered by the Residence Directive (section III of chapter 6).[169] Member States may adopt more favourable provisions concerning the family reunification of third-country nationals.[170]

Article 4(1) FRD determines which family members are eligible for family reunification. These are the spouse and minor children (including adopted children) of the sponsor and/or spouse. The children must be below the age of majority set in the Member State concerned and must not be married. Unaccompanied children over the age of 12 can be required to meet 'a condition for integration', as discussed in more detail below. In addition to the above categories, Member States may choose to authorise the entry and residence of the family members mentioned in Article 4(2) FRD. These are the dependent parents of the sponsor or spouse, providing they do not enjoy proper family support in the country of origin, and the adult unmarried children of the sponsor and/or spouse if they are objectively unable to care for themselves on account of their state of

[165] ibid, 4.

[166] ibid, 5.

[167] Art 3(1) FRD. Note that family reunification of people who are beneficiaries of international protection in accordance with the recast Qualification Directive (2011/95/EU) is regulated by that directive, provided the family already existed in the country of origin and the family members were present in the same Member State when the application for protection was made. The Qualification Directive does not allow the Member States to introduce integration requirements. See Art 2(j) and 23 Qualification Directive.

[168] Art 3(2) FRD.

[169] Art 3(3) FRD.

[170] Art 3(5) FRD.

health. Lastly, Member States may choose to authorise the entry and residence of the unmarried partner with whom the sponsor is in a duly attested, stable, long-term relationship or a registered partnership, as well as the unmarried minor children (including adopted children) and unmarried, adult but dependent children of that partner.[171]

Although Member States are not obliged to extend the right to family reunification to the categories of family members mentioned in Article 4(2) and (3) FRD, those which do so must then allow family reunification under the conditions laid down in the directive.[172] Article 4(4) FRD restricts the possibilities of family reunification in the event of a polygamous marriage. A sponsor can consequently only apply for family reunification with one spouse. Additionally, in the event of a polygamous marriage, Member States are entitled to limit the family reunification of minor children. Articles 4(5) and 4(6) allow certain conditions to be imposed regarding the ages of the family members with whom reunification is requested.

C. Conditions for Family Reunification

In principle, applications for family reunification must be made and examined while the family members are outside the host Member State.[173] As soon as the application is accepted, the Member State concerned must allow the family members to enter its territory and grant those family members 'every facility' for obtaining the requisite visas.[174] The host Member State must also grant the family members a renewable residence permit for at least one year.[175] Thus, once the application for family reunification has been accepted, the family members are entitled to entry and residence for at least one year.

The acceptance of the application, however, is subject to certain conditions. Of particular significance to this study is that the FRD expressly mentions the possibility of imposing integration requirements. The relevant provisions can be found in Article 4(1), final subparagraph, and Article 7(2) of the directive.[176] Both provisions are discussed in more

[171] Art 4(3) FRD.

[172] Art 4(2) and (3) FRD. See also Boeles et al 2009, 192.

[173] Art 5(3) FRD

[174] Art 13(1) FRD

[175] Art 13(2) FRD.

[176] Art 4(1), final subparagraph FRD reads:

> By way of derogation, where a child is aged over 12 years and arrives independently from the rest of his/her family, the Member State may, before authorising entry and residence under this Directive, verify whether he or she meets a condition for integration provided for by its existing legislation on the date of implementation of this Directive.

Art 7(2) FRD reads:

> Member States may require third country nationals to comply with integration measures, in accordance with national law.

detail below. It must be noted, however, that the provisions of Article 4(1), final subparagraph, are of little practical relevance. This is due to the standstill clause, which states that in order to be valid the integration conditions had to be provided in the existing national legislation of the Member States on the date of implementation of the directive. Only Germany fulfilled this requirement.[177] The focus of the discussion below is, therefore, on Article 7(2) FRD.

i. The Conditionality of Integration Requirements

It seems clear from the terms of the FRD that the integration requirements in Article 4(1), final subparagraph, and Article 7(2) may be imposed as conditions for the right to family reunification, implying that a failure to fulfil these requirements can lead to the application being refused.[178] Article 7 forms part of Chapter IV, entitled 'Requirements for the exercise of the right to family reunification'. Apart from integration requirements Article 7 mentions a number of other conditions – relating to income, accommodation and health insurance – that must be met if family reunification is to be granted. Evidence that these conditions are met must be provided when the application for family reunification is made.[179]

The integration requirements may moreover be imposed before family reunification is granted. This follows from Article 4(1), final subparagraph ('before authorising entry and residence') and *a contrario* from the second sentence of Article 7(2) FRD and from Article 15(3) of the Blue Card Directive. This also makes it plausible that the integration requirements in Article 7(2) FRD may be used as conditions for family reunification and not only as a way to improve the integration of those seeking admission before they enter the Member State. After all, it would seem rather premature to start the integration process in the country of origin if the application for family reunification could still be denied on other grounds (such as a lack of income).

Against this interpretation, it may be argued that the FRD aims to enable family reunification in order to create socio-cultural stability (section V.A). In remarks submitted to the Court of Justice, the European

With regard to the refugees and/or family members of refugees referred to in Article 12 the integration measures referred to in the first subparagraph may only be applied once the persons concerned have been granted family reunification.

[177] *Report from the Commission to the European Parliament and the Council on the application of Directive 2003/86/EC on the right to family reunification*, COM(2008) 610 final, 5. According to the same report, Cyprus also introduced integration conditions under Art 4(1), final subparagraph, FRD, but only after the implementation deadline.

[178] Unlike several other authors I do not believe that the term 'integration measures' can be distinguished from 'integration conditions', with the former allowing less room for coercive or conditional measures such as an integration test. My arguments on this point are explained in detail in section VI.D.v of ch 6.

[179] Art 7(1) FRD.

Commission, relying on this aim, expressed the view that Article 7(2) allows Member States to introduce integration requirements to ensure 'a minimum level of integration capacity' within the Member State concerned, but not to refuse admission to family members who fail to meet such requirements.[180] In the Commission's view, therefore, the FRD does not allow Member States to pursue a policy of 'integration through exclusion' (chapter 3, section II.C.). It is submitted, however, that although the aim of the FRD is to enable family reunification, this does not mean that requests for admission cannot be made subject to conditions or should be granted in each individual case.[181] As explained above, the actual provisions of the directive indicate that admission can be denied if the integration requirements set by Member States are not met. Hence, the Commission's interpretation cannot be followed.

Meanwhile, Article 7(2) FRD contains an exception for third-country nationals who are family members of refugees. This exception applies to the spouse and minor children of the sponsor and/or spouse.[182] These family members may be required to meet integration requirements only after family reunification has been granted. It is plausible to assume that, in this case, non-compliance with integration requirements cannot result in the right to family reunification being denied. This exception can be explained by the specific plight of refugee families, who are unable to exercise their family life in the country of origin.[183] With regard to integration requirements for children arriving independently of the rest of the family, as mentioned in Article 4(1), final subparagraph, an exception for children of refugees can be found in Article 10(1) FRD.

ii. The Relationship between Article 4(1), Final Subparagraph and Article 7(2) FRD

It may be asked what the relationship is between Article 4(1), final subparagraph and Article 7(2) FRD. At first sight the provisions appear to overlap: whereas Article 4(1), final subparagraph, applies specifically to children who are over 12 years of age and arrive independently from the rest of the family, Article 7(2) apparently covers all family members including unaccompanied children. Nevertheless it must be assumed that Article 4(1), final subparagraph, is not without significance and that both provisions have their own independent meaning.

[180] The remarks were submitted in the case of *Mohammed Imran*, C-155/11 PPU. The case was eventually closed without a decision on the merits, see section V.D.

[181] See also, with regard to Art 4(1), final subpara FRD, CoJ 27 June 2006, C-540/03 [2006] ECR I-5769 (*Parliament v Council*), paras 67–69.

[182] Art 7(2) read in conjunction with Art 12(1) and Art 4(1) FRD.

[183] See the preamble to the FRD, recital 8.

With regard to Article 4(1), final subparagraph, the preamble to the FRD explains that the reason why this provision was included was because of the assumption that children will integrate more easily at an early age and to ensure that they gain the necessary education and language skills at school.[184] Thus, it can be derived that Article 4(1), final subparagraph, was included so as to encourage parents to bring over their children as soon as possible rather than waiting until the children are older and may have more trouble integrating in the host Member State. If this is the case, however, it does not appear likely, on the basis of Article 7(2) FRD, that children younger than 12 could also be asked to comply with integration requirements. It must therefore be assumed that Article 7(2) FRD does not apply to children at all.[185]

To conclude, it is submitted that the FRD distinguishes three different groups for the purpose of imposing integration requirements. Adult family members may be required to comply with such requirements (providing they do not belong to a refugee family) on the basis of Article 7(2) FRD. Children who are over 12 years of age and arrive independently from the rest of the family may also be asked to comply with integration requirements, but only if the Member State concerned has met the standstill clause (section V.C above). Lastly, integration requirements may not be imposed on children who arrive with their family or are aged 12 or younger.

iii. Contents of the Integration Requirements

The Family Reunification Directive does not define what is to be understood by a 'condition for integration' or 'integration measures' in Articles 4(1) and 7(2). The same is true with regard to other directives in which these terms are used, in particular the Long-term Residents Directive (2003/109/EC) and the Blue Card Directive (2009/50/EC). It is therefore left to the Member States to determine the exact contents of these requirements. This also follows from the fact that Article 7(2) FRD allows Member States to impose integration requirements 'in accordance with national law'.

Nevertheless, some indications as to possible integration measures or conditions can be found in the directives. For instance, it becomes clear from Article 15(3) of the Long-term Residents Directive (LRD), which was adopted only shortly after the FRD, that integration requirements may entail the obligation to participate in language courses. The same can be

[184] Preamble FRD, recital 12.

[185] For a somewhat different approach, see Hailbronner et al 2010, 232–33, who maintain that Art 7(2) FRD does apply to children over 12 years of age. In my view this interpretation cannot be followed as it would presumably allow Member States to circumvent the standstill clause laid down in Art 4(1), final subparagraph.

derived from recital 23 of the preamble to the Blue Card Directive (BCD). In addition, the legislative documents pertaining to the LRD mention the possibility of integration programmes to increase the self-sufficiency of newly arrived immigrants, including language training, social orientation, vocational training and knowledge of the host state's society, as well as integration tests (section VI.D.iii of chapter 6). It was also considered that third-country nationals could be asked to pay the costs of the integration programmes.

On the basis of the above, it may be assumed that integration programmes and tests designed to improve or test immigrants' language abilities or their knowledge of the host society are in any case covered by the provisions of the Family Reunification Directive. Nevertheless, other types of integration requirements cannot be excluded in advance.

iv. Limitations to the Discretion of the Member States

Notwithstanding the above, the FRD also contains certain limitations to the discretion of EU Member States to apply integration requirements as a condition for family reunification. First of all, in examining an application under the directive, Member States must have regard to Articles 5(5) and 17 FRD. According to the former provision, Member States shall have due regard to the best interests of minor children. In addition, Article 17 obliges Member States, before rejecting an application, to take due account of 'the nature and solidity of the person's family relationships and the duration of his residence in the Member State and of the existence of family, cultural and social ties with his/her country of origin'.

It follows that, for each application, the Member States will need to have regard to the particular circumstances of the family members. Thereby the interests weighing in favour of family reunification being granted will need to be balanced against any grounds for rejecting the application.[186] Articles 5(5) and 17 FRD reflect, to a large extent, the criteria developed in relation to the right to family life in the ECHR and the ICCPR, which are discussed earlier in this chapter. The requirement of Article 5(5) also goes some way towards implementing Article 3 CRC, and Article 24(2) EU Charter of Fundamental Rights, within the framework of the directive. Unlike these provisions, however, the FRD does not require the best interests of the child to form a 'primary consideration'. Instead it obliges the Member States to have 'due regard' to these interests, which would appear a somewhat less demanding criterion.

In addition to the above, the EU Court of Justice (CoJ) ruled in its judgment in *Chakroun*, which concerned income requirements imposed by the Netherlands, that the scope left to Member States to maintain conditions

[186] See also Groenendijk 2006b, 366 and Boeles et al 2009, 186.

for family reunification under the FRD must be interpreted strictly. According to the Court, this follows from the fact that the general rule, as laid down in Article 4(1) FRD, is that family reunification should be authorised to the family members mentioned in that provision.[187] Earlier, the Court had already established that the directive went further than the provisions on the right to family life in international human rights law, which do not grant a right to exercise one's family life in the country where the sponsor resides.[188]

It may be claimed, in objecting to the Court's decision, that, by focusing on family reunification as the principal rule the CoJ tends to disregard the fact that the FRD allows the right to family reunification to be made subject to certain conditions. After all, the possibility of imposing these conditions is expressly foreseen by the directive. It may also be recalled that the purpose of the directive, as set forth in Article 1, is to determine the conditions under which the right to family reunification is to be exercised. There is therefore little in the FRD to suggest that it is the conditions to the right of family reunification that need to be interpreted restrictively. Nevertheless it is true, as the Court also stated, that the promotion of family reunification is stated as an objective in the directive's preamble. It can therefore be accepted that measures taken by Member States should not be of such a nature as to undermine this objective. Neither should such measures render the right to family reunification illusory and hence deprive the directive of its effectiveness.[189]

In the case of *Chakroun* it was argued that the Dutch regulations concerning income requirements were contrary to Article 7(1)(c) FRD, according to which the Member States may ask for evidence that the sponsor has sufficient resources to maintain him or herself and his or her family members without recourse to the social assistance system. The CoJ found that Member States are allowed, under Article 7(1)(c) FRD, to set a certain amount of income as a reference. However, they may not impose a minimum income level below which all requests for family reunification will be automatically refused, without examining the particular circumstances and actual financial needs of the applicants. The Court supported this interpretation by referring to Article 17 FRD which, as discussed above, also requires applications to be examined individually.[190]

As far as integration requirements are concerned, the standard imposed by Article 7(2) FRD can be seen as less specific than that imposed by Article 7(1)(c). As explained above, the directive does not state what is to be understood by integration, or how a sufficient level of integration is to

[187] CoJ 4 March 2010, C-578/08, [2010] *ECR*, p. I-01839 (*Chakroun*), paras 41–43.

[188] *Parliament v Council* (n 181), para 60.

[189] *Chakroun* (n 187), para 43; see also CoJ 26 April 2012, C-508/10 [2012] ECR 00000 (*Commission v the Netherlands*), para 65.

[190] *Chakroun* (n 187), para 48.

be measured. This implies that Article 7(2) provides few indications for the CoJ to find that integration requirements imposed by a Member State are contrary to the FRD. Nevertheless, the *Chakroun* judgment suggests that integration requirements, like income requirements, may not be such that they automatically exclude all those not complying with them. Although Member States are probably allowed to formulate a certain level of knowledge or language abilities that applicants ought to achieve, they still need to examine applications individually. Thereby regard must not only be had to the interests mentioned in Articles 5(5) and 17 FRD, but also to the relevance of the integration requirement in the particular case.

To illustrate the above it may be asked whether, for example, the Netherlands can lawfully require an applicant for family reunification to pass a Dutch language exam if the person concerned can demonstrate that he or she can also find a job working in English. Arguably, this will not be the case if it is established that the purpose of the integration requirement is to ensure that the applicant can engage in paid labour. However, as stated above, it remains up to the Member States to determine what is understood by integration and to define the contents of integration requirements. Thus, if the Netherlands maintains that language learning is meaningful regardless of economic self-sufficiency, the obligation to learn some Dutch would most likely fall within the boundaries set by the directive.

The requirement that an income or integration requirement must be necessary in the individual case is understood here as an element of the principle of proportionality, which is a general principle of EU law (chapter 1, section II.B.ii). In a later judgment, concerning the Long-term Residents Directive, the CoJ stated in more general terms that national measures transposing that directive must respect the principle of proportionality, which means that they must be suitable to achieve the objectives pursued and not go beyond what is necessary to attain them.[191] Surely, this also applies with regard to measures transposing the Family Reunification Directive.

In a report concerning the application of the FRD, the European Commission proposed several more specific criteria to determine the admissibility and proportionality of integration measures adopted by Member States under Article 7(2) FRD. According to the Commission,

> the objective of such measures is to facilitate the integration of family members. Their admissibility under the Directive depends on whether they serve this purpose and whether they respect the principle of proportionality. Their admissibility can be questioned on the basis of the accessibility of [such] courses or tests, how they are designed and / or organised (test materials, fees, venue, etc.), whether such measures or their impact serve purposes other than integration

[191] *Commission v the Netherlands* (n 189), para 75.

(e.g. high fees excluding low-income families). The procedural safeguard to ensure the right to mount a legal challenge should also be respected.[192]

Earlier in this chapter, it is argued that the criteria mentioned by the European Commission, such as the accessibility and the costs of integration courses or tests, are relevant to determine the proportionality of these requirements in relation to the right to family life. It seems plausible to assume that the same criteria also play a role in determining the proportionality of integration requirements under the Family Reunification Directive. It may furthermore be accepted that the purpose of the measures should indeed be to improve integration. However, as argued above, the aim of the integration requirements adopted under Article 7(2) need not (only) be to promote the integration of the family members for whom admission is sought. Instead, Article 7(2) leaves scope for requirements that deny access to those who do not meet the required level of integration, with the aim of supporting the integration process within the Member States.[193]

Lastly, the provisions of the FRD must be interpreted in such a way as to respect the fundamental rights laid down in the EU Charter of Fundamental Rights and recognised as general principles of EU law.[194] This is recalled in the preamble to the FRD (recital 2) and was confirmed by the CoJ in *Chakroun*.[195] The same applies to acts of the Member States that come within the scope of EU law (section II.B.ii of chapter 1). From the CoJ's judgment in *Parliament v Council*, it may be derived that these acts include national integration requirements as referred to in Article 4(1), final subparagraph, and Article 7(2) FRD.[196] With regard to the FRD, the right to respect for family life is of primary importance. Also relevant are the rights of the child, including the obligation to let the best interests of the child form a primary consideration, and the prohibition of discrimination.[197] Lastly, integration requirements adopted pursuant to Article 7(2) FRD will need to respect cultural, religious and linguistic diversity as well as the right to freedom of religion.[198]

[192] *Report from the Commission to the European Parliament and the Council on the application of Directive 2003/86/EC on the right to family reunification*, COM(2008) 610 final, 7–8. See also the Green Paper on the right to family reunification, COM(2011) 735 final, 4, and the European Commission's remarks in the case of *Mohammed Imran* (n 180).

[193] See also para 66 of the *Parliament v Council* judgment (n 181) where the CoJ held that the need to promote integration, as reflected in Art 4(1), final subparagraph, FRD could be brought under several of the legitimate aims mentioned in Art 8(2) ECHR.

[194] Arts 6(1) and (3) TEU.

[195] *Chakroun* (n 187), para 44.

[196] *Parliament v Council* (n 181), notably para 105. See also Battjes and Vermeulen 2007, para 6.

[197] See Arts 7, 21 and 24 EU Charter of Fundamental Rights. See also the CoJ's judgment in *Parliament v Council* (n 181), paras 35–37, where it is confirmed that the general principles of EU law include the fundamental rights laid down in the ECHR, the ICCPR and the CRC.

[198] See Arts 10 and 22 CFR and Art 9 ECHR.

As mentioned above, Article 5(5) FRD may fall somewhat short of the norm laid down in Article 3 CRC (and Art 24(2) CFR) as it does not require Member States to let the best interests of the child form a 'primary consideration'. Other than this, it can be derived from the discussion in this chapter and chapters 8 to 10 that the right to family life and the prohibition of discrimination do not, as such, preclude the introduction of integration requirements as a condition for family reunification. Nevertheless, where the FRD is applicable, Member States must respect these fundamental rights not only as a matter of international law, but also as a matter of EU law. It may be observed that decisions concerning the scope and meaning of these rights may be given by the CoJ, which in principle is not legally bound to follow the interpretations provided by other supervisory bodies such as the European Court of Human Rights or the UN Human Rights Committee.[199]

To date, however, the CoJ has not interpreted the above fundamental rights in a way that extends beyond the guarantees already laid down in the FRD. In particular, the Court found that Article 4(1), final subparagraph, FRD respects the right to family life because it does not grant Member States a larger margin of appreciation than that available to them under Article 8 ECHR. Thereby the Court also recalled that the directive requires Member States to balance the interests involved on the basis of Articles 5(5) and 17 which, as stated above, largely reflect the standards already set by the ECtHR and HRC.[200]

D. Dutch Case Law with Regard to the Family Reunification Directive

The Family Reunification Directive has thus far played only a limited role in Dutch case law concerning the Act on Integration Abroad. In one case before the District Court of Breda, an applicant for family reunification argued that imposing an integration exam as a condition for admission was contrary to Article 7(2) FRD. This argument was, however, rejected by the court on the grounds that the directive makes express provision for integration requirements and that the applicant had not argued why she considered the AIA to be unlawful.[201] Neither the applicant nor the court addressed the question of whether the obligation to pass the integration exam was proportionate considering the individual circumstances of the case.

[199] Toner 2004, 132–38; Boeles et al 2009, 185.

[200] *Parliament v Council* (n 181), paras 52–71.

[201] District Court of The Hague sitting in Breda 13 November 2007, case no 07/18500, para 2.9. An appeal was raised; however, the question concerning the compatibility of the AIA with the Family Reunification Directive was not addressed by the AJD; see AJD 16 May 2008, case no 200708934/1.

In another case, decided in appeal, the Administrative Jurisdiction Division (AJD) of the Council of State was asked whether a decision by the Dutch authorities to refuse permission for family reunification was in breach of Article 5(5) FRD (the obligation to have due regard for the best interests of the child). The case involved a mother whose request for admission had been denied because she had failed to pass the integration exam. Admission had however been granted to her two minor children. The AJD found that, assuming that Article 5(5) FRD was applicable, the only norm contained in this provision was that the interests of the children had to be taken into account, but that nothing could be said about the weight to be attached to these interests in a particular case. Arguably the obligation to take the best interests of the child into account also means that those interests must be given due regard as stated in the FRD; if not, the obligation would be rather meaningless. Thus it can be submitted that the AJD did not wrongly interpret the directive. This being said, however, it has already been observed that Article 5(5) FRD falls short of the standard set by Articles 3 CRC and 24(2) CFR, which require the best interests of the child to form a 'primary consideration'.

The compatibility of the AIA with the FRD was again contested in a case before the District Court of Zwolle in 2011.[202] In this case the applicant raised various objections to the AIA, including that the FRD does not leave room for integration conditions, that the Dutch authorities had failed to make the individual assessment required by the directive and that the integration exam abroad does not respect the EU principle of proportionality. These objections prompted the District Court to refer a number of questions for preliminary ruling to the CoJ. However, the applicant was consequently granted admission while the preliminary questions were pending. This led the CoJ to decide that it did not need to give a ruling.[203]

VI. INTERIM CONCLUSION: LEGAL STANDARDS CONCERNING INTEGRATION REQUIREMENTS AS A CONDITION FOR FAMILY REUNIFICATION

The previous sections investigate the legal standards that can be derived from the selected legal instruments concerning the admissibility of integration requirements as a condition for family reunification. Before applying these standards to the Dutch Act on Integration Abroad (AIA), it is useful to briefly recall the results of this investigation.

Firstly, it was established that each of the investigated instruments contains certain criteria applying to the admission of aliens for the purpose of

[202] District Court of The Hague sitting in Zwolle 31 March 2011, case no 10/9716.
[203] *Mohammed Imran* (n 180).

family reunification. The Family Reunification Directive grants a right to family reunification to third-country nationals coming within its scope. While a similar right is not included in the ECHR, ICCPR or CRC, each of these treaties may apply to cases involving family reunification in the event of certain circumstances. This is specifically the case in situations where family life cannot be exercised outside the Contracting State or where such exercise would be subject to severe difficulties or entail serious obstacles to a child's development.

Yet, even where the above instruments apply, the rights that are granted are not absolute. Each leaves scope for the states concerned to regulate the entry and residence of family migrants by means of immigration requirements. The possibility of requirements relating to integration is expressly foreseen in the Family Reunification Directive. The other instruments examined do not indicate what kind of immigration requirements may be imposed, leaving this to the discretion of the Contracting States. Nonetheless, the various treaty provisions set several criteria or conditions with which immigration requirements, including integration requirements, must comply.

To start with the criteria set by the FRD, it was established that integration requirements may not be applied where the person seeking family reunification is a minor child or the family member of a refugee. The requirements must furthermore be proportionate and must not render the right to family reunification illusory or ineffective. The need to apply integration requirements must also be assessed on a case-by-case basis, whereby regard must be had for the interests mentioned in Articles 5(5) and 17 FRD and the general principles of EU law, including the right to respect for family life.

Article 8 ECHR, which protects the right to family life, requires there to be a fair balance between the interests of the family and the interests of the state. Articles 17 and 23 ICCPR stipulate that integration requirements for family reunification meet the criteria of lawfulness and non-arbitrariness. Lastly, Articles 3, 9 and 10 CRC require applications for family reunification to be treated in a positive, humane and expeditious manner and for the best interests of the child to form a primary consideration. It is also argued that, in situations where a refusal to admit the applicant would cause the parents and the child to be separated, the CRC proscribes integration requirements that make family reunification effectively impossible.

Various factors have to be taken into account to determine whether integration requirements are in accordance with the above criteria, in particular the principle of proportionality. The factors to be considered and the weight to be attached to each factor may vary somewhat, depending on the interpretations provided by the various supervisory bodies. The Dutch courts must, however, respect the interpretations provided by the

ECtHR and the CoJ, while also giving due regard to the interpretations of the HRC and the CRC Committee.

The main factors identified in the previous sections concern the nature of the family relationship, the possibility of exercising family life elsewhere, the family's ties to the host state and the efforts that applicants must make to meet the integration requirements. With regard to the latter factor, it is argued that this will depend on circumstances such as the costs and level of the integration exam or programme, its accessibility, the availability of preparation facilities and the existence or absence of the possibility for an exemption if, despite the necessary efforts, the applicant does not succeed in meeting the integration requirement. Additionally, the effectiveness of the integration requirement should be taken into account.

VII. THE RIGHT TO FAMILY LIFE AND THE ACT ON INTEGRATION ABROAD

It can be concluded from the previous section that integration requirements for family reunification do not, as such, violate the right to family life as guaranteed by the provisions discussed in this chapter. Yet, it remains to be determined whether the Act on Integration Abroad (AIA) is also compatible with the standards set by these provisions. This is examined below.

A. Preliminary Remark: Family Members Eligible for Admission

Until 1 October 2012, family members eligible for family reunification under Dutch immigration law included not only the spouse and minor children of the sponsor, but also the unmarried partner and the parents and adult children of the sponsor and his or her spouse.[204] With the exception of minor children, the obligation to pass the integration exam abroad applied to each of these categories of family members under the same conditions. As of 1 October 2012, only the spouse or registered partner and minor children belonging to the family can apply for family reunification, other family members are not eligible to be admitted (chapter 2, section VI.B.i).

As explained above, the extension of the right to family reunification to family members other than the spouse and minor children means that applications by these family members are also subject to the provisions of the Family Reunification Directive (section V.B). The same is true with regard to Articles 17 and 23 ICCPR, which defer to the definition of a

[204] Arts 3.14(b) and 3.24–3.25 Aliens Decree 2000.

'family' in the national law of the Contracting State (section III.A). Article 8 ECHR applies to the relationships between couples (married or unmarried) and between parents and children. The provision also covers relationships with other family members when there are 'additional elements of dependence' (section II.A). Lastly, the scope of application of the CRC is limited to the relationship between parents and minor children.

B. The Requirement of Lawfulness

Where a right to family reunification exists in principle, integration requirements must meet the condition of lawfulness. This condition is expressly laid down in Article 17 of the ICCPR (section III.B). Of late, the ECtHR has also begun to examine whether immigration measures are 'prescribed by law', although this criterion did not previously form part of the fair balance test that is usually applied in admission cases (section II.B.ii). As explained in chapter 2, the existence of a legal basis for application of the integration exam abroad has been subject to legal debate in the Netherlands. Whereas the Aliens Act 2000 states that a residence permit (and hence an entry visa) may be refused if the applicant does not pass the exam, the Aliens Decree is formulated in such a way that this possibility is precluded in cases involving family reunification. However, it is submitted that, in view of the legislative history of the AIA, the failure to mention the integration exam in the Aliens Decree may be regarded as an evident mistake on the part of the legislator. It may therefore be assumed that the integration exam abroad has a legal basis in national law. The same conclusion was reached, albeit on different grounds, by the Administrative Jurisdiction Division of the Council of State, the highest court to decide in immigration cases.

The Aliens Act and the Aliens Decree provide a description of the contents of the integration exam abroad, as well as of the possibilities for exemption. In this respect the legislation can be qualified as sufficiently precise and circumscribed, as required under the ICCPR and ECHR. Lastly, decisions to refuse applications for family reunification on the grounds that the integration requirement has not been met are taken by a designated authority (the Aliens Affairs Minister) on a case-by-case basis.[205] It can therefore be concluded that the integration exam abroad is applied in accordance with the requirement of lawfulness.

[205] Art 14 (1) Aliens Act 2000.

C. The Requirement of a Legitimate Aim

It was established in chapter 3 that the purpose of the AIA is to further the integration process in the Netherlands by excluding those immigrants who do not meet certain integration standards. For those aliens who are eventually admitted, the AIA also aims to facilitate their integration by giving them a head start. It can therefore be stated that the objective of the AIA is to promote immigrant integration, partly by means of immigration control. As argued above, this can be considered a legitimate objective under Article 8 ECHR and Articles 17 and 23 ICCPR, as well as for the purposes of the Family Reunification Directive.[206]

It may be observed that the concept of 'integration' is still very open and leaves room for various definitions. How this concept is filled in is, in principle, a matter to be determined by the state concerned, as long as the integration objectives remain in accordance with the overall standards set by international and EU law. With respect to the Netherlands it has been established that, since the mid-1990s, integration policy has consistently sought to make immigrants self-sufficient and to promote their participation in the public domain, in particular in education and the labour market. In addition, however, the policy has also been directed towards cultural adaptation and, more recently, towards achieving a sense of commitment or emotional identification (chapter 3, sections III.A–III.C). Especially around the time when the AIA was adopted, when cultural adaptation was high on the integration agenda, immigrants were expected to become acquainted with 'Dutch society' and certain moral values and social norms portrayed as pertaining to 'the Dutch identity'. It is not entirely clear whether the latter also implied that these values and norms had to be accepted as being morally correct (chapter 3, section III.D.i).

From a legal perspective the above purposes are acceptable in principle, provided that immigrants are not asked to agree with particular norms, ideas or beliefs. It is argued earlier in this chapter (especially in section II.D.i) that requiring agreement or internalisation would amount to a form of indoctrination going beyond what can be regarded as legitimate. However, the contents of the integration exam abroad show that few of the questions contained therein appear to be specifically linked to this objective.[207] It must therefore be concluded that the above findings on the

[206] See sections II.D.i, III.C and V.C.iv.

[207] With regard to a few questions it could be argued that candidates are asked to take a normative stance rather than to produce factual knowledge. See, eg, question 62: 'Is it important to learn Dutch quickly?' (correct answer: yes), question 92: 'When should you start looking for work: as soon as possible or at a later date?' (correct answer: as soon as possible) and question 99: 'In the Netherlands, do you get social security benefits or does your partner provide for you?' (correct answer: your partner provides for you). If the latter question is meant to be factual, the answer would be incorrect. It must therefore be assumed that the question is a normative one.

purpose of the AIA do not call for any (far-reaching) alteration of the exam. A detailed investigation of the aims of the AIA would normally also go beyond the realm of the judiciary.[208] The more abstractly formulated objectives of promoting integration and controlling immigration generally support the conclusion that the Act serves a legitimate aim, in particular before an international court. Consequently, it is primarily up to the Dutch legislator to ensure that the objectives pursued by the AIA remain within the above limits.

In addition to the integration objectives identified in chapter 3, the Dutch government has referred to a number of the legitimate aims of Article 8(2) ECHR as being public interests served by the AIA. According to this argument, the Act aims to prevent marginalisation of certain segments of the population, which in turn is necessary to protect the economic well-being of the Netherlands, public order and public security and the rights and freedoms of others. This reasoning was supported by reference to the overrepresentation of ethnic minority groups in crime statistics. It was also claimed that marginalisation and segregation could cause people to turn their backs on society and be influenced by groups tending towards extremism and terrorism. The 9/11 terrorist attacks were mentioned in this respect, alongside other incidents of Islamic terrorism that occurred in the Netherlands and elsewhere in Western Europe. Lastly, it was stated that there was a real risk of immigrants becoming radicalised, adopting anti-Western attitudes and undermining generally accepted values such as the equality of the sexes and the freedom of expression.[209]

With regard to the above argument, it may be accepted that efforts to prevent marginalisation, radicalisation and terrorism constitute legitimate public interests within the context of Article 8 ECHR (and comparable provisions). Yet, as far as the prevention of crime or terrorism is concerned, it may be asked to what extent the integration exam abroad is able to contribute to these goals. In particular where the prevention of terrorism and radicalisation is concerned, it is submitted that the government's arguments are rather speculative. A more substantive motivation, if possible based on empirical evidence, would therefore be preferable.

D. Proportionality of the Integration Exam Abroad – Relevant Factors

As mentioned in section VI of this chapter, the proportionality of the obligation to pass the integration exam abroad needs to be assessed on an individual basis and cannot be determined on a general level. Nevertheless,

[208] cp Gerards 2002, 42–46 (on judicial review of legislative aims in equal treatment cases).
[209] *Parliamentary Papers II* 2003–2004, 29 700, No 3, 17; *Parliamentary Papers II* 2004–2005, 29 700, No 6, 47–48.

certain factors relevant to the proportionality assessment can be identified. These are discussed below.

i. Level of the Exam

When the AIA was enacted, the Dutch legislator paid particular attention to the Act's compatibility with Article 8 ECHR. The government took the view that the right to family life entailed that no one should a priori be excluded from the possibility of family reunification. It was consequently assumed that the integration exam abroad had to be achievable for everyone, taking into account that the government would not offer preparation facilities and that candidates would have to prepare themselves independently. Eventually the level of the exam was set at 'A1-minus' (chapter 2, section VI.C.i). To ensure that the exam would also be feasible for illiterate candidates, it was decided only to test oral skills.[210]

The evaluation conducted in 2009 showed that a large majority of candidates with little education were indeed able to pass the exam at the first attempt.[211] This suggests that the level of the exam was not unreasonably high. However, no information was available on the chances of illiterate candidates. The evaluation also indicated that those with little education were less likely to take the exam.[212] This may mean that such candidates were deterred by the burden of having to prepare for the exam. Still, case law of the ECtHR and the Dutch courts suggests that applicants for family reunification may, in principle, be required to make serious efforts to meet immigration requirements. Therefore, it cannot be concluded from the available information that an oral exam at the A1-minus level is disproportionately high.

On 1 April 2011, however, the level of the integration exam abroad was raised to A1 and the exam expanded to include a reading comprehension test (section VI.C.ii of chapter 2). To compensate for these changes, the study package now includes additional preparatory materials provided by the Dutch government. It remains the candidate's responsibility, however, to prepare for the exam independently.

In the government's view, the higher level of the integration exam abroad does not make it impossible for large groups of family members to be admitted for family reunification.[213] However, this stance appears at odds with the fact that the government earlier opted for an oral test, precisely so as not to exclude illiterate family members. In any case, it is submitted that the obligation to pass a reading comprehension test imposes

[210] *Parliamentary Papers II* 2003–2004, 29 700, No 3, 17; *Parliamentary Papers II* 2004–2005, 29 700, No 6, 18.

[211] Brink et al 2009, 37–38. On the effects of the AIA, see also section VI.D of ch 2.

[212] ibid, 37; Odé 2009, 289–90.

[213] *Bulletin of Acts and Decrees* 2010, 679, 3–4.

too great a burden on family members who are unable to read and write, also given that these persons have most likely not had much formal education. As far as the category of illiterate family members is concerned, it can be assumed that a reading test makes family reunification effectively impossible. To the extent that illiterate family members are not exempted, either as a category or on an individual basis (section VII.F), the reading test is therefore contrary to Article 7(2) of the Family Reunification Directive. The changes to the integration exam also mean that, in individual cases, the refusal to admit a family member is more likely to result in a violation of the ECHR, ICCPR or CRC.

ii. Availability of Preparation Facilities

Another factor influencing the admissibility of the integration exam abroad is the availability of preparation facilities, including language courses. As explained in chapter 2 (section VI.C.iv), the Dutch government has developed a study package that candidates may use to prepare for the 'Knowledge of the Netherlands' test and the reading comprehension test. Candidates can also use other study materials and the preparatory courses organised by private parties in several countries of origin, while some candidates can travel to the Netherlands on a short-term visa to prepare for the exam there.

Nevertheless, case law on the AIA indicates that there are situations in which the available facilities are insufficient. For instance, study materials may not be available in a language spoken by the candidate.[214] A candidate may also not have access to the infrastructure (such as a DVD player or the internet) needed to prepare for the exam.[215] To date, the Dutch courts have taken the stance that it is up to applicants and their family members to resolve these difficulties (section II.E.iii). It is submitted, however, that in circumstances such as the above it would be unreasonable to expect an applicant for family reunification to pass the integration exam abroad. This would, again, be contrary to the provisions of the Family Reunification Directive and increases the risk of a violation of Articles 8 ECHR, 17 and 23 ICCPR and 9 and 10 CRC.

iii. Accessibility of the Exam

A similar conclusion can be drawn with regard to the accessibility of the exam. Under normal circumstances, it would not be unreasonable to expect an applicant for family reunification to travel to the Dutch consu-

[214] President District Court of The Hague sitting in Middelburg 16 August 2007, case nos 07/30015 and 07/31032, LJN: BB3524.

[215] cp the facts in District Court of The Hague 21 October 2009, case no 09/5145, LJN: BK5782.

late or embassy in the country of origin to take the exam. However, this is different if, for instance, travelling is difficult or even impossible because of a conflict situation. In this respect, the 2009 evaluation also mentions the position of women in Afghanistan who are not allowed to travel independently.[216] In addition, there may be no exam location in the country of origin, as, for example, in Pakistan and Iraq.[217] In these cases it must be assessed whether the applicant can reasonably be expected to take the exam in another country. Where this possibility does not exist, it is again submitted that it would be disproportionate to refuse family reunification on the sole grounds that the integration requirement has not been met.

iv. Family Members of Former Asylum Seekers

As explained earlier (chapter 2,section VI.B.iii), the AIA does not apply to family members of persons holding an asylum permit. However, there are several categories of persons under Dutch immigration law who do not hold such a permit, but who may nevertheless be unable to exercise their family life in the country of origin because of a risk of persecution. These are, first of all, individuals granted an asylum permit and who have since obtained Dutch nationality. Additionally, a non-asylum-related residence permit used to be granted to people who had applied for asylum, but who had not received a decision on their application within three years (the *'driejarenbeleid'* or three-year-policy).

Family members of persons in the above categories are not exempted from the obligation to pass the integration exam abroad. During the enactment of the AIA, the government stated in relation to these family members that account would be taken of possible obstacles to the exercise of family life in the country of origin.[218] However, no express rule to this effect is included in the legislation or policy guidelines concerning the integration exam abroad. In individual cases, the circumstance that family life cannot be exercised in the country of origin may contribute to the finding that refusal to grant admission for family reunification is contrary to the right to family life as protected in the ECHR, ICCPR and CRC. This is particularly relevant with regard to applicants not falling within the scope of the Family Reunification Directive.[219]

[216] Lodder 2009, 71.

[217] ibid, 79.

[218] *Parliamentary Papers II* 2003–2004, 29 700, No 3, 9–10; *Parliamentary Papers II* 2004– 2005, 29 700, No 6, 36–37.

[219] It is as yet unclear whether the FRD also applies to third-country nationals who have become EU citizens through naturalisation.

v. Effectiveness of the Act on Integration Abroad

One more element playing a role in the proportionality assessment concerns the extent to which the AIA effectively contributes to the aims pursued. In chapter 2 (section VI.D) it was established that the effects of the integration exam abroad on the integration capacity of immigrants upon their arrival have thus far been rather limited, whereas the long-term effects cannot yet be measured.

In order to increase the effectiveness of the AIA, the Dutch government decided to raise the level of the exam to A1 and to include a reading test (chapter 2, section VI.C.ii). This can be expected to have a positive influence on the integration of those applicants coming to the Netherlands after passing the exam. However, as argued above, the fact that the exam has become more difficult also imposes a greater burden on applicants and may even exclude people who are illiterate from the possibility of family reunification. Overall, therefore, the increased level of the exam is not likely to have a positive effect on the AIA's proportionality.

E. The Obligation to Give Primary Consideration to the Best Interests of the Child

During the enactment of the AIA, the issue of its compatibility with the CRC was raised in parliament. In this context, the Dutch government stated that the introduction of the integration exam abroad would be in the best interests of the child. It argued that children's educational level could be adversely affected if their situation at home was not conducive to learning the Dutch language, which they need to use as a primary language in the Netherlands. In the government's view, the integration exam abroad would be a suitable instrument for reducing the risk of such adverse consequences.[220]

Clearly, the above argument is not without relevance. Nevertheless, the CRC also requires consideration to be given to the best interests of the child in the particular case. Therefore, if the government's argument is to be accepted, it has to be established that the integration exam serves the interest of the child in the individual case at hand and not just the general interests of migrant children living in the Netherlands. Moreover, the child's interest in learning Dutch needs to be weighed against the competing interest of not being separated from his or her parents or being forced to join the parents in another country.

[220] *Parliamentary Papers I* 2004–2005, 29 700, E, 5.

F. Exempted Categories and Individual Exemptions

It follows from the above that there are many circumstances affecting the compatibility of the integration exam abroad with the right to family life or family reunification. To a certain extent, these circumstances have been addressed by the creation of general categories of exemption (section VI.B.iii of chapter 2). It may be recalled that the AIA does not, for example, apply to children below the age of majority (18 years under Dutch law) or to those aged 65 or older. Also exempted are family members of people who have been granted a residence permit on asylum grounds, which includes the family members of (recognised) refugees.

Both the above exemptions are in conformity with the Family Reunification Directive. As the AIA entered into force after the implementation date of the directive, the standstill clause in Article 4(1), final subparagraph, FRD means that children older than 12 cannot be required to pass the integration exam abroad.[221] The exemptions can also influence the compatibility of the AIA with the ECHR, ICCPR and CRC in individual cases. For example, the exemption for family members of asylum permit holders means that the AIA will not stand in the way of family reunification in many cases where the exercise of family life would not be possible outside the Netherlands.

In addition to the above categories, the AIA does not apply to applicants who are durably unable to pass the exam owing to a physical or mental disability. Also exempted are those who, once in the Netherlands, would not be subject to compulsory integration on the grounds that they already have sufficient knowledge of Dutch language and society or because they are pursuing a relevant form of education. These exemptions ensure that the AIA does not preclude family reunification for those unable to take the exam because of disability, and that it does not impose an unnecessary burden. In view of the CoJ's judgment in *Chakroun*, the latter consideration is particularly relevant in relation to the Family Reunification Directive.

Even if they do not fall within any of the above categories, applicants may still be exempted on the grounds of individual circumstances (chapter 2, section VI.B.iii). This may happen, inter alia, if the applicant has failed to pass the integration exam abroad, but refusal of the application for family reunification would be eminently unreasonable. This ground may be invoked to ensure respect for the right to family life in certain cases, in particular where a candidate is unable to pass the exam owing to illiteracy. Another ground for individual exemption is that the refusal to allow family reunification would violate Article 8 ECHR. Provided that

[221] The AIA entered into force on 15 March 2006, whereas the implementation date of the Directive was 3 October 2005.

the assessment under Article 8 ECHR is correct, the above exemption clause can play an important role to ensure that the integration exam abroad respects the right to family life. However, it has been established that the Family Reunification Directive contains standards that are generally more protective than those of the ECHR. Some additional protective standards can also be found in the ICCPR and the CRC. These standards also need to be taken into account to ensure that the AIA is compatible with the right to family life. It is therefore suggested that the existing exemption clauses should be expanded so as to ensure compliance with the FRD, ICCPR and CRC, as well as with Article 8 ECHR. Lastly, such compliance also requires that the existing exemption clauses are not applied too rigidly (see again chapter 2, section VI.B.iii).

G. Summary: Compatibility of the Act on Integration Abroad with the Right to Family Life and Family Reunification

The previous sections assessed whether the AIA meets the standards set by international and EU law in relation to family reunification. On the basis of this assessment, it can be concluded that the obligation to pass the integration exam abroad is not as such incompatible with these standards. Nonetheless, a few remarks deserve to be made. First of all, it was argued that the aim of the AIA cannot be to make family migrants internalise particular norms or values, even if these norms or values are seen as pertaining to 'the Dutch identity'. While this finding does not call for changes to the exam in its current form, it should be taken into account if the curriculum is revised in the future.

Secondly, a number of factors were summed up that are relevant to determining the proportionality of the Act in individual cases. In particular, it was argued that the reading comprehension test makes it effectively impossible for illiterate family members to engage in family reunification. This test must therefore be considered disproportionate, at least under the standards set by the Family Reunification Directive. Other circumstances were also mentioned that may also result in a finding of disproportionality, either alone or in combination, such as the non-availability of preparation facilities or if the sponsor would risk persecution in the country of origin. These circumstances need to be assessed in every case, together with other factors such as the nature of the family relationship and the ties of the family members to the host state. Where children are involved, the best interests of the child need to be established on a case-by-case basis and must be given primary consideration. Thus far the latter standard has not yet been duly recognised by the Dutch authorities, including the courts.

Lastly, the possibilities were examined of being granted an exemption from the AIA in situations where the obligation to pass the integration exam abroad conflicts with the right to family life (including the right to family reunification in the FRD). Whereas exemptions may be granted on the basis of individual circumstances, it was submitted that the existing provisions are not formulated in sufficiently broad terms. In particular, more scope is needed to ensure respect for the ICCPR, the CRC and the FRD.

VIII. CONCLUDING OBSERVATIONS

On the basis of the examination in this chapter, it is concluded that the protection of family life by international legal instruments is relatively limited in situations where family members seek to be reunited across national borders. Although the existing standards for protection were raised by the adoption of the EU Family Reunification Directive, states, including the Netherlands, have retained the competence to make family reunification subject to immigration conditions, including requirements in the field of integration.

Integration requirements are imposed with the aim of improving the process of immigrant integration within the receiving state, which is in principle a legitimate objective. However, these requirements also constitute an obstacle for individuals seeking to be joined by their family members in the country where they hold legal residence or of which they are nationals. Consequently, persons belonging to transnational families are in a less favourable position than those whose family members happen to hold the same nationality. Given the increasing ease with which people are able to travel and establish and maintain contacts around the world, it may be doubted whether this differentiation ought to be upheld.

In my view, there is a strong argument to be made for legal recognition of the fact that family life is an international matter. Such recognition would imply that the right to family life includes a right to reunification and that restrictions to the latter right ought to be treated as exceptions to the rule. This was also the approach taken by the CoJ in the case of *Chakroun*. Arguably, however, such an approach is not as yet required by the Family Reunification Directive (which grants a right to family reunification only under certain conditions), nor by the various human rights treaties examined in this chapter or their interpretations by the respective supervisory bodies.

Recognition of a right to family reunification as part of the right to family life does not imply that this right must be all-encompassing or absolute. It is submitted that states may legitimately restrict the scope of the right to family reunification on the basis of criteria relating to the nature of the family relationship and/or the ties existing between one or more of the family members and the state concerned (notably nationality and duration of residence). Limitations to the right to family reunification may also be indicated on grounds relating to the general interest, including the interest of successful immigrant integration. However, as is already the case under the current legal framework in situations where a right to family reunification is taken to exist, such limitations must meet the requirement of proportionality. This brings me to another argument, which is of a more pragmatic nature.

As far as integration requirements are concerned, the example of the Dutch Act on Integration Abroad shows that it is difficult to establish the effect of such requirements on immigrant integration within the receiving state. However, as also recognised by the Dutch government, the effect of integration requirements will be less when the requisite level of the skills or knowledge is lower.[222] In this chapter, it is argued that the various legal instruments examined set limits on the efforts that applicants for family reunification may be required to make. This is especially true with regard to the Family Reunification Directive. Consequently, the effectiveness of integration requirements is necessarily limited by the fact that such requirements may not impose a disproportionate obstacle in situations where a right to family reunification has been established.

Given both the above limitation and the earlier argument about family reunification being part of the right to family life, it is suggested that it would be better for family reunification not to be made subject to the fulfilment of integration requirements. Instead, preference ought to be given to other measures to ensure that the arrival of family migrants does not adversely influence the process of immigrant integration in the host state. An example of such a measure is the Integration Act 2007, which is currently in force in the Netherlands, as well as the Newcomers Integration Act 1998 that preceded it. Obviously, however, other measures are possible.

Clearly, the above suggestion goes beyond what is required by the legal standards for family reunification identified in this chapter. Any decision to follow this suggestion will therefore be a political rather than a legal one. Even so, it was argued above that the said legal standards are not always respected by the Act on Integration Abroad in its current form. The changes proposed in section VII are therefore needed if the lawfulness of the Act is to be guaranteed.

[222] *Parliamentary Papers II* 2009–2010, 32 175, No 1, 9; *Bulletin of Acts and Decrees* 2010, 679, 3 and 5.

5

Freedom of Religion

I. INTRODUCTION

THIS CHAPTER CONSIDERS integration requirements in relation to the right to freedom of religion. While the connection between integration requirements as admission criteria and religious freedom may not be immediately obvious, the inclusion of this chapter was prompted by the fact that, at least in the Netherlands, religious servants form a specific target group of the Act on Integration Abroad (chapter 2, section VI.B.ii). This raises a number of questions, including whether the rights of religious servants or congregations may be affected by admission requirements such as the integration exam abroad and, if so, under which conditions limitations to these rights are allowed.

The examination conducted in this chapter addresses several provisions protecting the right to freedom of religion, starting with Article 9 of the European Convention of Human Rights (ECHR) and Article 18 of the International Covenant on Civil and Political Rights (ICCPR). As in chapter 4 on the right to family life, regard is given to relevant interpretations developed in the case law of the European Court of Human Rights (ECtHR) and the jurisprudence of the Human Rights Committee (HRC). In addition to these international provisions, attention is paid to Article 6 of the Dutch Constitution. With regard to each of the above provisions an attempt is made to establish legal criteria for their application in relation to integration requirements. Where available and relevant, account is also taken of interpretations supplied by the Dutch courts. Afterwards, the Act on Integration Abroad is evaluated in the light of the criteria identified.

Another question raised in this chapter is whether religious servants may be singled out as a particular target group for the purpose of applying integration requirements, or whether this constitutes discrimination on the grounds of religion. The above provisions regarding freedom of religion are therefore considered, together with those protecting the right to equal treatment (Arts 14 and 1 Twelfth Protocol ECHR, 2 and 26 ICCPR and 1 Dutch Constitution). An assessment of the Act on Integration Abroad in relation to this right is included in section VII.E. In view of the close connection with the right to freedom of religion, this issue is discussed here rather than in the chapters on equal treatment.

II. FREEDOM OF RELIGION AS PROTECTED BY ARTICLE 9 OF THE EUROPEAN CONVENTION OF HUMAN RIGHTS

Article 9(1) ECHR provides that everyone has the right to freedom of thought, conscience and religion. It is specified that 'this right includes freedom to change his religion or belief and freedom, either alone or in community with others and in public or private, to manifest his religion or belief, in worship, teaching, practice and observance'. Limitations to the freedom to manifest one's religion or beliefs are allowed, provided they are in conformity with the conditions set out in the second paragraph of the Article.

As discussed below, there is still little case law available on the applicability of Article 9 ECHR in cases involving the admission of aliens. Nevertheless it is argued that, in certain circumstances, a state's refusal to admit a religious servant because of failure to comply with an integration requirement can come within the scope of Article 9 ECHR. The conditions under which the freedom of religion may be limited are then assessed in order to formulate criteria for defining integration requirements for religious servants.

A. Scope of Article 9 ECHR – the Right of Religious Communities to Self-organisation and the Admission of Religious Servants

i. Individual and Collective Dimension of the Freedom of Religion

The freedom of religion as protected by Article 9 ECHR comprises various elements, including the right of the individual to hold (or not to hold) a religion or belief and to act in accordance with this religion or belief, for instance through the observance of religious customs or practices (such as praying, fasting or wearing a headscarf). Article 9 also protects the right to manifest one's religion or belief in community with others. This 'collective dimension' of the freedom of religion includes the right of religious congregations to organise themselves and to manifest their religion in organised settings.[1]

With regard to the admission of religious servants, it can readily be assumed that Article 9 ECHR does not protect the right of a non-national to be admitted to a State Party in order to exercise his or her freedom of religion on its territory as an individual.[2] This follows from the general

[1] For a more elaborate discussion of the scope of Art 9 ECHR see Van Dijk et al 2006, 752–67 and Harris et al 2009, 428–35.

[2] See also ACVZ 2005, 33, Vermeulen 2006, 251 and Kortmann 2008, 435. An exception to this rule may exist in case the manifestation of religion or belief is only possible in that State Party, eg, in case of pilgrimages or, perhaps, missionary activities.

assumption that the obligation of states to protect fundamental rights is normally limited to persons within their borders and that these fundamental rights do not entail an entitlement to exercise them anywhere in the world. Confirmation of this view can be found in ECtHR case law on the freedom of religion.[3]

However, the situation described above should be distinguished from one in which the admission of a religious servant is requested on behalf of a religious community in the receiving state. As mentioned above, the right to freedom of religion also has a collective dimension. Subjects of this right include ecclesiastical and religious bodies that are considered to exercise the right guaranteed by Article 9 ECHR on behalf of their adherents.[4] ECtHR case law acknowledges that religious communities traditionally exist in the form of organised structures and, therefore, that the freedom of religion includes the freedom to participate in religious communities. Where the organisation of such communities is concerned, Article 9 ECHR must be interpreted in the light of Article 11, which protects the freedom of association. Thus, religious communities must be allowed to operate freely and without unjustified interference from the state. The ECtHR regards the autonomous existence of religious communities as indispensable for pluralism in a democratic society and, therefore, as being at the heart of the protection afforded by Article 9 ECHR.[5]

With regard to the protection afforded to religious communities, the Court has recognised that the personality of religious leaders is of importance to the members of such communities. In this respect it has concluded on several occasions that state measures favouring a particular person as the leader of a divided religious community were in violation of Article 9 ECHR.[6] It can be inferred from this case law that the organisational autonomy of a religious community includes, in principle, the freedom to choose its own leadership. This brings us to the question of whether the

[3] See ECtHR 8 November 2007, app no 30273/03 (*Perry*), para 51; ECtHR (Grand Chamber) 20 December 2007, app no 25525/03 (*El Majjaoui and Stichting Touba Moskee*), para 32 and ECtHR 12 February 2009, app no 2512/04 (*Nolan and K*), para 62. See also the earlier decisions of the European Commission of Human Rights in the cases of *Omkarananda and the Divine Light Zentrum* (EComHR 19 March 1981, app no 8118/77, paras 5 and 6) and *Öz* (EComHR 3 December 1996, app no 32168/96).

[4] As confirmed recently in ECtHR 6 November 2008, app no 58911/00 (*Leela Förderkreis e.v. and others*), para 79. An overview of earlier case law on this topic can be found in Van Dijk et al 2006, 764–65.

[5] eg, ECtHR 26 October 2000, app no 30985/96 (*Hasan & Chaush*), para 62; ECtHR 16 December 2004, app no 39023/97 (*Supreme Holy Council of the Muslim Community*), paras 73 and 93; ECtHR 5 October 2006, app no 72881/01 (*The Moscow Branch of the Salvation Army*), para 58 and ECtHR 31 July 2008, app no 40825/98 (*Religionsgemeinschaft der Zeugen Jehovas and others*), paras 60 and 61.

[6] eg, ECtHR 14 December 1999, app no 38178/97 (*Serif*), para 52; *Hasan & Chaush* (n 5), para 62; ECtHR 13 December 2001, app no 45701/99 (*Metropolitan Church of Bessarabia and others*), para 117 and ECtHR 22 January 2009, app nos 412/03 and 35677/04 (*The Holy Synod of the Bulgarian Orthodox Church (Metropolitan Inokentiy) and others*), para 103.

refusal to admit a religious servant constitutes interference with the freedom of religion as protected by Article 9 ECHR or, in other words, whether this freedom includes the right to choose a religious leader who does not legally reside in the state where the community is based. This question is addressed below.

ii. Admission of Religious Servants

a. *El Majjaoui and Stichting Touba Moskee*: the Question Left Unresolved

This issue of the admission of religious servants in relation to the freedom of religion came up relatively recently in a decision by the ECtHR Grand Chamber in the case of *El Majjaoui and Stichting Touba Moskee*.[7] The facts leading up to this case concerned a Dutch religious foundation, the *Stichting Touba Moskee*, that wanted to employ Mr El Majjaoui, a foreign national, as a religious minister, but was refused the necessary work permit. Dutch immigration law prescribed that such a permit had to be obtained by all employers wishing to employ foreign nationals. The requirement applied, in principle, to all labour migrants in the Netherlands and was not directed specifically at religious workers. After the case had been referred to the Grand Chamber, it was struck out of the list because the Dutch authorities decided to grant the work permit after all.

Unfortunately, although the ECtHR in *El Majjaoui* made some observations concerning the scope of the protection granted by Article 9 ECHR, it failed to go to the heart of the matter. The Court held that Article 9 ECHR does not include a right for religious servants to be granted a work or residence permit; hence any requirements that have to be met before such a permit is granted do not constitute interference with the freedom of religion. It added that the Convention does not lay down for the Contracting States any given manner for ensuring its effective implementation and that the choice as to the most appropriate means of achieving this is in principle a matter for the domestic authorities.[8] The text of the judgment does not indicate whether the ECtHR considered only the existence of a right on the part of the applicant or also on the part of the religious foundation.[9] In any case, the Court did not address the actual question before

[7] *El Majjaoui and Stichting Touba Moskee* (n 3).

[8] ibid, para 32.

[9] On this point, the Court merely confirmed the statement made earlier by the European Commission of Human Rights that: '[Article 9 ECHR] does not guarantee foreign nationals a right to obtain a residence permit for the purposes of taking up employment in a Contracting State, even if the employer is a religious organisation'. See *El Majjaoui and Stichting Touba Moskee* (n 3), para 32. The same formulation was used by the EComHR in the cases of *Omkarananda and the Divine Light Zentrum* and *Öz* (n 3).

it, which did not concern the right to a work permit but instead the right of the religious foundation to appoint Mr El Majjaoui as its minister.[10]

This omission was pointed out by three members of the Court in a dissenting opinion. While these members agreed that Mr El Majjaoui was not, as an individual, entitled to be admitted to the Dutch domestic labour market, they stated that

> in certain circumstances a measure which results in a religious community being prevented from appointing the minister of religion of its choice may constitute an interference with that community's rights under Article 9, even if the minister concerned is a foreign national.[11]

According to the dissenters, the Grand Chamber should have examined whether the requirements maintained by the Netherlands for the issue of a work permit were compatible with the standards set by Article 9 ECHR, in particular the state's duty of neutrality. Thereby regard should have been had to 'the fact that in the choice of a religious minister/pastor/rabbi/imam much will depend on whether the religious community would have confidence in the person concerned'.[12]

It can be concluded that the ECtHR has not yet recognised that the appointment by a religious organisation of a minister from abroad may come within the scope of Article 9 ECHR. Nonetheless, the dissenters stated that this could be the case 'in certain circumstances'. It is argued below that there are at least two situations in which refusal to admit a religious servant from abroad can affect the freedom of a religious community as protected by Article 9 ECHR. The first situation is that in which admission is refused with the specific aim of limiting the freedom of religion. The second concerns cases in which denying admission makes it impossible for the community to continue its religious activities.

b. *Omkarananda* and Afterwards: Immigration Measures Used to Curb the Freedom of Religion

With regard to the argument that refusal to admit a religious servant constitutes an interference with Article 9 ECHR if it is specifically aimed at limiting the freedom of religion, support can be found in ECtHR case law and the decisions of the European Commission of Human Rights (EComHR). In *Omkarananda* and *Öz*, the Commission found that

[10] Compare the decision in *M.F.S. v Bulgaria* (ECtHR 12 February 2009 (admissibility decision), app no 33831/03), where the Court held that the granting of a residence permit was *normally* enough to secure the exercise of family life, but that it had to be examined whether this was also true in the case at hand. In doing so, the Court rightfully regarded the residence permit as a means to realise the right to family life rather than as a right in itself.

[11] *El Majjaoui and Stichting Touba Moskee* (n 3), dissenting opinion of judges Zupancic, Zagrebelsky and Myjer, para 3.

[12] ibid, paras 4–5.

> a measure of expulsion does not as such constitute an interference with the rights guaranteed by Article 9, unless it can be established that the measure was designed to repress the exercise of such rights and stifle the spreading of the religion or philosophy of the followers.[13]

Both cases concerned religious servants who worked or sought to work for religious organisations in the respondent states. In *Omkarananda* the applicant's residence permit was withdrawn and his deportation sought for reasons of public order. *Öz* concerned a religious servant of Turkish nationality who had been granted a residence permit to work for a particular religious organisation in Germany. The permit expired automatically upon the ending of his employment, after which he sought a new permit to work with another religious organisation. This request was denied on grounds of general immigration control and foreign policy (as the Turkish government had indicated that it wished the applicant to return to Turkey).

The Commission's approach was subsequently adopted by the ECtHR, as shown in the Court's judgments in *Perry* and *Nolan and K*. In *Perry*, the applicant (an American citizen) was granted a different residence permit that did not allow him to continue the religious activities he had been performing in Latvia for several years.[14] A similar situation occurred in *Nolan and K*, where the applicant, who had been working for a religious organisation in Russia, was refused re-entry into that country after travelling abroad.[15]

In both the above judgments, the ECtHR found that Article 9 ECHR had been violated because the measures taken by the state resulted in unjustified interference with the applicants' freedom of religion.[16] It appeared that in both cases the immigration measures had been taken precisely with the aim of ending the religious activities of the applicants, which were considered by the national authorities as constituting a threat to national security or public order. In *Nolan and K*, the Court repeated the criterion formulated by the Commission that

> deportation does not . . . as such constitute an interference with the rights guaranteed by Article 9, unless it can be established that the measure was designed to repress the exercise of such rights and stifle the spreading of the religion or philosophy of the followers.

Further on, it also stated that

[13] *Öz* (n 3), para 5 and *Omkarananda and the Divine Light Zentrum* (n 3).

[14] *Perry* (n 3).

[15] *Nolan and K* (n 3).

[16] See also the Court's admissibility decision in the case of *Lotter and Lotter* (ECtHR 6 February 2003, app no 39015/97) in which the applicants, both Jehovah's witnesses, complained that the withdrawal of their residence permits because of their religious activities constituted an interference with Art 9 ECHR. The case was deemed admissible by the Court, but was later struck out of the list.

> in so far as the measure relating to the continuation of the applicant's residence in a given State was imposed *in connection with the exercise of the right to freedom of religion*, such measure may disclose an interference with that right (emphasis added).[17]

It can be derived from the above case law that immigration measures taken against religious leaders constitute interference with Article 9 ECHR if their target is to impede religious activities. On the other hand it can be assumed that immigration measures taken for other reasons, such as common crimes committed by the applicant or a lack of income, will not be considered interference with the freedom of religion.

It may also be observed that the above decisions and judgments all concerned claims made by individual religious servants who had already been legally resident in the territory of the respondent states.[18] It is submitted that, in such situations, there may be interference with the freedom of religion, even with regard to the individual religious leader, because termination of the work or residence permit interferes with the exercising of religious activities in the respondent state for which permission had previously been given.[19] As argued above, this is not the case if the religious servant has not yet been admitted, as there is then normally no reason why he or she should be allowed to practise his or her religion in the particular state. However, the latter argument does not apply with regard to a religious organisation established in the respondent state. Therefore it may be assumed that the criterion formulated, inter alia, in the case of *Nolan and K* also applies to claims made by religious organisation seeking to appoint a foreign national as a religious leader: where it can be shown that admission is refused in connection with the exercising of religious freedom, such a refusal will come within the scope of Article 9 ECHR.

It is submitted that the above criterion can be justified from a theoretical perspective: it respects the competence of Contracting States to control immigration in principle, but provides a correction to ensure that this competence is not abused to restrict the freedom of religion. Yet it must be noted that the criterion may be more difficult to apply in practice. In particular there is a risk that states will be able to 'cover up' potential violations of Article 9 ECHR by stating that the refusal of admission was based

[17] *Nolan and K* (n 3), para 62.

[18] In *Öz*, *Perry* and *Nolan and K* the applicants were only the individual religious servants and not the organisations they worked for. This was different in *Omkarananda and the Divine Light Zentrum*, where the application was made on behalf of the religious servant *and* his community. In *Perry*, however, the Court reiterated its earlier case law about the right to associate under Art 9 ECHR and the importance that members of a religious community may attach to the personality of their religious leader, thus apparently also recognising that there was a collective interest involved.

[19] Compare the ECtHR's approach to immigration cases under Art 8 ECHR, in which the expulsion of legally resident family members is also regarded as an interference with the right to family life (as opposed to the expulsion of non-legally resident family members).

on reasons not related to religious freedom (but, for instance, to public order). In such cases, it may go beyond the (actual or legal) competence of the judiciary to establish the real reasons underlying the refusal.[20]

c. Impossibility for Religious Organisations to Continue their Activities

The second situation in which interference with the freedom of religion may be assumed is when the refusal to admit a religious servant would effectively prevent the organisation concerned from continuing its religious activities. This argument was put forward by Vermeulen and Aarrass.[21] According to these authors, measures not expressly touching upon the freedom of religion – such as immigration regulations – do not normally come within the scope of Article 9 ECHR unless they have the effect, in a particular case, of rendering the exercise of religious freedom impossible. This may be the case if a religious organisation is unable to find a suitable leader in the country in which it is established and is not allowed to bring in someone from abroad.

The above position has not been recognised as such by the ECtHR. Nevertheless, some support for it can be found in the Court's case law. A similar criterion appears to have been applied in the judgment in *Cha'are Shalom ve Tsedek*, which concerned a Jewish association prohibited from engaging in ritual slaughter. The Court, taking as a point of departure that the association was in fact seeking the right to obtain glatt meat, determined that the slaughter regulations of the respondent state did not constitute an interference with Article 9 ECHR because it was not made impossible for ultra-orthodox Jews to eat meat from animals slaughtered in accordance with their religious prescriptions. *In casu* it was established that the applicants could also obtain glatt meat from Belgium.[22]

A comparable approach can also be found in ECtHR case law on the right to family reunification under Article 8 ECHR. As discussed in chapter 4 (section II.C.ii), an important consideration in the fair balance test in admission cases is whether it would be possible for the family to exercise their family life elsewhere, notably in the country of origin. This consideration can be explained by the assumption that a refusal to allow family reunification should not make it totally impossible to enjoy family life. In cases where the Court found that family life could not reasonably be exercised elsewhere (as, for example, in the case of *Rodrigues Da Silva and Hoogkamer*) it held that denying permission for family reunification

[20] See Gerards 2002, 35–39.

[21] Vermeulen and Aarrass 2009, 78–79. See also Vermeulen 2006, 251 and ACVZ 2005, 33.

[22] ECtHR 27 June 2000, app no 27417/95 (*Cha'are Shalom ve Tsedek*), paras 80–81. It may be remarked that, instead on focusing on the right to eat glatt meat, the Court should have examined whether Art 9 ECHR covers the right to ritual slaughter. See Van Dijk et al 2006, 761.

resulted in a failure to comply with a positive obligation under Article 8 ECHR and thus in a violation of that provision.

A problem concerning the above approach is that it may be difficult to determine in practice when a religious organisation has no other choice but to engage someone from abroad. Such determination will be hampered by state authorities having to exercise restraint in relation to theological issues in order to maintain a sufficient level of state neutrality.[23] It is submitted that while the religious organisation may be expected to give reasons why it is seeking to employ a particular religious servant, the reasons provided will in principle have to be accepted by the responsible state body.

d. Final Remarks Concerning the Scope of Article 9 ECHR

As a final point, mention must be made of the argument put forward by Kortmann that the above criterion is too narrow. According to this author, generally applicable immigration rules should in principle be interpreted so as to respect as much as possible the freedom of religious organisations to appoint religious servants from abroad, subject to restrictions based on public order or similar grounds.[24] This stance appears to be based on the assumption that this freedom is in principle covered by the right to freedom of religion as protected inter alia by Article 9 ECHR, including when refusal to admit a religious servant would not make it impossible to continue the religious activities of the organisation concerned.

The approach favoured by Kortmann would imply a significant limitation of the legal competence of the Contracting States to the ECHR to control the immigration of religious servants. At the reverse of the question of whether such a limitation would be justified is the question of whether it is (still) reasonable to uphold that the opportunities available to religious communities to exercise their freedom of religion are in principle limited to the state in which they are established and, as far as their leadership is concerned, to that state's community of nationals and legal residents.

This is a fundamental question that cannot be given a definite answer here. Nonetheless, it may be noted that the ECtHR does not appear readily inclined to expand the scope of Article 9 ECHR so as to cover the admission of religious servants from abroad. It is submitted that this approach is acceptable as long as provision is made for exceptional situations such as those described above, in which immigration decisions are designed to curb the freedom of religion or in which the exercise of

[23] Vermeulen 2006, 251, see also Van Dijk et al 2006, 766 and Harris et al 2009, 430.

[24] Kortmann 2008, 435–36. By way of example the author refers to the *grundrechtfreundliche* (rights-friendly) approach applied by the German Constitutional Court (*Bundesverfassungsgericht*) in a case concerning the admission of a religious leader; see BVerfG 24 October 2006, 2BvB 1908/03 (*Moon*).

religious activities by a particular community would effectively be rendered impossible.[25]

B. Limitations to the Freedom of Religion: Article 9(2) ECHR

As mentioned above, limitations to the freedom to manifest religion or beliefs are allowed, providing they are in conformity with the conditions set out in the second paragraph of Article 9 ECHR. Under this paragraph, limitations to the manifestation of religion or belief must be 'prescribed by law' and be 'necessary in a democratic society in the interests of public safety, for the protection of public order, health or morals or for the protection of the rights and freedoms of others'. These conditions are briefly discussed here, with particular attention for criteria that may be relevant to integration requirements for the admission of religious servants.

The condition that a limitation of the freedom of religion must be 'prescribed by law' means it must have a basis in domestic law (including international or EU law applicable in the Contracting State). The ECtHR has not formulated any procedural requirements concerning the way in which national legislation must be adopted (for example, by a democratically elected body). Nevertheless, if they are to count as 'law' within the meaning of Article 9(2) ECHR, national rules must meet the requirements of 'accessibility' and 'foreseeability', both of which have been developed to a certain extent in ECtHR case law.[26]

Regarding the legitimate aims mentioned in Article 9(2) ECHR, it has been observed that these are relatively few compared to those in similar limitation clauses in other Convention articles.[27] The aims are all formulated in broad terms, whereby the meaning of 'protecting public order' does not differ substantially from that of 'preventing disorder' in Articles

[25] For a similar conclusion, see the *Guidelines for review of legislation pertaining to religion or belief*, prepared by the Office for Democratic Institutions and Human Rights (ODIHR) of the OSCE together with the European Commission for Democracy through Law (Venice Commission) of the Council of Europe and published by the OSCE/ODIHR. These guidelines state on p 19 that 'States properly have authority to impose regulations concerning entry into their country by foreigners. This typically involves granting visas of differing kinds. [. . .] If individuals from particular religious belief backgrounds fall within neutral criteria (such as by constituting security risks or likely criminal behaviour), they legitimately may be excluded. However, if a State creates purely religion-based categories for exclusion, this may be inconsistent with the required religious neutrality of the State. Moreover, since such restrictions may make it difficult for a particular belief community to staff its organization as it sees appropriate, such restrictions may in fact operate as an intervention in internal religious affairs'.

[26] Harris et al 2009, 344–48 and Van Dijk et al 2006, 336–39. On the application of the 'prescribed by law' criterion in cases concerning Art 9 ECHR, see Harris et al 2009, 435–36 and Van Dijk et al 2006, 768.

[27] Van Dijk et al 2006, 768.

8, 10 and 11 ECHR.[28] Nonetheless, the ECtHR emphasised in *Nolan and K* that 'the exceptions to the freedom of religion listed in Article 9(2) must be narrowly interpreted, for their enumeration is strictly exhaustive and their definition is necessarily restrictive'.[29] In this respect, the Court observed that the omission of the aim of protecting national security was not accidental but reflected

> the primordial importance of religious pluralism as 'one of the foundations of a "democratic society" within the meaning of the Convention' and the fact that a State cannot dictate what a person believes or take coercive steps to make him change his beliefs.[30]

Although ECtHR case law shows that limitations to the freedom of religion are not often found to lack justification because of not serving a relevant legitimate aim, the judgment in *Nolan and K* demonstrates that this possibility cannot be disregarded altogether.

Notwithstanding the above conditions, the validity of limitations to the freedom of religion will largely depend on their level of necessity. According to established ECtHR case law, the requirement that a limitation must be 'necessary in a democratic society' implies that it must serve a 'pressing social need' and be proportionate in relation to the aim pursued. Thereby the reasons adduced by the state to demonstrate the measure's necessity must be relevant and sufficient.[31]

In connection with the above criteria, regard must be had in cases involving the freedom of religion to the requirements of neutrality and impartiality that govern the relationship between church and state. The ECtHR has repeatedly emphasised the role of the state as a neutral and impartial organiser of religious pluralism.[32] It may be observed that the concept of neutrality is not uniform and can be applied in different ways, depending on the national context of the Contracting State.[33] Nevertheless, interference with Article 9 ECHR will not be considered necessary if, for instance, it favours one religious denomination over another or attempts to enforce religious unity.[34] Also, states should not adopt regulations (such as planning provisions) that are directed against minority groups and should ensure that education provided to children is sufficiently objective and pluralistic and does not amount to indoctrination.[35]

Before examining what the above criteria mean in relation to integration requirements for the admission of religious servants, one more

[28] ibid.
[29] *Nolan and K* (n 3), para 73, with references to further case law.
[30] ibid.
[31] Van Dijk et al 2006, 340–41.
[32] eg, *Supreme Holy Council of the Muslim Community* (n 5 above), para 93.
[33] Vermeulen 2010a, 52–57.
[34] Van Dijk et al 2006, 770 with references to case law.
[35] Harris et al 2009, 431, with references to case law. See also section II.D.i of ch 4.

remark must be made. As discussed in chapter 4 (section II.B), in cases concerning the admission of family members the ECtHR has mainly applied the 'fair balance' test instead of the 'necessity' test of Article 8(2) ECHR. The former makes no clear distinction between the question of whether the refusal to admit an alien comes within the scope of the right concerned and the question of whether a limitation to this right is justified. Instead, what takes place is a general balancing exercise between the interests of the individual applicants (*in casu* the religious community) and the public interests of the host state. In general, application of the 'fair balance' test leaves more scope for justification to the respondent state and hence makes it less likely that a violation of the Convention will be found.

In case law on Article 8 ECHR, the 'fair balance' test is usually applied in cases involving the admission of family members (which is often considered by the ECtHR as a (potential) positive obligation on the part of the state). It is possible that the Court would take the same approach in cases concerning the admission of religious servants. Thus far, however, the 'fair balance' test has not been applied in connection with the freedom of religion and the ECtHR has not devised any criteria to this effect. This chapter consequently proceeds on the assumption that, where Article 9 is applicable, requirements concerning the admission of religious servants must be in accordance with Article 9(2). It may be recalled, however, that admission cases will not normally come within the scope of Article 9 (section II.A); hence, it is not the case that religious servants are in principle entitled to admission, whereas family members are not. Rather, both under the 'fair balance' test of Article 8 and the interpretation of Article 9(1) proposed above, a primary issue will be whether the admission of the alien constitutes the only way in which the right to family life or to religious freedom can be exercised.

C. Margin of Appreciation

As explained in chapter 4 (section II.B.iii), the scope of the ECtHR's appraisal of state measures concerning the admission of religious servants is influenced by the margin of appreciation left to the respondent state. The breadth of this margin depends on a range of factors. As the Court regards freedom of religion as being of fundamental importance in a democratic society, limitations to this freedom are normally subjected to strict scrutiny, especially where 'the need to secure true religious pluralism' is at stake.[36] Nevertheless, there are some areas in which a wider margin

[36] ECtHR 29 August 1996, app no 18748/91 (*Manoussakis and others*), para 44. See also Van Dijk et al 2006, 769 and Arai-Takahashi 2002, 93–100.

of appreciation is applied, due for instance to the different traditions existing between the Contracting States. These include the regulation of relations between church and state.[37] Finally, as mentioned in chapter 4, there are also indications that the Court will grant a wider margin of appreciation where immigration or integration policy is concerned.

D. Article 9 ECHR in Relation to Integration Requirements

It appears beyond doubt that a general requirement for all religious servants appointed by a religious community to comply with integration conditions would come within the scope of the freedom of religion as protected by Article 9 ECHR. However, as explained above, this is not self-evident where the requirement applies to religious servants who are foreign nationals and have not yet been admitted to the state where the community is based. In this situation, a state decision to deny admission, including when based on failure to comply with an integration requirement, will not normally interfere with the religious freedom of the community, let alone with that of the individual religious servant. It has, however, been argued that there are two situations in which such a decision can nevertheless be covered by Article 9 ECHR.

One of these situations is when it can be established that the decision was in fact designed to curb the exercise of religious freedom. General immigration measures, such as the work permit requirement in the *El Majjaoui* case that applied to all labour migrants, will not easily fall foul of this exception. However this may be different with regard to measures specifically addressing religious servants. In this respect it may be recalled that religious servants constitute a specific target group of the Dutch Act on Integration Abroad because of the presupposed effect of their activities on the process of immigrant integration in the Netherlands. It is their position within the religious community that is believed to give them a certain influence in this integration process, and it is because of this influence that they are required to know the basics of Dutch language and Dutch society.

Where integration requirements for the admission of religious servants are based on arguments such as the above, it seems clear that they are not general measures that happen to touch upon the exercise of the freedom of religion, but instead measures specifically enacted in connection with that freedom.

Nonetheless, to determine whether integration requirements come within the scope of Article 9 ECHR, careful attention must be paid to the particular nature of such measures. One element to be taken into account

[37] Harris et al 2009, 437 and – critically – Arai-Takahashi 2002, 95–96.

is whether, in effect, their aim is to 'repress' the exercise of the freedom of religion, as stated by the ECtHR in *Nolan and K* (section II.A.ii.b). Where this is not the case, it must be asked whether less far-reaching aims, such as a wish to exercise control over the internal organisation of religious communities, are also capable of qualifying a measure as interfering with Article 9.[38] A second relevant factor is whether the activities that the state seeks to control or influence are of an essentially religious nature (such as ecclesiastical ceremonies or the interpretation of religious texts) or whether they correspond to tasks that can also be performed by secular bodies (such as social counselling or the provision of charity). Even though the distinction between these types of activities is not always easy to make, the freedom of religion is more likely to be affected if the state measures concern activities that are clearly of a religious nature.[39] On the other hand, where the same activities are also performed by secular bodies the question can be raised as to why the measures do not also apply to workers employed by those bodies (section VII.E).

The second situation in which, it is argued, admission criteria for religious servants may interfere with the rights conferred by Article 9 ECHR is when a religious community can only continue to exist by appointing a servant from abroad. This criterion can be applied equally with regard to integration requirements. Thus, whether a refusal of admission because of non-compliance with an integration requirement constitutes an interference with the freedom of religion will depend on the alternatives available to the community to find a religious servant within the country. However, the suitability of available candidates is a matter to be decided by the religious community itself as the principle of neutrality requires state authorities to be reticent on this point.

If it can be established that the integration requirements imposed by a state do in fact constitute a limitation of Article 9 ECHR, it then has to be determined whether this limitation can be justified. As explained above, this primarily requires there to be a domestic law that prescribes that admission can be refused in the event of non-compliance with integration requirements. This law must moreover be sufficiently accessible and foreseeable.

As a second condition, the integration requirements must pursue at least one of the legitimate aims set out in Article 9(2) ECHR (public safety, the protection of public order, health or morals or the protection of the rights and freedoms of others). Whether this condition is met has to be

[38] Of course, states seeking to control the internal organisation of religious communities may do this as a way of eventually undermining the existence of a particular religion or belief. Examples of such practices, which must clearly be qualified as a form of repression, are provided by De Jong (De Jong 2000, 443–51).

[39] The difference made by De Jong between the internal and external activities of religious organisations could perhaps be helpful in making this distinction, ibid, 423 and following.

judged in the light of the integration objectives pursued by the Contracting State. However, it is conceivable in principle for integration requirements to have been introduced in pursuit of one of the above interests. In this regard it may be observed that, despite the restrictive reading proposed by the ECtHR (section II.B), the concept of 'public order' has been interpreted to include more than the prevention of crime or disturbances of the physical environment. In the case of *Serif*, for instance, the respondent state (Greece) claimed that, by protecting the authority of a lawfully appointed religious leader (mufti), it sought to prevent disputes between different religious factions and to protect its international relations with Turkey. The ECtHR consequently accepted that the interference at stake served the protection of public order.[40] It has also been argued, on the basis of the *Leyla Sahin* case concerning the ban on Islamic headscarves at Turkish universities, that the concept of public order also includes the constitutional principles on which a state is founded (such as the principle of secularism in Turkey).[41]

In view of the above, it seems plausible that the notion of 'public order' in Article 9(2) ECHR would also cover integration objectives such as preserving social cohesion (including peaceful relations between different religious groups) and ensuring respect for the constitutional principles of the state concerned. It is also submitted that religious servants can be required to acquaint themselves with existing legal limitations on the freedom of religion (such as the right of individuals to leave a religious community) as a way of ensuring respect for the rights and freedoms of others. However, it is clear from the ECtHR's judgment in *Nolan and K* that a state may not seek to abolish or restrict religious pluralism or 'dictate what a person believes or take coercive steps to make him change his beliefs' (section II.B; see also section II.D.i. of chapter 4). The aim of the 'protection of the economic well-being of the state', which is often an important goal of integration policies, is also not mentioned in the second paragraph of Article 9 ECHR. It is therefore doubtful whether an integration measure solely directed towards economic aims (such as economic self-reliance) could constitute a legitimate restriction of the freedom of religion.[42]

Thirdly, it has to be determined whether integration requirements for the admission of religious servants are also 'necessary in a democratic

[40] *Serif* (n 6), paras 43, 45 and 47.

[41] See Vermeulen 2010b, 22–23. According to Vermeulen, the concept of 'public order' in Art 9(2) ECHR is interpreted extensively by the ECtHR to balance out the equally extensive interpretation of the scope of the freedom of religion in Art 9(1).

[42] It may be observed that the 'fair balance' test applied by the ECtHR under Art 8 ECHR does not require immigration requirements for family members to pursue one of the legitimate aims mentioned in the second paragraph of that provision (section II.B.i of ch 4). This is one point where the choice for the 'fair balance' or the 'necessity' test may, therefore, not be inconsequential.

society'. Again, the outcome of this determination will depend to a large extent on the particular features of the measure at stake and on the circumstances of the case. Some remarks can, nevertheless, be made.

As a first requirement, it will have to be established that the integration requirements are needed in order to address a 'pressing social need'. This criterion will probably be satisfied if the state can demonstrate the existence of problems relating to immigrant integration, for instance low levels of participation amongst immigrant groups. Still, the 'necessity' test also requires the interest of the state in addressing these problems to be balanced against the interference with the rights of the religious community. This proportionality test needs to be conducted not only *in abstracto*, but also with regard to the particular circumstances of the case.

The weight to be accorded to the interests of the religious community will depend, at least in part, on the extent to which the community is actually prevented from exercising its rights under Article 9 ECHR. Where it has already been established that the admission of a religious servant from abroad is the only way for the community to survive, the interference will be particularly significant. Other factors that ought to play a role in the proportionality assessment include the duration of the interference and the efforts required to meet the integration conditions. The latter will depend inter alia on the level of knowledge demanded, the costs of the integration requirement and the availability of courses or preparation materials (see also section II.D of chapter 4). Although in many cases these efforts will need to be made by the religious servant seeking admission and not by the religious community itself, they represent a hurdle for that community in the appointment of its desired leader.

The integration requirements will also need to constitute a suitable measure to achieve the aim pursued. While this criterion is normally not explicitly applied by the ECtHR, it is hard to see how a measure can be proportionate if it is not effective and therefore does not actually contribute to realising the interests of the state. With regard to integration requirements, it may be established whether the knowledge required is relevant and, where evidence is available, whether the requirements have actually contributed to reducing integration problems. There is some evidence that religious communities do indeed play an important role in the integration processes of immigrants and that, while safeguarding the cultural traditions of migrant groups, they also stimulate the migrants' social and cultural adaptation to the receiving society.[43] So far, however, it has not been established whether this role of religious communities is also enhanced if religious servants have to meet integration requirements before being admitted.

[43] ACVZ 2005, 26–27. The study concerned the role of migrant churches in the United States.

It is argued above that limitations to the freedom of religion should also be in conformity with the neutral and impartial role of the state towards religious organisations. This entails, in any case, that integration requirements should apply equally to all religious servants, irrespective of their denomination. A more difficult question is whether the principle of neutrality also means that state authorities should not concern themselves at all with the way in which religious servants conduct their tasks. While it can be submitted that integration requirements should, at any rate, not prescribe how religious servants must fulfil their duties (for example, what to preach or how to conduct a religious ceremony), they will normally not be so far-reaching. Instead, integration requirements will often be based on the assumption that a religious servant is not able to properly conduct his or her tasks without certain prior knowledge. Whether this is acceptable will depend, at least partly, on the type of knowledge required. It is argued that the contents of an integration course or exam should steer clear of any normative notions concerning religion or religious interpretations (at least to the extent that these notions do not correspond to legal norms). On the other hand, more neutral requirements, such as language proficiency, are not necessarily problematic. Here too, however, the question may arise as to why such requirements should apply only to religious servants.

III. ARTICLE 18 OF THE INTERNATIONAL COVENANT ON CIVIL AND POLITICAL RIGHTS

The right to freedom of thought, conscience and religion is also protected by Article 18 ICCPR. The first paragraph of this provision, which closely resembles Article 9(1) ECHR, protects 'the freedom to have or to adopt a religion or belief of one's choice, and freedom, either individually or in community with others and in public or private, to manifest his religion or belief in worship, observance, practice and teaching'. Under Article 18(3) ICCPR, limitations to the freedom of religion must be 'prescribed by law' and 'necessary to protect public safety, order, health or morals or the fundamental rights and freedoms of others'.

This section investigates whether any criteria can be inferred from Article 18 ICCPR with regard to integration requirements for the admission of religious servants in addition to those that stem from Article 9 ECHR. As explained in chapter 4, the ICCPR is not monitored by an international court or other body competent to issue binding decisions on the interpretation and application of the Covenant. Nevertheless some interpretational guidelines may be obtained from the jurisprudence of the Human Rights Committee (HRC), in particular its General Comments and Communications issued in individual cases. Additionally, for the purposes of interpretation, regard may also be had to the Declaration on the Elimination of All Forms of Intolerance and of Discrimination Based on Religion or Belief, which was adopted in 1981 by the United Nations General Assembly (the '1981 Declaration').[44]

A. Scope of Article 18 ICCPR

i. The Right of Religious Communities to Appoint Religious Leaders

Like Article 9 ECHR, Article 18(1) ICCPR protects the right to manifest one's religion or belief, both alone and in community with others. With regard to the collective dimension of this right, the HRC has specified that this includes the right of religious groups to choose their religious leaders, priests and teachers.[45] Support for this interpretation can also be found in Article 6(g) of the 1981 Declaration. According to the latter provision, the freedom of religion includes the freedom 'to train, appoint, elect or designate by succession appropriate leaders called for by the requirements and standards of any religion or belief'. It may therefore be accepted that the choosing by a religious community of its own leadership must be considered a manifestation of religion within the meaning of Article 18(1) ICCPR.

ii. Admission of Religious Servants

The next question then is whether Article 18(1) ICCPR also contains an obligation for the Contracting States to admit a religious servant, either on an individual basis or on behalf of a religious community. Although this question has not been expressly addressed by the HRC, there is reason to assume that such an obligation does not in principle exist. In its General Comment on the position of aliens, the HRC took the view that the ICCPR 'does not recognize the right of aliens to enter or reside in the territory of a State party', and that 'it is in principle a matter for the State to decide who it will admit to its territory'.[46] Additionally, during the deliberations on the draft (UN) Convention on the elimination of all forms of religious intolerance, a proposal to include a reference to the right to bring in (religious) teachers from abroad was rejected. This was based on the argument that to include the reference would amount to asking states to abandon their right to control the admission of foreigners to their terri-

[44] General Assembly resolution 36/55, adopted in the 73rd plenary meeting on 25 November 1981. The relevance of this Declaration for the interpretation of Art 18 ICCPR is confirmed in Joseph et al 2004, 501–02.

[45] HRC General Comment No 22 on the right to freedom of thought, conscience and religion (Art 18), adopted on 30 July 1993, ref no CCPR/C/21/Rev1/Add.4, para 4.

[46] HRC General Comment No 15 on the position of aliens under the Covenant, adopted on 11 April 1986, para 5.

tory.[47] These proceedings indicate that the UN Member States recognised that the freedom of religion could give rise to claims for admission but, at least at the time, did not want to recognise this as a right.[48]

Nevertheless, even if Article 18 ICCPR does not include a general right to admission for religious servants, the above considerations do not exclude the possibility that such a right could exist in exceptional circumstances. In the above General Comment the HRC also recognised that 'in certain circumstances an alien may enjoy the protection of the Covenant even in relation to entry or residence, for example, when considerations of non-discrimination, prohibition of inhuman treatment and respect for family life arise'.[49] It is argued that the admission of religious servants would come within the scope of Article 18(1) ICCPR in the same situations as described above in relation to Article 9 ECHR. These are situations in which immigration decisions are either designed to curb the freedom of religion or in which the exercise of religious activities by a particular community would effectively be rendered impracticable (section II.A.ii.d). These exceptions can therefore be seen as necessary to ensure that the right to freedom of religion is effective in practice, as well as to protect religious communities against abuse by the state of its powers in the field of immigration. There are no reasons why these considerations should not also be relevant in the context of the ICCPR.

An additional argument in favour of accepting that admission rights may sometimes be covered by the freedom of religion can be based on Article 18 ICCPR read in combination with Article 27.[50] The latter provision states that persons belonging to ethnic, religious or linguistic minorities shall not be denied the right to profess and practise their own religion in community with other members of their group. It may be assumed, however, that minority groups in particular may experience difficulties in finding religious leaders in the host country because of their size and, in the case of immigrant minorities, because they bring with them religious convictions that have not been historically present in the host state. Consequently, if Article 18(1) ICCPR did not allow the admission of religious servants from abroad, this would put minority groups at a

47 De Jong 2000, 429.

48 According to De Jong, the right to bring in religious teachers from abroad can nevertheless be derived from a combination of the right to train religious leaders and the right to maintain communications with individuals and communities in matters of religion at the national and international levels, both of which are included in the 1981 Declaration (Art 6(g) and (i)). See De Jong 2000, 429–30. In my view this argument is not convincing as the right to maintain cross-border communications is essentially different from the right to enter and reside in a state other than that of one's nationality.

49 HRC General Comment No 15 on the position of aliens under the Covenant, adopted on 11 April 1986, para 5.

50 On the relationship between Arts 18 and 27 ICCPR, see De Jong 2000, 254–57. It is assumed here, as argued by De Jong on 268–69, that Art 27 ICCPR applies also to immigrant minorities.

particular disadvantage. To avoid this outcome, it is submitted that Article 18(1) ICCPR should be read so as to include a right to admission of religious servants on behalf of minority groups who would otherwise be unable to practise their religion. Support for this argument can be found in the HRC's General Comment on Article 18, where it is stated that 'the Committee . . . views with concern any tendency to discriminate against any religion or belief for any reason, including the fact that they are newly established . . .'.[51]

B. Limitations to the Freedom of Religion: Article 18(3) ICCPR

If it is accepted that a religious community may, in special circumstances, be entitled to bring in a religious servant from abroad, the conditions under which limitations to this right may be justified need to be established. Under Article 18(3) ICCPR, limitations of the freedom of religion must firstly be prescribed by law. They must also be necessary in order to protect one of the specified aims: the protection of public safety, order, health or morals or the fundamental rights and freedom of others.

The requirement that limitations must be 'prescribed by law' means that they must have a basis in the national law of the Contracting State concerned. The precise contents of this requirement have not been specified by the HRC in relation to Article 18 ICCPR; however, it can be assumed that the criteria to be applied are similar to those included in the requirement of 'lawfulness' in Article 17 ICCPR. These criteria are outlined in section III.B of chapter 4.[52]

Concerning the aims enumerated in Article 18(3), the HRC has observed that the provision is to be strictly interpreted, meaning that restrictions are not allowed on other than the specified grounds even if they would be allowed as restrictions to other rights protected in the Covenant.[53] National security is mentioned as an example in this respect. Thus, like the ECtHR (section II.B), the HRC is of the view that measures to protect national security may not encroach upon the freedom of religion. Also, Article 18(3), like Article 9(2) ECHR, does not allow limitations designed to serve economic purposes.[54]

With regard to the aim of protecting public morals, the HRC has commented that 'the concept of morals derives from many social, philosophi-

[51] HRC General Comment No 22 on the right to freedom of thought, conscience and religion (Art 18), adopted on 30 July 1993, ref no CCPR/C/21/Rev.1/Add.4, para 2.

[52] It may be added that the term 'prescribed by law' excludes legislative measures enacted by local authorities, see De Jong 2000, 86.

[53] HRC General Comment No 22 on the right to freedom of thought, conscience and religion (Art 18), adopted on 30 July 1993, ref no CCPR/C/21/Rev.1/Add.4, para 8.

[54] On the limitation grounds of Art 18(3) ICCPR, see also De Jong 2000, 90—100 and Joseph et al 2004, 508–10.

cal and religious traditions; consequently, limitations on the [freedom of religion] for the purpose of protecting morals must be based on principles not deriving exclusively from a single tradition'.[55] It is submitted that the concept of morals, and therefore also the diversity of traditions reflected in this concept, is likely to vary among and even within different societies. Nevertheless, the HRC's comment may be understood as meaning that, where it is used to justify limitations to the freedom of religion, the concept of morals must express the actual views on morality existing within a society rather than seeking to change those views. Thereby the views of minority groups, as well as existing disagreements on the prevailing moral norms, will need to be given due regard. Also important to note is that Article 18(3) ICCPR (like Art 9(2) ECHR) refers to 'public morals' and therefore does not allow limitations to the freedom of religion that aim to influence the private moral views of individuals. Even so, the concept of morals remains a vague notion that is particularly liable to subjective interpretations and therefore should be applied with caution.[56]

The HRC has stated that, in interpreting the scope of the limitation clauses of the ICCPR, the Contracting States 'should proceed from the need to protect the rights guaranteed under the Covenant' and that limitations 'must not be applied in a manner that would vitiate the rights guaranteed in Article 18'.[57] As far as the requirement of necessity is concerned, it was specified that limitations should be applied only for a purpose mentioned in Article 18(3) and must be 'directly related and proportionate to the specific need on which they are predicated'.[58] Despite some slight variations, these criteria do not appear to differ substantially from the 'necessary in a democratic society' test applied by the ECtHR (section II.B).

The HRC has also stated that limitations to the freedom of religion should not discriminate, either in their purpose or in the way they are applied. From this it may be derived that, like Article 9(2) ECHR, Article 18(3) ICCPR stands in the way of limitations that do not apply equally to all religious denominations (see again section II.B). However, the HRC's comment is formulated in sufficiently broad terms so as also to cover limitations that are discriminatory on grounds other than religion. The prohibition of discrimination, in particular on grounds of nationality and racial or ethnic origin, is discussed in detail in chapters 8 to 10 of this study.

[55] HRC General Comment No 22 on the right to freedom of thought, conscience and religion (Art 18), adopted on 30 July 1993, ref no CCPR/C/21/Rev.1/Add.4, para 8.

[56] See also De Jong 2000, 97, who completely rejects the use of 'public morals' as a limitation ground.

[57] HRC General Comment No 22 on the right to freedom of thought, conscience and religion (Art 18), adopted on 30 July 1993, ref no CCPR/C/21/Rev.1/Add.4, para 8.

[58] ibid.

C. Article 18 ICCPR in Relation to Integration Requirements

It is concluded that, as far as integration requirements for the admission of religious servants are concerned, Article 18 ICCPR does not provide us with any standards substantially different from those stemming from Article 9 ECHR. Nevertheless some remarks can be made.

Firstly, it has been asserted that Article 18 read together with Article 27 ICCPR requires particular attention to be paid to the rights of religious minorities. To ensure that these minorities can effectively exercise their freedom of religion, it must be accepted that this freedom is infringed by a refusal to admit a religious servant while no suitable religious leader is available within the Contracting State. National measures concerning integration requirements for religious servants need to take this into account.

It is also argued that the concept of 'public morals' should be interpreted so as to take into account the different views and traditions existing within the Contracting States. As stated above, it is doubtful whether protection of public morals can serve as a relevant limitation ground in relation to integration requirements. However, if this is accepted, the above standard should be respected.

Thirdly and finally, it has been established that integration requirements that restrict the freedom of religion may not serve a discriminatory purpose, nor may they be applied in a discriminatory manner. This standard concerns not only discrimination between religious communities on account of their particular religion, but also discrimination on other grounds.

IV. ARTICLE 6 OF THE DUTCH CONSTITUTION

In the Netherlands, in addition to the guarantees provided in the above treaties, the freedom of religion and belief is protected by Article 6 of the Dutch Constitution.[59] Below it is examined whether this provision contains any relevant criteria concerning the issue addressed in this chapter – integration conditions for the admission of religious servants.

[59] Art 6(1) Dutch Constitution reads 'Ieder heeft het recht zijn godsdienst of levensovertuiging, individueel of in gemeenschap met anderen, vrij te belijden, behoudens ieders verantwoordelijkheid volgens de wet'. ('Everyone is free to manifest his religion or belief, alone or in community with others, subject to limitations provided by law'). Art 6(2) Dutch Constitution protects the freedom of religion and belief outside buildings and enclosed spaces and as such is not relevant to this study.

A. Scope of Article 6 Dutch Constitution

i. The Right of Religious Communities to Appoint Religious Leaders

Like Articles 9 ECHR and 18 ICCPR, Article 6 of the Dutch Constitution protects not only the religious freedom of individuals, but also that of collectivities. This can be derived from the first paragraph of the provision, which refers to the freedom to manifest one's religion or belief 'individually or in community with others'. The collective dimension of the freedom of religion in Article 6(1) also covers the right of religious communities to organisational freedom, including the right to choose their own leaders, teachers and other personnel.[60] Again, it has to be established whether this right also applies if the religious leader is a foreign national who has not yet been legally admitted to the Netherlands.

ii. Admission of Religious Servants

Thus far, the Dutch courts have not ruled on the above question with respect to Article 6(1) of the Constitution. Case law shows that the issue of admission of religious servants has come up several times.[61] However, the right to freedom of religion was either not alluded to at all in these cases or addressed only in relation to Articles 9 ECHR and 18 ICCPR. More importantly, where the freedom of religion played a role, the courts failed to deal with the question of its scope. In several judgments, the refusal to admit the religious servant was found to be lawful on the grounds that the freedom of religion does not grant religious communities a right to appoint a leader without having to comply with the prevailing immigration conditions.[62] On the basis of these decisions it cannot be established whether the court found the immigration conditions to constitute justified restrictions to the freedom of religion, or whether it considered this freedom not to be applicable at all. One exception concerns the judgment of the Amsterdam District Court, which expressly decided that – at least in the case concerned – Article 9 ECHR did not grant a right of admission either to the religious community or to the religious servant himself.

However, the Dutch government subscribes to the argument made earlier in this chapter (section II.A.ii.c) that the state may be under an obligation to admit a religious servant in the exceptional case where this is the

[60] Vermeulen 2000, 102–03.

[61] See AJD 2 July 1984, case no A-21798 (1982), LJN: AM8224; Pres AJD 2 July 1987, case nos R02.87.0624/S42 and R02.87.1133/S90, *KG* 1987/438; AJD 28 February 2003, case nos 200206325/1 and 200206347/1, para 2.7.1 and District Court of The Hague sitting in Amsterdam 23 March 2007, case no 06/37989, LJN: BA3169, para 6.4.

[62] AJD 2 July 1984, case no A-21798 (1982), LJN: AM8224 and AJD 28 February 2003, case nos 200206325/1 and 200206347/1, para 2.7.1.

only way for the religious community to continue its activities. This statement concerns Article 6(1) of the Constitution, as well as the relevant provisions of the ECHR and ICCPR.[63] A similar approach to the interpretation of Article 6(1) can be found in Dutch case law on matters not concerning immigration: in these cases, measures not prima facie affecting the freedom of religion are nevertheless considered to come within its scope in circumstances where the exercise of this freedom effectively becomes impossible.[64]

In addition to the foregoing, it may be asked whether Article 6(1) of the Constitution would also apply to immigration conditions for religious servants if it can be established that these conditions were imposed in direct connection with the exercise of the freedom of religion or even with the aim of repressing such exercise. Here an interesting parallel can be drawn with an earlier requirement of Dutch immigration law, which required an imam to be 'suitable to work as a religious servant for the Islamic community concerned'. Apparently this condition was introduced to avoid religious communities being subject to pressure from foreign states, which could in turn lead to cultural, political or religious conflicts within the Netherlands. The requirement was upheld by the court, which did not consider it a violation of Article 18 ICCPR.[65] However, this judgment was criticised by various authors on the grounds that the criterion of 'suitability' enabled the authorities to intervene in the appointment of religious servants for reasons relating to the content of their religious views or activities. This, it was argued, constituted an unjustified interference with the freedom of religion as protected inter alia by Article 6(1) of the Constitution.[66]

The requirement of 'suitability' for imams was eventually abolished. It is not clear, however, whether this was motivated by the assumption that there was an interference with the constitutionally protected freedom of religion. For this reason it cannot be said with certainty that the Dutch government has accepted that Article 6(1) also applies to immigration conditions imposed specifically in connection with the exercise of religious freedom.[67]

[63] *Parliamentary Papers II* 2005–2006, 19 637, No 1051, 4–5. This statement was made in reaction to a report issued by the Dutch Advisory Committee on Aliens Affairs (*Adviescommissie voor Vreemdelingenzaken*) concerning an immigration policy for religious servants (ACVZ 2005).

[64] See Vermeulen 2000, 100–01, with references to case law.

[65] AJD 2 July 1984, case no A-21798 (1982), LJN: AM8224.

[66] Vermeulen 1992, 127. See also Fernhout and Hofman in their case note on the judgment, published in *AB* 1985, 273.

[67] More recently, other requirements for the appointment of non-national religious servants were also abolished, in particular the obligations to notify vacancies to the *CWI* (the Dutch labour office) and to give priority to religious servants from EU/EEA Member States. Again, however, these changes were not expressly motivated on the grounds that the requirements interfered with the freedom of religion and more pragmatic reasons were provided instead. See *Government Gazette* 2007, 13825.

Before proceeding to the restriction clause, one more issue has to be discussed. This concerns an argument proposed by Vermeulen, to the effect that immigration matters do not fall under Article 6(1) of the Dutch Constitution because they are specifically addressed in Article 2(2).[68] The latter provision states that the admission and expulsion of aliens must be 'regulated by law', which means that legislation may be enacted on a sub-national level as long as there is a basis for it in a law made by the national legislator. This requirement is softer than that laid down in Article 6(1) which, as discussed below, provides that restrictions to the freedom of religion must be laid down in the national legislative act itself.

The Constitution itself does not state whether measures concerning both immigration and religious freedom come under Article 2(2) or Article 6(1); neither have the Dutch courts ruled on this issue. However, accepting that Article 2(2) is a *lex specialis* compared to the particular rights and freedoms expressed in the Constitution would imply that the government is free to act on the entire terrain of admission and expulsion without taking these rights and freedoms into account. This would be an unlikely outcome, also given that Article 2(2) is included in the first chapter of the Constitution, which concerns the protection of fundamental rights. It is, therefore, more plausible to consider Article 2(2) as the minimum norm (whereby regulations concerning the admission and expulsion of aliens must always have a basis in a national legislative act) and Article 6(1) as the *lex specialis* (where such regulations touch upon the freedom of religion, they must be laid down in the national legislative act itself). It is also recalled that the Dutch government itself recognised that the admission of religious servants may come within the scope of Article 6(1) (see above). The restriction clause in the latter provision is briefly addressed in the following section.

B. The Restriction Clause

According to Article 6(1) of the Dutch Constitution, restrictions to the freedom of religion are only permitted 'by law'. This means that such restrictions are unconstitutional unless they are laid down in a national legislative act (*wet in formele zin*, adopted by parliament and the government acting together as the legislator at the national level). The standard set by Article 6(1) is of a formal nature: it determines that only the national legislator may restrict the freedom of religion or belief, but it does not provide any criteria concerning the content of such restrictions. Meanwhile, Article 6(1) does not forbid decisions restricting the freedom of religion being taken by administrative bodies (ie the Aliens Affairs

[68] Vermeulen 2006, 253; see also ACVZ 2005, 39.

Minister). Such decisions must, however, be authorised in a specifically formulated national legislative act.

C. Article 6 Dutch Constitution in Relation to Integration Requirements

With regard to the scope of the freedom of religion, the above examination of Article 6(1) of the Dutch Constitution did not reveal any standards other than those proposed in sections II and III. Nevertheless, the Dutch government subscribes to the view that refusal to admit a religious servant constitutes interference with Article 6(1) if admission is sought by a religious community that would otherwise be unable to continue its activities. This stance confirms the argument made earlier with regard to Articles 9 ECHR and 18 ICCPR, but which has not (yet) been expressly adopted by the ECtHR and the HRC. It also applies when the refusal is based on the grounds that the religious servant has failed to comply with an integration requirement. On the other hand, it has not been established whether integration requirements for religious servants could also come within the scope of Article 6(1) of the Dutch Constitution on the grounds that they aim to exert control over the exercise of religious freedom.

It follows from the above that it remains unclear as to whether Article 6(1) of the Constitution could apply in all cases in which a religious community is denied the right to bring in a religious servant because of non-compliance with integration requirements, or only in exceptional circumstances. When it does apply, however, the standard with regard to restrictions is straightforward: the condition that admission is subject to fulfilment of integration requirements must be laid down in a national legislative act.

V. FREEDOM OF RELIGION AND EQUAL TREATMENT

Under the provisions discussed above, state actions resulting in interference with the freedom of religion are unlawful unless they meet the criteria set out in the respective restriction clauses. In addition, the principle of equal treatment prohibits discrimination of persons or groups of persons on the grounds of their religion. The legal framework concerning equal treatment is discussed in detail in chapter 8, but is also relevant in the context of this chapter. It follows from this framework that discrimination occurs when religious communities or their members are subject to unequal treatment without a reasonable and objective justification. Discrimination on the grounds of religion may occur if a distinction is made between different religious affiliations, but also if a religious community or its members are treated unequally by comparison with persons or organisations not belonging to any religion.

The principle of equal treatment can be found in each of the legal instruments discussed above: in the ECHR in Articles 14 and the Twelfth Protocol, in the ICCPR in Articles 2 and 26 and in Article 1 of the Dutch Constitution. Articles 14 ECHR and 2 ICCPR are of an accessory nature, which means they only apply to treatment coming within the scope of the rights and freedoms guaranteed in those treaties. However, this requirement has been broadly interpreted by the ECtHR, which applies Article 14 ECHR to treatment coming 'within the sphere' of the other rights of the Convention.[69] More importantly, the other equal treatment provisions apply independently of other rights and freedoms. Integration requirements for admission must consequently apply without discrimination on the grounds of religion, also when refusal of admission would not come within the scope of the freedom of religion.

VI. INTERIM CONCLUSION: LEGAL STANDARDS CONCERNING INTEGRATION REQUIREMENTS AS A CONDITION FOR THE ADMISSION OF RELIGIOUS SERVANTS

Before proceeding to assess the Dutch Act on Integration Abroad, it is useful to summarise the legal framework presented in the previous sections. With regard to each of the provisions examined (Art 9 ECHR, 18 ICCPR and 6 Dutch Constitution), the first question asked was whether they include a right for religious servants to be admitted to states of which they are not nationals. It was argued (section II.A.i) that in principle such a right does not exist for individual religious servants seeking admission for the purpose of exercising their freedom of religion alone. However, this situation is to be distinguished from one in which admission is sought by a religious organisation for the purpose of the collective exercise of religious freedom, for example in rites or ecclesiastical services.

Where the latter situation occurs, the freedom of religion also does not grant a general right to religious organisations to appoint servants from abroad. However, such a right may exist under particular circumstances. Firstly, if the appointment of the religious servant is a necessary condition for the organisation to be able to continue its activities. This possibility is recognised by the Dutch government (section IV.A.ii). It is also supported by case law from the Dutch courts and the ECtHR (section II.A.ii.c), where a similar approach can be recognised with regard to the freedom of religion in non-immigration contexts and the right to family life. Thus, in these particular circumstances, integration requirements for religious servants constitute interference with the freedom of religion. Nevertheless,

[69] eg, Arnardóttir 2003, 35–36.

a difficulty with this criterion is that state authorities need to be very reticent in judging whether a religious organisation cannot reasonably appoint another servant.

Secondly, integration requirements for religious servants may come within the scope of the above provisions if they are imposed in connection with the exercise of religious freedom. This can be derived from case law of the EComHR and the ECtHR; it was argued in section II.A.ii.b that this criterion also applies in admission cases. Even so, the exact scope of this criterion remains unclear: does it apply only to measures that aim to repress the freedom of religious organisations, or also to measures that aim to make such organisations subject to state control? With regard to integration requirements for religious servants, it was also argued that the applicability of the criterion will depend on the type of activities addressed by the requirements (section II.D).

In view of the above, it is useful to reiterate that integration requirements for the admission of religious servants do not necessarily come within the scope of the freedom of religion. Whether they do will have to be decided in the light of the particular nature of the measure, as well as the circumstances of the case. Only once it has been established that the freedom of religion has been limited do the criteria for justifying such limitations come into play.

Both Articles 9(2) ECHR and 18(3) ICCPR require limitations to the freedom of religion, *in casu* integration requirements, to be prescribed by law and to be proportionate in relation to an aim mentioned in those provisions (sections II.B and III.B). Both articles have been interpreted to exclude measures taken in the interests of national security or the economic well-being of the state. As far as the protection of public morals is concerned, it was argued that this aim does not cover the prescription of a particular set of morals or the regulation of morality outside the public domain. Nevertheless, integration objectives such as the maintenance of social cohesion or respect for constitutional principles can probably be brought under the aim of protecting public order or the rights and freedoms of others.

In addition to the requirement of proportionality, limitations to the freedom of religion must respect the principle of neutrality. This implies that integration requirements may not differentiate between religious organisations (which also follows from the principle of equal treatment) and may not be used to impose religious unity. In addition, it was argued that such requirements may not prescribe how religious servants are to fulfil their tasks, and that the contents of integration programmes or exams should steer clear of any normative notions concerning religion or religious interpretations (section II.D).

Article 6(1) of the Dutch Constitution states that limitations to the freedom of religion, regardless of their contents, are allowed, providing they are laid down in a specifically formulated national legislative act.

Integration requirements, irrespective of whether they constitute a limitation to the freedom of religion, may not amount to a form of discrimination on the grounds of religion. This means that, where these requirements result in the unequal treatment of individuals or religious organisations on the grounds of their religion, this distinction must be based on a reasonable and objective justification.

VII. THE ACT ON INTEGRATION ABROAD IN RELATION TO THE FREEDOM OF RELIGION AND THE RIGHT TO EQUAL TREATMENT

A. Religious Organisations in the Netherlands and Servants from Abroad

As explained above, the right to freedom of religion may be invoked by religious organisations seeking to appoint a servant from abroad. In the Netherlands there exists a variety of communities and organisations of a religious (or spiritual or philosophical) nature. Apart from the more traditional Christian and Jewish communities, these include various missionary organisations with origins in foreign countries, migrant churches and Islamic, Hindu and Buddhist communities. These groups' activities include worship and teaching, as well as more 'earthly' activities such as management and administration of the organisation.[70] In the past, various religious organisations have filed requests for the admission of religious servants. The number of requests from organisations belonging to ethnic minority groups has been rising since the 1950s, while since the 1970s growing numbers of Islamic groups have asked for imams and Islamic religious teachers to be admitted.[71] However, requests for admission have also been made by Catholic organisations confronted with an increasing lack of priests in the Netherlands.[72]

While every case has to be judged on its merits, there is no doubt that many of the aforementioned groups will count as religious organisations entitled to the protection offered by the ECHR, the ICCPR and the Dutch Constitution. It then remains to be seen whether the appointment of a particular religious servant also falls within a group's right to self-organisation. This will certainly be the case with regard to religious leaders and teachers (sections II.A.i and III.A.i). However, it could be argued that the organisational freedom of a religious community also includes the right to appoint people in other positions. In any case, the definition of 'religious servant' in Dutch legislation includes leaders and teachers, as

[70] See Hendrickx and De Lange 2004, 16–27; see also ACVZ 2005, 26.
[71] ACVZ 2005, 28.
[72] Hendrickx and De Lange 2004, 19.

well as other ecclesiastical personnel (chapter 2, section VI.B.ii). Hence, the appointment of persons who are qualified as religious servants (and thus subject to the requirement of integration abroad) can surely come within the scope of the right to religious self-organisation.

B. Does the Integration Exam Abroad Form a Limitation of the Freedom of Religion?

In principle, the right of religious communities to self-organisation does not extend to the appointment of religious servants from abroad; conditions for the admission of these servants do not, therefore, touch upon the freedom of religion. This is different, however, in the exceptional case where a religious organisation cannot find a suitable religious servant in the Netherlands and would be unable to function without one.

In this respect, Hendrickx and De Lange showed that many religious communities in the Netherlands have experienced problems as a result of immigration measures preventing them from engaging foreign nationals. Some communities have been hampered in the exercise of their religious activities, whereas others even felt that their continued existence was threatened. One example is that of the Buddharama temple, a Buddhist temple that needed a new monk because the current monk was ill and required assistance. Without a monk the temple could not continue to function. Other examples include Catholic weddings and funerals that have been forced to take place without a priest and Moroccan mosques that are temporarily or even permanently without an imam.[73]

Although these examples date back to before the adoption of the AIA, the effects of this Act may be the same. A religious servant who fails to pass the integration exam will be denied admission to the Netherlands. And even if the exam is eventually passed, the time, money and effort required to achieve this result may substantially delay such admission. The integration exam abroad can consequently constitute a limitation to the freedom of religion in particular circumstances such as those mentioned above.

Would it be possible to go further and argue that the obligation to pass the integration exam abroad always constitutes a limitation to the freedom of religion when applied to religious servants? This argument could be made on the grounds that the AIA is a measure that has been specifically enacted in connection with the exercise of religious freedom. Religious servants are not the only category of persons to whom the Act applies. However, the reasons why they have been included in its target group relate specifically to their position. Unlike family migrants, reli-

[73] Hendrickx and De Lange 2004, 98–101.

gious servants have not been brought under the AIA for the purposes of furthering their integration, but because of the role they are expected to play, in their capacity as clerics, in the integration process of the members of their community (chapter 2, sectionVI.C.ii). With regard to the freedom of religion, therefore, the AIA is not a general or neutrally formulated measure.

It is unclear, however, whether this also means that the integration requirement for religious servants as such limits the freedom of religion. As explained above, the criterion to be applied is not yet completely clear. On the one hand, it follows from the definition of who is a religious servant that the obligation to pass the integration exam is imposed in connection with activities of a religious nature. According to the Dutch government, this term applies specifically to persons for whom activities of a religious nature, such as conducting ecclesiastical services, attending marital or funeral ceremonies and teaching or explaining religious texts, are a primary activity. By contrast, those working for a religious organisation, but whose tasks are primarily administrative will not be considered to be religious servants.[74] Thus, the nature of the activities concerned does not detract from the conclusion that the AIA affects the freedom of religion.

On the other hand, it would go too far to say that the aim of the AIA is to 'stifle' or 'repress' the free exercise of religion. It may be assumed that the obligation to pass the integration exam, also since the level was raised on 1 April 2011, does not exert such pressure on religious organisations as to amount to repression. However the Act does exert a certain amount of control over the exercise of religious freedom, as the conditions set by the authorities for the appointment of religious servants relate to the fulfilment of their office.

Ultimately it would probably go too far, in view of existing ECtHR case law (such as *Nolan & K*), to argue that the integration exam abroad for religious servants as such constitutes a limitation of the freedom of religion. Nevertheless, it is clear that the specific targeting of the AIA towards religious servants is problematic in the light of the role played by the state vis-à-vis religious organisations. This matter is addressed again in paragraph VII.E, concerning the right to equal treatment.

C. Is the Limitation Justified?

It follows from the above that the integration exam for religious servants will not normally raise an issue under Articles 9 ECHR, 18 ICCPR and 6 Dutch Constitution. Still, in those cases where it does, a denial of admission on the grounds that the exam has not been passed will need to be

[74] *Parliamentary Papers II* 2005–2006, 19 637, No 1051, 2–4.

justified under the respective limitation clauses. This is assessed, in relation to Articles 9(2) ECHR and 18(3) ICCPR, in sections VII.C.i–VII.C.iii. In view of its different requirements, limitations to Article 6(1) Dutch Constitution are discussed separately in section VII.C.iv.

i. Prescribed by Law

Both Articles 9(2) and 18(3) ICCPR state that limitations to the freedom of religion must be prescribed by law. It is submitted that neither of these requirements differs substantially from the requirement of lawfulness in Article 17(1) ICCPR. This issue was discussed in section VII.B of chapter 4, where it was concluded that the obligation to pass the integration exam abroad has a sufficient basis in Dutch law.

ii. Legitimate Aim

To be justified under Articles 9(2) ECHR and 18(3) ICCPR, the integration exam abroad must serve one of the interests enumerated in those provisions, namely the protection of public safety, order, health or morals or the rights and freedoms of others. Arguably, to the extent that the integration exam abroad tests candidates' knowledge of the constitutional principles of the host state, it can be accepted as serving the protection of public order or the rights and freedoms of others (*cf* section II.D). This argument was also made by the Dutch government, which stated that religious servants have a role in determining the attitude of members of their communities towards the host society. For this purpose, religious servants need to be 'well aware of constitutional freedoms, such as the freedom of religion and of expression, and other universal values protected in human rights treaties, as well as the existence of other beliefs, homosexuality, the non-acceptability of honour killings, et cetera'.[75] The above aims are also reflected in some of the exam questions.[76]

As far as the requirement for Dutch language proficiency is concerned, it could probably be maintained that this serves to increase social cohesion (by improving communications between different groups in the population) and thus to protect public order.[77] However, with regard to the argument that integration is necessary in the interests of national security (to prevent terrorism and radicalisation, see chapter 4, section VII.C), it should be noted that this aim is not mentioned in Article 9(2) ECHR or

[75] *Parliamentary Papers I* 2004–2005, 29 700, E, 4.

[76] eg, question 56: 'Is homosexuality permitted or punishable by law?' (correct answer: permitted) and question 58: 'Is female circumcision permitted or punishable by law?' (correct answer: punishable by law).

[77] See also *Parliamentary Papers II* 2003–2004, 29 700, No 3, 4 and No 6, 47, where it is stated that the AIA aims to prevent the marginalisation of certain population groups.

18(3) ICCPR.[78] It may also be recalled that there is no justification for integration requirements that ask immigrants to denounce their identity (religious or otherwise) or to agree with particular views or ideas, even those widely held in the host society (see again section VII.C of chapter 4).

iii. Proportionality and Neutrality

To the extent that the above aims are accepted as legitimate, the next question is whether the AIA can also be considered proportionate in relation to those aims. In section VII.B, it was argued that refusal to admit a religious servant only comes within the scope of the freedom of religion if the religious community has no alternative means of continuing its activities. In these cases there will be a very weighty interest on the part of the religious community for the servant to be admitted. Consequently, it is argued that there will be a violation of Articles 9 ECHR and 18 ICCPR if failure to pass the integration exam results in the admission of the religious servant being permanently refused or delayed for a substantial period of time.[79]

Chapter 4 considered a number of factors that are of relevance in determining whether a religious servant can pass the integration exam abroad within a reasonable time and with a reasonable amount of effort. These include the accessibility of the exam, the availability of preparation facilities, the costs and the required level of knowledge or skills. What has been said about these circumstances in relation to the right to family life is equally applicable here. In particular, since the introduction of a reading comprehension test on 1 April 2011, the exam can be considered to present too great a hurdle for religious servants who are illiterate.

Another factor of relevance for the proportionality test is whether the integration exam abroad is an effective instrument to meet the objectives of the AIA; in other words whether it has a positive influence on religious servants' contribution to the integration process. Such influence is not easy to establish as the complex and abstract nature of this process means that the effectiveness of instruments such as the AIA is difficult to measure and is perhaps also necessarily limited. At the same time, the complexity of this policy field suggests that the effectiveness of the AIA is a matter that should not be intensively reviewed by national or international courts, but instead one in which a larger margin of appreciation should be granted to the national legislator. Nevertheless, it is unfortunate that the effect of the Act with regard to religious servants appears not

[78] This was not duly recognised by the Dutch Advisory Committee on Aliens Affairs, see ACVZ 2005, 39.

[79] What constitutes such a period of time is difficult to say in the abstract, but it is submitted that any period longer than some six months would not be obviously reasonable. However, the circumstances of the case may also play a role, for instance a shorter delay could also be disproportionate if a community is unable to bring in the religious servant before a particularly important religious event or festival.

to have been addressed at all during the 2009 evaluation.[80] In the absence of empirical data, the need for the integration requirement will be more difficult to maintain.

The requirement of neutrality does not raise a problem insofar as the AIA applies equally to all religious servants regardless of their faith or denomination. It was argued above that the principle of neutrality also means that the exam should not contain normative questions concerning religious topics or interpretations. In this respect, a problem may arise with regard, for example, to questions concerning the institution of marriage, same-sex partnerships or the position of women in the family and in society. To ensure compatibility with the freedom of religion, such questions should be limited to testing the candidate's knowledge of legal norms (such as the constitutionally guaranteed freedom of religion or equality of men and women). The integration exam abroad appears to be in accordance with this requirement.

iv. The Restriction Clause of Article 6(1) Dutch Constitution

To be justified under the restriction clause of Article 6(1), the obligation to pass the integration exam abroad must be laid down in a national legislative act. This criterion is met in Article 16(1)(h) of the Aliens Act 2000, which regulates the admission and expulsion of aliens in the Netherlands.[81] This provision states that a request for a residence permit can be denied if the applicant does not demonstrate a basic knowledge of the Dutch language and Dutch society. It follows from Article 16(1)(h) Aliens Act 2000, read in conjunction with Article 3(1)(b) of the Integration Act 2007, that religious servants must meet the requirement of integration abroad. The AIA is therefore compatible with Article 6(1) of the Dutch Constitution.

D. Possibilities for Exemption

Just like other aliens who have to pass the integration exam abroad, religious servants are eligible for exemptions in certain circumstances. In particular, it may be recalled that the AIA does not apply to applicants who are durably unable to pass the exam owing to a physical or mental disability, or who already have the required skills and knowledge.[82] Both exemptions add to the overall proportionality of the AIA. In addition, religious servants may be exempted on an individual basis if refusal of admission

[80] See ch 2, section VI.D.

[81] It may be recalled that the AIA amended the Aliens Act 2000 so as to include this condition; see ch 2, section VI.A.

[82] Art 3.71a(2)(c) Aliens Decree 2000 and Art 16 (1)(h) Aliens Act 2000 read in conjunction with Art 5 (1)(b)–(f) Integration Act 2007. See also ch 2, section VI.B.iii.

would be eminently unreasonable or disproportionate in the light of exceptional circumstances.[83]

The above possibilities for exemption probably suffice to prevent violations of the right to freedom of religion. Nevertheless, as is already the case with regard to the right to family life (section VII.F of chapter 4), it is recommended inserting a guideline in the Aliens Circular to the effect that admission will not be refused if the integration requirement would be contrary to any of the provisions discussed in this chapter. To establish whether this is the case, the legal standards formulated earlier need to be taken into account.

E. Discrimination on the Grounds of Religion?

Section V of this chapter briefly explained that unequal treatment on the grounds of religion amounts to discrimination – and is, therefore, prohibited – if it is not based on a reasonable and objective justification. This may concern unequal treatment between different religious affiliations, as well as unequal treatment of religious and non-religious groups or persons. This subsection focuses on the latter situation, by asking whether it is justified that the integration exam abroad applies specifically to religious servants.

As mentioned before, the AIA does not apply only to religious servants. However, in principle the Act applies only to aliens seeking admission to the Netherlands for a non-temporary residence purpose.[84] This can logically be explained on the grounds that integration only becomes an issue if a person is seeking to remain in the Netherlands for a longer period of time. Nevertheless, religious servants have been brought under the Act despite their residence purpose being qualified as temporary under the Aliens Decree.[85] In this respect, they are treated unequally compared to other aliens with a temporary residence purpose. We have already seen that this has been motivated on the grounds that it is not the integration of the religious servants themselves that is at issue under the AIA, but the role that these servants play in integration matters vis-à-vis the members of their religious communities.

It must then be assessed whether this motivation constitutes sufficient justification. This is not easy as the arguments supporting it are often expressed in rather abstract terms, referring to 'the great social interest served by the integration of religious servants' or 'the nature of [their]

[83] Art 3.71a (2)(d) Aliens Decree 2000 (as at 1 April 2011) and Art 4:84 General Administrative Act. See also section VI.B.iii of ch 2.

[84] Art 16(1)(h) Aliens Act 2000 read in conjunction with Art 3(1)(a) Integration Act 2007.

[85] Art 3.5(2)(d) Aliens Decree 2000.

function'.[86] Still, the government has stated that the task of religious servants is not limited to answering questions of a purely religious nature. Instead, they are also asked for guidance on 'matters relating to the socio-economic and socio-cultural integration process of ethnic minorities'.[87] Concrete examples mentioned included issues of everyday life such as finding a job, conflicts with neighbours and children dropping out of school.[88]

It may be argued that religious servants are not the only category of persons asked to advise on issues such as the above and who therefore play an influential role in the integration process of immigrant communities. The same can be said, for instance, with regard to teachers, social workers, journalists and members of migrant organisations. This argument was also raised in parliament when religious servants were brought under the 1998 Newcomers Integration Act.[89] In situations such as the above, however, conflicts may arise between religious norms and practices and the laws of the state.[90] The question then arises as to whether a state may apply integration measures, such as the AIA, to ensure that religious servants are aware of the prevailing legal norms and the legally established limitations to the freedom of religion.

It is submitted that this question must in principle be answered in the affirmative as states have a relatively large margin of appreciation where the area of church-state relations is concerned (section II.C). It follows that integration requirements specifically directed towards religious servants do not necessarily constitute discrimination on the grounds of religion. Arguably, this is also true with regard to the AIA. However, the exam should be a suitable measure to achieve the above purpose of informing religious servants about the place of religion in the Dutch legal order. As it is, most questions in the current test cannot be related to this purpose. The same is true with regard to the language test.[91] It is therefore proposed reconsidering the contents of the test so as to ensure compliance with the prohibition of discrimination on grounds of religion.

[86] See *Government Gazette* 2001, 247, 9. This regulation first brought religious servants within the scope of the integration legislation (the Newcomers Integration Act 1998, see ch 2, section V.C.ii). Arguments relating to the freedom of religion and the principle of equal treatment were discussed in some detail in the parliamentary debate preceding this regulation (see *Parliamentary Papers* 27 000); however, this did not stop it from being adopted.

[87] *Government Gazette* 2001, 247, 9, see also *Parliamentary Papers I* 2004–2005, 29 700, E, 4.

[88] *Proceedings I* 2000–2001, 34-1454.

[89] See, esp, *Parliamentary Papers II* 2000–2001, 27 000, No 6.

[90] Another example of a situation where such conflict arises concerns the wearing of religious clothing (eg, a headscarf) in public functions (eg, by judges or police officers).

[91] It could be argued that religious servants need to be able to speak Dutch in order to communicate with their followers. However, it has already been put forward that it is not very realistic to expect religious servants to learn Dutch at a sufficient level to communicate about philosophical questions within a reasonable period of time (*Proceedings I* 2000–2001, 34-1450).

F. Summary: Compatibility of the Integration Exam Abroad with the Right to Freedom of Religion and the Right to Equal Treatment

To summarise, the preceding assessment of the AIA leads us to observe firstly that the integration exam abroad for religious servants is not generally irreconcilable with the right to religious freedom. In most cases, requests by a religious community to bring in a servant from abroad will not be covered by the freedom of religion. Therefore the condition that religious servants must first pass the integration exam does not normally constitute interference with this freedom.

The right to freedom of religion may, however, be affected in individual cases where the religious community needs a servant from abroad to continue its activities. In such cases, the obligation to pass the integration exam abroad will be disproportionate if it has the effect of making the admission of the religious servant impossible or of delaying it for a substantial period of time. This may occur, for instance, in the case of illiterate applicants for whom the newly introduced reading comprehension test imposes a major obstacle. It needs to be ensured that the possibilities for individual exemption are applied in such situations so as to avoid violations of the right to freedom of religion.

With regard to the proportionality of the AIA, the effectiveness of the integration exam abroad in relation to the Act's objectives is also a factor of significance. So far this effectiveness has not been demonstrated and it has been argued that it may be very hard to do so. Given the complexity of the issue, the review conducted by national and international courts is likely to be less intense and a violation of the freedom of religion is unlikely to be found in an individual case on the grounds that the AIA is not effective. Nevertheless, it is submitted that the effectiveness of the integration exam for religious servants is a topic to be considered by the Dutch legislator and should at least have been addressed when the AIA was evaluated.

It has been established, regarding the right to equal treatment, that an integration exam abroad for religious servants does not amount to a form of discrimination on the grounds of religion. While religious servants are treated differently from other aliens with a non-temporary residence purpose, this differentiation is justified in principle by the need to protect the separation between church and state. However, the existing integration exam abroad is not suited to this purpose and needs to be reconsidered. If the relevant knowledge cannot be tested in Dutch because doing so would require a high level of language proficiency, the exam could be taken in the religious servants' own language.

VIII. CONCLUDING OBSERVATIONS

This chapter examines integration requirements for religious servants in relation to the right to freedom of religion and the right of religious groups and persons to equal treatment. In the course of this examination, two main issues were identified.

The first issue concerned the use of integration requirements as an immigration condition. If religious servants do not meet the integration requirements set by the receiving state, they will be denied admission to the territory and will not be able to be engaged by religious communities within that state. In this way integration requirements, like other immigration conditions, form a limitation to the freedom of religious servants and communities. However, it was established that such limitations normally fall outside the scope of the freedom of religion, which does not include a general right to admission for religious servants or a right for religious communities to appoint servants from abroad.

It follows that states are allowed, in principle, to regulate the admission of religious servants by means of integration requirements. Section II.A.ii.d discussed the question of whether or not such regulation should always be considered a restriction of religious communities' freedom to self-organisation. It was submitted, however, that the current approach is acceptable in principle. This position differs somewhat from that taken in chapter 4, for the reason that a religious community's choice for a particular leader or servant is not normally as exclusive as the relationship existing between family members, in particular parents and their children. Nevertheless, it was also argued that the state's competence to regulate the admission of religious servants may not be used to adopt measures that aim either to repress religious communities or effectively inhibit their activities. Support for these exceptions can be found in Articles 9 ECHR and 6 Dutch Constitution.

The second issue encountered concerned the relationship between the concept of integration as defined by the state and the values, norms and practices dictated by religious beliefs. In this respect, it was argued that integration requirements should steer clear of matters within the religious domain. This implies that integration programmes or exams should not concern the correctness or validity of religious prescriptions or interpretations. A fortiori, religious servants may not be asked to subscribe to such rules. This condition follows from the principle of state neutrality and must be met if limitations to the freedom of religion are to be justified, at least under Article 9(2) ECHR.

Nevertheless, it was also submitted that integration measures may be used as an instrument to guard the boundary between the religious domain and the secular or neutral domain of the state. To achieve this purpose, religious servants may be asked to become aware of the place of religion in the legal order of the receiving state and to acquaint themselves with legally established limitations to the freedom of religion. Integration requirements complying with this purpose do not go against the principle of neutrality. The need to protect the separation of church and state can also provide reasonable and objective justification for the unequal treatment occurring when integration requirements are directed specifically towards religious servants.

B. Integration Requirements, EU Law and International Agreements

6

The Right to Free Movement in European Union Law

I. INTRODUCTION

UNDER EUROPEAN UNION (previously European Community) law, nationals of EU Member States have long since had the right to move and reside in a Member State other than that of their nationality. This right has traditionally served to enable the free movement of persons which, together with the free movement of goods, capital and services, underpins the realisation of an internal market as a primary objective of the Union.[1] However, with the introduction of Union citizenship in the Treaty of Maastricht, nationals of EU Member States obtained the right to free movement independent of economic purposes. Together, EU citizenship and the free movement of persons currently provide the basis on which EU citizens are entitled to move and reside in EU Member States, subject to only very limited restrictions.

This chapter describes the legal framework regarding the right to free movement of EU citizens, as well as certain closely related rights. These include, first of all, the right of EU citizens to be accompanied by their family members. On the basis of this right, these family members are also entitled to move and reside in EU Member States regardless of their own nationality. Another closely related right is the right to free movement of nationals of Member States of the European Economic Area (EEA), which is laid down in the Agreement on the European Economic Area (the 'EEA Agreement').[2] For Swiss nationals, a similar right is guaranteed by the EC-Switzerland Agreement on the free movement of persons (the 'EC-Switzerland Agreement').[3]

Free movement rights have also been granted, at least to some extent, to certain categories of third-country nationals under Article 79 TFEU, formerly Article 63 of the Treaty establishing the European Community (TEC)). The latter article provides the legal basis for a common EU

[1] See currently Art 3(3) TEU and Art 26(2) TFEU.

[2] [1994] OJ L1/3.

[3] Agreement between the EC and its Member States, on the one part, and the Swiss Confederation, on the other, on the free movement of persons, [2002] OJ L114/6.

immigration policy, including measures concerning the right of third-country nationals to move between Member States. This extension of free movement rights to third-country nationals is based on a dual rationale. One aim is to promote the integration of third-country nationals by giving them rights comparable to those of EU citizens, while granting such rights to third-country nationals is secondly designed to foster the competitiveness of the EU economy by making the EU an attractive location for highly qualified workers.[4] This chapter discusses the free movement rights granted to third-country nationals by the Long-term Residents Directive (LRD) and the Blue Card Directive (BCD).[5] The Exchange Directive and the Researchers Directive are not taken into account as, given the temporary nature of the residence rights granted under these directives, they are less relevant for the issue of integration forming the object of this study.[6]

The aim of this chapter is to understand the contents and scope of the right of free movement provided for in EU law and of the restrictions imposed on the legislative competence of the Netherlands. In particular, it will be examined whether the relevant provisions of EU law leave Member States room to enact integration requirements, such as those laid down in the Dutch Act on Integration Abroad (AIA). At the end of the chapter, the AIA is assessed to see whether it respects the rights granted by EU law.

II. THE RIGHT TO FREE MOVEMENT OF EU CITIZENS

A. Citizenship and Free Movement of Persons in the TFEU

As stated in the introduction, the right of EU citizens to move and reside in the Member States is linked to the exercise of economic activities, as well as to the status of being an EU citizen. In order to achieve economic integration and an internal market, the TFEU guarantees the free movement of workers (Art 45 and the articles that follow), the right of establishment (Art 49 and the articles that follow) and the free movement of services (Art 56 and the articles that follow). These provisions allow EU citizens to enter and reside in another Member State as a worker, a self-employed person or a provider of services. The personal scope of these treaty provisions has been interpreted broadly so as also to include recipi-

[4] Iglesias Sánchez 2009a, 798–99. In addition, the Long-term Residents Directive also mentions the attainment of an internal market as an underlying motive of the right to free movement of third-country nationals. See also section VI.B below.

[5] Council Directive 2003/109/EC of 25 November 2003, [2004] OJ L16/44 and Council Directive 2009/50/EC of 25 May 2009, [2009] OJ L155/17.

[6] Council Directive 2004/114/EC of 13 December 2004, [2004] OJ L375/12 and Council Directive 2005/71/EC of 12 October 2005, [2005] OJ L289/15.

ents of services.[7] Nevertheless, the right to free movement under the above provisions remains tied to the exercise of some kind of economic activity. By contrast, Article 21 TFEU grants the right to move and reside freely in the territory of the Member States to all EU citizens.[8] This provision was introduced into EU law in the Treaty of Maastricht as part of the provisions on EU citizenship. It constitutes the right of free movement as a citizenship right, rather than as a corollary to economic freedoms.

The right to free movement of EU citizens is, nevertheless, subject to restrictions. As mentioned, Articles 45, 49 and 56 TFEU grant the right to enter and reside in another Member State only to those (economically active) EU citizens coming within the personal scope of these provisions. In addition, this right may be limited on grounds of public policy, public security or public health.[9] Under Article 21 TFEU, the right to free movement laid down therein is subject to the conditions and limitations laid down in the TEU and the TFEU and the measures adopted to give them effect.

Despite the differences in scope and content of the various treaty provisions, the right of EU citizens to free movement has over time become subject to a relatively uniform set of rules and interpretations.[10] The conditions governing this right are currently laid down in the Residence Directive, which is discussed in the following section.[11] First, however, it should be noted that, as a result of transitional measures following the accession of Bulgaria and Romania to the EU on 1 January 2007, the free movement of Bulgarian and Romanian nationals in the other Member States may be subject to restrictions for a limited period of time after their accession.[12] These restrictions concern the right of access to the labour

[7] Condinanzi et al 2008, 22–23. The personal scope of the provisions on free movement of services is also not restricted to EU nationals as it includes third-country nationals who are 'posted workers': persons employed by an undertaking in one Member State and then posted in another Member State in order to provide services there. See CoJ 9 August 1994, C-43/93 [1994] ECR I-03803 (*Vander Elst*), para 26. However, it must be noted that the provision or receipt of services is by definition of a temporary nature, see CoJ 30 November 1995, C-55/94 [1995] ECR I-4165 (*Gebhard*), paras 25–28 and CoJ 19 October 2004, C-200/02 [2004] ECR I-9925 (*Chen*), para 22. This means that the right of residence of service providers and recipients is also temporary, which makes it unlikely that this right would be conditioned upon fulfilment of integration conditions. The position of service providers and recipients (including posted workers) is consequently not addressed separately in this chapter.

[8] Some rights of free movement for economically inactive persons already existed before the introduction of EU citizenship, see Spaventa 2007, 114.

[9] See Arts 45(3), 52 and 62 TFEU.

[10] Condinanzi et al 2008, 22.

[11] Directive 2004/38/EC, [2004] OJ L158/77. This directive replaced the previously existing patchwork of directives relating to the free movement of EU citizens and their family members and to a large extent codified CoJ case law on this topic until the moment of its adoption. Boeles et al observed that the Residence Directive does not regulate the right of residence of recipients of services under Art 57 TFEU (Boeles et al 2009, 63). See, however, n 7.

[12] See Part 1 of Annexes VI and VII to the Act concerning the conditions of accession of the Republic of Bulgaria and Romania and the adjustments to the Treaties on which the European Union is founded, [2005] OJ L157. The Netherlands has made use of the

market and do not affect the right of Bulgarian and Romanian nationals to enter and reside in the other Member States.[13] The transitional measures governing the position of Bulgarian and Romanian nationals are, therefore, not of relevance for the purpose of this chapter and so are not discussed separately.

B. The Residence Directive

With regard to the right of EU citizens to move and reside in the Member States, the Residence Directive distinguishes between the rights of exit and entry, the right to short-term residence (up to three months), the right to residence for more than three months and the right to permanent residence. Considering the object of this study, the discussion in this section focuses on the provisions concerning the acquisition of the right to residence for more than three months.

The Residence Directive applies to all Union citizens who move or reside in a Member State other than that of which they are a national.[14] According to Article 20(1) TFEU, a Union citizen is every person with the nationality of an EU Member State. EU citizens are entitled to stay in another Member State for more than three months, subject to the conditions laid down in Article 7(1) of the Residence Directive. Basically, this provision grants the right of residence to EU citizens who are economically active (as workers or self-employed persons) or who have health insurance and sufficient resources to ensure that they will not become a burden on the social assistance system of the host Member State. Students are entitled to residence, provided they have health insurance and can assure the host Member State that they will not become a burden on the social assistance system.

With regard to the condition of having sufficient resources, Article 8(4) of the directive states that Member States may not require a fixed amount, but must take into account the personal situation of the person concerned. This provision reflects CoJ case law, according to which exceptions to the right to free movement of EU citizens must be interpreted in a restrictive

opportunity provided for in paras 2 and 7 to continue the transitional measures until 1 January 2012, after which they were further extended to 1 January 2014. See *Parliamentary Papers II* 2008–2009, 29 407, No 98, 3–4 and *Parliamentary Papers II* 2011–2012, 29 407, No 132, 3.

[13] Derogation from the provisions of the Residence Directive relating to entry and residence is possible only when these provisions 'cannot be dissociated from those of Regulation (EEC) No 1612/68 [on labour market access, *KV*] whose application is deferred to pursuant to paragraphs 2 to 5 and 7 and 8 [. . .], to the extent necessary for the application of [those paragraphs]'. See para 9 of Part 1 of Annexes VI and VII to the Act of Accession.

[14] Art 3(1) Residence Directive.

manner.[15] More specifically, in the case of *Baumbast*, the Court found that Article 18(1) TEC (now Art 21(1) TFEU) directly confers on all EU citizens the right to move and reside freely in the territory of the Member States and that the conditions and limitations governing the exercise of this right must be applied in compliance with the general principles of EU law, in particular the principle of proportionality.[16] It follows from this judgment that the conditions of Article 7(1) Residence Directive may not be applied more strictly than is necessary to prevent migrating EU citizens from becoming an unreasonable burden on the public finances of the host Member State.

Article 27(1) Residence Directive provides that the right of EU citizens to reside in the Member States may be restricted on grounds of public policy, public security or public health. Thus Member States may refuse the residence of EU citizens on the basis of one of these exceptions. Application of these exceptions must nevertheless be in compliance with the conditions and procedural safeguards laid down in Chapter VI of the Residence Directive, as well as with the general principles of EU law.[17] Article 27(1) explicitly provides that the specified grounds may not be invoked to serve economic ends.

For EU citizens falling within the scope of the Residence Directive, the acquisition of the right of residence is subject to no conditions other than the above. There is consequently no scope for Member States to make these persons' residence subject to an integration exam abroad, nor to any other conditions relating to their integration.

C. Situations not Covered by EU Law?

It follows from the previous sections that every EU citizen is, in principle, entitled to reside in another Member State on the basis of the treaty provisions relating to the right of free movement, in particular Article 21 TFEU. This right is subject only to limited conditions, which must moreover be applied in conformity with the general principles of EU law. It may therefore be concluded that, in most cases, the residence of EU citizens in another Member State will be a matter of EU law.

Nevertheless, there may be situations in which EU citizens do not meet the conditions for exercising the right of free movement under EU law.[18] In such situations it remains within the host Member State's power to

[15] Boeles et al 2009, 63–64.

[16] CoJ 17 September 2002, C-413/99 [2002] ECR I-7091 *(Baumbast and R)*, paras 81, 84 and 91. See also CoJ 7 September 2004, C-456/02 [2004] ECR I-7535 (*Trojani*), para 34 and *Chen* (n 7), para 32.

[17] Condinanzi et al 2008, 95. This was decided in, eg, CoJ 29 April 2004, C-482/01 and 493/01 [2004] ECR I-5257 (*Orfanopoulos & Oliveri*), paras 47 and 90–99.

[18] For an example of such a case, see the judgment in *Trojani* (n 16).

grant a right of residence as a matter of national law. This is explicitly provided for by Article 37 of the Residence Directive, which allows Member States to maintain or adopt more favourable national provisions.

Provided the granting of a national residence right does not come within the scope of any other provisions of EU law,[19] it must be assumed that this right is granted subject to national conditions, possibly including conditions of integration. However, as said above, this possibility only exists with regard to EU citizens who do not meet the limited conditions imposed by the Residence Directive or whose right of residence has been terminated on grounds of public policy, public security or public health. Apart from the fact that this situation will not frequently occur, it is also rather unlikely that, under these circumstances, Member States would be willing to grant a right of residence under national law. It must be concluded that, although the possibility of imposing integration conditions for the admission of EU citizens is perhaps not entirely non-existent, it is of little practical relevance.

III. FAMILY MEMBERS OF EU CITIZENS

A. Free Movement or Family Reunification?

EU law grants the right of residence in the Member States not only to EU citizens, but also to their family members. As in the case of EU citizens, the provisions relating to the residence of family members are laid down in the Residence Directive. However, the rights of family members do not have an explicit basis in the TFEU. Instead, these rights derive from the right to free movement of EU citizens, with the underlying assumption being that EU citizens could be deterred from exercising this right if they were not allowed to bring their family members with them.[20] In its case law concerning the admission of family members, the CoJ has relied not only on the provisions of the TFEU and of secondary legislation relating to the free movement of EU citizens, but also on the right to family life as a general principle of EU law.[21] It is concluded that the rights discussed in this section are better understood as constituting a right to family reunification of EU citizens than as a right to free movement of their family

[19] It may be observed that the CoJ has in the past determined the scope of EU law rather expansively. In *Trojani*, eg, the Court decided that the applicant fell within the personal scope of Art 18 TEC and hence of Art 12 TEC, despite the fact that his right of residence had been granted under national law. Where, however, the case concerns admission, this implies that the applicant does not yet have a right of residence; therefore the reasoning followed in *Trojani* cannot apply.

[20] Spaventa 2007, 30; Boeles et al 2009, 72.

[21] Boeles et al 2009, 73–74. See also Vermeulen 2008, 496.

members.[22] Nevertheless, because of their close relationship to the free movement of EU citizens, the rights of family members are discussed in this chapter.

The derivative character of the above rights means that family members of an EU citizen are only entitled to residence in the Member State in which that EU citizen resides.[23] Another consequence is that family members can only claim a right of residence in situations where refusal to admit them would impede the EU citizen's exercising his or her rights and freedoms granted by the TFEU.[24] This does not necessarily imply that the right to family reunification is limited to situations in which the EU citizen has physically moved to a Member State other than that of his nationality. In *Carpenter*, the CoJ accepted that EU citizens are entitled to be joined by their family members in their own Member State when they provide cross-border services in another Member State.[25] Additionally, the Court accepted that EU citizens are allowed to be accompanied by their family members when they move back to their own country after having exercised their right of free movement elsewhere in the EU. This right exists irrespective of whether the EU citizen is going to engage in economic activity in his or her own Member State upon his or her return.[26] More recently, it has become clear that national measures concerning family reunification can also impede the rights of EU citizens outside the free movement context. In *Ruiz Zambrano*, the CoJ formulated as a general criterion that Article 20 TFEU 'precludes national measures which have the effect of depriving Union citizens of the genuine enjoyment of the substance of the rights conferred by virtue of that status'. In that case, the Court found that the right of dependent children, who are EU citizens, to reside in the territory of the EU can be impeded if a right of residence is not granted to their parents or carers (see further section III.E).[27]

Notwithstanding this case law, there are still wholly or purely internal situations, in which the EU national remains in the Member State of his or her nationality and the exercise of his or her rights or freedoms granted by EU law would not be impeded if the admission of family members were to be refused. These situations fall outside the scope of EU law, consequently the EU citizens concerned cannot rely on EU law to claim a right to family reunification.[28] It is therefore possible (and this is also the case in

[22] cp CoJ 11 December 2007, C-291/05 [2007] ECR I-10719 (*Eind*), paras 23–24; CoJ 5 May 2011, C-434/09 [2011] ECR 0000 (*McCarthy*), para 42 and CoJ (Grand Chamber) 15 November 2011, C-256/11 [2011] ECR 00000 (*Dereci*), para 55.

[23] cp Art 3(1) Residence Directive.

[24] Luijendijk 2005, 156–57; CoJ 27 October 1982, C-35/82 and 36/82 [1982] ECR. 3723 (*Morson & Jhanjan*); *McCarthy* (n 22), para 54.

[25] CoJ 11 July 2002, C-60/00 [2002] ECR I-6279 (*Carpenter*), para 46.

[26] CoJ 7 July 1992, C-370/90 [1992] ECR I-4265 (*Surinder Singh*), para 21; *Eind* (n 22), paras 35–38.

[27] CoJ (Grand Chamber) 8 March 2011, C-34/09 [2011] ECR 0000 (*Ruiz Zambrano*), para 44.

[28] eg, *Morson and Jhanjan* (n 24), para 16; CoJ 5 June 1997, C-64/96 and 65/96 [1997] ECR

the Netherlands) that, within one Member State, nationals of that state who do not exercise the rights granted to them as EU citizens face tougher conditions for family reunification than nationals of other Member States. This situation is commonly referred to as 'reverse discrimination'. Notwithstanding the arguments made by various authors, neither the CoJ nor the EU legislator have as yet accepted that the right to family reunification is a general right that comes with the mere status of being an EU citizen.[29]

B. Family Members Entitled to Entry and Residence in the Member States

Family members of EU citizens have a right of residence in the Member State where the EU citizen resides, regardless of their own nationality. This follows logically from the fact that their rights derive from those of EU citizens: it is their capacity as family members that matters rather than their coming within the personal scope of the treaty provisions on free movement. Thus, the definition of who is a 'family member' in Article 2(2) Residence Directive covers EU citizens as well as third-country nationals.

Under the Residence Directive, the family members entitled to be admitted to the Member State where the EU citizen resides are:

- the spouse or registered partner (if the legislation of the host Member State treats registered partnerships as equivalent to marriage);
- the children, as well as the children of the partner or spouse, provided that they are under 21 or dependent on the parents;
- the dependent direct relatives in the ascending line, as well as those of the spouse or partner.[30]

The latter category of family members is not taken into account if the EU citizen is a student residing under the conditions set out in Article 7(1)(c)

I-3171 (*Uecker and Jacquet*), paras 16–20; CoJ (Grand Chamber) 1 April 2008, C-212/06 [2008] ECR I-1683 (*Government of the French Community and Walloon Government*), para 33; *McCarthy* (n 22), para 54; *Dereci* (n 22), para 60.

[29] Toner 2004, 75–77. For a comprehensive argument supporting the elimination of reverse discrimination, see Spaventa 2007, 113–34. See also Verschueren 2009 and Walter 2008. The issue of reverse discrimination is discussed in more detail in ch 10.

[30] It may be observed that the Residence Directive does not regulate the position of all persons entitled to entry and residence as family members of EU citizens since it only applies to family members of EU citizens who have moved to another Member State. As discussed in section III.A, a right to family reunification may also exist for EU citizens who have not moved to another Member State (cp the *Carpenter* case). It is assumed here that, in such a situation, the conditions governing the entry and residence of the family members (and the definition of who is a family member) are in principle the same as those laid down in the Residence Directive.

of the Residence Directive.[31] In that case, dependent relatives in the ascending line are covered by the provisions of Article 3(2) of the directive. According to this Article, the Member States shall 'facilitate' the entry and residence of certain categories of family members not covered by the definition of Article 2(2). The contents of the obligation to 'facilitate' entry and residence are discussed below (section III.D).

Lastly, the Residence Directive applies irrespective of whether a family member who is a third-country national had legal residence in the EU before joining the EU citizen. The requirement of previous lawful residence appeared to follow from the CoJ's judgment in *Akrich*, where the Court held that the Moroccan spouse of an EU citizen could not 'repair' his irregular residence status by moving with his wife to another Member State.[32] However, the Court later dismissed this position in *Metock*, where it concluded that the condition of previous lawful residence was incompatible with the Residence Directive.[33] In the same judgment the CoJ determined that the directive applies irrespective of when or where the marriage between the EU citizen and the third-country national took place or how the third-country national entered the host Member State.[34]

C. Conditions for the Entry and Residence of Family Members

The conditions for exercising the right of free movement by family members of EU citizens are also laid down in the Residence Directive. These conditions may differ depending on whether the family member has the nationality of an EU Member State or of a third country.[35] The discussion in this section again focuses on the conditions for residence of more than three months.

Family members of EU citizens are entitled to residence if they accompany or join an EU citizen satisfying the conditions set out in Article 7(1)(a), (b) or (c) Residence directive (see section II). This condition is the same for family members who are EU nationals themselves as for third-country nationals.[36] Furthermore, as is the case for EU citizens, the right of family members to enter and reside in the Member States may be restricted on grounds of public policy, public security or public health. Again, however,

[31] See Art 7(4) Residence Directive.

[32] CoJ 23 September 2003, C-109/01 [2003] ECR I-9607 (*Akrich*), para 50.

[33] CoJ (Grand Chamber) 25 July 2008, C-127/08, [2008] ECR I-6241 (*Metock and others*), para 80.

[34] ibid, para 99.

[35] Of course, a family member who is an EU national may well be entitled to entry and residence independently of the person to whose family he or she belongs. This is even more likely since the right of free movement is linked to the mere status of being an EU citizen and does not necessarily require the exercise of any economic activity. The conditions for exercising the right of free movement by EU citizens were discussed in section II.

[36] Art 7(1)(d) and (2) Residence Directive.

such restrictions are subject to compliance with the conditions and procedural safeguards provided in the Residence Directive, as well as with the general principles of EU law. The relevant provisions apply regardless of the nationality of the family member concerned.

For persons who are family members of EU citizens within the meaning of Article 2(2) Residence Directive, no residence conditions may be imposed other than those set out above. For these persons, therefore, Member States are not entitled to make admission to their territory dependent on integration conditions. The following subsections consider the position of family members not falling within the scope of Article 2(2) Residence Directive. Section III.D concerns family members coming within the scope of Article 3(2) Residence Directive, whereas section III.E deals with persons entitled to reside in a Member State because of being the primary carers of their children.

D. Article 3(2) Residence Directive: 'Facilitating' Entry and Residence

In principle, EU citizens are not entitled to family reunification with family members other than those mentioned in Article 2(2) Residence Directive. Nevertheless, Article 3(2) Residence Directive contains an obligation for Member States to facilitate, in accordance with their national legislation, the entry and residence of persons who are dependants or members of the household of EU citizens in the Member State of origin. Article 3(2) also covers family members who, because of serious health reasons, strictly require to be cared for by the Union citizen, the unmarried partner with whom an EU citizen has a durable and duly attested relationship and the dependent parents of EU citizens who are students (and the parents of their spouses or partners).[37]

Article 3(2) Residence Directive raises the question of what exactly the obligation to 'facilitate' entry and residence entails and, for the purposes of this study, whether this provision allows the admission of family members to be made dependent on integration conditions.[38] It may be derived from the wording of the provision, as well as from its context, that Member States are not required to grant those covered by Article 3(2) a right of

[37] Art 7(4) Residence Directive.

[38] Before the Residence Directive entered into force, similar obligations were laid down in Art 10(2) of Council Regulation 1612/68/EEC of 15 October 1968 on freedom of movement for workers within the Community (OJ Series I Chapter 1968(II), 475) and Art 1(2) of Council Directive 73/148/EEC of 21 May 1973 on the abolition of restrictions on movement and residence within the Community for nationals of Member States with regard to establishment and the provision of services ([1973] OJ L172/14). However these provisions have not been subject to interpretation by the CoJ, see Toner 2004, 51. At the time of writing, preliminary questions concerning the interpretation of Art 3(2) Residence Directive had been put to the CoJ in the case of *Rahman* (C-83/11). The Conclusions of the Advocate General were delivered on 27 March 2012.

entry and residence on the same footing as the family members referred to in Article 2(2). Instead, the reference to the national legislations of the Member States suggests that it remains up to those states to determine whether they choose to grant a right of entry and residence to the family members concerned and, if so, under which conditions.[39]

Nonetheless, if a request for family reunification is made with regard to a person covered by Article 3(2), the Member State concerned has to assess this request on an individual basis to see whether a right of entry or residence may be granted. This clearly follows from the provision itself, which states that 'the host Member State shall undertake an extensive examination of the personal circumstances of the persons concerned and shall justify any denial of entry or residence to these people'. Additionally, the preamble of the directive states that the situation of family members not covered by Article 2(2) must be 'examined by the host Member State on the basis of its own national legislation in order to decide whether entry and residence could be granted to such persons'.[40]

The term 'facilitate' suggests that the examination conducted by the Member State should, in principle, be aimed at granting a right of entry or residence on an individual basis. This implies that due weight must be given to the interests of the family and that refusal of entry or residence must be based on reasons of sufficient substance. All the circumstances of the case have to be taken into account in this respect, in particular the family member's relationship with, and his or her financial or physical dependence on the Union citizen. The legislation of a Member State that gives effect to Article 3(2) Residence Directive also has to be in conformity with EU fundamental rights and with the general principles of EU law. Here, the right to respect for family life is of particular relevance.[41] While this right does not offer any more specific criteria for the implementation of Article 3(2) than those set out above, it may serve as additional support for a decision in favour of family reunification.

It may be concluded that Article 3(2) Residence Directive does not, in principle, rule out Member States' competence to make the admission of persons covered by this provision dependent on integration conditions. However, requests for family reunification must always be assessed on an individual basis, with a view to granting a right of entry or residence. Thus if a family member does not meet the integration conditions imposed by a Member State, his or her request will still have to be individually examined to see whether the personal circumstances nevertheless require entry or residence to be granted. This examination and the possibility of

[39] See also Toner 2004, 67.

[40] Preamble, recital 6.

[41] The right to family life is laid down in Art 7 of the EU Charter of Fundamental Rights. It is also laid down in Art 8 ECHR and as such constitutes a general principle of EU law on the basis of Art 6(3) TEU.

granting residence have to be provided for in the national legislation of the Member State in the form, for example, of a hardship clause.

E. Additional Residence Rights for Carers: from *Baumbast* to *Ruiz Zambrano*

As a final observation with regard to the family members of EU citizens, attention may be drawn to a series of CoJ judgments that identify new rights of residence in addition to those covered by the Residence Directive. These judgments concern the rights of children, as well as those of the persons responsible for them as their primary carers.

First, in *Baumbast*, the Court addressed the position of an EU migrant worker's children who moved with that worker to another Member State and enrolled in the local school system. The CoJ decided that, in such circumstances, the children remained entitled to reside in that Member State under Article 12 of Regulation 1612/68 to pursue their education, even after their parent ceased to be a migrant worker. The Court also held that the children were entitled to be accompanied by the other parent, who was their primary carer, so that their right of residence would be facilitated. With regard to both the children and their carer, the right of residence was held to exist irrespective of their nationality.[42] In the recent cases of *Ibrahim* and *Teixeira* the CoJ not only confirmed its judgment in *Baumbast*, but also specified that the right of residence of the child's carer is based only on Article 12 Regulation 1612/68 and is not subject to the conditions laid down in the Residence Directive.[43] In particular, the Court held that the right continues to exist even if the parent has insufficient resources to avoid becoming a burden on the social assistance system of the host Member State. It did not matter in that respect that, in *Ibrahim*, the parent who was an EU migrant worker had only held that status for less than a year.

In *Chen* the situation was somewhat different as the child was an EU citizen who had a right of residence on the basis of Article 21 TFEU (then Art 18 TEC) instead of Article 12 Regulation 1612/68. However, as in *Baumbast*, the Court held that the person who was the child's primary carer (in this case her Chinese mother) was entitled to stay with her because otherwise the child's right of residence could not be effectively realised.[44] This decision was confirmed in *Ruiz Zambrano*, where the Court decided that a right of residence had to be granted to the father (a Columbian national) of two dependent children who had Belgian nation-

[42] *Baumbast* (n 16), paras 63 and 75.

[43] CoJ (Grand Chamber) 23 February 2010, C-310/08 [2010] ECR I-01065 (*Ibrahim*), para 50; CoJ (Grand Chamber) 23 February 2010, C-480/08 [2010] ECR I-01107 (*Teixeira*), paras 66–70.

[44] *Chen* (n 7), para 47.

ality and were therefore entitled to reside in the EU on the basis of Article 20 TFEU.[45]

The above case law shows that, in addition to the rights governed by the Residence Directive, Member States may be obliged to allow the residence in their territory of EU citizens and third-country nationals on the grounds that these persons are the primary carers of children who are EU citizens and whose rights would otherwise be impeded. The precise extent of this obligation is not yet clear.[46] Given the stance taken by the CoJ in *Ibrahim* and *Teixeira*, however, it seems almost certain that conditions relating to this right of residence (including integration requirements) will be considered incompatible with the relevant provisions (Art 12 Regulation 1612/68 and Art 21 TFEU). It does not seem to be relevant in this respect whether the parent was already residing in the Member State concerned when the child gained his or her right of residence, providing the parent is the primary carer and the child is not able to exercise his or her right independently.

IV. THE RIGHT TO FREE MOVEMENT OF NATIONALS OF THE EEA MEMBER STATES AND THEIR FAMILY MEMBERS

A third category of persons with free movement rights similar to those of EU citizens includes nationals of the States Parties to the Agreement on the European Economic Area (the EEA Agreement),[47] and the family members of those nationals, regardless of their nationality. The EEA Agreement, to which both the EU and its Member States are parties, contains provisions on the free movement of workers, the right to establishment and the free movement of services that are substantially the same as those laid down in the TFEU (section II).[48] On the basis of these provisions, nationals of EEA Member States are entitled to move and reside freely in the territories of the EU Member States. Family members of EEA nationals are not mentioned in the EEA Agreement. Like the family members of EU citizens however (section III), they derive their right of entry and residence from the right to free movement of the EEA nationals.

When the EEA Agreement was signed in 1994, its provisions regarding the free movement of persons corresponded to those of the *acquis*

[45] *Ruiz Zambrano* (n 27), para 45.

[46] See the Conclusions of the Advocate General in the case of *Iida*, C-40/11. This case concerns a Japanese father who relied on EU law to obtain residence in Germany, in order to be able to exercise his visiting rights to his daughter who lived with her mother in Austria.

[47] [1994] OJ L1/3. Apart from the 27 EU Member States, the states parties to this Agreement are Iceland, Norway and Liechtenstein. Iceland is currently a candidate Member State of the EU, negotiations on accession were opened on 27 June 2010 (see http://ec.europa.eu/enlargement).

[48] See Arts 28 and following, 31 and following and 36 and following of the EEA Agreement.

communautaire at that moment.[49] However, an EEA Joint Committee was created with the task of monitoring developments in EU law and incorporating them into EEA law.[50] In December 2007 this Joint Committee adopted a Decision incorporating the EU Residence Directive into the EEA framework. Consequently, the provisions of this directive are now equally applicable to EEA citizens and their family members, provided they come within the scope of the free movement provisions in the EEA Agreement.[51] The Joint Committee also monitors case law of the CoJ and of the European Free Trade Association (EFTA) Court to ensure the homogeneous application of provisions of the EEA Agreement with the corresponding provisions of EU law.[52]

A difference between the EEA Agreement and the TFEU is that the former does not contain any provisions on citizenship comparable to Articles 20 and 21 TFEU. As a result, EEA nationals are not entitled to free movement merely on the grounds of their nationality. The right to entry and residence is therefore available only to EEA nationals who move for the purpose of exercising economic activities, as foreseen by the Agreement.[53] Despite the CoJ's expansive interpretation of the economic free movement provisions, it follows that the rights of EEA nationals (and consequently those of their family members) are more limited than those of EU citizens. This difference may become more significant in the future if free movement rights are increasingly linked to EU citizenship instead of to market participation.[54]

Where EEA nationals and their family members have a right to enter and reside in EU Member States, it follows from the above that the conditions governing these rights are the same as for EU citizens and their family members. Consequently, it may be concluded that the admission of EEA nationals and their family members who are entitled to free movement may not be conditioned upon the fulfilment of integration conditions. For family members falling within the scope of Article 3(2) Residence Directive, the Member States are obliged to facilitate entry and residence subject to the conditions discussed in section III.D.[55]

[49] Luijendijk 2005, 155.

[50] Weiss and Wooldridge 2007, 207.

[51] Decision of the EEA Joint Committee No 158/2007 of 7 December 2007, [2008] OJ L124/20. The provisions of the directive have been incorporated into Annexes V and VIII to the EEA Agreement on the free movement of workers and the right to establishment.

[52] Art 105 EEA Agreement.

[53] This is confirmed in the preamble of the above Decision of the EEA Joint Committee concerning the Residence Directive. Recital 8 of this preamble states that 'the concept of "Union Citizenship" is not included in the Agreement'. In addition, both Annexes V and VIII to the EEA Agreement state that the Residence Directive shall apply 'to the fields covered by those annexes'; in other words, to the free movement of workers and the right to establishment.

[54] Luijendijk 2005, 155–56; Hedemann-Robinson 2001, 539–40.

[55] It is not entirely clear whether the reference to 'family members' in Decision 158/2007 of the EEA Joint Committee (n 51) also includes the family members meant in Art 3(2)

V. SWISS NATIONALS AND THEIR FAMILY MEMBERS

A. Free Movement of Swiss Nationals: the EC-Switzerland Agreement

For Swiss nationals and their family members, the right to free movement is regulated by the Agreement between the EC and its Member States on the one hand, and the Swiss Confederation on the other, on the free movement of persons (the 'EC-Switzerland Agreement').[56] This Agreement aims, inter alia, to accord to nationals of Switzerland a right of entry and residence in the territory of the EU Member States.[57] Provisions relating to the entry and residence of Swiss nationals and their family members are laid down in Articles 3–7 and in Annex I pertaining to the Agreement.

The right to free movement of Swiss nationals is clearly modelled on that of EU citizens and reflects the *acquis communautaire* as it stood when the EC-Switzerland Agreement was signed.[58] Article 16(1) provides that

> the Contracting Parties shall, in order to attain the objectives pursued by the Agreement, take all measures necessary to ensure that rights and obligations equivalent to those contained in the legal acts of the EC to which reference is made are applied in relations between them.

It is unclear whether this obligation also concerns the rights and obligations laid down in the EU Residence Directive. Although this directive was adopted after the entry into force of the EC-Switzerland Agreement and is not mentioned by it, it replaces a number of directives to which the Agreement refers.[59] Elements of the Residence Directive that are more favourable than those of the EC-Switzerland Agreement include, for example, the lack of a housing requirement for the family reunification of Swiss workers and a right of family reunification with registered partners.

Like the EEA Agreement, the EC-Switzerland Agreement does not include provisions on citizenship comparable to those of the TFEU. The CoJ has also held on several occasions that the objective of the

Residence Directive who are third-country nationals. According to the Joint Declaration attached to the decision, the EEA Agreement does not apply to third-country nationals. An exception is made for family members of EEA nationals 'as their rights are corollary to the right of free movement of EEA nationals', but the term 'family members' is not defined. Given that the obligation laid down in Art 3(2) Residence Directive also serves to remove obstacles for the free movement of EU citizens, it is assumed here that the same obligation exists under the EEA Agreement.

56 [2002] OJ L114/6.

57 Art 1(a) and (c) EC-Switzerland Agreement.

58 Luijendijk 2005, 155. See also Art 16(2) of the Agreement which states that, in so far as the application of the Agreement involves concepts of Community law, the case law of the CoJ prior to the signature of the Agreement shall be taken into account. On this provision, see Boillet 2010, 54–58.

59 Boillet 2010, 22.

EC-Switzerland Agreement is not for Switzerland to join the internal market of the EU, with the aim of removing all obstacles to an area of total free movement analogous to that provided by a national market. The Court therefore determined that 'the interpretation given to the provisions of Community law concerning the internal market cannot be automatically applied in analogy to the interpretation of the Agreement, unless there are express provisions to that effect laid down by the Agreement itself'.[60] It follows that the right to free movement of Swiss nationals will not necessarily develop in the same way as the right to free movement of EU citizens. Below, a summary is given of the provisions relating to the entry and residence of Swiss nationals and their family as they currently stand.

B. The Right to Entry and Residence of Swiss Nationals and their Family Members

Swiss nationals are entitled to enter EU Member States if they are in the possession of a valid identity card or passport. Family members who are not nationals of an EU Member State or Switzerland may require an entry visa. However, the Contracting Parties must grant these persons every facility for obtaining any necessary visas.[61] It is submitted that the issue of an entry visa to family members of Swiss nationals may not be subjected to any conditions other than those that must be fulfilled in order to qualify for entry or residence under the Agreement as this would clearly undermine the Agreement's effectiveness in relation to the stated objective of according a right of entry to Swiss nationals.

A right of residence is available to Swiss nationals who qualify as workers, self-employed persons or persons who are not economically active.[62] With the exception of workers employed for a period of less than one year, these persons must be granted a residence permit for at least five years.[63] For workers and self-employed persons the only conditions for the issue of a residence permit are possession of the document with which they

[60] CoJ 12 November 2009, C-351/08 [2009] ECR I-10777 (*Grimme*), paras 27 and 29; CoJ 11 February 2010, C-541/08 [2010] ECR I-0000 (*Fokus Invest*), paras 27 and 28 and CoJ 15 July 2010, C-70/09 [2010] ECR I-0000 (*Hengartner and Gasser*), paras 41 and 42.

[61] Art 1(1) of Annex I to the EC-Switzerland Agreement.

[62] Art 4 and 6 EC-Switzerland Agreement. A right of residence also exists for providers and recipients of services under Art 5 EC-Switzerland Agreement. However, this right exists only for the duration of the service and is therefore necessarily temporary. This follows from the CoJ's judgment in *Gebhard* (n 7), which predates the signing of the EC-Switzerland Agreement and is therefore relevant to its interpretation (cp Art 16(2) of the Agreement). As stated above, the right to temporary residence is unlikely to be made subject to integration conditions. Therefore the residence rights of providers and recipients of services are not discussed in this chapter.

[63] Arts 6(1), 12(1) and 24(1) of Annex I EC-Switzerland Agreement.

entered the EU Member State and proof of their employment or self-employment. Persons who are not economically active must demonstrate that they have sufficient financial means not to have to apply for social benefits during their stay and comprehensive health insurance. Students, who are also included in the Agreement as not economically active persons, must demonstrate that they have sufficient financial means to ensure that neither they nor their family members will make any claim for social security, that they are registered for a vocational training course at an approved establishment and that they have comprehensive health insurance.[64]

Swiss nationals with the right to reside in an EU Member State are entitled to be joined by their family members, regardless of their nationality.[65] Consequently, as for family members of EU and EEA nationals, the right of residence of family members of Swiss nationals depends on the exercising of the right of free movement by those Swiss nationals. According to the definition in the EC-Switzerland Agreement, family members are:

- the spouse and relatives in the descending line, the latter if they are under the age of 21 and dependent;
- dependent relatives in the ascending line of the Swiss national and his or her spouse;
- in the case of a student, the spouse and dependent children.[66]

With regard to the family members of workers, the EC-Switzerland Agreement requires the worker to have adequate housing.[67] Other than that, the only conditions for the residence of family members of Swiss nationals are that they must possess the document with which they entered the territory and proof of their family relationship and, if applicable, their dependency.[68]

As is the case for EU citizens and their family members (sections II.B and III.C), Swiss nationals and their family members may be refused entry and residence on the grounds of public policy, public security and public health.[69] However, it may be concluded from the above that the enacting of integration conditions would be contrary to the provisions of the EC-Switzerland Agreement on the right of entry and residence of Swiss

[64] Art 24(4) Annex I EC-Switzerland Agreement.

[65] Arts 7(d) and 3 of Annex I EC-Switzerland Agreement.

[66] Art 3(2) Annex I EC-Switzerland Agreement. It may be observed that this definition is more limited than that in the EU Residence Directive as it does not mention persons with whom the Swiss national has entered into a registered partnership (section III). As mentioned above (section V.A), it is unclear whether the right to family reunification must be applied in accordance with the Residence Directive as this directive is not explicitly referred to in the Agreement.

[67] Art 3(1) Annex I EC-Switzerland Agreement. Again, it is unclear whether this requirement is still valid as it is not included in the Residence Directive.

[68] Art 3(3) Annex I EC-Switzerland Agreement.

[69] Art 5 Annex I EC-Switzerland Agreement.

nationals and their family members. Consequently, such conditions may not be imposed on persons coming within the scope of this Agreement.

C. Other Family Members: the Obligation to Facilitate Entry and Residence

As a final observation, it must be mentioned that Article 3(2) Annex I to the EC-Switzerland Agreement contains a clause similar to Article 3(2) Residence Directive (section III.D). According to this provision, the Contracting Parties have agreed to facilitate the admission of family members who do not have a right to free movement, but who are dependent on the Swiss national or who lived with that national in the country of origin. It is submitted that this 'obligation to facilitate' corresponds to that laid down in the Residence Directive. This means that EU Member States may set conditions (including integration conditions) for the entry and residence of the family members covered by this provision, but that requests for family reunification must always be subject to an individual assessment with a view to granting admission.

VI. THIRD-COUNTRY NATIONALS WHO ARE LONG-TERM RESIDENTS AND THEIR FAMILY MEMBERS

A. The Long-term Residents Directive

One more category of beneficiaries of the right to free movement in the EU is that of third-country nationals who have obtained the status of 'long-term resident'. Unlike EU citizens, long-term resident third-country nationals ('long-term residents') do not derive their right of free movement from the provisions of the TFEU on citizenship or the free movement of persons. Instead, a legal basis can be found in the treaty provisions concerning policies on border checks, asylum and immigration.[70]

Before the Lisbon Treaty entered into force, Article 61 TEC provided for the Council to adopt a number of measures 'in order to establish progressively an area of freedom, security and justice'. These included measures 'in the fields of . . . immigration and safeguarding the rights of third country nationals', more specifically measures regarding 'conditions of entry and residence' and 'defining the rights and conditions under which nationals of third countries who are legally resident in a Member State may reside in other Member States'.[71] The wording of the relevant provi-

[70] Part III, Title V, Chapter 2 TFEU (formerly Part III, Title IV TEC).
[71] Arts 61(b) and 63(3) and (4) TEC.

sions of the TFEU is slightly different, as Articles 67(2) and 79(1) TFEU provide for the Union to develop a common immigration policy which is fair towards third-country nationals and ensures the fair treatment of third-country nationals legally residing in the Member States. For this purpose, measures are to be adopted concerning 'the conditions of entry and residence' and 'the definition of the rights of third country nationals residing legally in a Member State, including the conditions governing freedom of movement and of residence in other Member States'.[72] Article 45(2) of the EU Charter of Fundamental Rights also provides that the right of free movement and residence may be granted, in accordance with the Treaties, to third-country nationals who are legally resident in the territory of a Member State. This illustrates that the right to free movement is considered in the EU legal order as a fundamental right, which is available to EU citizens but may also be extended to third-country nationals.

The right of free movement of long-term resident third-country nationals is regulated in the Long-term Residents Directive (LRD), which was adopted on the basis of Articles 63(3) and (4) TEC.[73] The deadline for implementing this directive expired on 23 January 2006. The LRD sets out both the terms under which third-country nationals must be granted the status of long-term resident in a Member State and the conditions governing the right of residence in another Member State.[74] The terms relating to the conferral of long-term resident status are not of interest for the purpose of this study as this status can only be obtained after five years of legal residence. Instead, the discussion in this chapter focuses on the conditions under which third-country nationals with long-term resident status are entitled to enter and reside in another Member State. Although more restricted, the right of long-term residents to some extent resembles the right of free movement of EU citizens. Like EU citizens, long-term residents who move to another Member State are entitled to be joined by their family members. Their position is discussed in section VI.E.

B. Objectives

The LRD thus determines the terms under which long-term residents may take up residence in another Member State. The preamble provides some information as to the underlying objectives pursued by the directive. Recital 2 refers to the Conclusions of the European Council held in Tampere in 1999, where it was stated that the legal status of third-country

[72] Art 79(2)(a) and (b) TFEU.

[73] Council Directive 2003/109/EC of 25 November 2003, [2004] OJ L16/44, as amended by Directive 2011/51/EU of the European Parliament and the Council of 11 May 2011, [2011] OJ L132/1.

[74] Art 1 LRD.

nationals should be approximated to that of EU citizens and that long-term residents should be granted a set of uniform rights in the Member State where they reside which are as close as possible to those enjoyed by EU citizens. As the aim to grant uniform rights is limited to the Member State where the third-country national resides, this aim can be understood as not referring to the right of free movement between the Member States. Nevertheless, the statement regarding the approximation of the legal status of third-country nationals to that of EU citizens is framed in general terms and may therefore be taken to include EU citizens' right of free movement.

The preamble furthermore states that the treatment of long-term residents should be equal to that of citizens of the Union 'in a wide range of economic and social matters' in order to achieve the integration of those long-term residents, which is, in turn, a key element in the fundamental EU objective of promoting economic and social cohesion.[75] In *Commission v the Netherlands*, the CoJ stated that 'the principal purpose of [the LRD] is the integration of third-country nationals who are settled on a long-term basis in the Member States'.[76] The legislative history of the LRD shows that long-term residents' right to reside in other Member States is to be seen as one of the instruments for such integration.[77] Notably, this concept of integration differs from that underpinning Dutch integration policy. The assumption underlying the LRD would appear to be that the integration of long-term residents will be furthered by a secure residence status.[78] Nevertheless, as shown below, the directive creates a possibility to make the residence of long-term residents conditional upon integration requirements. Consequently, like the Family Reunification Directive (chapter 4, section V.A), the Long-term Residents Directive incorporates different and even contradictory conceptions of integration. Lastly, the preamble also indicates that establishing conditions governing the right of long-term residents to reside in another Member State should also contribute to the effective attainment of an internal market as an area in which the free movement of persons is ensured and constitute a major factor of mobility in the Union's employment market.[79]

[75] Preamble, recitals 4 and 12.

[76] CoJ 26 April 2012, C-508/10 [2012] ECR 00000 (*Commission v the Netherlands*), para 66; see also CoJ (Grand Chamber) 24 April 2012, C-571/10 [2012] ECR 00000 (*Kamberaj*), paras 81, 86 and 90.

[77] Iglesias Sánchez 2009a, 799, referring to the Proposal for the Directive, COM (2001) 127 final, [2001] OJ C240 E24/79.

[78] Groenendijk 2004, 122; see also the *Report from the Commission to the European Parliament and the Council on the application of Directive 2003/109/EC concerning the status of third-country nationals who are long-term residents*, COM(2011) 585 final, 1.

[79] Preamble, recital 18.

C. The Right of Long-term Residents to Reside in Another Member State

Article 14(1) LRD grants third-country nationals who have obtained long-term resident status in one Member State the right to reside in another Member State for a period of more than three months. This right may be exercised for the purpose of undertaking an economic activity as an employed or self-employed person, for studies or vocational training or for other purposes.[80] The right of residence in another Member State is not granted to posted workers or providers of cross-border services, while Member States also remain free to determine, in accordance with their national legislation, the conditions concerning the residence of seasonal and cross-border workers.[81]

The LRD does not contain any provisions relating to the right of long-term residents to enter the second Member State. Instead, this right can be found in Article 21(1) of the Schengen Implementing Convention,[82] which provides that third-country nationals holding a valid residence permit issued by one of the Contracting Parties may move freely in the territory of the other Contracting Parties for up to three months. Long-term residents wishing to take up residence in the second Member State for a longer period must apply for a residence permit within those three months.[83] To be granted a residence permit, the long-term resident must meet the conditions set out in Article 15 LRD. Of particular relevance for the purpose of this study is the possibility for Member States to require third-country nationals to comply with integration measures (Art 15(3) LRD). This possibility exists unless the third-country national has already had to comply with integration conditions in order to obtain long-term resident status in the first Member State.[84] In the latter case the long-term resident can only be required to attend language courses.[85]

[80] Art 14(2) LRD.

[81] Art 14(5) LRD. The possibility of instituting a quota for long-term residents coming from another Member State, as foreseen by Art 14(4) LRD, is not relevant for the Netherlands as no such limitation was included in its national legislation at the time when the directive was adopted.

[82] [2000] OJ L239/19.

[83] Art 15(1) LRD. According to this provision, Member States may accept applications for residence permits made by long-term residents who are still in the first Member State, but they are not obliged to do so.

[84] See Art 5(2) LRD.

[85] The full text of Art 15(3) LRD reads:

> Member States may require third country nationals to comply with integration measures, in accordance with national law.
>
> This condition shall not apply where the third country nationals concerned have been required to comply with integration conditions in order to be granted long-term resident status, in accordance with the provisions of Article 5 (2).
>
> Without prejudice to the second subparagraph, the persons concerned may be required to attend language courses.

The scope and contents of Article 15(3) LRD are examined in more detail in the following subsections. The first questions discussed are whether the right of residence in the second Member State depends on the long-term resident's compliance with integration requirements and when such requirements may be imposed (before or after residence is granted). The other questions are what type of integration requirements may be imposed, and whether any limitations to Member States' discretion follow from the directive or from other rules of EU law. In this connection it may be recalled that acts of the Member States that come within the scope of application of EU law must be in conformity with fundamental rights and other general principles of EU law. Arguably these acts include integration requirements adopted pursuant to Article 15(3) LRD.[86]

D. Compliance with Integration Measures as a Condition for Residence in the Second Member State: the Meaning of Article 15(3) LRD

i. Integration as a Condition for Residence?

The first issue to be addressed is whether it follows from Article 15(3) LRD that compliance with integration requirements, as laid down in the Member State's national legislation, is a condition for entitlement to residence in a second Member State. In this respect, the text of Article 15(3) is not very precise as it merely states that 'Member States may require third country nationals to comply with integration measures, in accordance with national law'. This does not reveal anything about the consequences of such requirements not being fulfilled. However, Article 15 LRD is headed 'Conditions for residence in a second Member State', whereas Article 14(1) LRD clearly states that long-term residents will acquire the right to reside in the second Member State 'provided that the conditions set out in this chapter are met'. In addition, it follows from Articles 19(2) and 22(1)(b) LRD that Member States may refuse, withdraw or refuse to renew a residence permit if the conditions provided for in Articles 14, 15 and 16 are not or no longer fulfilled. These provisions make it clear that non-compliance with the said conditions, including national conditions relating to integration, may result in the loss or non-acquisition of the right of residence in the second Member State.[87]

A different reading of Article 15(3) LRD has been proposed by De Heer, who argues that it follows from the overall system and purpose of the directive that non-compliance with integration requirements may be

[86] See section V.C.iv of ch 4.

[87] See also Iglesias Sánchez 2009a, 800.

sanctioned by a fine, but cannot result in a loss of residence rights.[88] In support of this argument, De Heer points out that Member States may require compliance with integration requirements as a condition for acquisition of long-term resident status, which is the strongest residence right granted by the LRD. He concludes that it would be contrary to the system of the directive if the same requirement had to be fulfilled (again) to obtain residence in the second Member State, while adding that such a requirement would also be contrary to the directive's objective of attaining an internal market.[89]

In my view these arguments cannot be maintained. Firstly they are not compatible with the clear wording of the above provisions (Arts 14(1), 19(2) and 22(1)(b) LRD), which make it plain that the right to residence is conditional upon the fulfilment of integration requirements. Secondly I do not believe that the acquisition of long-term resident status must be qualified as a 'stronger' right than the right to move to a second Member State or that these rights in any way overlap. There is, therefore, no reason to assume that the same conditions cannot apply to the acquisition of both rights, except where this is explicitly stated in the directive (as in Art 15(3), second paragraph). Lastly, it is submitted that enacting a right for third-country nationals to move to another Member State constitutes a step towards the further realisation of an internal market, even if this right is subject to certain conditions or limitations. Nevertheless, as discussed below, the objectives of the LRD (including the attainment of an internal market) are not without relevance for the further interpretation of Article 15(3).

ii. When May Compliance with Integration Requirements be Demanded?

Another matter not expressly stated in the text of Article 15(3) LRD is the moment at which a Member State may ask a long-term resident to comply with integration requirements. Can such compliance be demanded before a residence permit is granted, or only afterwards (as a condition for preserving or prolonging the right of residence)? As shown above, Article 14(1) LRD states that long-term residents shall *acquire* the right of residence in the second Member State if the relevant conditions are met. Article 19(2) LRD also provides that a residence permit must be granted 'if the conditions in Articles 14, 15 and 16 are met'. This suggests that Member States may ask for compliance with integration requirements before granting a residence permit. On the other hand, Article 22(1)(b)

[88] De Heer 2007, 278.

[89] De Heer also assumes that the consequence of the non-acquisition of residence rights in the second Member State is incompatible with the use of the term 'integration measures' (instead of 'integration conditions') in Art 15(3) LRD, first paragraph. This argument is addressed in section VI.D.v.

LRD provides that the residence permit may be withdrawn 'when the conditions of Articles 14, 15 and 16 *are no longer met*' (emphasis added). This suggests that compliance with the said conditions is something that can continue to be required after the residence permit has been granted. This could apply, for example, if a long-term resident is asked to participate in an integration programme or language course. It thus appears that Article 15(3) allows LRD long-term residents to be asked to meet integration requirements, both before and after a right of residence has been granted in the second Member State.

The finding that integration requirements may be imposed before residence is granted is, however, subject to an exception. As mentioned earlier, third-country nationals who have already had to comply with integration requirements to obtain long-term resident status in the first Member State can only be asked to attend language courses.[90] This requirement cannot always be easily fulfilled in a Member State other than the one in which the long-term resident is expected to integrate. For instance, it may not be feasible in practice to ask a person holding long-term resident status in Estonia to take a Dutch course in that country before moving to the Netherlands. Arguably, therefore, the exemption in Article 15(3) LRD implies that long-term residents who have already complied with integration requirements in the first Member State cannot be asked to meet such requirements again before moving to the second Member State. It also follows that, for this group of long-term residents, the acquisition of residence in the second Member State cannot be conditioned upon the fulfilment of integration requirements.[91]

iii. Contents of Integration Requirements

The Long-term Residents Directive does not give an overall definition of the terms 'integration measures' or 'integration conditions'. The same is true with regard to other directives in which these terms are used, the Family Reunification Directive (2003/86/EC) and the Blue Card Directive (2009/50/EC). From the text of Article 15(3) LRD it can be derived that the integration requirements referred to in this provision may include, but are not limited to attendance at language courses. However, in the absence of any further definition, it is left to the Member States to determine the contents of integration requirements. This also follows from the wording of

[90] Art 15(3), second and third paragraphs LRD.

[91] As explained in section VI.C, long-term residents are allowed to remain in the second Member State for a period of up to three months before a residence permit is granted. However, Art 15(1) LRD also obliges long-term residents to apply for a residence permit as soon as possible after they have entered the second Member State. It is therefore assumed that the Member States cannot expect long-term residents to use the three-month period after their arrival to comply with integration requirements (ie to attend language classes) before applying for residence.

Article 15(3) LRD, which states that third-country nationals may be required to comply with integration measures 'in accordance with national law'.

Considering the many possible understandings of the concept of 'integration' (see chapter 3), 'integration requirements' could in principle be used to pursue a variety of different objectives. These may include participation in the social, economic, cultural or political life of the host society, the creation of a sense of commitment to the host country or, for example, the promotion of interethnic contacts. Integration requirements can also take different forms: long-term residents may be required to participate in a course or programme, to provide proof of certain skills or knowledge (through an exam or by other means), to attend a ceremony or submit a declaration of loyalty.[92] At first sight, Article 15(3) LRD and the provisions in other directives referring to integration requirements do not exclude any of these possibilities. Lastly, these provisions do not indicate how the financial and organisational responsibilities for fulfilling integration requirements are to be divided between the long-term resident and the host Member State. In other words, it is not stated who should pay for the integration course or exam or whether the host Member State has to provide study materials or other facilities.

The legislative history of the LRD provides some insight into the kind of integration requirements foreseen by the negotiating parties.[93] It shows that the inclusion of integration requirements in the directive was proposed by Austria, Germany and the Netherlands. These Member States wanted to create scope in the directive for the integration requirements already existing in their national legislation, whereby newly arrived immigrants were obliged to follow integration programmes from the moment they obtained legal residence. The Netherlands also wanted to introduce an obligation for certain groups of third-country nationals to pay the costs of the integration programme before being admitted. According to these three Member States, such requirements were necessary to promote the full participation and self-sufficiency of third-country nationals. It was specified that knowledge of the country and of the language of the host Member State were considered essential, including for improving the opportunities available to third-country nationals in the labour market, in education and in other areas of society, and that integration programmes could include language training, as well as social orientation and vocational training.[94]

[92] cp the declaration of loyalty that must be made to obtain Dutch citizenship in the Netherlands, see Art 6(2) and 8(1)(e) of the Dutch Nationality Act (*Rijkswet op het Nederlanderschap*).

[93] For an extensive overview of this history, see Carrera 2009, 175–83.

[94] Council doc. 12271/02 of 23 September 2002. A study conducted by Michalowski in 2003 shows that, at that time, at least seven EU Member States other than the Netherlands had some form of integration programme for immigrants, often focusing on language abilities and sometimes on knowledge of the host society. See Michalowski 2003.

Another Council document shows that the possibility of an integration test was also considered.[95] As stated above, the final text of the LRD does not mention either integration tests or programmes. However, in the absence of any indications to the contrary, it must be assumed that the requirements that Member States may impose under Article 15(3) LRD include both integration tests and programmes (and payment of the costs thereof by the long-term resident). Nevertheless, long-term residents who have already complied with integration requirements in the first Member State in accordance with Article 5(2) LRD can only be required to attend language courses (section VI.C). Council documents show that this exception was introduced because it was deemed undesirable for third-country nationals to have to pass an integration test twice: once to acquire long-term resident status and again for residence in the second Member State.[96] The limitation of the exception clause to language courses seems somewhat surprising, given that other types of integration courses (such as social orientation and vocational training) are not necessarily less country-specific. Nevertheless, the LRD does not preclude Member States from offering such courses to long-term residents on a voluntary basis.

iv. Limitations to the Discretion of the Member States

In spite of the discretion that the LRD leaves to the Member States to determine the contents of integration requirements, a number of limitations can also be identified. These follow both from the directive itself and from other instruments and provisions of EU law. Firstly, it can be assumed that the terms 'integration conditions' and 'integration measures' do not cover requirements already covered by other provisions of the LRD, for example those relating to income or public policy and public security.[97] Although the term 'integration' is in itself broad enough to include such requirements, such an interpretation would run counter to the system of the directive and deprive its other provisions of their meaning.

Secondly, integration requirements cannot be of such a nature as to undermine the objective or effectiveness of the LRD.[98] It is recalled that the purpose of the directive is not only to improve the integration of long-term residents by granting them a legal status similar to that of EU citizens, but also to contribute to the attainment of an internal market and to form a factor of mobility in the Union's employment market (section VI.B). Consequently, integration requirements must not have the effect of undermining the free movement of third-country nationals who are long-

[95] Council doc. 12624/02 of 9 October 2002, 2.
[96] Council doc. 12624/02 of 9 October 2002, 2.
[97] See Arts 15(2) and 17 LRD.
[98] *Commission v the Netherlands* (n 76), para 65.

term residents.[99] It follows that integration requirements imposed by Member States may not be of such a nature that long-term residents cannot reasonably be expected to comply with them. In addition, integration requirements enacted by the Member States will need to respect the EU principle of proportionality. While it is up to the Member States to decide on the integration objectives pursued, integration requirements thus have to meet the criteria of suitability and necessity.[100]

Although the above criteria necessarily remain rather abstract, they could imply, for example, that integration tests must be set at a sufficiently low level, that study materials must be easily available or provided by the Member State, that long-term residents may not be required to pay high fees for integration tests or programmes and that mandatory integration programmes may only be of limited duration (see also, with regard to the Family Reunification Directive, section V.C.iv of chapter 4). Also, following the CoJ's approach in *Baumbast* and *Chakroun* (section II.B above and section V.C.iv of chapter 4), an individual assessment will need to be made, taking into account the personal circumstances of the applicant including factors such as illiteracy, medical problems or a limited learning capacity.[101] With regard to national integration measures, a possibility for exemption will have to be included, for instance in the form of a hardship clause. As a final element, the effectiveness of these measures should be considered.

Lastly, integration requirements imposed by Member States for exercising the right of residence in a second Member State must be in conformity with fundamental rights, including those laid down in the EU Charter of Fundamental Rights and the European Convention on Human Rights.[102] Apart from the right to free movement, which is discussed above, relevant provisions may be those concerning the freedom of religion, respect for cultural, religious and linguistic diversity and the prohibition of discrimination.[103] While the precise content of these provisions clearly lends itself to extensive discussion, it seems obvious that long-term residents may not be asked to relinquish their religious or cultural identity, to refrain from

[99] See also Peers 2004, 442–43.

[100] *Commission v the Netherlands* (n 76), para 75.

[101] A relevant difference with the situation in *Chakroun* could be that Art 17 FRD explicitly requires individual examination of the application for family reunification, whereas a similar provision is not included in the LRD. Nevertheless, the CoJ appears in *Chakroun* to base its interpretation not only on Art 17 FRD, but also on the purpose of the directive, the fact that it grants a right to family reunification (to which the income requirement constitutes an exception) and the right to respect for family life as protected by the CFR and as a general principle of EU law (paras 41–47 of the judgment). Consequently, a similar interpretative approach could be taken with regard to Art 15(3) LRD on the basis of the purpose of that directive, the fact that it grants a right to free movement and Arts 79(2)(b) TFEU and 45 (2) CFR.

[102] cp Arts 6(1) and (3) TEU. See also *Kamberaj* (n 76), para 79.

[103] See Arts 10, 21 and 22 CFR and Arts 9, 14 and 1 Twelfth Protocol ECHR. The prohibition of discrimination is addressed in detail in chs 8 to 10.

speaking their mother tongue or to subscribe to the religious norms prevailing in the host Member State (see also chapter 4, section V.C.iv).

v. 'Integration Measures' Versus 'Integration Conditions'?

The interpretation of Article 15(3) LRD proposed above has been contested in the literature. In particular, it has been argued that certain limitations to the discretionary power of the Member States to impose integration requirements follow from the use of the term 'integration measures' instead of ' integration conditions'. Several authors have stated that non-compliance with 'integration measures' may not result in a refusal of the right of residence in the second Member State.[104] Other authors, notably Groenendijk, have contended that the term 'integration condition' allows for a higher level of obligation or responsibility to be placed on the long-term resident. According to Groenendijk, provisions using the term 'integration conditions' allow Member States to require immigrants to pass an integration test to demonstrate that they have attained knowledge or skills at a certain level. Immigrants may also be required to bear the costs of following an integration programme. By contrast, the term 'integration measures' merely allows Member States to require a certain effort on the part of the individual, such as participating in language or integration courses.[105] Carrera goes even further by saying that the term 'integration measures' precludes any kind of obligatory character or binding effect of the measures to be taken.[106]

To support these interpretations, the above authors rely on the legislative history of the Long-term Residents Directive, which shows that the term 'integration conditions' was favoured by those Member States supporting a restrictive integration policy (notably Austria, Germany and the Netherlands).[107] These Member States specifically proposed replacing the words 'integration measures' in Article 15(3) LRD by 'integration conditions'.[108] This proposal was not, however, supported by a majority of the delegations and did not make it into the final text of the directive. This led the above authors to conclude that Article 15(3) LRD does not allow for integration requirements such as those proposed by the three Member

[104] De Heer 2007, 278; Carrera 2009, 195 and Pascouau 2010, 445.

[105] Groenendijk 2004, 122–24; Groenendijk 2006, 224. This argument is repeated by other authors, including Brinkmann 2008, 40, Iglesias Sánchez 2009b, 215 and Pascouau 2010, 445–46. The European Commission, in its report on the application of the LRD (n 78), also suggests that 'integration measures' of Art 15(3) differ from the integration conditions of Art 5(2), in that long-term residents who have already been subject to integration conditions in the first Member State can thereafter only be asked to attend language courses (p 7 of the report). As explained above, this follows from the text of Art 15(3), second and third paragraphs, LRD, rather than from the use of the term 'measures' as such.

[106] Carrera 2009, 195.

[107] Groenendijk 2004, 122–24; Carrera 2009, 175–83.

[108] See Council doc. 7393/1/03 of 14 March 2003, 5.

States, notably integration tests or mandatory participation in integration programmes.

In my view, there are several reasons why the terms 'integration measures' and 'integration conditions' cannot be assumed to have the specific meaning proposed by Groenendijk and Carrera. Indeed, the legislative history of the LRD indicates that the negotiating parties made a distinction between the two terms. Still, this can only be a relevant factor of interpretation if this distinction is also expressed in the text of the relevant legal instruments. When looking at different language versions of the LRD and the other migration directives in which reference is made to integration requirements, this does not appear to be the case.[109] The terms are sometimes used interchangeably, whereas at other times they are replaced in some language versions by different terms altogether.[110]

The legislative history of the LRD or the other Directives furthermore does not support the attribution of any specific meaning to 'integration measures' or 'integration conditions'. The relevant Council documents do not define the contested terms, nor do they explain the reasons why the use of either term was supported or rejected by the delegations involved in the negotiations. To derive any particular definition from the negotiation process as described above therefore seems somewhat far-fetched. The reading proposed by Carrera – that integration measures cannot be of an obligatory character – is also hard to reconcile with the text of Article 15(3) LRD, which states that long-term residents may be required 'to comply with integration measures'. Besides, if it is accepted that integration measures cannot be of a binding nature, it is hard to see why a legal basis in the directive would be required at all.

It is thus concluded that the mere use of the term 'integration measures' or 'integration conditions' does not indicate the possible contents of the integration requirements to be enacted by the Member States.[111] Nevertheless, as discussed above, Member States' discretion is restricted in several other ways. As a result, integration requirements that impose too large a burden on long-term residents are, in my view, contrary to Article 15(3) LRD regardless of the wording used in that provision.

[109] See also Vermeulen 2010, 95.

[110] To give some examples: the term 'integration conditions' is used in Art 4(1) FRD in some language versions, whereas others refer to an 'integration criterion'. Furthermore, the Spanish version of the LRD uses the term 'integration measures' both in Art 5(2) and 15(3) first paragraph, whereas all the other language versions use 'integration conditions', and both the Swedish and Dutch versions of Art 15(3) second paragraph use 'integration conditions', while the others use 'measures' (even though the Swedish version also uses 'measures' in Art 7(2) FRD). Finally, the German version of Art 33 Qualification Directive uses the term 'integration measures' where other language versions use terms such as 'integration facilities', 'instruments for integration' or 'mechanisms of integration'.

[111] See also Van Dam 2008, 71 and 79.

E. Family Members of Long-term Residents

i. Definition of 'Family Members' in the Long-term Residents Directive

Long-term resident third-country nationals who move to another Member State are entitled to be joined or accompanied by their family members, subject to the conditions of Article 16 LRD. According to the definition provided in Article 2(e) LRD, the term 'family members' refers to those third-country nationals who reside in the Member State concerned in accordance with the Family Reunification Directive (FRD). It must be assumed that this definition does not require the family members actually to have been *granted admission* under the FRD, as this would exclude all family members who were admitted before the implementation of that directive. Since the LRD specifically concerns third-country nationals who have resided in a Member State for some time, it may be supposed that in many cases these third-country nationals will have family members who were already living with them before the FRD came into being.[112]

It is, nevertheless, conceivable that the EU legislator wanted the definition of family members in the LRD to be consistent with other directives, notably the FRD. A reasonable interpretation therefore seems to be that the reference to the FRD in Article 2(e) LRD indicates which family relationships are included under the latter directive. The term 'family members' in the LRD thus covers those family members who are mentioned in Article 4 FRD, regardless of when they were admitted. Support for this interpretation is found in the Commission proposal for the LRD, where Article 4 FRD is explicitly referred to.[113] Where the latter article contains optional provisions (with regard, for example, to the inclusion of unmarried and registered partners), it is submitted that these must be applied by each Member State in the same way with regard to family members of long-term residents as for the purposes of allowing family reunification.

ii. The Right to Reside in a Second Member State

As mentioned above, the right of residence of family members in a second Member State is regulated by Article 16 LRD. This provision requires, first of all, that the family was already constituted in the first Member State.[114] Where this is not the case, the entry and residence of family members in the second Member State are subject to the provisions of the Family Reunification Directive (FRD), which was discussed in chapter 4.[115] Family

[112] The deadline for implementation of the FRD was 3 October 2005, whereas the LRD had to be implemented by 23 January 2006.

[113] COM(2001) 127 final, 11.

[114] Art 16(1) LRD.

[115] Art 16(5) LRD.

members coming under the Long-term Residents Directive must apply for a residence permit within three months of entering the territory of the second Member State.[116] Conditions relating to their right of residence are laid down in Articles 16(4), 17 and 18 LRD. On the basis of these provisions the second Member State may, for example, require evidence of sufficient resources or refuse the right of residence on the grounds of public policy, public security or public health.

The LRD does not expressly mention the possibility of imposing integration requirements. However, Article 16(1) LRD states that family members must meet the conditions referred to in Article 4(1) FRD.[117] Since Article 4(1) mentions the conditions laid down in Chapter IV of the FRD, it could be argued that family members who move to a second Member State must meet all the conditions of that Chapter, including the integration requirement laid down in Article 7(2) FRD. However, acceptance of this argument would be hard to reconcile with other provisions of the LRD, in particular the conditions laid down in Articles 16(4), 17 and 18. These conditions overlap, at least in part, with those in Articles 6 and 7(1) FRD.[118] It is therefore unlikely that Article 16(1) LRD would make the conditions of Chapter IV FRD equally applicable to the family reunification of long-term residents who move to a second Member State.

[116] Art 16(3) in conjunction with Art 15(1) LRD. As for long-term residents, the right of family members to enter the second Member State and to reside there for up to three months is based on Art 21 of the Schengen Implementing Convention.

[117] Art 4(1) FRD reads:

The Member States shall authorise the entry and residence, pursuant to this Directive and subject to compliance with the conditions laid down in Chapter IV, as well as in Article 16, of the following family members:

(a) the sponsor's spouse;
(b) the minor children of the sponsor and of his/her spouse, including children adopted in accordance with a decision taken by the competent authority in the Member State concerned or a decision which is automatically enforceable due to international obligations of that Member State or must be recognised in accordance with international obligations;
(c) the minor children including adopted children of the sponsor where the sponsor has custody and the children are dependent on him or her. Member States may authorise the reunification of children of whom custody is shared, provided the other party sharing custody has given his or her agreement;
(d) the minor children including adopted children of the spouse where the spouse has custody and the children are dependent on him or her. Member States may authorise the reunification of children of whom custody is shared, provided the other party sharing custody has given his or her agreement.

The minor children referred to in this Article must be below the age of majority set by the law of the Member State concerned and must not be married.

By way of derogation, where a child is aged over 12 years and arrives independently from the rest of his/her family, the Member State may, before authorising entry and residence under this Directive, verify whether he or she meets a condition for integration provided for by its existing legislation on the date of implementation of this Directive.

[118] Both Art 16(4)(c) LRD and Art 7(1)(b) and (c) FRD set requirements relating to income and health insurance, whereas Arts 17–18 LRD and Art 6 FRD provide for exceptions relating to public policy, public security and public health.

It is submitted instead that the reference to Article 4(1) FRD aims to determine which family members are entitled to move with the long-term resident to the second Member State.[119] Article 4(1) FRD mentions, in short, the spouse and the minor (adopted) children of the sponsor (ie the long-term resident) and/or the spouse. It follows that the circle of family members who may move to a second Member State is narrower than the definition of family members in Article 2(e) LRD, as the latter may also cover family members mentioned in Article 4(2) and (3) FRD (in short: dependent parents, adult unmarried children and unmarried or registered partners). However, Article 16(2) LRD provides that the Member States may authorise long-term residents to bring along family members other than those mentioned in Article 4(1) FRD. The proposed reading of Article 16(1) LRD thus results in an interpretation that is consistent with the Family Reunification Directive. Under both directives, Member States are obliged to admit the spouse and minor (adopted) children (Arts 4(1) FRD and 16(1) LRD), whereas they have discretion with regard to the admission of other family members (Arts 4(2) and (3) FRD and 16(2) LRD).

A remaining question is whether the second Member State may require children of long-term residents, who are over 12 years of age and arrive independently of the family, to comply with the integration requirement laid down in Article 4(1), final subparagraph, FRD. It is submitted that this does indeed follow from Article 16(1) LRD. However, Article 4(1), final subparagraph, FRD contains a standstill clause which states that the integration requirement must have existed in the legislation of the Member State concerned on the date of the implementation of the directive. Only Germany meets this condition.[120]

Oosterom-Staples suggests that family members of long-term residents may be subjected to integration requirements when they move to the second Member State because Article 15(3) LRD speaks of 'third country nationals' in general and not of 'long-term residents'.[121] This interpretation is, however, contradicted by a systematic argument: Article 15 concerns the conditions for free movement of long-term residents, whereas their family members are covered by Article 16.[122] Where Article 15 is also applicable to family members this is explicitly indicated, as in Article 16(3). It must thus be assumed that the integration requirement of Article 15(3) applies only to the long-term residents themselves and not to their family members. This reading is supported by the preamble to the LRD, which states that the right of family members to move to another Member State is meant to preserve family unity and to avoid hindering the exercis-

[119] See also Boeles et al 2009, 221.
[120] See ch 4, section V.C.
[121] Oosterom-Staples 2004, 71.
[122] See also Van Dam 2008, 76.

ing of this right by the long-term resident.[123] These objectives would be hampered if family member could be refused residence on the grounds that they failed to comply with integration requirements. It is concluded that the right of family members of long-term residents to reside in another Member State cannot be conditioned upon the fulfilment of integration requirements. Member States are not, however, prevented from offering integration programmes to family members on a voluntary basis.

iii. Family Members Other than those Referred to in Article 4(1) Family Reunification Directive

As mentioned above, Article 16(2) LRD states that Member States may authorise the residence on their territory of family members other than those referred to in Article 4(1) FRD, provided the family was already constituted in the first Member State. Consequently, where the family members do not fulfil the conditions of Article 4(1) FRD, it is left to the discretion of the second Member State to determine whether a right of residence will be granted. It is, nonetheless, submitted that a right of residence granted pursuant to Article 16(2) LRD may not be conditioned upon requirements other than those laid down in that directive. Otherwise, if Member States were allowed to set conditions according to their national law, this would hamper the development of a common immigration policy as prescribed by Article 79(1) TFEU. The proposed interpretation is also consistent with the system of Article 4 FRD, which provides that a Member State may admit additional categories of family members (as mentioned in paras 2 and 3 of that provision) under the conditions set forth in the Family Reunification Directive. Thus, while Member States remain free to deny the right of residence to family members who are not included under Article 4(1) FRD, where they do authorise such residence this must be on the terms of the LRD and so without imposing integration requirements.

VII. THIRD-COUNTRY NATIONALS WHO ARE HOLDERS OF AN EU BLUE CARD AND THEIR FAMILY MEMBERS

A. The Blue Card Directive

Lastly, there is the category of third-country nationals who have been issued an EU Blue Card in accordance with the Blue Card Directive (BCD). This directive was adopted in 2009 and had to be implemented by the Member States by 19 June 2011. Like the Long-term Residents Directive,

123 Recital 20.

the Blue Card Directive was adopted on the basis of Articles 63(3)(a) and (4) TEC (currently Arts 79(2)(a) and (b) TFEU) and thus forms part of EU immigration policy. The objectives of the Blue Card Directive are primarily of an economic nature. The directive was enacted with the aim of making the EU more attractive to highly qualified labour migrants from third countries in order to address shortages in the European labour market and make the European economy more competitive.[124] To achieve this aim, the BCD regulates the entry and residence (for more than three months) of third-country nationals for the purposes of highly qualified employment, as well as the right of these persons to enter and reside in another Member State. It also regulates the entry and residence of their family members, both in the first and the second Member State.[125]

The rights of entry and residence for EU Blue Card holders and their family members are briefly discussed below. Since this chapter concerns the right of free movement in EU law, the discussion is limited to the rights of entry and residence in the second Member State. The initial admission of highly qualified labour migrants and their family members is dealt with in the following chapter. The BCD is without prejudice to more favourable provisions of bilateral or multilateral agreements concluded between the EU and/or the Member States and one or more third countries or of other instruments of EU law.[126]

B. The Right of EU Blue Card Holders to Enter and Reside in Another Member State

The right of EU Blue Card holders to move to another Member State is regulated in Article 18 BCD. According to Article 18(1), the right to free movement is granted after the person concerned has resided for 18 months in the first Member State on the basis of an EU Blue Card. This right may be exercised for the purpose of highly qualified employment, as defined in Article 2(b) BCD. The right of residence in the second Member State is, however, without prejudice to the right of that Member State to determine the numbers of highly qualified third-country nationals permitted to enter its territory.[127]

As in the case of long-term residents, the right of EU Blue Card holders to enter the second Member State and to reside there for up to three months follows from Article 21 of the Schengen Implementing Convention.[128] Under Article 18(2), however, Blue Card holders (or their

[124] See the preamble of the directive, notably recital 7.
[125] Art 1 BCD.
[126] Art 4(1) BCD.
[127] Art 18(7) in conjunction with Art 6 BCD.
[128] On the basis of the Blue Card issued by the first Member State.

employers) must apply for a Blue Card in the second Member State within one month of entry. The issue of the Blue Card is subject to the conditions laid down in Article 5 BCD. These conditions mostly relate to the qualifications for employment, as well as to the protection of public policy, public security and public health. Integration requirements are not mentioned.

It follows that EU Blue Card holders have a right of residence in a second Member State, provided they meet the conditions set by the BCD and the second Member State has not set a quota. Where such a right exists, Member States no longer have the possibility of making the admission dependent on integration requirements.

C. The Right of Family Members of EU Blue Card Holders to Enter and Reside in Another Member State

The Blue Card Directive also applies to family members of the EU Blue Card holder. According to the BCD, 'family members' are 'third country nationals as defined in Article 4(1) of Directive 2003/86/EC' (the 'Family Reunification Directive').[129] As explained above (section VI.E.ii), Article 4(1) FRD mentions the spouse and the minor (adopted) children of the sponsor (ie the EU Blue Card holder) and/or the spouse. It follows that other family members, such as dependent parents and adult children or unmarried or registered partners, are not covered by the BCD. The same is true for children who do not meet the conditions set out in the second and third subparagraphs of Article 4(1) FRD.[130]

Family members are entitled to accompany or join the EU Blue Card holder in the second Member State, provided the family was already constituted in the first Member State.[131] Like the Blue Card holders themselves, the family members are entitled to enter the second Member State and reside there for up to three months on the basis of the residence permit granted by the first Member State.[132] However, they (or the Blue Card holder) must apply for a residence permit in the second Member State within one month of entry.[133] The issue of the residence permit is subject to a number of conditions to be met by the family members or the Blue Card holder, but integration requirements may not be imposed.[134]

[129] Art 2(f) BCD.

[130] As explained above, the final subparagraph of Art 4(1) FRD includes an integration requirement for children aged over 12 who arrive independently of the rest of the family. However, this requirement is of no relevance to the Dutch situation because of its standstill clause. Moreover, discussion of this requirement would be out of place here since it is not directly related to the right of residence in the second Member State.

[131] Art 19(1) BCD.

[132] Art 21 Schengen Implementing Convention.

[133] Art 19(2) BCD.

[134] Arts 19(3) and (4) BCD.

This is different in cases where the family was not already constituted in the first Member State. In these cases, the family reunification of the Blue Card holder in the second Member State is subject to Article 15 BCD.[135] The latter declares the Family Reunification Directive applicable, although with a number of derogations. The possibility of imposing integration requirements is laid down in Articles 4(1) and 7(2) of the FRD (chapter 4, section V). However, it must be observed that, for family members of EU Blue Card holders, integration requirements can only be applied after family reunification has been granted.[136] It follows that the BCD does not allow 'integration abroad' and that the right to family reunification cannot be made conditional upon compliance with integration requirements. According to the preamble, the purpose of this derogation is to create favourable conditions for family reunification in order to make the EU more attractive for highly qualified third-country nationals. It is explicitly stated that the derogation does not preclude Member States from maintaining or introducing integration requirements, including language learning, for family members of EU Blue Card holders.[137] Yet these integration requirements can only be imposed after admission and therefore fall outside the scope of this study.

VIII. THE RIGHT TO FREE MOVEMENT AND THE ACT ON INTEGRATION ABROAD

The previous sections describe the right of free movement within EU law, examining which persons are entitled to move and reside freely within the EU Member States and whether this right may be conditioned upon fulfilment of integration requirements. Where specific provisions relating to integration requirements were found, their contents were examined in order to determine more specifically the boundaries of the discretion available to the Member States. In the final section of this chapter the findings with regard to the right to free movement are summarised and discussed. Firstly, however, it is examined whether the Dutch Act on Integration Abroad (AIA) is in compliance with this right, as set out in the relevant instruments of EU law.

A. Nationals of the Member States of the EU, the EEA and Switzerland and their Family Members

Under the Dutch Aliens Act (*Vreemdelingenwet 2000*), aliens may be required to pass the integration exam abroad if they want to obtain a tem-

[135] Art 19(6) BCD.
[136] Art 15(3) BCD.
[137] Preamble BCD, recital 23.

porary residence permit (*verblijfsvergunning bepaalde tijd regulier*).[138] However, persons belonging to the category of 'Community citizens' (*gemeenschapsonderdanen*) do not need a residence permit in order to reside legally in the Netherlands.[139] This category consists of:

- nationals of the EU Member States and their family members who are entitled to entry and residence in another Member State on the basis of the TEC (now TFEU) or EU secondary legislation;
- nationals of the Member States of the EEA and their family members who are entitled to entry and residence in the EU Member States on the basis of the EEA Agreement; and
- Swiss nationals and their family members who are entitled to reside in an EU Member State on the basis of the EC-Switzerland Agreement.[140]

Since the above persons do not need a residence permit, they are also not required to pass the integration exam abroad. As far as EU citizens and their family members are concerned, the right to free movement is thus respected. The same is true for nationals of EEA Member States and Switzerland and their family members.

As the category of 'Community citizens' is defined by reference to the rights of entry and residence granted under the treaties, it is sufficiently flexible to accommodate developments such as the adoption of new instruments of secondary legislation or the interpretation of existing provisions by the CoJ. By way of example, when the AIA was adopted the Dutch government initially proceeded on the assumption that family members of EU citizens who were third-country nationals were not entitled to the right of free movement under the Residence Directive unless they had already been lawfully admitted to the EU.[141] As described in section III.B, the CoJ later rejected this stance in *Metock*. This judgment made it clear that third-country nationals who are family members of EU citizens are also 'Community citizens' within the meaning of the Aliens Act, even if they have not held previous lawful residence in the EU.

i. Family Members not Entitled to the Right of Free Movement

As set out above, the right of free movement under the Residence Directive, the EEA Agreement and the EC-Switzerland Agreement is available only to certain categories of family members (notably the spouse,

[138] Art 16(1)(h) Aliens Act.

[139] Art 8(e) Aliens Act.

[140] Art 1(e) Aliens Act.

[141] *Parliamentary Papers II* 2003–2004, 29 700, No 3, 17–18. In view of doubts regarding the legal position of these third-country nationals, the government eventually decided to wait until the CoJ passed judgment in the case of *Jia* (C-1/05), which was pending at the time. See *Parliamentary Papers I* 2004–2005, 29 700, E, 3. In the end, third-country nationals/family members of EU citizens were never brought under the AIA.

minor children and dependent parents). In addition, the Netherlands is also obliged to facilitate the entry and residence of other categories of family members who are not entitled to free movement. In this respect the Residence Directive mentions:

- family members other than those mentioned in Article 2(2) Residence Directive who, in the country from which they have come, are dependants or members of the household of the EU citizen, or who because of serious health grounds strictly require the personal care of the EU citizen;
- the partner with whom the EU citizen has a duly attested durable relationship; and
- the dependent parents of EU citizens who are students, as well as the dependent parents of the spouse or partner (section III.D).

By virtue of Decision No 158/2007 of the EEA Joint Committee, the relevant provisions of the Residence Directive are equally applicable to the family members of nationals of the EEA Member States (section IV). With regard to family members of Swiss nationals, the obligation to facilitate entry and residence applies to those who are dependent on or who lived with the Swiss national in the country of origin (section V.C).

It has been argued that integration requirements may be enacted for the admission of the above categories of family members, as long as requests for family reunification are always subject to an individual assessment with the view to granting admission. However, the Dutch government has chosen to admit these family members under the same conditions as EU citizens (and nationals of an EEA Member State or Switzerland) themselves.[142] No integration requirements are therefore imposed.

B. Long-term Residents and their Family Members

Third-country nationals who are long-term residents may move to the Netherlands in accordance with the provisions of the Long-term Residents Directive. Their right of residence may be conditioned upon fulfilment of integration requirements, provided they have not already complied with such requirements to obtain long-term resident status in the first Member State (section VI.D). Family members of long-term residents may not be required to comply with integration requirements, provided the family was already constituted in the first Member State.

Here, too, the Dutch legislator has chosen not to make use of the discretion available under the LRD. Long-term residents and their family members are exempted from the requirement to obtain a long-term visa and

[142] Arts 8.7(2), (3) and (4) of the Aliens Decree (*Vreemdelingenbesluit 2000*).

hence also from the obligation to pass the integration exam abroad (chapter 2, section VI.B.iii). It is observed that the wording of the relevant provisions of the Aliens Act does not entirely correspond with that of the LRD, as Article 17(1)(h) Aliens Act mentions only the spouse and minor children of the long-term resident. This leaves out the minor children of the spouse, who are also covered by the LRD providing the spouse has custody or shared custody and the children are dependent on him or her.[143] However, as seen in chapter 2, the AIA does not in any case apply to children who have not yet reached the age of majority.

As a matter of Dutch immigration policy, the exemption from the integration exam abroad is extended to the registered partner of the long-term resident, as well as to his or her children.[144] This extension is in conformity with Article 16(2) LRD, which allows Member States to accept other family members of the long-term resident for family reunification under the conditions provided in the directive (section VI.E.iii).

C. EU Blue Card Holders and their Family Members

Lastly, the position of EU Blue Card holders and their family members is discussed. Under Dutch immigration rules, the residence of EU Blue Card holders and their family members is regarded as temporary for the purposes of the integration legislation.[145] Since aliens whose residence permit is issued for a temporary purpose are not obliged to comply with integration requirements, either abroad or in the Netherlands, EU Blue Card holders and their family members are exempted from the AIA.[146] This is in conformity with the provisions of the Blue Card Directive (section VII).

IX. CONCLUDING OBSERVATIONS

This chapter examines the right of free movement in the law of the European Union. For EU citizens, the right to move to other Member States (and to bring along their family members) is instrumental to the achievement of economic integration within the EU and to the realisation of an internal market. At the same time, the right to move and reside freely in the Member States forms an essential element of the concept of EU citizenship. Under the existing legal framework, EU citizens and their family members are now entitled to reside in any other Member State, subject

143 Art 16(1) LRD in conjunction with Art 4(1)(d) FRD.
144 Para B1/4.1.1 Aliens Circular (*Vreemdelingencirculaire 2000*).
145 Art 2.1(1)(a) and (p) Integration Decree (*Besluit inburgering*).
146 Art 16(1)(h) Aliens Act in conjunction Art 3(1)(a) Integration Act 2007 (*Wet inburgering*).

only to limited restrictions, even when their family members are third-country nationals who did not previously have lawful residence in the EU. The situation of nationals of the EEA Member States and Switzerland bears a strong resemblance to that of EU citizens. Despite the lack of an underlying notion of citizenship, the legal conditions governing their right of residence in the Member States are largely similar.

The legal instruments governing the free movement of EU citizens and their family members do not foresee the possibility of making their right of residence in another Member State subject to integration requirements such as those enacted in the Netherlands. In general, the only conditions pertaining to the right of free movement are that immigrants must attain a certain level of economic self-sufficiency and must not pose a threat to the public policy, public security or public health in the receiving Member State. No other limitations, including conditions intended to select immigrants with a view to their participation in or commitment to the receiving society, are allowed. The Member States remain competent to regulate the admission of those EU citizens, nationals of EEA Member States or Switzerland and family members of the above categories who are not entitled to free movement under the legal instruments discussed in this chapter. However, the broad scope of the right of free movement and the low threshold set for its exercise mean that the extent of this competence has been strongly reduced. With regard to the admission of EU citizens in particular, the discretion still available to the Member States is of very little practical relevance.

For third-country nationals not falling into the above categories, the situation is less straightforward. It can still be argued that, as a general rule, these third-country nationals are only entitled to reside in the Member State to which they have been admitted and do not enjoy a right of free movement comparable to that of EU citizens. Nevertheless, a right of long-term residence in another Member State is included in both the LRD and the BCD. These directives regulate the intra-EU movement of third-country nationals who are long-term residents, EU Blue Card holders and their family members, provided the family was already constituted in the first Member State. Interestingly, the directives allow the Member States to impose integration requirements only for the admission of long-term residents.

It has been argued that Member States' discretion with regard to integration requirements for long-term residents is not unlimited: such requirements may not undermine the objectives or effectiveness of the Long-term Residents Directive and must, moreover, be proportionate. This implies that integration requirements enacted by the Member States must be such that they can be met by long-term residents with a reasonable amount of effort. Nevertheless, the possibility of imposing integration requirements on long-term residents represents an exception to the overall picture emerging from this chapter, which is that the right of free movement under EU law cannot be restricted by such conditions.

In this way a sort of three-step ladder is created: on top are those immigrants entitled to free movement without being subjected to integration conditions; these include EU citizens, but also EU Blue Card holders and their family members. Then come long-term residents, who may be asked to comply with integration requirements, but only within the limits set by the LRD. Family members of long-term residents may also be placed in this category: although they may not be asked to comply with integration requirements themselves, their right of residence is dependent on that of the long-term resident. Thirdly, there is the category of persons who are not entitled to free movement as a matter of EU law and whose admission may therefore be subjected to integration requirements determined by the individual Member States, subject of course to obligations under international law.

It was concluded that the Dutch legislation concerning the integration exam abroad is compatible with the right of free movement as regulated by EU law. It can even be argued that Dutch legislation is more consistent, as it does not impose integration requirements on long-term residents seeking to exercise their right of free movement. Nonetheless, a tension can be observed between the EU right of free movement and the Dutch integration policy, to the extent that the latter is based on a national conception of integration. Whereas the AIA identifies knowledge of the Dutch language and Dutch society as factors indicative of a person's capacity to integrate in the Netherlands, beneficiaries of the right to free movement cannot be required to demonstrate such knowledge in order to be admitted.

7

International Relations and Labour Migration

I. INTRODUCTION

THIS CHAPTER DEALS with immigration provisions in international (often bilateral) agreements between states. Such agreements may be concluded for a variety of reasons, for example to promote international trade or other forms of (economic) cooperation, to enhance diplomatic relations or to give expression to the ties stemming from a colonial past. Included in these agreements there may be a right of residence for nationals or certain categories of nationals of the Contracting States, who are thereby placed in a privileged position vis-à-vis other aliens. For the Netherlands, relevant immigration provisions are not only to be found in the agreements that it has concluded itself but also in those concluded by the EU (and its Member States) with third countries. The latter category of agreements is also discussed in this chapter.[1]

Apart from aliens who benefit from international relations this chapter deals with another privileged category of immigrants, namely those admitted for the purpose of performing paid labour. Like most states, the Netherlands is willing to admit (mostly highly qualified) aliens who can compensate for shortages in the labour market and contribute to economic growth. However, the admission of labour migrants is not only a matter of national law. As seen in the previous chapter, the admission of highly qualified labour migrants is regulated at an EU level by the Blue Card Directive. Also of relevance are the European Convention on the Legal Status of Migrant Workers and the European Social Charter, which have been concluded within the framework of the Council of Europe. The latter agreement contains a provision concerning family reunification of labour migrants. Where the admission of family members is linked to the admission of labour migrants or aliens admitted under bilateral agreements, their position is also discussed in this chapter.

[1] These agreements include the EEA Agreement and the EC-Switzerland Agreement concerning the free movement of persons. Given, however, the close resemblance between these agreements and the provisions of EU law regarding the right to free movement, these agreements are discussed in ch 6.

Like the previous chapters, this chapter examines the scope of the admission rights granted by the above legal instruments, and whether those instruments allow for immigrants to be selected on the basis of integration-related criteria.

II. INTERNATIONAL AGREEMENTS CONCLUDED BY THE EUROPEAN UNION

Over time the European Union (often together with the Member States) has concluded a large number of agreements, also known as association agreements, with third countries.[2] Although the relationship between the EU (and the Member States) and third countries is governed by public international law, the association agreements also form part of the EU legal order.[3] As such, these agreements are capable of creating rights and obligations for the Member States (*cf* Art 216 (2) TFEU), as well as for individuals in relation to those Member States.[4] Most of the existing association agreements do not create any rights of admission for third-country nationals to the EU Member States.[5] An important exception, however, is the Association Agreement between the EEC and Turkey. This Agreement, and the decisions adopted to give it effect, is discussed below in section II.A. In addition, some potentially relevant provisions are included in the Stabilisation and Association Agreements concluded with several countries in the Western Balkans that are, along with Turkey, actual or potential candidates for membership of the EU. The latter agreements are briefly discussed in section II.B.

A. The Association Agreement between the EEC and Turkey

The Association Agreement between the EEC and Turkey ('EEC-Turkey Agreement') entered into force in the Netherlands on 1 December 1964.[6] Articles 12–14 of the Agreement provide that the Contracting Parties shall be guided by the relevant provisions in the EC Treaty (now the TFEU) in order to gradually bring about the free movement of workers and to

[2] The competence for concluding these agreements is laid down in Art 217 TFEU (formerly Art 310 TEC).

[3] eg, CoJ 30 April 1974, C-181/73 [1974] ECR 449 (*Haegeman*), para 5.

[4] Chalmers et al 2010, 652–53, see also Hailbronner 2000, 216–20.

[5] Boeles et al 2009, 92–95 and Wiesbrock 2010, 97–109. The latter author also mentions the partnership and cooperation agreements concluded with several former USSR states on the basis of Art 133 TEC (now Art 207 TFEU). A full overview of the international agreements concluded by the EU can be found in the European Commission's Treaties Office Database, at http://ec.europa.eu/world/agreements/default.home.do.

[6] [1964] OJ 217/3687 (no English version available), approved by Council Decision 64/732/EEC of 23 December 1963, [1964] OJ L217/3685.

eliminate restrictions on the right to establishment and the free movement of services. More specific provisions can be found in the Additional Protocol to the EEC-Turkey Agreement[7] and in the decisions adopted by the EEC-Turkey Association Council pursuant to Article 36 of the Protocol. A distinction can be made between the legal regime applying to the free movement of workers and that applying to the right to establishment.[8]

According to Article 41(2) of the Additional Protocol it is up to the Association Council, established pursuant to Article 6 of the Agreement, to determine the timetable for the progressive abolition of existing restrictions on the freedom of establishment. So far, however, the Association Council has not acted upon this assignment. With regard to workers, Article 36 Additional Protocol provides that the Association Council shall take the necessary measures to secure, progressively and in accordance with the principles set out in Article 12 of the Association Agreement, their free movement between the EU Member States and Turkey. The Council has adopted several decisions pursuant to this provision, of which Decision 1/80 is most relevant to the topic discussed here. Articles 6 and 7 of this decision grant Turkish workers and their family members a right of access to the labour market that is established gradually after several years of lawful employment.

The EEC-Turkey Agreement and the related instruments do not expressly grant Turkish nationals or their family members a right of entry or residence in the EU Member States. In the interpretation of the CoJ, Articles 6 and 7 of Decision 1/80 grant Turkish workers and their family members a right of residence as a corollary to the right of access to the labour market, so as not to render the latter right ineffective. However, this right of residence exists only after the Member State concerned has permitted the Turkish worker and/or his family members to enter its territory and to take up employment there. Consequently, the power of the Member States to regulate the entry and initial residence of Turkish workers and their family members is unaffected by the said provisions.[9] Nevertheless, the legal instruments pertaining to the association with Turkey contain a number of standstill and non-discrimination clauses that are of relevance for the admission of Turkish nationals. These clauses are discussed in the following subsections, followed by a brief review of the position of family members of Turkish workers and self-employed persons.

[7] [1972] OJ L293/4 (English-language version [1977] OJ L361/60).

[8] The EEC-Turkey Agreement also concerns the freedom to provide services. However, as remarked in the previous chapter, any right of residence deriving from this freedom is by definition temporary and thus less relevant to the purposes of this study. The following sections therefore mention only the right to establishment, even if the legal rules discussed also concern the freedom to provide services.

[9] CoJ 16 December 1992, C-237/91 [1992] ECR I-6781 (*Kus*), para 25; CoJ 17 April 1997, C-351/95 [1997] ECR I-2133 (*Kadiman*), paras 31 and 32; more recently CoJ 24 January 2008, C-294/06 [2008] ECR I-203 (*Payir and others*), para 36.

i. Standstill Clauses: No New Restrictions for the Admission of Turkish Workers and Self-employed Persons

The first paragraph of Article 41 Additional Protocol states that 'the Contracting Parties shall refrain from introducing between themselves any new restrictions on the freedom of establishment and the freedom to provide services'. A similar standstill clause is laid down in Article 13 of Decision 1/80 with regard to the free movement of workers: the Member States may not introduce new restrictions on the conditions of access to employment applicable to workers and their family members legally resident and employed in their respective territories. According to the CoJ, these provisions prohibit the Contracting Parties from introducing new restrictions on the free movement of workers or the freedom of establishment as from the date of entry into force of the respective legal instruments (the Additional Protocol and Decision 1/80).[10] The Court has held both provisions to be directly effective; Turkish nationals can consequently rely on it before the courts of the Member States.[11]

Importantly, the standstill clauses do not, in themselves, grant Turkish nationals a right of establishment, access to the labour market or entry or residence in the Member States of the EU. The CoJ has repeatedly stressed that the provisions pertaining to the EEC-Turkey Association 'do not encroach upon the competence retained by the Member State to regulate both the entry into their territory of Turkish nationals and the conditions under which they may take up their first employment'.[12] Nevertheless, when regulating on this matter, Member States may not adopt any rules that have the object or effect of making the establishment or employment of Turkish nationals subject to stricter conditions than those existing before the standstill clauses entered into force.[13] In recent case law, the CoJ clarified that the scope of the standstill clauses covers not only rules relating to the exercise of an economic activity (as an employed or self-employed person), but also rules relating to the initial admission of Turkish nationals to a Member State where they intend to exercise such activity. This was decided, with regard to Article 41(1) Additional Protocol, in the case of *Tum and Dari* and, with regard to Article 13 Decision 1/80, in *Commission v the Netherlands*.[14]

[10] CoJ 11 Ma 2000, C-37/98 [2000] ECR I-2927 (*Savas*), para 46; CoJ 21 October 2003, C-317/01 and 369/01 [2003] ECR I-12301 (*Abatay & Sahin*), para 74.

[11] *Savas* (n 10), paras 46–54; *Kadiman* (n 9), para 28.

[12] *Savas* (n 10), paras 58 and 64; *Abatay & Sahin* (n 10), paras 62–63; CoJ 20 September 2007, C-16/05 [2007] ECR I-7415 (*Tum & Dari*), paras 52 and 58; more recently CoJ 21 January 2010, C-462/08 [2010] ECR I-00563 (*Bekleyen*), paras 35 and 36.

[13] *Abatay & Sahin* (n 10 above), para 66.

[14] *Tum & Dari* (n 12), para 63; CoJ 29 April 2010, C-92/07 [2010] ECR I-03683 (*Commission v the Netherlands*), para 49. In *Tum & Dari* the Court made the proviso that EU law may not be relied upon in cases of abuse or fraudulent conduct on the part of the persons concerned, see para 64.

As far as Article 13 is concerned, it may be claimed that the CoJ's judgment in *Commission v the Netherlands* neglects the wording of this provision, which expressly mentions 'workers and their family members *legally resident* and employed in [the Member States]' (emphasis added). The Court supported its decision with the argument that the standstill clause of Article 13 is of the same kind as that of Article 41(1) Additional Protocol and serves an identical objective; hence both provisions must be interpreted in the same way.[15] However, it may be argued, conversely, that the wording of Article 13 Decision 1/80 specifically indicates that the scope of this provision is narrower than that of Article 41(1) Additional Protocol, thus denoting that the Contracting Parties were more reluctant to give up control over the position of workers than over that of self-employed persons.[16] More generally, it may be remarked that there is an obvious tension between the CoJ's stance that the EU Member States remain competent to rule on the initial admission of Turkish nationals and its interpretation of the standstill clauses, whereby Member States are not allowed to impose any new restrictions with regard to such admission. In fact, the CoJ appears to have expanded the scope of the relevant legal instruments beyond that attributed to them in its earlier case law, without explaining the reasons for this expansion.[17]

Despite these objections, it is clear from current case law that admission criteria adopted by EU Member States may be contrary to the standstill clauses of the EEC-Turkey Association. In principle, Member States are precluded from adopting any measures that have the object or effect of making the admission of Turkish workers or self-employed persons subject to more restrictive conditions than those applying when the respective standstill clauses entered into force. Nonetheless, the CoJ has ruled that the standstill clauses allow for the enactment of new measures where such measures are also applicable to EU citizens. This is derived from Article 59 of the Additional Protocol, which provides that Turkey may not receive more favourable treatment than that granted by the EU Member States to one another under the TFEU. In the CoJ's view, Article 59 read in conjunction with the standstill clauses implies that the admission of Turkish workers and self-employed persons may not be subject to new obligations that are disproportionate compared with those applying to EU citizens.[18]

[15] See also CoJ 17 September 2009, C-242/06 [2009] ECR I-8465 (*Sahin*), para 65.

[16] As was the case with regard to the accession of Bulgaria and Romania to the EU: transitional measures were adopted in this context concerning the right of access to the labour market, but not the right of establishment (section II.A of ch 6). Compare also the Stabilisation and Association Agreements discussed in section II.B.

[17] See also Groenendijk 2010, point 3.

[18] *Sahin* (n 15), para 71; *Commission v the Netherlands* (n 14), para 55. It is recalled that the admission of EU citizens is regulated by EU law (the Residence Directive) and is subject only to limited conditions, see ch 6, section II.B.

The Court has also specified that the term 'restrictions' in Article 41(1) Additional Protocol and Article 13 Decision 1/80 covers both procedural and material conditions for admission.[19] Moreover, with regard to short-stay visa requirements, the Court held that these were liable to constitute a restriction to free movement not only because denying a visa would prevent such movement altogether, but also because of the 'additional and recurrent administrative and financial burdens' involved in obtaining a visa.[20] These considerations suggest that the standstill clauses are equally prohibitive of the introduction of integration requirements, such as the obligation to pass an integration exam abroad, provided such requirements did not already exist in the legislation of the Member State concerned. Consequently, such requirements may not be adopted by the Member States in relation to Turkish nationals seeking admission for the purposes of engaging in economic activity, either as a worker or as a self-employed person.

ii. Non-discrimination

Apart from the standstill clauses, the legal instruments pertaining to the EEC-Turkey Association also contain a number of provisions prohibiting discrimination between Turkish nationals and nationals of EU Member States. Article 9 of the Association Agreement contains a general clause that prohibits any kind of discrimination on the grounds of nationality within the scope of the Agreement, in accordance with the principle laid down in Article 7 EEC Treaty (now Art 18 TFEU). Additionally, Article 10 of Decision 1/80 prescribes that Member States shall not discriminate between Turkish workers and EU workers as regards remuneration and other conditions of work.[21]

It follows from their wording that the scope of the above provisions is limited to matters falling within the scope of the Association Agreement (Art 9 Agreement) or to remuneration and other conditions of work (Art 10 Decision 1/80). Hence, for a long time it could be assumed that these non-discrimination clauses did not apply to the admission of Turkish workers and self-employed persons to the territory of the EU Member States. However, as described above, the CoJ has in recent years expanded the scope of the legal instruments pertaining to the EEC-Turkey Association so as also to cover initial admissions. Given this case law, the criteria relating to the admission of Turkish workers and self-employed persons would also seem to come within the scope of Article 9 of the Association Agreement. Indeed, this was confirmed by the CoJ in

[19] *Tum & Dari* (n 12), para 69; *Sahin* (n 15), para 65.

[20] CoJ 19 February 2009, C-228-06 [2009] ECR I-1031 (*Soysal & Savatli*), para 55. This case concerned the freedom to provide services.

[21] See also Art 37 of the Additional Protocol.

Commission v the Netherlands, where the Court considered discriminatory the administrative charges levied by the Dutch authorities for the acquisition and extension of residence permits by Turkish nationals. The Court also held that, for Turkish workers, the charges constituted a condition of work that was discriminatory and hence contrary to Article 10 of Decision 1/80.[22]

It follows that conditions imposed by EU Member States for the admission of Turkish workers and persons wishing to avail themselves of the freedom of establishment must be compatible with Article 9 Association Agreement and Article 10 Decision 1/80. It is not entirely clear from the Court's case law whether this excludes all conditions that are not also imposed on EU citizens. In any case, however, the conditions imposed on Turkish nationals may not be disproportionate compared to those imposed on EU citizens. The proportionality test applied by the CoJ in this respect appears to be strict: in *Commission v the Netherlands*, for example, the Court considered the charges levied on Turkish nationals to be disproportionate since the difference between these charges and those levied on EU citizens was more than minimal.[23]

The non-discrimination clauses of Article 9 Association Agreement and Article 10 Decision 1/80 would consequently seem to limit the competence of Member States regarding the admission of Turkish nationals even further than the standstill clauses discussed in the previous section. Effectively, the former oblige Member States to regulate the admission of Turkish workers and self-employed persons in the same (or almost the same) way as the admission of EU citizens. As described in the previous chapter, this leaves very little scope for Member States to impose requirements for residence. The possibility of imposing integration requirements also appears to be excluded. Lastly, it may be observed that Turkish nationals can in all likelihood rely on the non-discrimination clauses vis-à-vis the Member States. The direct effect of Article 10 of Decision 1/80 has already been established by the Court.[24] With regard to Article 9 of the Association Agreement the Court has not yet established that it has direct effect; it follows, however, from *Commission v the Netherlands* that this provision is sufficiently precise and unconditional to determine whether a given condition must be considered discriminatory in a particular case.[25]

[22] *Commission v the Netherlands* (n 14), para 75. It can be objected that it is stretching the term 'condition of work' too far to hold that it also covers conditions for admission to the territory. However, if such conditions fall outside the scope of Art 10 Decision 1/80, they will arguably still be covered by the general non-discrimination clause of Art 9 of the Agreement.

[23] *Commission v the Netherlands* (n 14), para 74. In this case the lowest charges were more than two-thirds higher than the charges imposed on EU citizens, a difference which the Court did not consider to be 'minimal'.

[24] CoJ 8 May 2003, C-171/01 [2003] ECR I-410 (*Wählergruppe Gemeinsam*), paras 54–67.

[25] *Commission v the Netherlands* (n 14), paras 75–76, see also Groenendijk 2010, point 7.

iii. Family Members of Turkish Workers and Self-employed Persons

Attention must also be paid to the position of family members of Turkish workers and self-employed persons. The legal instruments adopted in the context of the EEC-Turkey Association do not contain a right to family reunification. With regard to Decision 1/80, this was confirmed by the CoJ in the case of *Demirel*.[26] However, recent case law contains a number of indications that the admission of family members of Turkish nationals may nevertheless be regulated, at least to a certain extent, by the said instruments.

A first indication can be found in the CoJ's judgment in *Abatay & Sahin*, where the Court stated that

> Decision 1/80 does not make the access to the territory of a Member State of family members of a Turkish worker already legally present in that state in order to join the rest of the family conditional on the exercise of paid employment.[27]

Here, the Court seems to proceed on the assumption that the admission of family members of Turkish workers is subject to the provisions of Decision 1/80. This was later confirmed in the case of *Commission v the Netherlands*, where the Court found the administrative charges levied on Turkish workers *and their family members* to be contrary to the non-discrimination clause of Article 10 of Decision 1/80. The same conclusion was also drawn, in the light of Article 9 Association Agreement, with regard to family members of Turkish nationals seeking to establish themselves in a Member State.[28]

Family members of Turkish workers and self-employed persons are not mentioned in Article 10 of Decision 1/80, nor indeed in Article 9 of the Agreement or Article 41(1) of the Additional Protocol. This raises the question of why the Court nevertheless found that it could examine the conditions relating to the admission of these family members. One answer to this question could be that the Court did not consider the position of the family members themselves, but instead considered family reunification as one of the conditions of work or establishment in respect of which Turkish workers and self-employed persons are entitled to be treated without discrimination compared with Community nationals. This would be reminiscent of the Court's approach under EU law, whereby the right to family reunification is considered to be inherent in the right of free movement of EU citizens (chapter 6, section III.A).[29] If this is indeed

[26] CoJ 30 September 1987, C-12/86 [1987] ECR 3719 (*Demirel*), paras 22 and 28.

[27] *Abatay & Sahin* (n 10), para 82.

[28] *Commission v the Netherlands* (n 14), paras 75–76.

[29] See also CoJ 29 March 2012, C-7/10 and 9/10 [2012] ECR 00000 (*Kahveci & Inan*), para 3, where the Court confirmed that Art 7 of Decision 1/80 'seeks to enable family members to be with a migrant worker, with a view to thus furthering, by means of family reunification, the

the view taken by the Court, it would also imply that the admission of family members of Turkish self-employed persons is a condition of establishment, to which the standstill clause of Article 41(1) Additional Protocol is applicable. With regard to family members of Turkish workers, the standstill clause of Article 13 Decision 1/80 applies in any case as family members are expressly mentioned in this provision.

As the CoJ did not give reasons for applying the above provisions to family members of Turkish workers and self-employed persons, it cannot be said with certainty that the above explanation is correct. If it is, this would mean another step in the process whereby the position of Turkish nationals is increasingly being put on a par with that of EU citizens, as well as another limitation to the competence of the EU Member States in the field of immigration regulation. Arguably, this expansion is not in itself contrary to the objectives of the Association Agreement, which include the realisation of the free movement of workers and the right of establishment by reference to the EEC Treaty (now TFEU).[30] However, as the Court itself has held in previous case law, the provisions setting out these objectives only constitute programmatic clauses that are incapable of directly governing the position of Turkish nationals.[31] The implementation of these provisions is a task for the Association Council, which is a common organ of the Contracting Parties and hence cannot be substituted by the CoJ.

B. Stabilisation and Association Agreements with the Western Balkan Countries

The EU and its Member States have concluded Stabilisation and Association Agreements ('SAAs') with four countries in the Western Balkans, namely Macedonia, Croatia, Albania and Montenegro.[32] The aims of these association agreements include the promotion of harmonious economic relations and the gradual development of a free trade.[33] At the time of writing, Albania, Macedonia and Montenegro were (potential) candidate countries, whereas Croatia was an acceding country, expected

employment and residence of the Turkish worker who is already legally integrated in the host Member State'.

[30] Arts 12 and 13 of the Association Agreement.

[31] *Demirel* (n 26), para 23. See also Hailbronner 2000, 229–31.

[32] [2004] OJ L84/1 (Macedonia, entry into force on 1 April 2004); [2005] OJ L26/3 (Croatia, entry into force on 1 February 2005); [2009] OJ L107/166 (Albania, entry into force on 1 April 2009) and [2010] OJ L108/3 (Montenegro, entry into force on 1 May 2010). Stabilisation and Association Agreements have also been signed with Serbia and Bosnia and Herzegovina; however these agreements have not yet entered into force. See http://ec.europa.eu/enlargement/countries/check-current-status/index_en.htm.

[33] See Art 1 of the respective agreements.

to join the EU on 1 July 2013. The SAAs contain very few provisions of relevance to the admission of nationals of the said countries to the EU Member States. In this respect, the agreements are even less 'generous' than the Europe Agreements concluded with various Central and Eastern European countries preceding their accession to the EU in 2004 and 2007.[34] Still, a number of provisions are useful to mention. The contents of each of the agreements are largely identical; where relevant differences exist this will be stated.

Each of the agreements contains a prohibition of discrimination for workers who are nationals of the respective third countries and legally employed in the territory of a Member State.[35] This prohibition concerns discrimination with regard to working conditions, remuneration or dismissal compared to the nationals of the Member State. The wording of the relevant provisions strongly indicates that the admission of third-country nationals is not included within their scope; in other words, such nationals cannot rely on them in order to be granted entry or residence in an EU Member State.[36] Admittedly, this interpretation is subject to some doubt, given the CoJ's judgment in *Commission v the Netherlands* (section II.A.ii above), where it was held that administrative charges for acquiring a residence permit came within the meaning of Article 10 of Decision 1/80 pertaining to the EEC-Turkey Agreement. The wording of the latter provisions is similar to that of the non-discrimination clauses in the SAAs. However, the meaning of these clauses must be assessed in their own context, taking into account the object and purpose of the agreements in which they are included.[37] In this connection it is observed that the objectives of the SAAs are less far-reaching, where the freedom of movement of workers is concerned, than those of the EEC-Turkey Agreement. In particular, the SAAs do not contain any clauses comparable to Article 12 of the EEC-Turkey Association Agreement, which calls for the progressive realisation of the freedom of movement of workers to be guided by the relevant provisions of the EEC Treaty (now TFEU). The SAAs moreover do not include a general non-discrimination clause, as laid down in Article 9 EEC-Turkey Agreement.

As regards establishment, the SAAs primarily contain provisions relating to the establishment of companies from the associated third countries in the EU Member States. Such companies are entitled to treatment no less favourable than that accorded by the Member States to their own companies or to any company of any third country, whichever is better.[38] The

[34] On these agreements see, eg, Staples 1999, 239–70 and Hailbronner 2000, 239–53.

[35] Art 44(1) SAA Macedonia, Art 45(1) SAA Croatia, Art 46(1) SAA Albania and Art 49(1) SAA Montenegro.

[36] See also Hailbronner 2000, 241–43 and Hedemann-Robinson 2001, 570–72 with regard to similar provisions in the Europe Agreements.

[37] eg, CoJ 27 September 2001, C-257/99 [2001] ECR I-6557 (*Barkoci & Malik*), paras 51–52.

[38] Art 48(3) SAA Macedonia, Art 49(3) SAA Croatia, Art 50(3) SAA Albania and Art 53(2) SAA Montenegro.

Contracting Parties have also agreed not to adopt any new regulations or measures that would introduce discrimination as regards the establishment or operation of companies of the other party, compared to their own companies.[39] The SAAs provide for the above provisions eventually to be extended to the establishment of natural persons. The modalities for such extension are to be determined by the Stabilisation and Association Councils, four or five years after the entry into force of the respective agreements.[40] For Croatia and Macedonia, the relevant dates have already passed (1 February 2009 for Croatia, 1 April 2009 for Macedonia); at the time of writing, however, no action had yet been taken. Given that the relevant articles of the SAAs require implementation by the Stabilisation and Association Councils, it must be assumed that these provisions do not have direct effect.[41] Hence, until action is taken by the Councils, nationals of Croatia and Macedonia will not be able to rely on the SAAs to obtain a right of establishment in the EU Member States.[42]

Each of the SAAs contains a clause stating that

> nothing in this Agreement shall prevent the Parties from applying their laws and regulations regarding entry and stay, employment, working conditions, establishment of natural persons and supply of services, provided that, in so doing, they do not apply them in such a manner as to nullify or impair the benefits accruing to any Party under the terms of a specific provision of this Agreement.[43]

With regard to similar clauses in the Europe Agreements, the CoJ held that, in any case, rights of entry and residence conferred on third-country nationals by those agreements could not be regarded as 'absolute privileges' inasmuch as their exercise could be limited by rules of the host Member State. On the other hand, such limitations may not be of such a nature as to make it impossible or excessively difficult to exercise the rights granted by the agreements.[44] For the time being, however, this case

[39] Art 49(2) SAA Croatia, Art 50(2) SAA Albania and Art 53(3) Montenegro. The SAA Macedonia only contains an obligation on the part of Macedonia vis-à-vis EU companies, see Art 48(2).

[40] Art 48(4) SAA Macedonia, Art 49(4) SAA Croatia, Art 50(4) SAA Albania and Art 53(4) SAA Montenegro. The provision in the Macedonia Agreement differs from the other provisions in that it requires the SAA Council to examine whether to extend the provisions on establishment to natural persons, in the light of the CoJ case law and the situation in the labour market.

[41] Compare *Savas* (n 10), paras 39–45, with regard to Art 41(2) Additional Protocol to the EEC-Turkey Agreement.

[42] A right of residence does exist with regard to 'key personnel' of companies from the associated countries that are established in an EU Member State, see Art 53 SAA Macedonia and the corresponding articles in the other agreements. However, this right of residence is by definition temporary (see the relevant provisions) and therefore not relevant for the purposes of this study.

[43] Art 62 SAA Macedonia, Art 63 SAA Croatia, Art 64 SAA Albania and Art 66 SAA Montenegro.

[44] eg, *Barkoci & Malik* (n 37), para 83; CoJ (Grand Chamber) 16 November 2004, C-327/02 [2004] ECR I-11055 (*Panayotova*), para 39.

law is not relevant in respect of the SAAs because the latter do not (yet) grant any admission rights to third-country nationals.

C. International Agreements Concluded by the EU and the Act on Integration Abroad

Having looked at several international agreements concluded at the EU level, the AIA is now considered in relation to those agreements. As established in section II.B, the Stabilisation and Association Agreements with Macedonia, Croatia, Albania and Montenegro do not as yet grant any residence rights to nationals of those countries. Consequently, the power of the Dutch authorities to apply the AIA to these nationals remains unaffected. The same cannot be said, however, with regard to Turkish nationals who come within the personal scope of the Association Agreement between the EEC and Turkey. With regard to these nationals, the standstill and non-discrimination clauses of the Association Agreement, the Additional Protocol and Decision 1/80 have to be taken into account.

Until August 2011, Dutch immigration law did not contain a general clause to the effect that Turkish nationals were exempted from the integration exam abroad. However, as explained in chapter 2 (section VI.B.iii), such an exemption has since been introduced in response to a judgment of the Central Appeals Tribunal (*Centrale Raad van Beroep*). The Tribunal ruled that Turkish nationals falling under the scope of the EEC-Turkey Association Agreement cannot be subjected to compulsory integration under the Integration Act 2007 (the integration exam in the Netherlands).[45] Consequently, because the target group of the AIA is linked to that of the Integration Act, Turkish nationals were also exempted from the integration exam abroad.[46] The latter decision was based on national law, rather than on a finding of incompatibility of the AIA with the EEC-Turkey Association Agreement, the Additional Protocol or Decision 1/80. However, it follows that these instruments are now also respected.

III. INTERNATIONAL AGREEMENTS CONCLUDED BY THE NETHERLANDS

This section examines a number of bi- and multilateral treaties to which the Netherlands is a party and that contain provisions relating to the entry and/or residence of aliens. While it has been argued that similar provisions can be found in several other treaties, it would go beyond the scope

[45] Central Appeals Tribunal 16 August 2011, case nos 10/5248, 10/5249, 10/6123 and 10/6124, LJN: BR4959.

[46] *Parliamentary Papers II* 2011–2012, 31 143, No 89.

of this chapter to discuss each of these agreements separately.[47] In this regard, it is observed that most of these treaties are rarely or never invoked in practice. It is also submitted that, at least where the possibility of imposing integration requirements is concerned, the treaties concluded between the Netherlands and other Member States of the EU or the EEA do not offer any guarantees additional to those already stemming from the TFEU and the EEA Agreement (see chapter 6).[48] For these reasons, the examination in this chapter is limited to four agreements with countries that do not belong to the EU/EEA and from which relatively high numbers of immigrants come to the Netherlands. These are the bilateral treaties concluded with the United States, Japan and Suriname. In addition, the European Convention on Establishment, which is mainly relevant in relation to Turkish nationals, is also considered.

A. The Dutch-American Friendship Treaty

The Dutch-American Friendship Treaty and its Protocol contain limited provisions regarding the entry and residence of American nationals in the Netherlands.[49] In the context of this study the main provision of the Treaty is Article II(1), which grants a right of entry and residence in the Netherlands to American nationals for two specifically defined purposes. These purposes are:

(a) to trade between the territories of the two Contracting Parties and engage in related activities in the area of trade (traders), or
(b) to develop and lead the operation of an enterprise in which they have invested a substantial amount of capital or if they are actually in the process of realising such an investment (entrepreneurs).

Although the Treaty itself does not make the admission of American traders or entrepreneurs subject to any conditions, Article II(4) states that the Contracting Parties retain the right to take 'measures that are neces-

[47] For an overview of approximately 30 bilateral treaties concluded by the Netherlands and their consequences for Dutch immigration law, see Roelofs 2004.

[48] These include the Agreement concerning the Implementation of Articles 55 and 56 of the Treaty concerning the Establishment of the Benelux Economic Union (*Overeenkomst inzake de tenuitvoerlegging van de artikelen 55 en 56 van het Verdrag tot instelling van de Benelux Economische Unie*) and the Agreement on Establishment between the Netherlands and Germany (*Nederlands-Duits Vestigingsverdrag*). The same applies to the Revised Agreement between the Netherlands and Switzerland (*Gewijzigd Nederlands-Zwitsers Traktaat*) in view of the EC-Switzerland Agreement on the free movement of persons (ch 6, section V).

[49] Treaty concerning Friendship, Commerce and Navigation between the Kingdom of the Netherlands and the United States of America (*Verdrag van vriendschap, handel en scheepvaart tussen het Koninkrijk der Nederlanden en de Verenigde Staten van Amerika*), signed in The Hague on 27 March 1956. *Treaty Series* 1956, 40 and following, entry into force for the Netherlands on 5 December 1957. On this treaty, see Steenbergen et al 1999, 369–71; Kuijer and Steenbergen 2005, 246–48 and Roelofs 2003.

sary to maintain public order and to protect public health, public morals or security'.

It follows that the above provisions leave scope for introducing immigration requirements, provided these requirements are necessary in order to meet one of the aims enumerated in Article II(4). Of particular interest in this regard is how the aim of 'maintaining public order' is to be understood. If a narrow definition is adopted, it can be argued that this aim includes only the prevention of criminal acts. Arguably, however, a broader definition of 'public order' would also allow for measures in the field of integration, including measures aiming to promote social cohesion or to create awareness about the legislation and constitutional structure of the host state.

From the preamble of the Dutch-American Friendship Treaty it may be derived that its primary purpose is to reinforce international relations between the US and the Netherlands, rather than to create individual immigration rights for Dutch and American nationals. It is consequently submitted that the aim of 'maintaining public order' must be understood in a broad sense, going beyond the mere prevention of criminal acts.[50] It follows that the admission of American traders and entrepreneurs to the Netherlands could, in principle, be made dependent on integration conditions. Such conditions must however be 'necessary' for the maintenance of public order.[51] It is submitted that this implies that the aim pursued must have a certain weight and that the integration requirement must be reasonably suited to meeting this aim.

According to Article 1 of the Protocol to the Dutch-American Friendship Treaty, the spouse and the unmarried, minor children of an American national entitled to admission under Article II(1)(a) or (b) of the Treaty will also be admitted to the Netherlands if they accompany that national or if they join him or her later for the purpose of family reunification. The wording of Article 1 of the Protocol does not limit the category of beneficiaries to American nationals; hence, it must be assumed that the entitlement to admission also concerns spouses and children with another nationality, subject to the measures referred to in Article II(4).[52]

[50] This is also the view expressed by the Dutch government during the parliamentary deliberations on the ratification of the Treaty. In this debate it was stated that 'measures to maintain public order . . . do not only include incidental government actions for the prevention of imminent threats to that order, but also legislative provisions that have been adopted with the aim of enforcing public order in the widest possible meaning of the word'. See *Parliamentary Papers I* 1956–1957, 4338 (R38), No 140a, 2. For a different view, see Roelofs 2003, 190.

[51] As argued in ch 5 (section II.D), integration measures that aim to create awareness about legislation or constitutional principles could probably be subsumed under the interest of 'protecting public order'. Presumably, however, the interest of maintaining public order is broader and could also cover requirements aiming to promote social cohesion and/or enable the participation of immigrants in various aspects of public life.

[52] See also Roelofs 2003, 190.

Article 2 of the Protocol specifies that the provision of Article II(1)(b) also applies to American nationals representing an American business or entrepreneur and working for that business in a 'responsible' position ('key personnel'). Article II(1)(c) of the Treaty provides that admission shall also be granted for purposes other than those mentioned under (a) or (b), but with respect for the laws of the Contracting State concerning the admission and residence of aliens. It follows that the Dutch-American Friendship Treaty does not preclude the application of national immigration rules, including integration requirements, to American nationals who are not traders or entrepreneurs within the meaning of Article II(1)(a) and (b). Lastly, Article II(2) contains an obligation to facilitate the admission, stay and departure of American tourists and other visitors. However, because of the temporary nature of their stay, this provision is not relevant for the purpose of this study.

B. The Treaty on Commerce and Navigation between the Netherlands and Japan

The Treaty on Commerce and Navigation between the Netherlands and Japan (*Verdrag van handel en scheepvaart tussen Nederland en Japan*) entered into force on 9 October 1913.[53] The Treaty was suspended during the course of the Second World War, but reactivated in 1953.[54] In 2008 the Administrative Jurisdiction Division (AJD) of the Dutch Council of State confirmed that the Treaty was still in force.[55] In the same judgments, the AJD also confirmed that Article 1(1°) of the Treaty may be relied upon by Japanese nationals seeking to be admitted to the Netherlands. According to this provision, Japanese nationals are entitled, where the rights to free movement and residence are concerned, to be treated equally to the nationals of the most favoured nations. Consequently Japanese nationals are entitled to admission under the same conditions as American nationals under the Dutch-American Friendship Treaty (section III.A).[56] It follows that a limited right of admission exists for Japanese traders and entrepreneurs and for their family members, whereby the latter do not need to have Japanese nationality. Nevertheless, it was argued above that this right does not preclude the introduction of integration requirements, provided those requirements are necessary for maintaining public order or for protecting public morals.

[53] *Bulletin of Acts and Decrees* 1913, 389. An English translation of this treaty was published in *The American Journal of International Law*, Vol 8:3, Supplement Official Documents (July 1914), 228–36.

[54] Roelofs 2004, 150.

[55] AJD 8 August 2008, case no 200800099/1 and AJD 8 August 2008, case no 200800100/1.

[56] AJD 8 August 2008, case no 200800099/1, para 2.4.2 and AJD 8 August 2008, case no 200800100/1, para 2.4.2. See also Roelofs 2004, 149.

C. Agreements between the Netherlands and Suriname

After Suriname's independence from the Netherlands in 1975, the two countries concluded the Agreement concerning residence and establishment (*Overeenkomst inzake het verblijf en de vestiging van wederzijdse onderdanen*).[57] This agreement remained in force for five years, until 25 November 1980. In 1982 it was replaced by the Agreement concerning entry and residence (*Overeenkomst inzake de binnenkomst en het verblijf van wederzijdse onderdanen*).[58] A protocol to the latter agreement establishes a right to family reunification for persons granted residence in the Netherlands before 25 November 1980. Considering the time that has since passed, however, it may be assumed that this protocol no longer has much relevance. It is therefore not discussed any further.

Annex I to the 1982 Agreement sets out a number of conditions relating to the entry and residence of Surinamese nationals, including for the purpose of family reunification. Article 9 of the Agreement states that changes to the policy laid down in the Annex should only be effectuated after the Surinamese authorities have been notified of these changes and have had the opportunity to ask for deliberations. In 2000, however, the District Courts' Aliens Affairs Legal Uniformity Chamber (*Rechtseenheidskamer*) decided that Article 9 of the 1982 Agreement was only binding for the Netherlands in its relation to Suriname. The Court pointed out that Article 8 of the Agreement explicitly affirmed the autonomy of both the Netherlands and Suriname with regard to the entry and residence of each other's nationals. Therefore, the Netherlands was not bound by the Agreement to grant admission to Surinamese nationals under the conditions set out in Annex I, even if it had altered these conditions without following the prescribed procedure of notification.[59]

It follows that the 1982 Agreement does not grant any rights of entry or residence in the Netherlands to nationals of Suriname. Article 9, however, obliges the Netherlands to notify the Surinamese authorities of any changes in its immigration policy with regard to Surinamese nationals. It is submitted that the introduction of the integration exam abroad, which applies to Surinamese applicants for family reunification (and religious servants), constitutes such a change (even if in practice nearly all Surinamese nationals are exempted on the grounds that they have received their primary education in Dutch; see section VI.B.iii of chapter 2). To the best of my knowledge, no notification has been given. However,

[57] *Treaty Series* 1975, 133.

[58] *Treaty Series* 1981, 35, entry into force for the Netherlands on 1 December 1982. On both treaties, see Steenbergen et al 1999, 373–78 and Kuijer and Steenbergen 2005, 178.

[59] District Court of The Hague (Aliens Affairs Legal Uniformity Chamber), 30 May 2000, case no 99/18 S1813, *JV* 2000/156, paras 24–25.

it would be up to the Surinamese authorities to decide whether to raise this issue with the Netherlands.

D. The European Convention on Establishment

Unlike the treaties discussed in the previous subsections, which are all bilateral agreements, the European Convention on Establishment (ECE) was concluded within the framework of the Council of Europe.[60] With the exception of Turkey, all the States Parties to the Convention are also Member States of the EU and / or the EEA. While the ECE contains a number of provisions concerning the entry and residence of nationals of other States Parties, these do not grant any rights of free movement additional to those already granted under EU law or the EEA Agreement (chapter 6). The ECE is therefore only relevant with regard to the position of Turkish nationals, who may, in addition, also be covered by the standstill or non-discrimination provisions of the EEC-Turkey Agreement (section II.A).

Article 1 ECE obliges the States Parties to the Convention to facilitate the entry into their territory by nationals of other States Parties, but only for the purpose of temporary visits. In addition Article 2 states that the States Parties must facilitate the prolonged or permanent residence of nationals of the other Parties on their territories. This obligation only exists, however, 'to the extent permitted by the economic and social conditions' of the State Party concerned. Article 2 also indicates that the obligation to facilitate prolonged or permanent residence is subject to the conditions set out in Article 1, which means that it does not apply if this would be contrary to the *ordre public* or to national security, public health or morality. The Protocol to the ECE shows that the application of these grounds is subject to national criteria, as is the determination of the economic and social conditions that may prevent a State Party from admitting nationals of other Parties for prolonged or permanent residence.[61]

Lastly, the Protocol determines that regulations of the States Parties governing the admission and residence of aliens 'shall be unaffected by the Convention in so far as they are not inconsistent with it'.[62] The formulation used here suggests that this stipulation applies only to regulations that already existed when the ECE entered into force. Nevertheless, it is clear from Article 2 of the Convention and the explanatory remarks in the Protocol that the ECE does not grant nationals of the States Parties a right

[60] *Treaty Series* 1956, 20 and following, entry into force for the Netherlands on 21 May 1969. On this treaty, see Steenbergen et al 1999, 97–102.

[61] See Section I(a)(1)-(3) of the Protocol. See also Section III(a), which clarifies that the concept of *ordre public* is to be understood in a wide sense allowing, eg, the exclusion of nationals of another party for political reasons or because they are unable to pay the costs of their stay.

[62] Section II(a) of the Protocol.

to be admitted to the territory of another Party, let alone preclude such a right from being made subject to integration requirements. Instead, it is submitted that the obligation to 'facilitate' prolonged or permanent residence merely requires the States Parties to favourably consider adopting legislation allowing nationals of other Parties to apply for long-term residence, and only in so far as this would not be contrary to the general interests enumerated in Article 1 (see also section IV.C). In doing so, the States Parties must pay due regard to family ties.[63] It follows from the above, however, that the ECE does not provide a legal basis for an actual right to family reunification.

E. International Agreements Concluded by the Netherlands and the Act on Integration Abroad

In conclusion, none of the four international agreements examined above preclude the introduction of integration requirements for the admission of third country nationals per se. The Agreement concerning entry and residence between the Netherlands and Suriname does not contain any restrictions on the introduction of integration requirements, even if it requires the Surinamese authorities to be notified of any such change.

Some limitations to integration requirements do follow from the Dutch-American Friendship Treaty and, by consequence, via the 'most favoured treatment' clause, from the Treaty on Commerce and Navigation with Japan. These limitations are, however, limited in scope as they apply only to American and Japanese traders and entrepreneurs and their family members. It has also been argued that both treaties leave room for integration measures that are 'necessary to maintain public order and to protect public health, public morals or security'. It is submitted that the AIA meets this criterion, at least to the extent that it aims to further the participation of immigrants in various areas of the public domain (and so to improve social cohesion) or to inform them about certain aspects of Dutch legislation or the constitutional structure. Whether all elements of the integration exam abroad (and in particular the 'Knowledge of the Netherlands' test) are equally suitable for this purpose is a question that is not discussed in detail here. After all, as seen in chapter 2 (section VI.B.i), nationals of the United States and Japan are in any case exempted from the AIA. It follows that the Act respects the bilateral treaties concluded with these countries.

Lastly, it was established that the European Convention on Establishment may be of some relevance to the position of Turkish nationals. As the Convention does not grant Turkish nationals a right to be

[63] Section III(b) of the Protocol.

admitted to the Netherlands, however, it is unlikely that they could rely on it before the Dutch courts. In addition, it can be plausibly maintained that the integration exam abroad is a measure aiming to contribute to the safeguarding of the *ordre public*, or that is justified in view of the economic and social conditions of the Netherlands. It is therefore concluded that, in bringing Turkish nationals under the AIA in 2006, the Dutch government did not act contrary to its obligation to facilitate their prolonged or permanent residence as required by Article 2 ECE. As explained earlier in this chapter section II.C), Turkish nationals are currently exempted from the integration exam abroad because this was required by national law.

IV. LABOUR MIGRATION

The final part of this chapter deals with international instruments concerning labour migration to which the Netherlands is a party. As announced in the introduction, the first instrument discussed is the EU Blue Card Directive concerning the admission of highly qualified labour migrants from third countries. Some attention is then paid to the provisions relating to family reunification of labour migrants in the European Convention relating to the Legal Status of Migrant Workers (ECMW) and the European Social Charter (ESC). The revised ILO Convention (No 97) on Migration for Employment is not discussed because it does not contain any provisions relating to entry or residence.

A. The EU Blue Card Directive

The EU Blue Card Directive (BCD) is discussed in chapter 6 in respect of the right of free movement in the law of the European Union. It may be recalled that the aim of this directive is to make the EU more attractive to highly qualified labour migrants from third countries. To this end, the directive sets the conditions of entry and residence (for more than three months) of third-country nationals in EU Member States for the purpose of highly qualified employment, as well as the conditions governing the right of EU Blue Card holders to move to another Member State.[64] The free movement rights of EU Blue Card holders are examined in section VII of the previous chapter. This chapter focuses on the conditions under which a Blue Card must be issued by the first Member State (section IV.A.i), with the conditions for family reunification of EU Blue Card holders, which are also laid down in the Blue Card Directive, being discussed in section IV.A.ii.

[64] Art 1 BCD.

i. The EU Blue Card for Highly Qualified Third-country Nationals

The EU Blue Card is a combination of a work and residence permit that allows third-country nationals to enter and reside in a Member State and take up highly qualified employment there under the terms of the Blue Card Directive.[65] Article 5 of the directive sets the criteria to be met by third-country nationals applying for a Blue Card. The issue of a Blue Card is not dependent on fulfilment of integration requirements. Most of the criteria relate directly to the residence purpose (for example, a valid work contract or binding job offer, proof of relevant higher qualifications and a salary above a minimum threshold). In addition, the applicant must have valid travel and entry documents and evidence of health insurance and must not be considered to pose a threat to public policy, public security or public health.

It follows that the BCD restricts the competence of the Member States to set integration requirements for the admission of highly qualified third-country nationals. Nonetheless, the Blue Card Directive has only limited scope. Article 3 BCD mentions several categories of third-country nationals who are not covered by the directive. These include persons benefiting from various forms of international protection, EU long-term residents and family members of EU citizens exercising their right of free movement. Moreover, third country nationals who meet the above criteria cannot obtain a right of residence without a positive decision from the Member State.[66] Article 8 BCD sets out a number of grounds on which an application for a Blue Card may be refused even if the criteria of Article 5 are met. These include the availability of workers in prioritised categories (such as the national or Community workforce) and the need to ensure ethical recruitment in countries of origin. The Member States also remain entitled to determine the numbers of third-country nationals admitted for the purpose of highly qualified employment.[67] Lastly, the directive does not preclude the right of the Member States to issue residence permits other than an EU Blue Card for any purpose of employment.[68] It is, therefore, concluded that the extent to which the Blue Card Directive effectively constrains the discretion of the EU Member States with regard to the admission of (highly qualified) labour migrants is not very large.

ii. Family Members of EU Blue Card Holders

Third-country nationals who have been issued an EU Blue Card are entitled to bring along their family members. Article 15 BCD declares that the

[65] Art 2(c) BCD.
[66] See also Boeles et al 2009, 231.
[67] Art 6 BCD.
[68] Art 3(4) BCD.

Family Reunification Directive (FRD) is equally applicable to the family reunification of Blue Card holders, subject to a number of derogations. The conditions set by this directive, in particular the requirements relating to integration, are discussed in detail in chapter 6. In the case of family members of EU Blue Card holders, however, integration requirements may only be applied after the persons concerned have been granted family reunification.[69] This implies that a residence permit may not be refused because of the family members failing to comply with integration requirements, which is an important difference from the FRD. This difference is explained by the fact that the BCD aims to create an attractive setting for highly qualified labour migrants, including favourable conditions for family reunification.[70] The preamble to the BCD expressly confirms that the derogation of Article 15(3) does not preclude Member States from maintaining or introducing integration conditions and measures, including language learning, for family members of EU Blue Card holders.[71] However, as established in chapter 6, these requirements fall outside the scope of this study as they can only be imposed after admission has been granted.

B. The European Convention Relating to the Legal Status of Migrant Workers

The European Convention relating to the Legal Status of Migrant Workers (ECMW) was concluded in the framework of the Council of Europe and entered into force for the Netherlands on 1 May 1983.[72] The Convention has been ratified by several EU Member States, as well as Norway and Turkey. In 2006 and 2007 three more countries acceded: Albania, Moldova and Ukraine.

The ECMW does not apply to all migrant workers. Instead its personal scope is limited to those nationals of the Contracting Parties who have been authorised by another Contracting Party to reside in its territory in order to take up paid employment.[73] The criteria governing the granting of authorisation are not laid down in the Convention; hence, the admission of migrant workers is left to the competence of the Contracting Parties. However, Article 12 grants migrant workers a right to family reunification. This provision grants family members of migrant workers a right to be admitted to the territory of the Contracting State where the migrant

[69] Art 15(3) BCD.
[70] Preamble of the BCD, recital 23.
[71] ibid.
[72] CETS No 93, *Treaty Series* 1978, 70 and 1983, 45.
[73] Art 1(1) ECMW. Those excluded from the scope of the Convention also include frontier workers, artists, sailors, persons following an education, seasonal workers and employees of a company established outside the host state, see Art 1(2).

worker is employed. 'Family members' within the meaning of Article 12 are the spouse and the unmarried minor children of the migrant worker, the latter as long as they are dependent.[74] The Convention does not require the family members to have the same nationality as the migrant worker.

The residence right of family members is subject to the same conditions as those set by the Convention for migrant workers themselves.[75] According to Article 9 ECMW, migrant workers and their family members are entitled to a residence permit for the duration of the employment, but this may be withdrawn for reasons of national security, public policy or public morals, because the holder refuses to comply with measures prescribed by an official medical authority or if a condition essential to its issue or validity is not fulfilled. In the case of family reunification, the migrant worker must have normal housing available for the family and may be required to meet certain income requirements.[76] Lastly, the Contracting Parties may impose a waiting period of up to 12 months before granting authorisation for family reunification.[77] The Convention does not, however, leave scope for the Contracting Parties to make family reunification dependent on fulfilment of integration requirements.[78]

Article 12(1) ECMW states that family members of migrant workers 'are authorised . . . to join the migrant worker in the territory of the Contracting Party' if the conditions for this are met. Given the formulation of this provision and the fact that the conditions are laid down in the Convention itself, it is submitted that Article 12(1) ECMW is self-executing in the sense of Article 93 Dutch Constitution (*een ieder verbindend*). This reading is supported by the preamble of the Convention, which refers to the 'rights and privileges' granted to nationals of the Contracting Parties. This means that migrant workers and their family members can rely on this provision before the Dutch courts. For migrant workers who are nationals of Member States of the EU or the EEA the ECMW will be of little relevance, as their situation is already governed by more favourable provisions in the TFEU and the EEA Agreement (chapter 6).[79] However, the Convention does create an additional right of family reunification for nationals of Albania, Moldova and Ukraine. Lastly, it cannot be excluded that the provisions on family reunification in the ECMW are in some respects more favourable than those in the Association Agreement between the EEC and Turkey (section II.A).

[74] Art 12(1) ECMW.

[75] Art 12(1) ECMW.

[76] Art 12(1) and (2) ECMW. Before imposing income requirements the Contracting Parties must send a declaration to the Secretary General of the Council of Europe.

[77] Art 12(1) ECMW.

[78] See also Groenendijk 2007, 113.

[79] Art 32 ECMW provides that the Convention does not preclude more favourable treatment granted by provisions of national law or of any bilateral or multilateral treaties, both anterior and posterior.

C. The European Social Charter (Revised)

The European Social Charter (ESC), in its revised form, entered into force in the Netherlands on 1 July 2006.[80] Like the ECMW, the Charter is also a Council of Europe instrument.[81] The States Parties must agree to be bound by at least a certain number of articles of the Charter, including at least six of the nine designated articles setting out the most important social rights.[82] The Netherlands is bound by the entire Charter, subject to two reservations that are not relevant for the purpose of this study.[83]

Article 19 ESC concerns the right of migrant workers and their families to protection and assistance. According to paragraph 6 of this article, the Contracting Parties undertake 'to facilitate as far as possible the reunion of the family of a foreign worker permitted to establish himself in the territory [of those Parties]'. Article 19(10) ESC extends the scope of this obligation to the family reunion of self-employed migrants.[84] For the purpose of this chapter, the meaning of this provision is analysed and, in particular, the question of whether it stands in the way of integration requirements being imposed on the family reunion of migrant workers.

To begin with, it can be assumed that Article 19(6) ESC does not contain a right to admission for family members, nor does it preclude the family reunion of migrant workers being made subject to conditions or requirements. This follows from the wording of Article 19(6) which states that family reunion must be 'facilitated as far as possible'. This formulation allows more scope for the Contracting Parties than if family reunion were to be 'granted' or 'allowed'.[85] Nevertheless, it is submitted, also on the basis of the wording, that Article 19(6) does place an obligation on the Contracting States to make an effort to reduce obstacles to family reunion to the minimum required by the public interest. This implies that requirements for family reunification are allowed, to the extent that they can be shown to serve a public interest and to be necessary to achieve that objective.

Additionally, with regard to integration requirements, the obligation to facilitate may be taken to mean that the Contracting States must assist

[80] *Treaty Series* 2004, 13 and 2006, 128. Before this date the Netherlands was bound by the original version of the European Social Charter, the provisions of which are largely similar.

[81] CETS No 163.

[82] Art A(1) of Part III ESC.

[83] These reservations are included in the instrument of acceptance deposited with the Secretary General of the Council of Europe, see www.conventions.coe.int.

[84] Hence, references in the rest of this section to migrant workers also include self-employed migrants.

[85] See, however, the conclusions of the European Committee on Social Rights (ECSR) on the Netherlands, in which the Committee refers to the 'right to family reunion', as well as to migrant workers being 'entitled' to be reunited with their spouse. See ECSR Conclusions XVII-1 – Netherlands (Kingdom in Europe) and Aruba, 26, available at www.coe.int. It is submitted that the Committee's approach is not supported by the text of the Charter.

applicants for family reunion in complying with those requirements by, for example, ensuring the availability of preparation materials for an integration test. The Advisory Division of the Dutch Council of State referred to Article 19(6) ESC in support of its stance that the Netherlands should supervise the development of suitable course materials for the integration exam abroad.[86] Article 19(6) can thus be read as calling for a shared responsibility with regard to integration requirements for family reunion, instead of placing the responsibility entirely on the migrant workers and their family members.

A few remarks can be made with regard to the personal scope of Article 19(6) ESC. First of all, Article 19(6) applies only to migrant workers who are nationals of a Contracting State. With regard to most provisions of the Charter a statement to this effect is included in the Appendix. Although Article 19 is not included in this statement, its limitation to nationals of the Contracting Parties nevertheless follows from the wording of this provision, which refers to 'the right of migrant workers and their families to protection and assistance in the territory *of any other Party*' (emphasis added).[87] Furthermore, with regard to family members, the Appendix to the ESC specifies that Article 19(6) covers at least the worker's spouse and unmarried children, the latter as long as they are minors according to the law of the receiving state and dependent on the migrant worker. The family members are not required to have the same nationality as the migrant worker.

As far as the family reunion of migrant workers is concerned, it may be observed that Article 19(6) ESC does not create any obligations for the Contracting Parties beyond those stemming from the TFEU and the EEA Agreement (chapter 6, sections II–IV). Nevertheless, the ESC has been accepted by a number of countries that are not EU or EEA Member States.[88] With regard to migrant workers who are nationals of these countries, the ESC creates an additional obligation. This does not mean, however, that individual migrant workers or their family members can also rely on the Charter provisions before the Dutch courts. The Appendix to Part III of the (revised) ESC states that 'it is understood that the Charter contains legal obligations of an international character, the application of which is submitted solely to the supervision provided for in Part IV'. This seems to exclude the possibility that the Charter also contains obligations of the Contracting Parties vis-à-vis individuals, which could be enforced through the courts.[89] However, even if this statement in the Appendix is

[86] *Parliamentary Papers II* 2003–2004, 29 700, No 4, 5.

[87] See also Steenbergen et al 1999, 106–07 and Wiesbrock 2010, 186.

[88] At the time of writing these countries were Albania, Andorra, Armenia, Azerbaijan, Bosnia and Herzegovina, Georgia, Macedonia, Moldova, Montenegro, Russia, Serbia, Turkey and Ukraine. See http://conventions.coe.int.

[89] Hailbronner 2000, 348.

not taken to exclude direct effect, the contents of the individual provisions are still relevant. The Dutch Central Appeals Tribunal (*Centrale Raad van Beroep*) has held that most provisions of the ESC contain 'generally formulated social objectives which the Contracting Parties have bound themselves to pursue through their legislation, rather than recognized rights which can be relied upon by individuals'.[90] As stated above, Article 19(6) ESC lays down a duty for the Contracting States to facilitate family reunion for migrant workers. Given the lack of a clearly formulated right and the need for the Contracting States to take appropriate measures, it is argued that Article 19(6) ESC is not self-executing (*een ieder verbindend*) and does not have direct effect in the Dutch legal order.

D. Labour Migration and the Act on Integration Abroad

i. Standards Set by International Instruments

The above instruments – the EU Blue Card Directive, the European Convention on Migrant Workers and the revised European Social Charter – all have a limited personal scope. Nevertheless, each contains some standard with regard to integration requirements for certain categories of migrant workers or their family members. Such requirements may not be imposed as a condition for the admission of applicants for an EU Blue Card or their family members, nor for family members of migrant workers falling under the ECMW. With regard to the family reunification of migrant workers who are nationals of the Contracting Parties, the revised ESC integration requirements are not forbidden; however, their enactment must be in conformity with the obligation to facilitate family reunion as far as possible. The same applies with regard to the family reunification of self-employed migrants. It has been submitted that this implies that integration requirements must be necessary in order to attain a public interest. In addition, where possible, the Contracting Parties must share the responsibility of ensuring that the integration requirements can be met, for example by guaranteeing the availability of course materials or by taking on responsibility for some of the costs.

ii. The Situation of Labour Migrants and their Family Members under the AIA and Compliance with International Instruments

The AIA does not apply to aliens applying for a residence permit for a temporary purpose. As a consequence, migrant workers, self-employed

[90] eg, Central Appeals Tribunal 5 December 2003, case no 01/4843 and Central Appeals Tribunal 22 December 2008, case nos 08/4535 and 08/4540, para 4.2. A case in which a provision of the ESC was found to be self-executing is HR 30 May 1986, *NJ* 1986/688 regarding Art 6 (4) ESC (the right to strike).

migrants and their family members are all in principle exempted from the obligation to pass the integration exam abroad.[91] This includes applicants for an EU Blue Card, and their family members. It follows that the situation of labour migrants and their family members under the AIA is, in principle, compatible with the international instruments examined earlier in this chapter.

Nevertheless, situations may occur in which the above exemptions prove to be too narrow. This will be the case when a person qualifies as a migrant worker within the meaning of the ECMW or the ESC, but is admitted to the Netherlands for a non-temporary residence purpose or obtains a permanent residence permit after five years. The ESC, unlike the ECMW, does not require a person to have been admitted for the purpose of employment in order to qualify as a migrant worker. In the above situation, family members will be required to pass the integration exam unless another exception applies. It seems that this possibility was not recognised by the Dutch government when the AIA was adopted.[92]

As explained above (section IV.B) Article 12 ECMW fully precludes the possibility of integration requirements for the family reunification of migrant workers. This provision could be breached if, for example, the AIA were to be applied to the family reunification of a Turkish or Ukrainian national who has been admitted for the purpose of taking up employment and has obtained a permanent residence permit. With regard to Article 19(6) ESC, the question arises as to whether the obligation to pass the integration exam is necessary to attain a public interest. Given the arguments provided by the government (chapter 3, section II.B.ii), it is submitted that such an interest has been sufficiently established.[93] It has been argued, however, that the obligation to facilitate family reunion implies that the Netherlands must do more to support family members of migrant workers who have to pass the integration exam abroad. One way to do this would be by ensuring that adequate and affordable means of preparation are available in all the countries where the exam is administered and by reducing the costs of the exam. As things stand, the responsibility for taking and passing the exam is left entirely to the migrant workers and their family members.

[91] Art 16(1)(h) Aliens Act read together with Art 3(1)(a) Integration Act 2007 and Art 2.1(1) Integration Decree.

[92] See *Parliamentary Papers II* 2004–2005, 29 700, No 6, 48–49, where the government states that Art 19(6) ESC is respected because labour migrants and their family members are exempted from the AIA.

[93] The government has also argued that the civic integration exam abroad is justified under the restriction clause of Art 31 ESC (Art G revised ESC). See *Parliamentary Papers II* 2004–2005, 29 700, No 6, 49. It is submitted that this restriction clause has no relevance with regard to Art 19(6) ESC as the latter provision does not contain a right to family reunification and the obligation 'to facilitate' already allows for restrictions deemed necessary in the public interest, see section IV.C above.

V. CONCLUDING OBSERVATIONS

This chapter examines a number of international agreements, concluded at a European and national level, as well as several legal instruments concerning labour migration. As far as the possibility to impose integration requirements is concerned, the most far-reaching standards are found in the EEC-Turkey Agreement. According to recent CoJ case law, this agreement leaves no scope for the Netherlands to impose integration requirements on the admission of Turkish workers and self-employed persons, or their family members. In addition, integration requirements are also precluded by the provisions of the Blue Card Directive and Article 12 of the ECMW. However, it should be noted that the personal scope of each of these instruments is rather limited, with their application being restricted to specific categories of economic migrants and/or family members of those migrants. Moreover, apart from the BCD, they apply only to immigrants (or family members of immigrants) who are nationals of the states that are party to the agreement concerned. Apart from EU and EEA nationals these are only the nationals of Turkey, Albania, Moldavia and Ukraine.

Besides the above instruments, other treaties require the Netherlands (and other Contracting Parties) to facilitate the admission of certain categories of immigrants (Turkish nationals under the ECE, family members of labour migrants under the ESC) or even grant them a right of admission (traders and entrepreneurs under the bilateral agreements with the United States and Japan). However, each of these treaties leaves the states concerned considerable discretion to make such admission subject to conditions, if this is required by the public interest. The possibility to introduce integration requirements therefore remains largely unaffected, even if it is argued that the States Parties to the ESC should, as much as possible, ensure that responsibility for compliance with these requirements does not rest solely with the immigrant family members.

Regarding the AIA, it was recalled that labour migrants and their (accompanying) family members are exempted from the obligation to pass the integration exam abroad, as are nationals of the United States and Japan. Consequently, the Act is largely compatible with the international instruments examined in this chapter. Nonetheless, the exemptions in national legislation are sometimes narrower than required by the treaties. Article 19(6) ESC also seems to require more efforts to be made by the Netherlands to support family members of migrant workers in preparing for the integration exam, for instance by increasing the availability of preparation materials or reducing the costs of the exam.

On a somewhat more abstract level, it is observed that most of the instruments discussed in this chapter broadly pursue two purposes: the admission of immigrants for economic reasons or the reinforcement of international relations between states. Unless integration is understood in a strictly economic sense (as performing paid labour or being financially independent), there is no reason to assume that immigrants who are admitted on the above grounds are prima facie more likely to integrate successfully than those coming for other purposes. For this reason, it is submitted that there are no grounds for arguing that integration requirements are not relevant for labour migrants or migrants admitted under international agreements. It is also submitted that, in the situations discussed in this chapter, the alien's interest in being admitted is less imperative than where admission is sought for the purpose of family reunification or to obtain international protection (see also chapter 3, section II.C.i). It follows that, in principle, integration requirements may be imposed as a means to improve the integration process in the host state.

Nonetheless, the interests of integration need to be balanced against the (economic or diplomatic) interests served by admitting labour migrants or nationals of befriended states (see also chapter 8). As this chapter has shown, the outcome of this balancing exercise is not always the same. Another possible reason for introducing integration requirements, especially in the case of labour migrants, could also be that such requirements may help immigrants in performing their work. Requirements regarding language proficiency or awareness of social conventions in the host state may, for instance, help immigrants to function more easily in the labour market (see also chapter 3, section III.D.i). Where this is meant to be the purpose of integration requirements, however, such requirements are more likely to take the form of facilitative measures (such as an integration programme or course) than of conditions for admission.

Lastly, this chapter has shown that instruments concerning the admission of labour migrants and nationals of befriended states often also grant a privileged position to family members of these aliens. As the Blue Card Directive shows, this may be a way to attract labour migrants from abroad so as to promote the economic interest of the host state. In this case, as stated above, the decision to introduce integration requirements (or not) will depend on a balancing of these economic interests against the interests of integration. However, apart from the economic interests, regard must also be had for the right to respect for family life. In this connection, it is submitted that there is no reason why the family reunification of labour migrants should be subject to a more favourable regime than that existing for other persons. However, as argued in chapter 4, once labour migrants (or other immigrants) have built up strong ties to the host state, they should be entitled to family reunification in that state. In that situation, integration requirements should no longer function as grounds for the non-admission of family members.

C. *Integration Requirements and Equality*

8

The Right to Equal Treatment: Direct Differential Treatment on Grounds of Nationality and Residence Purpose

I. INTRODUCTION

AS EXPLAINED IN chapter 2 (section VI.B) the Act on Integration Abroad does not apply to all immigrants alike. Whereas some aliens have to pass the integration exam abroad in order to be admitted to the Netherlands, others are exempted from this condition. This chapter, together with chapters 9 and 10, investigates how this difference in treatment should be assessed in relation to the right to equal treatment and the prohibition of discrimination. More specifically the following topics are addressed: the differential treatment of immigrants on the grounds of their nationality and residence purpose; the indirect differential treatment of immigrants and their family members on the grounds of racial or ethnic origin; and the 'reverse discrimination' of Dutch nationals who are not entitled to family reunification under EU law.

A general overview of the legal framework concerning the right to equal treatment is provided in section II, followed by an examination in sections III and IV of the relevance of nationality and residence purpose as criteria for differentiating between immigrants when applying integration requirements. In the course of this examination several possible justifications for making distinctions on these grounds are considered. Lastly, in section V, the findings of the previous sections are applied to the Act on Integration Abroad. The issue of indirect differential treatment on the grounds of race or ethnic origin is discussed separately in chapter 9, while the 'reverse discrimination' of Dutch nationals is addressed in chapter 10.

II. LEGAL FRAMEWORK CONCERNING THE RIGHT TO EQUAL TREATMENT

A. The Principle of Equal Treatment

The principle of equal treatment is generally recognised as a fundamental legal principle. This principle is often conveyed by the formula that 'equal situations must be treated in the same way and unequal situations must be treated differently to the degree of their inequality'.[1] Yet the meaning of the equal treatment principle does not lend itself to precise definition. As various authors have noted, the requirement for equal situations to be treated the same way is of a formal nature and does not tell us when two cases are equal or what equal treatment consists of.[2] The determination that situations are equal or unequal always, therefore, rests on a value judgement that is external to the equal treatment principle itself.[3] The same is true with regard to the question of whether a particular form of unequal treatment is nevertheless acceptable because of being based on a reasonable justification (section II.C). Because of this 'normative indeterminacy',[4] the equal treatment principle as such provides little guidance with regard to the issues addressed in this chapter. Nevertheless, the principle has been translated into a number of legal norms, including provisions in human rights treaties. Through the formulation and application of such norms, the equal treatment principle has gained content. The relevant legal provisions are described below.

B. The Right to Equal Treatment – Relevant Legal Provisions

i. International Human Rights Treaties

The most relevant provisions for the Netherlands with regard to equal treatment as a human rights norm are laid down in Article 14 of the European Convention on Human Rights (ECHR) and Article 26 of the

[1] Vierdag 1973, 7; Loenen 1998, 19; Arnardóttir 2003, 8–9. The formula can be traced back to Aristotle's *Ethica Nicomachea*, where it was phrased in a somewhat more complicated way; see Gerards 2002, 9.

[2] Vierdag 1973, 8; Gerards 2002, 9. A slightly different view is taken by Loenen, who supports the characterisation of the equal treatment principle as being of a formal nature, but emphasises that when a decision is taken in one particular case, the principle of equal treatment gains substance in that it then prescribes that equal cases must be treated in the same way. See Loenen 1998, 19.

[3] Vierdag 1973, 15; Arnardóttir 2003, 13.

[4] This term is used by Arnardóttir, see Arnardóttir 2003, 10.

International Covenant on Civil and Political Rights (ICCPR).[5] Article 14 ECHR is of an accessory nature, which means that it can only be invoked in combination with one of the substantive rights or freedoms laid down in the Convention or its Protocols. For Article 14 to be applicable it is sufficient for the alleged discrimination to come within the ambit of one of those rights or freedoms; the finding of a violation is not required.[6] Thus, where integration requirements for family migrants or religious servants are concerned, Article 14 can be relied on in combination with Article 8 (respect for family life) or Article 9 (freedom of religion). Since 1 April 2005 the ECHR also contains an autonomous provision on equal treatment in Article 1 of its Twelfth Protocol.[7] This article is not accessory to the other Convention rights, but extends to any right granted under national law. Although case law on Article 1 Twelfth Protocol is still scarce, the ECtHR has indicated that its interpretation of this provision will be guided by the same concepts and principles that are used to interpret Article 14. The only difference will therefore be the variety in scope.[8]

The right to equal treatment is also guaranteed in Articles 2(1) and 26 of the ICCPR. Like Article 14 ECHR, Article 2(1) guarantees equal treatment in relation to the substantive rights and freedoms protected by the Covenant. These include the right to respect for family life (Arts 17 and 23) and the freedom of religion (Art 18). Article 2(1) also applies if the substantive right has not been violated.[9] Article 26 ICCPR, on the other hand, can be invoked independently of the other articles of the Covenant. Because of its autonomous character Article 26 ICCPR has often been invoked in proceedings before the Dutch courts.

In addition to the equal treatment rights guaranteed by the ECHR and the ICCPR, a prohibition of discrimination specifically on the grounds of race is laid down in the Convention on the Elimination of All Forms of Racial Discrimination (CERD).[10] It is argued below (section III.A.ii) that the definition of racial discrimination in this Convention does not cover differential treatment on the grounds of nationality, which means that the CERD is not relevant to the examination conducted in this chapter. Its provisions are, however, discussed in more detail in chapter 10.

[5] Both provisions are formulated in terms of a prohibition of discrimination instead of a right to equal treatment. For the purposes of this study, it is assumed that equal treatment and non-discrimination are both expressions of the same concept (cp Loenen 1998, 33 and Arnardóttir 2003, 6–8).

[6] Gerards 2002, 103–06; Van Dijk et al 2006, 1028–31.

[7] The Twelfth Protocol entered into force for the Netherlands on 1 April 2005, *Treaty Series* 2001, 18 and 2004, 302.

[8] ECtHR (Grand Chamber) 22 December 2009, app nos 27996/06 and 34836/06 (*Sejdić and Finci*), paras 55–56. On the interpretation of Art 1 Twelfth Protocol ECHR see also Arnardóttir 2003, 33–35.

[9] HRC 9 April 1981, No 35/78 (*Aumeeruddy-Cziffra and others v Mauritius*), para 9.2 (b) 2 (i) 8.

[10] UNTS Vol 660, p 195, *Treaty Series* 1966, 237 and following, entry into force for the Netherlands on 4 January 1969.

ii. EU Law

The right to equal treatment is also guaranteed by provisions of EU law, in particular Articles 18 and 19 of the Treaty on the Functioning of the European Union (TFEU) and Article 21 of the EU Charter of Fundamental Rights. Both Article 18 TFEU and Article 21(2) of the Charter prohibit any discrimination on grounds of nationality within the scope of application of the EU Treaties.[11] It is generally assumed, however, that these provisions apply only to EU citizens and not to third-country nationals (persons who are not nationals of an EU Member State).[12] Several authors have argued in recent years that this interpretation is too narrow, especially since the Treaty of Amsterdam introduced a treaty basis for EU legislation concerning third-country nationals in the fields of immigration and asylum.[13] Yet the EU Court of Justice (CoJ) has so far not appeared inclined to adopt a broader reading.[14] In this chapter, therefore, Articles 18 TFEU and 21 (2) of the Charter are not taken further into account.

Other authors have suggested meanwhile that nationality-based differential treatment of third-country nationals could possibly be examined under the principle of non-discrimination, which has been designated by the CoJ as a general principle of EU law.[15] Again, however, there are no indications that the scope of this principle is broader than that of the non-discrimination provisions of the TFEU and the Fundamental Rights Charter.

Article 19 TFEU prohibits discrimination on a limited number of grounds that are not relevant to the topics raised in this chapter. Article 21(1) of the Charter, on the other hand, applies to discrimination on 'any ground'. While it can be derived *a contrario* from Article 21(2) that this does not include nationality-based discrimination, it is submitted that Article 21(1) does in principle apply to differential treatment on the grounds of residence purpose. It may further be recalled that the provisions of the Charter apply to acts of the EU institutions, as well as to acts of the Member States, when they implement EU law.[16]

[11] The TFEU and the TEU, see Art 1(2) TFEU. Arts 18 TFEU and 21(2) CFR state that: 'Within the scope of the Treaties, and without prejudice to any special provisions contained therein, any discrimination on grounds of nationality shall be prohibited'.

[12] eg, Bell 2002, 37–38; De Schutter 2009, 26 and 33 and Chalmers et al 2010, 555.

[13] See Boeles 2005 and Hublet 2011.

[14] See recently CoJ 4 June 2009, C-22/08 and 23/08 [2009] ECR I-4585 (*Vatsouras & Koupatantze*), para 52. In this judgment the CoJ stated that Art 12 TEC (now Art 18 TFEU) concerns discriminatory treatment of EU nationals in relation to other EU nationals and that it was not intended to apply to differences in treatment between EU nationals and third-country nationals.

[15] De Schutter 2009, 78–79 and Wiesbrock 2010, 543.

[16] Art 51(1) CFR.

iii. The Dutch Constitution

The right to equal treatment is also laid down in Article 1 of the Dutch Constitution, which provides that all who are present in the Netherlands shall be treated equally in equal cases and prohibits discrimination on 'any ground'.[17] Article 1 applies independently of other rights and freedoms and covers each of the issues discussed in this chapter. However, while the scope of this provision is rather broad, its requirements are not very specific. More detailed norms regarding equal treatment have been laid down in a number of national legislative measures, but these are not applicable to the field of immigration policy.[18] The relevance of Article 1 of the Dutch Constitution is also limited by the fact that the Dutch courts are not allowed to assess the constitutionality of legislation at the national level.[19] As a result, judicial interpretation has added little clarity to the meaning of Article 1 of the Dutch Constitution.

iv. Applicability of the Above Provisions in Admission Cases

Before moving on, it should be noted that the above provisions apply to persons who are present on the territory or who are subject to the jurisdiction of the states concerned. Yet the AIA primarily differentiates between aliens who have not yet been admitted to the Netherlands and are still in the territory of another state. This could mean that these aliens are simply not entitled to the right of equal treatment as laid down in the said provisions, or that it should at least first be established whether their request for admission falls under Dutch jurisdiction. For the purposes of the present chapter, however, this question can be left aside. As Vermeulen has already argued, the AIA affects not only aliens seeking to be admitted to the Netherlands, but also persons in the Netherlands who have an interest in their presence.[20] In the context of the AIA, these persons will most often be family members and, in a small number of cases, members of a religious community (chapters 4 and 5). For as long as the alien is unable, whether permanently or temporarily, to enter the Netherlands because of not passing the integration exam abroad, the family or religious community in the Netherlands will be unable to experience their family life or exercise their religion in community with that person. This is a disadvantage that is not experienced by family members and religious

[17] The Dutch text of Art 1 of the Constitution reads: 'Allen die zich in Nederland bevinden, worden in gelijke gevallen gelijk behandeld. Discriminatie wegens godsdienst, levensovertuiging, politieke gezindheid, ras, geslacht of op welke grond dan ook, is niet toegestaan'.

[18] See notably the Equal Treatment Act (*Algemene wet gelijke behandeling*), *Bulletin of Acts and Decrees* 1994, 230.

[19] Art 120 Dutch Constitution.

[20] Vermeulen 2010a, 103–04.

communities of persons who do not have to pass the exam. Hence, the AIA results in differential treatment of persons both within and outside the territory of the Netherlands.

C. Justification of Differential Treatment

As discussed in the previous section, the right to equal treatment is protected by a number of different provisions in human rights treaties, EU law and the Dutch Constitution. Clearly however, not all differential treatment constitutes a violation of these provisions. Law-making typically entails the use of distinctions and categorisations, and it is therefore hard to see how a legal system could be maintained without any form of differential treatment.[21] When, for example, implementing measures in the field of education, distinctions may be made between children with and without disabilities or with different learning capabilities. Such forms of differential treatment are not normally regarded as problematic from a legal perspective because they are based on reasons considered acceptable. Consequently, the right to equal treatment only prohibits differential treatment that cannot be justified.[22]

This leads to the question of when justification for differences in treatment can be said to exist. Here a distinction can be made between 'open' and 'closed' provisions containing a right to equal treatment.[23] Closed provisions prohibit circumscribed forms of differential treatment, for example differentiations based on the grounds of sex or disability. They prescribe that such treatment is always unjustified, unless it comes under an exception explicitly stated in the provision. Open provisions, on the other hand, apply to any form of differential treatment, regardless of the ground for differentiation. They are also 'open' in the sense that they do not define the reasons why the differential treatment may be considered justified.

The equal treatment provisions of the ECHR, the ICCPR and the Dutch Constitution and Article 21(1) of the EU Charter of Fundamental Rights

[21] Compare the statement of the European Court of Human Rights in ECtHR 23 July 1968, app nos 1474/62, 1677/62, 1691/62, 1769/63, 1994/63 and 2126/64 (*Belgian Linguistic Case*), para 10, as well as the UN Human Rights Committee's General Comment No 18 of 10 November 1989 on non-discrimination.

[22] Another possibility is that differential treatment is considered acceptable because it concerns situations that are not equal. A determination of the comparability of the situations concerned normally precedes the question of justification. Often, however, the same circumstances may provide grounds for arguing either that there is no unequal treatment because there are no equal cases, or that there is unequal treatment which is, however, justified. In the example provided above it could be argued, for instance, that children with disabilities cannot be compared to children without disabilities. This argument would have led to the same outcome, namely that the difference in treatment was acceptable. On comparability and justification, see Gerards 2002, 28–79.

[23] Gerards 2002, 16–17.

are all open provisions: although some of these articles list a number of grounds for differentiation, the way in which they are formulated makes it clear that these listings are not exhaustive.[24] Whether justification exists is then left to be determined by the courts or other bodies applying the provisions. For a difference in treatment to be justified, the differentiation will generally need to pursue a valid or legitimate aim and to be proportionate in relation to that aim. This is known in ECtHR case law as the 'reasonable and objective justification test'.[25] Similar criteria have been applied – in varying degrees of detail – by the Human Rights Committee (HRC) and the CoJ in equal treatment cases.[26] Importantly, whether a particular instance of differential treatment is justified will depend on the review that is conducted. This issue is discussed in the following subsection.

D. Scope of Review and the Relevance of 'Suspect Grounds'

When a complaint of unjustified differential treatment or discrimination is assessed by an international court or other supervisory body, the outcome of the case will be influenced by the scope of the review. Depending on the extent of this review, the respondent state will have more or less discretion in determining whether a particular difference in treatment is based on a reasonable and objective justification. In ECtHR case law this is known as the doctrine of the 'margin of appreciation', which plays a role in cases concerning Article 14 ECHR as well as in relation to other Convention rights.[27]

In general the extent of the margin of appreciation can be determined by a variety of factors, including the nature of the protected rights or interests, the aim being pursued and the existence of consensus between the Contracting States. These factors are also of relevance in equal treatment cases.[28] In addition, a specific factor determining the margin of

[24] With regard to Art 1 Twelfth Protocol ECHR, the Explanatory Report shows that it was expressly decided not to add new grounds in comparison with Art 14, both because this was considered unnecessary and because it could have given rise to 'unwarranted *a contrario* interpretations' as regards discrimination based on grounds not included. See Arnardóttir 2003, 34.

[25] Van Dijk et al 2006, 1041–43. This test was first formulated by the ECtHR in the *Belgian Linguistic Case* (n 21). See also Gerards 2002, 120–64 and Arnardóttir 2003, 42–51.

[26] On the approach of the HRC, see Joseph et al 2004, 700–28 and Vandenhole 2005, 46–56. On the CoJ, see Gerards 2002, 236–306. Note, however, that Art 21(1) of the EU Charter of Fundamental Rights only gained legally binding force on 1 December 2009. Case law regarding this particular provision is, therefore, still scarce.

[27] Van Dijk et al 2006, 1043–46. On the margin of appreciation in relation to the right to family life and the freedom of religion, see section II.B.iii of ch 4 and section II.C of ch 5.

[28] Gerards 2002, 169–97. The formula typically used by the Court in Art 14 cases is that 'the scope of the margin of appreciation will vary according to the circumstances, the subject matter and its background'; see, eg, ECtHR 28 November 1984 (*Rasmussen v Denmark*), para 40 and ECtHR 11 July 2006 (admissibility decision), app no 8407/05 (*Savoia and Bounegru*).

appreciation in relation to Article 14 ECHR is the ground on which the differential treatment is based. The ECtHR has held in various cases that differentiations based on certain 'suspect grounds', such as sex, race or religion, can only be justified by 'very weighty reasons'.[29] This 'very weighty reasons' test leaves the respondent state little or no margin of appreciation, with the cases in which it was applied almost invariably resulting in the finding of a violation of the Convention.[30]

While the ECtHR has not provided any clear guidelines for deciding which differentiation grounds are 'suspect' and hence require application of the 'very weighty reasons' test, some indications can be found in case law. In *Abdulaziz* this determination was based on the existence of common ground among the Contracting States concerning the importance of promoting the equality of the sexes.[31] More recently, in the case of *Carson and others*, the Court stated that a high level of protection is needed in relation to 'differences [of treatment] based on an inherent characteristic, such as gender or racial or ethnic origin'. [32] However, it should also be noted that the 'suspectness' of a particular ground is not absolute, but may differ according to the context in which the differentiation is made. This is especially clear with regard to nationality as the ground for differentiation (section III.B). A second, related remark is that the differentiation ground is not the only factor determining the scope of the margin of appreciation. A strict review may be indicated even when a suspect differentiation ground is lacking, for example when the differential treatment affects a particularly important aspect of a Convention right.[33] By contrast, the strict level of review that would normally follow from the existence of a suspect differentiation ground may also be 'levelled down' because of the disputed measure being taken in a policy area where states traditionally have a certain amount of discretion, such as social or economic policy.[34]

[29] Loenen 1998, 35–44. The term 'suspect grounds' is derived from the case law of the US Supreme Court.

[30] Gerards 2004, 184. On the 'very weighty reasons' test, see Gerards 2002, 197–207 and Van Dijk et al 2006, 1046–49.

[31] Schokkenbroek 1998. The use of the 'common ground' argument for the application of the 'very weighty reasons' test is also mentioned – and criticised – by Gerards, see Gerards 2004, 186–88.

[32] ECtHR 4 November 2008, app no 42184/05 (*Carson and others*), para 80.

[33] See ECtHR 10 March 2009, app no 45413/07 (*Anakomba Yula*), para 37. The applicant in this case wanted to institute court proceedings in order to ensure the recognition of her daughter by the biological father, but was refused financial assistance on the grounds that she did not have a residence permit. In relation to the complaint under Art 14 ECHR the Court stated that ' les questions en jeu devant les tribunaux internes en l'espèce étaient des questions graves liées au droit de la famille. Les décisions que les tribunaux allaient rendre marqueraient de manière définitive la vie privée et familiale non seulement de la requérante elle-même mais de plusieurs autres personnes. Il devrait donc y avoir des raisons particulièrement impérieuses pour justifier une différence de traitement entre personnes possédant une carte de séjour et personnes n'en possédant pas, telle la requérante '.

[34] eg, ECtHR 27 November 2007, app no 77782/01 (*Luczak*), para 52 and *Carson and others* (n 32), para 61.

While the doctrine of the margin of appreciation has been developed quite elaborately in relation to Article 14 ECHR, differentiations in the scope of review are also indicated with regard to other equal treatment provisions. With regard to Article 26 ICCPR, the HRC has indicated that stricter scrutiny is required when the differential treatment is based on one of the grounds expressly mentioned in that provision.[35] The CoJ has also previously applied variations in its scrutiny of various equal treatment provisions in EU law. These variations could be related to different factors, including the differentiation ground at issue.[36] With regard to Article 21(1) of the EU Charter, it is expected that a similar approach will be followed and that the discretion left to the EU institutions and the Member States to justify differential treatment will depend on the differentiation ground at stake, as well as on other interests and circumstances of the case.

E. Formal and Substantive Equality and Indirect Differential Treatment

Lastly, when examining whether a particular legal classification is justified from an equal treatment perspective, the outcome will depend on how 'equality' is defined. One distinction that is frequently made in this respect is that between formal and substantive equality: the concept of formal equality focuses on equal treatment, whereas substantive equality is more concerned with obtaining equal results.[37] By way of example, imagine an integration policy whereby the same integration course is offered to all participants, regardless of their skills and previous education. In this case there is equal treatment and hence no problems arise when viewed from a formal conception of equality. However, a substantive equality approach would be more concerned with enabling all participants to reach the same final level. Such an approach would require a differentiated course offer, adapted to the varying needs of the participants.

Related to the concept of substantive equality is the concept of indirect differential treatment. This type of treatment is considered to occur when

[35] Joseph et al 2004, 693; Vandenhole 2005, 113.

[36] Gerards 2002, 306–41. The CoJ has in principle applied strict scrutiny with regard to distinctions based on the grounds of sex and nationality. However, as noted above, the prohibition of nationality-based discrimination in EU law has thus far not been applied in cases involving third-country nationals. As also noted earlier, the relevance of a particular differentiation ground may vary depending on the context. It follows that nationality-based distinctions may be assessed even more strictly when the purpose of the equal treatment provisions is to establish an internal European market than when they concern the right to equal treatment as a human rights norm (cp Gerards 2002, 359).

[37] Loenen 1998, 19–30; Gerards 2002, 12. On different conceptions of equality, see also Arnardóttir 2003, 20–29.

a measure formulated in neutral terms nevertheless has disproportionate effects on a particular group of persons.[38] It may be that those effects were also foreseen by the legislator and that the neutral formulation is in fact meant to disguise a form of differential treatment that would otherwise be forbidden.[39] However, the concept of indirect differential treatment is currently mostly effective in combating the unintended adverse effects of seemingly neutral measures.[40] In the context of open provisions, the use of this concept can result in stricter scrutiny being applied if it is established that the disputed measure disproportionately affects a group characterised by a suspect differentiation ground (section II.D). Additionally, the concept of indirect differential treatment can be used to enable the application of closed provisions that prohibit differential treatment on a limited number of grounds.[41]

The understanding that the right to equal treatment also covers situations of indirect differential treatment may follow directly from the formulation of the legal provision, as is the case with Article 1(1) CERD ('any distinction . . . which has the purpose *or effect*') (emphasis added).[42] The other provisions mentioned in section II.B are less clear in this respect; however, the concept of indirect differential treatment has been accepted by the ECtHR, the HRC and the CoJ.[43] The concept is discussed in more detail in chapter 9 in relation to the issue of indirect differential treatment on the grounds of racial or ethnic origin.

[38] More precisely the concept of indirect differential treatment implies substantive equality as it is grounded in the recognition that equal treatment may nevertheless lead to unequal results. See Gerards 2002, 13. Thereby it should be taken into account that 'equal' always means 'equal in relation to a particular ground or characteristic'. The requirement, eg, that applicants for a particular job must be proficient in Dutch excludes non-Dutch speakers from the range of candidates and therefore prescribes a form of unequal treatment (on the grounds of language). The requirement is, however, neutral with regard to ethnicity as it does not prescribe differential treatment on this ground. Nevertheless, the effect of the requirement may be that it excludes members of ethnic minority groups, in which case indirect differential treatment on the grounds of ethnicity is said to take place.

[39] An example provided by Gerards is that of a literacy requirement that was attached to the right to vote in the United States and which served to exclude the black population from elections, see Gerards 2002, 24.

[40] Loenen 1998, 49–50.

[41] Gerards 2004, 180–81.

[42] cp General Recommendation No 14 of the CERD Committee on the definition of discrimination (Art 1, para 1), dated 22 March 1993, available at www.ohchr.org. In para 2 the Committee states that 'in seeking to determine whether an action has an effect contrary to the Convention, it will look to see whether that action has an unjustifiable disparate impact upon a group distinguished by race, colour, descent, or national or ethnic origin'. See also Thornberry 2005, 256.

[43] On the use of the concept by the ECtHR and the CoJ, see notably Gerards 2002, 113–15 and 227–28. The HRC uses a definition of discrimination similar to that of Art 1(1) CERD, except in respect of the limitation to the race-related grounds, see HRC General Comment No 18 on Non-discrimination, para 7 (available at www.ohchr.org). See also Joseph et al 2004, 693–99 and Vandenhole 2005, 58–59, with references to HRC jurisprudence.

III. DIFFERENTIAL TREATMENT ON THE GROUNDS OF NATIONALITY

This section examines the legal standards set by the above provisions on differential treatment on the basis of nationality, especially in admission cases. First, however, a preliminary remark is made about the meaning of the term 'nationality'. In section III.A a distinction is drawn between nationality and the related concepts of alienage and national origin. It is also argued that nationality – unlike national origin – is not a forbidden discrimination ground within the meaning of the International Convention on the Elimination of All Forms of Racial Discrimination (CERD). Section III.B then assesses whether nationality qualifies as a 'suspect ground', which would imply that differentiations based on this ground will require very strong justification. Next, the reasons for justification are discussed in section III.C. As the reasons that could be adduced to justify differential treatment are in principle unlimited, this chapter focuses on the reasons provided by the Dutch government in relation to the AIA. Section III.D discusses Dutch case law with regard to differential treatment on the grounds of nationality, in particular where the AIA is concerned.

A. Preliminary Remark: Nationality, Alienage and National Origin

Before examining the legal framework standards set by the above provisions on differential treatment on the basis of nationality, it is useful to briefly clarify the meaning of this term. In the following two subsections a distinction is drawn between nationality and the related concepts of alienage and national origin. It is also argued that nationality – unlike national origin – is not a forbidden discrimination ground within the meaning of the International Convention on the Elimination of All Forms of Racial Discrimination (CERD).

i. Nationality and Alienage

Differential treatment on the grounds of nationality may take various forms. In the first place, a state may differentiate between persons who are nationals of that state and persons with the nationality of other states ('aliens'). It is generally accepted under international law that such distinctions are justified, at least within the context of immigration policy.[44]

[44] See, eg, the judgments of the ECtHR in *Moustaquim* (ECtHR 18 February 1991, app no 12313/86), para 49 and *A and others v the United Kingdom* (ECtHR (Grand Chamber) 19 February 2009, app no 3455/05), para 186. See also Art 3 Fourth Protocol ECHR and Art 12(4) ICCPR, which guarantee the right to enter the state of which one is a national and prohibit

However, states can also differentiate between aliens of different nationalities, as is the case under the Act on Integration Abroad. In this situation the differentiation ground is also nationality, but the distinction is not between nationals and non-nationals. It is this latter form of differential treatment that is investigated in this section. To avoid terminological confusion, however, the first type of differential treatment (between nationals and non-nationals) is henceforth referred to as 'differential treatment on the grounds of alienage'. Where mention is made of 'differential treatment on the ground of nationality', this refers to a differentiation between aliens.

ii. Nationality and National Origin

The term 'nationality' can also be confusing because it can be understood both as 'a politico-legal term, denoting membership of a state', and as a 'historico-biological term, denoting membership of a nation'. Nationality in the latter sense is a sociological or ethnographical, rather than a legal concept.[45] For the purposes of this study, however, the term 'nationality' is used to indicate the legal bond between a person and a state.[46]

From a legal perspective the distinction made above is significant because, as is submitted here, nationality as a legal status is not included in the definition of 'racial discrimination' provided in Article 1(1) of the CERD.[47] While this definition mentions 'national origin', this term does not refer to the legal bond between a person and a state. Instead, it follows from the *travaux préparatoires* of the Convention that the term 'national origin' should be understood in conjunction with 'descent' and 'ethnic origin' to indicate nationality in the ethnographical sense. In addition the US representative suggested that 'national origin' could also refer to a person's previous nationality, thereby apparently referring to legal status.[48] If accepted, this interpretation could be used, for instance, to cover distinctions between persons who obtained their nationality through

the expulsion of a state's own nationals; similar rights are not granted to aliens. The latter is confirmed in the HRC's General Comment on the position of aliens under the Covenant, which states that 'The Covenant does not recognize the right of aliens to enter and reside in the territory of a State party. It is in principle a matter for the State to decide who it will admit to its territory' (HRC General Comment of 11 April 1986, para 5).

[45] Schwelb 1966, 1006, citing Weis 1956, 3.

[46] cp Art 2(a) of the European Convention on Nationality (ECN), where nationality is defined as 'the legal bond between a person and a State [that] does not indicate the person's ethnic origin'.

[47] According to this definition, racial discrimination means 'any distinction, exclusion, restriction or preference based on race, colour, descent, or national or ethnic origin which has the purpose or effect of nullifying or impairing the recognition, enjoyment or exercise, on an equal footing, of human rights and fundamental freedoms in the political, economic, social, cultural or any other field of public life'.

[48] Schwelb 1966, 1007.

birth and those who received it through naturalisation. For the purposes of this chapter, however, national origin as a previous legal status is not relevant.

While it follows from the above that Article 1(1) CERD does not refer to nationality as a legal status, Article 1(2) CERD states that differentiations between nationals and non-nationals do not amount to racial discrimination. It is submitted that this provision serves to confirm the right of states to distinguish between nationals and aliens and to avoid such differentiations being qualified as (indirect) discrimination on the grounds of race, descent or ethnic or national origin. Hence, Article 1(2) should not be read *a contrario* so as to bring the distinction between nationals and non-nationals (and hence nationality) within the scope of Article 1(1).[49] The same is true with regard to Article 1(3) CERD, which was introduced to allow some of the States Parties to maintain their existing legislation regarding, amongst other things, favourable conditions for the reacquisition of nationality by former nationals, which would otherwise have to be classified as discrimination on the grounds of national origin.[50] Again, it follows that Article 1(3) must not be understood to imply that the CERD also covers discrimination on the basis of nationality.

The monitoring body of the CERD, the Committee on the Elimination of Racial Discrimination ('CERD Committee'), has issued a General Recommendation on discrimination against non-citizens, in which it states that:

> Under the Convention, differential treatment based on citizenship or immigration status will constitute discrimination if the criteria for such differentiation, judged in the light of the objectives and purposes of the Convention, are not applied pursuant to a legitimate aim, and are not proportional to the achievement of this aim.[51]

The reference to citizenship led Terlouw to conclude that nationality is a differentiation ground covered by the CERD.[52] However, regardless of whether this was in fact the Committee's intention, adding nationality in

[49] Nevertheless, Vandenhole observes that the CERD Committee has adopted an increasingly restrictive interpretation of Art 1(2) and has rejected differential treatment of non-nationals in relation to all but a limited number of human rights (Vandenhole 2005, 90–92). It is hard to see how this interpretation can be reconciled with the text of the Convention.

[50] Schwelb 1966, 1009–11. Art 1(3) CERD states that 'nothing in this Convention may be interpreted as affecting in any way the legal provisions of States Parties concerning nationality, citizenship or naturalization, provided that such provisions do not discriminate against any particular nationality'.

[51] CERD Committee General Recommendation No 30 on Discrimination Against Non Citizens, dated 1 October 2004, para 4. General recommendations are issued by the Committee on the basis of Art 9(2) CERD. Although such recommendations are not binding, they do have a certain authority as guidelines for interpreting the Convention.

[52] Terlouw 2005, 121–22. This author concludes that the CERD is applicable to the distinction between aliens of different nationalities under the AIA and that this distinction is contrary to the Convention because it lacks sufficient justification. See further section III.C.

the legal sense as a ground to the definition of racial discrimination would be incompatible with the text and history of Article 1 CERD. The same is true with regard to immigration status. The General Recommendation therefore cannot support the conclusion that differentiations on the grounds of nationality should henceforth be brought under the CERD. Such differentiations do, however, fall within the scope of the open non-discrimination provisions of the ECHR, the ICCPR and the Dutch Constitution. The following subsections therefore examine the question of when the differential treatment of aliens can be said to be based on a reasonable and objective justification. Firstly, however, it will be examined whether nationality is a 'suspect' differentiation ground, implying that this differential treatment would need to be justified by very weighty reasons.

B. Is Nationality a 'Suspect Ground'?

Both the ECtHR and the HRC have been asked on a number of occasions to decide on complaints concerning differential treatment on the ground of nationality.[53] As far as the classification of this differentiation ground is concerned, these cases have led to varying results. In various judgments the ECtHR has stated that distinctions based 'exclusively on the ground of nationality' must be justified by very weighty reasons in order to be compatible with the Convention.[54] It follows that, at least in these cases, nationality was regarded as a 'suspect ground' (section II.D). In other cases, however, the Court did not consider a difference in treatment between persons of different nationality to require very weighty reasons, or even conducted a rather lenient review.[55] The HRC meanwhile has accepted that nationality is a differentiation ground that can be considered under Article 26 ICCPR, even if it is not expressly mentioned in that provision. It has not, however, commented on the scope of the review to be conducted or stated that differentiations based on nationality require an additional justification compared to differentiations on other grounds.[56]

[53] Some of these cases (also) involved a difference in treatment between nationals and non-nationals, which was qualified earlier in this chapter as a differentiation on the grounds of alienage (section III.A.i). The decisions in these cases will be taken into account insofar as they contain considerations that are also relevant to distinctions between non-nationals. On the ECtHR's case law on differential treatment on grounds of nationality see also Lawson 2005, 124–29.

[54] See ECtHR 16 September 1996, app no 17371/90 (*Gaygusuz*), para 42; ECtHR 30 September 2003, app no 40892/98 (*Koua Poirrez*), para 46; *Luczak* (n 34), para 48 and ECtHR (Grand Chamber) 18 February 2009, app no 55707/00 (*Andrejeva*), para 87.

[55] ECtHR 18 February 1991, app no 12313/86 (*Moustaquim*), para 49; ECtHR 27 June 1996, app no 21794/93 (*C v Belgium*), para 38 and ECtHR 28 May 2009, app no 26713/05 (*Bigaeva*), para 40.

[56] See, eg, HRC 6 April 1989, no 196/1985 (*Gueye*), para 9.4 and HRC 29 April 2002, No 965/2000 (*Karakurt*), para 8.4. See also Vandenhole 2005, 128–29.

The ECtHR itself has not explained why it has treated nationality as a suspect classification on some occasions, but not on others. Some authors have argued that the 'very weighty reasons' test does not apply to differentiations between EU citizens and third-country nationals.[57] Indeed, it seems that this possibility cannot be excluded. A more apparent explanation, however, would be that the variation in the Court's approach is due to the policy context.[58] All the cases in which the 'very weighty reasons' test was applied concerned differentiations in the context of social security. By contrast, two of the cases in which the 'very weighty reasons' test was not used concerned immigration policy.[59] The third case concerned the right to practise as a lawyer, which, as the Court found, is a profession with a certain public interest.[60]

With regard to differentiations based on nationality in the immigration context, Vermeulen argued that the power to control immigration typically belongs to the sovereign domain of the state. For this reason, states have a large margin of appreciation in the field of immigration policy and measures adopted in this field are generally not subject to strict scrutiny by an international body such as the ECtHR.[61]

Some support for this explanation can be found in other ECtHR case law. First of all, the Court has repeatedly stressed in immigration cases that the Contracting States are entitled to regulate the entry of aliens into their territory.[62] Moreover, the Court has stated in rather general wording that its subsidiary role vis-à-vis the Contracting States is 'fully applicable in the field of immigration'.[63] However, there is also evidence that immigration cases do not always involve a (large) margin of appreciation for the respondent state. In particular, in *Abdulaziz* the Court applied the 'very weighty reasons' test despite the fact that the case concerned the admission of aliens to the United Kingdom. It did so because it found the differential treatment at issue in this case to be based on a suspect

[57] See Schokkenbroek 1998, 22 and Human Rights Watch 2008, 25.

[58] See also Gerards 2004, 185–86; Van Dijk et al 2006, 1049 and Vermeulen 2010a, 100.

[59] *Moustaquim* (n 55) and *C v Belgium* (n 55). See also the earlier decision of the European Commission of Human Rights in the case of *X, Y & Z v the United Kingdom* (EComHR 6 July 1982, app no 9285/81). In this decision the Commission found that the immigration policy of the United Kingdom did not violate Arts 8 and 14 ECHR, despite the fact that it differentiated between Commonwealth citizens and other aliens. It would appear that the Commission did not apply very intense scrutiny.

[60] *Bigaeva* (n 55).

[61] Vermeulen 2010a, 99–100; in the same vein see Gerards 2004, 185–86.

[62] See, eg, ECtHR 28 May 1985, app nos 9214/80, 9473/81 and 9474/81 (*Abdulaziz, Cabales & Balkandali*), para 67 and, more recently, ECtHR 31 July 2008, app no 265/07 (*Darren Omoregie and others*), para 54.

[63] ECtHR 12 February 2009 (admissibility decision), app no 33831/03 (*M.F.S. v Bulgaria*): 'La Cour rappelle que le mécanisme de sauvegarde des droits fondamentaux institué par la Convention revêt un caractère subsidiaire par rapport aux systèmes nationaux *et que ce principe s'applique pleinement en matière d'immigration*' (emphasis added).

ground, *in casu* sex.[64] It follows that the 'very weighty reasons' test may also apply in cases concerning immigration policy.

Nevertheless it seems that the 'common ground' between the Contracting States to the ECHR, which led the Court to qualify sex as a suspect ground in *Abdulaziz* (see also section II.D), does not exist with regard to differentiations based on nationality, at least not in the immigration context. For the time being, therefore, it will be assumed that in the field of immigration policy nationality is not a suspect classification and differentiations on this ground are not in principle subject to the 'very weighty reasons' test. It is submitted that this approach is acceptable, at least where nationality is perceived as a legal bond between a person and a state. Nonetheless, a heightened level of scrutiny – and thus strong justification – may still be required because of factors other than the differentiation ground.[65] This could apply in, for instance, situations involving young children.[66]

C. Is the Differential Treatment Based on a Reasonable and Objective Justification?

As mentioned above, this section does not discuss all possible justifications for nationality-based distinctions regarding the admission of aliens. Instead, the examination is limited to those justifications put forward by the Dutch legislator in relation to the Act on Integration Abroad, which is briefly described here. The following sections assess whether the reasons advanced constitute a legitimate aim and whether the difference in treatment is proportionate in relation to that aim.

It may be recalled that the AIA does not apply to nationals of some economically developed, mostly Western countries, including nationals of Member States of the EU or EEA (section VI.B.i of chapter 2). With regard to the latter group, the Dutch government argued that their exemption was required by EU law as these nationals have the right of free movement within the European Union.[67] The ensuing difference in treatment

[64] *Abdulaziz, Cabales & Balkandali* (n 62), para 78.

[65] cp Arnardóttir 2003, 151, who argues that a strict review is indicated where nationality refers to national origin (see also section III.A.ii), but not necessarily in cases involving differential treatment between aliens and nationals or EU citizens. She adds that, in the latter type of cases, the strictness of review will more easily be influenced by factors other than the differentiation ground.

[66] See section II.B.iii of ch 4. Compare also the judgments of the ECtHR in *Anakomba Yula* (n 33) and *Niedzwiecki* (ECtHR 25 October 2005, app no 58453/00), para 33. In the latter case the Court found a violation of Arts 8 and 14 ECHR in respect of a difference in treatment on the grounds of residence status in relation to the granting of child benefits.

[67] *Parliamentary Papers II* 2003–2004, 29 700, No 3, 19. It could be argued that the above exemption also concerns the family members of nationals of EU/EEA member states and that, in fact, the differentiation ground at stake is not nationality, but whether a person is a

was consequently motivated by the aim of ensuring compliance with international obligations.

In addition to this objective several reasons were put forward to justify the preferential treatment granted to nationals of non-EU/EEA countries such as the United States, Australia and Japan (see again section VI.B.i of chapter 2). Some variations exist regarding the formulation of these reasons in subsequent phases of the legislative process.[68] Nevertheless, two main arguments can be distinguished, and these are used as the basis for discussion in this chapter. Firstly, it was submitted that the exemption from the AIA applied to 'a limited number of countries' which were 'comparable to the Netherlands in socio-economic and social terms'. For this reason it was expected that immigration from these countries would not lead to substantial problems in the sphere of integration and that nationals of these countries did not have a strong interest in taking the integration exam abroad.[69] As a second argument, it was emphasised that nationals of the designated countries were already exempted from the long-term visa requirement. To make them subject to the AIA would therefore make their admission to the Netherlands dependent on prior permission, which was not previously the case. The government feared that setting conditions for the admission of these nationals would have an adverse impact on the 'foreign and economic relations' of the Netherlands with the countries concerned.[70]

On top of the above arguments, the Dutch government also stated that the exempted countries did not create any 'large-scale or uncontrolled' migration influxes.[71] While it is not entirely clear how this statement is to be understood, it is submitted that the fact that a certain country does not generate large numbers of immigrants does not imply that those who do come are more likely to integrate. In other words, there is no logical connection between the number of immigrants from a particular country and the individual integration capacity of each of them. The level of

beneficiary of the right of free movement within the EU. Although this is a valid argument, it is also the case that the right of free movement can only be invoked by persons who are nationals of an EU or EEA member state and that the rights of family members derive from this right (section III.A of ch 6). It follows that nationality is still a decisive factor with regard to the differential treatment concerned. Lastly, although they were not expressly mentioned, it may be observed that the exemption on the basis of international obligations also applies to Swiss nationals and their family members who are entitled to the right to free movement, see Art 16(1)(h) read in conjunction with Art 17(1)(b) and Art 1(e) Aliens Act.

[68] Compare *Parliamentary Papers II* 2003–2004, 29 700, No 3, 19 and *Parliamentary Papers II* 2004–2005, 29 700, No 6, 31–32.

[69] *Parliamentary Papers II* 2003–2004, 29 700, No 3, 19 and *Parliamentary Papers II* 2004–2005, 29 700, No 6, 32. The first report speaks of 'a limited number of western (oriented) third countries [that are] comparable to European countries in socio-economic, social and political terms'.

[70] *Parliamentary Papers II* 2004–2005, 29 700, No 6, 32.

[71] *Parliamentary Papers II* 2003–2004, 29 700, No 3, 19 and *Parliamentary Papers II* 2004–2005, 29 700, No 6, 32. The first report refers to 'undesired and unrestrained' migration influxes'.

immigration from a particular country does not, therefore, justify a difference in treatment with regard to integration requirements.

The thrust of the government's argument, however, appears to be different: namely that exempting certain nationalities from the AIA does not undermine the effect of the integration requirement abroad because immigration from the exempted countries is in any event minimal and does not have a significant impact on the integration process in the host country. Read in this way, the argument concerns the proportionality of the difference in treatment rather than its purpose. This issue is addressed in more detail in section VI.

i. Compliance with International Obligations: EU Law and Bilateral Agreements

a. Preliminary Remarks: International Obligations and State Responsibility

The question of the extent to which the need to comply with international obligation constitutes a reasonable and objective justification for differential treatment on the ground of nationality is examined below. Firstly, however, some brief remarks are made about states' responsibility under public international law for acts that are required by international legal instruments, *in casu* the TFEU and the EU Residence Directive. The question of responsibility has come up before the ECtHR on several occasions, including in the cases of *Matthews* and *Bosphorus*.[72] In these cases the respondent governments argued that the impugned acts fell outside their responsibility as defined by Article 1 ECHR, either because they resulted directly from an act of European Community law (*Matthews*) or because they constituted the implementation of an EC regulation that left no discretion to the Member States (*Bosphorus*). This raises the question of whether a state could, in a similar vein, argue that it is not responsible for differences in treatment that result from its legislation because it was forced to make these distinctions so as to comply with its international obligations.

It is submitted here that this is not the case. For one, the above arguments were not accepted by the ECtHR. However the position in situations such as the one at issue here also differs from those in *Matthews* and *Bosphorus* because the differential treatment is not as such required by international agreements. While EU law does indeed impose an obligation to grant a right of admission to EU nationals without subjecting them to integration conditions, it does not require such conditions to be imposed

[72] ECtHR 18 February 1999, app no 24833/94 (*Matthews*), para 26 and ECtHR (Grand Chamber) 30 June 2005, app no 45036/98 (*Bosphorus Hava Yollari Turizm ve Ticaret Anonim Sirketi*), para 109.

on other aliens. EU Member States may therefore also choose to avoid the differential treatment by not imposing integration requirements at all. Consequently, the responsibility of these states for the differential treatment is beyond doubt. This reasoning also applies equally in situations where the differential treatment results from international obligations other than those concerning the EU right of free movement.

Nevertheless, the fact that exempting certain categories of aliens from integration requirements is motivated by the desire to comply with international agreements is not inconsequential. As discussed below, compliance with international obligations has previously been characterised by the ECtHR as a legitimate interest that may justify some nationalities being given preferential treatment.

b. International Obligations as a Justification Ground

Formulated in general terms, the purpose of the Act on Integration Abroad is to improve the integration of immigrants in the Netherlands. Nevertheless, the nationals of certain states are exempted from the conditions imposed by the Act because such exemption is required by international agreements. It follows that the purpose of this exemption (and hence of the differential treatment) is to ensure compliance with these agreements. It is the latter purpose (rather than the purpose of integration) which must be considered when examining whether the differential treatment resulting from the exemption is justified.

ECtHR Case Law on Obligations of EU Law

In this respect, it is worthwhile mentioning two ECtHR judgments in which a difference in immigration rules for EU citizens and third-country nationals was found to be based on a reasonable and objective justification: *Moustaquim* and *C v Belgium*.[73] Both cases involved Moroccan nationals who faced deportation from Belgium for reasons of public order and who were thereby prevented from continuing the exercise of their family life. Both applicants relied on Articles 8 and 14 ECHR, claiming that their deportation constituted discrimination because EU nationals in a similar situation would not have been deported. However, the Court held that the alleged differential treatment was based on a reasonable and objective justification because Belgium belonged, together with the other Member States of the EU (then the EC), to a 'special legal order', which had 'in addition, established its own citizenship'.[74]

[73] *Moustaquim* (n 55) and *C v Belgium* (n 55).

[74] *Moustaquim* (n 55), para 49 and *C v Belgium* (n 55), para 38. The reference to European citizenship is made only in *C v Belgium*, but was later confirmed in ECtHR 21 June 2011, app no 5335/05 (*Ponomaryov*), para 54.

The above judgments do not explicitly refer to the existence of international obligations; however, the justification for the differential treatment relates to the existence of the EU as a legal order. In several other judgments, the ECtHR also accepted that compliance with obligations of EU law constitutes a legitimate aim for the purposes of limiting the rights and freedoms laid down in the ECHR. In particular, in the aforementioned *Bosphorus* case (concerning Article 1 First Protocol ECHR), the Court decided that 'compliance with legal obligations flowing from [the] membership of the European Community' constituted 'a legitimate interest of considerable weight'. It also recognised 'the growing importance of international cooperation and of the consequent need to secure the proper functioning of international organisations', in particular in relation to a supranational organisation such as the EC.[75] Finally, in *S.A. Dangeville*, the ECtHR acknowledged that the purpose of bringing domestic legislation into line with an EC directive was 'clearly a legitimate objective consistent with Article 1 Protocol 1'.[76] This case also concerned a difference in treatment, which was, however, not examined separately by the Court.

ECtHR Case Law on Bilateral Agreements

The ECtHR has also considered differences in treatment that did not result from obligations of EU law, but instead from bilateral agreements concluded by the respondent state. One of these cases, *Koua Poirrez*, concerned an Ivory Coast national who resided in France, but was denied an invalidity pension on the grounds of his nationality. In this respect he was treated differently from French nationals or nationals of countries with which France had signed a reciprocity agreement. As mentioned above (section III.B) the ECtHR applied the 'very weighty reasons' test. It then concluded that the differential treatment was not based on any 'objective and reasonable justification'.[77]

In the case of *Carson and others*, however, the ECtHR did accept a difference in treatment resulting from the existence of bilateral agreements. This case concerned the uprating of pensions paid by the respondent state (the United Kingdom) to its nationals who were living abroad. Under United Kingdom law, pensions of nationals living in foreign countries were only uprated if this was provided for in a bilateral treaty. This led to a complaint by a number of pensioners who were living in countries with which no agreements had been concluded and claimed that the British legislation violated their rights under Article 1 First Protocol and Article 14 ECHR. The ECtHR found, however, that the applicants were not in a relevantly similar position to pensioners living in countries *with* bilateral

[75] *Bosphorus Hava Yollari Turizm ve Ticaret Anonim Sirketi* (n 72), para 150.
[76] ECtHR 16 April 2002, app no 36677/97 (*S.A. Dangeville*), para 55.
[77] *Koua Poirrez* (n 54), para 49.

agreements and hence concluded that there had been no violation of the Convention. The following considerations merit being cited at length:

> Those living in reciprocal agreement countries are treated differently from those living elsewhere because an agreement had been entered into; and an agreement has been entered into because the United Kingdom considered it to be in its interests.
>
> States clearly have a right under international law to conclude bilateral social security treaties and indeed this is the preferred method used by the Member States of the Council of Europe to secure reciprocity of welfare benefits [. . .]. Such treaties are entered into on the basis of judgments by both parties as to their respective interests and may depend on various factors, among them the number of people moving from one country to the other, the benefits available under the other country's welfare scheme, how far reciprocity is possible and the extent to which the advantages to be gained by an agreement outweigh the additional expenditure likely to be incurred by each State in negotiating and implementing it. [. . .] It is the inevitable result of such a process that different conditions apply in each country depending on whether or not a treaty has been concluded and on what terms.
>
> The Court agrees [. . .] that it would be extraordinary if the fact of entering into bilateral arrangements in the social security sphere had the consequence of creating an obligation to confer the same advantages on all others living in all other countries. Such a conclusion would effectively undermine the right of States to enter into reciprocal agreements and their interest in so doing.[78]

In the above judgments, the ECtHR did not say whether compliance with bilateral agreements may be regarded as a legitimate aim as such. In *Koua Poirrez* it merely concluded that the difference in treatment was not based on an objective and reasonable justification.[79] On the other hand, it may be derived from *Carson* that the aim of the differential treatment was not so much compliance with international obligations, but rather the pursuit of economic interests that led the British government to enter into these obligations. Although the ECtHR was clearly very reticent in assessing these interests, it could nevertheless be the case that the extent to which bilateral agreements can justify a difference in treatment depends, at least partly, on the reasons why those agreements were concluded.

Communications of the Human Rights Committee

Back in 1997, the HRC was asked to review a complaint resembling that in the *Carson* case referred to above. This complaint was filed by two former Dutch citizens, Mr and Mrs Van Oord, who had emigrated to the United States of America, but received their pensions from the Netherlands. The amount of these benefits was regulated in a bilateral treaty between the Netherlands and the US, which contained less favourable provisions for

[78] *Carson and others* (n 32), paras 87–89.
[79] *Koua Poirrez* (n 54), para 49.

the applicants than similar treaties concluded by the Netherlands with Australia, New Zealand and Canada. The applicants, who had in the meantime obtained American nationality, claimed that they were subject to discrimination on the basis of their nationality as they were treated differently from former Dutch nationals who had become Australians, New Zealanders or Canadians. However, the HRC found that 'the categories of persons being compared are distinguishable and . . . the privileges at issue respond to separately negotiated bilateral treaties which necessarily reflect agreements based on reciprocity'. It concluded that the differentiation was based on reasonable and objective criteria and did not amount to prohibited discrimination within the meaning of Article 26 ICCPR.[80]

The Committee later made it clear, however, that the above justification did not apply with regard to all forms of differential treatment. This was decided in the case of Mr Karakurt, a Turkish national who lived and worked in Austria. Unlike Austrian nationals and nationals of other Member States of the EEA, Mr Karakurt was not eligible to be a member of the work council of the association of which he was an employee. The Austrian government expressly claimed that the distinction between EEA nationals and other aliens was the result of an international law obligation entered into by Austria on the basis of reciprocity, and which pursued the legitimate aim of abolishing differences in the treatment of workers within the EU (then EC) and EEA Member States.[81] However, the HRC found that the distinction between aliens of different nationalities was not based on a reasonable justification. Thereby it took into account that the differential treatment concerned the capacity to stand for election to a work council, which had the task of promoting staff interests and supervising compliance with work conditions. The Committee moreover expressly stated that no general rule could be drawn from its earlier decision in *Van Oord* to the effect that international agreements as such constitute a sufficient justification in relation to Article 26 ICCPR.[82]

International Obligations: Concluding Observations

The above judgments and communications suggest that the extent to which differences in treatment between aliens of different nationalities may be justified by international obligations depends, to an important extent, on the nature of the right at issue. As the admission of aliens is by definition a matter involving different states (the sending and the receiving states), it is submitted that international obligations may reasonably

[80] HRC 14 August 1997, No 658/1995 (*Van Oord*), para 8.5.

[81] *Karakurt* (n 56), para 5.5.

[82] ibid, para 8.4. In view of a reservation made by Austria, the HRC found that it was precluded from assessing the difference in treatment between Austrian nationals and aliens. This finding was however disputed – rightfully in my view – by two members of the Committee, see the partly dissenting opinion of Sir Nigel Rodley and Mr Martin Scheinin.

play a role in determining the criteria for such admission. Support for this view can be found in the ECtHR judgments in *Moustaquim* and *C v Belgium*. While both these cases concerned deportation, it is argued that there is no relevant difference compared to admission cases. Importantly, both judgments also concerned aliens with family ties in Belgium, which implies that international obligations can in principle also justify differences in treatment in the area of family reunification.

The next question is whether the existence of international obligations always constitutes a relevant and sufficient reason to justify differences in treatment between aliens of different nationalities. In this respect, it may be observed that the judgments in *Moustaquim* and *C v Belgium* concerned obligations stemming from EU law. In these judgments, the ECtHR considered that the EU (then the EC) constitutes a 'special legal order' which has moreover established its own citizenship. While the Court did not clarify the relevance of these remarks, it could be the case that the judgments in *Moustaquim* and *C v Belgium* reflect the fundamental importance of the right to free movement in the EU legal order, a right which is currently linked to the concept of EU citizenship (chapter 6). Additionally, in *Bosphorus*, the Court specifically mentioned the supranational character of the EC.[83] These remarks raise the question of whether, in the view of the ECtHR, the need to comply with international obligations gains added weight if those obligations stem from EU law.

In the absence of a more detailed motivation, it is difficult to say whether the ECtHR would have reached the same outcome if the differential treatment in *Moustaquim* and *C v Belgium* had been based on international obligations other than EU law, for instance on bilateral agreements. It is submitted, however, that such agreements could in principle justify a difference in admission criteria for aliens of different nationalities. As the ECtHR and HRC acknowledge, bilateral agreements are normally concluded between states on the basis of reciprocity. Consequently a state may wish to negotiate a bilateral agreement to secure favourable treatment for its nationals abroad, in return for which it guarantees similar treatment to the nationals of the other state party. It is argued that this is a legitimate interest, not only in the field of social security, but also in respect of immigration. Hence, one of the topics that states may seek to address in a bilateral agreement concerns the conditions under which they will grant admission to each other's nationals, including the maintenance of visa or other admission requirements.[84]

[83] *Bosphorus Hava Yollari Turizm ve Ticaret Anonim Sirketi* (n 72), para 150.

[84] In this respect, it may be observed that the Dutch Advisory Committee on Aliens Affairs proposed concluding reciprocal bilateral agreements on admission with those states whose nationals were to be exempted from the Act on Integration Abroad. In the Committee's view, the existence of such agreements could have served as justification for the exemption as required by international provisions on the right to equal treatment. See ACVZ 2004a, 33.

Where a state seeks to negotiate bilateral agreements with the purpose of ensuring favourable treatment for its own nationals abroad, the viability of such agreements will inevitably depend on the extent to which reciprocity is possible.[85] For this reason, states will conclude bilateral treaties with some countries but not with others. In *Carson and others*, the ECtHR held that a state which has entered into a bilateral agreement with another state is not thereby obliged to grant the same benefits to nationals of other states. According to the Court, 'such a conclusion would effectively undermine the right of States to enter into reciprocal agreements and their interest in so doing'.[86] Thus it can be concluded that the existence of bilateral agreements to secure favourable treatment by states of each other's nationals in the field of immigration in principle constitutes a reasonable and objective justification for the differential treatment resulting from such agreements.

ii. Foreign and Economic Relations

As explained in section III.C, the Dutch government stated that one reason why some nationalities are exempted from the AIA is because the Netherlands did not want to thwart its foreign and economic relations with the countries concerned. While it is possible for such relations to be expressed by means of (bilateral) legal agreements and thus correspond to international obligations, this is not necessarily the case. In any case, the objective of maintaining good foreign and economic relations can be distinguished from the objective, as discussed in the previous subsection, of securing advantages for one's own nationals abroad on the basis of reciprocity. For this reason the former objective is addressed separately here.

In general, the wish to maintain good foreign (diplomatic) and economic (eg trade) relations can be accepted as a legitimate state interest. This is supported by the ECtHR judgments in *Bosphorus* and *Al-Adsani*, in which the Court recognised, in general terms, the importance of international cooperation and of comity and good relations between states.[87] It can moreover reasonably be argued that foreign and economic relations between states serve other interests which are expressly recognised as legitimate aims in the ECHR or ICCPR, such as the economic well-being of the state and perhaps also national security and territorial integrity.[88]

It is also accepted that the foreign and economic relations existing between two states can be influenced by many different circumstances,

[85] See also the ECtHR in *Carson and others* (n 32 a), para 88.

[86] ibid, para 89. The same argument was made by Vermeulen, see Vermeulen 2010a, 104–05.

[87] *Bosphorus Hava Yollari Turizm ve Ticaret Anonim Sirketi* (n 72), para 150 and ECtHR 21 November 2001, app no 35763/97 (*Al-Adsani*), para 54.

[88] eg, Arts 8(2) and 10(2) ECHR and Arts 19(3) and 21 ICCPR.

including the treatment granted by one state to the nationals of the other state in the field of immigration.[89] Whether and how the introduction or continuation of immigration requirements for nationals of another state affect the foreign and economic relations with that state will depend on the specificities of the relationship at issue. It must therefore be assumed that the state authorities responsible for external relations (for example, the Foreign Affairs Minister) have a large margin of appreciation to decide whether preferential treatment should be granted to certain nationalities, as they are better placed than (international) judiciary bodies to assess the effects of those decisions.[90] However such preferential treatment is not an automatic or necessary consequence of the existence of foreign or economic relations. It is consequently submitted that states may be required to give reasons why their external relations require them to treat some aliens differently from others, whereby it must be assessed whether these reasons are not manifestly unfounded.

Lastly, Kortmann suggested that an exemption from integration requirements cannot be justified by the aim of maintaining good foreign and economic relations because this aim is not related to the purpose of integration.[91] It is submitted, however, that such a relationship is not necessarily required. Even where there is a general rule to the effect that aliens must meet an integration requirement before being admitted, exceptions to this rule may be justified if the interest of integration is outweighed by the competing interest of maintaining good external relations. Where this is the case, it will be the latter interest and not the interest of integration that constitutes the (legitimate) aim of the difference in treatment.[92] If, however, the scope of the exemption(s) is too large, the proportionality of the differential treatment may be at issue. This matter is addressed below in section III.C.iv.

iii. Comparability of Countries of Origin

The Dutch government provided another justification for the nationality-based difference in treatment regarding the integration requirement

[89] See also Wiesbrock 2010, 545, who states that 'the ECtHR is likely to accept the existence of strong economic ties between two countries as a legitimate aim for the exemption from integration abroad requirements'.

[90] cp Vierdag 1973, 24–25. This author argues that the international legal principle of 'equality of States' leaves 'an enormous discretion to the States in their mutual relations', which is due to 'the particularized character of the relations of States vis à vis other States in international law'. He does not, however, address the consequences which the differentiated relations between states may have for the nationals of those states.

[91] Kortmann 2009, 24.

[92] It may be noted that Kortmann himself conducts a similar reasoning, where he maintains that an exemption from the integration requirement can be justified by the need to comply with international obligations (Kortmann 2009, 23). Arguably, this exception does not serve the purpose of integration either.

abroad. As described at the beginning of section III.C, the government held that some countries of origin were comparable to the Netherlands in 'socio-economic, social and political terms' and therefore there would be no major problems concerning integration as far as nationals of those countries were concerned.

Considering that the purpose of the integration exam abroad is to address problems in the field of immigrant integration, it makes sense to apply this requirement only in situations where such problems are expected to occur. It is therefore submitted that the above justification corresponds to a legitimate aim. It is also, however, subject to a number of objections.[93]

As in the case of the arguments discussed in sections III.C.i and III.C.ii (international obligations and foreign and economic relations), the argument addressed in this subsection provides a justification for differential treatment of aliens of different nationalities. Nonetheless, there is a difference. When an exemption from immigration requirements is created because of international obligations or international relations, this exemption logically applies to nationals of those states to which the obligations apply or which are involved in those relations. It follows that, in these cases, the differentiation ground of nationality reflects the immigrants' legal membership of an entity (the state) which has negotiated favourable immigration conditions on their behalf. On the other hand, when the exemption is motivated by the assumed comparability of countries of origin, the existence or absence of inter-state relations does not play a role. Instead, the differentiation ground of nationality is used here as a 'proxy' for the capacity to integrate, that is to say for certain personal characteristics of immigrants that are considered to be of relevance for their integration in the host society.

This brings us to the first problem regarding the justification ground at issue. The Dutch government appears to assume that immigrants from countries that are comparable to the Netherlands will integrate more easily into Dutch society. Nationals of these countries are therefore exempted from the integration exam abroad. However, that fact that a person has the nationality of a particular country does not necessarily imply that he or she has also lived in that country and is familiar with its society. On the other hand, a person may have lived in an exempted country without having its nationality. This can be illustrated by means of an example. In the Dutch government's view, Canada is a country comparable to the Netherlands, whereas the Democratic Republic of Congo (DRC) is not. Yet Canadians born and bred in the DRC are exempted from the AIA, whereas Congolese nationals who have lived all or most of their lives in Canada

[93] Some of the arguments presented below are also made by Walter 2008, 56 and Kortmann 2009, 23–24.

are not. It follows that the exemption is both too wide and too narrow. To the extent that the comparability of countries of origin is indeed considered a relevant indicator for integration potential, it would be better therefore to use the duration of residence in those countries, instead of nationality, as a criterion for exemption. However, as argued below, such comparability does not in any case provide a relevant justification.

Insofar as it is possible to identify criteria useful for determining whether someone will successfully integrate in another country, the nature of those criteria will necessarily depend on the definition of integration employed. As seen in chapter 3, the concept of 'integration' can be given various meanings, including, for example, economic self-reliance, interaction with persons belonging to different social groups or a sense of loyalty or commitment to the host country. However, despite the plurality of possible understandings of integration, it is not easily conceivable as to how the (social, socio-economic or political) comparability of countries of origin to the host country indicate how persons coming from those countries will fare in the host society. While the criterion as it stands is too abstract to be applied, it also does not lend itself to further concretisation. On the one hand, this is due to the fact that many features that can be identified as characteristics of countries of origin (such as the existence of a market economy, a democratic form of government or high levels of unemployment) are not connected to the integration of nationals or residents of those countries elsewhere.[94] Arguably, such a connection may exist with regard to certain other features, such as social conventions or the prevalence of certain languages. Often, however, such characteristics will be bound to particular regions or groups of the population and will therefore be subject to differentiation not only between, but also within countries.

To illustrate the difficulties surrounding the criterion of comparability, mention can be made of two remarks made during the parliamentary debate on the Dutch Act on Integration Abroad. With regard to the exemption for nationals of the United States and Japan, Tiny Kox, a member of parliament for the Socialist Party (*SP*), stated that

> First of all not all Americans and Japanese speak good English. Secondly the exemption does not apply to many citizens of this world who do speak good

[94] Compare Joppke's view on the differential treatment under the AIA, where he says that 'the cut is between rich and poor countries' (Joppke 2010, 41). The author does not appear to consider this distinction as problematic as (he contends) it does not amount to 'dubious, quasi-racial discrimination'. From a legal perspective, however, the important question is whether such a distinction is relevant in view of its purpose. In this connection I would submit that there is no reason to believe that aliens coming from poor countries will integrate less well than those from rich countries. In the same vein, see also Human Rights Watch 2008, 27 ('There is no evidence that the declared social and economic level of a country is a reliable indicator of the capability, inclination or willingness of a potential individual migrant to integrate').

> English, such as those who are residents of the former British colonies. Thirdly, even for immigrants from the United States or other English-speaking countries a command of the Dutch language will still be relevant for the purposes of communication in everyday life.[95]

In addition Tof Thissen, a member of parliament for the Green party (*GroenLinks*), stated that

> At this moment, the United States is torturing people in Afghanistan and in Iraq and the death penalty still exists in many American states. Extreme forms of poverty also occur in the United States. Yet American citizens do not have to pass the integration exam abroad to come to the Netherlands and marry the man or woman of their choice, whatever their sexual preference.[96]

It follows from the above that the 'comparability of countries of origin' is not a useful criterion for indicating the integration capacity of immigrants and cannot be used to justify differences in treatment with regard to integration requirements. A related disadvantage of this criterion is that it carries with it the risk of stereotyping or even stigmatisation of certain groups of immigrants. These groups risk being considered as 'inherently unfit for integration' because of their national background. The existence of such stereotypes is not likely to have a positive effect on the integration process.[97]

iv. Final Remarks Concerning Justification

The previous subsections examined the justification grounds presented by the Dutch government with regard to the differential treatment of aliens under the Act on Integration Abroad. It was established that an exemption from integration requirements for certain nationalities can be justified in the light of competing interests, including the need to comply with EU law or bilateral agreements or to maintain good foreign and economic relations with other states. Such competing interests may constitute a legitimate reason to provide for an exception from an otherwise generally applicable rule. Nevertheless, as more immigrants are exempted from integration requirements, the effect of those requirements will normally be less. It is submitted that this diminishes the relevance of the integration measures at stake and consequently the proportionality of the differential treatment. This is a factor to be taken into account in determining whether the differential treatment is justified.[98]

[95] *Proceedings I* 2005, No 12, 605.

[96] *Proceedings I* 2005, No 12, 601.

[97] Groenendijk 2005, 15.

[98] cp the argument made by Vermeulen 2010a on 104–05. Vermeulen concludes here that the differential treatment between Dutch nationals and other EU citizens with regard to family reunification (the 'reverse discrimination' discussed in chapter 10) is justified. However, he says 'That third country family members of EU citizens are exempted from the [AIA]

Lastly, the proportionality of the differential treatment also depends on the extent of the disadvantage suffered by those aliens required to comply with integration requirements. This disadvantage needs to be balanced against the interest served by the differential treatment. Relevant factors in determining the extent of the disadvantage include, inter alia, the level of an integration exam, the availability of preparation facilities and the personal circumstances of the candidates.[99] An example of a case where the ECtHR considered the interference with the applicant's right to equal treatment disproportionate can be found in the judgment in *Luczak*.[100] In *Moustaquim*, however, the ECtHR did not find there to have been a violation of Article 14 ECHR, despite the significant interests at stake for the applicants.[101] This may indicate that the Court attached considerable weight to the interest of compliance with EU law and/or that it granted a large margin of appreciation because of the immigration context (section III.B).

D. Dutch Case Law

This section examines whether any further criteria can be derived from Dutch case law with regard to integration requirements and the right to equal treatment, especially of aliens of different nationalities. It also assesses how this case law treats the arguments made in the previous sections, concerning the justification provided for the differential treatment.

Thus far two judgments by Dutch district courts have addressed the issue of nationality discrimination under the Act on Integration Abroad.[102]

must be regarded as a specific exception to the general rule, in practice concerning only a very limited number of persons and justified as a consequence of EU law'. It may be derived that the argument would not be maintained if the difference in treatment concerned a larger number of migrants or even the majority of them (in which case the exemption would become the general rule).

[99] See also section II.D of ch 4, on the proportionality of integration requirements in relation to the right to family life.

[100] *Luczak* (n 34), paras 52–60.

[101] In this case the Court concluded that deportation of the applicant would amount to a violation of his right to family life as protected by Art 8 ECHR, see *Moustaquim* (n 55), para 46. However, an explicit proportionality test was not conducted regarding the complaint concerning differential treatment.

[102] District Court of The Hague sitting in Rotterdam 23 April 2008, case no 07/35128 and District Court of The Hague sitting in Utrecht 29 June 2009, case no 08/39827. A complaint that the AIA violated the right to equal treatment as protected by the ICCPR was also made in District Court of The Hague sitting in Breda 8 January 2009, case nos 08/9327 and 08/32918; however, this complaint was not addressed by the court. Finally, in one case the court decided that Art 14 ECHR was not applicable because the applicant's right to family life under Art 8 ECHR had not been violated, see District Court The Hague sitting in Amsterdam 8 March 2011, case nos 10/23459 and 10/23449. As explained above, such a violation is not required by the ECtHR (section II.B.i). This part of the judgment was not, however, addressed in appeal.

However, the preferential treatment of certain nationalities already existed in Dutch immigration legislation before the AIA was introduced, as those aliens currently exempted from the integration requirement were already exempted from the obligation to obtain a long-stay visa (*machtiging tot voorlopig verblijf*, see section VI.B.i of chapter 2). In 2006, the Administrative Jurisdiction Division of the Council of State (AJD), the highest court in immigration cases, accepted that the latter exemption was justified by the need to protect the Dutch economic order and therefore did not violate Article 26 ICCPR.[103] The same reasoning was later applied by the District Courts of Rotterdam and Utrecht in relation to the AIA. Consequently, these courts found that the differential treatment regarding the integration exam abroad was also justified because of the need to protect the Dutch economic order.

Despite the above judgments, it is submitted that the AJD's reasoning with regard to the long-stay visa requirement cannot automatically be applied to the requirement of integration abroad. Firstly, the visa requirement and the integration requirement are different conditions serving different purposes. In respect of the visa requirement, the AJD found the difference in treatment to be justified by the need to protect the Dutch economic order. Yet the reasoning provided in this judgment is very brief and does not explain what is to be understood by this objective. While it may include economic relations with other states, it could also concern the need to control the immigration of persons with insufficient resources. Arguably, if the AJD meant that the aim of maintaining economic relations with other states justified an exemption from the visa requirement, this would also apply with regard to the integration exam (section III.C.ii). However, as already stated, the judgment does not provide clarity on this point.

Moreover, even if it could be derived from the AJD's decision that the exemption from the integration requirement serves a legitimate aim, the courts should still have assessed whether this aim was also sufficiently important to outweigh the disadvantage suffered by the applicants. The introduction of the AIA made the conditions for admission to the Netherlands more stringent. As a consequence, the difference between

[103] AJD 31 January 2006, case no 200508648/1, para 2.3. Other judgments mention additional justifications for the difference in treatment with regard to the long-stay visa requirement, namely 'the upholding of foreign relations', 'national security' and '[the prevention of? *KV*] illegal immigration'. See District Court of The Hague sitting in Breda 13 November 2007, case no 07/18500, para 2.6. and District Court of The Hague sitting in Breda 8 April 2008, case no 07/42458, para 2.7. In one judgment the court also held that in general an exemption from the visa requirement could be justified on the basis of international obligations or even 'considerations of opportunity', see District Court of The Hague sitting in Rotterdam 21 July 2005, case no 04/49309, para 4.5.8. Lastly, the above judgments of the District Court of Breda mention that the differentiation was based on bilateral agreements concerning the abolishment of visa requirement for certain countries. However, no further details or evidence as to the existence of these agreements were provided.

aliens who have to meet these conditions and those who do not has become more significant, and the disadvantage experienced by the former has become greater.[104] It follows that the differential treatment under the AIA requires a separate proportionality test, with the additional burden of having to pass the integration exam being taken into account.

As a last remark, it is noted that the courts did not apply the 'very weighty reasons' test in the above judgments.[105] As suggested above (section III.B), this test does not normally apply in immigration cases when the differential treatment is based on nationality. Hence, there is no reason to assume that the approach of the Dutch courts at this point is incompatible with the standards of the equal treatment provisions of the ECHR and the ICCPR.

IV. DIFFERENTIAL TREATMENT ON THE GROUNDS OF RESIDENCE PURPOSE

The criteria used by states to decide on the admission of aliens are commonly connected to the reasons why admission is sought. For instance, family members may be expected to demonstrate their family ties to someone residing in the host state, whereas labour migrants may be asked to show that they have either already found employment or that they are capable of doing so within a reasonable time. Criteria such as these differentiate between potential immigrants on the grounds of their residence purpose.

Residence purpose is not mentioned as a differentiation ground in any of the equal treatment provisions discussed in this chapter (section II.B). Arguably, however, it counts as 'any other ground' or 'status' within the meaning of those provisions. Consequently distinctions based on residence purpose must be based on a reasonable and objective justification.[106] At the same time, the reason why someone chooses to move to another country is not of such a nature that it must be qualified as a 'suspect' ground for differentiation. The justification provided will therefore be subject to a certain margin of appreciation (section II.D).

As far as integration requirements are concerned, it can readily be seen that these may be more relevant in relation to some residence purposes than others. Certain categories of immigrants, such as seasonal labour migrants, exchange students or au pairs, can reasonably be exempted from

[104] See also Vermeulen 2010a, 101.

[105] cp *a contrario* AJD 3 September 2008, case no 200706325/1 (*Verwijsindex Antillianen*), para 2.11.3.

[106] As far as Art 21(1) of the EU Charter of Fundamental Rights is concerned this applies to those distinctions that result from acts of EU institutions or of the Member States when they implement EU law, see section II.B.ii.

integration requirements on account of the temporariness of their stay. Less obvious, but not implausible is the argument that certain categories of immigrants have a higher capacity for adjustment or participation because of their residence purpose. Clearly, the validity of this argument will depend on the particular integration objectives pursued. If, for example, integration is primarily perceived as a matter of economic participation, it may be legitimate to foresee an exemption from integration requirements for labour migrants or entrepreneurs. Another possibility is that existing family ties in the host country may be considered an important factor in preventing social isolation. Thus, where prevention of this is the primary integration objective there may be grounds for creating an exemption for family migrants.[107] Often, however, the objectives pursued by integration requirements will be more diverse and complex and it will be less easy to connect exemptions to the choice for a particular residence purpose.

Lastly, it could be argued that integration requirements are harmful to the economic interests of the host state because they make that state a less attractive destination for labour migrants and investors and thus lead to a reduction in economic migration. Like the international obligations and external relations discussed earlier in this chapter (sections III.C.i and III.C.ii), the need to protect the economy does not relate directly to the purpose of integration, but represents another, conflicting interest. This interest could be put forward to support a more lenient immigration regime for (certain groups of) labour migrants, as has been the case with the EU Blue Card Directive (section VII of chapter 6 and section IV.A of chapter 7). The example of this directive also shows that the same argument may be used to support an exemption for family members of these labour migrants. It is submitted that this argument is valid in principle and that exemptions based on the economic interests of the state will normally fall within its margin of appreciation. Nonetheless, as mentioned above (section III.C.iv), the proportionality of such exemptions will depend on various factors, including the extent of the disadvantage for those who are not exempted and the effectiveness of the integration requirement if it is not applied to all immigrants alike.

V. THE RIGHT TO EQUAL TREATMENT AND THE ACT ON INTEGRATION ABROAD

In the foregoing it has been discussed to what extent nationality and residence purpose constitute relevant criteria for deciding which aliens must

[107] For instance, Canadian immigration legislation assesses the 'adaptability' of certain categories of labour migrants on the basis of a number of factors, including whether the person has a relationship with a person living in Canada, see http://www.cic.gc.ca. Note, however, that the criterion of adaptability does not apply in relation to family migrants.

be subjected to integration requirements. This section examines the Act on Integration Abroad in the light of the arguments developed in that discussion, with a specific focus on whether the differences in treatment that result from this Act are proportionate to the reasons why these distinctions are made.

A. Differential Treatment on Grounds of Nationality

The reasons why the AIA differentiates between aliens according to their nationality are discussed in section III.C above. It was concluded there that the 'comparability of countries of origin' argument does not constitute a relevant justification for this difference in treatment. It was also found, however, that an exemption for certain nationalities may be justified by the need to ensure compliance with international obligations (including both EU law and bilateral agreements) and/or in the interests of maintaining good foreign and economic relations with other states.

As far as the AIA is concerned, it has already been established that the exemption from the integration exam abroad for EU nationals is motivated by obligations of EU law. Similarly, an exemption has to be maintained for certain categories of third-country nationals in order to comply with bilateral agreements. This is the case notably with regard to certain groups of economic migrants from the United States and Japan, who are entitled to admission on the basis of the (friendship) treaties concluded between these countries and the Netherlands (section III of chapter 7). While these treaties have not been expressly mentioned by the Dutch government in relation to the differential treatment under the AIA, it is submitted that they provide a valid reason for that treatment.

With regard to other categories of third-country nationals the exemption from the AIA cannot be justified by reference to international obligations. It must therefore be assumed that the only (relevant) reason why these aliens are exempted from the integration exam abroad is to protect the foreign and economic relations of the Netherlands with the countries concerned. As argued earlier, these relations in principle constitute a valid objective. Nonetheless, where the AIA is concerned, two remarks deserve to be made. The first is that the Dutch government has in no way shown that the foreign and economic relations of the Netherlands would in fact be harmed if the integration exam abroad were to be imposed on nationals of the exempted countries. There are no indications that this possibility has been discussed with the authorities of the states concerned or that negative reactions have been received from abroad. In other words, the expected negative influence on the foreign and economic relations of the Netherlands has not as yet been confirmed.

The second remark is that third-country nationals who are exempted from the AIA are not exempted from other requirements for residence in the Netherlands, such as the income requirement or the condition that they must not represent a danger to Dutch public order.[108] As they are not subject to the obligation to obtain a visa before admission, these third-country nationals do not need to demonstrate their compliance with the said conditions before their arrival. They do, however, have to meet these conditions in order to be granted a residence permit once they are in the Netherlands. Apparently, these residence conditions are not perceived as an obstacle to the Dutch foreign and economic relations. This raises the question of why this would be different where integration requirements are concerned. Surely, the difference in treatment caused by the AIA would be less significant if all aliens who are not exempted on the basis of international obligations were obliged to pass the exam at some stage in the immigration process, either before or after admission. Arguably this would also increase the effectiveness of the integration requirement. This latter point is discussed in more detail in section V.C.

B. Differential Treatment on Grounds of Residence Purpose

In principle, the Act on Integration Abroad is meant to apply only to those aliens who are to become permanent or at least long-term residents of the Netherlands. For this reason the Act distinguishes between aliens whose residence purpose is temporary and those whose residence purpose is non-temporary.[109] Under Dutch immigration legislation, aliens admitted for a non-temporary residence purpose become eligible for a permanent residence permit after five years.[110] Aliens with a temporary residence purpose cannot obtain a permanent residence permit, which means they have to leave the Netherlands when the reason for which they were admitted ceases to exist. The latter category includes, for example, students, interns and au pairs. Given the limited duration of their stay these aliens do not have to pass the integration exam abroad before being admitted to the Netherlands. As observed in chapter 2 (section VI.B.i), the main category of aliens whose residence purpose is qualified as non-temporary and who are therefore subject to integration requirements consists of family migrants.[111]

[108] Art 16(1)(c) and (d) Aliens Act.
[109] Art 16(1)(h) Aliens Act read in conjunction with Art 3(1)(a) Integration Act 2007.
[110] Art 21(1)(b) Aliens Act.
[111] Another numerically important group of non-temporary immigrants consists of persons who have been admitted on asylum grounds. However, international and EU asylum law (in particular the principle of *non-réfoulement*) forbids the admission of these aliens being made subject to integration requirements. It is submitted that the non-applicability of the AIA to this group is based on an evidently valid and ponderous justification which does not

In section IV of this chapter it is argued that exemptions from integration requirements for immigrants whose stay in the host state will be temporary can readily be seen as justified in view of the objective of those requirements. Consequently, the fact that the AIA distinguishes between temporary and non-temporary residents is not as such problematic with regard to the right to equal treatment. Nevertheless, the Dutch legislation shows an important inconsistency where the position of labour migrants (and their accompanying family members) is concerned. Under the Act on Integration Abroad labour migration is qualified as a temporary residence purpose. As a result, labour migrants and their family members do not have to pass the integration exam abroad. The Aliens Act, however, designates labour migration as a non-temporary residence purpose, which means that labour migrants and their family members may apply for permanent residence after five years.[112] In view of this possibility, the exclusion of labour migrants and their family members from the AIA cannot be explained by the limited duration of their residence.[113]

It follows that the difference in treatment between family migrants and labour migrants, both of whom are in principle eligible for permanent residence, must be based on an alternative justification. As suggested in section IV, one possible argument could be that labour migrants are specifically admitted to the Netherlands to accede to the labour market. Their capacity for economic participation and self-reliance can therefore be taken as a given. However, this argument does not explain why not only labour migrants, but also their accompanying family members are exempted from the integration exam abroad as the admission of family

require detailed discussion. Meanwhile, the AIA does apply to religious servants despite this group not being eligible for permanent residence (section VII.E of ch 5). Given the close connection to the freedom of religion, the inclusion of religious servants under the AIA is discussed separately in ch 5.

[112] This follows from the fact that labour migration is not mentioned as a temporary residence purpose in Art 3.5(2) of the Aliens Decree.

[113] With regard to the foregoing it must be observed that certain categories of labour migrants are required to obtain a work permit. From Art 11(1) of the Labour Migration Act (*Wet arbeid vreemdelingen*) it follows that work permits are initially granted for a maximum of three years. If, after that period, the work permit is not renewed, the holder will not be able to remain in the Netherlands as a labour migrant. This is why labour migrants were originally excluded from the scope of the Newcomers Integration Act 1998 (ch 2, section IV.D.iv). This is explained by Van der Winden 2006, 26–27. The exemption for labour migrants was later 'copy-pasted' into the Integration Act 2007, see *Parliamentary Papers II* 2003–2004, 29 700, No 3, 7 and No 6, 32–33. However, there is no legal impediment preventing work permits from being extended after the initial three-year period. Moreover some categories of labour migrants, notably highly skilled migrants, are exempted from the work permit requirement altogether (see Art 3 Labour Migration Act and Art 1-1i Labour Migration Decree [*Besluit uitvoering Wet arbeid vreemdelingen*]). In summary, there is no legal or practical rule that necessarily makes the residence of labour migrants temporary. Lastly, as far as family members are concerned, it may be observed that the nature of their residence purpose (temporary or non-temporary) is determined by reference to that of the principal applicant (Art 3.5(2)(a) Aliens Decree).

members is not conditioned upon labour market participation. Moreover, as explained in chapter 3, the objectives of Dutch integration policy are not limited to economic participation. This appears clearly from the legislative history of the AIA, where the government states that:

> Basic knowledge of the Dutch language and society are so essential to further integration in the Netherlands that the lack of it cannot be compensated by, for example, work experience in a non-Western society or the perspective of low-skilled labour in the Netherlands. The consequences of the attraction of immigrant labour in the 1960s should present a strong warning in this respect. We must prevent the repeated formation in our society of large groups of non-integrated aliens, who work but who are otherwise insufficiently equipped to fully participate in our society.[114]

Lastly, it was suggested above that imposing integration requirements on labour migrants and their family members could lead to a reduction in labour migration, which could in turn be harmful to the economic interests of the Netherlands. It was submitted that the protection of these interests constitutes a legitimate aim, which may justify a difference in treatment between labour migrants and family migrants. This argument would moreover explain why family members of labour migrants are also exempted from integration requirements, as the existence of such requirements could make the Netherlands a less attractive destination for the labour migrants themselves.[115]

The extent to which the wish to protect Dutch economic interests was one of the reasons why the Dutch legislator decided to exempt labour migrants and their family members from the integration exam abroad is not entirely clear. The argument was briefly touched on during the parliamentary discussion of the AIA, however no substantial reasoning was provided.[116] Similarly, the legislative history does not indicate that the economic interests that would be served by exempting labour migrants were offset against the interests of their integration. It is therefore submitted that the differential treatment of labour migrants compared to other non-temporary migrants (notably family migrants) at least requires additional reasoning. The fact that labour migrants and their family members do not have to pass the integration exam abroad is also relevant with regard to the overall proportionality of the AIA. This issue is addressed below.

[114] *Parliamentary Papers II* 2004–2005, 29 700, No 6, 8.

[115] Note that, for labour migrants and their family members who are entitled to admission on the basis of the EU Blue Card Directive, integration conditions are precluded as a matter of EU law (section VII of ch 6 and section IV.A of ch 7). The above argument only applies therefore to labour migrants whose admission is regulated by Dutch domestic law.

[116] See *Parliamentary Papers II* 2004–2005, 29 700, No 6, 33.

C. Scope of the Exemption and Effectiveness of the Integration Requirement

As explained above (section III.C.iv), the relevance of integration measures diminishes if large numbers of immigrants are exempted from those measures because of international obligations or external relations. It is, therefore, important to establish the share of immigrants to the Netherlands that actually has to pass the integration exam abroad. Unfortunately, the figures needed to answer this question are not readily on hand. Nonetheless, data that are available include the total numbers of (legal) immigrants to the Netherlands over the past few years, as well as the numbers of immigrants falling within the target group of the AIA. A comparison of these figures shows that immigrants required to pass the integration exam abroad constituted approximately 15 per cent of the total number of applicants for admission over the years 2007–2010:

Table 2. Target group of the AIA in relation to total number of applicants for admission

	Total applicants for admission[1]	**Target group AIA**[2]
2007	80,257	12,258 (15.3%)
2008	102,872	15,025 (14.6%)
2009	104,411	15,773 (15.1%)
2010	110,234	13,679 (12.4%)

[1] Figures obtained from Statistics Netherlands (*Centraal Bureau voor de Statistiek*), http://statline.cbs.nl, table *Immigratie van niet-Nederlanders; migratiemotief, geboorteland, leeftijd*.

[2] Figures taken from the Monitor of the Integration Exam Abroad (*Monitor Inburgeringsexamen Buitenland*) (ch 2, section VI.D). The figures presented concern aliens between 18 and 65 years who come to the Netherlands for a residence purpose qualified as non-temporary under the Integration Act 2007 and who must be in possession of a long-stay visa (*machtiging tot voorlopig verblijf*). The figures for 2007–09 include aliens who may still be exempted from the integration exam abroad because, for instance, they belong to the family of someone holding an asylum permit or because of a medical indication (ch 2, section VI.B.iii). From 2010 onwards it was possible to take these exemptions into account, which shows that the actual numbers of immigrants having to pass the exam were even lower. Obviously, one must be careful when comparing figures from different sources as different definitions may have been used. The percentages presented in the table above must therefore be regarded as approximations. For the purpose of the argument here, however, they present a sufficiently clear picture.

Earlier in this chapter, it was established that the criteria of nationality and residence purpose, which are used to define the target group of the AIA, do not constitute relevant indicators of the capacity for integration of persons seeking admission to the Netherlands. It must therefore be assumed that the risk of integration-related problems also exists with regard to those aliens who are exempted on these grounds. Given this assumption, the fact that 15 per cent or less of all applicants are obliged to pass the integration exam abroad raises serious doubts about the proportionality of this difference in treatment.[117] After all, it is reasonable to expect that the expected positive effect of the AIA on the integration process in the Netherlands will be much less significant if the exam is taken by only 15,000 immigrants (and not by 85,000 others) than if it is taken by all. In this situation, it can be wondered whether the advantage to be gained by continuing the integration requirement still outweighs the disadvantage caused by the interference with the right to equal treatment. In this respect, it is noteworthy that the share of persons having to take the integration exam abroad is likely to decrease even further, due to the increased level of the exam from 1 April 2011 onwards (section VI.C.ii of chapter 2) and the exemption for Turkish nationals (section II.C of chapter 7).[118]

Notwithstanding the above, it is primarily up to the Dutch legislative authorities to determine the weight to be attached to the interest of integration (and hence to the significance of the AIA, even when limited in scope). These authorities enjoy a certain margin of appreciation, which, as established earlier in this chapter, is relatively large as far as differentiation on the grounds of nationality or residence purpose is concerned (sections III.B and IV). It is therefore submitted that the AIA, considered *in abstracto*, is not incompatible with the right to equal treatment as protected by national and international human rights norms.

VI. SUMMARY AND CONCLUDING OBSERVATIONS

This chapter analyses how differences in treatment in the field of integration requirements must be assessed in relation to the right to equal treatment. At the beginning of the chapter, a general overview was given of the criteria used to determine whether a difference in treatment is compatible with the relevant legal instruments. Subsequently, more specific criteria were formulated with regard to differences in treatment based on nationality or residence purpose. Possible justifications for these kinds of differential treatment were also examined.

In respect of differentiations based on nationality it was firstly established that, at least in the immigration context, nationality does not qualify as a suspect classification that would significantly narrow the available room for justification. Next, different reasons were examined as possible

[117] See also Groenendijk 2011, 28–29.

[118] According to the 2011 Monitor of the Integration Exam Abroad, the number of applicants for admission belonging to the target group of the AIA decreased in the second half of 2011, from 1500 to 1000 applications per month.

explanations of why states may apply integration requirements to aliens of certain nationalities but not to others. Here it was argued that nationality does not provide a relevant indicator of a person's integration capacity. However, a difference in treatment between aliens of different nationalities could be justified because of a need to maintain good international relations with other states or because of international obligations. The latter include obligations of EU law, as well as bilateral agreements concluded on the basis of reciprocity. These justification grounds apply equally in the case of integration requirements. Nonetheless the criterion of a 'reasonable and objective justification' implies that the aim pursued must be sufficiently important to outweigh the disadvantage suffered by aliens who have to meet the requirement on account of the differential treatment. States do, however, have a certain margin of appreciation to determine whether a particular difference in treatment is proportionate. In the context of the Netherlands, this margin is moreover left to the legislator, which means that the review conducted by the courts is not very strict.

Regarding differentiations based on residence purpose it was also argued that no suspect classification is at stake. It was furthermore submitted that distinctions on the grounds of residence purpose may be relevant in connection with integration requirements, in particular where only temporary residence is pursued. Potentially a relationship could also be drawn between residence purpose and the capacity to integrate; however, it was submitted that this would only be possible in the case of a limited and narrowly formulated definition of integration. Lastly, the economic interests of the receiving state could justify an exemption from integration requirements for labour migrants and their family members. Again, the lawfulness of this justification ground depends on a balancing of interests, whereby states have a certain margin of appreciation.

Based on the criteria set out above it was determined that the difference in treatment resulting from the AIA must in principle be considered justified. Nonetheless, two problems were observed. First, as far as the distinction on the grounds of residence purpose is concerned, insufficient reasons were found to explain why labour migrants and their family members are exempted from the integration exam abroad. Secondly, as a result of the various exemptions created, only a small percentage of those migrating to the Netherlands and whose integration cannot be taken for granted are required to pass the exam before being admitted. Consequently, the suitability or adequacy of the AIA as a measure to further the integration process is impaired. Lastly, with regard to the case law concerning the Act, it was remarked that it is not sufficient for Dutch courts to refer to earlier decisions concerning the long-stay visa requirement. Instead, the differential treatment under the AIA must be examined separately, with due regard for the reasons why these distinctions are made and for their proportionality.

This chapter also shows that defining the target group of integration requirements is a complex process, involving a variety of often competing interests. Where states create exemptions – for instance, because of international obligations or to attract highly skilled labour migrants – immigration policies can give the impression of differentiating between 'desirable' and 'non-desirable' or 'wanted' and 'not-so-wanted' aliens. From the perspective of the right to equal treatment, however, such distinctions are not always problematic. The legal instruments discussed in this chapter do not in principle preclude states from refusing admission to certain aliens or making their entry subject to conditions in accordance with their national interest. Nonetheless, what is required is for these distinctions to be made on the basis of objective and neutral criteria and to be justified by legitimate and sufficiently weighty interests.

Where such justification is not provided, there is a risk that the difference in treatment will be based, at least partly, on subjective criteria or prejudice. This risk is particularly pressing in the field of integration policy because 'integration' is in itself a rather abstract concept and often used to address perceived or ascribed as well as actual differences between groups in the population. Hence, there is a danger that legislative measures aimed at improving integration will in fact serve to reinforce existing stereotypes ('non-Western aliens are just different from Western aliens'). It was remarked earlier in this chapter that such a development is not likely to promote relationships between different communities. However, it was also established that national and international courts tend to leave a certain margin of appreciation to the national or legislative authorities when examining whether a difference in treatment is justified. While understandable in view of considerations of subsidiarity or constitutionally divided powers, this margin makes it more difficult to determine whether stereotypes or prejudices have – explicitly or implicitly – played a role in the enactment of the legislation the courts are asked to assess. The task of guarding against the influence of such subjective criteria lies primarily, therefore, with the legislator.

In this respect, as far as the AIA is concerned, it has already been observed that no (convincing) explanation has been provided of the reasons why labour migrants and their family members are exempted from the integration exam abroad. The same is true with regard to third-country nationals who are not entitled to admission on the basis of international agreements and whose exemption is based, without any further motivation, on the grounds that this is required by the 'international and economic relations of the Netherlands'. More specific and cogent justification would be needed to explain the preferential treatment enjoyed by these groups. If such justification is not available, these groups ought to be brought under the scope of the Act on Integration Abroad, unless the difference in treatment is abolished in another way.

9

The Right to Equal Treatment: Indirect Differential Treatment on the Grounds of Racial or Ethnic Origin

I. INTRODUCTION

THE PREVIOUS CHAPTER established that the Dutch Act on Integration Abroad distinguishes between different groups of aliens on the basis of their nationality. This chapter investigates whether this distinction also amounts to differential treatment on the grounds of racial or ethnic origin. Clearly, the Act does not expressly mention racial or ethnic origin as a criterion to determine which aliens must pass the integration exam abroad. As asserted earlier however, the right to equal treatment also entails protection against indirect discrimination. Such discrimination may occur when a certain group of persons is disproportionately affected by a particular measure, even if the measure is not directly aimed at that group (section II.D. of chapter 8).

An important objective of the legal provisions forbidding racial and ethnic discrimination is to protect persons against actions or practices inspired by racism or ethnic intolerance (section II.E). However, the concept of indirect racial or ethnic discrimination does not presuppose the existence of racist intentions or beliefs. Instead, it may be used to render visible the unintended effects that an apparently neutral measure – such as the Act on Integration Abroad – can have on particular ethnic or racial groups and that would have remained invisible if only forms of direct differential treatment were addressed. It is for this purpose that the concept of indirect discrimination is applied in this chapter.

A general overview of the legal framework concerning the right to equal treatment is provided in chapter 8. The current chapter firstly examines the legal standards concerning differential treatment on grounds of race and ethnic origin and indirect differential treatment (section II). Particular attention is paid to the applicability and significance of these standards in relation to integration conditions for the admission of (certain groups of) aliens. Next, in section III, the legal framework established in section II is used to conduct an assessment of the Act on Integration Abroad.

II. LEGAL STANDARDS REGARDING INDIRECT DIFFERENTIAL TREATMENT ON GROUNDS OF RACIAL OR ETHNIC ORIGIN

This section examines a number of legal norms that prohibit (indirect) discrimination on the grounds of race or ethnic origin. Various legal provisions and their applicability to the topic of this study are discussed in section II.A. After that, attention is paid to race and ethnic origin as differentiation grounds (section II.B), to the concept of indirect differential treatment (section II.C), the criteria for justification (section II.D) and the scope of review (section II.E). Lastly, in section II.F, some criteria are formulated concerning the prohibition of indirect racial and ethnic discrimination in relation to integration requirements for the admission of aliens.

A. Relevant Legal Provisions

i. (Inter)national Human Rights Provisions

The equal treatment provisions of the ECHR, the ICCPR and the Dutch Constitution are discussed in some detail in chapter 8 (section II.B). It was established that each of these instruments contains open provisions on equal treatment that forbid discrimination based on any grounds or status, including race and ethnic origin.[1] Discrimination on the grounds of race and ethnic origin is also prohibited under the Convention on the Elimination of All Forms of Racial Discrimination (hereafter CERD). The CERD prohibits racial discrimination, which is defined in Article 1(1) as:

> Any distinction, exclusion, restriction or preference based on race, colour, descent, or national or ethnic origin which has the purpose or effect of nullifying or impairing the recognition, enjoyment or exercise, on an equal footing, of human rights and fundamental freedoms in the political, economic, social, cultural or any other field of public life.

It follows that the CERD does not cover all forms of differential treatment on the above grounds, but only those negatively affecting a person's enjoyment of his or her human rights or fundamental freedoms. A list of such rights and freedoms is laid down in Article 5 CERD. Although this

[1] See Art 14 (and 1 Twelfth Protocol) ECHR, Arts 2 and 26 ICCPR and Art 1 Dutch Constitution. While all these provisions expressly mention 'race' as a differentiation ground, this term is commonly understood also to include ethnic origin. See, eg, ECtHR 13 December 2005, app nos 55762/00 and 55974/00 (*Timishev*), para 56 and various Concluding Observations of the HRC cited in Vandenhole 2005, 126–27. Art 1 of the Dutch Constitution was adopted with the aim of ensuring compliance with the obligations stemming from the CERD (*Parliamentary Papers II* 1970–1971, 11 051, No 3, 10–11). It must therefore be assumed that the term 'race' in this provision includes the various racial discrimination grounds mentioned in Art 1(1) of that Convention (see below).

list is non-exhaustive, it may be observed that it does not include a general right to be admitted to a state of which one is not a national. Such a right is also not mentioned in several important human rights instruments, such as the Universal Declaration of Human Rights (UDHR), the ICCPR and the ECHR. It can therefore be questioned whether the CERD also applies to differential treatment in the field of immigration requirements. However, as shown in chapters 4 and 5, state measures concerning the admission of family migrants and religious servants may in certain cases come within the scope of national or international human rights obligations. It is therefore submitted that such measures are in principle covered by the CERD.[2] This outcome is in line with ECtHR case law concerning Article 14 ECHR, in which the relationship between the prohibition of discrimination and the enjoyment of other rights and freedoms is also construed rather loosely and it is sufficient if the alleged discrimination comes 'within the ambit' of one of the other ECHR provisions (section II.B.i of chapter 8).

Meanwhile several other limitations to the definition of Article 1(1) can be found in Articles 1(2), 1(3) and 1(4) CERD. According to these provisions, racial discrimination does not result from unequal treatment between citizens and non-citizens, from legal provisions concerning nationality, citizenship or naturalisation (provided they do not discriminate against a particular nationality) or from 'positive discrimination' measures.

ii. EU Law

Discrimination on the grounds of race and ethnic origin is also addressed in various instruments of EU law, in particular Article 19 TFEU and Article 21(1) of the EU Charter of Fundamental Rights. Article 19(1) TFEU served as the legal basis for the adoption of the EU Racial Equality Directive (RED), which affords protection against racial and ethnic discrimination in various fields such as employment and education.[3] Although the directive itself states that it does not apply to differences in treatment that are based on nationality, it may be argued that this exception does not concern differences amounting to indirect differential treatment on grounds of racial or ethnic origin.[4] More important, for the purposes of this chapter, is that the directive also does not apply to provisions and conditions

[2] See also General Recommendation No 30 on Discrimination Against Non-Citizens, dated 1 October 2004, para 9 (available at www.ohchr.org) in which the CERD Committee declared that states should 'ensure that immigration policies do not have the effect of discriminating against persons on the basis of race, colour, descent, or national or ethnic origin'. This statement confirms that discrimination as defined in Art 1(1) CERD may also occur in the context of immigration measures.

[3] Council Directive 2000/43/EC of 29 June 2000, [2000] OJ L180/22.

[4] Busstra 2010, 42–45; De Schutter 2009, 73–75.

concerning the entry and residence of third-country nationals and stateless persons in the territory of Member States.[5] As EU nationals in any case do not have to comply with integration requirements (chapter 6, section II), it must be understood that the RED is of little relevance for the examination conducted in this chapter.

On the other hand, Article 21(1) of the Charter of Fundamental Rights is not subject to such limitations. This provision prohibits 'any discrimination', including on the grounds of race and ethnic origin.[6] The prohibition is addressed to the institutions of the European Union, as well as to the Member States when they are implementing EU law.[7] It follows that, within the context of this study, Article 21(1) of the Charter is of relevance with regard to integration requirements for third-country nationals who apply for family reunification under the Family Reunification Directive (FRD) or who move to a second Member State in accordance with the Long-term Residents Directive (LRD) (section V of chapter 4 and section VI of chapter 6).

B. Discrimination Grounds

Race and ethnic origin are difficult concepts, which are closely related to social and cultural identity. No definition of these concepts is provided in any of the legal instruments mentioned above. However, in *Timishev*, the ECtHR stated that:

> Ethnicity and race are related and overlapping concepts. Whereas the notion of race is rooted in the idea of biological classification of human beings into subspecies according to morphological features such as skin colour or facial characteristics, ethnicity has its origin in the idea of societal groups marked by a common nationality, tribal affiliation, religious faith, shared language, or cultural and traditional origins and backgrounds.[8]

It can be derived from this definition, as well as from academic literature on the subject, that both race and ethnic origin are socially constructed concepts which are based on the presumption that people can be divided into distinguishable groups or communities.[9] This presumption may be

[5] Art 3(2) Racial Equality Directive.

[6] Unfortunately, the CoJ failed to clarify the scope of this provision in the case of *Kamberaj* (CoJ (Grand Chamber) 24 April 2012, C-571/10 [2012] ECR 00000). In this case, which concerned differential treatment of long-term resident third-country nationals, as compared to EU citizens, in respect of housing benefits, the CoJ confirmed that such treatment falls outside the scope of the RED (paras 49–50). The question of compatibility with Art 21(1) of the Charter was raised by the referring court (para 39) but not addressed by the CoJ.

[7] Art 51(1) EU Charter of Fundamental Rights.

[8] *Timishev* (n 1), para 55. This definition was repeated (with some slight alterations) in ECtHR (Grand Chamber) 22 December 2009, app nos 27996/06 and 34836/06 (*Sejdić and Finci*), para 43.

[9] Busstra 2010, 30–32; Bulmer and Solomos 1998, 822; De Schutter 2009, 17–20.

held by outsiders, as well as by the members of the group themselves. As the ECtHR noted in *Timishev*, racial and ethnic categorisations are commonly linked to particular features or characteristics (Busstra uses the term 'proxies'), whereby the term 'race' is generally used for categorisations on the basis of physiological features (notably skin colour) and 'ethnicity' refers to categorisations based on cultural or sociological characteristics (such as language or religion).[10] However, it must be observed that such features and characteristics cannot be equated to race or ethnic origin, but only form an indication thereof.[11]

Given that race and ethnicity refer to perceptions of belonging, rather than to actual behaviour or physical features, one particular difficulty in the legal context is how a person's racial or ethnic origin is to be established.[12] Probably the most reliable way of doing this is by means of self-identification.[13] Alternatively, a person's racial or ethnic origin can be determined by someone else on the basis of the above proxies. Importantly however, racial and ethnic classifications are not static, but subject to change and contestation.[14] It follows that the proxies by which racial and ethnic groups are designated cannot be established once and for all, and that regard must be had to the particular social context. In this connection Busstra pointed out that international human rights law has come to recognise an increasing number of characteristics as proxies for race or ethnicity, including geographical affiliation and even social origins and class.[15]

The use of proxies can also be a relevant instrument for establishing whether a particular measure leads to a difference in treatment between persons on account of their race or ethnic origin. This may be the case, in particular, where the applicability of a measure is determined by a criterion that is also a proxy for race or ethnicity. Much will depend, however, on the nature of the criterion, as well as on the context in which the measure is taken. For example where a distinction is based on skin colour, there will most likely be differential treatment on the grounds of racial origin as skin colour has historically functioned as a proxy for race and is not likely

[10] See also Howard 2008, 11.

[11] By way of illustration, if someone wears a *djellaba* in the context of the Netherlands, this indicates that they are of Moroccan ethnic origin. Clearly, however, whereas the fact of wearing a *djellaba* is a way of dressing, being Moroccan refers to an element of one's identity. A similar example can be given with regard to gender: although wearing a skirt is something which (in the European context) is mostly done by women, wearing a skirt is obviously not the same as being a woman.

[12] See Terlouw 2009, 609–11.

[13] cp the CERD Committee's General Recommendation No 8 of 22 August 1990 on Identification with a particular racial or ethnic group (ref no A/45/18), available at www.ohchr.org. In this recommendation the Committee states that, for the purposes of reporting by the State Parties, individuals shall be recognised as belonging to a particular racial or ethnic group or groups by means of self-identification unless a justification exists to the contrary.

[14] Bulmer and Solomos 1998, 822.

[15] Busstra 2010, 30–33.

to be relevant in any other way. On the other hand, the situation often becomes more complicated if other criteria are used as grounds for differentiation. In the context of the Netherlands, for example, someone may be refused a job because he or she speaks Arabic or because he or she does not speak Dutch. In both cases the difference in treatment is based on language. However, the fact of speaking Arabic can be taken as a proxy for belonging to a particular ethnic group (in other words, Muslims or Moroccans). With regard to the fact of not speaking Dutch, such a connection is much more difficult to make. Yet it may be that this criterion, even if not directly indicative of racial or ethnic origin, nevertheless entails indirect differential treatment on these grounds. The issue of indirect differential treatment is discussed in more detail in section II.C below.

Several of the legal provisions referred to in section II.A mention national origin as a potential differentiation ground, sometimes in addition to race and/or ethnic origin. In the previous chapter it is argued that this ground refers primarily to nationality as an ethnographical category.[16] In this sense, the term 'national origin' does not differ to any relevant extent from 'ethnic origin' and therefore does not require separate discussion.[17]

C. Indirect Differential Treatment

The concept of indirect differential treatment was briefly introduced in the previous chapter (section II.V). In short, indirect differential treatment occurs if a measure formulated in neutral terms nevertheless disproportionately affects a particular group of persons falling under a relevant differentiation ground. As mentioned earlier, this effect may be caused intentionally, for example where a measure distinguishes between groups on account of their nationality in order to circumvent the prohibition of discrimination on the ground of race or ethnicity. In the context of the legal provisions discussed in this chapter, however, no evidence of discriminatory intent is required: it is the effect rather than the aim of the measure that is relevant.[18] By using the concept of indirect indiscrimina-

[16] See section III.A.ii of ch 8. See also Vierdag 1973, 101 and Vandenhole 2005, 126–27 and 139–40, who discuss the use of the term 'national origin' in legal instruments other than the CERD.

[17] cp De Schutter 2009, 13, who states that national origin 'is a concept close to, and at times indistinguishable from' racial and ethnic origin. See also Thornberry 2005, 258, who points out that the *travaux préparatoires* concerning Art 1(1) CERD indicate that there may be overlaps between the various grounds mentioned in that provision.

[18] See Art 1(1) CERD ('any distinction . . . which has the purpose or effect'); a similar definition is used by the HRC, see HRC General Comment no 18 on Non-discrimination, para 7 (available at www.ohchr.org). See also the judgment of the ECtHR in *DH and others v the Czech Republic* (ECtHR (Grand Chamber) 13 November 2007, app no 57325/00), para 194, where it was stated that 'where it has been shown that legislation produces such a discriminatory effect, the Grand Chamber considers that ..., it is not necessary in cases in the educa-

tion in this way it becomes possible to pursue a more substantive concept of equality (see again section II.V of chapter 8) and to address structural inequalities including, but not limited to those resulting from a history of intentional discrimination.[19]

In cases of alleged indirect discrimination, it is normally up to the applicant to demonstrate that a particular measure has a disproportionate effect on the group to which he or she belongs. If this succeeds, a presumption of indirect discrimination is thereby established. The burden of proof then shifts to the respondent state, which has to show that the difference in treatment is based on a reasonable and objective justification (section II.D).[20] The determination of the existence of a disproportionate effect is nonetheless a complex issue, which raises many questions. While an in-depth examination of these questions goes beyond the scope of this study, some of the main difficulties involved are highlighted below.

i. Standard of Proof

A primary issue relating to the establishment of a presumption of indirect discrimination is of course the standard of proof that is required. In EU law, where the concept of indirect discrimination has been well developed, different criteria have been devised in this regard. In the field of nationality discrimination the CoJ has accepted that indirect differential treatment occurs when a particular measure is 'intrinsically liable' to affect migrant workers more than national workers, for example because it differentiates on the basis of geographic elements.[21] This is a rather light standard, which does not require the applicant to demonstrate that the measure has actually produced an adverse effect, but merely that it is, by its nature, likely to do so.

By contrast, in cases of sex discrimination, the Court has asked applicants to show that the contested measure has in fact resulted in a disadvantage for a substantially higher proportion of the members of one sex than the other.[22] This criterion requires much stronger evidence of a disproportionate effect, which will often involve statistics (see below).[23]

tional sphere to prove any discriminatory intent on the part of the relevant authorities'. Finally a requirement of discriminatory intent is also lacking in the definition of indirect discrimination in Art 2(2)(b) RED.

[19] On the concept of indirect discrimination, see also Busstra 2010, 203–04.

[20] See, eg, in relation to Art 14 ECHR, Van Dijk et al 2006, 1039–40. See also Henrard 2008.

[21] Gerards 2002, 258–60; Tobler 2005, 225–28; Busstra 2010, 214.

[22] Schiek 2002, 296; Gerards 2002, 246–48; Tobler 2005, 228–33; Busstra 2010, 214.

[23] The difference between the standards applied by the CoJ can be explained by the fact that the abolition of distinctions on the grounds of nationality is directly linked to the purpose of market integration, which constitutes an uncontested fundamental objective of the EU. Yet this is or has been less obvious with regard to the promotion of fundamental rights, which provides the primary context for the promotion of gender equality. The different rationales underlying EU anti-discrimination law are elaborately analysed in Bell 2002.

Lastly, the Racial Equality Directive states that indirect differential treatment occurs where a particular measure 'would put persons of a racial or ethnic origin at a particular disadvantage compared with other persons'.[24] As explained above (section II.A.ii), this directive is not applicable to the issues raised in this chapter. However, from the viewpoint of consistency of EU law and in the absence of obvious arguments to the contrary, the CoJ may be expected to apply the same criterion when treating cases of indirect racial or ethnic discrimination under Article 21(1) of the Charter of Fundamental Rights. It may be derived from the words 'would put' that the RED does not require evidence of actual adverse effects, but that it is sufficient to demonstrate that such effects are liable to occur.[25] In this respect the standard of proof required by the RED resembles the lighter criterion formulated by the CoJ with regard to nationality discrimination.[26]

The above standards for establishing a presumption of indirect discrimination differ primarily with regard to the type of evidence to be adduced.[27] If it is enough for a particular group to risk being disproportionately affected, the applicant may rely on qualitative evidence to prove such a risk. Such evidence may consist of facts of general knowledge.[28] For example, it may be submitted that the socio-economic position of Turkish and Moroccan communities in the Netherlands is generally less favourable than that of the majority population. Where necessary, these facts may be complemented or backed up by other materials such as scientific or other reports, policy evaluations or judicial decisions.[29] In some cases the risk of disproportionate effects may also be directly related to the criterion used. For instance, a rule that applies only to persons needing a residence permit automatically entails indirect differential treatment on the grounds of alienage (section III.A.i of chapter 8).[30]

Meanwhile, proof of actual disproportionate effects on a particular group has to be demonstrated by means of quantitative (statistical) evidence. One practical problem relating to this type of proof is that statistical data will not always be available. In addition, the evidence must be significant, and this may be problematic if the disputed measure concerns

[24] Art 2(2)(b) RED.

[25] Busstra 2010, 219.

[26] Schiek assumes that the threshold for evidence of indirect discrimination in the RED is 'slightly higher' than in the original draft, which stated that a measure had to be 'liable' to produce adverse effects. See Schiek 2002, 296.

[27] Busstra 2010, 214.

[28] Schiek 2002, 296; Gerards 2002, 260; Tobler 2005, 231.

[29] Gerards 2002, 584–85.

[30] ibid, 585–86. The author argues that in cases where the criterion is so closely related to the indirect differentiation ground, it may be better to assume direct differential treatment. This could be a way to prevent situations where 'neutral' differentiation criteria are employed to 'cover up' differences in treatment that are actually based on suspect grounds (section II.D of ch 8).

only a small group.[31] The latter problem is not likely to play a role with regard to generally applicable legislation. Nevertheless a presumption of indirect discrimination is clearly more difficult to demonstrate where statistical evidence is required.

Related to the type of proof is the level of disparity that is demanded to establish a case of indirect differential treatment. In other words, it must be determined when a certain effect can be considered 'disproportionate'. This aspect is particularly relevant where statistical evidence is used or required. As discussed above, the RED demands that persons belonging to a racial or ethnic group would be put 'at a particular disadvantage'. This term is not further explained. In cases involving differential treatment on the grounds of sex, the CoJ has previously required the percentage of women affected to be 'considerably' higher than the percentage of affected men. Additionally, the Court also accepted that there could be indirect differential treatment in the case of a 'lesser but persistent and relatively constant' level of disparity over a long period of time.[32] While these criteria provide some indications, they are clearly not very specific. As a reference, it could be assumed that a disproportionate effect exists when the percentage of persons belonging to a particular racial or ethnic group that is disadvantaged by a particular measure is at least 1.5 times as high as the percentage of disadvantaged persons not belonging to that group.[33] As argued below, however, other comparisons are possible. Alternatively, especially in cases where significant figures are indeterminate or not available, the statistical information may be looked at in combination with qualitative evidence.[34]

The case law and comments of the other monitoring bodies (the ECtHR, the HRC and the CERD Committee) do not display a clear choice for any of the above standards, let alone a further specification of them. In earlier cases the ECtHR set a very high standard for evidence of indirect discrimination, which made a presumption thereof almost impossible to prove.[35] This approach was significantly mitigated, however, in later judgments. In *DH and others v the Czech Republic*, the ECtHR stated that in order to 'guarantee those concerned the effective protection of their rights, less strict evidential rules should apply in cases of alleged indirect discrimination'.[36] In this case it was explicitly accepted that a presumption of indirect discrimination could be derived from statistical evidence,

[31] Sjerps 1999, 245–47; Gerards 2002, 580–81; Busstra 2010, 214.

[32] Gerards 2002, 248; Busstra 2010, 218. Both authors refer to the CoJ's judgment in *Seymour-Smith*, CoJ 9 February 1999, C-167/97 [1999] ECR I-623.

[33] As used by the Dutch Equal Treatment Commission (*Commissie Gelijke Behandeling*), see Gerards 2002, 587–88. A similar criterion is mentioned in Busstra 2010, 219 (with further references).

[34] Gerards 2002, 587–88; Busstra 2010, 219.

[35] Arnardóttir 2003, 79–84; Van Dijk et al 2006, 1040–41.

[36] *DH and others v the Czech Republic* (n 18), para 187.

provided the statistics presented were 'reliable and significant'.[37] As to the level of disparity, the Court considered in *DH and others* that a presumption of indirect discrimination had been established, considering that the disputed education measures had had 'considerably more impact' on children of Roma origin.[38] In the same judgments, however, the ECtHR declared that 'there are no procedural barriers to the admissibility of evidence or pre-determined formulae for its assessment' and that 'the level of persuasion necessary for reaching a particular conclusion [is] intrinsically linked to the specificity of the facts, the nature of the allegation made and the Convention right at stake'.[39] It follows that the type of proof that can be accepted as evidence of indirect differential treatment and the standard of evidence will vary from case to case.

It follows that, in EU law as under Article 14 (and 1 Twelfth Protocol) ECHR, there is scope to assume a presumption of indirect racial or ethnic discrimination in the absence of 'hard' statistical evidence proving actual adverse effects on persons of a particular racial or ethnic origin. However, no very specific evidential standards have been formulated, and what is considered sufficient proof may therefore differ from one situation to another. In the view of the ECtHR, such differentiations are also required because of the varying circumstances of each case.

With regard to the Racial Equality Directive, Busstra proposes applying lenient standards when determining the existence of a presumption of indirect discrimination so as to maximise the number of situations that may be scrutinised under the directive. She argues that this inclusive interpretation is balanced by the objective justification test, which is also prescribed by the directive and allows for the consideration of interests that may validate the difference in treatment.[40] This is a useful approach, which may also be applied in relation to other non-discrimination norms, provided the existence of a possible justification is assessed. The justification test and the scope of review to be applied are discussed in sections II.D and II.E below.

ii. Which Comparison to Make?

In order to establish whether a racial or ethnic group is disproportionately affected by a particular measure, the effects of the measure on that group must be compared to the effects on other groups. This raises the question of which comparison must be made and which groups are to be com-

[37] ibid, para 188.

[38] ibid, para 193. Statistical evidence presented in this case revealed that in the region concerned only 1.8% of non-Roma children were placed in special schools, compared to 50.3% of Roma children (para 190).

[39] *DH and others v the Czech Republic* (n 18), para 178; ECtHR 5 June 2008, app no 32526/05 (*Sampanis et autres*), para 71.

[40] Busstra 2010, 205–06.

pared.[41] Again, this question primarily arises in cases involving statistical evidence.

As far as the identification of relevant groups is concerned, it has been argued that the comparison should be made among all persons addressed by the disputed measure.[42] With regard to immigration requirements, however, this criterion does not resolve all the questions that may arise. If the requirement applies to all immigrants seeking admission, it could be assumed that the comparison must be made within this group, by comparing those able to meet the requirement with those unable to do so. Yet, as the Dutch Act on Integration Abroad shows, it may also be the case that immigration requirements apply only to certain categories of immigrants and not to others. If the comparison in such cases is limited to those having to meet the requirement, it will be unable to take account of any indirect differential treatment resulting from the criteria used to define the target group.[43] In this type of situation, therefore, the comparison should include all applicants for admission rather than just those who have to meet the requirement.[44] Even then, however, the comparison will still not identify the effects on those who may have wished to apply for admission, but who refrained from doing so because they knew or believed that the requirement would stand in their way. To address this omission, the comparison needs also to include all potential immigrants, which in turn can make it more difficult to obtain reliable data.[45]

[41] eg, Loenen 1998, 50–51; Sjerps 1999, 245–46.

[42] Busstra 2010, 220–21.

[43] In this respect Busstra differentiates between formal and material differences in treatment. The former concern situations in which a difference in treatment is made on one ground (eg, nationality), but results in (indirect) differential treatment on another ground (eg, race or ethnic origin). Material differences in treatment occur when a particular measure applies equally to everyone (eg, the obligation to pay municipal taxes), but nonetheless has a different effect on some groups than on others (eg, certain ethnic groups experience a greater disadvantage because of their socio-economic position). See Busstra 2010, 206–07.

[44] Both Gerards and Busstra also argued that comparability arguments should not normally play a role in determining which groups to compare. An example of such an argument would be that family migrants and labour migrants are not comparable groups (because, eg, integration-related problems occur mostly in relation to family migrants) and therefore the comparison should be limited to family migrants. Instead, the argument that labour migrants do not experience the same level of integration-related problems should be dealt with in the context of the justification test. See Gerards 2002, 248–50 and Busstra 2010, 221–22.

[45] As Loenen pointed out, another consequence of restricting the comparison to a limited group (eg, the workforce within a particular company or persons actually seeking admission) is that the finding of indirect differential treatment will depend on the particular (ethnic or other) composition of that group and that the outcome may be different if the same measure is applied to another group in a similar situation (eg, the workforce within another company or persons applying for admission in another country). However, it is submitted that, to the extent the concept of indirect differential treatment is used to enable the visibility of actual adverse effects, such a consequence would not be problematic. For instance, if persons belonging to ethnic group X migrate to country A but not to country B, an immigration requirement adopted by country A will affect that group, whereas the same requirement adopted by country B will not. In this situation, country B should arguably not be held responsible for the disadvantage suffered by members of group X (cp Loenen 1998, 51, who

Once the relevant group of comparators has been identified, the next question is which comparison should be made. By way of illustration, we can imagine an immigration rule that requires aliens who want to be admitted to have a secondary education diploma. The comparison is made between all aliens applying for admission (*n* = 10,000). Of these aliens, 1500 belong to ethnic group A, whereas 8500 belong to ethnic group B. Admission is refused to 6000 aliens, of whom 1000 belong to ethnic group A, on the grounds that they lack the required diploma. These figures can be represented as follows:

Table 3. Establishing a presumption of indirect discrimination

	Secondary education diploma	**No secondary education diploma**
Ethnic group A	500	1,000
Ethnic group B	3500	5000

On the basis of the above information, it can be established that the admission rate among persons belonging to ethnic group A is one-third (33.3 per cent) whereas two-thirds (66.6 per cent) will be denied admission. On the other hand, 41.2 per cent of the persons belonging to ethnic group B will be admitted and admission will be denied to 58.8 per cent. The next question is whether the difference between the groups is significant (which is not the case if the 1.5-criterion is used, see section II.C.i).

Alternatively, it is possible to compare the percentage of persons belonging to ethnic group A in the overall pool with their share of the group that is admitted. This shows that, although persons belonging to ethnic group A constitute 15 per cent of the overall pool (1500 out of 10000), they only constitute 12.5 per cent of the group that is admitted. By contrast, persons belonging to ethnic group B constitute 85 per cent of the overall pool and 87.5 per cent of the group that is admitted.[46] Hence this form of comparison also shows that persons belonging to ethnic group A are relatively more affected by the immigration requirement than those belonging to ethnic group B, thus leaving the question of when a difference is sufficiently significant to prove a presumption of indirect discrimination.

The above comparison is made between only two groups. In reality, however, the ethnic diversity among immigrants seeking admission to a

uses a different example). Of course, the above argument does not hold if there is reason to believe that the immigration requirement is precisely the reason why members of group X do not move to country B. As mentioned above, this effect can only be properly measured if the group of potential immigrants is also included in the comparison.

[46] This type of comparison is proposed by Busstra 2010, 224.

particular state will normally be much greater, which means that group A will not only have to be compared to group B, but also to groups C, D, E and so on. If the latter form of comparison is used, it may turn out that persons belonging to ethnic groups A, B, C and D all constitute approximately 25 per cent of the overall pool, while 5 per cent of the group admitted belongs to group A, 7 per cent to group B, 25 per cent to group C and 63 per cent to group D. In my view, the admission rate of each group in this situation needs to be considered separately in relation to the share they represent of the overall pool. In the example provided here, this would lead to the conclusion that a presumption of indirect discrimination can be established with regard to ethnic groups A and B, but not with regard to ethnic groups C and D.

D. Justification of Indirect Differential Treatment

It follows from the above that establishing a presumption of indirect racial or ethnic discrimination can be a complex undertaking. Once such a presumption has been established, the next question is whether the difference in treatment is nevertheless based on an objective and reasonable justification. This test requires the differential treatment to pursue a legitimate aim and also to be in a reasonable relationship of proportionality to that aim (section II.C of chapter 8). With regard to indirect differential treatment, the requirement for a reasonable and objective justification moreover entails that the measure must not be intended to distinguish between groups of different racial or ethnic origin, even where this is not explicitly put forward as a differentiation ground.[47]

In cases of indirect differential treatment, the nature of the justification provided may also be different than in situations involving direct differential treatment. The fact that a particular group is disproportionately affected by a certain measure may be due to social circumstances that cannot easily be changed by the legislator (for example, the socio-economic position of some ethnic groups may be worse than that of others, which means they will be hit harder by a measure that imposes a financial burden). In such situations, the question of justification will not primarily concern the aim of the measure or its suitability, but rather whether another measure could have been adopted with less adverse effects on the group concerned and whether the advantage gained through the measure is of sufficient importance to outweigh these effects.[48]

With regard to the prohibition of racial discrimination in the CERD, it is observed that a justification test is not foreseen in the Convention. Article

[47] *DH and others* (n 18), para 195. On the test used by the Court in this judgment, see Henrard 2008, 246–47 and Busstra 2010, 226.

[48] Gerards 2008, 922; see also Busstra 2010, 229–31.

1(1) CERD constitutes a 'closed provision' (section II.C of chapter 8), which implies that differences in treatment falling under its definition of racial discrimination are prohibited unless they are covered by one of the exceptions of Article 1(2)–(4). Nevertheless, the CERD Committee has accepted that differential treatment does not amount to racial discrimination if it is justified in relation to the objectives and purposes of the Convention.[49]

Although the Committee's interpretation goes against the wording of Article 1(1) CERD, its approach is not without its merits. In the absence of a possibility for justification, the definition of racial discrimination can be expected to be interpreted in a restrictive way so as to preclude reasonable and legitimate state actions from falling foul of the prohibition laid down in the Convention. Such a restrictive interpretation would, however, necessarily limit the scope of the Convention, with the result that protection against racial discrimination may not always be available even if the action concerned is not based on a reasonable and objective justification. The introduction of a justification test thus allows for a more refined examination in cases where a difference in treatment is based on grounds of racial or ethnic origin.[50] It is therefore submitted that the CERD Committee's approach is defensible in view of the purpose of the Convention, which is to eliminate racial discrimination in all its forms and manifestations.[51] It may also be noted that the acceptance of the possibility of justification is in line with the approach taken by the ECtHR with regard to racial discrimination under Article 14 ECHR and with the definition in the Racial Equality Directive.[52]

Despite accepting a justification test, the CERD Committee has not yet provided detailed criteria for determining whether, in a particular case, a difference in treatment is justified in relation to the objectives and purposes of the Convention. However, the Committee has on occasions stated that the criteria for differentiation must be applied pursuant to a legiti-

[49] CERD Committee General Comment No 14 on the Definition of Discrimination (Art 1, para 1), of 22 March 1993.

[50] cp the argument made in section II.C.i above concerning the need to apply lenient standards when establishing a presumption of indirect differential treatment. See also Arnardóttir 2003, 146–47. Commenting on the reticence of the ECtHR to treat complaints concerning differences in treatment as being based on race (and thus requiring strict scrutiny), this author states that 'the seriousness of the allegation seems to have begun to function to the detriment of effective protection against such discrimination'. Arguably, if there were scope for justification (or, in the case of the ECtHR, for differentiation in the level of scrutiny, section II.E), the Court would be more willing to qualify these differentiations as instances of potential racial discrimination.

[51] cp the preamble to the CERD which reads: 'The States Parties to this Convention . . . resolved to adopt all necessary measures for speedily eliminating racial discrimination in all its forms and manifestations, and to prevent and combat racist doctrines and practices in order to promote understanding between races and to build an international community free from all forms of racial segregation and racial discrimination'.

[52] Art 2(2)(b) RED.

mate aim and that they must be proportional to the achievement of that aim.[53]

E. Scope of Review

The issue of the scope of review in equal treatment cases was already addressed in a general manner in chapter 8 (section II.D), when it was established that the scope of review is determined by various factors, specifically including the differentiation grounds at stake. Differences in treatment that are based on grounds of racial or ethnic origin are generally held to require strict scrutiny.[54] This view finds confirmation in the case law of the ECtHR, which has held on various occasions that such differentiations constitute a violation of Article 14 ECHR, unless they are based on a very strong justification. In several cases, the Court stated that where differences in treatment are based on race, colour or ethnic origin, 'the notion of objective and reasonable justification must be interpreted as strictly as possible'.[55] Another formulation used by the Court is that 'no difference in treatment which is based exclusively or to a decisive extent on a person's ethnic origin is capable of being objectively justified in a contemporary democratic society built on the principles of pluralism and respect for different cultures'.[56] Although the latter criterion appears even more stringent than the former, the Court itself does not seem to make a clear distinction as, in several judgments, both criteria are used alongside each other.[57] Nevertheless it is clear that the Court considers differentiations based on race or ethnic origin to be a particularly serious form of discrimination, which can even amount to inhuman or degrading treatment.[58]

The importance of the prohibition of racial discrimination is also stressed by Article 4(1) ICCPR, which states that this prohibition is one of the norms from which no derogation is possible in times of emergency.

[53] Vandenhole 2005, 38.

[54] eg, Loenen 1998, 35; Gerards 2002, 85; Arnardóttir 2003, 146.

[55] See, eg, ECtHR (Grand Chamber) 16 March 2010, app no 15766/03 (*Oršuš and others*), para 156.

[56] *Timishev* (n 1), para 58.

[57] See *DH and others* (n 18), paras 176 and 196 and ECtHR (Grand Chamber) 22 December 2009, app nos 27996/06 and 34836/06 (*Sejdić and Finci*), para 44. See also para 149 of the Grand Chamber judgment in *Oršuš and others*, where the Court, while expressly referring to *Timishev*, simply stated that 'very weighty reasons would have to be put forward before the Court could regard a difference in treatment based exclusively on the ground of ethnic origin as compatible with the Convention'.

[58] See, amongst other judgments, *Timishev* (n 1), para 56, where the Court qualified racial discrimination as 'a particularly invidious kind of discrimination'. In the *Cyprus v Turkey* case the ECtHR found the discriminatory treatment of Greek Cypriots to be so severe as to amount to a violation of Art 3 ECHR (see ECtHR (Grand Chamber) 10 May 2001, app no 25781/94, paras 306–11.

Arguably, this supports the view that differentiations on the grounds of race or ethnic origin should in principle be subject to intense scrutiny. The HRC has also stated that its review will be stricter when a differentiation is based on one of the grounds mentioned in Article 26 ICCPR, which include race, colour and national origin (section II.D of chapter 8).

Nevertheless, it is submitted that the scope of review should also be determined in relation to the nature of the differential treatment and that alleged indirect discrimination on grounds of race or ethnic origin will not always require an equally strong justification as when the difference in treatment is directly based on these grounds.[59] One important reason underlying the prohibition of racial or ethnic discrimination is the wish to combat racism or racist ideologies and the acts or practices resulting from them.[60] As Howard explains, the concept of racism is 'based on the belief that some races are superior to others'.[61] Busstra similarly relates the term racism to the belief that persons belonging to a certain group are 'unreliable' or 'less intelligent' than others.[62] Racist ideologies and practices are therefore inherently contrary to the principles of equality and human dignity that lie at the basis of human rights instruments in general and the right to equal treatment in particular.[63] However, the link between racism and racial discrimination can be assumed much more easily in situations where the difference in treatment is directly (and hence intentionally) based on racial or ethnic origin. On the other hand, where the difference in treatment consists of an unintended disproportionate effect on a particular racial or ethnic group, it will be more easily justified on the grounds of other general interests that are served by the measure at stake (see also section II.D). In such cases, a less stringent level of review would be indicated.

Support for the above argument can be found in the RED, which leaves considerably more scope for justification in situations of indirect differential treatment than when direct differential treatment is concerned.[64] At first sight it appears from ECtHR case law that strict scrutiny is also required in cases involving indirect differential treatment on grounds of

[59] See also Loenen 1999, 204; Arnardóttir 2003, 124–25 and Gerards 2008, 921.

[60] See, eg, the preamble to the CERD, cited in n 51. See also, amongst other judgments, *DH and others* (n 18), para 176: 'the authorities must use all available means to combat *racism*, thereby reinforcing democracy's vision of a society in which diversity is not perceived as a threat but as a source of enrichment' (emphasis added).

[61] Howard 2008, 11–14.

[62] Busstra 2010, 30–31 and 34. See also the General Policy Recommendation No 7 of the Council of Europe's European Commission against Racism and Intolerance (ECRI), which defines racism as 'the belief that a ground such as race, colour, language, religion, nationality or national or ethnic origin justifies contempt for a person or group of persons, or the notion of superiority of a person or a group of persons'.

[63] cp Art 1 of the Universal Declaration of Human Rights, as well as the preambles to the CERD and the ICCPR.

[64] Art 2(2) RED. An exception to the prohibition of direct differential treatment is laid down in Art 4.

racial or ethnic origin. However, in *Sampanis* as well as in *Oršuš*, the Court noted the occurrence of racist incidents involving non-Roma parents who did not want their children to be placed in classes with Roma children.[65] In *DH and others* no mention was made of such incidents, but the Court referred more generally to the vulnerable and disadvantaged position of Roma in Europe, which resulted from 'a history of rejection and persecution' culminating in 'their attempted extermination by the Nazis, who considered them an inferior race'.[66] It follows that in these cases the groups concerned (in all three cases Roma) were already in a disadvantaged position due to earlier racism and/or at a particular risk of being stigmatised or excluded from the mainstream society. It is submitted that this social context provides a valid reason for applying a stricter level of review, even in the absence of a discriminatory intent on the part of the respondent state.[67] Arguably, however, ECtHR case law leaves scope for less strict scrutiny in situations where there is no evidence of stigmatisation or a history of racial intolerance. In this connection it is also noted that the findings of a violation of Article 14 ECHR in *DH* and *Oršuš* were subject to considerable controversy within the Court, with as many as eight of the seventeen judges stating that no discrimination on the grounds of race had occurred in the latter judgment.

F. The Prohibition of Indirect Racial and Ethnic Discrimination in Relation to Integration Requirements

i. Effects of Integration Requirements

What can be derived from the above with regard to integration requirements for the admission of immigrants? According to the criteria set out above, such requirements constitute a form of indirect racial or ethnic discrimination if they have a disproportionate effect on a particular racial or ethnic group (or groups) and if no reasonable and objective justification is available. In the case of integration requirements this effect can occur in various ways. First of all, unless the integration requirement targets all immigrants alike, there will be a distinction between those persons or

[65] *Sampanis et autres* (n 39), para 82; *Oršuš and others* (n 55), paras 154–55.

[66] *DH and others* (n 18), paras 13 and 182. In this judgment the Court also referred to various sources confirming the existence of racism and intolerance vis-à-vis Roma, see paras 54–59.

[67] See also Gerards 2002, 88–89 and Hendriks 2008, 66–67. The latter author states that systematic forms of racial discrimination cannot be properly eliminated without taking account of the particular social circumstances, including disadvantages suffered by particular groups and the causes thereof, as these circumstances play a role in determining the effects of the policy measures and legislation adopted by the state concerned. He warns, however, that courts must also be careful not to interpret such circumstances in a wrong manner.

groups of persons who are affected by it and those who are not. In this situation the former will experience the disadvantages that come with having to meet the requirement, including inter alia the costs of the integration exam or programme and the time and effort involved in preparation. A second possible effect, which is particularly likely to occur if the integration requirement is enacted as an obligation of result (in other words, the obligation to pass an exam or to obtain a certain level of skills or knowledge), is that it will be more difficult for some persons or groups of persons to achieve this result. This may be due to different factors, including for example a lower average level of education or a larger difference between the native language of the persons concerned and the language of the host country. Lastly, it may be the case that certain persons or groups of persons are more heavily affected by the integration requirement because they have fewer financial resources. In the latter two situations, even if the persons concerned are not precluded from meeting the integration requirement altogether, the burden of doing so will be relatively high compared to that faced by others.

ii. Establishing a Presumption of Indirect Discrimination

When determining whether a particular racial or ethnic group is disproportionately disadvantaged by the integration requirement, the question arises as to how such an effect can be established. As shown above, the requirements regarding evidence and the standard of proof will depend to a large extent on the circumstances of the case and on the information available; therefore this question cannot easily be answered in the abstract. In some situations it may be possible to prove a presumption of indirect discrimination on the basis of qualitative evidence. It could be relevant, for example, to see whether the case law concerning integration requirements in a particular state shows that the applicants in those cases always or nearly always belong to the same racial or ethnic group. Alternatively, it could be argued, on the basis of assumed facts of general knowledge, that the criteria used to delimit the target group of the integration measure are inherently more likely to affect persons belonging to a particular racial or ethnic group. It could be submitted, for instance, that these persons more often belong to transnational families (if the integration requirement applies specifically to family migrants), that they often have the nationality of one of the countries to which the integration requirement applies and/or that they are already in a disadvantaged position which makes the burden of having to meet the integration requirement especially heavy (section II.F.i). Such arguments are not without relevance, especially in situations where more specific evidence cannot be obtained. They are also, however, rather general, and facts of general knowledge may be subject to dispute. Additional evidence will therefore normally be necessary. Given the nature of the issue at stake, there is no reason to assume a priori that such evidence cannot be required.

If statistical evidence is used, a relevant comparison must be made. It may be observed that, in principle, the group affected by integration requirements includes aliens who apply for admission and also persons in the host state who have an interest in their being admitted ('host state residents').[68] It is submitted that, in principle, these categories may be combined and compared, as a group, to those applicants for admission and host state residents who are not affected by the integration requirement. Alternatively, the situation of applicants and that of host state residents may be considered separately if, for instance, data on one of the two groups are more difficult to obtain, In that case, however, any presumption of indirect discrimination found will apply only to the category under consideration and the effects of the integration requirement will only be taken partly into account.

In section II.C.ii, it was argued that the situation of applicants for admission who have to meet an immigration condition is best compared with that of all applicants for admission. This applies also in the case of integration requirements. In order to demonstrate the deterrent effect of such requirements, the comparison should be extended to persons for whom the integration requirement constituted a reason not to apply for admission. In practice, however, identifying this group will be very difficult. As far as the group of host state residents is concerned, it is arguably even more difficult to determine which groups must be compared. To take the situation of family members, one possibility would be to make a comparison within the group of persons bringing in a family member from abroad; in other words, between those whose incoming family members must meet an integration requirement and those for whom this is not the case. However, the comparison could also include host state residents who enter into a family relationship with someone who is already in the host state. While this would make the pool of comparators very large, it is not obviously relevant for the purposes of establishing a presumption of indirect discrimination whether family relationships are created within the

[68] Who exactly belongs to the latter group of persons is a question in itself, and one to which the answer is not immediately obvious. It is submitted that this group in any event includes the family members of aliens who seek admission for the purpose of family reunification. Arguably, however, it may also include members of a religious organisation (if the person seeking admission is a religious servant) or employers who want to bring in labour migrants from abroad, provided of course the granting of admission is made dependent on integration requirements. With regard to the latter group it will also make a difference if the employer is a large multinational (in which case it will be difficult to maintain that anyone is personally affected by the non-admission of a future employee) or a small business with only a few employees (eg, a Turkish restaurant seeking to bring in a new chef). Although discussing these intricacies here in detail would go beyond the scope of this chapter, they clearly illustrate the difficulties involved in proving a presumption of indirect discrimination.

host state or across the border (although this may be a factor to be taken into account in the justification phase). The feasibility of the latter comparison will depend to a large extent, however, on the availability of evidence concerning family relationships entered into within the host state.

The comparisons proposed above are particularly geared towards proving a potential discriminatory effect resulting from the fact that the integration requirement does not apply to all immigrants alike. As explained above, however, a discriminatory effect may also arise from the fact that it is more difficult for persons belonging to specific racial or ethnic groups to meet the requirement because they have fewer resources – educational, financial or other – than those belonging to other groups. In order to prove this type of effect, making a comparison with persons – applicants for admission or host state residents – who have not had to meet the integration requirement will not be useful. Instead, one reasonable (and probably feasible) comparison would be between applicants for admission who are able to comply with the integration requirement and those who are not.[69] Beyond this, however, determining whether an integration measure hits certain groups harder than others risks becoming a rather complex statistical operation because the burden imposed by such measures will depend on a number of variable factors, such as income levels and previous education. This will make it difficult to trace the disadvantage caused by the integration requirement back to a particular ethnic or racial group.

iii. Justification

It was already submitted that, in principle, the aim of improving immigrant integration constitutes a legitimate state interest. Another requirement of the justification test, in the context of this chapter, is that integration measures should not have the objective of distinguishing between groups of the population on account of their racial or ethnic origin. This implies that the definition of integration formulated by the host state must, as far as possible, be racially and ethnically neutral, and that the fact of belonging to a particular racial or ethnic group should not be perceived as an impediment to successful integration.

The above requirement of neutrality entails that immigrants should not be obliged to relinquish their own ethnicity or to identify with the culture and/or values of the majority population of the host state. Any requirement for a declaration to this effect will consequently be contrary to the prohibition of racial or ethnic discrimination, even if the measure is not targeted at a specific racial or ethnic group. In addition, it is argued that

[69] If the integration requirement consists of an integration exam, it may also be useful to distinguish between applicants who pass the exam at the first attempt and those who need repeated attempts.

integration requirements may not prohibit the use of immigrants' own language. Beyond these kinds of obligations, however, the standards following from the requirement of neutrality become less clear. It remains the case that integration conditions will always entail at least a minimum level of adaptation to the standards and legislation of the host state, which necessarily reflect the values and culture of majority population.[70] Examples include the obligation to learn the language of the host state and to respect restrictions on religious clothing in certain areas of public life. Determining the acceptability of such obligations will ultimately entail a negotiation between the need for unity and integration and the interest of ethnic pluralism, which must also take account of the social and historical context of the state concerned and whereby states therefore enjoy a certain margin of appreciation.

Besides the requirement for integration measures to pursue a legitimate and non-discriminatory aim, the reasonable and objective justification test also entails that this aim could not have been reached by other means that would have produced less of a discriminatory effect and that the disadvantage suffered by the racial or ethnic group concerned is not disproportionate compared to this aim. It has been submitted that this determination is normally subject to a certain margin of appreciation on the part of the state concerned. Nevertheless, this margin will be forfeited in situations where the discriminatory effect of the integration measure concerns a group that is already in a disadvantaged position and/or at a particular risk of being stigmatised and excluded from mainstream society. One relevant factor to be taken into account in this connection is the nature of the public discourse on immigrants and integration in the host state: where this discourse is already geared towards exclusion and non-acceptance of differences, integration requirements are arguably more likely to reinforce rather than help bridge ethnic divides.[71]

As explained earlier, indirect differences in treatment may not only result from integration requirements as such, but also from the fact that certain groups of immigrants are exempted from those requirements. Chapter 8 shows that such exemptions may have been created for reasons not directly related to the aim of improving integration, for example to ensure compliance with international law or to protect the economic well-being of the host state. In this situation, efforts to determine whether the integration requirement is justified despite its discriminatory effect must also take account of why certain groups are exempted from that requirement. Again, the 'reasonable and objective justification' test requires these reasons to be both legitimate and not designed to distinguish between

[70] Kymlicka 1995, 108–15.

[71] On the consequences of public discourse for the political incorporation of immigrants, eg, see Bloemraad 2006, 236–42.

persons on account of their racial and ethnic origin, while there must also be a reasonable relationship of proportionality between the exemption (and the ensuing discriminatory effect) and the interests it is meant to serve.[72]

The above remarks do not concern situations where an integration measure is explicitly directed towards a particular ethnic or racial group with the aim of improving their position. This is the case where, for instance, members of one ethnic group are made to follow a language programme on the grounds that this group is especially likely to experience problems in the field of integration. Such a distinction could be legally justified, subject to certain conditions, as a form of positive discrimination.[73] In such cases, however, the difference in treatment is intentional and falls outside the legal framework concerning indirect discrimination presented in the above sections. The possibility of positive discrimination is not discussed in this study.

III. INDIRECT DIFFERENTIAL TREATMENT ON GROUNDS OF RACIAL OR ETHNIC ORIGIN AND THE ACT ON INTEGRATION ABROAD

The previous section investigates the legal standards stemming from the prohibition of indirect racial and ethnic discrimination in relation to integration requirements for the admission of aliens. These standards are currently applied to the Act on Integration Abroad. Arguably, the compatibility with the prohibition of racial and ethnic discrimination constitutes one of the most complex legal issues regarding this Act, partly due to the fact that the applicable legal framework remains relatively open and undefined, as well as to the lack of relevant (statistical) evidence. It is, therefore, not possible to draw very strong conclusions. Nevertheless, an attempt is made to provide an initial, general assessment serving as a basis for further investigations.

[72] In this connection, it may be observed that the CERD Committee has been critical about legislation differentiating between EU/EEA nationals and nationals of other countries. The Committee has expressed concern about the immigration legislation of Estonia, which contained restricted immigration quotas for 'citizens of most countries in the world, except those of the European Union, Norway, Iceland and Switzerland' (Concluding Observations on Estonia dated 19 April 2000, doc no CERD/C/304/Add.98, para 11). Denmark was also criticised for not offering subsidised mother-tongue teaching to third-country nationals on a par with nationals of EU and EEA countries (Concluding Observations on Denmark, 2006, GA Doc A/61/18, 55). It is possible that the above measures were adopted to ensure compliance with the respective states' obligations under EU law or the EEA Agreement. In the absence of any explanation, however, the relevance of the Committee's comments for other exemptions or preferential treatment concerning EU/EEA nationals cannot be established.

[73] See, eg, Art 1(4) CERD and Art 5 RED.

A. Racial or Ethnic Groups Affected by the AIA

As discussed in chapter 2, the target group of the AIA is primarily determined through the criteria of nationality and residence purpose. In addition, certain exemptions have been created, including for persons who cannot be required, under international obligations, to pass the integration exam abroad. The Act thus does not directly distinguish between persons on account of their racial or ethnic origin and the target group appears to be characterised by a relatively high degree of ethnic diversity, both regarding the applicants for admission and their family members in the Netherlands.[74] Nevertheless, this does not exclude the possibility of certain racial or ethnic groups being disproportionately affected by the obligation to pass the integration exam abroad.

It would go beyond the scope of this chapter to investigate whether a disproportionate effect can be established with regard to all the different ethnic groups represented among immigrants to and in the Netherlands. Instead, the examination focuses on the position of the two biggest groups of migrant minorities, being persons of Turkish or Moroccan descent. The fact that these groups are relatively large also makes it easier to collect statistically significant evidence that may serve to prove a presumption of indirect discrimination. It is, however, worth mentioning that, as of August 2011, persons with Turkish nationality no longer belong to the target group of the AIA (chapter 2, section VI.B.iii). As far as this group is concerned, the analysis in this chapter is thus limited to the situation pertaining before that time. It is, nonetheless, still illustrative in showing how the criteria found in section II of this chapter are to be applied.

The choice to consider the Turkish and Moroccan minorities as ethnic groups raises the question as to how persons can be identified as belonging to these groups and thus as being of Turkish or Moroccan ethnic origin. Earlier in this chapter, it was stated that a person's ethnicity is preferably established by means of self-identification. However, no overview of ethnic groups in the Netherlands based on self-identification is available. Instead, persons are defined as belonging to an ethnic minority on the basis of their country of birth (for first-generation immigrants) or the country of birth of their parents (for second-generation immigrants).[75]

[74] Apart from family migrants, religious servants are also subject to the AIA (section VI.B.ii of ch 2); hence, the Act affects not only family members in the Netherlands but also religious communities. Numerically, however, religious servants constitute a much smaller share of the target group than family migrants. For this reason, the examination in this section is restricted to the latter category.

[75] In the definitions used by Statistics Netherlands (*Centraal Bureau voor de Statistiek*), a person is regarded as a second-generation immigrant if at least one of the parents was born outside the Netherlands. Second-generation immigrants are assigned to an ethnic minority group according to the country of birth of the mother. If the mother was born in the Netherlands, the country of birth of the father is used. See http://statline.cbs.nl (table *Bevolking; generatie, geslacht, leeftijd en herkomstgroepering per 1 januari*).

According to these definitions, the Turkish minority consisted in 2011 of 388,967 persons, while the Moroccan minority comprised 355,883 persons.[76]

Applicants for admission are not registered as belonging to a particular ethnic minority. The ethnicity of these applicants can therefore only be established indirectly (and hence imprecisely), on the basis of information concerning their nationality and/or country of origin or birth.[77]

The possible discriminatory effect of the AIA on Turkish and Moroccan migrant communities has previously been highlighted by the non-governmental organisation Human Rights Watch. This organisation also asserted that the AIA (indirectly) discriminates against 'non-Western migrants' on account of their ethnic origin and nationality.[78] In the same vein, the CERD Committee in 2010 published Concluding Observations on the Netherlands, in which it expressed concern that 'the application of the [AIA] results in discrimination on the basis of nationality, particularly between so-called "Western" and "non-Western" state nationals'.[79]

It was argued in chapter 8 (section III.A.ii) that discrimination on the grounds of nationality is not covered by the CERD and does not constitute a form of racial or ethnic discrimination. It follows that a difference in treatment between Western and non-Western migrants on account of their nationality is not as such incompatible with the CERD and does not come within the scope of this chapter. Nevertheless, the observations made by Human Rights Watch and the CERD Committee raise the question of whether non-Western migrants (or non-Western nationals) should be qualified as a separate racial or ethnic group.

The answer to this question is not immediately obvious. It may be assumed that the term 'non-Western migrants' concerns persons who come from or are nationals of non-Western countries. However, this includes a large diversity of cultures, languages, religions, lifestyles and migration patterns. It is therefore not plausible to claim that non-Western migrants all belong to a single ethnic group. Still, they may be perceived as such within Dutch society. As remarked above (section II.B), race and

[76] See http://statline.cbs.nl (table *Bevolking; generatie, geslacht, leeftijd en herkomstgroepering per 1 januari*). Information is also available on third-generation immigrants (persons of whom at least one of the grandparents was born outside the Netherlands); see http://statline.cbs.nl (table *Bevolking; niet-westerse derde generatie*). This information shows that, in 2010, there were between 8320 and 8533 third-generation immigrants belonging to the Turkish minority and between 5752 and 5858 belonging to the Moroccan minority.

[77] See http://statline.cbs.nl (table *Migratie: land van herkomst/vestiging, geboorteland en geslacht*). Information concerning the nationality of applicants for admission is provided by the Dutch Immigration and Naturalisation Service (*Immigratie- en Naturalisatiedienst*), see www.ind.nl. Additional information can also be found in the evaluation of the AIA conducted in 2009, see Brink et al 2009 and Lodder 2009.

[78] Human Rights Watch 2008, 26–30.

[79] Concluding Observations of the CERD Committee concerning the Netherlands, 16 March 2010, CERD/C/NLC/CO/17–18, para 5.

ethnic origin are socially constructed concepts that depend on the perceptions of outsiders, as well as on those of the members of the group themselves. In this connection, it is observed that non-Western migrants (or 'non-Western allochthones') are often regarded as a separate category in data compiled by Statistics Netherlands (*Centraal Bureau voor de Statistiek*). The same category is used to determine the target group of Dutch integration policy, although other categories increasingly seem to play a role.[80] It has been argued that these categorisations contribute to a process of culturalisation that is quite similar to racialisation (ie the construction of a racial group).[81] It is questionable, however, whether non-Western migrants are also regarded as a separate racial group outside this policy context – including by themselves. The extent to which a process of racialisation or categorisation must have advanced before a particular group of persons can be legally qualified as a racial group is also uncertain.

In the light of the above, it is submitted that the question of whether 'non-Western migrants' constitute a particular racial or ethnic group cannot be answered within the confines of this study. This would require further investigation into the use of this category and the legal definition of the terms 'race' and 'ethnic origin'. The assessment conducted below is limited to examining the specific position of the Turkish and Moroccan migrant communities.

B. A Presumption of Indirect Racial or Ethnic Discrimination?

Does the AIA have a disproportionate effect on persons of Turkish or Moroccan ethnic origin? In answering this question, the first issue to be examined is whether persons of Turkish or Moroccan origin have a significantly higher chance of being confronted with the integration requirement abroad as an obstacle to family reunification. This examination looks at persons applying to be admitted to the Netherlands, as well as Dutch residents seeking to bring in a family member from abroad.

During the legislative process leading up to the adoption of the AIA, it was observed that men and women of Turkish and Moroccan origin often marry a partner from their country of origin.[82] To the extent that family migrants from Turkey and Morocco are obliged to pass the integration exam abroad, it can be assumed that their family members in the

[80] *Parliamentary Papers II* 2009–2010, 31 268, No 25 (*Integratiebrief*), 15.

[81] Schinkel 2008.

[82] *Parliamentary Papers II* 2003–2004, 29 700, No 3, 4; *Parliamentary Papers II* 2004–2005, 29 700, No 6, 3–4. All the information I was able to retrieve about the family reunification of Dutch residents concerned adult married couples; I was not able to find any information on family reunification with children, parents or other relatives. For this reason, only family reunification with spouses is examined here. As indicated in section III.A, the qualification 'of Turkish or Moroccan origin' refers to persons who were born or who have at least one parent born in Turkey or Morocco.

Netherlands are also affected.[83] In 2001, five years before the AIA was adopted, slightly fewer than 60 per cent of Turkish men and women living in the Netherlands and getting married brought in a marriage partner from Turkey or Morocco.[84] This number subsequently declined quite strongly, especially among the second generation. By 2006 it had fallen to around 25 per cent and in 2009 to below 20 per cent.[85]

When compared to persons belonging to other ethnic groups who also bring over a marriage partner from the country of origin, there is no reason to assume that Dutch residents of Turkish or Moroccan origin are more frequently affected by the AIA. Arguably, some ethnic groups will be affected to a lesser degree because persons belonging to these groups often have the nationality of an EU Member State, in which case their incoming spouses do not have to pass the integration exam abroad (chapter 6, section III). However, this exemption on the grounds of obligations of EU law applies regardless of ethnic origin.[86] The effect of this exemption on the ethnic composition of the group affected by the AIA cannot therefore easily be predicted.

Even so, despite the decline in the number of 'migration marriages' amongst Dutch residents of Turkish or Moroccan origin, these groups still marry a partner from the country of origin relatively often compared to persons belonging to other ethnic groups. In 2009, for example, the number of people of Turkish descent marrying a partner from Turkey was about five times as high as the number of Surinamese marrying a partner from Suriname and about eight times as high as the average number of immigrants from Western countries (*westerse allochtonen*) who married a partner from their country of origin. In the same year, the number of people of Moroccan descent marrying a partner from the country of origin was approximately four times as high as that of Surinamese and roughly six times as high as the average for immigrants from Western countries.[87]

[83] Of course, Dutch residents of Turkish or Moroccan origin will also be affected by the AIA if they marry a partner from another country (not being their country of origin) to which the Act applies. Unfortunately, the available information is insufficiently specific to be able to take this group into account. Nevertheless, an earlier study suggests that this group is probably not very large: as at 1 January 2000, only 1.3% of persons of Turkish or Moroccan origin married a partner who migrated from a country other than the country of origin. See Hooghiemstra 2003, 23.

[84] See the table in Annex 2 to *Parliamentary Papers II* 2004–2005, 29 700, No 6, 55. For Moroccan women the percentage was somewhat lower: 51.9%.

[85] The figures for 2006 are taken from the 2008 annual report on integration (*Jaarrapport Integratie*), see Table 2.7 of the annex to the report. The figures for 2009 come from the 2010 report, at 51–53. Both reports were published by Statistics Netherlands and are available at www.cbs.nl.

[86] This means, eg, that a French national of Moroccan origin will also be covered by this exemption, as will a German national of Turkish origin.

[87] See the 2010 annual report on integration, at 51–53 (n 85). Figures for migration marriages among the native Dutch population are not available, which makes it impossible to include this group in the comparison.

When comparing Dutch residents of Turkish or Moroccan origin and other Dutch residents entering into a marriage, persons belonging to the former groups are consequently more likely to marry a partner from abroad and are thus to be affected by the AIA.[88] A presumption of indirect ethnic discrimination can, therefore, be established, at least where the Turkish and Moroccan communities in the Netherlands are concerned.

Next, it may be asked whether Turks and Moroccans are also overrepresented among immigrants applying for admission to the Netherlands and who have to pass the integration exam abroad. As indicated above, one problem in answering this question is that figures concerning immigration to the Netherlands mostly categorise immigrants according to their nationality.[89] While it may be assumed that, at least in the context of Turkish and Moroccan immigrants to the Netherlands, the correlation between nationality and ethnicity is rather strong, the information that can be gathered from these immigration statistics does not provide a very precise picture of the effects of the AIA on different ethnic groups. Nevertheless, where large differences are observed, this may still suffice to prove that particular groups are disproportionately affected compared to others.

The 2009 evaluation of the AIA shows that in 2006, 2007 and 2008 nationals of Turkey and Morocco constituted the two largest groups amongst those who took the integration exam abroad, with figures of approximately 21 per cent (Turks) and 15 per cent (Moroccans).[90] Unfortunately, no figures are readily available on the relative share of Turkish and Moroccan nationals among the total number of applicants. However, the annual reports of the Dutch immigration service (*IND*) show that, in 2007 and 2008, Turkish nationals constituted only 9 per cent of all applicants for a long-stay visa (*mvv*) and 8–9 per cent of all applicants for a residence permit (*verblijfsvergunning regulier*). For Moroccan nationals the figures were 5–6 per cent.[91] The reports also show that neither Turks nor Moroccans are in the top 10 of applicants for asylum, which is the main immigration category for which no long-stay visa is required.

Together, these pieces of information suggest that persons of Turkish or Moroccan nationality have a much higher chance of having to pass the integration exam abroad than (certain) other categories of aliens seeking to be admitted to the Netherlands. This makes it quite likely that a similar

[88] This is not to say that the same conclusion does not also apply to certain other non-Western immigrant communities (eg, Afghans or Somalis). However, as stated above, the examination in this chapter focuses on the position of persons of Turkish and Moroccan origin.

[89] Although Statistics Netherlands gives immigration figures by country of birth, these statistics do not provide the information necessary to determine whether persons do or do not fall under the AIA (notably residence purpose).

[90] Section VI.D of ch 2.

[91] The annual reports of the *IND* are available at www.ind.nl.

effect occurs with regard to persons of Turkish or Moroccan ethnic origin. It follows that a presumption of indirect ethnic discrimination also exists with regard to persons of Turkish or Moroccan origin who apply for admission to the Netherlands.[92]

Thirdly, it is examined whether persons of Turkish or Moroccan origin also have more difficulty passing the integration exam abroad than candidates belonging to other ethnic groups. To this end, the pass rates of Turkish and Moroccan exam candidates are compared with the average pass rates of all candidates. Again, the available figures only distinguish according to the nationality of the candidates and not their ethnicity. They do not, therefore, give a very precise indication of the effects on different ethnic groups. Nevertheless, the comparison shows that the pass rate of Moroccan nationals was consistently higher than the average pass rate between 15 March 2006 (when the AIA entered into force) and 30 June 2010. Throughout this period, the pass rates among Moroccan nationals varied between 92 and 95 per cent, whereas the average pass rates varied between 87.5 and 90.4 per cent. On the other hand, the comparison shows the pass rates of Turkish nationals to have been consistently lower than the average pass rates, ranging from 86.5 to 89 per cent.[93] The percentage of Turkish nationals who do not pass the exam is consequently between 11 and 13.5 per cent, compared to the average of between 9.6 and 12.5 per cent. If the 1.5-criterion is taken as a point of departure (section II.C.i), it must be concluded that this difference is not in itself sufficient to establish a presumption of indirect ethnic discrimination. This conclusion could be revised, however, if the difference continued to exist over a longer period of time.

Lastly, Human Rights Watch claimed that the Turkish and Moroccan communities in the Netherlands are disproportionately affected by the AIA because their disadvantaged (socio-economic) position makes it harder for persons in these groups to bear the costs of the integration

[92] Earlier (section II.F.ii) it was asserted that it will often be too difficult to measure whether an integration requirement also has a deterrent effect on certain ethnic or racial groups, to the effect that persons belonging to those groups refrain from applying for admission altogether. Nevertheless, the researchers who conducted the 2009 evaluation of the AIA were able to show that the share of Turkish and Moroccan nationals who applied for a long-stay visa after the AIA entered into force was not significantly lower than before (the percentage of Turkish nationals remained at 18%, whereas Moroccans went from 18% to 14%). This suggests that any deterrent effect of the AIA on these groups is not very strong. See Brink et al 2009, 61–62 and Odé 2009, 289–90.

[93] The figures in this section are based on the evaluation of the AIA conducted in 2009 (Brink et al 2009) and on the Monitor of the Integration Exam Abroad (*Monitor inburgeringsexamen buitenland*), see section VI.D of ch 2. These sources concern the period between 15 March 2006 to 1 September 2008 (the evaluation period), the years 2008 and 2009 and the first half of 2010 (the period between 1 September and 31 December 2008 is included in the evaluation and in the monitor for 2008). The average pass rate was calculated on the basis of the numbers presented in these sources, excluding the results obtained by Turkish and Moroccan nationals.

exam and of the necessary preparation. The report referred to statistical evidence showing, inter alia, that 30 per cent of Turkish and Moroccan households live below the poverty line compared to 8 per cent of native Dutch households.[94] While this evidence is not without significance, a more specific comparison is required to establish a presumption of indirect ethnic discrimination on these grounds. In particular, more relevant evidence could be obtained by making the comparison between households seeking to bring in a family member from abroad.[95] In the absence of such information, a presumption of indirect ethnic discrimination cannot be assumed. It is submitted, however, that the report by Human Rights Watch signals a need for further research into the financial effects of the AIA.

i. *Evidence of Discriminatory Intent?*

Human Rights Watch has also drawn attention to the Turkish and Moroccan communities being 'uppermost in the mind of [Dutch] policymakers when the overseas integration test legislation was introduced'.[96] Although not expressly stated, this claim may be understood to suggest a discriminatory intent on the part of the Dutch legislator. As explained above (section II.C), evidence of discriminatory intent is not necessary to establish a presumption of indirect discrimination. For the purpose of this chapter, therefore, such evidence can be disregarded. Nevertheless, the parliamentary history of the AIA does indeed reveal that the problems designed to be resolved by the Act were considered to be especially prevalent among certain ethnic groups (in particular Turks, Moroccans and other non-Western migrant communities).[97] Although it may well be the case that some ethnic groups are more affected by particular problems (such as high unemployment or elevated crime rates) than others, two remarks can be made.

The first is that care must be taken to ensure that data concerning levels of integration are gathered in an ethnically neutral manner.[98] Secondly, where a correlation is found between, for instance, ethnic background and unemployment levels, this does not necessarily imply that ethnicity is

[94] Human Rights Watch 2008, 30–31.

[95] As it stands, the evidence provided by Human Rights Watch leaves open the possibility that it is mostly 'richer' persons within the Turkish and Moroccan communities who engage in family reunification, while among the native Dutch those living below the poverty line are overrepresented among the group seeking to bring in a partner from abroad. If so, the AIA could still affect native Dutch persons to the same extent as (or even more strongly than) persons of Turkish or Moroccan origin.

[96] Human Rights Watch 2008, 16–17 and 30. See also Groenendijk 2011, 29.

[97] See *Parliamentary Papers II* 2003–2004, 29 700, No 3, 4–5 and *Parliamentary Papers II* 2004–2005, 29 700, No 6, 3 and 5–6.

[98] Schinkel has argued that, in the Netherlands, this is not always the case, see Schinkel 2008.

also a causal factor in determining someone's chances of finding employment. Other factors may well play a role, including for instance the immigrants' level of education, their financial position, the economic climate in the Netherlands at the time of their arrival or prejudices on the part of the receiving population. Hence, unless a causal relationship can be established (and perhaps even then), ethnic origin should not be one of the criteria determining who has to meet an integration requirement and who does not.[99]

C. Justification

The issue of potential indirect discrimination on ethnic grounds was not raised during the legislative procedure leading to the adoption of the AIA. Several years later, in response to the above report by Human Rights Watch, the Dutch government denied that Turkish and Moroccan migrant communities were disproportionately affected by the Act.[100] Consequently, no justification for this effect was provided. Nonetheless, it was established in the previous subsection that the AIA does have a disproportionate effect on Turkish and Moroccan migrant communities in the Netherlands, as well as on persons of Turkish or Moroccan origin who apply for admission. The question of whether these effects can be justified by a reasonable and objective justification is examined below.

A discriminatory effect of the AIA was shown to exist, first of all, with regard to Dutch residents of Turkish or Moroccan origin because these people are more likely to marry a partner from the country of origin. The discriminatory effect thus results from the greater prevalence among persons of Turkish or Moroccan origin of 'migration marriages'. This raises the question of whether there exists a justification for the fact that the AIA applies only to migration marriages and not to marriages where both partners already live in the Netherlands.

Such justification is not hard to find. One reason why the AIA applies only to immigrants is because it is assumed that they are not proficient in Dutch and lack the knowledge about the Netherlands considered necessary for successful integration. It is argued in chapter 3 (section II.B.iii) that the AIA also functions as a selection mechanism, to ensure that immigrants admitted to the Netherlands have a certain minimum level of education. Such a selection mechanism is not needed, however, if both partners are already Dutch residents. In other words, the AIA is an immigration requirement, rather than a condition for marriage, which explains why only immigrants are affected by it. It is concluded that the discrimi-

[99] The issue of intentional discrimination is taken up in more detail in De Vries 2012.
[100] *Parliamentary Papers II* 2007–2008, 29 700, No 56, 4.

natory effect of the AIA on Dutch residents of Turkish or Moroccan origin does not amount to a violation of the prohibition of racial or ethnic discrimination.

Another effect of the AIA, established in section III.B, is that persons of Turkish or Moroccan origin who apply to be admitted to the Netherlands are more likely than others to have to pass the integration exam abroad. Presumably, this effect is primarily caused by the two main criteria used to define the target group of the AIA, namely nationality and residence purpose (section VI.B.i of chapter 2). Most immigrants of Turkish or Moroccan origin who seek admission to the Netherlands are family migrants. Moreover, unlike EU citizens and certain third-country nationals, Moroccan nationals and (until August 2011) Turkish nationals are not exempted from the AIA on the grounds of their nationality.

The previous chapter argues that the difference in treatment, under the AIA, of aliens of different nationalities can be considered to serve a legitimate interest (compliance with international obligations and the protection of the foreign and economic relations of the Netherlands). Regarding the distinction on the grounds of residence purpose, the Dutch authorities have thus far not adequately explained why the AIA applies primarily to family migrants and not to labour migrants.[101] Even if such an explanation were provided, however, the question would remain as to whether the AIA could not be replaced by another measure that would not have a discriminatory effect. Arguably, the current Act could be replaced by an exam or an educational requirement that would apply to labour migrants and family migrants alike. Alternatively, it would be worthwhile considering whether the aim of improving integration could not be furthered by integration measures that would apply only after arrival and would not constitute a requirement for admission. The advantage of such measures is that they could apply to EU citizens and third-country nationals alike.

Whether the AIA is justified in its current form or should be replaced by a measure with less or no discriminatory effect is a question that must be answered through a balancing exercise, with regard for the various interests involved (including the interest of compliance with international law and the protection of the external relations of the Netherlands), for the (expected) effect of the AIA and of alternative measures in achieving better integration results and for whether the discriminatory effect on certain ethnic groups can be eradicated fully or only in part. In assessing these interests the Netherlands has a certain margin of appreciation, which in principle is larger in cases involving indirect differential treatment than where direct differential treatment has occurred. Nevertheless, it is argued above that there are grounds for stricter scrutiny in situations involving alleged indirect ethnic or racial discrimination if the group affected is

[101] Section V.B of ch 8.

already in a disadvantaged position or is especially vulnerable to stigmatisation or exclusion from mainstream society.

It is submitted in this respect that the position of the Turkish and Moroccan migrant minorities in the Netherlands does raise some concerns. Contrary to what the ECtHR stated in *D.H. and others* regarding the Roma population in the Czech Republic (section II.E), Turks and Moroccans in the Netherlands do not have a 'history of rejection and persecution'. Incidents of racist violence against these groups, although not non-existent, are also relatively uncommon.[102] However, compared to the majority population, the Turkish and Moroccan communities continue to face problems in several areas of socio-economic integration, including education, labour market participation and housing.[103] As explained above (section III.B.i), the Dutch legislator recognised this when the AIA was adopted. There also exists a prevalent political discourse in the Netherlands that is critical of 'mass immigration', 'un-integrated immigrants' and 'the "Islamisation" of Dutch society'.[104] There seems little doubt that this discourse is at least in part directed towards the Turkish and Moroccan migrant communities. Lastly, a survey shows that persons belonging to these groups indicate that they have experienced discrimination on account of their ethnic origin.[105]

Given this situation, it is not unlikely that a measure primarily affecting persons of Turkish or Moroccan origin – even in the absence of discriminatory intent – will have the effect of putting these groups at a further distance from the majority population, at least in perception. Whether this effect will in fact occur as a result of the adoption of the AIA is, of course, very difficult to determine. Nevertheless, it is submitted that the position of the Turkish and Moroccan minorities in the Netherlands is such that the existence of a justification for the disproportionate effect of the integration exam abroad must be subject to strict scrutiny. It will be up to the Dutch authorities in this respect to demonstrate that the objectives of the AIA cannot be reached as well (or even better) by means of measures with less or no discriminatory effect. If such justification cannot be provided, it must be concluded that the differential treatment of Turkish and Moroccan immigrants is not reasonably and objectively justified and hence that the AIA violates the prohibition of indirect ethnic discrimination.

[102] Wagenaar and Van Donselaar 2010, 30–32. The authors noted 148 incidents of racially motivated violence (against persons or objects) in 2009, of which 52 were classified as 'anti-Islamic'. In 2008 the number of manifestations of 'anti-Islamic' violence stood at 89. Turkish and Moroccan migrants constitute two of the largest Islamic communities in the Netherlands.

[103] See the 2010 annual report on integration (*Jaarrapport Integratie*), available at www.cbs.nl.

[104] See also Human Rights Watch 2008, 7–11. A primary exponent of this discourse is Geert Wilders, the leader of the Dutch Freedom Party (*PVV*), which managed to win 24 of the 150 seats in the Dutch Parliament in the June 2010 general elections.

[105] See the *European Union Minorities and Discrimination Survey (EU MIDIS) 2009 (Main Results Report)* published by the EU Fundamental Rights Agency and available at www.fra.europa.eu.

IV. CONCLUDING OBSERVATIONS

This chapter considers the compatibility of integration requirements with the prohibition of indirect racial and ethnic discrimination. As explained earlier, the concept of indirect discrimination can be used to reveal and assess the unintended effects of legislative measures on particular racial or ethnic groups. The second section of this chapter examines how this concept is to be applied in relation to integration requirements for the admission of aliens, with particular regard for the different effects or disadvantages that such requirements may produce and how it can be established whether those effects amount to a presumption of indirect racial or ethnic discrimination. It was argued in this respect that integration requirements can amount to indirect differential treatment of persons applying for admission, as well as of host state residents. In practice, however, it can be rather difficult to determine whether a particular measure disproportionately affects one or more racial or ethnic groups: qualitative evidence often provides insufficient proof, whereas more specific statistical evidence can be difficult to obtain.

Another difficulty lies in determining the level of scrutiny to be applied by judicial bodies. It was argued that, although differential treatment resulting from racism or ethnic intolerance must be strictly reviewed, strict scrutiny is not necessarily indicated in situations where the differential treatment consists of unintended effects. Instead, the level of scrutiny needs to be determined in the light of the social context and the existence of factors making the specific racial or ethnic group particularly vulnerable to exclusion. It was submitted that such factors played a role in the indirect discrimination cases ruled on by the ECtHR concerning the position of Roma in the education system. However, no general criteria for determining the level of scrutiny in indirect discrimination cases have so far been provided. All in all, it can be concluded that the existing legal framework concerning indirect racial or ethnic discrimination is not easy to apply in practice.

It was nevertheless attempted in section III to evaluate the AIA against the background of the above legal framework, with particular regard for the position of the Turkish and Moroccan migrant communities in the Netherlands and persons of Turkish or Moroccan origin who apply for admission. Since there is hardly any information concerning these groups that is based on self-identification, use was made of data where persons of Turkish or Moroccan origin were identified as such on the basis of their nationality or country of birth. These data showed that these groups are not disproportionately affected by the AIA in the sense of having lower pass rates for the integration exam abroad (although Turks pass less often than Moroccans). However, both groups are more likely to have to take the exam than persons belonging to other ethnic groups. Dutch residents of Turkish or Moroccan origin are also more likely to be confronted with the consequences of the AIA because they are more likely to marry someone from abroad than persons belonging to the majority population are.

The final subsection of this chapter examines whether the above effects are nevertheless justified in view of the interests that the AIA aims to pursue and the reasons why the Act was adopted in its current form. Several problems were identified in this respect. The first, which was already signalled in the previous chapter, is that the Dutch legislator has not adequately explained why the AIA does not apply to labour migrants and their family members. It is likely, however, that the disproportionate effect of the AIA on immigrants of Turkish or Moroccan origin is caused at least in part by the fact that the Act applies primarily to family migrants. A second problem is that the Dutch legislator has not explored whether the aims of the AIA could also have been reached through alternative measures that would not have had a discriminatory effect on persons of Turkish or Moroccan origin. The need to conduct such an investigation is recognised as constituting a very strict requirement, which does not allow the Dutch authorities much margin of appreciation. It is argued in this case, however, that a high level of scrutiny is indicated because of the already vulnerable position of the Turkish and Moroccan migrant communities in the Netherlands, which means that they require particular protection against indirect ethnic discrimination.

10

The Right to Equal Treatment: 'Reverse Discrimination'

I. INTRODUCTION: THE PROBLEM OF REVERSE DISCRIMINATION

AS EXPLAINED IN chapter 6, EU law operates on the premise that the right of free movement between EU Member States will be obstructed if it does not also include a right to family reunification. Family members of EU nationals who move to another Member State – or who return to their own Member State after having moved within the EU – are consequently also entitled to be admitted to that state. This right exists regardless of the nationality of those family members or whether they have previously had legal residence in the EU. It is subject to very limited conditions and does not depend on the fulfilment of integration requirements. In addition, it has recently become clear that EU nationals can be entitled to family reunification under EU law if refusal to admit their family members would impede the exercise of the rights to which they are entitled as EU citizens.[1]

On the other hand, in cases where EU nationals' enjoyment of their rights under the TFEU is not obstructed by a Member State's national legislation concerning family reunification, that legislation remains applicable (chapter 6, section III.A). Where this legislation imposes more stringent conditions for family reunification, such as integration conditions, this will result in a disadvantage for those EU nationals who are not entitled to family reunification under EU law.[2] This situation is commonly referred to as 'reverse discrimination' because it contrasts with the traditional pattern whereby states treat their own nationals more favourably than

[1] CoJ (Grand Chamber) 8 March 2011, C-34/09 [2011] ECR 0000 (*Ruiz Zambrano*), see also section III.A of ch 6.

[2] By way of example, imagine a Dutch and a French national who are both living in the Netherlands. Both want to bring over a spouse from Morocco. The situation of the French national falls under EU law, which means that the family reunification is not subject to integration conditions. The situation of the Dutch national, however, is covered by Dutch immigration law, which means that the spouse must pass the integration exam abroad. A situation of this sort occurred in the case of *McCarthy* (CoJ 5 May 2011, C-434/09 [2011] ECR 0000), concerning a British national who unsuccessfully sought to rely on EU law to obtain a right of residence for her Jamaican husband. See also CoJ (Grand Chamber) 15 November 2011, C-256/11 [2012] ECR 00000 (*Dereci*).

nationals of other states.[3] This traditional pattern reflects a notion commonly found in political theory, which entails that nationality (or citizenship) corresponds to the highest level of inclusion in a community.[4]

The examination in chapter 4 shows that the right to family life does not include a general right to family reunification for nationals. Still, to the extent that nationality is perceived as a privileged status, reverse discrimination will be seen as problematic because nationals are treated less favourably than aliens. Evidence of this perception is found in the parliamentary debate on the AIA, where members of parliament spoke negatively about the Act resulting in 'discrimination by the Netherlands of its own citizens'.[5] Nevertheless, it is argued below that there is no legal norm requiring states to grant their own nationals a status at least equally strong as that granted to aliens (section II). It follows that the unfavourable treatment by a state of its own nationals is in principle subject to the same legal standards as other forms of differential treatment (section II of chapter 8). Some additional remarks concerning these standards in relation to reverse discrimination are made in section III. Subsequently, case law of the Dutch courts concerning reverse discrimination in family reunification cases is briefly reviewed in section IV. Section V assesses whether the reverse discrimination resulting from the AIA is compatible with national and international legal standards on the right to equal treatment.

II. THE RELEVANCE OF NATIONALITY: A 'MOST FAVOURED' STATUS?

Nationality, as a legal status, expresses a formal bond between a person and a state (chapter 8, section III.A.ii). As such, the concept of nationality is not without relevance in international (human rights) law. Three categories of legal provisions can be distinguished in this respect.

Firstly, there are provisions that grant specific rights only to nationals. These include notably the right to political participation (Art 25 ICCPR)[6]

[3] To present a complete picture it is noted that, pursuant to the entry into force of the Family Reunification Directive, reverse discrimination of 'non-moving' EU nationals occurs not only in relation to 'moving' EU nationals (of the same or a different nationality), but also in relation to third-country nationals. While the directive leaves room for integration requirements, it also provides guarantees for family reunification that are not available under Dutch immigration law, notably through the supervision of the CoJ and the application of general principles of EU law (section 5 of ch 4). For an overview of different situations of reverse discrimination in relation to family reunification, see Verschueren 2009, 77–78.

[4] Bosniak 2006, 3.

[5] *Proceedings II*, 2004–2005, No 60, 3894–95; *Proceedings I*, 2005–2006, No 13, 662. See also Vermeulen, who qualifies reverse discrimination as 'the most problematic aspect' of the AIA. The author maintains, however, that the difference in treatment is compatible with international equality norms (Vermeulen 2010a, 102–04).

[6] See also Art 16 ECHR, which states that the provisions concerning freedom of expression, freedom of association and the prohibition of discrimination do not impede the right of

and the right to enter, remain in and leave the state of one's nationality (Art 3 Fourth Protocol ECHR, Art 12 ICCPR and Art 10(2) CRC).[7] Secondly, there are provisions that guarantee the right to a nationality or protect persons from not having a nationality. The right to obtain a nationality can be found in Article 24(3) of the ICCPR, Article 7 CRC and Article 4(a) of the European Convention on Nationality (ECN).[8] Articles 4(b) and (c) ECN moreover provide that statelessness shall be avoided and that no one shall be arbitrarily deprived of his or her nationality. The prevention of statelessness is also the object of a number of other treaties, including the UN Convention on the Reduction of Statelessness.[9] A third category of provisions consists of those that grant aliens the same rights as nationals. This type of provision is included, for example, in the Refugee Convention, the UN Convention on the Status of Stateless Persons[10] and the European Social Charter (with regard to migrant workers). Through these instruments, the legal status of the national is taken as the standard by which the status of the alien is defined.

It follows that nationality is a status to which particular rights are attached and to which everyone is entitled. In addition some treaties contain equal treatment clauses requiring certain groups of aliens (refugees, stateless persons and migrant workers) to be granted particular rights on an equal footing with nationals. However, these rules do not require nationality – implicitly or explicitly – to be treated as a 'most favoured' status, meaning that nationals should always be treated at least equally to aliens and prohibiting reverse discrimination. In certain contexts, international law (other than EU law) also provides for certain privileges to be accorded specifically to aliens. This is the case notably with regard to diplomats and staff members of international organisations.

states to restrict the political activities of aliens. It follows, *a contrario*, that political activities conducted by nationals are protected by the Convention. Lastly, Art 3 First Protocol ECHR obliges the Contracting States to organise elections so as to ensure the free expression of 'the people'. It is as yet unclear whether this article grants the right to vote only to nationals or also to aliens, see Van Dijk et al 2006, 919–21.

[7] It may be observed that the relevance of the latter provisions extends beyond the mere right to enter and remain as a person's (lawful) presence in the territory of a state in turn makes them eligible for rights other than those mentioned above. See, for instance, Art 2(1) ICCPR: 'Each State party to the present Covenant undertakes to respect and to ensure to all individuals *within its territory* and subject to its jurisdiction the rights recognized in the present Covenant, without distinction of any kind, such as race, colour, sex, language, religion, political or other opinion, national or social origin, property, birth or other status'. Additionally the right to political participation ensures that nationals cannot only passively enjoy rights, but may also actively contribute to deciding on the content of those rights and the conditions on which they are granted.

[8] CETS No 166, *Treaty Series* 1998, 10 and following, entry into force for the Netherlands on 1 March 2000.

[9] UNTS Vol 989, 175, *Treaty Series* 1967, 124 and following, entry into force for the Netherlands on 13 December 1975.

[10] UNTS Vol 360, 117, *Treaty Series* 1955, 42 and following, entry into force for the Netherlands on 11 July 1962.

As long as the above provisions are respected, states are of course free to award 'most favoured' treatment to their own nationals as a matter of national law. With regard to the Netherlands, it is noted that a general legal norm to this effect is not included in the Dutch Constitution or in other legislation. However, when the Integration Act 2007 was enacted (section V.D of chapter 2), the Council of State found that it would be contrary to the right to equal treatment if (non-moving) Dutch nationals were made to pass an integration exam, while other EU nationals would be exempted from this obligation. In particular the Council, acting as advisory body to the legislator, found that such a distinction could not be justified by 'the mere presence or absence of a Community law context'.[11] This finding eventually led the Dutch legislator to exempt all Dutch nationals from the obligation to pass the integration exam so as to ensure that their status was equal to that of other nationals of the EU Member States.[12] The preferential treatment of EU nationals, however, was not considered problematic in relation to third-country nationals, even though this difference in treatment was equally based on obligations stemming from EU law. On this point, the Council of State declared that 'the integration requirement for third-country nationals can be justified by the fact that, unlike Dutch nationals, they do not have a special relationship with the Netherlands'.[13] It can be derived that, at least for the purposes of the Integration Act 2007, Dutch nationals were in fact accorded a sort of 'most favoured' status.

Interestingly, however, the Council of State did not address the issue of reverse discrimination in its commentary on the proposal for the AIA.[14] Vermeulen suggests that this omission may be due to the presumption that the differential treatment under this Act takes place outside the jurisdiction of the Netherlands, as the AIA requires aliens to pass an integration exam in their home countries. However, he points out that such a presumption would be mistaken because the integration exam abroad affects family members both in and outside the Netherlands (section II.B.iv of chapter 8).[15] Still, while Dutch nationals are treated on a par with EU nationals with regard to integration obligations, this is not the case in respect of the right to family reunification. It is submitted that in this

[11] *Parliamentary Papers II* 2005–2006, 30 308, No 4, 3–4.

[12] For an overview of the legislative process leading up to the Integration Act 2007, in particular the discussions concerning the right to equal treatment, see De Vries 2006, 278–81.

[13] *Parliamentary Papers II* 2005–2006, 30 308, No 106, 2. For a good understanding of the Council's position, it may be pointed out that it did not argue that Dutch nationals should always be exempted from integration requirements. In fact, the Newcomers Integration Act of 1998 also applied to Dutch nationals who had previously lived abroad (section IV.D.iv of ch 2). However, the Council of State found that integration obligations could not be imposed on (certain groups of) Dutch nationals if EU nationals would be exempted. The argument thus criticised the proposed differential treatment rather than the obligation as such.

[14] *Parliamentary Papers II* 2003–2004, 29 700, No 4.

[15] Vermeulen 2010a, 103–04.

respect the Dutch integration legislation is incongruent. However, this in itself does not mean that the reverse discrimination of Dutch nationals under the AIA is also contrary to the right to equal treatment. Whether this is the case must be assessed in the light of the legal standards set out in chapter 8 (section II). Below, some remarks are made concerning the applicability of these standards in relation to reverse discrimination.

III. THE RIGHT TO EQUAL TREATMENT IN SITUATIONS OF REVERSE DISCRIMINATION

A. Applicability of EU Non-discrimination Provisions

An overview of various legal provisions guaranteeing the right to equal treatment (or the prohibition of discrimination), including several provisions of the TFEU and the EU Charter of Fundamental Rights (Arts 18 and 19 TFEU and Art 21 CFR), is provided in chapter 8 (section II.B). The applicability of the latter provisions is, however, limited to situations within the scope of application of EU law. As explained above, the occurrence of reverse discrimination results precisely from the fact that many EU nationals do not use their right of free movement (and are not impeded in the exercise of their citizenship rights) and thus do not establish a connection with EU law. As a consequence, these nationals are also barred from invoking the non-discrimination provisions of the TFEU or the Charter to obtain a right to family reunification under the same conditions as EU nationals who can rely on EU law.[16]

This restriction of the scope of EU law mainly to cross-border situations and the ensuing phenomenon of reverse discrimination have often been criticised in the literature. In particular, it has been argued that, after the introduction of EU citizenship and the increasing communitarisation of immigration law, it would be inconsistent to continue treating the family reunification of certain categories of EU citizens as a matter falling outside the scope of EU law.[17] However, this alleged inconsistency has not thus far been resolved by the EU legislator or the CoJ. Since the provisions of EU law on non-discrimination are not applicable, the question remaining is whether reverse discrimination by a state of its own nationals is compatible with standards of equal treatment in international law (notably Art 14 and 1 Twelfth Protocol ECHR) and, for the Netherlands, with Article 1 of the Dutch Constitution.

[16] CoJ 25 July 2008, case no C-127/08 [2008] ECR I-6241 (*Metock and others*), para 78; see also *Dereci* (n 2), paras 70–72.

[17] See notably Spaventa 2007, Walter 2008 and Verschueren 2009.

B. Differentiation Ground: Migrating Versus Non-migrating EU Nationals

As established earlier in this study (chapter 8, section II) differences in treatment must be based on a reasonable and objective justification so as not to amount to prohibited discrimination. In determining whether such a justification exists, states have a margin of appreciation that depends, for a large part, on the differentiation ground at stake. As explained in the introduction, reverse discrimination entails differential treatment between EU nationals who have and those who have not made use of their right to free movement. Consequently, it can be said that the differentiation ground is whether or not one is a 'migrating EU national'.[18]

Alternatively, it could be argued that reverse discrimination is a form of differential treatment on the grounds of nationality as the distinction will mainly be between a state's own nationals and nationals from other EU Member States.[19] However, the right to family reunification under EU law is also available to nationals who return to their own state after having exercised the right to free movement elsewhere in the EU (chapter 6, section III.A). Conversely, there is as yet no evidence that a right to family reunification exists for EU nationals born in a Member State other than that of their nationality and who have always lived there.[20] Therefore it is concluded that nationality constitutes, at most, an indirect differentiation ground. In either case, there is no reason to assume that reverse discrimination must be treated as a suspect classification with little or no room for justification (chapter 8, sections II.D and III.B).

C. Justification: Compliance with Obligations of EU Law

Reverse discrimination occurs when family members of migrating EU nationals are exempted from integration requirements because such requirements are not permitted under EU law. Consequently, the reason behind this exemption is to ensure that national integration requirements do not contravene EU law obligations. In chapter 8 (section III.C.i.b) it is argued that this constitutes a reasonable and objective justification for dif-

[18] In exceptional cases EU nationals can also engage the right to free movement without actually migrating to another Member State, as happened, eg, in the *Carpenter* case (section III.A of ch 6). A right to family reunification under EU law also exists for EU nationals who would otherwise be impeded in the exercise of their right to reside in the EU (as in the case of *Ruiz Zambrano*, see again section III.A of ch 6). For the purpose of this chapter, the term 'migrating EU nationals' must be understood also to include these situations.

[19] As Walter seems to assume, see Walter 2008, 55–57 and Verschueren 2009, 83.

[20] With the exception of children dependent on the care of their parents, see ch 6, section III.E.

ferences in treatment in the field of immigration requirements. Support for this argument was found in the ECtHR's judgment in *Moustaquim*, where the Court held that the differentiation between EU citizens and third-country nationals was justified because the EU constitutes a 'special legal order'.

According to Verschueren, the ECtHR's reasoning in *Moustaquim* does not apply to differential treatment between EU nationals. In this author's view, EU citizens all belong to the EU special legal order. Hence, he finds that their position is not comparable to that of third-country nationals even if the EU nationals have not made use of the right to free movement.[21] It is submitted, however, that this argument cannot be maintained. While the decision in *Moustaquim* concerned a difference in treatment between EU nationals and third-country nationals, the ECtHR found this differentiation to be justified because it was based on the need to comply with obligations of EU law. Consequently, it was the applicability of EU obligations that validated the preferential treatment of EU nationals, rather than their nationality as such. The scope of these obligations remains to be determined by the EU institutions. As explained above, reverse discrimination exists precisely because the EU legal order does not apply to certain situations, including the family reunification of non-migrating EU nationals. From the judgment in *Moustaquim*, it can therefore be derived that such distinctions are compatible with Article 14 ECHR, provided they are also proportionate.

The Dutch Advisory Committee on Aliens Affairs (*ACVZ*) has argued that the Netherlands is not only allowed, but actually *obliged* to bring family members of non-migrating EU nationals under the AIA.[22] In the Committee's view, this follows from the fact that the exemption of these family members is not required by obligations of EU law. Consequently, the right to equal treatment requires them to be treated in the same way as others to whom no such obligations apply.

It is submitted that this is a valid observation, assuming there are no alternative reasons – other than compliance with EU law – to justify an exemption for family members of non-migrating EU nationals. This raises the question, however, of whether it is acceptable for states to create such an exemption with the purpose of putting their own nationals in a privileged position. In other words, whether states can enact a more favourable family reunification régime for their own nationals than for aliens. In

[21] Verschueren 2009, 84. Contrary to what this author states, the ECtHR in *Moustaquim* did not find that the situation of EU nationals was incomparable to that of third-country nationals (in other words that they did not constitute equal cases), but that the differential treatment of EU nationals and third-country nationals was based on a reasonable and objective justification. By contrast the Court found in the same case that the situation of third-country nationals was incomparable to that of Belgian nationals, which made the search for a justification unnecessary. See ECtHR 18 February 1991, app no 12313/86 (*Moustaquim*), para 49.

[22] ACVZ 2004a, 32–33.

my view, such a distinction can in principle be justified on the grounds that nationals have a particular interest in being able to live with their own family members in the country of their nationality (section II.C of chapter 3). However, this argument applies equally to aliens with strong ties to the state concerned, notably through long-term residence.[23] It was already observed, moreover, that the suitability of integration measures will be jeopardised if too many immigrants are exempted from these measures on grounds unrelated to their integration capacity (section III.C.iv of chapter 8).

IV. DUTCH CASE LAW

No case law is yet available from the Dutch courts concerning reverse discrimination resulting from the Act on Integration Abroad. Before the AIA entered into force, the Roermond District Court ruled on a case concerning reverse discrimination in relation to the obligation to obtain a long-stay visa. In this case, the court found that the difference in treatment was justified by the need to comply with obligations under EU law and that the exemption of family members of (migrating) EU nationals from the visa requirement constituted a reasonable exception to an overall restrictive immigration policy. Accordingly, it was found that there had been no violation of the right to equal treatment (Art 26 ICCPR).[24]

This judgment suggests that the district court considered compliance with EU law as a legitimate objective, which can in principle justify the reverse discrimination of non-migrating Dutch nationals. This outcome is compatible with the international legal standards concerning equal treatment that were formulated above (section III.C) and earlier in chapter 8. Nevertheless, it should again be noted that the integration exam abroad imposes a heavier burden on applicants for admission than the visa

[23] Likewise, in the case of *Abdulaziz*, the respondent state argued that more lenient rules for family reunification applied to women with close ties to the United Kingdom so as to avoid the hardship that these women would suffer if they were forced to move abroad. In the view of the ECtHR this aim was 'unquestionably legitimate'. Contrary to what was argued above, however, the Court found that a relevant relationship to the United Kingdom could not be assumed on the grounds of residence alone. See ECtHR 28 May 1985, app nos 9214/80, 9473/81 and 9474/81 (*Abdulaziz, Cabales & Balkandali*), para 88.

[24] District Court of The Hague sitting in Roermond 26 October 2004, case no 03/26987, LJN: AR3411. See also District Court of The Hague sitting in Amsterdam 29 April 2009, case no 08/6690 and following. The latter case involved a Moroccan national seeking to be admitted to the Netherlands to remain with her Dutch son. She claimed that both she and her son were subject to discrimination because she could not obtain a right of residence under EU law. The court, however, found that there had been no violation of the right to equal treatment (Art 14 ECHR) as the applicant could have applied for family reunification under Dutch law. It is not clear whether the court simply did not consider the difference between the conditions for family reunification under EU law and under domestic law, or whether it implicitly considered this difference to be justified.

requirement alone. The Dutch courts will therefore have to conduct a separate proportionality test to determine whether reverse discrimination with regard to integration requirements is also based on an objective and reasonable justification (section III.D of chapter 8).

V. REVERSE DISCRIMINATION UNDER THE ACT ON INTEGRATION ABROAD

It is concluded that the exemption from the AIA for family members of migrating EU nationals – including Dutch nationals – serves a legitimate objective (to respect the obligations stemming from EU law). What remains, then, is the question of whether this exemption and the ensuing reverse discrimination of non-migrating Dutch nationals are also proportionate. Regard must be had in this respect for the purpose of the distinction (compliance with obligations stemming from EU law), as well as for the interests served by the integration exam abroad and the unequal treatment endured by non-migrating Dutch nationals.

As discussed above, the Roermond District Court found that the exemption of family members of migrating EU nationals from the long-term visa requirement constitutes a proportionate exception to the general immigration rules. However, the introduction of the integration exam abroad raised the threshold for family reunification under Dutch law, thus widening the gap between those affected by domestic law and those falling under the more lenient rules of EU law. This means that the disadvantage of being treated differently from migrating EU nationals has become more significant. This disadvantage was amplified even further by the increased exam requirements introduced on 1 April 2011.

As already discussed in chapter 8 (section V.C), the scope of the exemption must be taken into account to determine whether the AIA can still be considered a suitable measure for promoting immigrant integration in the Netherlands. In this connection, it is observed that the Roermond District Court considered preferential treatment of migrating EU nationals to be justified as an exception to a generally restrictive immigration policy (section IV).[25] Arguably, this qualification still applies.[26] Nevertheless, as a consequence of developments in EU law, the circle of family members who are eligible for admission without being subject to integration

[25] A similar reasoning is followed by Vermeulen, who described the exemption from integration requirements for (third-country) family members of EU nationals as 'a specific exemption to the general rule, in practice concerning only a very limited number of persons and justified as a consequence of EU law'. See Vermeulen 2010a, 104.

[26] Unfortunately, I have not been able to retrieve figures concerning the number of aliens admitted as family members of migrating EU nationals. It is therefore not possible to specify the share of total admissions that these family members represent.

requirements has increased in recent years.[27] Family members of migrating EU nationals are also not the only group of persons exempted from the AIA because of international obligations or other reasons not related to their integration capacity. The same applies to the migrating EU nationals themselves, to the nationals of certain third countries, to labour migrants and their family members and, as of August 2011, to Turkish nationals (chapter 2, section VI.B.iii). The limited scope of the AIA casts doubts on its effectiveness as an integration measure and hence on its proportionality.

Even so, it was also considered earlier that the choices made by the Dutch legislator remain within the margin of appreciation granted by the applicable legal standards and therefore do not constitute a violation of the right to equal treatment. There is no reason to assume a different outcome in respect of the issue of reverse discrimination. The reverse discrimination of non-migrating Dutch nationals under the AIA can therefore not be regarded as unlawful. Nevertheless, this conclusion does not discharge the legislator from the responsibility to make a careful assessment of the proportionality of the Act, also in the light of new legal or factual developments.

VI. CONCLUDING OBSERVATIONS

Following the examination in chapters 8 and 9, this chapter highlights one more aspect of the relationship between integration requirements for the admission of aliens and the right to equal treatment. The central question addressed is whether states may enact integration requirements as a condition for family reunification of their own nationals, while certain groups of aliens (in particular migrating EU nationals) are not faced with such requirements.

One special element characterising situations of reverse discrimination is that the nationals of a state are entitled to fewer rights vis-à-vis that state than others who possess a different nationality. This raises questions about the meaning attached in that particular state to the (political) concept of nationality (or citizenship) and the relationship between national citizenship and citizenship of the EU. In section II it is argued that the way in which this relationship has been implemented in different areas of the Dutch integration legislation is inconsistent: as far as the integration exam in the Netherlands is concerned, the rights of Dutch nationals have been equalised with those of (migrating) EU nationals, but this has not happened with regard to family reunification and the integration exam

[27] In addition to the adoption of the Residence Directive, these developments include CoJ case law such as the judgments in *Metock and others*, *Ibrahim*, *Teixeira* and *Ruiz Zambrano*. For further details, see ch 6. The circle of beneficiaries has also increased as a result of the accession of new Member States to the EU.

abroad. If this inconsistency is to be resolved, the Dutch approach towards integration will need to be reconsidered, taking into account the existence of EU citizenship and the privileged position of EU nationals and their family members. A more facilitative and less coercive policy will be less likely to run into the barriers raised by EU law and will therefore lend itself more easily to being applied to all persons at risk of experiencing integration-related problems.

It has also been established that there are no international legal standards requiring states to grant their own nationals at least the same rights as aliens. The question of whether reverse discrimination is lawful must therefore be answered on the basis of the general legal framework concerning the right to equal treatment, whereby differential treatment is allowed, providing it is based on a reasonable and objective justification.

Earlier in this study it was concluded that the wish to comply with obligations of EU law can in principle constitute such justification (chapter 8, section III.C.i.b). In situations of reverse discrimination, however, states must strike a fine balance. On the one hand, they must provide justification if certain groups of aliens are treated more favourably than their own nationals. On the other hand, there is no self-evident reason why nationals should be entitled to family reunification under more lenient conditions than aliens. It was submitted that such preferential treatment could be considered lawful because of the close ties that nationals (and long-term residents) can be assumed to have developed with the state concerned (and that result in a greater interest in their being able to live in that state). However, when large groups of immigrants are exempted from integration conditions, the effectiveness of those conditions (and hence the proportionality of the distinction) will be diminished.

Notwithstanding the above, the legal standards concerning equal treatment discussed in this study do not state that reverse discrimination in the field of integration requirements is either forbidden or required. When appraising the various interests concerned, states are entitled to a certain amount of discretion. As far as the AIA is concerned, it was concluded that the Dutch legislator has not surpassed the boundaries of this discretion. It was also submitted that the interference with the right to equal treatment that currently results from the reverse discrimination of non-migrating Dutch nationals would not be resolved if family members of these nationals were henceforth exempted from the AIA, as there would then still be a difference in treatment between (migrating and non-migrating) EU nationals on the one hand and third-country nationals on the other. However, the existence of the problem of reverse discrimination can be seen as an additional argument in support of an alternative solution to the existing integration problems in the Netherlands and one that does not result – or only to a lesser extent – in differential treatment of aliens, Dutch nationals or both.

11

Conclusions

UNDER THE ACT on Integration Abroad, integration has become a condition for immigration to the Netherlands. Non-compliance with this condition results in the non-admission of aliens and, therefore, in their exclusion from Dutch territory. This study assessed how such integration conditions relate to the rights of immigrants as laid down in (inter)national immigration law, including the law on fundamental rights. In addition, some standards have been formulated regarding the contents of integration requirements and the different integration objectives that can be pursued. This chapter considers the findings from the various chapters of this study and presents some concluding observations.

I. INTEGRATION REQUIREMENTS AS A CONDITION FOR ADMISSION

A. Integration as a Ground for Exclusion

Chapter 3 examined how the connection between integration and immigration was conceptualised in the Netherlands. As shown in Chapter 2, the adoption of the Act on Integration Abroad followed the enactment, in 1998, of the Newcomers Integration Act, which obliged certain categories of immigrants to participate in integration programmes upon arrival. Given this history, it is not surprising that the AIA was at least partly defended as an instrument designed to prepare immigrants, before their arrival, for further integration in the Netherlands. It was also recognised, however, that the Act would function as an instrument of exclusion as its application would result in the non-admission of immigrants who did not pass the integration exam abroad. The AIA was thus also meant to function as a selection mechanism, so as to ensure that immigrants are not admitted unless they are likely to integrate successfully. This objective was qualified as 'integration through exclusion'.

This objective, meanwhile, still leaves room for different approaches. When the AIA was first adopted, its stated purpose was to select immigrants on the basis of their willingness to integrate. A consequence of this chosen objective was that the integration exam had to be reasonably feasible for everyone who was sufficiently motivated. Later, the level of the exam was raised and the AIA became more focused on selecting immigrants on the basis of their proven ability to learn Dutch, and thus indirectly their learning capacity and previous education. At this stage, immigrants no longer had to be only 'willing', but also 'able'.

It may be argued that whether an exam selects on the basis of motivation or on linguistic ability is not very significant. After all, in both cases the efforts that are required will depend, to a large extent, on the capacity of the candidate, and immigrants with stronger learning capacities or more education will be able to pass the exam more easily. In addition, the determination of the effort that can reasonably be required of immigrants necessarily includes an element of arbitrariness. Nevertheless, the choice for a selection criterion influences the way in which the integration exam is implemented, for instance, with regard to the level of knowledge required, the role of the government in providing preparation facilities and the possibility of exemptions for candidates who are unable to pass despite demonstrated efforts. Ultimately, an exam aiming to select on the basis of motivation should take the form of an obligation of effort that all immigrants are able to meet. On the other hand, an exam selecting of the basis of ability implies acceptance of the fact that some immigrants will be unable to fulfil the conditions and will therefore be ineligible for admission.

B. Integration Versus Admission: a Balancing of Interests

It follows from the above that integration requirements are not merely a barrier to the entry of non-nationals, but also an instrument to support the integration process in the host state. The acceptability of such requirements therefore has to be determined through a balancing of interests, taking into account their contribution to successful integration (as part of the public interest of the host state) and the effects of non-admission on individual immigrants, host state residents and/or competing public interests. Chapter 3 argued that, in this respect, states have a certain amount of discretion to decide on the acceptability of integration requirements in case of labour migration and, to a lesser extent, in case of family reunification. The analysis in the second part of this book showed that this notion is also expressed in the legal instruments regulating the admission of aliens in international law. This outcome is discussed in more detail below.

As regards admission for the purposes of family reunification, chapter 3 argued that individuals have a strong interest in being able to enjoy their family life in the country with which they have strong ties, through nationality, long-term residence or other relevant factors. As far as the EU Member States are concerned, this interest is now expressed in the Family Reunification Directive, which grants a right to admission to family members of third-country nationals who are eligible to reside in a Member State for at least one year.

In addition, a right to family reunification can exist under international human rights law (the ECHR, ICCPR and CRC), in particular in situations where the exercise of family life in the country of origin is impossible or very difficult. Arguably, international human rights treaties give special consideration to family members of persons who were admitted to the host state to obtain protection from persecution or inhuman treatment in their country of origin. The same applies if the exercise of family life in the country of origin is thwarted by other barriers, such as severe medical conditions or the presence of children who are rooted in the host state and would suffer from displacement. However, under international human rights law, the threshold for accepting the existence of such barriers is relatively high. A right to family reunification is therefore not easily found to exist.

The existence of a right to family reunification, be it under the Family Reunification Directive or – in exceptional circumstances – under international human rights treaties, moreover does not imply that this right is absolute. With the exception of refugee families, the Family Reunification Directive expressly allows the admission of family members to be made dependent on the fulfilment of integration requirements. This is also the general rule under Article 8 ECHR, Articles 17 and 23 ICCPR and Articles 9 and 10 CRC. Integration requirements must, however, meet the criteria set by the above instruments. In particular, there must be a relationship of proportionality between the interest of integration (the public interest of the host state) and the interests of the individual family members. This proportionality depends on the personal situation of the family members, the efforts they must make to meet the integration requirements (which in turn depends on factors such as the level of the exam, circumstances in the country of origin and so on), and on the necessity and effectiveness of those requirements.

More specifically it was argued that, once a right to family reunification has been established, integration requirements will be disproportionate if they make the exercise of this right effectively impossible. As said before, this will depend in part on the circumstances of the case. Nevertheless, to return to the distinction made above, it follows that integration requirements may reasonably oblige family members to make a certain effort, but may not indefinitely exclude them on the grounds of their inability to reach a particular level. This implies that the level of integration requirements must not be set so high as to exclude persons with little education or learning capacities, and that there should be a possibility for individual exemptions (for instance, a hardship clause).

Another group of aliens who may be faced with integration requirements for admission is religious servants. Chapter 5 concluded that the right to freedom of religion does not normally include a right of religious servants to be admitted to a state of which they are not nationals or a right of religious communities to appoint religious servants from abroad. It follows that, in principle, states preserve full discretion to make the admission of religious servants dependent on the fulfilment of integration requirements and to decide on the contents of those requirements. Two exceptions to this rule were nevertheless identified. One concerns the situation in which refusal to admit a religious servant would effectively prevent the religious community in the host state from continuing its religious activities. The second situation is when the decision to refuse admission in fact serves to control the exercise of religious freedom.

Where one of the above situations occurs, it does not automatically follow that the religious servant has an absolute right to be admitted and that integration requirements are thereby precluded: limitations to the freedom of religion are allowed. It was argued that the public interest of integration can provide grounds for such limitations. Nevertheless, the limitation clauses of Articles 9 ECHR and 18 ICCPR also require integration conditions to be proportionate and this will depend on their effectiveness and on the burden imposed on the religious servant (or on the religious community in the host state). Again, it is submitted that such conditions may not be such that they cannot reasonably be fulfilled. However, substantive criteria for limitation are not included in Article 6(1) of the Dutch Constitution, by which the freedom of religion is also protected. According to this provision, the freedom of religion can always be restricted, providing the restriction has been ordered by the national legislator.

Several other grounds for the admission of aliens were discussed in chapters 6 and 7. The legal instruments examined in these chapters concern immigration for economic purposes (labour migration) and the admission of aliens who are nationals of states with which the host state maintains friendly diplomatic relations. In many cases these grounds are combined, as illustrated, for example, by the EEC-Turkey Association Agreement and the Dutch-American Friendship Treaty. Both agreements regulate the international movement of certain categories of economically active nationals of the Contracting Parties, including workers, entrepreneurs and other self-employed persons. Similarly, with regard to the EU, the right of free movement was originally limited to EU nationals who migrated for economic purposes. Later, however, this right was extended to include all EU nationals, a development that was supported by the ongoing European integration and the creation of EU citizenship.

Whereas some of the legal instruments discussed in chapters 6 and 7 do not affect the competence of the Contracting States to introduce integration requirements into their immigration legislation, others make such requirements subject to conditions or exclude them altogether. In particular, the extent to which states can enact integration requirements is greatly limited by the rules of EU law on the right to free movement (including the very similar regulations applying to nationals of the EEA Member States and Switzerland). Additional limitations stem from the EEC-Turkey Association Agreement, the Blue Card Directive and the European Convention on the Legal Status of Migrant Workers. Other instruments, such as the Long-term Residents Directive, the European Convention on Establishment or the Dutch-American Friendship Treaty, allow states to make the admission of foreign nationals, at least to a certain extent, subordinate to considerations of integration. It is concluded that the balancing act, between the interest of integration and the competing interests that led to the adoption of the above instruments, such as the wish to attract (highly skilled) labour and maintain diplomatic relations or promote European integration, does not always lead to the same outcome.

What causes these different outcomes is primarily a political question that has not been addressed in this study. What has been examined, however, is how the resulting differentiations should be judged in view of the right to equal treatment. The results of this assessment are reviewed in the following section.

C. Integration and Equality

The overall framework regarding the right to equal treatment in international human rights instruments (and the Dutch Constitution) was outlined in chapter 8. It was established that integration measures may lawfully result in differential treatment of immigrants and/or host state residents, provided such differential treatment is based on a reasonable and objective justification. Such justification can be taken to exist when a group of persons is exempted from integration requirements on the grounds that they are less likely to experience problems in the field of integration. In most cases, however, a criterion by which this 'capacity for integration' can be determined will not be easy to find.

In any case, such a criterion will depend on the particular integration objectives being pursued. It was argued that, for example, it would be justified to exempt labour migrants from the scope of application of an integration measure if the purpose of that measure is to ensure that immigrants participate in the labour market or to prevent unemployment. Where the integration requirement includes a test of the language of the host state, it would also be reasonable to exempt those immigrants who can show – through other reliable means – that they are already sufficiently proficient in this language. A similar ground for exemption is included in the AIA (chapter 2, para section VI.B.iii). On the other hand, it was concluded that an immigrant's nationality or the 'social, socio-economic and political comparability of the country of origin' are not suitable criteria to determine the integration capacity of the person concerned.

Besides differences in integration capacity, differences in treatment with regard to the application of integration requirements can be justified by the existence of competing public interests. Interests already mentioned in this connection are the economic interest of the host state (including the need to attract labour migrants from abroad), the protection of economic and foreign relations with other states and compliance with obligations stemming from international law (including EU law and bilateral agreements). It was argued that, at least where the resulting differentiations are based on the grounds of nationality or residence purpose, the host state has a certain margin of appreciation, meaning that these differentiations will not rapidly amount to prohibited discrimination.

Nevertheless, the requirement for a reasonable and objective justification entails that differences in treatment must be proportionate. This proportionality will be endangered if a majority of the immigrants entering a country are exempted from the obligation to comply with integration requirements on grounds not related to their integration capacity. This is because, in that situation, the effectiveness of the integration measure will be diminished and it will contribute less to the purpose of improving integration. Consequently, the utility of the integration measure will no longer outweigh the difference in treatment that it causes. A problem of this nature can occur both with regard to distinctions made between immigrants seeking admission (chapter 8) and with regard to the 'reverse discrimination' of a state's own nationals (chapter 10). With regard to the latter, it was also noted that the preferential treatment of large groups of aliens compared to a state's own nationals raises questions of a political nature about the meaning of nationality (or citizenship) in those states.

Concerning the relationship between integration and equality, attention was also paid to the issue of indirect differential treatment, in particular on grounds of racial or ethnic origin (chapter 9). When a state includes integration requirements in its immigration legislation, it must be aware that – even if this is not intended – such legislation may create a greater disadvantage for some racial or ethnic groups than for others. If this disadvantage is sufficiently strong (amounting to a 'disproportionate effect'), it will result in a presumption of indirect discrimination that must again be based on a reasonable and objective justification. In particular, this requirement of justification means that the purpose of the integration requirement could not have been reached by other measures that would have had less or no discriminatory effect. While the host state may have a margin of appreciation in this regard, the scope of this margin will depend on the social circumstances of the racial or ethnic group concerned and on the risk that it runs of being excluded from mainstream society.

II. INTEGRATION OBJECTIVES AND THE CONTENT OF INTEGRATION REQUIREMENTS

A. Concepts of Integration

In addition to integration requirements functioning as instruments to control the admission of immigrants, this study also considered the integration objectives that these requirements are meant to help achieve. Traditionally, 'integration' is often understood as the coming together of a group of persons or the abolition of social, economic and cultural divides between different sections of the population in a particular state. Understood in this way, integration is a process that involves society as a whole. In the context of integration requirements, however, the concept of integration refers to something else. Inherent in the idea of such requirements is that integration constitutes a standard or norm that immigrants must adapt to. This does not exclude the possibility of support being provided by the government or other institutions of the host state (in the form, for example, of preparation facilities); hence, integration requirements are not necessarily incompatible with the idea of shared responsibility for the integration process. Nevertheless, they are based on the premise that integration refers to certain attitudes, behaviours and/or skills on the part of immigrants, the existence of which integration requirements are meant to test or enhance.

Notwithstanding this qualification, the concept of integration remains open and subject to different interpretations. The description in chapter 3 of this study showed how the ideal of integration (or citizenship) in the Netherlands continued to evolve over time, including after the Act on Integration Abroad was adopted. Different elements of this ideal that can be distinguished include (economic) self-reliance and participation in various areas of the public domain, in particular in education and the labour market; adaptation to the culture (language, norms and values) of the majority population and a psychological or emotional commitment to the host state.

The same chapter assessed these various integration objectives from a normative-political perspective, arguing that the aim of integration measures should not be to make immigrants accept or subscribe to particular norms or values or to ensure their exclusive loyalty to the receiving state. In addition, it was submitted that purely cognitive requirements, such as that immigrants must know about the history, geography or traditions of the host state, are of little use unless they serve an underlying purpose, such as political or economic participation in society or the creation of a sense of commitment. States may, however, require immigrants to respect existing legislation and to contribute to the preservation of the welfare state. Cognitive requirements, including the obligation to learn the language of the host state, are therefore acceptable if they are directed towards these aims. Lastly, states may seek to promote emotional identification of immigrants with the host state in order to create a sense of belonging and solidarity. Such identification may not (and cannot), however, be enforced.

B. Legal Standards Concerning Integration Objectives and the Contents of Integration Requirements

The analysis in the second part of this study found that the objectives and contents of integration requirements are generally not governed by any specific legal standards. Where the enactment of integration requirements for admission is allowed, most of the relevant legal instruments do not state anything other than that such requirements must be aimed at 'integration', at the 'protection of public order or the rights and freedoms of others' or even more generally that they must be in 'the public interest'. Since a more specific definition of acceptable integration objectives has not been provided, the range of objectives that may be pursued is not clearly demarcated.

It was argued, however, that integration requirements must in any case respect the boundaries set by human rights treaties. As such, the pursuit of social unity or cohesion through integration policies must not include the objective of abolishing or restricting religious or ethnic diversity. Integration tests or programmes directed towards such objectives have to be rejected. Although this criterion may not always be easy to apply in practice, it was submitted that integration tests should not in any case contain normative questions or prescriptions regarding religious or cultural practices (such as dress codes or conventions concerning relations between the sexes), unless these reflect actual legal standards that are in themselves compatible with human rights norms. Integration requirements must, moreover, respect the freedom of thought, which means that immigrants must not be asked to agree with particular values, ideas or beliefs and that information conveyed through integration programmes or tests (for example, about the constitutional principles of the state or the customs and conventions of the host society) must be presented in an objective and pluralistic manner so as not to amount to indoctrination.

In chapter 5, some standards were formulated concerning integration requirements for religious servants. It was argued that these servants must not be asked to answer normative questions relating to the contents of their faith or to comply with instructions regarding the exercise of their religious duties. Nonetheless, integration requirements may be used to inform religious servants about regulations pertaining to the separation of church and state with the aim of protecting this separation. The same objective can also provide grounds for imposing integration requirements specifically on religious servants as a target group.

The above standards, in particular the condition that integration requirements must respect human rights provisions, remain at a rather general level. As already stated, more specific legal criteria have not yet been formulated. Such criteria are likely, however, to be developed in the future, through the adoption of more specific legislative rules (at the EU level, for example) or through legal challenges against integration measures.

III. THE ACT ON INTEGRATION ABROAD IN RELATION TO (INTER)NATIONAL IMMIGRATION LAW

One of the purposes of this study was to determine whether the AIA respects the right of aliens and Dutch residents as protected by international immigration law and the Dutch Constitution. In the course of the examination several incompatibilities were identified, which are presented below.

A first issue concerns the compatibility of the AIA with the right to family life and family reunification, which was examined in chapter 4. It was argued that the existence of integration requirements is not as such contrary to this right. Nevertheless, several features of the AIA were identified which make it very probable that application of the Act will be disproportionate, and hence unlawful, in individual cases or in respect of particular groups of aliens. A first element concerns the level of the exam (which was increased on 1 April 2011) and the introduction of a reading comprehension test, which make the integration requirement reasonably impossible to meet for immigrants who are illiterate. Other factors that are likely to result in the disproportionality of the requirement (alone or in combination) are a lack of adequate preparation facilities, circumstances in countries of origin influencing the accessibility of the exam and the fact that no exemption has been created for the family members of persons who came to the Netherlands in search of international protection, but who were granted a residence permit for purposes other than asylum. Unless more lenient use is made of the available exemption clauses, there will be individual cases in which application of the Act violates international human rights treaties (the ECHR, ICCPR and CRC) or the EU Family Reunification Directive. This will also occur, more generally, in cases involving illiterate applicants. Furthermore, as there is no procedural guarantee to ensure that due weight is given to the best interests of children, which must form a 'primary consideration', the AIA does not meet the standard set by Article 3 CRC.

Next, it was found that the integration requirement for the admission of religious servants is generally compatible with the legal norms concerning the freedom of religion (chapter 5). Nonetheless, a violation may occur in exceptional circumstances, if the situation is such that admission of the religious servant is necessary to enable a religious community in the Netherlands to continue its activities and the burden placed upon the religious servant by the integration requirement is disproportionate (if, for example, the servant is illiterate or there is no access to preparation facilities). To prevent such violations, the application of the AIA to religious servants in individual cases should be examined under Article 9 ECHR and Article 18 ICCPR.

Also in chapter 5, it was argued that the fact that religious servants form a specific target group of the AIA is not as such contrary to the prohibition of discrimination on the grounds of religion. It may be justified to make the admission of religious servants dependent on the fulfilment of integration requirements so as to protect the separation between church and state. However, the contents of the integration exam abroad, in its current form, are not particularly suited to this purpose. It is therefore recommended reconsidering the contents of the exam for religious servants. Bearing in mind the purpose of the exam and the complexity of the subject at stake, it could be preferable to administer the exam in religious servants' own language.

Chapter 7 argued that application of the integration exam abroad to Turkish nationals and their family members is precluded by the standstill and non-discrimination clauses of the EEC-Turkey Association Agreement, its Additional Protocol and Decision 1/80, as interpreted by the CoJ, to the extent that they come within the scope of these instruments. Although the Dutch legislator has thus far failed to recognise the full meaning of the Association Agreement, Turkish nationals have, in the meantime, been exempted from the AIA on grounds derived from national law. A similar exemption applies to their family members. An incompatibility remains, however, as regards the application of the AIA to family members of labour migrants who are nationals of Albania, Moldavia, Turkey or Ukraine, as these family members are entitled to admission on the basis of the European Convention on the Legal Status of Migrant Workers (ECMW). Lastly, Article 19(6) of the revised European Social Charter (ESC) obliges the Netherlands to facilitate compliance with the AIA by family members of labour migrants who are covered by this agreement, which may be understood as an obligation to assist them in preparing for the exam.

As a final issue, the compatibility of the AIA with the right to equal treatment was assessed. It was concluded that differentiations on the grounds of nationality and residence purpose do not, as such, amount to prohibited discrimination and that the Dutch authorities have generally remained within their margin of appreciation inasmuch as the proportionality of the integration requirement is concerned. Nonetheless, the Dutch legislator has not convincingly explained why labour migrants and their family members are exempted from the obligation to pass the integration exam abroad. An issue was also raised regarding the possibility of indirect discrimination on the grounds of ethnic origin. In this connection, it is recalled that the legal framework concerning indirect ethnic discrimination, especially in the immigration context, is far from well-established. In particular, no clear standards have so far been developed regarding the evidence needed to prove a presumption of indirect discrimination and the margin of appreciation to be applied by the courts. The assessment of the effects of the AIA is also complicated by the fact that the available statistical evidence does not specify the ethnic origins of the persons concerned. Nevertheless, on the basis of the existing legal standards and factual information, it was concluded that the AIA disproportionately affects immigrants of Moroccan (and previously also Turkish) origin and that no sufficient justification for this effect has been provided. In the absence of such justification and given the already vulnerable position of the Turkish and Moroccan migrant communities in the Netherlands, it was argued that the AIA does not respect the prohibition of indirect ethnic discrimination.

In summary, it is concluded that continuing the AIA in its current form presents some problems from a legal perspective. Of these, the issue of indirect ethnic discrimination is arguably the most difficult to resolve, as this will require at least a thorough reconsideration of the target group. From the perspective of equality, extending the AIA to all immigrants seeking to be admitted to the Netherlands, or at least to the majority of them, is recommended. However, this study has shown that such a broadening of the scope of the Act's application would run into a variety of legal barriers.

A similar problem exists with regard to the effectiveness of the integration exam abroad. Chapter 2 established that the effect of the AIA on the integration capacity of new immigrants remains rather limited. This fact is of both legal and political significance, as the Act's contribution to successful integration is what justifies its infringement on the individual interests of immigrants and Dutch residents. The effect of the exam will probably become more significant if the level is raised, which is why the exam was made more difficult on 1 April 2011. However, this change has also increased the probability of the integration requirement constituting a disproportionate limitation to the right to family life in individual cases.

A successful integration policy requires legislation that is both effective and respectful of the rights of immigrants and Dutch residents. However, the growing body of legal standards governing the admission of immigrants means that the legislator's room for manoeuvre in this field is increasingly constrained. As a measure to promote immigrant integration in the Netherlands, integration requirements at the border clearly have their limits.

Bibliography

Adviescommissie voor Vreemdelingenzaken (ACVZ), *Inburgeringseisen als voorwaarde voor verblijf in Nederland* (The Hague, ACVZ, 2004a)

——, *Voorbij de horizon van 'Amsterdam'. Een advies over het Europese beleid inzake asiel, arbeids- en gezinsmigratie na 1 mei 2004, ten behoeve van het Nederlandse voorzitterschap* (The Hague, ACVZ, 2004b)

——, *Toelating en verblijf voor religieuze doeleinden* (The Hague, ACVZ, 2005)

——, *Briefadvies huwelijks- en gezinsmigratie* (The Hague, ACVZ, 2010a)

——, *Advies inzake de conceptwijziging van het Vreemdelingenbesluit 2000 in verband met de wijziging van het basisexamen inburgering* (The Hague, ACVZ, 2010b)

Anderson, B, *Imagined Communities* (London / New York, Verso 2006, first printed in 1983)

Arai-Takahashi, Y, (*The Margin of Appreciation Doctrine and the Principle of Proportionality in the Jurisprudence of the ECHR* (Antwerp / Oxford / New York, Intersentia, 2002)

Arnardóttir, OM, *Equality and Non-Discrimination under the European Convention on Human Rights* (The Hague / London / New York, Martinus Nijhoff, 2003)

Battjes, H, *European asylum law and its relation to international law* (diss. VU University) (Amsterdam, VU University, 2006)

Battjes, H and Vermeulen, BP, case comment to CoJ (Grand Chamber) 27 June 2006, C-540/03, (*Parliament* v *Council*) (2007) *Administratiefrechtelijke Beslissingen* 16

Bauböck, R and Joppke, C (eds), *How Liberal Are Citizenship Tests?*, EUI Working Paper RSCAS 2010/41 (San Domenico di Fiesole, European University Institute, 2010)

Bell, M, *Anti-Discrimination Law and the European Union* (Oxford, Oxford University Press, 2002)

Benhabib, S, *The Rights of Others. Aliens, Residents and Citizens* (Cambridge, Cambridge University Press, 2004)

Bloemraad, I, *Becoming a Citizen. Incorporating Immigrants and Refugees in the United States and Canada* (Berkeley / Los Angeles / London, University of California Press, 2006)

Boeles, P, 'Europese burgers en derdelanders: wat betekent het verbod van discriminatie naar nationaliteit sinds Amsterdam?' (2005) *Tijdschrift voor Europees en Economisch Recht* 12, 500–13

Boeles, P and Lodder, GG (eds), *Integratie en uitsluiting* (The Hague, Sdu uitgevers, 2005)

Boeles, P, Den Heijer, M, Lodder, G and Wouters, K, *European Migration Law* (Antwerp / Oxford Portland, Intersentia, 2009)

Boillet, V, *L'interdiction de discrimination en raison de la nationalité au sens de l'Accord sur la Libre Circulation des Personnes* (diss. Université de Lausanne) (Basel, Helbing Lichtenhahn, 2010)

Bonjour, S, 'Between Integration Provision and Selection Mechanism. Party Politics, Judicial Constraints, and the Making of French and Dutch Policies of Civic Integration Abroad' (2010) *European Journal of Migration and Law* Vol 12:3, 299–318

Bosniak, L, *The Citizen and the Alien. Dilemmas of Contemporary Membership* (Princeton / Oxford, Princeton University Press, 2006)

Brink, M, Van Rossum, S, Visser, T and Van den Berg, N, *Evaluatie inburgeringsbeleid voor nieuwkomers* (Amsterdam, Regioplan, 1997)

Brink, M, Does, B, Odé, A and Tromp, E, *Verscheidenheid in integratie. Evaluatie van de effectiviteit van de WIN* (Amsterdam, Regioplan, 2002)

Brink, M and Tromp, E, *Evaluatie eindtermen maatschappijoriëntatie* (Amsterdam, Regioplan, 2003)

Brink, M, Van Gent, MJ, Klaver, JFI and Odé, AWM, *De Wet inburgering buitenland. Een onderzoek naar de werking, de resultaten en de eerste effecten* (Amsterdam, Regioplan, 2009)

Brinkmann, G, 'The Transposition of the Family Reunification Directive in Germany' in Böcker, A et al (eds), *Migration law and sociology of law. Collected essays in honour of Kees Groenendijk* (Nijmegen, Wolf Legal Publishers, 2008) 35–41

Bulmer, M and Solomos, J, 'Introduction: Re-thinking Ethnic and Racial Studies' (1998) *Ethnic and Racial Studies* Vol 21:5, 819–37

Busstra, MJ, *The implications of the Racial Equality Directive for minority protection within the European Union* (diss. EUR) (Utrecht, Eleven International Publishing, 2010)

Carrera, S, *In Search of the Perfect Citizen? The Intersection between Integration, Immigration and Nationality in the EU* (Leiden / Boston, Martinus Nijhoff, 2009)

Carrera, S and Wiesbrock, A, *Civic Integration of Third-Country Nationals. Nationalism versus Europeanisation in the Common EU Immigration Policy* (Centre for European Policy Studies, 2009)

Centraal Bureau voor de Statistiek (CBS), *Allochtonen in Nederland*, annual reports published between 1995 and 2004 (Voorburg, CBS, 1995–2005)

Chalmers, D, Davies, G and Monti, G, *European Union Law* (Cambridge, Cambridge University Press, 2010)

Condinanzi, M, Lang, A and Nascimbene, B, *Citizenship of the Union and Free Movement of Persons* (Leiden / Boston, Martinus Nijhoff, 2008)

Craig, P and De Búrca, G, *EU Law. Text, Cases and Materials* (Oxford, Oxford University Press, 2008)

De Hart, B, 'Love Thy Neighbour: Family Reunification and the Rights of Insiders' (2009) *European Journal of Migration and Law* Vol 11:3, 235–52

De Heer, C, 'De status van langdurig ingezeten derdelander (1). Achtergrond en inhoud van richtlijn 2003 / 109 / EG' (2007) *Migrantenrecht* Vol 22:7, 272–80

De Jong, CD, *The Freedom of Thought, Conscience and Religion or Belief in the United Nations (1946-1992)* (Antwerp / Groningen / Oxford, Intersentia – Hart, 2000)

De Schutter, O, *Links between migration and discrimination*, report prepared for the European Commission (Luxembourg, Publications Office of the European Union, 2009)

Detrick, S (ed), Doek, J and Cantwell, N (contributors), *The United Nations Convention on the Rights of the Child. A Guide to the 'Travaux Préparatoires'* (Dordrecht / Boston / London, Martinus Nijhoff, 1992)

De Vries, KM, 'Het nieuwe Nederlandse inburgeringsstelsel' (2006) *Migrantenrecht* Vol 21:8, 272–82

——, case comment on AJD 2 December 2008, case no 200806120/1, (2009) *Administratiefrechtelijke Beslissingen* 36

——, 'The Dutch Act on Integration Abroad: a case of racial or ethnic discrimination?' in Morano-Foadi, S and Malena, M (eds), *Integration for Third-Country Nationals in the European Union. The Equality Challenge* (Cheltenham/Northampton, Edward Elgar Publishing, 2012) 324–45

Dhondt, NML and Geursen, WW, 'Over gedeelde bevoegdheden en hiërarchie in interpretatiemethoden' (2008) *Nederlands Tijdschrift voor Europees Recht* 10, 276–84

Dixon, M and McCorquodale, R, *Cases & Materials on International Law* (Oxford, Oxford University Press, 2003)

Driouichi, F, *De casus Inburgering en Nationaliteitswetgeving* (Amsterdam, Amsterdam University Press, 2007)

Durmus, A and Köse, E, ' Het Associatierecht EEG-Turkije en de verplichte inburgering' (2009) *Migrantenrecht* Vol 24:8, 353–62

Entzinger, HB, *Het minderhedenbeleid* (diss. Leiden University) (Amsterdam/Meppel, Boom, 1984)

Fermin, A, *Nederlandse politieke partijen over minderhedenbeleid 1977–1995* (Amsterdam, Thesis Publishers, 1997)

——, *Burgerschap en integratiebeleid*, report prepared for the Home Affairs Ministry (Utrecht, European Research Centre on Migration & Ethnic Relations, 2000)

——, 'Inburgering en eigen verantwoordelijkheid' in Gowricharn, R (ed), *Falende instituties. Negen heikele kwesties in de multiculturele samenleving* (Utrecht, De Graaff, 2006)

——, 'Burgerschap en multiculturaliteit in het Nederlandse integratiebeleid' (2009) *Tijdschrift voor beleid, politiek en maatschappij* Vol 36:1, 13–27

Forder, CJ, 'Positieve verplichtingen in het kader van het Europees verdrag tot bescherming van de rechten van de mens en de fundamentele vrijheden' (1992) *NJCM-Bulletin* Vol 17:6, 611–37

——, 'Family Rights and Immigration law: a European Perspective' (2003) *Irish Journal of Family Law* 3, 2–18

——, 'Over de kern en de grensgevallen van het familierecht' in Van Den Eeckhout, V, Forder, CJ, Hooghiemstra, E, Nicolai, E and Van Walsum, SK (eds), *Transnationale gezinnen in Nederland* (The Hague, Boom Juridische uitgevers, 2005)

Gerards, JH, *Rechterlijke toetsing aan het gelijkheidsbeginsel* (The Hague, Sdu Uitgevers, 2002)

——, 'Gelijke behandeling en het EVRM. Artikel 14 EVRM: van krachteloze waarborg naar 'norm met tanden'?' (2004) *NJCM-Bulletin* Vol 29:2, 176–98

——, case comment to ECtHR 5 June 2008, app no 32526/05 (*Sampanis and others*) (2008) *European Human Rights Cases* 2008/92, 919–22

——, 'Samenloop van nationale en Europese grondrechtenbepalingen – hoe moet de rechter daarmee omgaan?' (2010) *Tijdschrift voor Constitutioneel Recht* Vol 1:3, 224–55

Godeschalk, M, 'Het assimilatie-beleid voor Indische Nederlanders: de overheid en het maatschappelijk werk gedurende de eerste jaren van de repatriëring' (1990) *Jambatan. Tijdschrift voor de geschiedenis van Indonesië* Vol 8:1, 39–47

Goodwin-Gill, GS, *The refugee in international law* (Oxford, Clarendon Press, 1996)

Groenendijk, K, 'Legal Concepts of Integration in EU Migration Law' (2004) *European Journal of Migration and Law* Vol 6:2, 111–26

——, 'Integratie en uitsluiting in het Nederlandse vreemdelingenrecht' in Boeles, P and Lodder, GG (eds), *Integratie en uitsluiting* (The Hague, Sdu uitgevers, 2005) 9–31

——, 'Family Reunification as a Right under Community Law' (2006a) *European Journal of Migration and Law* Vol 8:2, 215–30

——, 'Nieuw inburgeringsrecht strijdig met Gemeenschapsrecht' (2006b) *Migrantenrecht* Vol 21:10, 366–68

——, 'Inburgeren in het buitenland: de Gezinsherenigingsrichtlijn biedt meer bescherming dan artikel 8 EVRM' (2007) *Migrantenrecht* Vol 22:3, 111–13

——, case comment on CoJ 29 April 2010, C-92/07 (*Commission* v *The Netherlands*) (2010) *Jurisprudentie Vreemdelingenrecht* 2010/237

——, 'Pre-departure Integration Strategies in the European Union: Integration or Immigration Policy?' (2011) *European Journal of Migration and Law* Vol 13:1, 1–30

Guild, E, Groenendijk, K and Carrera, S (eds), *Illiberal Liberal States. Immigration, Citizenship and Integration in the EU* (Farnham/Burlington, Ashgate, 2009)

——, 'Understanding the Contest of Community: Illiberal Practices in the EU?' in Guild, E, Groenendijk, K and Carrera, S (eds), *Illiberal Liberal States. Immigration, Citizenship and Integration in the EU* (Farnham/Burlington, Ashgate) 1–25

Hailbronner, K, *Immigration and Asylum Law and Policy of the European Union* (The Hague/London/Boston, Kluwer Law International, 2000)

—— (ed), *EU Immigration and Asylum Law. Commentary on EU Regulations and Directives* (Munich, C.H. Beck/Oxford, Hart Publishing, 2010)

Halleskov, L, 'The Long-Term Residents Directive: A Fulfilment of the Tampere Objective of Near-Equality?' (2005) *European Journal of Migration and Law* Vol 7:2, 181–201

Harris, DJ, O'Boyle, M, Bates, EP and Buckley, CM, *Law of the European Convention on Human Rights* (Oxford, Oxford University Press, 2009)

Hathaway, JC, *The law of refugee status* (Markham etc, Butterworths Canada, 2001)

Hedemann-Robinson, M, 'An overview of recent legal developments at Community level in relation to third country nationals resident within the European Union, with particular reference to the case law of the European Court of Justice' (2001) *Common Market Law Review* 525–86

Hendrickx, I and De Lange, T, *Toelating van vreemdelingen voor verblijf bij religieuze organisaties* (Nijmegen/Tilburg, Wolf Legal Publishers, 2004)

Hendriks, AC, case comment to ECtHR (Grand Chamber) 13 November 2007, app no 57325/00 (*DH and others* v *the Czech Republic*) (2008) *European Human Rights Cases* 2008/5, 65–70

Henrard, K, 'Een zoektocht naar een beter begrip van en een adequaat toetsingsmodel voor indirecte discriminatie', case comment to ECtHR (Grand Chamber) 13 November 2007, app no 57325/00 (*DH and others* v *the Czech Republic*) (2008) *NJCM-Bulletin* Vol 33:2, 234–50

Hooghiemstra, E, *Trouwen over de grens. Achtergronden van partnerkeuze van Turken en Marokkanen in Nederland* (The Hague, Sociaal en Cultureel Planbureau, 2003)

Howard, E, 'Race and Racism – Why does European Law have Difficulties with Definitions?' (2008) *The International Journal of Comparative Labour Law and Industrial Relations* Spring issue, 5–30

Hublet, C, 'La portée de l'article 12 du traité instituant la Communauté européenne vis-à-vis des ressortissants de pays tiers: une evolution?' in Snyder, F and Thym, D (eds), *Europe: a Continent of Immigration? Legal Challenges in the Construction of European Migration Policy. Europe: un continent d'immigration? Défis juridiques dans la construction de la politique européenne de migration* (Brussels, Bruylant, 2011)

Human Rights Watch, *The Netherlands: Discrimination in the Name of Integration. Migrants' Rights under the Integration Abroad Act* (Human Rights Watch, 2008)

Iglesias Sánchez, S, 'Free Movement of Third Country Nationals in the European Union? Main Features, Deficiencies and Challenges of the new Mobility Rights in the Area of Freedom, Security and Justice' (2009a) *European Law Journal* Vol 15:6, 791–805

——, 'Free Movement as a Precondition for Integration of Third-Country Nationals in the EU' in Guild, E, Groenendijk, K and Carrera, S (eds), *Illiberal Liberal States. Immigration, Citizenship and Integration in the EU* (Farnham / Burlington, Ashgate, 2009b) 205–19

Jones, G, *Tussen Onderdanen, Rijksgenoten en Nederlanders* (Amsterdam, Rozenberg Publishers, 2007)

Joppke, C, 'Immigration and the identity of citizenship: the paradox of universalism' (2008) *Citizenship Studies* Vol 12:6, 533–46

——, 'How Liberal Are Citizenship Tests? A Rejoinder' in Bauböck, R and Joppke, C (eds), *How Liberal Are Citizenship Tests?* EUI Working Paper RSCAS 2010/41 (San Domenico di Fiesole, European University Institute, 2010)

Joseph, S, Schultz, J and Castan, M, *The International Covenant on Civil and Political Rights. Cases, Materials and Commentary* (Oxford, Oxford University Press, 2004)

Klaver, JFI and Odé, AWM, *Civic Integration and Modern Citizenship* (Groningen, Europa Law Publishing, 2009)

Kortmann, CAJM, 'Toelating en verblijf van vreemde bedienaren' in Böcker, A et al (eds), *Migration law and sociology of law. Collected essays in honour of Kees Groenendijk* (Nijmegen, Wolf Legal Publishers, 2008) 433–39

——, *Staatsrecht en raison d'Etat* (Deventer, Kluwer, 2009)

Kostakopoulou, D, 'The anatomy of civic integration' (2010) *The Modern Law Review* Vol 73:6, 933–58

Kuijer, A (ed), *Nederlands vreemdelingenrecht* (The Hague, Boom Juridische uitgevers, 2005)

Kymlicka, W, *Multicultural Citizenship* (Oxford, Clarendon Press, 1995)

Lawson, R, 'Positieve verplichtingen onder het EVRM: opkomst en ondergang van de "fair balance"-test – Deel I' (1995a) *NJCM-Bulletin* Vol 20:5, 558–73

——, 'Positieve verplichtingen onder het EVRM: opkomst en ondergang van de "fair balance"-test – Deel II' (1995b) *NJCM-Bulletin* Vol 20:6, 727–50

——, 'Taaleisen en discriminatieverboden in het Europese recht. Over het alledaagse leven als maatstaf' in Boeles, P and Lodder, GG (eds), *Integratie en uitsluiting* (The Hague, Sdu uitgevers, 2005) 115–34

Lodder, GG, *Juridische aspecten van de Wet Inburgering Buitenland* (Leiden, Instituut voor Immigratierecht, 2009)

Loenen, T, *Het gelijkheidsbeginsel* (Nijmegen, Ars Aequi Libri, 1998)

——, 'Indirect Discrimination: Oscillating Between Containment and Revolution' in Loenen, T and Rodrigues, PR (eds), *Non-Discrimination Law: Comparative Perspectives* (The Hague / London / Boston, Martinus Nijhoff, 1999) 195–211

Lucassen, J and Penninx, R, *Nieuwkomers, Nakomelingen, Nederlanders. Immigranten in Nederland 1550-1993* (Amsterdam, Het Spinhuis, 1994), an English translation of this book is available: Lucassen, J and Penninx, R (translation by Wintle, M), *Newcomers: immigrants and their descendants in the Netherlands 1550-1995* (Amsterdam, Het Spinhuis, 1997)

Luijendijk, H, *Nederlandse gemeenten en het Europese personenverkeer: een onderzoek naar de consequenties van het personenverkeer voor de beleidsterreinen burgerzaken en ruimtelijke ordening en huisvesting* (Deventer, Kluwer, 2005)

Mak, G, 'Het huishouden als strijdtoneel. De inburgering van Indische Nederlanders' in Captain, E, Hellevoort, M and Van der Klein, M (eds), *Vertrouwd en vreemd. Ontmoetingen tussen Nederland, Indië en Indonesië* (Hilversum, Verloren, 2000) 241–56

Michalowski, I, *An overview on introduction programmes for immigrants in seven European Member States,* report commissioned by the Advisory Committee on Aliens Affairs (The Hague, ACVZ, 2003)

——, 'Required to assimilate? The content of citizenship tests in five countries' (2011) *Citizenship Studies* Vol 15:6–7, 749–68

Odé, A, 'De Wet inburgering buitenland: zelfselectie belangrijker dan selectie' (2009) *Migrantenrecht* Vol 24:7, 288–92

Odé, A and De Vries, K, 'De geschiedenis van inburgering in Nederland' in Odé, A, Dagevos, J, Van der Leun, J and De Valk, H (eds), *Jaarboek minderheden 2010. Inburgering in Nederland* (The Hague, Sdu uitgevers, 2010) 15–32

Onafhankelijke adviescommissie normering inburgeringseisen (Commissie Franssen), *Inburgering getoetst. Advies over het niveau van het inburgeringsexamen in het buitenland,* (advisory report commissioned by the Aliens Affairs and Integration Minister, 2004)

Oosterom-Staples, H, *Europeesrechtelijke grenzen aan inburgeringsverplichtingen,* report prepared for the Research and Documentation Centre of the Justice Ministry (Tilburg, University of Tilburg, 2004)

Oosterom-Staples, H and Vazquez Muñoz, A, 'Burgerschap van de Unie' (2004) *Tijdschrift voor Europees en Economisch Recht* 12, 494–506

Oosterom-Staples, H and Woltjer, A, *Toelatings- en verblijfsvoorwaarden onderdanen Turkije,* report prepared for the Research and Documentation Centre of the Justice Ministry (Tilburg, University of Tilburg, 2009)

Ovey, C and White, RCA, *European Convention on Human Rights* (Oxford, Oxford University Press, 2002)

Pascouau, Y, *La politique migratoire de l'Union européenne. De Schengen à Lisbonne* (Paris, Fondation Varenne, 2010)

Peers, S, 'Implementing equality? The Directive on long term resident third country nationals' (2004) *European Law Review* Vol 29:4, 437–60

Penninx, R, *Naar een algemeen etnisch minderhedenbeleid?*, preparatory study conducted for the Scientific Council for Government Policy (The Hague, Staatsuitgeverij, 1979)

Prins, B, *Voorbij de onschuld. Het debat over de multiculturele samenleving* (Amsterdam, Van Gennep, 2000)

Puts, JHL, *Asielzoekers tussen Rijk en gemeenten. Onderhandelingen over de huisvesting van migranten* (The Hague, VNG-uitgeverij, 1995)

Reneman, M, 'Het Kinderrechtenverdrag krijgt tanden. Over hoe het VN Verdrag inzake de Rechten van het Kind via het EU-recht en het EVRM binnendringt in het Nederlandse vreemdelingenrecht' (2011) *Asiel- en Migrantenrecht* Vol 2:8, 349–62

Ruitenberg, GCAM, *Het Internationaal Kinderrechtenverdrag in de Nederlandse rechtspraak* (Amsterdam, Uitgeverij SWP, 2003)

——, case comment to AJD 23 September 2004, case no 200404485/1 (2004) *Rechtspraak Vreemdelingenrecht* 25

Roelofs, SHJM, 'De toepassing van het Nederlands-Amerikaans vriendschapsverdrag' (2003) *Migrantenrecht* Vol 18:6, 184–91

——, 'Vriendschaps- en handelsverdragen. Een doos van Pandorra voor de toelating van vreemdelingen?' (2004) *Migrantenrecht* Vol 19:4, 147–56

Schiek, D, 'A New Framework on Equal Treatment of Persons in EC Law?' (2002) *European Law Journal* Vol 8:2, 290–314

Schinkel, W, *De gedroomde samenleving* (Kampen, Klement, 2008)

Schokkenbroek, JGC, *Toetsing aan de vrijheidsrechten van het Europees verdrag tot bescherming van de rechten van de mens* (diss. Leiden University) (Leiden University, 1996)

——, 'The Prohibition of Discrimination in Article 14 of the Convention and the Margin of Appreciation' (1998) *Human Rights Law Journal* Vol 19:1, 20

——, 'Methoden van interpretatie en toetsing: een overzicht van beginselen toegepast in de Straatsburgse jurisprudentie' katern *EVRM Rechtspraak & Commentaar* (loose leaf-edition) (The Hague, Koninlijke Vermande, 2000)

Schwelb, E, 'The International Convention on the elimination of all forms of racial discrimination' (1966) *International and Comparative Law Quarterly* 996–1068

Sjerps, I, 'Effects and Justifications. Or how to Establish a Prima Facie Case of Indirect Sex Discrimination' in Loenen, T and Rodrigues, PR (eds), *Non-Discrimination Law: Comparative Perspectives* (The Hague/London/Boston, Martinus Nijhoff, 1999) 237–47

Sociaal en Cultureel Planbureau (SCP) *Rapportage minderheden 1993* (Rijswijk, SCP, 1993)

——, *Oudkomers in beeld. De schatting van een mogelijke doelgroep* (The Hague, SCP, 2001)

Spaventa, E, *Free Movement of Persons in the European Union. Barriers to Movement in their Constitutional Context* (Alphen aan den Rijn, Kluwer Law International, 2007)

Spijkerboer, T, *Zeker weten. Inburgering en de fundamenten van het Nederlandse politieke bestel* (The Hague, Sdu Uitgevers, 2007)

——, 'Structural Instability: Strasbourg Case Law on Children's Family Reunion' (2009) *European Journal of Migration and Law* Vol 11:3, 271–93

Spijkerboer, TP and Vermeulen, BP, *Vluchtelingenrecht* (Nijmegen, Ars Aequi Libri, 2005)

Staples, H, *The Legal Status of Third Country Nationals Resident in the European Union* (The Hague/London/Boston, Kluwer Law International, 1999)

Steenbergen, JDM, Spijkerboer, TP, Vermeulen, BP and Fernhout, R, *Internationaal immigratierecht* (The Hague, Sdu Uitgevers, 1999)

Struijs, AJ, *Minderhedenbeleid en moraal. Erkenning van culturele identiteit in het perspectief van de liberale moraal* (diss. VU University) (Amsterdam, VU University, 1998)

Terlouw, A, 'Discriminatie op grond van nationaliteit. Algemene Aanbeveling 30 van het Committee on the Elimination of Racial Discrimination en haar betekenis voor Nederland' (2005) *NJCM-Bulletin* Vol 30:1, 119–27

——, 'Etnische registratie van risicojongeren en het verbod van rassendiscriminatie' (2009) *NJCM-Bulletin* Vol 34:6, 608–22

Tholen, JHMM, *Vreemdelingenbeleid en rechtvaardigheid?* (diss. Nijmegen University) (Nijmegen University, 1997)

Thornberry, P, 'Confronting Racial Discrimination: A CERD Perspective' (2005) *Human Rights Law Review* Vol 5:2, 239–69

Tobler, C, *Indirect discrimination. A case study into the development of the legal concept of indirect discrimination under EC law* (Antwerp / Oxford, Intersentia, 2005)

Toner, H, *Partnership rights, free movement, and EU law* (Oxford / Portland, Hart, 2004)

Van Blom, K and Van Schilt-Mol, T, *Aardappels leren eten . . . Een verkenning van het inburgeringsbeleid in Nederland* (Katholieke Universiteit Brabant, 2001)

Van Dam, D, *Een ander kader dan immigratie. Onderzoek naar overeenkomstige begrippen in de Gezinsherenigingsrichtlijn, Langdurig ingezetenenrichtlijn en Unieburgersrichtlijn* (master's thesis Radboud University) (Nijmegen, RU, 2008)

Van den Berg, MJM, *Eenheid en verscheidenheid. Vormgeving van basiseducatie voor volwassenen* (diss. Erasmus University) (De Lier, Academisch Boeken Centrum, 1992)

Vandenhole, W (2005) *Non-Discrimination and Equality in the View of the UN Human Rights Treaty Bodies* (Antwerp / Oxford, Intersentia)

Van der Winden, JH, *Wet inburgering in het buitenland* (The Hague, Sdu Uitgevers, 2006)

Van der Zwan, A and Entzinger, HB, *Beleidsopvolging minderhedendebat* (The Hague, Home Affairs Ministry, 1994)

Van Dijk, P and Van Hoof, GJH (eds), *Theory and practice of the European Convention on Human Rights* (The Hague, Kluwer Law International, 1998)

Van Dijk, P, Van Hoof, F, Van Rijn, A and Zwaak, L (eds), *Theory and Practice of the European Convention on Human Rights* (Antwerp / Oxford, Intersentia, 2006)

Van Gunsteren, H, 'Burgerschap in Nederland 1992-2008: voortschrijdend inzicht?' (2009) *Tijdschrift voor beleid, politiek en maatschappij* Vol 36:1, 41–49

Van Huis, I and De Regt, A, 'Tussen dwang en dialoog. Maatschappijoriëntatie in inburgeringscursussen' (2005) *Sociologie* Vol 1:4, 382–406

Van Oers, R, 'Citizenship Tests in the Netherlands, Germany and the UK' in Van Oers, R, Ersbøll, E and Kostakopoulou, D (eds), *A Re-definition of Belonging? Language and Integration Tests in Europe* (Leiden / Boston, Martinus Nijhoff, 2010) 51–105

Van Oers, R, Ersbøll, E and Kostakopoulou, D (eds), *A Re-definition of Belonging? Language and Integration Tests in Europe* (Leiden / Boston, Martinus Nijhoff, 2010a)

——, 'Mapping the redefinition of belonging in Europe' in Van Oers, R, Ersbøll, E and Kostakopoulou, D (eds), *A Re-definition of Belonging? Language and Integration Tests in Europe* (Leiden / Boston, Martinus Nijhoff, 2010b) 307–31

Van Praag, CS, 'Het Overheidsbeleid inzake allochtone groepen' in Verwey-Jonker, H (ed), *Allochtonen in Nederland* (The Hague, Staatsuitgeverij, 1973) 21–46

Van Walsum, SK, *De schaduw van de grens* (Gouda, Quint, 2000)

——, *The Family and the Nation. Dutch family migration policies in the context of changing family norms* (Newcastle upon Tyne, Cambridge Scholars Publishing, 2008)

Verhallen, S, *Lessen Nederlands voor anderstalige volwassenen in Nederland. Een inventarisatie van cursussen naar doel en opbrengst* (The Hague, Stichting Bibliographia Neerlandica, 1986)

Vermeulen, BP, 'Artikel 6' in Akkermans, PWC and Koekkoek, AK (eds), *De Grondwet. Een artikelsgewijs commentaar* (Zwolle, WEJ Tjeenk Willink, 1992) 106–45

——, 'Artikel 6' in Koekkoek, AK (ed), *De Grondwet. Een systematisch en artikelsgewijs commentaar* (Deventer, W.E.J. Tjeenk Willink, 2000) 93–109

——, 'Het uitzetten van radicale imams' (2006) *Migrantenrecht* Vol 21:6–7, 250–54

——, 'Akrich, Commissie / Spanje, Jia. Nog steeds geen *Eind* aan de onduidelijkheid over eerste toelating van derdelanders / gezinsleden van EU-migranten' in Böcker, A et al (eds), *Migration law and sociology of law. Collected essays in honour of Kees Groenendijk* (Nijmegen, Wolf Legal Publishers, 2008) 495–502

——, 'On freedom, equality and citizenship. Changing fundamentals of Dutch minority policy and law (immigration, integration, education and religion)' in Foblets, M-C, Gaudreault-Desbiens, J-F and Dundes Renteln, A (eds), *Cultural Diversity and the Law. State Responses from Around the World* (Brussels, Bruylant, 2010a) 45–143

——, 'The freedom of religion in Article 9 of the European Convention on Human Rights: historical roots and today's dilemma's' in Van de Beek, A, Van der Borght, EAJG and Vermeulen, BP (eds) *Freedom of Religion* (Leiden / Boston, Brill, 2010b) 9–29

Vermeulen, BP and Aarrass, B, 'De reikwijdte van de vrijheid van godsdienst in een pluriforme samenleving' in Nieuwenhuis, AJ and Zoethout, CM (eds), *Rechtsstaat en religie* (Nijmegen, Wolf Legal Publishers, 2009)

Verschueren, H, 'Enkele denkpistes ter oplossing van het probleem van de omgekeerde discriminatie bij gezinshereniging' (2009) *Migrantenrecht* Vol 24:3, 76–86

Vierdag, EW, *The Concept of Discrimination in International Law* (The Hague, Martinus Nijhoff, 1973)

Wagenaar, W and Van Donselaar, J, 'Racistisch en extreemrechts geweld in 2009' in Rodrigues, PR and Van Donselaar, J (eds), *Monitor Racisme & Extremisme. Negende rapportage* (Amsterdam, Anne Frank Stichting / Amsterdam University Press, 2010) 15–36

Walter, A, *Reverse discrimination and family reunification* (Nijmegen, Wolf Legal Publishers, 2008)

Weis, P, *Nationality and Statelessness in International Law* (London, Gibson Press, 1956)

Weiss, F and Wooldridge, F, *Free Movement of Persons within the European Community* (Alphen aan den Rijn, Kluwer Law International, 2007)

Wetenschappelijke Raad voor het Regeringsbeleid (WRR), *Etnische minderheden* (The Hague, Staatsuitgeverij, 1979)
——, *Allochtonenbeleid* (The Hague, Sdu uitgeverij, 1989)
——, *Eigentijds burgerschap* (under the supervision of Van Gunsteren, HR) (The Hague, Sdu uitgeverij, 1992)
——, *Nederland immigratiesamenleving* (The Hague, WRR, 2001a)
——, *Nieuwe kansen voor taalonderwijs aan anderstaligen* (The Hague, WRR, 2001b)
——, *Identificatie met Nederland* (Amsterdam, Amsterdam University Press, 2007)
Wiesbrock, A, *Legal Migration to the European Union. Ten Years After Tampere* (diss. Maastricht University) (Nijmegen, Wolf Legal Publishers, 2010)

Index